Comprehensive Computer Learning (CCL)

by

Bittu Kumar

Published by:

F-2/16, Ansari road, Daryaganj, New Delhi-110002
☎ 23240026, 23240027 *Fax:* 011-23240028
info@vspublishers.com www.vspublishers.com

Online Brandstore: amazon.in/vspublishers

Regional Office : Hyderabad
5-1-707/1, Brij Bhawan (Beside Central Bank of India Lane)
Bank Street, Koti, Hyderabad - 500 095
☎ 040-24737290
vspublishershyd@gmail.com

Follow us on:   

BUY OUR BOOKS FROM: AMAZON FLIPKART

ISBN 978-93-505701-4-2
New Edition

DISCLAIMER

While every attempt has been made to provide accurate and timely information in this book, neither the author nor the publisher assumes any responsibility for errors, unintended omissions or commissions detected therein. The author and publisher makes no representation or warranty with respect to the comprehensiveness or completeness of the contents provided.

All matters included have been simplified under professional guidance for general information only, without any warranty for applicability on an individual. Any mention of an organization or a website in the book, by way of citation or as a source of additional information, doesn't imply the endorsement of the content either by the author or the publisher. It is possible that websites cited may have changed or removed between the time of editing and publishing the book.

Results from using the expert opinion in this book will be totally dependent on individual circumstances and factors beyond the control of the author and the publisher.

It makes sense to elicit advice from well informed sources before implementing the ideas given in the book. The reader assumes full responsibility for the consequences arising out from reading this book.

For proper guidance, it is advisable to read the book under the watchful eyes of parents/guardian. The buyer of this book assumes all responsibility for the use of given materials and information.

Printed at : Param Offsetters, Okhla, New Delhi–110020

Publisher's Note

After successfully publishing youth-oriented books and getting commendable appreciation from students, teachers and parents alike, V&S Publishers is venturing into the arena of student and job-oriented books with a series of computer books on various important subjects for readers of all ages. Written and presented in lucid language and simple terms, without any computer jargon, these books are an easy-to-follow manual for readers. For the convenience of readers the information is set out in an easy to understand, step-by-step format, with clear illustrations and detailed explanations to accompany each action. Besides, every book is accompanied with video tutorials on Youtube for better understanding of the readers.

Today we live in a world of computers. The present scenario is that computers are used in every field be it education, business, trade and commerce, home and hobby, or even our ordinary day-to-day life. The importance of computers is an undeniable fact in today's world. In fact, we can't think of a world without computers.

Realising this indisputable fact, we are coming up with the series of **"Comprehensive Computer Learning (CCL)"** books. The series currently includes –

1. Comprehensive Computer Learning (CCL) Hindi
2. Comprehensive Computer Learning – Concise Computer Course
3. Comprehensive Computer Learning – Microsoft Office 2010
4. Comprehensive Computer Learning – Desktop Publishing (DTP)
5. Comprehensive Computer Learning – Adobe Photoshop

Key features of these books:

- Written in simple and lucid language
- Presented in step-by-step, easy-to-understand format with detailed explanations with appropriate images & screenshots, charts & tables
- Useful tips and notes given in every chapter as additional information

This book **"Comprehensive Computer Learning"** has been explicitly written keeping in mind the needs of Youngsters and explains the basics of computer in simple & precise manner.

While every effort has been made to minimise printing and other errors, it may be possible that a few might have managed to escape the wakeful eyes. We would like to request the readers to bring these errors to our notice so that we can rectify the same in subsequent editions.

Contents

Section–III Getting Down to Business

Section–IV Going Digital with Music, Photos, & Video

Section–V Tapping the Power of the Internet

Section–VI Maintaining/Troubleshooting your Computer

Section–VII Add-Ons

SECTION-I
INTRODUCTION TO
COMPUTER

An Introduction

What is a Computer?

Computers are machines that perform tasks or calculations according to a set of instructions, or programs. The first fully electronic computers, introduced in the 1940s, were huge machines that required teams of people to operate. Compared to those early machines, today's computers are amazing. Not only are they thousands of times faster, they can fit on your desk, in your lap, or even in your pocket.

Types of computers

Computers range in size and capability. At one end of the scale are supercomputers, very large computers with thousands of linked microprocessors that perform extremely complex calculations. At the other end are tiny computers embedded in cars, TVs, stereo systems, calculators, and appliances. These computers are built to perform a limited number of tasks.

The personal computer, or *PC*, is designed to be used by one person at a time. This section describes the various kinds of personal computers: desktops, laptops, handheld computers, and Tablet PCs.

Desktop computers

Desktop computers are designed for use at a desk or table. They are typically larger and more powerful than other types of personal computers. Desktop computers are made up of separate components. The main component, called the system unit, is usually a rectangular case that sits on or underneath a desk. Other components, such as the monitor, mouse, and keyboard, connect to the system unit.

Desktop computer

Laptop computers

Laptop computers are lightweight mobile PCs with a thin screen. They are often called notebook computers because of their small size. Laptops can operate on batteries, so you can take them anywhere. Unlike desktops, laptops combine the CPU, screen, and the keyboard in a single case. The screen folds down onto the keyboard when not in use.

Laptop computer

Handheld computers

Handheld computers, also called personal digital assistants *(PDAs)*, are battery-powered computers small enough to carry almost anywhere. Although not as powerful as desktops or laptops, handhelds are useful for scheduling appointments, storing addresses and phone numbers, and playing games. Some have more advanced capabilities, such as making telephone calls or accessing the Internet. Instead of keyboards, handhelds have touch screens that you use with your finger or a stylus (a pen-shaped pointing tool).

Handheld computer

Tablet PCs

Tablet PCs are mobile PCs that combine features of laptops and handhelds. Like laptops, they're powerful and have a built-in screen. Like handhelds, they allow you to write notes or draw pictures on the screen, usually with a tablet pen instead of a stylus. They can also convert your handwriting into typed text. Some Tablet PCs are "convertibles" with a screen that swivels and unfolds to reveal a keyboard underneath.

What can you do with computers?

- In the workplace, many people use computers to keep records, analyze data, do research, and manage projects. At home, you can use computers to find information, store pictures and music, track finances, play games, and communicate with others—and those are just a few of the possibilities.

- You can also use your computer to connect to the Internet, a network that links computers around the world. Internet access is available for a monthly fee in most urban areas, and increasingly, in less populated areas. With Internet access, you can communicate with people all over the world and find vast information.

Here are some of the most popular things to do with computers:

The web

The World Wide Web (usually called the Web, or web) is a gigantic storehouse of information. The web is the most popular part of the Internet, partly because it displays most information in a visually appealing format. Headlines, text, and pictures can be combined on a single webpage—much like a page in a magazine—along with sounds and animation. A website is a collection of interconnected webpages. The web contains millions of websites and billions of webpages.

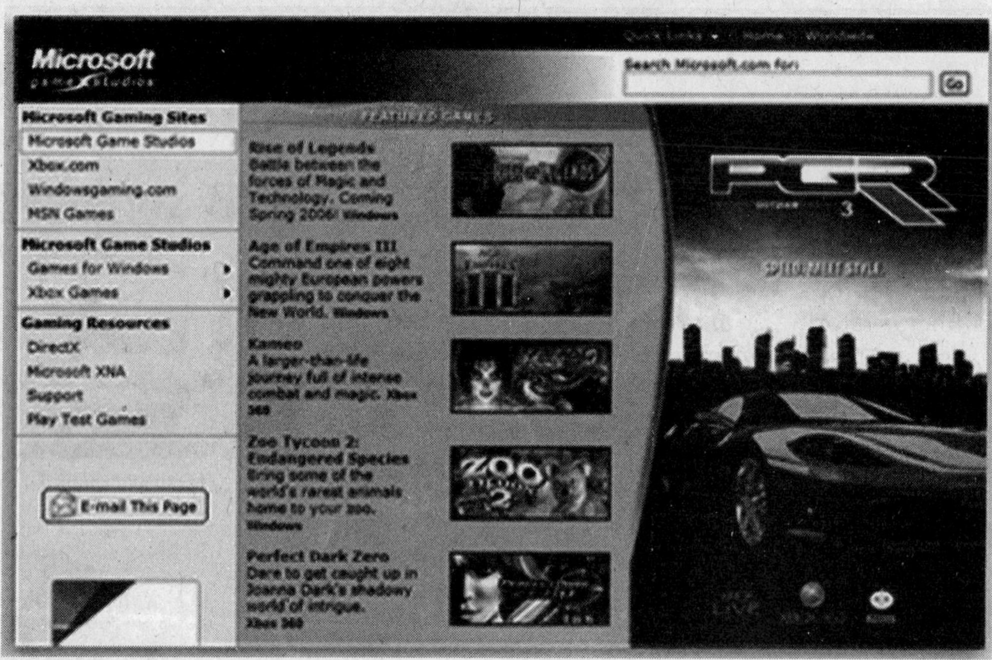

. A Webpage (Microsoft Game Studios)

Surfing the web means exploring it. You can find information on the web about almost any topic imaginable. For example, you can read news stories and movie reviews, check airline schedules, see street maps, get the weather forecast for your city, or research a health condition. Most companies, government agencies, museums, and libraries have websites with information about their products, services, or collections. Reference sources, such as dictionaries and encyclopedias, are also widely available.

The web is also a shopper's delight. You can browse and purchase products—books, music, toys, clothing, electronics, and much more—at the websites of major retailers. You can also buy and sell used items through websites that use auction-style bidding.

Email

Email (short for electronic mail) is a convenient way to communicate with others. When you send an email message, it arrives almost instantly in the recipient's email inbox. You can send email to many people simultaneously, and you can save, print, and forward email to others. You can send almost any type of file in an email message, including documents, pictures, and music files. And with email, you don't need a stamp!

Instant messaging

Instant messaging is like having a real-time conversation with another person or a group of people. When you type and send an instant message, the message is immediately visible to all participants. Unlike email, all participants have to be online (connected to the Internet) and in front of their computers at the same time. Communicating by means of instant messaging is called chatting.

Pictures, music, and movies

If you have a digital camera, you can move your pictures from the camera to your computer. Then you can print them, create slide shows, or share them with others by email or by posting them on a website. To learn more about what you can do with photos, You can also listen to music on your computer, either by importing (transferring to your computer) music from audio CDs or by purchasing songs from a music website. Or, tune in to one of the thousands of radio stations that broadcast over the Internet. If your computer comes with a DVD player, you can watch movies.

Gaming

Do you like to play games? Thousands of computer games in every conceivable category are available to entertain you. Get behind the wheel of a race car, battle frightening creatures in a dungeon, or control civilizations and empires! Many games allow you to compete with other players around the world through the Internet.

History of Computers

A Computer history timeline is described as follows:

Counting aids →Manual caculators → Mechanical calculators → Programmable calculators → Programmable computers

The Table below explains the History of Computers in detail:

Date	Inventor	Device	Details
3000 B.C	Babylonians	Abacus	Simple counting and calculating aid. Thought to have first been invented around this time.
1200 A.D	unknown	Chinese abacus	In widespread use in China by this time (according to textbook).
1600	unknown	Japanese abacus	In widespread use in Japan by this time (according to textbook).
1600	John Napier	Napier's Bones	Multiplication and division tool based on logarithms.

Date	Inventor	Device	Details
1621	William Oughtred	Slide Rule	Similar in purpose and function to Napier's Bones. Based on logarithms also. Popular up until the 1960's.
1623	Wilhelm Schickard	Shickard's Calculator	Interlocking geared wheels. Not much known about it.
1642	Blaise Pascal	Pascaline	Could add, subtract, multiply and divide.
1673	Gottfried Wilhelm von Leibniz	Leibniz Calculator	Similar to Pascaline. A mechanical calculating device.
1801-1804	Joseph Jacquard	Jacquard Loom	Weaving machine that could be "programmed" with punched cards.
1820	Thomas deColmar	deColmar's Arithometer	First mass-produced mechanical calculator.
1822-1833	Charles Babbage	Difference Engine	(Never completed) Steam powered. For calculating large tables of numbers for astronomy and engineering. Would have had > 4000 gears levers and wheels.
1834	Charles Babbage	Analytical Engine	(Never completed) Embodied many of ideas of modern computers: memory, programmable processor, input/output capabilities. Was to use punched cards, probably got that idea from Jacquard. Ada Lovelace (daughter of the poet Lord Byron) also contributed and is considered the world's first programmer.
1890	Herman Hollerith	Hollerith Tabulating Machine	Punched card tabulating machine created to tabulate results of the 1890 US Census. He incorporated as "The Tabulating Machine Company" which later became "International Business Machines" (a.k.a. IBM)
1937-1942	John V. Atanasoff and Clifford E. Berry	Altanasoff-Berry Computer (ABC)	First computer prototype to use vacuum tubes instead of mechanical switches. Also used the binary number system like a modern computer.
~1942-1945	Konrad Zuse	Z3	A binary computer. Based on electromechanical relay switches. But working under the Nazi regime in Germany, his work was unknown until much later.
1939	Howard Aiken (IBM sponsored)	Harvard Mark I	Electromechanical relay computer with many moving parts. Used decimal number system.
1943	A British team incl. Alan Turing	COLLOSUS	Electronic device made to decode encrypted ENIGMA messages. Made with vacuum tubes and based on binary arithmetic.
1943-1945	John W. Mauchly and J. Presper Eckert	ENIAC	General purpose computer. Vacuum tubes. Designed to calculate trajectory tables for the US Army, but wasn't finished until shortly after the war. Programmed via switches and patch cables.

Date	Inventor	Device	Details
1951	Eckert-Mauchly Computer Corp.	UNIVAC	First commercially successful digital computer. Also used magnetic tape for storage. Took punched cards too. Remington-Rand is the corp that actually marketed and sold UNIVAC, because Eckert-Mauchly ran out of money.
Late 1950's	Various	Various	"Second generation computers", based on transistors.
1965	RCA	RCA Spectra 70	One of the first "Third Generation Computers" based on integrated circuits (IC)
1965	IBM	IBM 360	Another of the first "Third Generation Computers". Based on IC technology.
1965	Digital Equipment Corp. (DEC)	PDP-8	First commercially successful minicomputer (also IC-based).
1971	Ted Hoff (INTEL)	Intel 4004	First "Fourth Generation Computer", i.e. first micro-processor. That is, the first complete processor on a single chip built using integrated circuit technology. Followed by 8008, 8085, 8080, 8086, 8088, 80286, 80386, 80486, 80586 (a.k.a "Pentium), Pentium II, Pentium III, Pentium IV.
1974	Motorola	6800	Early predecessor of processor first used in Macintosh computers, the 68000.
1976	Zilog	Z80	Based on Intel's 8080, versions still used today in embedded computing tasks.
1974	Jonathan A. Titus	Mark-8	Early hobbyist personal computer.
1975	Ed Roberts	MITS Altair	First truly commercial hobbyist microcomputer.
1977	Steve Wozniak and Steve Jobs	Apple I	Another early microcomputer kit for hobbyists.
1978	Steve Wozniak and Steve Jobs	Apple II	Early personal computer with colour graphics and actually useful software (VisiCalc).
1981	IBM	IBM PC	Predecessor of the most popular personal computer platform in use today.
1983	Apple Computer	Lisa	First commercial personal computer with a Graphical User Interface (GUI) based on ideas from Xerox PARC research lab.
1984	Apple Computer	Macintosh	First commercially successful computer with a GUI.

Photographs of some computers described below:

ancient abacus

Napier's Bones

Intel 4004

Leibniz Calculator

deColmar's Arithometer

Univac

ENIAC

RCA spectra 70

We shall now look at working of a computer

Tip....

Charles Babbage is known as the Father of Computers.

Working of a computer

First question that might strike your mind is how do computer works, here is a brief explanation:

Powering on the computer

When you first press the power button the computer sends a signal to the computer power supply, which converts the alternating current (AC) into a direct current (DC) to supply the computer and its components with the proper amount of voltage and electricity.

Once the computer and its components have received ample power and the power supply reports no errors it sends a signal (using transistors) to the motherboard and the computer processor (CPU). While this is happening, the processor will clear any leftover data in the memory registers and give the CPU program counter a F000 hexadecimal number. This number is the location of the first instruction and tells the CPU that it's ready to process the instructions contained in the basic input/output system (BIOS).

BIOS and the POST

When the computer first looks at the BIOS, it begins the power-on self-test (POST) sequence to make sure the components in the computer are present and functioning properly. If the computer does not pass any of these tests, it will encounter an irregular POST. An irregular POST is a beep code that is different from the standard one or two beeps. For example, an irregular POST could generate no beeps at all or a combination of different beeps to indicate the cause of the failure.

If the computer passes the initial POST, it will next look at the first 64-bytes of memory located in the complementary metal oxide semiconductor (CMOS) chip, which is kept alive by the CMOS battery even when the computer is turned off. This chip contains information such as the system time and date and information about all the hardware installed in your computer.

After loading the CMOS information, the POST will begin inspecting and comparing the system settings with what is installed in the computer. If no errors are found it will then load the basic device drivers and interrupt handlers for hardware such as the hard drive, keyboard, mouse, floppy drive. These basic drivers allow the CPU to communicate with these hardware devices and allow the computer to continue its boot process.

Next, the POST will check the real-time clock (RTC) or system timer and the computer system bus to make sure both of these are properly working on the computer. Finally, you'll get a picture on your display after the POST has loaded the memory contained on the display adapter and has made it part of the overall system BIOS.

Next, the BIOS will check to see if it's currently performing a cold boot or warm boot (reboot) by looking at the memory address 0000:0472, if it sees 1234h the BIOS knows that this is a reboot and will skip the remainder of the POST steps.

If 1234h is not seen, the BIOS knows that this is a cold boot and will continue running additional POST steps. Next, it tests the computer memory (RAM) installed in the computer by writing to each chip. With many computers, you'll know it's performing this step if you see the computer counting the total installed memory as it's booting.

Finally, the POST will send signals to the computer floppy, optical, and hard drive to test these drives. If all drives pass the test, the POST is complete and instruct the computer to start the process of loading the operating system.

Booting the operating system

After the computer has passed the POST, the computer will start the boot process. This process is what loads the operating system and all of its associated files. Because Microsoft Windows is the most commonly used operating system, this section will cover the process of loading Microsoft Windows.

The BIOS first hands control over to the bootstrap loader, which looks at the boot sector of the hard drive. If your boot sequence in CMOS setup is not setup to look at the hard drive first, it may look at the boot sector on any inserted floppy disk drive or optical disc first before doing this.

In this example, the Microsoft Windows XP NT Loader (NTLDR) is found on the boot sector and tells the computer where to find the remaining code on the hard drive. Next, Windows loads the ntdetect.com file, which displays the Windows splash screen and loads the Windows registry. After loading the registry, Windows begins to load dozens of low-level programs that make up the operating system into memory. Many of the initially loaded programs are what allow Windows to communicate with the essential hardware and other programs running on the computer.

After the registry has loaded the initial basic hardware devices, it begins to load Plug and Play devices, PCI, and ISA devices. After loading all these devices, Windows then moves to loading full support of the hard drive, partitions, and any other disk drives and then moves to all other drivers that have been installed.

Finally, after successfully completing the above steps any additional required services are loaded and Windows starts.

Hardware devices communicating with the computer

After the computer has loaded the operating system, hardware attached to the computer must be able to communicate with the CPU. Hardware communication is done by using an interrupt request (IRQ). Each time a hardware device needs the attention of the computer the interrupt controller sends the request (INTR) to the CPU so it temporarily stops what it is doing to process the request of the hardware device. Anything that was being currently done by the CPU is put on hold and stored as a memory address in the memory stack and is returned to after the interrupt request is processed.

Hardware and Software

Computers work through an interaction of hardware and software. Hardware refers to the parts of a computer that you can see and touch, including the case and everything inside it. The most important piece of hardware is a tiny rectangular chip inside your computer called the central processing unit (CPU), or microprocessor. It's the "brain" of your computer—the part that translates instructions and performs calculations. Hardware items such as your monitor, keyboard, mouse, printer, and other items are often called hardware devices, or devices.

Software refers to the instructions, or programs, that tell the hardware what to do. A word processing program that you can use to write letters on your computer is a type of software. The operating system (OS) is software that manages your computer and the devices connected to it. Two well-known operating systems are Windows and Macintosh operating system. Your computer uses the Windows operating system.

Parts of a Desktop Computer

Here is the description of an average desktop computer.

Parts of a computer

If you use a desktop computer, you might already know that there isn't any single part called the "computer." A computer is really a system of many parts working together. The physical parts, which you can see and touch, are collectively called hardware. (Software, on the other hand, refers to the instructions, or programs, that tell the hardware what to do.)

The illustration below shows the most common hardware in a desktop computer system. Your system may look a little different, but it probably has most of these parts. A laptop computer has similar parts but combines them into a single notebook-sized package.

Focusing on Key PC Components

Let's explore different components of PC

System unit

The system unit is the core of a computer system. Usually it's a rectangular box placed on or underneath your desk. Inside this box are many electronic components that process information. The most important of these components is the central processing unit (CPU), or microprocessor, which acts as the "brain" of your computer. Another component is random access memory (RAM), which temporarily stores information that the CPU uses while the computer is on. The information stored in RAM is erased when the computer is turned off.

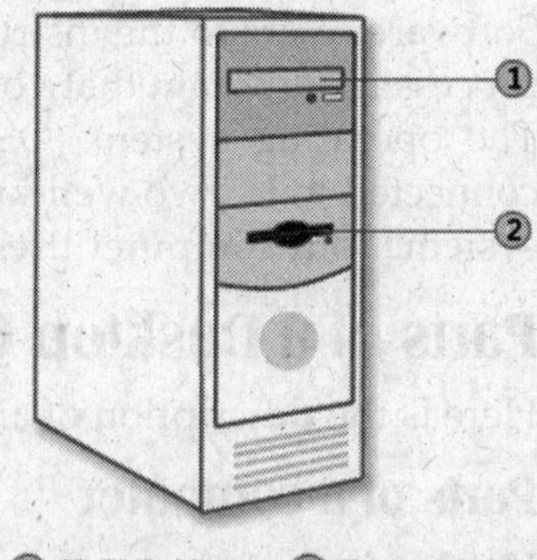

System unit

Almost every other part of your computer connects to the system unit using cables. The cables plug into specific ports (openings), typically on the back of the system unit. Hardware that is not part of the system unit is sometimes called a peripheral device or device.

Central Processing Unit (CPU)

The central processing unit (CPU, occasionally central processor unit is the hardware within a computer system which carries out the instructions of a computer program by performing the basic arithmetical, logical, and input/output operations of the system. CPU consists of RAM(Random Access Memory), Processors & BIOS Chips.

Microprocessor SSOP

Monitor

A monitor displays information in visual form, using text and graphics. The portion of the monitor that displays the information is called the screen. Like a television screen, a computer screen can show still or moving pictures.

There are two basic types of monitors: CRT (cathode ray tube) monitors and LCD (liquid crystal display) monitors. Both types produce sharp images, but LCD monitors have the advantage of being much thinner and lighter. CRT monitors, however, are generally more affordable.

LCD monitor (left); CRT monitor (right)

IO Devices – Keyboard/Mouse

Keyboard

Keyboard

A keyboard is used mainly for typing text into your computer. Like the keyboard on a typewriter, it has keys for letters and numbers, but it also has special keys:

- The *function keys*, found on the top row, perform different functions depending on where they are used.
- The *numeric keypad*, located on the right side of most keyboards, allows you to enter numbers quickly.
- The *navigation keys*, such as the arrow keys, allow you to move your position within a document or webpage.

You can also use your keyboard to perform many of the same tasks you can perform with a mouse.

Mouse

Mouse

A mouse is a small device used to point to and select items on your computer screen. Although mice come in many shapes, the typical mouse does look a bit like an actual mouse. It's small, oblong, and connected to the system unit by a long wire that resembles a tail. Some newer mice are wireless.

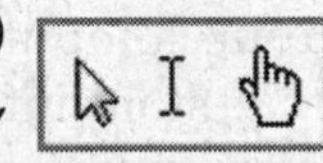

A mouse usually has two buttons: a primary button (usually the left button) and a secondary button. Many mice also have a wheel between the two buttons, which allows you to scroll smoothly through screens of information.

When you move the mouse with your hand, a pointer on your screen moves in the same direction. (The pointer's appearance might change depending on where it's positioned on your screen.) When you want to select an item, you point to the item and then *click* (press and release) the primary button. Pointing and clicking with your mouse is the main way to interact with your computer.

Scanner

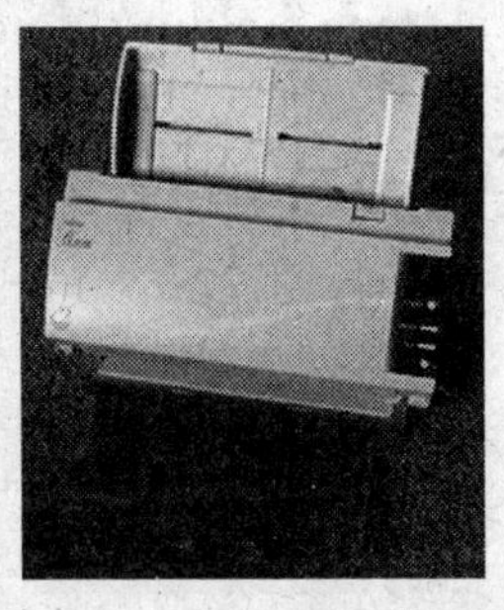

scanner—is a device that optically scans images, printed text, handwriting, or an object, and converts it to a digital image. Common examples found in offices are variations of the desktop (or flatbed) scanner where the document is placed on a glass window for scanning. Hand-held scanners, where the device is moved by hand, have evolved from text scanning "wands" to 3D scanners used for industrial design, reverse engineering, test and measurement, orthotics, gaming and other applications. Mechanically driven scanners that move the document are typically used for large-format documents, where a flatbed design would be impractical.

Printer

A printer transfers data from a computer onto paper. You don't need a printer to use your computer, but having one allows you to print email, cards, invitations, announcements, and other materials. Many people also like being able to print their own photos at home.

Laser printer

The two main types of printers are – inkjet printers and laser printers. Inkjet printers are the most popular printers for the home.

They can print in black and white or in full colour and can produce high-quality photographs when used with special paper. Laser printers are faster and generally better able to handle heavy use.

Inkjet printer

Webcam

A webcam is a video camera that feeds its images in real time to computer or computer network, often via USB, ethernet, or Wi-Fi.

Their most popular use is the establishment of video links, permitting computers to act as videophones or videoconference stations. The common use as a video camera for the World Wide Web gave the webcam its name. Other popular uses include security surveillance, computer vision, video broadcasting, and for recording social videos .

Hard Drive

Your computer has one or more disk drives—devices that store information on a metal or plastic disk. The disk preserves the information even when your computer is turned off.

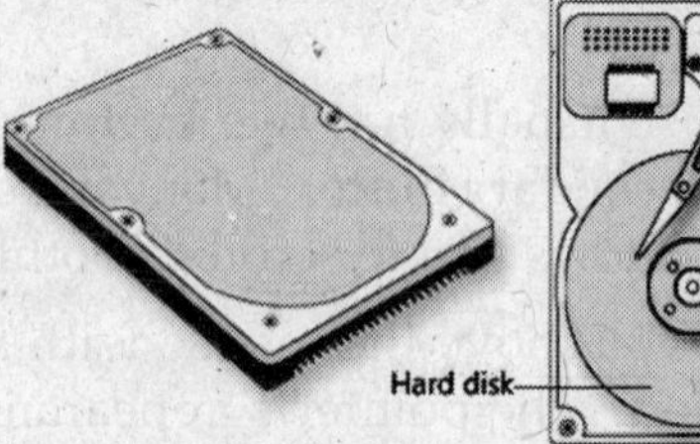

Hard disk drive

Hard disk drive

Your computer's hard disk drive stores information on a hard disk, a rigid platter or stack of platters with a magnetic surface. Because hard disks can hold massive amounts of information, they usually serve as your computer's primary means of storage, holding almost all of your programs and files. The hard disk drive is normally located inside the system unit.

Optical Drive for CDs and DVDs

Nearly all computers today come equipped with a CD or DVD drive, usually located on the front of the system unit. CD drives use lasers to read (retrieve) data from a CD, and many CD drives can also write (record) data onto CDs. If you have a recordable disk drive, you can store copies of your files on blank CDs. You can also use a CD drive to play music CDs on your computer.

CD/DVD

DVD drives can do everything that CD drives can, plus read DVDs. If you have a DVD drive, you can watch movies on your computer. Many DVD drives can record data onto blank DVDs.

Floppy disk drive

Floppy disk

Floppy disk drives store information on floppy disks, also called floppies or diskettes. Compared to CDs and DVDs, floppy disks can store only a small amount of data. They also retrieve information more slowly and are more prone to damage. For these reasons, floppy disk drives are less popular than they used to be, although some computers still include them.

Video Adapter

A video Adapter (also called a display card, graphics card, graphics board, display adapter or graphics adapter) is an expansion card which generates a feed of output images to a display. Most video cards offer various functions such as accelerated rendering of 3D scenes and 2D graphics, MPEG-2/MPEG-4 decoding, TV output, or the ability to connect multiple monitors (multi-monitor).

Sound Card

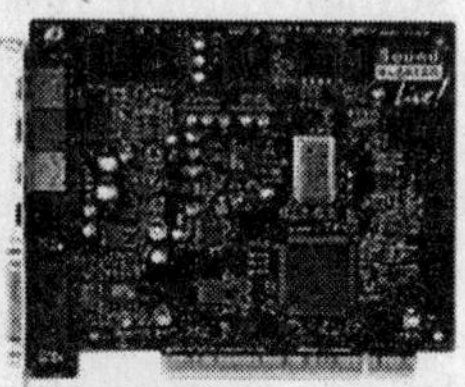

A sound card (also known as an audio card) is an internal computer expansion card that facilitates the input and output of audio signals to and from a computer under control of computer programs. The term sound card is also applied to external audio interfaces that use software to generate sound, as opposed to using hardware inside the PC. Typical uses of sound cards include providing the audio component for multimedia applications such as music composition, editing video or audio, presentation, education and entertainment (games) and video projection.

Sound functionality can also be integrated onto the motherboard, using basically the same components as a plug-in card. The best plug-in cards, which use better and more expensive components, can achieve higher quality than integrated sound. The integrated sound system is often still referred to as a "sound card".

Ports and Jacks

In computer hardware, a port serves as an interface between the computer and other computers or peripheral devices. Physically, a port is a specialized outlet on a piece of equipment to which a plug or cable connects. Electronically, the several conductors making up the outlet provide a signal transfer between devices.

Modem

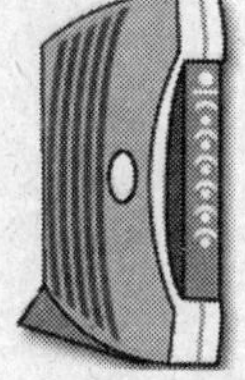

Cable modem

To connect your computer to the Internet, you need a modem. A modem is a device that sends and receives computer information over a telephone line or high-speed cable. Modems are sometimes built into the system unit, but higher-speed modems are usually separate components.

Bluetooth Wireess Adapter

Bluetooth Adapter

Desktop devices using Bluetooth technology are available. With a base station that connects via cables to the fixed-line telephone and also the computer via soundcard, users with any Bluetooth headset can pair their headset to the base station, enabling them to use the same headset for both fixed-line telephone and computer VoIP communication. This type of device, when used together with a multiple-point Bluetooth headset, enables a single Bluetooth headset to communicate with a computer and both mobile and landline telephones.

Touchpad

Touchpad

A touchpad (or trackpad) is a pointing device featuring a tactile sensor, a specialized surface that can translate the motion and position of a user's fingers to a relative position on screen. Touchpads are a common feature of laptop computers, and are also used as a substitute for a mouse where desk space is scarce. Because they vary in size, they can also be found on personal digital assistants (PDAs) and some portable media players. Wireless touchpads are also available as detached accessories.

Speakers, Mics & Headphones

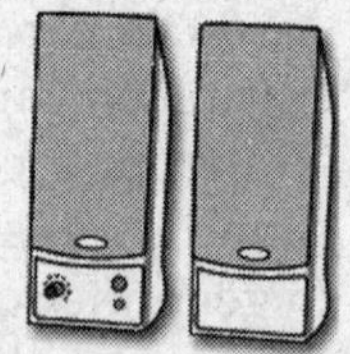
Computer speakers

Speakers are used to play sound. They may be built into the system unit or connected with cables. Speakers allow you to listen to music and hear sound effects from your computer. While Mics are used to record/send voice.

A microphone (colloquially called a mic or mike is an acoustic-to-electric transducer or sensor that converts sound into an electrical signal. Microphones are used in many applications such as telephones, tape recorders, karaoke systems, hearing aids, motion picture production, live and recorded audio engineering, FRS radios, megaphones, in radio and television broadcasting and in computers for recording voice, speech recognition, VoIP, and for non-acoustic purposes such as ultrasonic checking or knock sensors.

The First Steps

Buying the Right Computer for You

When buying a PC, you have much more to consider than simply whether you want a desktop PC, notebook, or netbook. You need to think not only about portability, but also processor type and speed, disk storage capacity, memory, CD/DVD drives, audio, video, operating system, and a whole lot more. In addition, you want to find the right PC at the best price.

Well, you've come to the right place. This chapter explains key considerations, provides guidance on making the right choices for your needs, and shows you how to shop for great deals on PCs.

Assessing Your Computing Needs

Your choice of PC hinges on the reasons you're getting a new PC and how you plan to use it. Check all items that apply.

Focusing on Mobility

If you need or want to travel with your PC, mobility is the first and most important consideration. You can rule out entire categories of computers based solely on how portable you need your PC to be. The following sections describe your options from least to most mobile/portable.

Desktop PC

Desktop PCs are the largest, sturdiest, heaviest, and least portable of the bunch, but they offer three major advantages:

- ❒ **More bang for your buck:** A comparably equipped portable PC costs several thousands more.
- ❒ **More suitable for meeting advanced needs:** A top-of-the-line desktop model can do things a top-of-the-line portable PC may not, such as play the latest video games at warp speed and produce theater-quality video and sound.

- ❒ **More room to grow:** Desktop models typically offer more upgrade options to meet future needs.

Desktop models also come as space-saving all-in-one PCs that look like a monitor with a mouse and keyboard attached (with cables or without). All-in-one models often have touch-screens to make them even easier to use.

Notebook (Laptop)

Notebook PCs, also called laptops, include everything most users need in a single, compact unit that typically weighs less than 1kilogram.

Tablet PC

A tablet PC is like a notebook with a screen that pivots, folds back, and allows you to write on it. It's perfect for people who need to jot down handwritten notes, sign digital documents, or pivot the screen to show something to clients. Real estate agents, financial planners, investment brokers, and others who must travel, present information to clients, and have them sign documents often find a tablet PC the ideal solution.

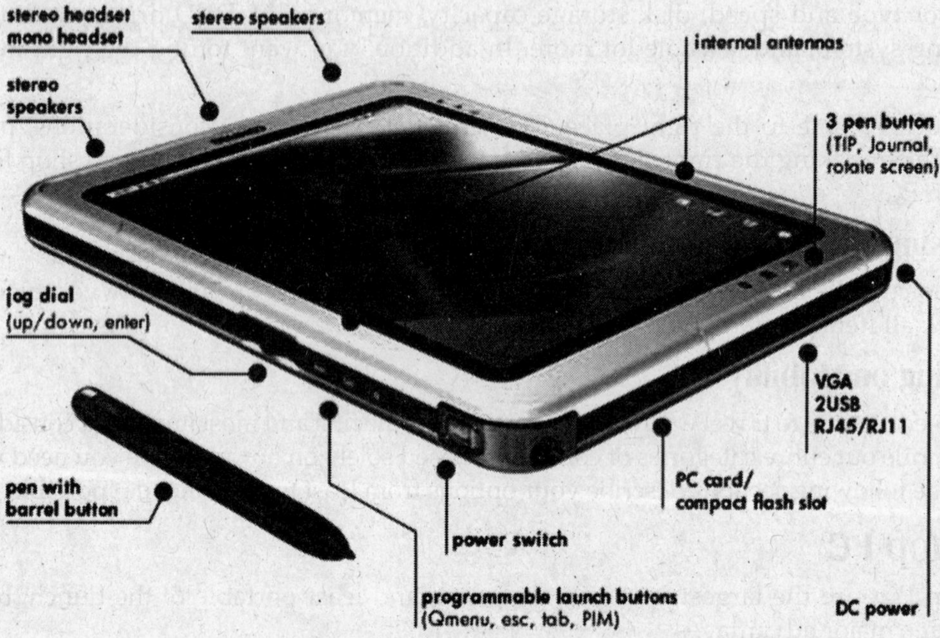

Netbook

Netbooks are streamlined notebooks designed primarily to use the Internet and perform basic tasks. They typically have smaller screens and keyboards, weigh about ½ kg or less, and are very affordable. The biggest drawback may be the lack of an internal CD or DVD drive. You can add an external CD or DVD drive, but it just isn't quite the same.

Recommendation

Netbook

I always recommend notebooks, tablet PCs, or larger netbooks over desktop models. Why? Because you can connect a mouse and a full-size keyboard and monitor to a portable computer to make it more like a desktop model, but you can't make a desktop model any smaller or lighter. Some portable PCs even have optional docking stations to enable you to quickly and easily connect the PC to any and all external devices.

Buying Key Components

A PC is a collection of components designed to work as a unit. When you start shopping, you'll encounter lists of components along with specifications for each component. The following sections describe the most important components and what to look for based on your needs.

❒ **Central Processing Unit (CPU)**

The central processing unit (CPU) or processor is the computer's brain; it performs all the calculations for the computer. When choosing a CPU, consider the following factors:

- **Architecture:** This is the overall design of the CPU. One of the most important design considerations is the number of cores the CPU has. Multi-core processors, including dual- and quad-core processors, are like having two, three, or four processors built into a single CPU.
- **Clock speed:** Measured in gigahertz (GHz), clock speed indicates how fast the CPU processes instructions.
- **L2 cache:** Also known simply as cache, L2 cache is temporary storage built into the chip for recently or frequently used data and instructions. It helps the CPU function at top speed.
- **Front side bus:** This is the path that connects the CPU to other key components, including memory. Front side bus speed is measured in gigabytes—the faster, the better.

❒ **Operating System**

You can tell a lot about a computer by checking the version of Windows 7 that's installed on it. First, check whether the PC has a 32- or 64-bit version of Windows 7. The 32-bit version is fine for most needs and may be best if you have older 32-bit hardware or software you want to use. If you're looking for a performance boost or starting from scratch, lean toward a PC that runs the 64-bit version of Windows. The 64-bit PCs and software handle larger amounts of memory (4GB and higher). All computers that have the Windows 7 Compatible logo can run either the 32- or 64-bit version.

After choosing between the 32- and 64-bit version, you have another choice to make: Windows Starter, Home Premium, Professional, or Ultimate edition.

- **Windows Starter**: This is a streamlined version exclusively for netbooks.

- **Home Premium**: Windows 7 Home Premium can handle all your basic needs, simplify the process of setting up a home network, and manage all your media and entertainment needs, including managing and sharing photos, videos, and music; watching, recording, and copying DVDs; listening to, recording, and copying CDs; and watching and recording TV shows (with the addition of a TV tuner).
- **Professional:** Windows Professional has everything Home Premium has, plus a few features typical for businesses: Running Windows XP productivity programs in Windows XP Mode, automatically backing up files to your home or business network, and connecting easily and securely to your company network from remote locations.
- **Ultimate**: Windows Ultimate has everything included in the Professional edition, plus the ability to encrypt data on a portable PC or portable storage device, features for IT professionals, and support for 35 different languages.
- **Windows Vista:** Earlier Version of Windows available in many Variants as of Windows 7
- **Windows XP:** Earlier Version of Windows comes without Driver Support, Still used in Many systems with Low Grade Configuration.

Random Access Memory (RAM)

Random access memory (RAM), often referred to simply as memory, stores all the data and instructions the PC requires to perform its job while it's on. When you turn off your PC, everything is erased from memory. When shopping for RAM, consider the following:

- **Amount**: I recommend at least 2GB for most users and 4GB for serious media, entertainment, and gaming junkies. If the PC comes with the 32-bit version of Windows, don't bother with more than 4GB.
- **Type and speed**: Look for DDR2 or DDR3 SDRAM and compare speeds, measured in gigabytes. DDR stands for "double data rate," and SDRAM stands for "synchronous dynamic random access memory." Just remember that DDR2 is good, DDR3 is better, and higher speed translates into better performance and higher cost.
- **Upgradeability:** Make sure you can add more RAM later to meet your future needs. See "Shopping for a PC with Room to Grow" later in this chapter for details.

Hard Drive

The computer's hard drive is a disk inside the computer that stores data permanently; when you turn the computer off, the data remains on the disk. When comparing hard drives in different PCs, consider the following factors:

- **Storage capacity:** Size or storage capacity is measured in gigabytes. 250GB is usually more than enough. Photographers, videographers, serious gamers, and game designers require more space—at least 500GB.
- **Speed:** Speed is measured in revolutions per minute (RPMs) and is directly related to the rate at which the drive can read data from the disk. A speed of 5400 RPMs is standard and sufficient for most needs. High-end users should consider speeds of at least 7200 RPMs.

- **Interface:** The Serial ATA (SATA) interface is standard and sufficient for most needs. A SATA drive coupled with motherboard that supports it can transfer data at up to 300MB per second. Steer clear of the older ATA (also called IDE) interface. SCSI is another high-performance option.
- **Buffer:** A buffer is memory built into the drive to store data temporarily so the system doesn't need to wait for the relatively slow-spinning disk to read frequently accessed data and instructions. Most hard drives have an 8MB buffer, which is sufficient for most needs; 16MB or more is better.

❒ **Optical Drive for CDs and DVDs**

Optical drive is another name for CD or DVD drive. When comparing optical drives, consider the following features:

- **Multi-format:** Most optical drives are multi-format, meaning you can use them to store computer data and play or record CDs or DVDs. Opt for a multi-format DVD+RW—a single drive that can handle all of these tasks.
- **Speed:** Speed is expressed as X (times), which describes how fast the drive can write data to the disc. 8X is standard, but I recommend 16X or faster. Recording with an 8X drive is pretty slow, even if you don't burn discs all that often.
- **Interface:** You have the same choices here as you do with hard drives: ATA (IDE) or SATA. Again, I recommend going with a SATA interface, but in the case of optical drives, ATA (IDE) is sufficient and very common.
- **Slot or tray load:** With a slot-load drive, you insert the disc like a quarter in a pop machine, which is cool, easy, and efficient. Traditional drives require you to eject a tray, place a disc on it, and then load the tray.
- **Dual-layer support:** Some optical drives can read from and write to both sides of a dual-layer disc, essentially doubling its storage capacity. If you plan to back up files, dual-layer DVD+RW are great; otherwise, this feature isn't all that important.
- **Laser disc labelling:** Many optical drives (often referred to as LightScribe burners) can print labels on discs designed to have labels printed on them, which is pretty cool but not all that important.
- **Blu-ray support:** Planning to watch high-definition movies on your computer? Then consider a Blu-ray drive. In addition to being able to play Blu-ray video, these drives can store up to 50GB on a single disc. If you're planning to copy a lot of CDs or DVDs, having two drives makes the job much easier.

❒ **Video Adapter**

A video adapter processes the data required to display images on a monitor. Many computers include integrated video (part of the motherboard) supporting one or more of the following standards:

- **Digital Visual Interface (DVI):** DVI enables you to play high-definition video.
- **High-Definition Media Interface (HDMI):** Like DVI, HDMI is designed for high-definition video. The only difference is that HDMI carries both video and sound, whereas DVI carries only video. Computers typically support one or the other.

- **Blu-ray support:** Blu-ray discs are copy-protected by AACS technology, so if you're planning to watch high-definition video, make sure the PC supports High-Bandwidth Digital Content Protection (HDCP) decoding. Most important is that the PC you buy have the right port (DVI or HDMI) for the monitor you choose. You may encounter some older PCs and monitors that support the VGA standard, but this is obsolete. Top-line PCs have a separate video card (or two). If you're a hardcore video game player, look for a PC that has a separate video card.
- **Video Standard:** PCIe (Peripheral Component Interconnect Express) is a big step up in speed and performance from the older Accelerated Graphics Port (AGP) standard.
- **Memory:** Graphics cards have their own memory to improve display quality and performance. 256MB is standard; 1GB is better for serious game players, photographers, or videographers.
- **Dual display support:** Look for a PC that allows you to connect two monitors so you have the option of a dual-display configuration. This allows you to expand your desktop, so that you can, for example, have your e-mail displayed in one window while you're working on a document in the other.
- **Multiple display support:** Hardcore game players often opt for systems with multiple video cards (as many as four) linked together for optimum display quality and performance. If this is what you have in mind, look for systems that support the nVidia Scalable Link Interface (SLI) or ATI Crossfire technology.
- **DirectX 10:** Newer graphics cards support DirectX 10 (DX10), Microsoft's multimedia technology for displaying realistic images with complex lighting and shading effects.
- **DVI or HDMI support with HDPC decoding:** DVI or HDMI is essential for playing Blu-ray DVDs and taking advantage of advanced graphics and animation in video games.

❒ **Monitor**

A monitor displays everything so you can see what you're doing. Make sure the monitor you're getting is large enough for your needs and clear enough for your eyes. The following list describes the most important characteristics to consider:

- **Size:** Size is the most important consideration. Don't settle for anything smaller than 15 inches, unless you're shopping for a netbook PC. A 19- or 21-inch monitor is usually sufficient for working and for watching TV or DVDs, as long as you sit really close. You may also want to consider a widescreen monitor to work on two documents side by side.
- **Interface:** Newer monitors support DVI or HDMI, both of which send a digital signal directly to the monitor for better performance and quality.
- **Aspect ratio:** Aspect ratio is the ratio of width to height. For standard monitors, the aspect ratio is 4-to-3. Newer, wide-screen monitors have an aspect ratio of 16-

to-9, which is ideal for viewing documents side by side and watching HDTV and DVD movies in wide-screen format.

- **Maximum resolution:** Maximum resolution is a measure of the number of coloured dots (pixels) that comprise the screen. Generally, the more dots, the clearer the picture. Typical resolution for a 17- or 19-inch flat-panel LCD is 1280 1024 dpi (dots per inch). Comparable wide-screen models have a resolution of 1440 900 dpi. Unless you're in the market for a small portable PC, don't settle for anything less than 1280 960 dpi.
- **Contrast ratio:** The contrast ratio is the difference in brightness between white and black. Look for a contrast ratio of at least 500-to-1 for a clearer, crisper display.
- **Response time:** Response time, measured in milliseconds (ms), expresses the time it takes a pixel to change colours. For most purposes, a response time of 8ms is sufficient. Game players should look for response times of 5ms or less.
- **Ergonomics:** If you plan to sit in front of the computer for several hours a day, make sure you can adjust the monitor's height and angle for maximum comfort. Some monitors also swivel from side to side, which comes in handy if you need to show something to a colleague, client, or family member sitting beside you.
- **Gloss:** Some portable PCs come with glossy screens designed to produce a sharper display, but some users don't like the reflective nature of these screens.
- **Touch-screen:** Touch-screens, available for both desktop and portable PCs, are a standard option on tablet PCs. A touch-screen enables you to interact with your computer by pointing and tapping the screen with your finger, instead of or in addition to using a mouse. If you're in the market for a touch-screen, look for a multi-touch model or ask the dealer whether the PC supports Windows Touch.

Sound Card

Sound goes hand in hand with video. Standard models come with integrated audio, which often produces high-quality surround sound output—5.1, meaning five speakers plus a subwoofer. If you can't settle for less than bone-rattling, theater-quality sound or you're using your PC to record and mix audio, you'll need to step up to a midlevel or high-end dedicated sound card. When comparing sound cards, consider the following characteristics:

- **Surround sound:** Midlevel sound cards support 5.1 surround sound. High-end sound cards support 7.1 surround sound—seven speakers plus a subwoofer, to really immerse you in sound.
- **Interface:** Newer sound cards are built with a PCI interface for improved performance. Steer clear of older IDE versions.
- **ampling rate:** Sampling rate determines how fast the sound card pulls data from an analog (sound wave) signal to convert it into a digital signal. The higher the sampling rate, the clearer the digital recording.

- **Bit depth:** Bit depth is the amount of data recorded for each sample and directly corresponds to the resolution or richness of the sound. All you really need to know is that CD-quality audio is 16-bit, whereas higher-quality DVD audio is 24-bit.
- **Number of voices:** When reading specs, you're likely to encounter the numbers 32 and 64, as in AWE32 or AWE64. This has nothing to do with bit depth. It refers to the number of distinct "voices," or sounds, the card can play simultaneously.
- **Signal-to-noise ratio:** This is the ratio of the power of the signal to the power of undesirable background noise. The higher the ratio, measured in decibels (dB), the less noticeable the background noise. Look for this number to be 105dB or higher.
- **Blu-ray support:** Blu-ray discs are copy-protected by AACS technology, so if you're planning to watch high-definition video, make sure the computer is equipped with a sound card that has a decoder for Dolby Digital and DTS surround sound formats. Without the appropriate decoder, the soundtrack still plays, but not in theater quality.

Some sound cards are specifically designed for home theater, gaming, or recording and mixing music. If you have any of these high-end needs, be sure to ask the dealer about available sound card upgrades.

❒ **Ports and Jacks**

All PCs have ports and jacks into which you plug your peripheral devices, including a monitor, printer, mouse, keyboard, digital camera, webcam, phone line, networking cable, and scanner. Any PC you choose should have the following ports and jacks:

- **Universal Serial Bus (USB):** USB ports enable you to easily connect all sorts of external devices (over 100) to a single port, including external hard drives, CD and DVD drives, mouse, keyboard, webcam, and so on. Make sure the PC has at least two, and preferably four, USB 2.0 ports.
- **Graphics port:** A DVI or HDMI port that's suitable for the monitor you plan to use is essential.
- **Audio input (microphone):** Almost all PCs include a microphone jack, for voice communications over the Internet and speech recognition—you talk, it types.
- **Audio output:** Even if you purchase a portable PC with built-in speakers, make sure it includes an audio output and headphone jack so you can connect external speakers and headphones.
- **Modem (optional):** An internal dial-up modem enables you to connect to the Internet over a standard phone line. As broadband Internet (via cable, satellite, or Wi-Fi) becomes more popular and accessible, dial-up modems are becoming obsolete, but a dial-up modem is useful if broadband options are not available or as a backup if you lose your broadband connection. To take advantage of cutting-edge technologies, I also recommend that you purchase a PC with the following ports:
    - **eSATA:** An eSATA port is a nice addition if you're planning to use highspeed external storage devices, but USB 2.0 is plenty fast enough for most users' needs.

- **ExpressCard:** An ExpressCard slot is particularly beneficial on portable PCs because it enables you to easily add and remove devices, including a TV tuner, memory card reader (for cards like those used in digital cameras), wireless broadband Internet device, Wi-Fi, an eSATA port, and even extra RAM or a hard drive. Standard ExpressCards are 54mm wide and can accept 34mm cards. The 34mm slots are often used on smaller portable PCs, to save space and consume less battery power.

❒ **Networking, Wi-Fi, and Wireless Broadband**

Almost all computers include the following networking options, but make sure both are available:

- **Local area network (LAN) port:** Also called an Ethernet port, a LAN port enables you to connect the computer via cable to a network. The port looks like an oversized phone jack.
- **Wi-Fi:** Wi-Fi is for wireless networking either in your home or business or in Wi-Fi hotspots, including some hotels, coffee shops, airports, and Internet cafes and kiosks. Opt for the latest Wi-Fi standard (802.11n as I was writing this book), which is typically backward compatible with earlier standards, including 802.11b and 802.11g.

  Many portable PCs also come equipped with support for wireless broadband Internet, but you can add it later with a wireless broadband USB or ExpressCard modem.

❒ **Bluetooth Wireless Connectivity**

Bluetooth is a wireless technology that enables any two Bluetooth-enabled devices within range to communicate without cables. For example, you can connect a Bluetooth keyboard, mouse, webcam, and headset to the computer or exchange data between your cellphone and PC. I recommend purchasing a computer with Bluetooth support.

❒ **Webcam**

A webcam is a small (sometimes tiny) camera that can capture a photo or video of you as you sit in front of your computer. Many computers come with a built-in webcam, which I consider an essential component of any portable PC. If you purchase a desktop model, it may not include a webcam, but a quality webcam is inexpensive and very easy to add later. When comparing webcams, consider the following:

- **Resolution:** Resolution determines image size and quality. A resolution of 640 480 is sufficient for most uses; 960 720 is better, especially if you're going to be video recording yourself to share with others.
- **Autofocus:** An autofocus lens keeps you in focus as you move around.
- **Frame rate:** Frame rate is a measure of the number of frames in each second of video. For smooth video, look for a webcam that supports at least 30 frames per second (fps).
- **Low-light support:** Low-light conditions can negatively affect frame rates and quality, so make sure the webcam has built-in technology to correct for this.

- **Built-in microphone:** Webcam microphones are great for videoconferencing because they're directional and noise-cancelling.
- **Skype support:** Skype is a popular service that enables you to make free PC-to-PC "phone" calls, make affordable PC-to-phone calls, and videoconference using your PC. Make sure the webcam wears the Skype logo, for optimum quality and performance.
- **Connection:** For portable PCs, built-in is best. For desktop models, look for a Bluetooth or USB webcam.
- **Size:** Generally, the smaller the better. The camera need not be large to produce high-quality images.
- **Design and adjustments:** Some webcams are designed to sit on a desk; others clip onto the monitor. This is pretty much a personal preference, but if the webcam is not built in, make sure you can adjust it easily up and down and side to side.

❒ Keyboard

A keyboard enables you to type and enter commands. You don't have much choice here unless you purchase a keyboard separately. Two features I recommend are wireless (Bluetooth), so you have one less cable to deal with, and full size, so you don't have to type on a dinky keyboard.

❒ Mouse or Touchpad

A mouse or touchpad enables you to enter commands simply by pointing to what you want and clicking a button or tapping the touchpad. A mouse is a fairly standard piece of equipment, so you don't have much choice here. However, if the computer you choose supports Bluetooth, get a wireless mouse.

Almost all portable PCs have a built-in touchpad instead of a mouse, although you can disable the touchpad and connect a mouse. A touchpad translates finger motion into pointer position on the screen. Unfortunately, I can't provide any guidelines here. Try before you buy, if possible, and read reviews to see if any users have had trouble using a particular PC's touchpad.

❒ Additional Portable PC Considerations

Portable PCs are a different species entirely. As you shop, keep the following factors in mind:

- **Battery life:** How long do you need the PC to operate on battery power alone? Some portable PCs are designed to run for eight hours or more on a single charge.
- **Weight:** Some portable PCs are lighter than others. How heavy of a PC are you willing to lug around—3 pounds, 5 pounds, 7 pounds? Expect to pay a premium or surrender features and functionality for the lightest of the bunch.

❒ Printer

Printers are usually sold separately. Following are key considerations:

- **Laser or inkjet**: Laser printers are typically faster, pricier, and a better choice for business use. Inkjet printers tend to be slower, more affordable, and more versatile, making them better for home use. If you're planning to print photos, opt for an inkjet.

- **Printer only or multi-function**: Choose a multi-function printer that can print, copy, fax, and scan documents and images. You may not think you need all these functions now, but you'll miss them later if you choose a printer that doesn't have them.
- **Print quality:** Print quality is typically measured in dots per inch (dpi). 600dpi is sufficient for most users, but if you think you'll need higher-quality output, choose a printer with a resolution of 1200dpi or higher. These can print in lower resolutions, to conserve ink or toner.
- **Speed:** Print speed is measured in pages per minute (ppm). If you're buying the printer to share among multiple network users, you may need something that's superfast (more than 20ppm). For home use, 10ppm is usually fast enough.
- **Connection:** Printers can connect to PCs in a variety of ways. Most connect via a USB port, but some connect wirelessly via Bluetooth or via Wi-Fi access points with built-in print servers. If you plan to share the PC on a network, Wi-Fi is best, but you can still share a USB printer by connecting it to a wireless router.
- **Consumables:** Paper and ink can get very expensive. Consider paying extra for a printer designed to use less ink. Also check the prices and capacity of the replacement ink or toner cartridges the printer uses.
- **Memory card slots:** Many newer printers have memory card slots on the front that provide a convenient way to transfer photos from a digital camera to your printer. Some printers also include a USB port for transferring images directly from the camera.

Shopping for a PC with Room to Grow

Most computers are not all they can be. They're fine for now, but as technology and your individual needs change, they may not keep up. Fortunately, you can upgrade most computers by installing a bigger hard drive or a second hard drive, adding RAM, or installing a faster and more powerful video card. If you're shopping for a desktop model, check for the following:

- **Two open drive bays:** These enable you to add a hard disk, DVD, or backup drive to your computer later.
- **Two or three open PCI expansion slots:** If you want to plug in extras later (a sound card, external drive, scanner, or TV tuner card), you'll need some open expansion slots.
- **Two to four USB 2.0 ports:** You can string together over 100 devices on one USB port, making upgrades a snap.
- **Expandable memory:** Make sure you can add memory modules without removing the existing modules. If the computer has a 1GB RAM module in each of its two RAM slots, you'll have to remove one of the modules to add more memory. It's

better if one slot has a 2GB RAM module and the other is open. Portable PCs are more difficult and expensive to upgrade, so you're better off buying a portable PC that has more than what you need right now. You can forget about expansion slots, because portable PCs don't have any, but USB ports and an Express Card slot provide you with many upgrade options.

Warranty and Technical Support

Almost all computers come with a limited warranty, and many include limited tech support for a set amount of time. For the rank beginner, I recommend paying extra for an extended warranty, preferably with onsite service, so you don't have to take the computer "into the shop" or ship it to the dealer. I also recommend paying extra for technical support so that you have someone on call if anything goes wrong. While you're at it, check the dealer's return policy.

Going Shopping

Shopping for a computer is a process of narrowing your choices down to one computer. The following sections lead you through the process many follow when shopping for a new computer.

Finding a Manufacturer and Line of PCs You Like

After deciding on a type of computer (desktop, notebook, tablet, or netbook), narrow your selection by manufacturer. Visit a few of these manufacturers' websites to check out the products they offer. Also visit your local electronics or office supply store so that you can see and touch a few makes and models.

Exploring Different Models and Packages

Within every product line, PC manufacturers offer several models and packages that typically range from low-budget, bare-bones versions to top-of-the-line models that are the most powerful, the fastest, and the most feature packed.

Check out the different models and packages to see what the pricier models have that the lower-cost models are missing. Pricier models typically have a faster CPU, more RAM, a larger and faster hard drive, a better video card, and sometimes a larger monitor or more and/or better software, but you may not need all those extras. Look for a model/package that meets your needs with room to grow.

When shopping online, you typically choose a model and then have the option to customize it; for example, you may want additional memory, a larger monitor, more hard drive space, and a better sound system.

Researching Your Options

After narrowing your selection to a few candidates, research each of them on the web. If you don't have a computer with Internet access, borrow one. A manufacturer can claim anything it wants about a product, but only a product's reviews and ratings provide an unbiased view, and the best place to find these ratings and reviews is the web. Visit Google at www.google.com and search for the make and model followed by the phrase "rating review" (without the quotation marks).

You may also find valuable ratings and reviews at the following websites:

Manufacturer's website: Websites of any stores that sell the specific make and model

- CNET, at reviews.cnet.com
- *PC Magazine*, at www.pcmag.com (click **Reviews** in the menu)
- *PC World*, at www.pcworld.com/reviews.html
- Computer Shopper, at computershopper.com

Shopping for the Best Price

Fortunately for you, competition in the PC market keeps profit margins slim, but it's still a good idea to shop around for the best price. Following are some tips:

- Check with your school, the company you work for, and any organizations you belong to, to determine whether they receive any special deals on PCs or have a PC purchase program in place to help cover the cost.
- Shop online. Head to Google at www.google.com and search for the make and model. You'll find plenty of dealers online, along with comparison shopping sites that can help you track down the best price. If you don't have a computer connected to the Internet, borrow one.
- Shop offline. Visit local electronics and office supply stores and Target to see whether they're offering any special deals. It's not likely, but you may find a better deal offline than online.

Points to Remember

- ☆ **Minimum requirements netbook PC**: 1GHz CPU; 1GB RAM with room for one additional GB; 80GB hard drive; 10-inch display; full-size keyboard; built-in microphone, speakers, and 480 640 webcam; two USB 2.0 ports; 802.11 b/g wireless card; Bluetooth support; Windows 7 Starter.
- ☆ **Minimum requirements basic PC**: 1.6GHz CPU, 1–2GB RAM with room for more,120MB hard drive, 8X DVD+RW drive, integrated audio and video, 802.11 b/g wireless networking, 15- or 17-inch flat-panel monitor, two USB 2.0 ports, Windows 7 32-bit Home Premium.
- ☆ **Minimum requirements intermediate PC**: Dual-core CPU a step or two down from the highest speed available, at least 2GB RAM with room for more, 250GB hard drive, 16X DVD+RW drive, 5.1 surround sound audio, 802.11 b/g wireless networking, 17- or 19-inch flat-panel monitor, four USB 2.0 ports, Bluetooth support, Windows 7 32-bit Professional or Ultimate.
- ☆ **Minimum requirements advanced PC**: Quad-core CPU, 4GB RAM with room for more, 500GB hard drive, 16X Double-Layer DVD+RW drive, high-definition audio card, 512MB or more PCI video card with DVI or HDMI support, 802.11 b/g/n wireless networking, 20-inch flat-panel monitor or larger, four USB 2.0 ports, two FireWire ports, Bluetooth support, Windows 7 64-bit Professional or Ultimate.

Unpacking Your Equipment

You don't need detailed instructions to know how to open boxes, but be careful and be aware of the following precautions:

- ❒ Take your time.
- ❒ Clear all drinks from your work area.
- ❒ Unpack on the floor, to avoid dropping anything.
- ❒ Don't cut open the boxes. You can easily scratch something inside or hack
- ❒ through a cable.
- ❒ For any large part, such as a system unit or monitor, check the box for guidance on how to unpack it. The box usually includes some indication of which side is up and whether to lift the part out of the box or slide it out from the side.
- ❒ Save all the packing material. Many manufacturers accept returns only in the original packing. The packing material is also useful if you ever need to move.
- ❒ Read the packing list(s) thoroughly to be sure you received everything you ordered. If something is missing, contact the manufacturer or dealer *immediately*.
- ❒ Inspect the cables for cuts and check for bent pins on the connectors. If you find a bent or damaged pin, call the manufacturer instead of trying to fix it yourself, which could void the warranty. (You'll find out more about connectors and pins later in this chapter.)
- ❒ Let the computer sit for two or three hours to adjust to the room temperature and humidity.
- ❒ Don't turn on *anything* until *everything* is connected. On some PCs, you can safely plug in devices when the power is on, but check the manual to be sure.
- ❒ Remove any spacers or packing materials from the disk drives and printer. These materials are commonly used to keep parts from shifting during shipping.
- ❒ Complete and submit any registration or warranty forms. This can save your money down the road.

Finding a Comfortable Home for Your PC Connecting Everything

Choose a place for your PC that's convenient and comfortable. To keep your PC healthy, make sure the location meets the following criteria:

- ❒ A cool, dry, well-ventilated area away from direct sunlight.
- ❒ As free of dust, smoke, and pet hair as possible.
- ❒ Near a properly grounded outlet that's not on the same circuit as an appliance that draws a lot of electricity, such as an air conditioner. You can buy an inexpensive three-prong outlet tester at your local hardware store to determine whether outlets are properly grounded.
- ❒ Near a phone jack or cable-Internet outlet, depending on how you plan to connect to the Internet.
- ❒ On a sturdy surface.

Setting Up, Starting Your PC

If you purchased a desktop PC, you may have several components you need to connect to the system unit—the box that contains the CPU and other central components.

Before you start connecting anything, set all the parts where you want them to be. (Moving the parts around after you connect them tends to tangle the cables.) Fortunately, many PCs come with illustrated instructions on how to connect the various components and/or use colour-coded plugs and ports.

Turning It On

Turning on a laptop or an all-in-one desktop model is a snap. All you do is press and release the power button, and your PC comes to life. Starting a standard desktop PC is a little more involved because you have more than one component to power up.

Here's standard operating procedure for starting a desktop PC:

- Press and release the power button on your monitor.
- If your PC is connected to a cable modem for Internet service, turn it on and wait for the indicator lights to show that a connection with the Internet service provider (ISP) is established.
- If your PC is connected to a router, turn on the router.
- Turn on any other devices connected to your PC that you plan to use this session, such as a printer or scanner.
- Turn on your speaker system. If it has an audio control, turn it to about quarter volume so you don't burst your eardrums when the PC comes to life.
- Press and release the power button on the system unit. At this point, the monitor may display some startup messages as it reads its startup instructions and performs its preflight checks.

Dealing with the First-Time Startup Ritual (Booting a Computer)

When you start your PC for the first time, it leads you through several preliminary tasks. Just follow the onscreen clues and instructions. The usual routine includes the following:

- **Activate and register Windows**. Assuming that your PC is connected to the Internet, Windows contacts Microsoft's website and leads you through the process of activating and registering Windows. Activation is required. Registration is optional.
- **Adjust your regional settings.** Windows asks you a series of questions so it can properly set the date and time.
- **Install or configure new hardware.** If you connected any peripheral devices to your PC, Windows identifies the devices and installs the drivers required to use those devices. You may be asked to insert a disc that came with the device.

- **Install Windows updates.** Microsoft is constantly improving Windows. If your PC is connected to the Internet, Windows may download and install the latest updates to make it more reliable and secure. This may take a long time depending on the number of updates and the speed of your Internet connection.

Turning It Off, Shutting It Down

When you're done using your PC, you may want to shut it down to reduce wear and tear and conserve electricity. Although you can shut down most components, including the printer and monitor, by pressing and releasing or holding down the power button for a second or two, you should never do this with the system unit. Instead, let Windows power it down for you:

- ❒ Click the Start button, in the lower-left corner of the screen, as shown in figure below

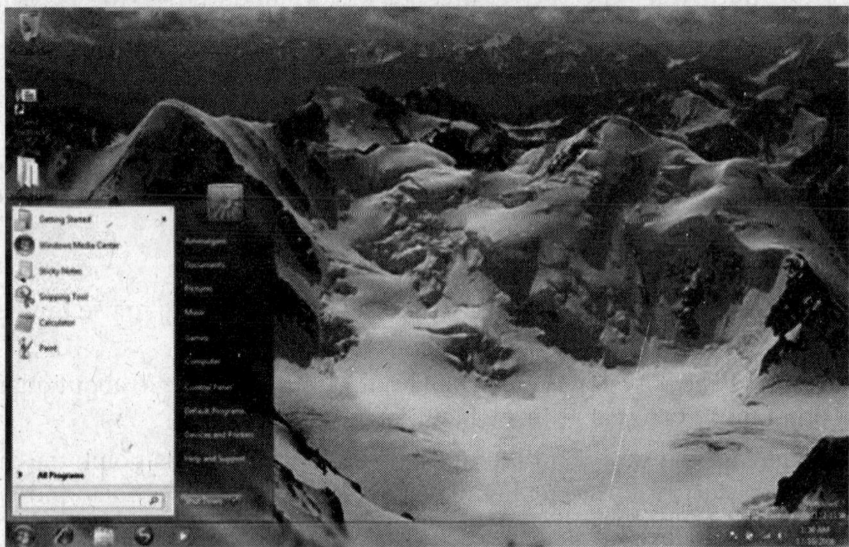

- ❒ Click **Shut down**. Windows logs you off and powers down your PC.
- ❒ Turn off everything else.

Windows features several other options for logging off your PC or shutting it down. To access these options, click the arrow to the right of the Shut down button:

- ❒ **Log off**: If Windows is set up for more than one user you can log off the current user so that another user can log on. Logging off clears everything from your desktop and displays the Windows log-on screen so that you or another user can log on. (It's a good idea to save whatever you're currently working on before logging off so that you don't lose some or all of your work.)
- ❒ **Switch user**: Switch user allows a different user to log on while keeping the current user's applications running. The current user can then log on later and pick up where he or she left off.
- ❒ **Sleep**: Click Sleep, press and release the power button on your PC, or close the lid of a portable PC, and Windows puts the PC to sleep—a power-saving mode similar to

pressing pause on a DVD player. You can wake up your PC by pressing and releasing your PC's power button.

- **Hibernate:** Hibernate saves what you're doing to the hard disk and then turns off the PC. When you turn it back on, Windows restores what you were doing so that you can resume. Hibernation uses the least amount of power of all the power-saving modes.
- **Restart:** Restart exits and starts Windows. You may need to restart your PC after you install a new program or device, change a Windows setting, or fix a problem.
- **Lock:** Lock returns you to the log-on screen. If you password-protect your PC, you can lock it whenever you step away from it, to prevent other people from using it. Windows automatically powers down newer PCs after a certain period of inactivity, to conserve power. You can adjust the power-saving settings to suit your preferences.

Points to Remember

- ☆ Be careful unpacking your PC and peripheral devices.
- ☆ Put all your equipment in place before connecting anything.
- ☆ To figure out where to plug in all the cables, check the manual or setup instructions that came with your PC and match the shape and configuration of the connectors with the ports.
- ☆ When starting your PC, turn on all the peripheral devices before turning on power to the system unit.
- ☆ To turn off your PC, click the Windows **Start** button, click **Shut down**, and then turn off anything that's connected to the system unit, including the monitor.

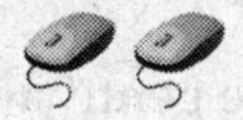

Mastering I/O Devices

Taking Control with Input Devices

A mouse is a two-button device (sometimes with a wheel between the two buttons or other variations with more buttons) that allows you to point and click commands and options, and drag and drop items on the screen. To use a mouse effectively, master the following basic mouse moves:

Wired Mouse

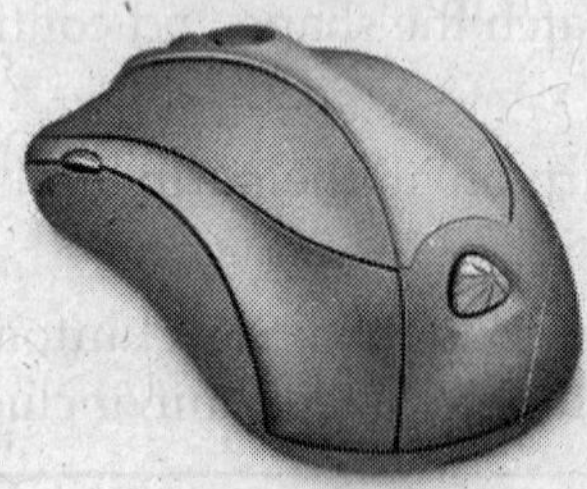

Wireless Mouse

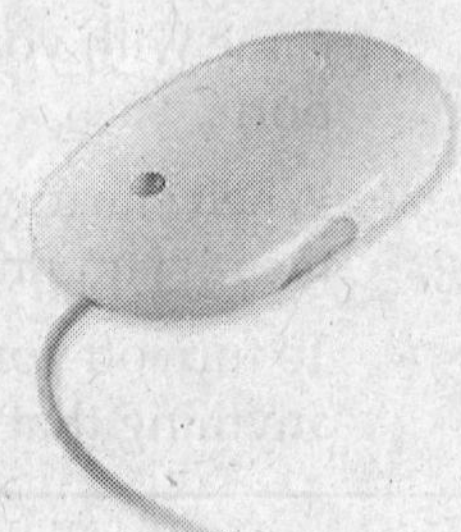

Mouse used with Mac

Mastering Basic Mouse Moves

- **Moving the mouse**: Hold the mouse gently with your index finger on the main mouse button (left for righties and right for lefties). Slide the mouse over a clean, smooth surface slowly in the direction you want the onscreen pointer to move. If you run out of room, lift the mouse, move it in the direction opposite of where you need to go, and then set it down and continue sliding the mouse in the direction you want the mouse pointer to go.
- **Point**: Move the tip of the mouse pointer over an object or command. The mouse pointer may change appearance when it's over an object. If it's over an object you can click, the pointer may appear as a pointing hand. If it's over text, it appears as an I-beam, which indicates where the insertion point will be moved if you click the left mouse button.
- **Rest (Hover):** Rest the tip of the mouse pointer over a menu item to open a submenu or over an object to view information about it.
- **Click:** Press and release the left mouse button, typically to select an object or command.
- **Double-click**: Press and release the left mouse button twice in quick succession, typically

to execute a command or run a program.

- **Right-click**: Press and release the right mouse button once, typically to open a context-sensitive menu—a menu that contains commands exclusively for this particular object.
- **Drag:** Hold down the left mouse button while moving the mouse. You may drag to move something, draw something, select text, or change the size or shape of an object.
- **Drag and drop**: Click the left mouse button on an object to select it and keep it down while dragging an object from one location to another, and then release the button to drop it in place. If your mouse has a wheel between the two buttons, you can use the wheel to perform some additional maneuvers.
- **Scroll:** Rotate the wheel forward to scroll down or backward to scroll up.
- **Pan**: Click and hold the wheel while moving the mouse forward or back. (Panning is sort of like scrolling, but smoother.)
- **Autoscroll:** Click the wheel and then move the mouse forward or back. This is sort of like panning, except that you don't have to hold down the wheel. When you're done autoscrolling, click the wheel again to disable it.
- **Zoom in or out**: Hold down the Ctrl key while rotating the wheel forward to zoom in or backward to zoom out.

Pecking Away at the Keyboard

Computer keyboards are populated with more than just the standard letter and number keys required for typing:

- **Function keys:** The 10 or 12 "F" keys at the top of the keyboard (F1, F2, F3, and so on) enable you to quickly enter common commands without moving your hands from the keyboard.
- **Arrow keys:** The arrow keys—Page Up, Page Down, Home, and End— move the cursor or insertion point in a document to wherever you want to type or enter a correction.
- **Numeric keypad:** The numeric keypad contains a group of number key positioned like the keys on an adding machine. With Num Lock off, they function as arrow keys.
- **Ctrl and Alt:** The Ctrl (Control) and Alt (Alternate) keys make the other keys on the keyboard act differently from the way they normally act. For example, you can press Ctrl+C (hold down the Ctrl key while pressing C) to copy a selection.
- **Esc:** The Esc (Escape) key in most programs backs you out of or quits whatever you're currently doing.
- **PrtSc:** PrtSc (Print Screen) sends the screen image to the Windows Clipboard so that you can paste it into a document.

Navigating with a Touchpad

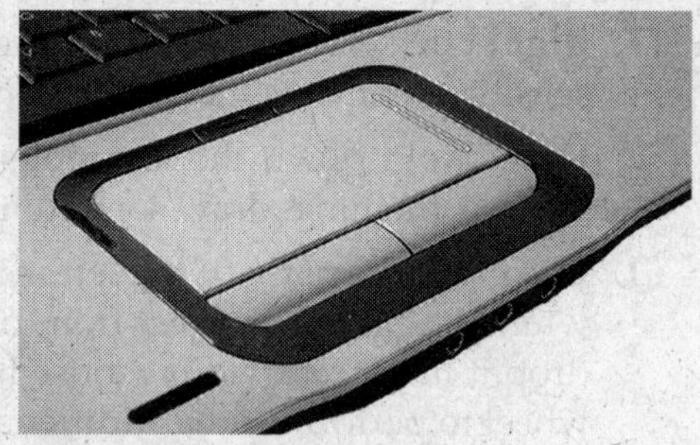

The purpose of a touchpad, a standard feature on mobile PCs, is the same as that of a mouse, but instead of moving the mouse to move the onscreen pointer, you slide your finger across the touchpad. The touchpad has left and right buttons that correspond to the left and right mouse buttons. However, most touch pads also let you use the touchpad itself to click, double-click, and drag:

- **Click:** Tap the touchpad once to select an object.
- **Double-click:** Tap the touchpad twice in quick succession to execute a command or run a program.
- **Drag:** Tap the touchpad twice, as if you're double-clicking, but keep your finger on the touchpad the second time down and slide your finger across the touchpad. (This move can be tough to execute.)
- **Scroll Lock:** Scroll Lock (ScrLk) is a rarely used key left over from older PCs. It locks scrolling up or down.
- **Volume controls:** Many newer keyboards feature controls to adjust speaker and microphone volume and other common computer settings.
- **Programmable buttons:** Most keyboards include special programmable buttons that enable you to quickly open your Internet home page, navigate the Internet, check e-mail, and put your computer in sleep mode. If you don't use one of the buttons for its designated function, you can reprogram it to perform some other frequent task.

Settings – Keyboard and Mouse

Browse settings for Keyboard & Mouse

Pressing Key+Key Combinations

Many keys can perform additional tasks when used in tandem with other keys. For example, you can press Alt+F4 to close the currently active window. To execute a key combination, hold down the first key(s) while pressing and releasing the last key, and then release the first key.

Cutting Corners with the Windows Key

Press

- Windows - Open the Start menu
- Windows+Tab - Cycle through running programs in the taskbar
- Windows+F - Find a file
- Ctrl+Windows+F - Find a computer on a network

- Windows+F1 - Display the Windows Help window
- Windows+R - Display the Run dialog box (for running programs)
- Windows+Pause/Break- Display the System Properties dialog box
- Windows+E - Run Windows Explorer for managing folders and files
- Windows+D or Windows+M - Minimize or restore all program windows
- Shift+Windows+M - Undo minimize all program windows

Using Dual-Function Keys on Portable PCs

Portable computers, especially netbooks, may lack the space for a full set of keys plus buttons to turn on the computer, adjust the display, and move the mouse pointer. To fit all the keys and buttons into this limited space, many keys are assigned double duty. For example, a key may be used with another key to adjust the speaker volume. In most cases, the keyboard includes a key labelled Fn, Keys that perform double-duty have their primary functions displayed in black or white, and their secondary functions displayed in the colour that matches the Fn key (typically blue). To take advantage of the secondary function of the key, hold down the Fn key while pressing the key labelled with the desired function; for example, on my netbook PC, Fn+Up Arrow cranks up the volume.

Keyboard

Getting in Touch with Your Touch-Screen

Thanks to the iPhone, touch-screens have become the latest fad in the world of personal computers. With a touch-screen and Windows 7, you can now navigate your computer, its resources, and just about everything the Internet has to offer by touching, tapping, and flicking the screen:

- **Tap:** Tapping an object is like clicking it.
- **Grab:** Press your finger against an object, slide your finger to drag the object, and then release to drop it in place.
- **Scroll:** Scroll a document up or down by sliding your finger up or down over the contents of the document. Scroll left or right using two fingers.
- **Flick**: Slide your finger quickly left or right over a page to "flip" to the next or previous page as you would do in a book or newspaper.
- **Select text**: Select text in a document by dragging your finger over the text from lower right to upper left or vice versa. You can then grab the text and drag it wherever you like.
- **Right-click**: To right-click an object, hold one finger against it and tap the screen with a second finger. You can also press and hold the object until a circle appears around your finger and then release.

Screenshot of desktop

- **Zoom in or out**: Press one finger against the upper-left corner of the area, press a second finger against the lower-right corner, and then slide your fingers apart to zoom in or closer together to zoom out.
- **Two-finger tap**: Tap with two fingers, one on either side of the object you want to work with, to expand that section of the screen.

Customizing Your Mouse, Touchpad, and Keyboard

Windows gives you some control over the way your mouse, keyboard, and touchpad behave. The following sections show you how to access these settings.

Adjusting Your Mouse Settings

If you're a lefty or you have trouble clicking fast enough to execute a double-click, you can customize your mouse to accommodate the way you work. Click the **Start** button (in the lower-left corner of the screen) and then click **Control Panel**, **Hardware and Sound**, **Mouse** (under Devices and Printers). This opens the Mouse Properties dialog box. If your PC has a touchpad, Your Mouse Properties dialog box may look a little different

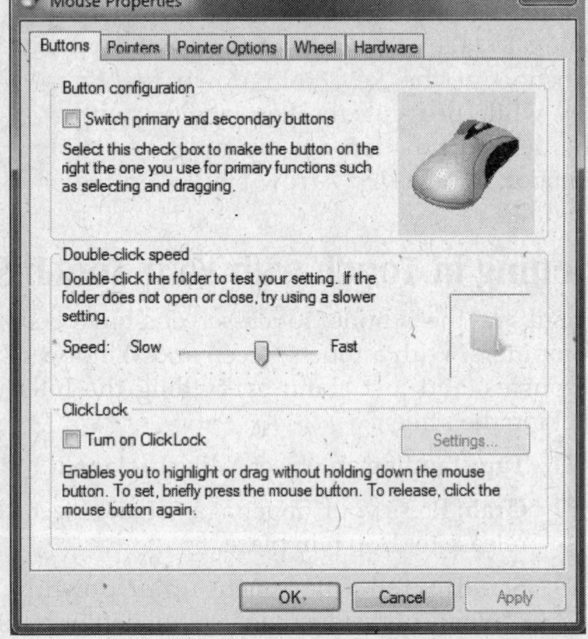

Adjusting Mouse Settings

Adjusting Your Keyboard Settings

If you hold down a key on your keyboard, Windows automatically "types" the character repeatedly. You can adjust the key repeat delay (how long you have to hold down the key before it starts to repeat), the repeat speed (how fast the characters are repeated), and the cursor blink rate (how fast the insertion point blinks):

- Click Start, Control Panel.
- Click the View by Category option (upper right) and click Large Icons.
- Click Keyboard.
- Enter your preferences and click OK.

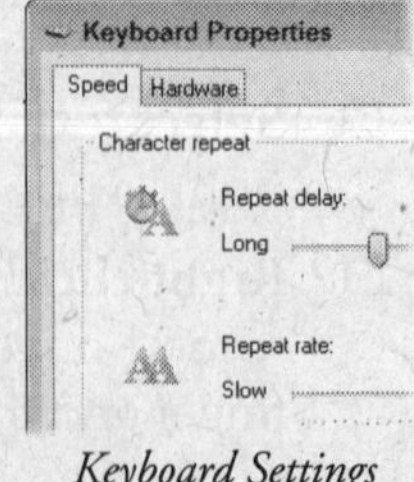

Keyboard Settings

Enabling Windows Accessibility Features

If you have a physical, vision, or hearing impairment that makes your mouse, keyboard, or monitor difficult to use, click Start, Control Panel, Ease of Access, Ease of Access Centre. Click the following options to enable one or more of the ease of access features.

- Start Magnifier zooms in on an area of the screen. After starting Magnifier, open its Views menu and choose the desired option: Full screen magnifies the entire screen, pushing some of the contents off-screen; move the mouse pointer to the edge of the screen to scroll off-screen content into view. Lens displays a rectangle that magnifies the area of the screen the mouse is over. Docked allocates the top of the screen to display the magnified area.
- Start Narrator activates a narrator who describes what's displayed onscreen and any actions you perform using the keyboard so that you can hear what you're doing. After clicking Start Narrator, enter your preferences and then click the minimize button to shrink the window. You can exit Narrator at any time by clicking its icon in the taskbar and clicking Exit.
- Start On-Screen Keyboard displays a picture of a keyboard so that you can type by clicking keys with your mouse, touchpad, or other pointing device.
- Set Up High Contrast allows you to turn on a high-contrast display to ease eyestrain and improve readability. To turn high contrast on or off, press Left Shift+Left Alt+Print Screen.

Below these four main options is a section called "Explore all settings," with additional options for making your PC easier to use. Each of these options enables you to activate and configure several accessibility options to achieve the desired goal. For example, if you click **Make the computer easier to see**, you can enable high contrast, Magnifier, and Narrator; turn off unnecessary animations; and hide background images.

Barking Out Commands with Speech

Recognition

With a good microphone (preferably a headset microphone) and Windows Speech Recognition, you can literally tell your computer what to do. To enable Speech Recognition, click **Start**, **Control Panel**, **Ease of Access**, **Speech Recognition**. The first time you run Speech Recognition, Windows leads you through a process of setting up your microphone and tuning the feature to recognize your voice. Simply follow the onscreen instructions.

After setting up Speech Recognition, Windows enables you to take an onscreen tutorial on how to use it and provides a list of commands the feature is set up to recognize, such as Start Listening (turn on Speech Recognition), Start Notepad, Scroll Up, Scroll Down, and Stop Listening (turn off Speech Recognition).

Points to Remember

- ☆ Click an object to select it; double-click to open or run it.
- ☆ Key+Key means you press and hold the first key while pressing and releasing the second key.
- ☆ To adjust the mouse settings, click **Start, Control Panel, Hardware and Sound, Mouse;** enter your preferences; and click **OK**.
- ☆ To enable any of Windows' accessibility features, click **Start, Control Panel, Ease of Access, Ease of Access Centre**.
- ☆ To enable Speech Recognition, click **Start, Control Panel, Ease of Access, Speech Recognition.**

SECTION–II
MANAGING YOUR
COMPUTER

Windows, GUI & Operating System

To accomplish anything with your PC, you need to master some essential Windows maneuvers, including running programs, selecting menu commands, and switching between open windows. This chapter takes you on a tour of Windows, reveals its most important features, and shows you how to communicate with your computer through Windows.

Getting Around in Windows 7

After you start your PC and log on, Windows appears. The opening screen consists of four main components—the Windows desktop, Start button, taskbar, and notification area.

Note....

The appearance and functionality of your Windows desktop depend on whether your computer supports the Aero desktop experience. If it does, any windows on the desktop feature a translucent glass design so that you can see what's behind each open window.

Exploring the Windows Desktop, Start Menu, and Taskbar

The Windows desktop is your designated area for work and play. Whenever you run a program, it appears in a separate window on your desktop. Like the actual top of a desk, the Windows desktop can become very cluttered with all sorts of stuff:

- Desktop icons to run programs you frequently use; gadgets to tell you what time it is and report the weather; files, folders, and programs; and even desktop accessories—Notepad, Calculator, and so on. (Initially, the desktop contains only one item—the Recycle Bin icon. Whenever you delete anything, Windows places it in the Recycle Bin so you can restore something if you accidentally delete it.

Start Button

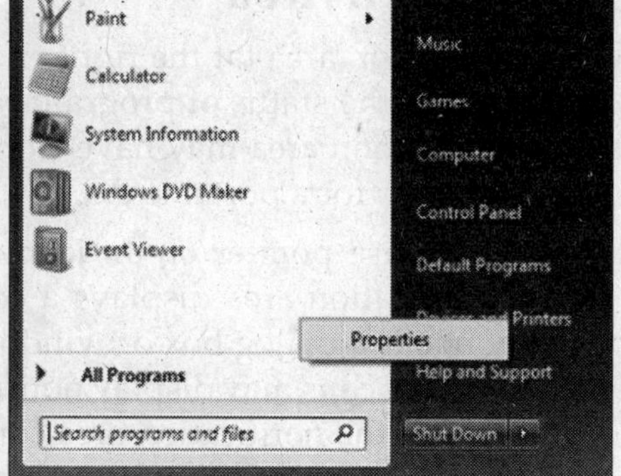

Whenever you need to start doing anything, click the Start button to open the Start menu. The Start menu is divided into three sections: Search box (just above the Start button); left pane for running programs; and right pane for accessing folders, the Control Panel, Windows Help, and Shut down options.

From the Start menu, you can perform any of the following common activities:

- **Start a program:** Click the **Start** button and click the program you want to run. If you don't see the program, rest the mouse pointer on **All Programs** to view more programs and program folders. (Windows adds frequently used programs to the Start menu's left pane so you don't need to open All Programs to find them.)

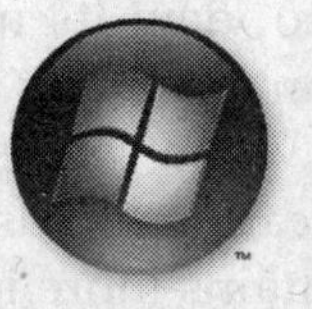

- **Search for files, folders, and programs:** Just above the Start button is a search box. Simply type a word or two describing what you're looking for and press **Enter** to have Windows help you find it.
- **Open frequently used folders:** The right side of the Start menu contains a list of frequently used folders, including your personal folder (at the top), Documents, Pictures, Music, Games, and Computer (providing access to all the disks on your computer).
- **Access the Control Panel:** The Windows Control Panel gives you access to all of your computer's settings and enables you to install and remove programs.
- **Get help with Windows:** On the right side of the Start menu, near the bottom, is an option to access the Windows Help system called Help and Support.
- **Shut down or log off:** In the lower-right corner of the Start menu is the Shut down button, for turning off your PC. You can click the arrow to the right of the Shut down button to access additional options. If you click **Start**, **All Programs** and then click a folder, a Back button replaces All Programs. You can click the **Back** button to return to the previous list of Start menu.

Taskbars

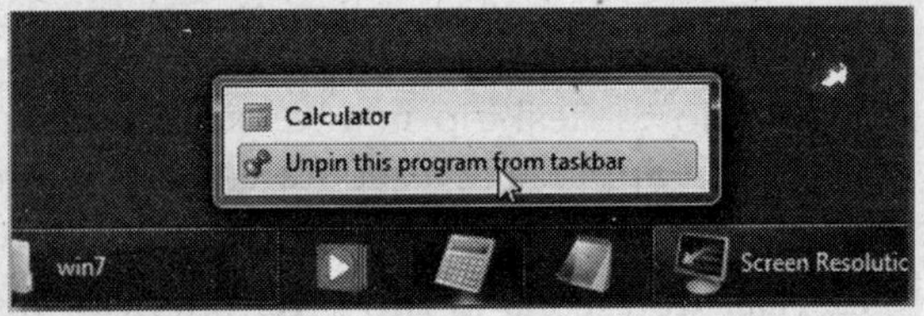

Taskbar

The taskbar is the horizontal bar at the bottom of the screen. It contains the Start button (on the left), Quick Launch buttons (to the right of the Start button), and notification area (on the right). (See Figure) Unlike the desktop, which can be hidden by open windows, the taskbar always remains in front. Whenever you run a program or open a file, a button for it appears in the taskbar. The button for the currently active program is darker than buttons for inactive windows, which appear faded. You can quickly access an open program or file by clicking its button. If you rest the mouse pointer on a button, a thumbnail image of the window appears above the button to remind you what's going on in that window. (Thumbnails appear only if your computer supports Aero desktop features. If your computer does not support Aero, you'll see a tooltip with a brief description of the item.) You can add toolbars and buttons to the taskbar to place frequently used programs and other items within easy reach.

Notification Area

The notification area (at the right end of the taskbar) includes the time, the date, and icons that indicate the status of programs and services running in the background. For example, your notification area may have icons for an antivirus program, your network connection, battery power for a portable PC, or USB devices connected to your PC.

Rest the mouse pointer on an icon to view its name or status. Right-clicking most icons in the notification area displays a context menu with additional options. Double-clicking usually opens a dialog box or window you can use to enter preferences for the program or device. Some icons may display notifications occasionally to call your attention to something important. If the notification area contains more icons than can fit in its limited space, click the arrow pointing up (the **Show hidden icons** button to the left of the navigation area) to access the additional icons.

Managing Windows on Your Desktop

Each time you run a program or open a file in Windows, a new window appears on your desktop. After several hours of work, your desktop can become very cluttered, making it difficult to find what you need. Fortunately, Windows provides several methods to control open windows, as described in the following sections.

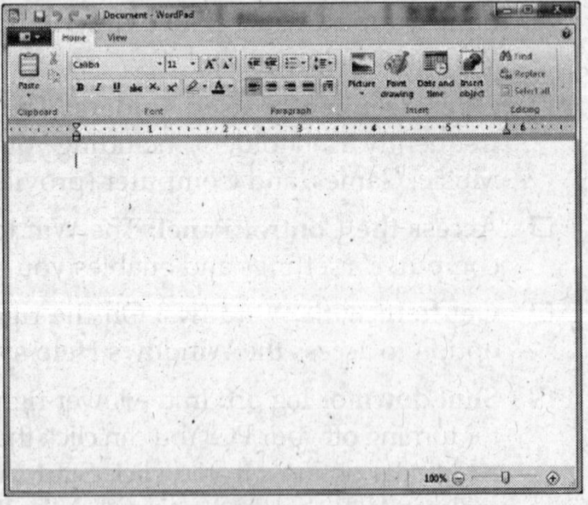

Resizing windows

Resizing a Window

Windows provides several methods for resizing Windows:

- ❒ Click the **Maximize** button or double-click the title bar to display the window full screen.

- ❐ Click the **Restore** button or double-click the title bar to return a maximized window to its former size.
- ❐ Click the **Minimize** button or the window's taskbar button to clear the window from the desktop. You'll still see the window's button in the taskbar.
- ❐ Rest the mouse pointer over the window's border or corner so the mouse appears as a double-headed arrow, and then drag to make the window larger or smaller.

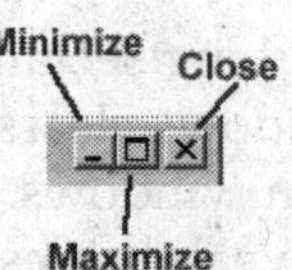

Moving a Window

To move a window, drag its title bar.

Moving and Resizing Windows with Snap

The Windows Snap feature enables you to move and resize windows by snapping them to the edges of the desktop. (When dragging to the edge of the desktop, you must drag all the way until the mouse pointer hits the edge.)

- ❐ **Arrange two windows side by side:** Drag a window's title bar so the mouse pointer touches the left or right edge of the screen. An outline appears displaying the future position and dimensions of the window. Release the mouse button, and the window is resized to consume the left or right half of the desktop.
- ❐ **Expand a window vertically:** Drag the window's top border up or bottom border down to the edge of the screen and release the mouse button to expand the window to the full height of the desktop without changing its width.
- ❐ **Maximize a window:** Drag the window's title bar to the top of the desktop and release the mouse button to expand it to fill the entire desktop.
- ❐ **Switching to a Window**
- ❐ The easiest way to switch to a specific window is to click its taskbar button. This moves the window to the front of the stack. If a program has more than one document open, rest the mouse pointer on the button to display thumbnails of the documents and then click the one you want. (Your computer displays thumbnails only if it supports the Aero desktop features.) If you can see any portion of the window you want to change to, click it to move the window to the front of the stack.

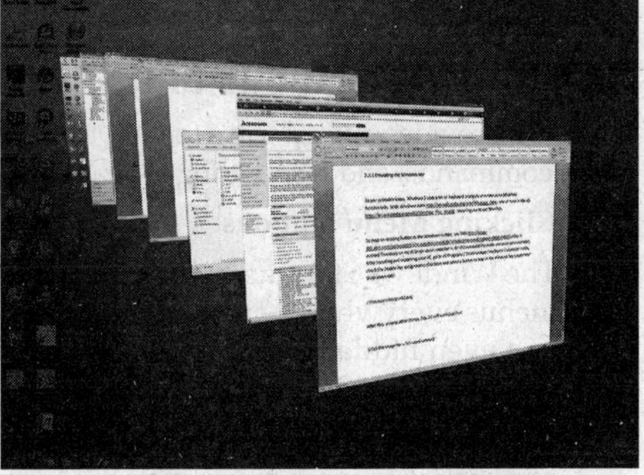

Moving and resizing windows with snap

Closing a Window

If you're done with a program or document, click its **Close** button or right-click its taskbar button and click **Close window**. This closes the document and/or exits the program and removes the window from the desktop. If you close a document you haven't saved, Windows prompts you to save the document first.

Clearing the Desktop

At the far right end of the taskbar is a long rectangular box, which is the Show desktop button. When you click the button, Windows clears everything off the desktop. When you click it again, Windows restores all open windows. Hover the mouse over the button, and all open windows turn transparent to reveal the desktop.

Shaking a Window into Focus

If your computer supports the Aero desktop features, you can shake a window to make it the centre of attention and clear any other open windows off the desktop (minimize them). To shake a window, quickly drag its title bar left and right.

Seeing More with Scrollbars

If a window cannot display everything it contains, a scrollbar appears along the right side and/or bottom of the window. The scrollbar on the right enables you to scroll up and down; the scrollbar at the bottom lets you scroll left and right. You can use the scrollbar to bring the hidden contents of the window into view, as follows:

- Drag the scroll box (inside the bar) to the area of the window you want to view. For example, to view the middle of the window's contents, drag the scroll box to the middle of the bar.
- Click inside the scrollbar on either side of the scroll box, to move the view one window at a time. For example, if you click once below the scroll box, you'll see the next window of information.
- Click a scroll arrow (at each end of the scrollbar) to scroll incrementally in the direction of the arrow. You can hold down the left mouse button to scroll continuously.

Ordering from Menus and Dialog Boxes

Windows provides several ways for you to "talk" to your computer by clicking buttons, selecting menu commands, and responding to dialog boxes (onscreen fill-inthe- blank forms).

- **Clicking Menu Options**

  The Windows Start menu isn't the only menu you'll encounter in Windows. You'll find menus everywhere—in menu bars near the top of most program windows, in toolbars, and even hidden inside objects (context menus). You click a menu's name to open it and then click the desired option or command.

  If a double-headed, downward-pointing arrow appears at the bottom of a menu, you can click it to view more options. As you choose options, Windows may move them closer to the top of the menu so the options you use most frequently are within easy reach.

- ❐ **Using Context Menus**

  Context menus provide convenient access to commands and options available only for a specific object. You right-click the object to display the context menu and then click the desired option.

Talking with a Dialog Box

If you choose a menu command that's followed by a series of dots (...), the program displays a dialog box requesting additional information, as shown in Figure. You must then enter your preferences and give your okay.

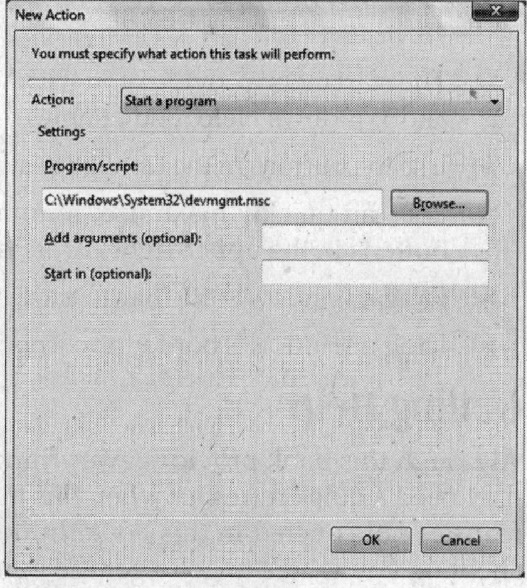

Bypassing Menus by Using Toolbar Buttons

Although menus contain a comprehensive list of available options, they can be a bit clunky. To help you bypass the menu system, most programs include a ribbon or toolbars with buttons for the most frequently used commands. To perform a task, you simply click the desired button.

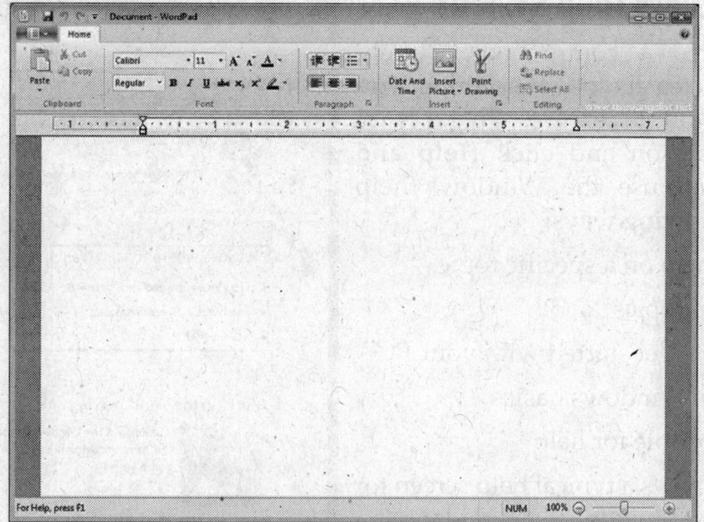

Checking Out Windows Accessories and Games

Chances are good that your computer came loaded with all sorts of software. If you purchased a home PC, it probably includes Microsoft Works or some other program suite (package) and a couple of computer games. But even if your computer wasn't garnished with additional programs, Windows has several desktop accessories, including Calculator, WordPad, Paint, and Sound Recorder. To run any of these programs, click **Start**, **All Programs**, **Accessories**, and then click the program you want to run.

Windows also features several games you can play to limber up your mouse fingers and have some fun, including Chess Titans, FreeCell (very addictive), Hearts, Mahjong Titans, Minesweeper, and Solitaire. Click **Start**, **All Programs**, **Games**, and click the game you want to play.

Points to Remember

- ☆ The Start menu provides you with access to all of your programs, PC settings, documents, and Windows Help, and enables you to log off Windows or shut down your PC.
- ☆ Use the buttons in the taskbar to switch to the program or document window you want.
- ☆ You can quickly maximize, minimize, restore, and close windows by using the three buttons in the upper-right corner of every window.
- ☆ Drag a window's title bar to move it.
- ☆ Drag a window's border or corner to resize it.

Getting Help

Although this book provides everything you need to know to use your Windows 7 PC, you may need a quick refresher when this book isn't nearby or help using programs or Windows features not covered in this book. In this chapter, my goal is to make you self-sufficient by showing you where to go to get the guidance and instructions you need.

Using the Windows Help System

Windows features a comprehensive help system that can teach you everything you need to know about its features. To get help, click the **Start** button and click **Help and Support**. You can use the Windows help system in the following ways:

- ❒ Search for help on a specific topic
- ❒ Browse help topics
- ❒ Learn how to get started with your PC
- ❒ Brush up on Windows basics
- ❒ Ask other people for help

Adjacent figure shows a typical help screen for a specific topic and provides some guidance on how to navigate Windows Help and Support.

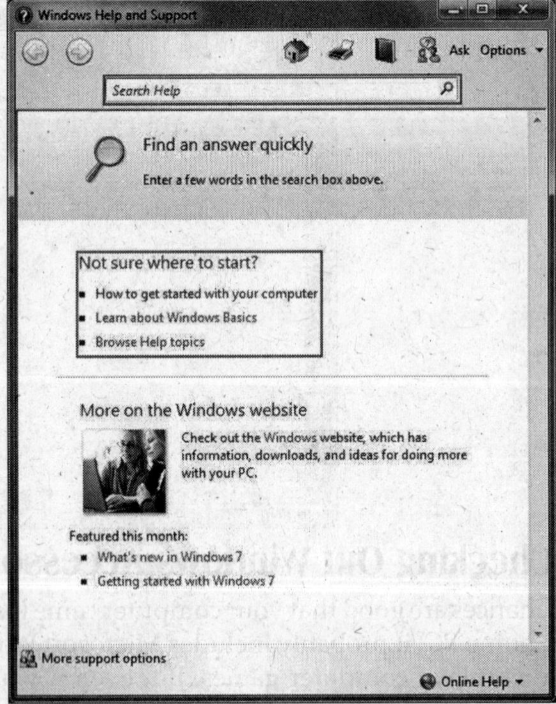

Windows help and support

Searching for Specific Help

The easiest and fastest way to get help with a specific task is to search the help system:

- ❒ Click in the Search Help box.
- ❒ Type one or more words to describe what you need help with.

- ❒ Press Enter or click the magnifying glass to the right of the box. This displays a list of help topics that match the description you typed.
- ❒ Click the desired help topic.

Browsing the Help System

You can browse the help system's table of contents for the assistance you need:

- ❒ Click the **Browse Help** button (the book icon in the upper right) to display the help system's equivalent of a table of contents.
- ❒ Click a heading to display a list of topics related to that heading.
- ❒ Follow the trail of links to the answer or instructions you need. (Links appear as blue text that's underlined when you rest the mouse pointer on them.)

Learning How to Get Started with a New PC

On the Help and Support window's Home page (the page that appears when you first run Help and Support), click **How to get started with your computer** to learn common tasks for the first few weeks you begin using a new computer, including protecting your computer and installing new hardware and programs.

Brushing Up on Windows Basics

On the Help and Support window's Home page (the page that appears when you first run Help and Support), click **Learn about Windows Basics** to get up to speed on the basic Windows maneuvers covered in Chapters earlier already.

Getting Context-Sensitive Help

Windows knows what you're doing at any given time and is always ready to lend a hand. When you need assistance, simply head to the desktop and press the **F1** key.

(If you press **F1** when one of your application windows is active, you'll get context sensitive help for that application.) The Windows Help and Support window pops up, offering information and instructions related to the activity in which you're currently engaged. If this isn't quite the help you were looking for, you can use the Help and Support window to search or browse for additional help. In many dialog boxes and some windows, you'll see a question mark icon, shown in the adjacent figure. Click the icon for help with this particular dialog box or window.

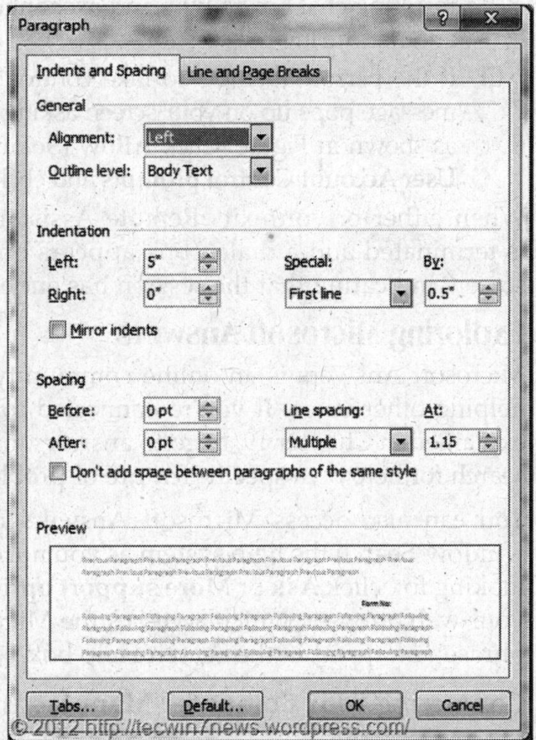

Paragraph Setting

Getting Help from Other People

If you can't find the help you need *inside* Windows, you may need to consult a resource *outside* Windows. Click **Ask** (upper right) or **More support options** (lower left) to learn how to get help from other people over the Internet. In the following sections, I cover these additional support options.

Getting Remote Assistance from a Friend

Most people have a computer-whiz friend or family member they can call on when they run into trouble. Unfortunately, your personal PC guru may live across town or in another state, but you may be able to use Remote Assistance to enlist that person's assistance. With Remote Assistance, your assistant can connect to your computer, view your computer screen, chat with you about what you're both looking at, and even take control of your PC (with your permission, of course) to show you how to perform a task or to troubleshoot a problem.

- ❒ Click **Start, All Programs, Maintenance, Windows Remote Assistance.**
- ❒ Follow instructions as Windows leads you through the process. If you choose to send an invitation via e-mail, Remote Assistance e-mails the recipient a file and generates a password you can send to the person in a separate e-mail message, via a chat session, or over the phone. The recipient runs the attached file and enters the password, and then can view your computer.
- ❒ You can talk with your assistant over the phone or use the resulting chat box to type and exchange messages with one another during the session.
- ❒ If the person attempts to take control of your computer, a message pops up on your screen asking for your permission, as shown in Figure. Click **Allow [So-and-So] to respond to User Account Control prompts** and click **Yes.**

When either of you exits Remote Assistance, the connection is terminated and a dialog box appears on the other person's screen, indicating that the session has ended.

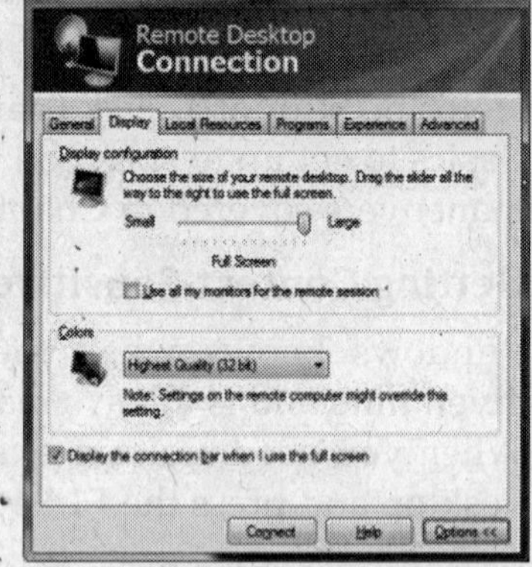

Getting remote assistance

Exploring Microsoft Answers

Microsoft Answers is an online community of Microsoft tech support personnel and users helping other users. If you're connected to the Internet, you can use your web browser, as explained in Chapter 19, to go to answers.microsoft.com and then browse answers by topic or search for help on a specific feature or problem.

You can also access Microsoft Answers directly from the Windows Help and Support window. Search the help system as you normally would. If it doesn't have the answer you're looking for, click **Ask** or **More support options** and then click **Microsoft Answers.** This runs your web browser, which accesses the Microsoft Answers site and searches for the word or phrase you typed in the Search Help box.

Contacting Your Computer Manufacturer or Microsoft Support

For solving more mystifying problems, you may need to call in the big guns— Microsoft Customer Support or your computer manufacturer. Most manufacturers have very useful sites for troubleshooting hardware and software issues and obtaining any software updates your PC may need.

To connect with Microsoft Customer Support or your computer manufacturer, run Windows Help and Support, click **More support options** (lower left), and then, under Contact technical support, click **computer manufacturer** or **Microsoft Customer Support** and follow the onscreen cues and clues to find what you're looking for. If you choose **computer manufacturer**, Microsoft provides links and phone numbers for all major PC manufacturers.

Getting More Windows Help on the Web

Microsoft offers much more help with Windows via its website. If your computer is connected to the Internet, head to windows.microsoft.com/en-s/windows7/help for how-to videos, tutorials, and more.

For assistance with a technical issue, search Microsoft's Knowledge Base at support.microsoft.com/search/. When you get there, click **Show more search options** (below the Search box) so you can narrow the search to a specific Microsoft product, such as Windows 7.

Getting Help with Applications and Games

Most applications and games don't include printed instructions on how to use them. Software developers provide instructions via help systems, in much the same way Windows does. To obtain help with a particular application or game, use its Help menu, as shown in the adjacent figure, or press **F1** while in the application.

Applications and games

Points to Remember

- To get help with using Windows, click **Start, Help and Support.**
- The quickest way to get help is to display the Help and Support window and use the Search Help box to find what you're looking for.
- To obtain context-sensitive help (for what you're currently doing), press the **F1** key.
- To obtain help from other people, click **Start, Help and Support, More support options** (lower left), and then click the link for the desired option and follow the onscreen cues.

Personalizing windows

If you're like most people, you enjoy decorating your home or office to add your own personal touch. You might paint the walls a different colour, hang a few photos of friends or family members, or populate your shelves with knickknacks and family photos. In similar ways, you can customize and decorate the Windows desktop. This chapter shows you how.

Microsoft ships Windows with default settings that control its appearance, but eventually, every user's version of Windows starts to look a little different as the individual personalizes it to suit his or her tastes. Here you discover several adjustments for injecting a little of your personality into Windows.

Personalizing Appearance

- Click Start, Control Panel, Appearance and Personalization, Personalization or right-click a blank area of the Windows desktop and click Personalize.
- Scroll through the collection of themes and click the one you want.
- Click Desktop Background (below the themes).
- Scroll through the collection of background pictures and click the one you want. If you click more than one, Windows will cycle through them as a slide show.
- Click the Picture position button and choose the desired position. For example, you can choose to have the picture centreed or fill the entire desktop.
- If you chose more than one background picture, click the Change picture every button and choose how often you want Windows to change background pictures. You can also choose to shuffle the pictures for random display and/or pause the slide show when the PC is running on battery power, to conserve power.
- Click Save changes.
- Click Window Colour.
- Click the desired colour or click Show colour mixer (near the bottom of the window) and mix your own custom colour.
- If your PC supports Aero, you can click Enable transparency to enable (checked) or disable (unchecked) the window transparency feature.

- ❒ Drag the Colour intensity slider left or right to set the desired brightness of the selected colour.
- ❒ Click Save changes.
- ❒ Click Sounds.
- ❒ Click the button directly below Sound Scheme and click the desired scheme.
- ❒ Under Program events, you can double-click an event to play the sound assigned to that event.
- ❒ When you've settled on a scheme you like, click OK.
- ❒ Click Screen Saver.
- ❒ Click the Screen Saver button and click the screen saver you want to use. Windows displays a preview of the screen saver in action.
- ❒ Enter your preferences to specify the amount of time your PC is inactive before the screen saver kicks in and whether you want Windows to display the log-on screen when you resume use.
- ❒ For some screen savers, you can click the Settings button and enter additional preferences, such as how fast the design moves across the screen.
- ❒ Click Save changes.
- ❒ When you're done making changes, scroll to the top of the theme gallery, click Save theme at the bottom of My Themes, type a name for your theme, and click Save. Your theme is now part of your theme gallery.

  You can now close the Control Panel or leave it open to customize Windows even more. Click Appearance and Personalization in the top bar to return to this screen.

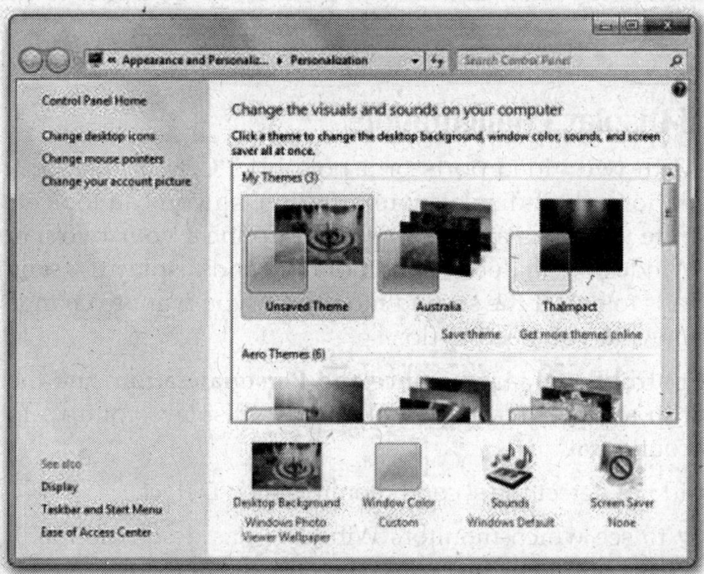

Personalizing appearance of windows

Note.... ✍

If you see a photo or other image on your computer or on a web page that you'd like to use as your background image, right-click it and click Set as desktop background or Set as Background.

Adjusting the Display Settings

You can adjust display settings in Windows to fit more on the screen, make text more readable, or connect to a projector or external display, as explained in the following sections.

Changing Text and Object Size

You can make everything on your desktop smaller (to fit more) or larger (to see it better):

- ❒ Click **Start**, **Control Panel**, **Appearance and Personalization**.
- ❒ Under Display, click **Make text and other items larger or smaller**.
- ❒ Click the desired size.
- ❒ Click **Apply**.

Adjusting the Screen Resolution

In Windows 7, you can adjust size and screen resolution to fit more stuff on the screen or display larger objects and text:

- ❒ Click **Start, Control Panel, Appearance and Personalization.**
- ❒ Under Display, click **Adjust screen resolution.**
- ❒ If more than one monitor is connected, click the **Display** button and select the monitor you want to adjust.
- ❒ Click the **Resolution** button and drag the slider up or down to the setting marked **(recommended)**.
- ❒ Click **Apply**.

Managing a Dual-Display Configuration

If you have a PC with two video ports or a portable PC with one video port, you have everything you need for a dual-display configuration, so you can look at two programs or documents in separate windows at the same time. Connect your two monitors to your PC and turn them on. Windows will detect both monitors and display the same thing on both of them. If Windows fails to detect the second monitor or you want to change the dual-display configuration, here's what you need to do:

- ❒ Click **Start**, **Control Panel**, **Appearance and Personalization**, and then, below Display, click **Connect to an external display**. Windows displays controls for managing your dual-display configuration.
- ❒ If Windows did not detect the second monitor, click **Detect**.
- ❒ Click **Identify** to see which monitors Windows has designated as 1 and 2. Windows briefly displays the number 1 on one screen and 2 on the other.

- To rearrange the displays, drag and drop one of the monitor images to the far side of the other image.
- Open the Multiple displays box and choose how you want Windows to configure your dual display:
    - **Duplicate these displays:** Displays the same thing on both monitors, which is useful if you're giving a presentation.
    - **Extend these displays:** Extends the desktop across both screens so that you have more room to spread out.
    - **Show desktop only on 1:** Shows Windows only on display 1.
    - **Show desktop only on 2:** Shows Windows only on display 2.

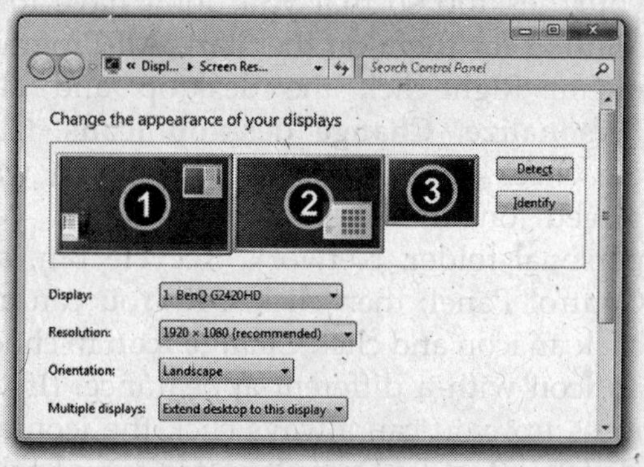

Dual display configuration

- You can use the **Display** and **Resolution** drop-down lists to set the resolution for each display independently.
- Click **Apply**.

Note....

*On most portable PCs, you can press **Fn+F5** to switch between using the display screen, the external monitor, or both.*

Connecting a Projector to Your PC

When giving a presentation, you may need or want to connect a projector to your PC to display the presentation on a larger screen:

- Turn on the projector and plug it into a VGA, DVI, or USB port on your computer.
- Click **Start, Control Panel, Appearance and Personalization.**
- Under Display, click **Connect to a projector.**
- Click the option that best describes how you want your desktop to be displayed: **Computer Only, Duplicate, Extend,** or **Projector only.**

Taking Control of Desktop Icons

Initially, Windows displays only one desktop icon—the Recycle Bin. For easy access to the programs, games, files, and folders you use most frequently, you can create additional desktop icons. The following sections show you how to add icons to the desktop and manage them.

Adding Desktop Icons

You can add desktop icons for programs, files, pictures, and other items. Find the item you want to create a desktop icon for. This can be a program on the Start, All Programs menu; a disk, file, or folder icon; or an icon for a specific hardware device. Right-click the item, point to **Send to,** and click **Desktop (create shortcut).**

You can quickly add some standard icons to your desktop so that you don't have to go hunting for them on the Start, All Programs menu: Right-click the desktop and click **Personalize**, **Change desktop icons**. Click the check box next to each icon you want placed on the desktop: Computer, your personal folder, Network, Recycle Bin, and Control Panel; then click **OK**. You can also click an icon and click **Change icon** to choose an icon with a different appearance. (If you mess up, you can always click the icon and click the **Restore Default** button to go back to the original icon.)

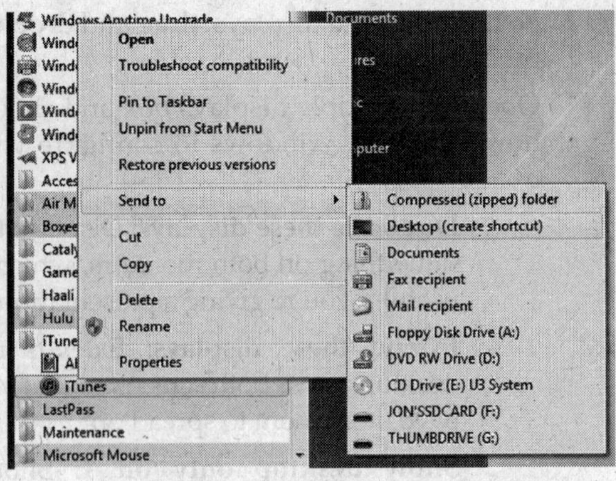

Controlling desktop icons

Deleting Desktop Icons

Most desktop icons are shortcuts, small images that merely link to the items they represent. Deleting the shortcut doesn't delete the file or other item it's linked to. If you delete a file's original icon, however, Windows deletes the file by moving it to the Recycle Bin. To flag an icon as a shortcut, Windows displays the icon with an arrow in its lower-left corner, as shown in the Figure.

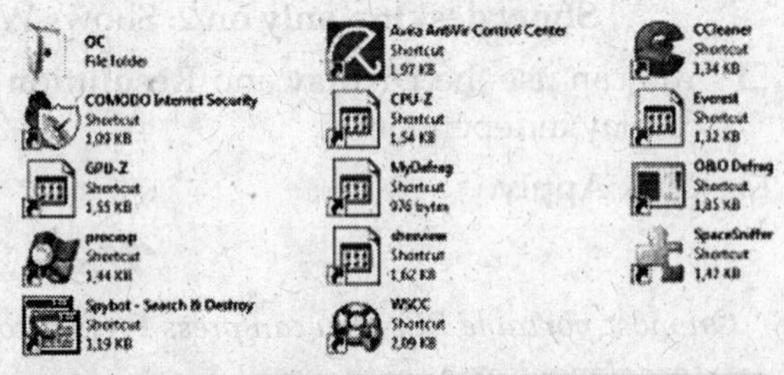

To delete a desktop icon, right-click the icon, click **Delete**, and, when prompted for confirmation, click **Yes**.

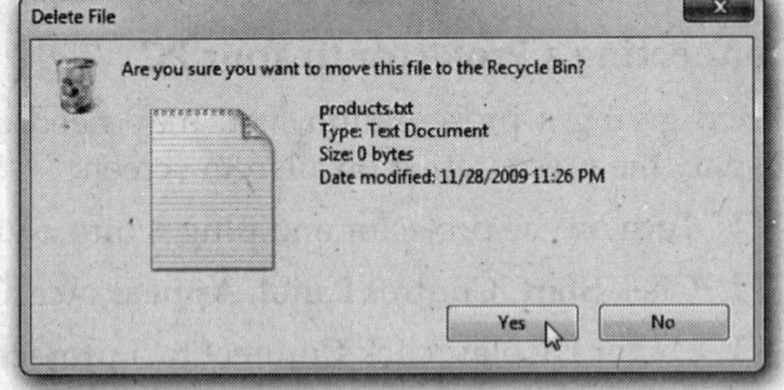

Deleting desktop icons

Hiding All Desktop Icons

To toggle the display of desktop icons on or off, right-click the desktop, point to **View**, and click **Show desktop icons**.

Renaming Icons

To rename an icon, right-click it and click **Rename** (or click the icon twice slowly, not a double-click), type the new name, and press **Enter**.

Rearranging Icons

If your desktop gets too cluttered or unmanageable, Windows has several tools to help you control the size and arrangement of the desktop icons. To move an icon, drag and drop it to the desired location.

To change the appearance or position of all icons on the desktop, right-click a blank area of the desktop and point to **View** or **Sort by**, and choose the desired option. For example, you can choose **View, Large Icons** and **View, Auto Arrange** to bump up the icon size and have Windows arrange the icons on the desktop for you.

Adding Gadgets to Your Desktop

Windows provides quick access to customizable mini-applications called *gadgets*, which include a calendar, clock, news headlines (from the Internet), weather updates, and more. To turn on a gadget, right-click the desktop, click **Gadgets**, and double click the gadget you want to use, as shown in Figure

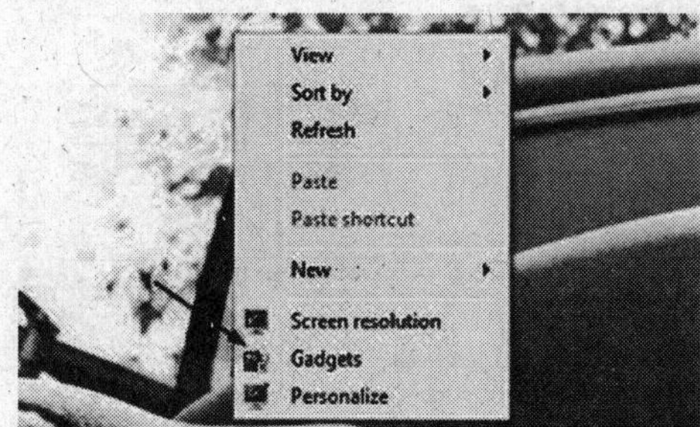

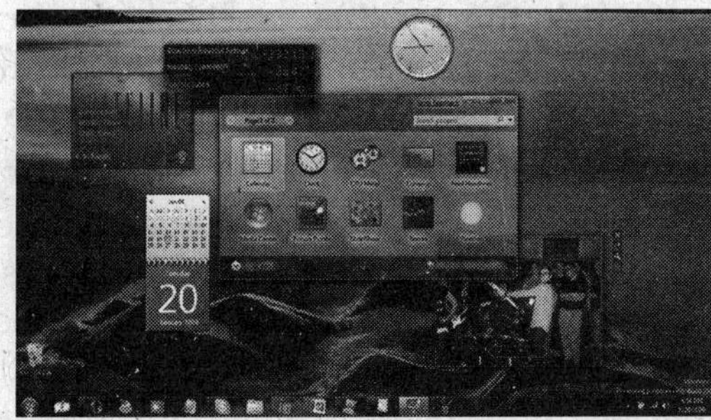

Adding gadets to desktop

Windows provides several controls for manipulating your gadgets. Rest the mouse pointer on the gadget to display its controls. Then, depending on the gadget, you can do the following:

- Drag the gadget to move it. (You can simply drag the gadget or use the drag handle that appears when you mouse over the gadget.)
- Click **X** to close the gadget.
- Click the size icon and choose the desired size.
- Click the wrench to enter gadget preferences. For example, the weather gadget enables you to enter a location to get your local weather updates. To toggle the display of all gadgets on or off, right-click the desktop, point to **View**, and click **Show desktop gadgets.**

Note....

If your PC is connected to the Internet, you can add more gadgets to your gadget gallery. In the lower-right corner of the gadget gallery, click Get more gadgets online. Be careful, however—gadgets can be memory hogs.

Configuring the Taskbar

Your taskbar may not look like much, but it has a lot of potential. In the following sections, you will see how to customize the toolbar to fully tap its power.

Adjusting the Taskbar Properties

Right-click a blank area of the taskbar, click **Properties**, and use the resulting dialog box to enter your preferences, as shown in Figure. Most of the properties are self-explanatory, but a couple are a little vague:

- Lock the taskbar prevents you from accidentally moving or resizing the taskbar.
- **Auto-hide the taskbar** minimizes the taskbar when you're not using it. To bring the hidden taskbar back into view, move the mouse pointer to the edge of the screen where the taskbar usually hangs out.

Moving and Resizing the Taskbar

The taskbar is not an immovable object. To move it, right-click a blank area of the taskbar and, if **Lock the taskbar** is checked, click it to remove the check mark and unlock the taskbar. Now you can use your mouse to drag the taskbar to any edge of your screen.

To resize the taskbar, rest the mouse pointer over the edge that's closest to the desktop so that the mouse pointer appears as a double-headed arrow. Then drag the edge toward the middle of the desktop to make the taskbar bigger. You can always make it smaller by dragging in the opposite direction.

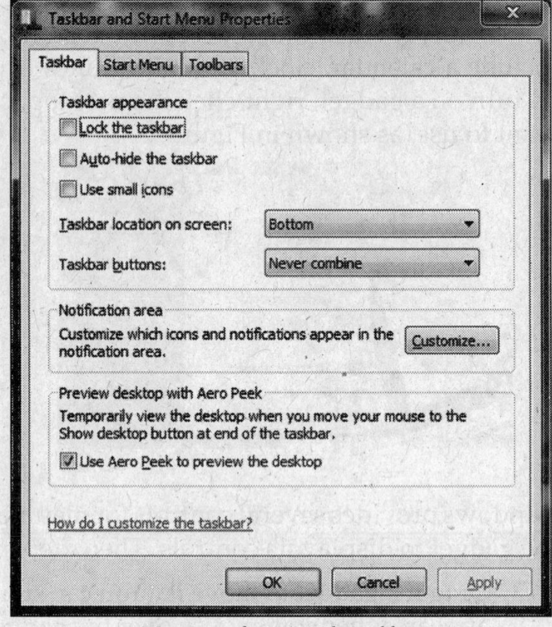

Moving and resizing the taskbar

Adding Icons

Just as you can add icons to the desktop, you can add icons to the taskbar. Simply drag an icon over the place on the taskbar where you want it to appear and drop it in place. You can also right-click an icon and click **Pin to taskbar**. To remove an icon, right-click it and click **Unpin from taskbar**.

Adding a Toolbar

You can add an entire collection of buttons and other controls to the taskbar by adding a toolbar. Right-click a blank area of the toolbar, point to **Toolbars**, and click the toolbar you want to use. You can move a toolbar by dragging it to the other side of another toolbar. To resize a toolbar, drag its handle, as shown in Figure. You can remove a toolbar by right-clicking it and choosing **Close toolbar**.

Changing the Date and Time

At the right end of the taskbar, Windows displays the current date and time. To change the date or time, click the date or time, click **Change date and time settings**, **Change date and time**, and then use the resulting dialog box to enter your changes.

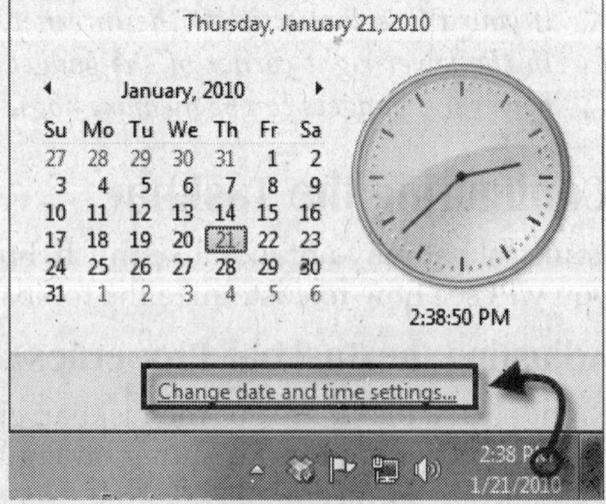

Changing date and time

To change the date, click the arrow button on either side of the month to display the current month, and then click today's date. To change the time, click the hour, minute, or second you want to change and then click the up or down arrow to the right of the time to make your change. When you're done, click **OK**.

Personalizing Your Start Menu

The Start menu is designed to put everything within easy reach, but it doesn't always succeed. Fortunately, you can step in and optimize the Start menu for the way you work.

Pin a Program to the Start Menu

Pinning an item places it at the top of the Start menu so it's always within easy reach.

To pin an item, right-click its icon and click **Pin to Start Menu**. Another way to pin something to the Start menu is to drag it over the Start button and then, when the menu opens, drag it up into the menu area and drop it in place.

You can change the order of pinned items by dragging them up or down. To remove a pinned item from the Start menu, right-click it and choose **Unpin from Start Menu**.

Removing Programs from the Start Menu

To remove a program from the Start menu, right-click it and click **Remove from this list**. Removing the program from the Start menu does not remove it from the All Programs list or from your computer. You need to uninstall the program

Clear Recently Opened Files

Windows keeps track of your recently opened programs and documents and displays a list of them in the Start menu's left pane for easy access. To clear this list and prevent Windows from keeping track of recently opened items in the future, follow these steps:

- ❒ Right-click a blank area of the taskbar and click **Properties**.
- ❒ Click the **Start Menu** tab.
- ❒ Click the following options to uncheck them: **Store and display recently opened programs in the Start menu** and **Store and display recently opened items in the Start menu and taskbar**.
- ❒ Click **OK**.

Customize the Appearance of Start Menu Items

You can further customize the Start menu to include or exclude certain items, change their appearance, and change the size of the Start menu to display more or fewer recent programs and items. Right-click the taskbar, click **Properties**, click the **Start Menu** tab, enter your preferences, and click **OK**.

You can restore the Start menu to its original state by clicking the Use Default Settings button at the bottom of the dialog box.

Configuring Power-Saving Features

Windows conscientiously helps you conserve energy (and battery power if you're using a portable PC). Unless you adjust the settings, Windows places your PC on a balanced plan—balancing performance with energy. If you want to be more or less aggressive in cutting back on energy consumption, you can change plans and/or adjust specific settings:

- ❒ Click **Start, Control Panel, Hardware and Sound, Power Options**.
- ❒ Click the power plan you want to use. (Power plan availability depends on what your PC supports.)
- ❒ Next to the selected power plan, click **Change plan settings**.
- ❒ Use the resulting options to specify the number of minutes or hours of inactivity that must pass before Windows dims the display, turns off the display, and puts the computer to sleep, as shown in the adjacent Figure
- ❒ Drag the **Adjust plan brightness** slider (if it has one) to increase or decrease your display's brightness. (Different PCs may have different options.)
- ❒ (Optional) Click **Change advanced power settings**, use the Power Options dialog box to enter more detailed power settings, and click **OK**.
- ❒ Click **Save changes**.

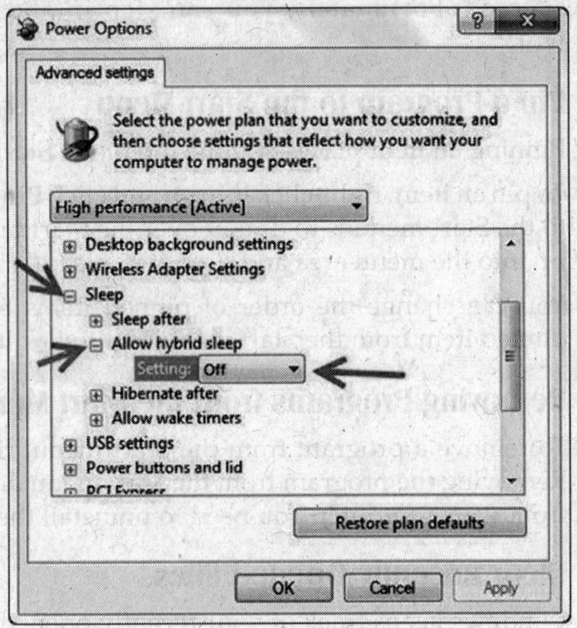

Power-saving features

Adjusting Your PC's Speaker Volume

The trick to adjusting the volume on a computer is to start with the obvious controls first: any volume dials on the computer, sound card, or speakers. Set these controls to the desired level. If you're not sure which way to turn them, set them at the halfway point so that when your computer starts to play audio, it won't burst your eardrums.

Note....

If you're working on a notebook PC or have a newfangled keyboard, you may have volume controls for both the speaker and the microphone within easy reach of the keys. Look around the periphery of the keyboard area for volume controls. You may also have a volume control in the notification area that allows you to drag a slider.

Next, check the volume control in Windows. Click **Start, Control Panel, Hardware and Sound, Adjust system volume**. Windows displays a Volume Mixer with one or more sliders that control volume for different components. Drag the **Device** slider to the desired volume level. To mute a device, click the speaker icon below its slider.

Points to Remember

- ☆ To personalize Windows, right-click a blank area of the desktop, click Personalize, and use the resulting dialog box to enter your preferences.
- ☆ To add an icon to the desktop, right-click the icon, point to Send to, and click Desktop (create shortcut).
- ☆ To pin an item to the Start menu, right-click the item and click Pin to Start Menu.
- ☆ To access settings for your taskbar and Start menu, right-click the taskbar and click Properties.
- ☆ To access the Windows power-saving settings, click Start, Control Panel, Hardware and Sound, Power Options.

Creating & Managing User Accounts

Sharing a computer is like sharing a car. When you share a car, each driver adjusts the seat and steering wheel for individual comfort, adjusts the mirrors to see out the back, and stores the garage door opener in a unique hiding place. Likewise, some computer users like a plain, uncluttered desktop, whereas others prefer to populate their desktops with dozens of icons, a sidebar, and other accessories. Fortunately, Windows enables you to set up a separate user account for each person so that each person can customize Windows without affecting the appearance and function of Windows for other users. In addition, user accounts enable each user to keep a separate e-mail account, which means the messages for all users don't get mixed up in the same mailbox. User account passwords also provide privacy in a shared environment.

Adding a New User to Your PC

When you or your computer's manufacturer installed Windows, the setup program automatically created a user account, so that Windows could greet you on startup. To add a user account, click **Start**, **Control Panel**, **Add or remove user accounts** (under User Accounts and Family Safety), and then **Create a new account**. Use the resulting dialog box to name the

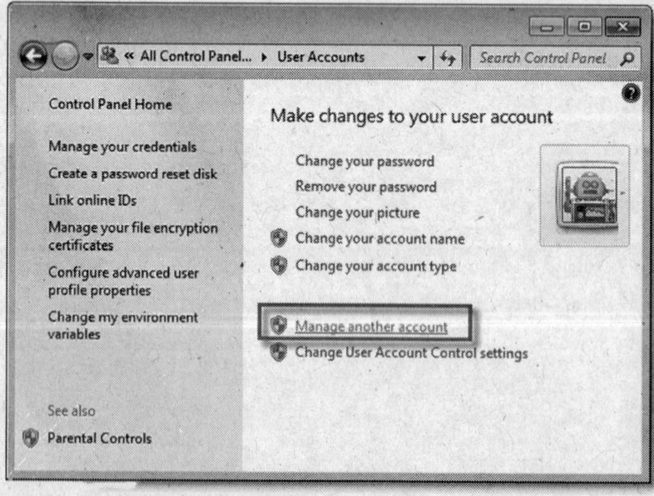

Adding a new user

new account and specify the account type: Standard user or Administrator. When you click **Create Account**, Windows takes you to the Manage Accounts window, where you'll see a new icon for the account you created.

Making Changes to a User Account

You can edit a user account to change its name, protect the account with a password, change the picture that represents your account, and more. To get started, click **Start, Control Panel, Add or remove user accounts**, and then click the account you want to configure. Windows displays several options for configuring the account, as shown in figure below:

- **Change the account name**: Simply click this option, type a new name, and click Change Name.
- **Create a password or Change the password**: To prevent unauthorized access to a user account, password-protect it. Click this option, type your password in the two designated boxes, enter a password hint (optional), and click Create password.
- **Remove the password**: An administrator can remove user account passwords.

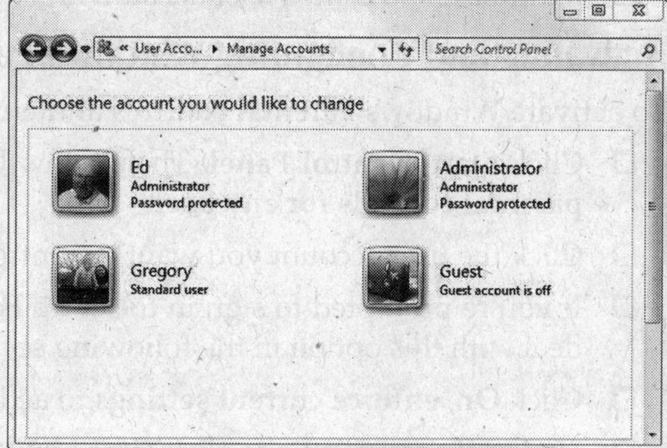

Making changes to a user account

- **Change the picture:** This option enables you to change the picture that represents you. You can even use the **Browse for more pictures...** option to choose a digital image, such as a photo, stored on your PC.
- **Change the account type:** An administrator can change an account type from Standard user to Administrator.
- **Delete the account:** This option enables an administrator to remove an account that is no longer in use.

Enabling or Disabling the Guest Account

If you have guests who occasionally use your computer to check their e-mail, browse the web, or play games, you can enable the Guest Accounts feature to let them log on as guests without having to enter a password. They can then run programs and perform other tasks, but they cannot install new software or change any account settings.

In short, guest users can use your PC without messing it up.

To enable or disable the guest account, click **Start**, **Control Panel**, **Add or remove user accounts**, and then click either **Turn On** or **Turn off the guest account**.

Setting Parental Controls for a User

If you're setting up a user account for a child or teenager, consider activating Windows Parental Controls. You can prohibit computer use during certain days or times of day, and limit or block access to certain games or programs. With the addition of Windows Live Family Safety (a free add-on), you can also monitor and restrict a child's activity on the web.

Before activating Windows Parental Controls, perform the following tasks to prevent users from signing on using an unprotected user account:

- Make sure the guest account is off.
- Make your account a password-protected administrator account. Always password-protect administrator accounts; otherwise, it's easy for anyone to log on as an administrator and change settings, possibly locking you out of your own PC!
- Make sure the child's user account is set to Standard user.

Activating and Configuring Windows Parental Controls

To activate Windows Parental controls and enter your preferences, follow these steps:

- Click **Start**, **Control Panel**. Then below User Accounts and Family Safety, click **Set up parental controls for any user**.
- Click the user account you want to control.
- If you're prompted to sign in to set up Family Safety, close the window for now. You'll deal with this option in the following section.
- Click **On, enforce current settings** to activate Parental Controls.
- Under Windows Settings, click **Time Limits**, drag over the time blocks that indicate the days and times this user is prohibited from using the PC, and click **OK**. (See figure below)
- Click **Games**, enter your preferences to restrict this user from playing certain games, and click **OK**.
- Click **Allow and block specific programs**, and then do one of the following:
  - Click **User can use all programs** and click **OK**.
  - Click **User can only use the programs I allow**, select any programs you want for this user, and click **OK**.
- Click **OK** to close the Parental Controls window and then exit the Control Panel.

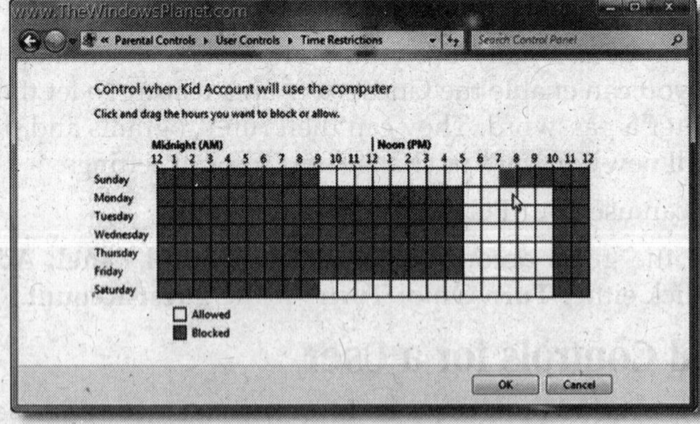

Windows parental controls

Using Windows Live Family Safety

Windows Live Family Safety is a part of the free Windows Live add-on. If your PC is connected to the Internet, go to Windows Live Family Safety (at explore.live.com/windows-live-family-safety), click the **Download** button, and follow the onscreen instructions to download (copy to your PC) and install Windows Live and create a free Windows Live account.

After installing Windows Live, click Start, Control Panel, and then Set up parental controls for any user. Near the bottom, open the Select a provider list and click Windows Live Family Safety. The first time you choose this option, Windows prompts you for the e-mail address and password you use for your Windows Live account. After you log in, Windows prompts you to choose which user accounts to monitor. Click the check box next to each user account you want to monitor, click Save, and click OK when Windows indicates the setup is complete. From this point on, you use the Windows Live Family Safety website to monitor and configure the safety settings for all of your user accounts. Go to home.live.com, log in, click More (in the top menu bar), and click Family Safety. Windows displays icons for all user accounts on your PC. For each user, you can click Edit settings to bring up the different options.

Logging Off Windows

Always log off or lock your computer when you step away from it. This prevents other users from changing your settings, snooping in your e-mail account, and performing other sinister or careless acts.

Points to Remember

- ☆ To add or remove a user account, click **Start**, **Control Panel**, **Add or remove user accounts**, and use the resulting screen to make your changes.
- ☆ To prevent others from logging on to your Windows account, add a password to your account.
- ☆ To enable Windows Parental Controls for a user, click **Start**, **Control Panel**, **Set up parental controls for any user**, and use the resulting screen to make your changes.
- ☆ If you share your PC with other users, be sure to log off or lock your PC before you step away from it to prevent others from messing with your stuff.

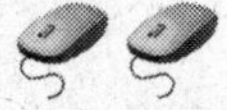

Managing Disk, Folders & Files

Every computer has one or more disk drives for permanent storage of programs, documents, music, video, and content. These disk drives can read content from disks and write (record) content to disks, assuming that the disks are recordable. This chapter introduces you to the types of disks and disk drives you're likely to encounter and shows you how to access and manage everything stored on the various disks inside your PC.

Disk Drives: Easy as A-B-C

Your computer assigns a letter to each disk drive to identify it. Most new PCs come with two drives: C for the hard drive inside the PC, and D for the CD or DVD drive. A and B are reserved for floppy drives, which are relics of the past. The important thing to remember is that disk drives are identified by letters, as shown in the figure below:

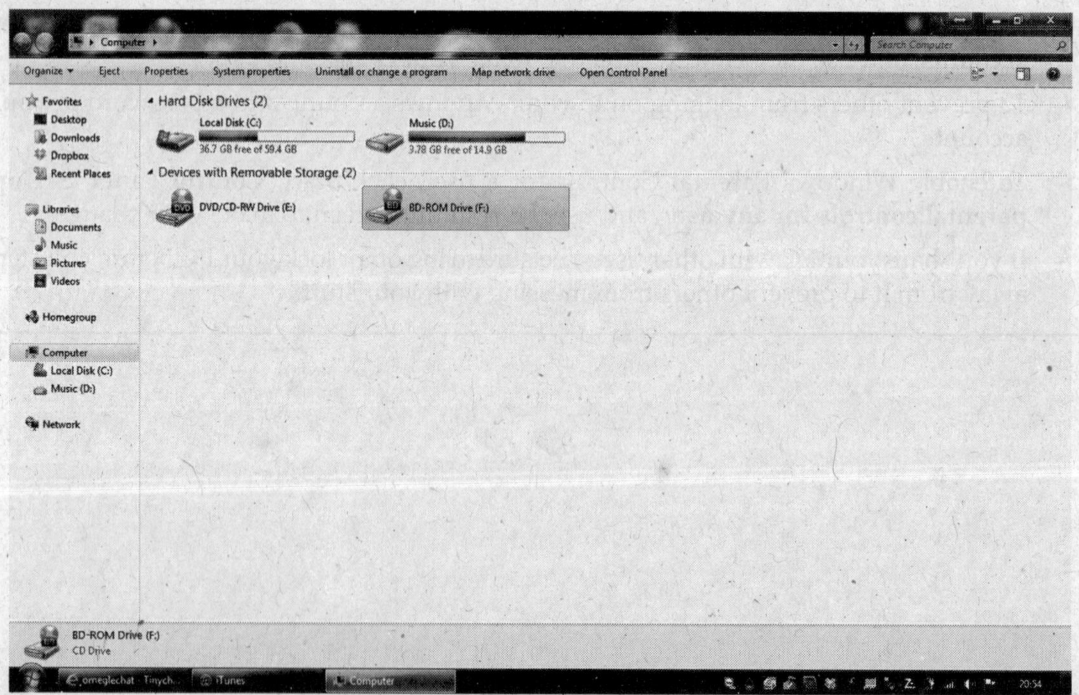

The Hard Disk Drive: C

The drive inside the computer is the internal hard disk drive (hard drive for short), usually called drive C. With hard drives, you don't handle the disk; it's hermetically sealed inside the drive, which is inside the PC.

Note....

A hard disk drive can be partitioned (divided) into one or more drives that the computer refers to as C, D, E, and so on.

The CD or DVD Drive: Usually D

A CD (compact disc) or DVD (digital video disc) drive is standard equipment on every new computer. It's usually located on the front of the system unit on a desktop PC or on the right side of a portable PC. The computer usually refers to it as D. Be sure you purchase the right discs for the drive and your intended purpose:

- **CD-R:** Use CD-R (CD-Recordable) discs to make music CDs so that you can play the CD not only on your PC, but also on most audio CD players.
- **CD-RW:** Use CD-RW (CD-Re Writable) if you plan to store computer files on the discs and perhaps erase files and add other files later.
- **DVD-R or DVD+R:** Use -R or +R (Recordable) discs to make video DVDs that play not only on your PC, but also on most standard TV DVD players. -R and +R work the same but use different symbols because they are competing technologies. Check the front of the disc drive or its documentation or look up the drive on the web to see which formats it supports.
- **DVD-RW or DVD+RW:** Use -RW or +RW (Re Writable) discs if you plan to store computer files on the discs and perhaps erase files and add other files later. RW discs can be rewritten a thousand times.
- **Speed:** Recordable discs and drives are rated by speed, so make sure the maximum speed of the disc is equal to or greater than that of the drive.
- **Printable:** The latest craze is to print labels right on the disc. If your drive supports this feature, you may want to buy printable discs compatible with the labeling technology—for example, LightScribe, *www.lightscribe.com.*
- **Dual-layer:** If your drive supports dual-layer discs, it can store double the amount of data on each disc, which is especially useful for backing up large amounts of data.
- **Blu-ray:** Most newer optical drives can play Blu-ray DVDs but aren't built to record to them. However, if you have a drive that can record Blu-ray discs and you're planning to make your own Blu-ray DVDs, make sure the discs support Blu-ray, too.

External Drives and Other Anomalies

Although internal hard drives and optical drives are standard fare on PCs, other types of drives are very popular for use in backing up files or taking files on the road:

- **External hard drives:** These drives sit outside the computer and connect to the system unit by a data cable, typically a USB cable.
- **USB flash drives:** Commonly referred to as thumb drives, these drives are small enough to fit on a keychain and plug right into your computer's USB port.

External HDD *USB Flash Drive* *Memory Cards*

- **Memory cards:** These cards are primarily used in digital cameras and printers designed to print digital photos.
- **PC card drives:** Many portable PCs come with a PC card slot into which you can plug various devices, including a disk drive.

Loading and Unloading CDs and DVDs

If you've ever loaded a CD into your audio CD player or a DVD into your DVD player, you have all the technical expertise required to load discs into your PC's CD or DVD drive. Just be sure to handle the disc only by its edges so you don't scratch the surface or get any dirt or fingerprints on it. The technique for loading a disc into a CD or DVD drive differs depending on the drive:

- If the drive has an open slot on the front, slide the disc, shiny side down or left, into the slot, just as you would insert a coin into a pop machine. If the drive has a drive tray, press the load/eject button on the front of the drive to open it; then lay the disc in the tray, shiny side down, and press the load/ eject button. (Don't push in the tray to close it, as this may damage the loading mechanism.)

Tip....

If you ever have trouble playing a CD or DVD, the disc might be dirty. To clean the disc, wipe it off with a soft, lint-free cloth from the centre of the disc out to its edges, never in a circular motion. (Wipe the side without the picture or printing on it, because this is the side that the drive reads; some discs are two-sided.) If something sticky gets on the disc, dampen the cloth with a little distilled water and wipe it dry. Let the disc dry thoroughly before inserting it into the drive.

The Windows AutoPlay feature attempts to identify the contents of the disc and find the right program to play it. Windows does a pretty good job of matching disc contents to programs, but if it needs help, it prompts you to select an AutoPlay option, as shown in Figure. You can select one of the options Windows suggests or click **View more AutoPlay options in Control Panel** to select a program from a more comprehensive list.

If Windows automatically performs the wrong action on this type of disc, you can specify a different action by clicking **Start**, **Control Panel**, **Hardware and Sound**, **AutoPlay**. Next to the type of disc whose AutoPlay setting you want to change, open the drop-down list and click the action you want Windows to perform whenever a disc of this type is inserted.

To eject a disc, you usually have two options. You can either press the eject button on the drive itself or save wear and tear on the button by having Windows eject the disc for you. Click **Start**, **Computer**, right-click the drive's icon, and click **Eject**.

Using an External USB or Flash Drive

To use a USB drive, simply plug it into one of your PC's USB ports. What happens next varies depending on what's on the drive:

Using external USB or flash drive

- Windows may identify the drive as a storage device and assign it a letter so that you can use it as any other drive on your PC. Windows may prompt you to choose an AutoPlay option, as it does sometimes when you load a CD or DVD.
- The drive may come with its own software that launches as soon as you connect the device. Follow the onscreen prompts and clues to determine how best to proceed. The only drawback of a USB drive is that it's easier to lose data by removing the drive before Windows is done writing to it. Before unplugging the drive from the USB port, click the **Safely Remove Hardware and Eject Media** icon in the notification area, click the **Eject** option for the device, and wait for Windows to display the Safe To Remove Hardware notification.

Exploring Your Disks, Folders, and Files

All the programs, documents, and other data on your PC is stored on disks as files organized (grouped) into various folders. To see what's on one of your PC's disks, click **Start**, **Computer**, and then double-click one of the disk icons. Windows displays the contents of the selected disk drive, as shown in the figure below:

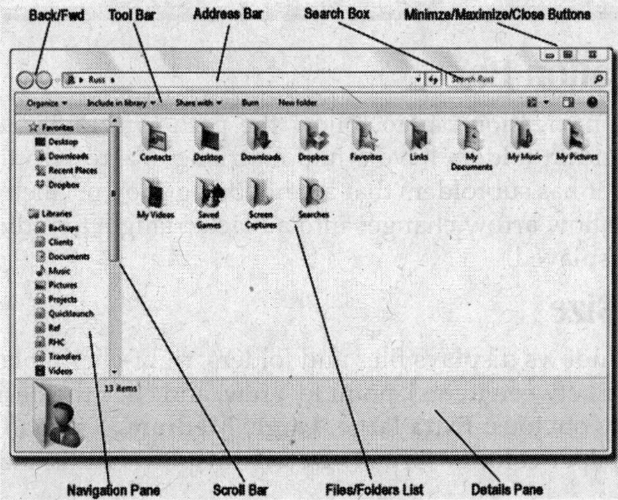

Exploring your computer

To navigate your disks and folders, double-click the disk on which the file or folder is stored and then double-click folder after folder to follow the trail to the folder or file you're looking for. (You can double-click folders in the navigation or library pane.) You can always use the **Back** button to go back to the previous folder or click **Forward** if you go back and then want to return to a folder. To open a file or run a program, double-click its icon.

The trail to a file is actually called a *directory path* that starts with the drive letter (sometimes called the *root directory*) and ends with whatever folder or file name you're looking for.

Figure shows the directory path as it appears near the top of every Windows Explorer Window. You can click a folder in the path to change to that folder or click the **Back** button to back up to the previous folder.

Tip

You can make a disk, folder, file, or program more accessible by placing an icon for it on the Windows desktop. Right-click the icon, point to ***Send To****, and click* ***Desktop (create shortcut)****.*

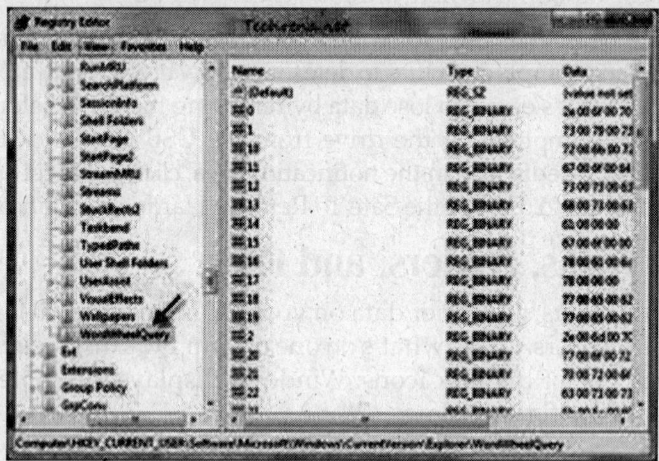

Using the Navigation Bar

You can also use the navigation bar to follow the path to a folder or file. Notice in the navigation bar that certain folders have a hollow triangle/arrow to the left of them. This indicates that the folder has subfolders that are not being shown. Click the arrow to display the subfolders. The hollow arrow changes into a black triangle to indicate that the folder's subfolders are now displayed.

Changing Icon Size

To change the way Windows displays files and folders, right-click a blank area in the folder pane (above, below, or between items), point to **View**, and click the desired option. The first four options are pretty obvious: **Extra large**, **Large**, **Medium**, or **Small icons**. **List** displays tiny icons in a newspaper-column format; **Details** displays additional information about each file, including, size, type, and date modified; **Tiles** is sort of like List, but with larger icons; and **Content** displays tile-size icons followed by larger names and date modified.

Rearranging Items

Windows arranges icons by name from A to Z. To sort by some other criterion, right-click a blank area in the folder pane, point to **Sort by**, and click the desired sort order: **Name**, **Date Modified**, **Type**, or **Size**. You can also choose to sort items in **Ascending** order (A to Z or 1 to 10) or **Descending** order (Z to A or 10 to 1). To display items in groups, right-click a blank area in the folder pane, point to Group by, and click **Name**, **Date Modified**, **Type**, or **Size**. You can also choose to display groups in **Ascending** or **Descending** order.

Applying View Preferences to All Folders

Changing the view settings and sort order for one folder does not change the settings for all folders. To change the view settings and sort order for all folders of the same type (for example, all picture folders), follow these steps:

- ❐ Enter your view and sort order preferences for a folder, as explained in the previous two sections.
- ❐ Click **Organize** (left end of the toolbar, as shown in Figure) and click **Folder and search options**.
- ❐ Click the **View** tab.
- ❐ Click **Apply to Folders** and click **OK**.

Choosing Single-Click or Double-Click Navigation

Unless you choose otherwise, Windows has you click files or folders to select them and double-click to open files or run programs. That's a lot of clicking. To reduce the amount of clicking, click **Organize** (left end of the toolbar) and click **Folder and search options**. Click **Single-click to open an item (point to select)** and click **OK**. Now you just have to get used to it.

Adjusting More Folder Options

You can change numerous settings to control the appearance and behaviour of folders, but this book doesn't really have the space to cover all the options. To explore on your own, click **Organize** (left end of the toolbar) and then click **Folder and search options**. You should be aware of two advanced settings on the View tab. Under Hidden files and folders, consider turning on **Show hidden files, folders and drives**. Windows hides some files to protect them, but this can cause problems when you're troubleshooting and need to find a particular Windows file. Also consider turning off **Hide extensions for known file types**. Almost all file

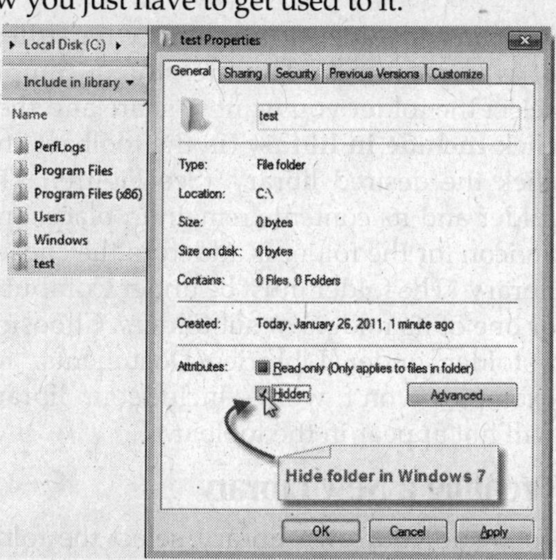

Adjusting folder options

names have a period at the end, followed by a three-character extension that indicates the file type—.doc (file created in Microsoft Word), .jpg (a special type of graphic file), .exe (an executable program file), and so on. These can come in mighty handy when you're instructed to look for a file with a certain file extension.

Managing Your Files Using Windows

Libraries

Windows 7 is designed to help you track down files wherever they happen to be stored on your PC. If you're obsessively organized, you probably need to know where everything is and you're likely to carefully construct your own filing system that makes sense to you. If you're not well organized, you can stick files and folders anywhere and use the Windows Libraries and its Search feature to find the needles in your haystack.

Understanding Windows Libraries

Initially, every user has four libraries: Documents, Music, Pictures, and Videos. You can see your libraries in the navigation pane. Libraries are folders with a twist. The twist is that each library acts more as an index of files and folders stored anywhere on your PC, so the actual files and folder don't have to actually be stored inside the library folder. For example, your Pictures library might include digital photos stored inside the library itself, in a different folder (such as C:\Photos), or even in a folder on an external hard drive (such as D:\VacationPhotos).

Browsing a Library's Contents

To browse a library's contents, click **Start**, **Computer**, and then click the library you want to browse. For convenience, Windows lists a few libraries on the right pane of the Start menu, so you can click **Start**, **Documents** (for example) to access the Documents library directly. You can then open folders and documents stored in the library as described earlier in this chapter.

Adding Folders to a Library

You can add folders to any library, regardless of where those folders are stored. Simply select the folder you want to share and then click **Include in library** (in the toolbar) and click the desired library. (See Figure.) The folder and its contents remain in place, and an icon for the folder is added to the chosen library. (The folder must be under Computer or one of its folders or subfolders. Choosing a folder under Libraries/Documents, for example, won't work—Include in library will not appear in the toolbar.)

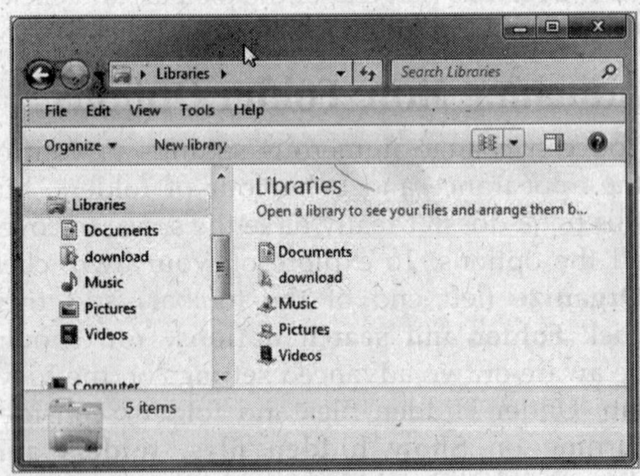

Adding folders to library

Creating a New Library

To create your own library, select the folder you want to share, and then click **Include in library** (in the toolbar) and click **Create new library**. Windows creates a new library and assigns it the same name as the folder you selected. To rename the library, right-click it in the navigation bar, click **Rename**, type the new name, and press **Enter**.

Arranging a Library's Contents

In addition to being able to sort items in the library as you sort items in a folder, you can arrange a library's contents. Open the library or a folder inside a library and then click the button next to **Arrange by:** (upper right) and click the desired arrangement.

You can also rearrange the library locations. When you're in one of the libraries, click the **locations** link below the library's name (in the upper left of the folder pane, not in the navigation pane). Click a location and then right-click it and choose **Move up** or **Move down**. Click **OK**.

Changing the Default Save Location

When you begin using programs to create documents and other types of files, you eventually save your work to disk for safekeeping. When you choose the **File**, **Save** command to save a document, the program displays a dialog box asking you to name the file and choose the folder in which you want it saved. Most Windows programs are set up to save files in the Documents folder (also called My Documents in some programs) or in one of the other standard Windows libraries, such as Pictures. You can choose a different drive and folder to save this particular file, but the next time you create and save a file, Windows will default to the Documents folder again. In some programs, you can choose a different default location, usually through the Tools, Options command.

Here's an easier way to change the default save location through Windows: When you're in one of the libraries, click the **locations** link below the library's name. Click the location you want to use as the default save location, and then right-click it and choose **Set as default save location**. Click **OK**.

Finding Files and Folders

The more files and folders you store on your PC, the more likely you'll lose or misplace something. Fortunately, Windows can help you find just about anything in about the time it takes to type a description of what you're looking for. The following sections show you how to perform different types of searches in Windows.

Searching Your Entire PC

To perform the easiest and broadest search, click **Start** and type a word or two describing the item you're looking for. As you type, Windows displays a list of items that match the description you typed so far. Keep typing to narrow your search. Type less to broaden your search.

Searching a Library or Folder

To perform a more targeted search, search the library or folder where you think the item is likely to be. Windows will search all locations in that library or folder:

- ❐ Open the library or folder you want to search. For example, click **Start, Documents**. (To search all libraries, click **Start, Computer, Libraries**.)

- Click in the **Search** box (upper-right corne the file or folder. As you type, Windows searches and displays all the items that have the entry you typed in their names or content. The more you type, the fewer items you see as Windows narrows the search. For each item in the list, Windows highlights the text that matches what you've typed.
- If you see a file that may be the one you're looking for, click it and then click the **Show preview pane** button (the middle button below the Search box). Windows opens the preview pane on the right. If your PC has a program that can open the file, a portion of the file's contents appears in the preview pane.
- To open the file, double-click it. If you don't see the file you're looking for, scroll to the bottom of the search results and click one of the **Search again** in options. For example, you can perform the same search in Libraries or Computer.

Searching Your Entire PC

Using Search Filters

Regardless of whether you search for a specific word, you can narrow the list of files displayed in the folder pane by selecting a search filter. For example, you can choose to filter by date and then limit the results to files modified yesterday, last week, earlier this week, or on a specific date.

Click in the **Search** box to display the Search menu, and then click one of the search filters at the bottom of the Search menu: **Authors**, **Type**, **Date modified**, or **Size**. Use the resulting options to specify your filter criteria, as shown in figure.

Searching a library or folder

Selecting Files and Folders

Before you can do anything with a file or folder, you must select it:

- ❒ Click a file or folder to select it. (Remember, if single-click access is on, you select the file by resting the tip of the mouse pointer on it.) Selected items appear highlighted, as shown in Figure.
  - To select non-neighboring (noncontiguous) items, select one item and then hold down the **Ctrl** key and select each additional item. (You can deselect a selected item by selecting it again.)
  - To select neighboring (contiguous) files and folders, select the first file or folder and hold down the **Shift** key while selecting the last one in the group.
  - You also can select a group of items by dragging a box around them. Point to a blank area above and to the left of the block of items you want to select, and then hold down the left mouse button while dragging down and to the right until the box surrounds all the items you want. When you release the mouse button, all the items within the box's borders are highlighted.

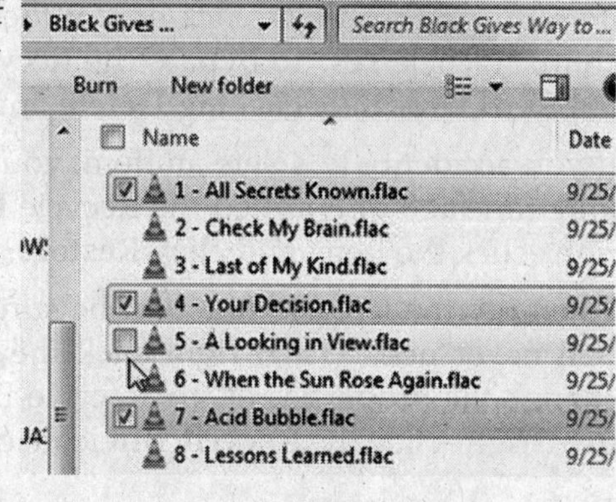

Selecting files and folders

Tagging and Rating Files

Tagging and/or rating certain files, including music and photos but not documents, can make finding them much easier later and help you recall a file's contents. To rate a file, select it in Windows File Manager; then, at the bottom of the window, click the desired rating star. To tag the file, click **Add a tag** and type one or more descriptive words or phrases separated by semicolons.

Making Your Own Folders

If you want to store your files in an independent folder of your choosing, create a new folder:

- ❒ Click **Start, Computer**.
- ❒ Change to the disk or folder in which you want the new folder located.
- ❒ Click **New folder** in the toolbar or right-click a blank area in the folder pane, point to **New**, and click **Folder**.
- ❒ Type a name for the folder (255 characters or fewer). As you start typing, the **New folder** name is deleted and is replaced by what you type. You can use any character or number, but you cannot use any of the following characters:

  \ / : * ? " < > |.
- ❒ Press **Enter**.

Deleting and Recovering Files: The Recycle Bin

Windows comes complete with its own trash compactor, called the Recycle Bin, conveniently located in the upper-left corner of your desktop. Whenever a file or folder has outlived its usefulness, either drag it over the **Recycle Bin** and release the mouse button, or select the item(s) and then right-click one of the selected items and click **Delete**. When prompted to confirm, click **Yes**. To bypass the Recycle Bin and permanently delete an item, hold down the **Shift** key while clicking **Delete** and then click **Yes** to confirm. Be careful with this!

If you accidentally delete an item, you can usually recover it, unless you deleted the item a long time ago or emptied the Recycle Bin. To recover an item, double-click the Recycle Bin, right-click the item, and click **Restore**.

To empty the Recycle Bin, first be sure the Recycle Bin contains only files and folders you will never need. Then right-click the **Recycle Bin** icon and click **Empty Recycle Bin**. To change the properties of the Recycle Bin, including the maximum amount of disk space it uses, right-click the **Recycle Bin** icon, click **Properties**, enter your preferences, and click **OK**.

Folders and Files

To rename a file or folder, right-click the item's name, click **Rename**, type the new name, and press **Enter**.

Moving and Copying Folders and Files

The most straightforward way to move items is to open two windows: one that shows the item(s) you want to move and another that shows the future destination of the items. Then simply drag any one of the selected items over the destination and release the mouse button to drop the items in place. Hold down the **Ctrl** key while dragging to copy the items instead of moving them. When you hold down the Ctrl key, a plus sign appears next to the mouse pointer, indicating that the items will be copied, not moved.

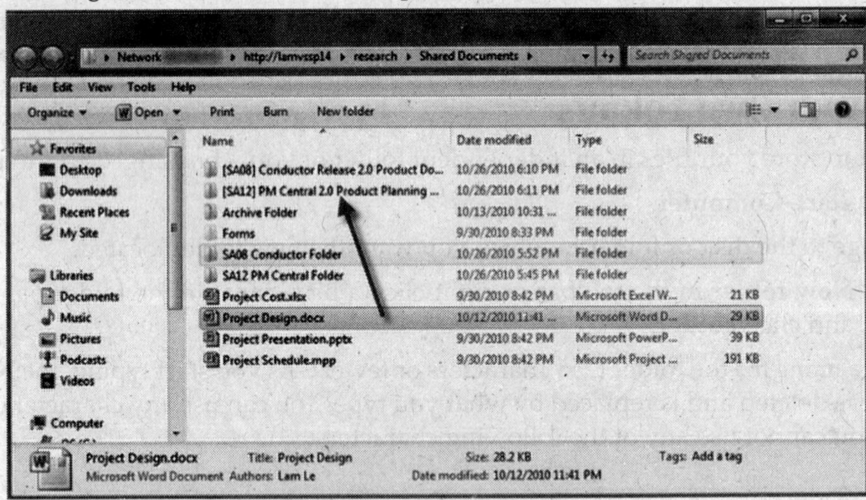

Moving and copying folders and files

Here's a quicker way to copy or move files:

- ❐ Select the items you want to copy or move in the folder pane.
- ❐ Display the desired destination folder in the navigation pane. You may need to click arrows to the left of items in the navigation pane to display the destination folder.

- Drag any one of the selected items over the destination folder and drop it inplace, keeping the following important information in mind:
  - If you drag an item to a *different disk,* Windows assumes that you want to *copy* the item instead of move it. To move the item, hold down the **Shift** key while dragging.
  - If you drag a folder or file to a different folder on the *same disk,* Windows assumes that you want to *move* the item to the new destination. To copy the item, hold down the **Ctrl** key while dragging.
  - If you're not sure, use the right mouse button instead of the left while dragging. When you release the button, a menu appears asking whether you want to move or copy the items. Sometimes the easiest way to move a file or folder is to cut and paste it (especially if you don't have the benefit of a two-paned Explorer window). Right-click the icon for the item you want to move and click **Cut** (to move the item) or **Copy** (to copy it). (To copy the objects instead, right-click an object and click **Copy**.) Change to the disk or folder in which you want the cut item placed. Right-click the disk or folder icon (or right-click a blank area in its contents window) and click **Paste**.

Copying Files to a CD or DVD

Copying files to a CD or DVD requires a slightly different approach than copying files on a hard disk drive, because the blank disc must first be prepared to store files and may then need to be properly "closed" so it can play on other computers and devices. Windows can burn files to a disc using either the Windows Live File System format or the Mastered format.

- **Windows Live File System:** Live File System discs are generally better for storing computer files, because you can add and remove files after burning files to the disc.
- **Mastered:** Mastered discs are generally better for storing music and pictures, because they're more compatible with regular CD, DVD, and Blu-ray players. To burn files to a disc using Live File System, follow these steps:
  - Insert a blank disc. The AutoPlay dialog box appears, displaying Blank CD or DVD options.
  - Click **Burn files to disc**. The Burn a Disc dialog box appears.
  - Type a name for this disc in the Disc title box, click **Like a USB flash drive**, and click **Next**. Windows formats the disc (which can take some time) and then displays the AutoPlay window.
  - Click **Open folder to view files**. Windows opens an empty disc folder window for that disc.
  - Copy files or folders to the disc as explained earlier in this chapter, or select a group of items you want to copy, right-click one of the items, point to **Send to**, and click the disc drive that contains the blank disc. As you add files to the disc, Windows automatically burns them to the disc.
  - Eject the disc as explained earlier in this chapter (see "Loading and Unloading CDs and DVDs"). Windows automatically "closes" the session and ejects the disc.

To burn files to a disc using Mastered, follow these steps:

- ❐ Insert a blank disc. The AutoPlay dialog box appears, displaying Blank CD or DVD options.
- ❐ Click **Burn files to disc** and click **OK**. The Burn a Disc dialog box appears.
- ❐ Type a name for this disc in the Disc title box, click **With a CD/DVD player**, and click **Next**. Windows displays an empty disc folder window.
- ❐ Copy files or folders to the disc as explained earlier in this chapter, or select a group of items you want to copy, right-click one of the items, point to **Send to**, and click the disc drive that contains the blank disc. As you copy items to the disc, a notification appears indicating that you have files waiting to be burned to the disc.
- ❐ When you're done copying items, click the notification balloon to display the window that contains the files waiting to be written to the disc.
- ❐ Click **Burn to disc** (in the toolbar near the top of the window), and then follow the wizard's instructions to burn the files to the disc and eject it.

Sharing Folders and Files with Other Users

Normally, each user's libraries remain off-limits to other users on this computer or on other computers that comprise a network. Windows provides two ways to share folders or files in your library with other users.

- ❐ Share among members of the same homegroup, Copy the files or folders you want to share to the Windows Public folder,

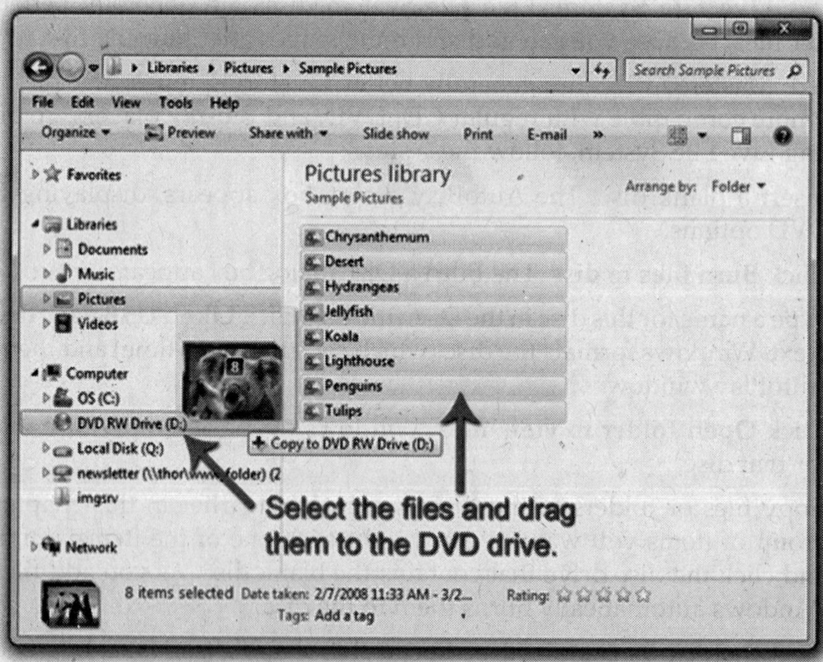

Sharing folders and files

To make sure Public folder sharing is enabled, click **Start, Control Panel, Choose homegroup and sharing options** (under Network and Internet), **Change advanced sharing settings.** Scroll down until you see **Public** and click the down arrow to the right. If the following is not enabled, select it: **Turn on sharing so anyone with network access can read and write files in the Public folders.** Click **Save changes.**

Points to Remember

- To display the disks, folders, and files on your PC, click **Start, Computer.**
- To move a file, drag it over the destination disk or folder icon and drop it in place. To copy a file, hold down the **Ctrl** key while dragging.
- To add a folder to a library, right-click the folder, point to **Include in library**, and click the desired library.
- To perform a quick search for anything on your PC, click **Start** and start typing one or more words to describe what you're looking for.
- To burn computer files to a blank CD or DVD, insert the disc, follow the onscreen cues, and remember that Live File System is usually best for burning computer files.

Running installing & Re-installing programs

Without programs, a computer is just a fancy box packed with electronic circuitry. Programs enable you to harness the power of that circuitry and use it to perform specific tasks such as typing a letter, keeping your checkbook balanced, surfing the World Wide Web, playing video games, and much more. This chapter shows you how to take control of programs. Here you learn how to run programs already installed on your computer, buy and install programs, and uninstall programs you no longer use.

Running Your Programs

Whenever you install a program, the installation utility places the program's name on the Start, All Programs menu or one of its submenus. To run the program, you simply click **Start**, **All Programs**, click the desired program group (if necessary), and click the program's name. (See figure) If you don't see the program you want to run, start typing its name in the **Search** box, and Windows will help you find it.

As you run programs, Windows automatically adds them to the Start menu's left pane so you can find them more easily next time. Programs you use often stay put, while those you use less often may get bumped off the menu, but you can still always find them on the All Programs menu or one of its submenus.

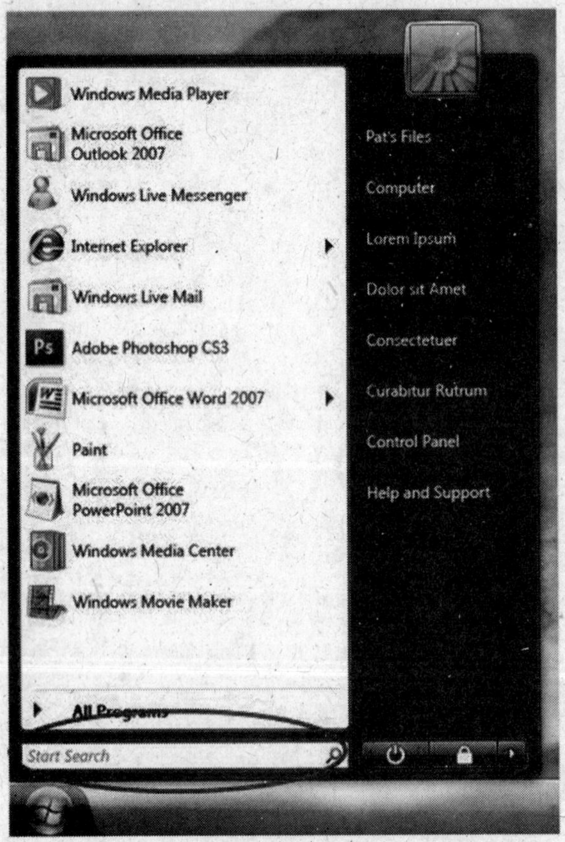

Run a program

Tip...

You can quickly run a program and open a document simply by double-clicking the document. Windows runs the program associated with that document type, and the program opens the document

Using Jump Lists for Quick Access to Programs and Files

As you use various programs to create, save, and edit documents (see Part 3), Windows keeps track of what you're doing and creates a jump list for every program, which contains the names of the files you worked on most recently. To access a program's jump list, do this:

- **From the Start menu:** Jump lists appear only for pinned or recently used programs that appear in the Start menu's left pane. To view a program's jump list, click **Start** and then mouse over the program.
- **From the taskbar:** Jump lists appear only for pinned or currently running programs that appear in the taskbar. To view a program's jump list, right click a program's icon in the taskbar.

After displaying a program's jump list, you can perform any of the following tasks:

- **Open an item:** Click the item to open it in the program associated with it.
- **Remove an item:** Right-click the item and click **Remove from this list**.
- **Copy an item:** Drag the item off the jump list and drop it wherever you want. For example, you can drag an item from its jump list into an e-mail message to attach the file to your message. (**Pin an item to the list:** Pinning an item to the jump list moves it to the top portion of the list, where it remains until you remove it. This is useful for documents you frequently open and work on. Right-click the item and click **Pin to this list**.
- **Unpin an item from the list:** To unpin an item, right-click it and click **Unpin from this list**. You can clear the history of recently opened programs, files, folders, and websites from the Start menu and taskbar. You may want to do this if you share a computer with someone and don't want that person to be able to see what you've been doing.

To clear the history, follow these steps:

- Right-click a blank area of the taskbar and click **Properties**.
- Click the **Start Menu** tab.
- Under Privacy, click the check box (to remove the check mark) next to **Store and display recently opened files in the Start menu** and **Store and display recently opened items in the Start menu and the taskbar**.
- Click **OK**.

Buying Software Your Hardware Can Run

Before you purchase any program, read the minimum hardware requirements printed on the outside of the package to determine whether your computer has what it takes to run the program. Be sure to note the following information:

- ❒ **Operating system:** Your PC can probably run older programs, but you're better off with Windows 7 versions.
- ❒ **Free hard disk space:** Be sure your hard disk has enough free disk space. To find out how much free disk space your computer has, Click **Start**,
- ❒ **Computer**. Windows displays the amount of used and free storage space on each disk drive.
- ❒ **CPU requirements:** CPU stands for central processing unit, and it's the brain of your computer. If the program requires at least a 1.5GHz 64-bit (x64) processor and you have a 1GHz 32-bit (x32) processor, your computer won't be able to run the application effectively, if at all.
- ❒ **Type of monitor:** All newer monitors support DVI and/or VGA. Some may support HDMI, too. See Chapter 2 for more about different types of monitors.
- ❒ **Graphics card:** Some games and graphics programs require a specific type of graphics card (display adapter).
- ❒ **Joystick:** Although most computer games allow you to use your keyboard and mouse, games are usually more fun if you have a joystick or something else that's a little more versatile.
- ❒ **CD or DVD drive:** Because of their size, many newer software packages (including Windows Vista) come on DVDs. Check for the required speed of the drive, too.
- ❒ **Sound card:** Games and programs for recording and mixing audio may require a special sound card or other recording equipment.
- ❒ **Amount of memory:** If your computer does not have the required memory (also known as RAM, short for "random access memory"), it might not be able to run the program, or the program might cause the computer to crash (freeze up). You can find out most of what you need to know about your computer from the System Information utility. Click **Start**, **All Programs**, **Accessories**, **System Tools, System Information**. The System Information window appears (see Figure), displaying the operating system name and version number, the type and speed of your processor, and the amount of RAM—physical (actual RAM) and virtual (hard drive space used as RAM).

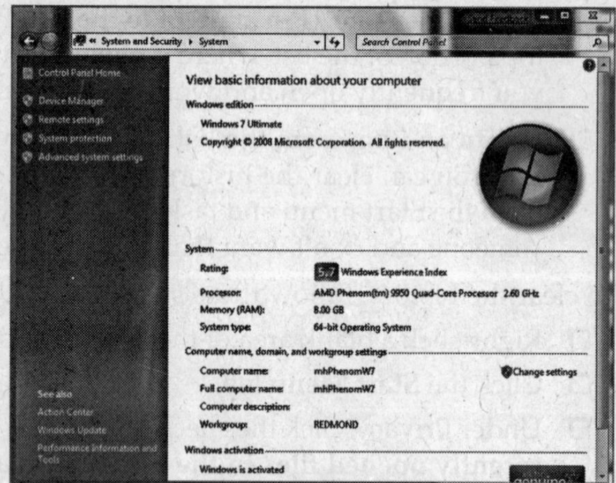

System information window

Click the plus sign next to Components to explore information about other components of your computer, including the CD-ROM drive, sound device, display, hard drives (under Storage), and so on.

Where to Find Programs

You can find programs and games online and offline. The following sections point out some of the most common methods of acquiring programs and some of the pros and cons of each.

The Usual Places You Shop

You can find programs and games online and offline. Following are some of the most common places to go to acquire programs and some of the pros and cons of each:

- **Offline retail stores:** You can find PC-based programs just about anywhere you can buy computers and office supplies.
- **Software developers:** Most software developers, including Microsoft, sell their programs directly to consumers online and usually let you try before you buy. You usually have the option to download the program and start using it right away or order the "media version" (on CD or DVD).
- **Shareware/Freeware sites:** Shareware sites, like download.cnet.com, are the ultimate in try-before-you-buy. You download the program and use it for the specified trial period; if you like it, you buy it. Freeware is like shareware, but you're not expected to pay … ever. (To avoid viruses and other malware, download only from trusted, well-established sites.) Security settings in your browser may prevent you from downloading or installing a file. If this happens, you usually see a security message at the top of the browser window indicating what's going on and how to proceed.

Installing Your New Program

Nearly every program on the market comes with an installation file (usually called Setup or Install) that does everything for you. If the program is on CD or DVD, you can usually pop the disc into the appropriate drive, and Windows will automatically initiate the installation routine. You click a few options to tell the installation utility that it can install the program according to the default settings, and then you can kick back and watch the installation routine do its thing.

Note....

Windows may prompt you for permission before installing a program. If you're not logged onto Windows as an administrator, you may need an administrator to enter a password before you can continue. If the installation doesn't start automatically when you insert the disc, here's what you do:

- If you haven't inserted the program disc into the drive, insert it now.
- Click **Start**, **Computer**.
- Double-click the icon for the drive that contains the disc. This displays a list of files and folders on the disc.
- Double-click the file named **Setup**, **Install**, or its equivalent. This starts the installation utility.
- Follow the onscreen instructions to complete the installation. If you downloaded a program, it may come as a compressed file (often called a *zip file*), which typically appears as a folder with a zipper

Installing a new program

on it and .zip in the file name. In most cases, you open the folder as you usually do, double-click the **Setup** or **Install** file, and proceed with the installation. If that doesn't work, try extracting the contents of the folder first. Right-click the compressed folder, click **Extract all**, and then click **Extract**. Windows extracts the contents and displays it in a separate window, where you can launch **Setup** or **Install**.

Removing a Program You Never Use

Your hard disk isn't an ever-expanding universe on which you can install an unlimited number of programs. As you install programs, create documents, send and receive e-mail messages, and view web pages, your disk can quickly become overpopulated.

One of the best ways to reclaim a hefty chunk of disk space is to remove (uninstall) programs you don't use.

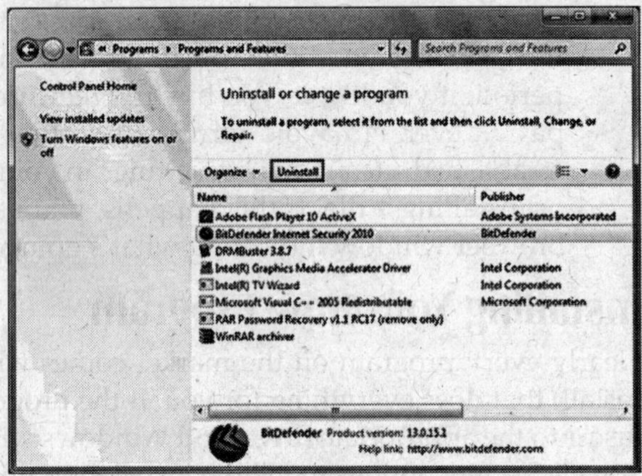

To remove a program safely and completely, always use the Windows Add/Remove Programs utility:

- ❐ Click **Start**, **Control Panel**.
- ❐ Under **Programs**, click **Uninstall a program**.
- ❐ Click the program you want to uninstall and then, in the toolbar (near the top of the window), click **Uninstall**. (See Figure)
- ❐ Click **Yes** to confirm.

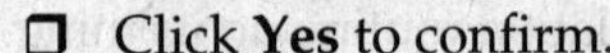

Removing a program

Some programs enable you to install or uninstall various components of the program. For example, you can install Microsoft Office without installing one of its programs, such as Access. In such cases, when you click a program to uninstall, you may see additional options in the toolbar, including Change and Repair.

Points to Remember

- ☆ To run a program, click **Start**, **All Programs**, click the desired program group, and click the program's icon.
- ☆ Not all programs run on all computers. Before buying a program, be sure your PC meets the requirements printed on the program's box.
- ☆ To access details about the components that comprise your computer, click **Start**, **All Programs**, **Accessories**, **System Tools**, **System Information**.
- ☆ To install a program, insert its installation disc or locate and double-click its **Setup** or **Install** file.
- ☆ To remove a program you no longer use, open the Windows **Control Panel**, click **Uninstall a program** under **Programs**, and follow the onscreen prompts.

Installing & Managing Additional Hardware Devices

Even if you purchased a PC with everything you thought you needed, you may discover new gadgets you simply can't live without. In addition, over time, you may want to take advantage of newer technology that your older PC is ill equipped to deal with. Instead of buying an entirely new PC, you may be able to upgrade your PC for a fraction of the cost. This chapter shows you how.

Upgrade or Buy a New PC?

I generally prefer upgrading my old PC to buying a new one for several reasons, including the fact that transferring programs, documents, e-mail, and everything else from an old PC to a new one is a hassle. I'm also not too fond of our throw-away culture. I'd rather repair than replace, even when repairing costs a little more. However, sometimes it makes sense to replace the entire PC:

- The upgrades cost more than half as much as a brand-new PC.
- You currently have a portable PC with limited upgrade options.
- Your PC is more than three years old (or less for a portable PC, because it's likely to get banged around a bit more). If you upgrade and then a major component of the PC goes belly up, that old PC can turn into a money pit.
- In addition, some of the newer software can have trouble with the older hardware.
- Someone you know could really put your old PC to good use.
- Even with all the upgrades you want, your PC still wouldn't be able to do what you want it to do. Make a list of all the upgrades you plan to make, shop around to determine the cost of each upgrade, total the amount, and compare it with the price of a new PC. The comparison may be enough to convince you to move up to a newer model.

Tip...

If you're thinking of replacing or upgrading your PC simply because it's slow, consider giving your PC a tune-up first and troubleshooting for performance issues.

Exploring Upgrades and Optional Accessories

When you're ready to soup up or accessorize your PC, you may want to know what your options are. The following list presents the most popular and useful upgrades and accessories:

- **Memory (RAM):** If your system has a meager 1GB RAM, adding another gigabyte or 3 can give it an instant performance boost.
- **External hard drive:** External hard drives are easy to install and are great for backing up files. Also, if you're running out of storage on your internal hard drive, you can move your photos, video, and other large files to the external drive to clear some space.
- **Internal hard drive:** If your PC has a vacant drive bay (a place for mounting another drive), you can significantly boost available storage by installing another internal drive.
- **Optical disc drive:** You may want to install a new disc drive to take advantage of a newer disc format, such as Blu-ray; upgrade from -R to +RW; or have two disc drives to simplify the process of copying discs.
- **Wi-Fi and/or Bluetooth adapter:** If your PC doesn't support wireless connectivity (Wi-Fi for wireless Internet or Bluetooth for wireless devices, such as a wireless keyboard or mouse), you can add this functionality. You can purchase a single adapter that supports both Wi-Fi and Bluetooth.
- **Webcam:** A webcam enables you to videoconference with your PC and take snapshots and record video of yourself while sitting at your PC.
- **Video card:** When you're upgrading to a new monitor (say, from VGA to DVI) or adding a second monitor, you may need to add a video card. Newer video cards typically have several ports for VGA, DVI, and perhaps even HDMI.
- **TV tuner:** Planning to watch TV on your PC? Then you'll need to add a TV tuner card or add a video card that includes a built-in tuner.
- **Memory card reader:** A memory card reader enables you to transfer data from flash memory cards commonly used to store photos in digital cameras and other devices.
- **Network adapter:** Most newer PCs have a local area network (LAN) port, as described in Chapters 1 and 2. If your PC has no LAN port, you can add one.
- **Sound card:** If you've decided to transform your PC into your family entertainment system, you may want to change or add a sound card to produce theater-quality sound.
- **Digital media server:** Media servers store, organize, and distribute digital media, including movies and music, throughout the house. The server is usually part of the home network (cable or wireless) and may be a specialized device or a full-featured computer. It usually has a multiformat disc player for transferring music and video to the server's hard drive, which is usually massive compared to that of a standard PC. The media server also includes a remote control.

- **Media centre extender:** A media centre extender enables you to place your digital media server in a separate room and stream the audio or video to the home theater or stereo system.

Installing External Devices

The easiest upgrades are those you can make simply by plugging an external device into one of your PC's existing ports or bringing a wireless device within range of the wireless adapter.

USB

You can add a webcam, hard drive, optical disc, wireless modem, TV tuner, card reader, Wi-Fi adapter, Bluetooth adapter, printer, keyboard, mouse, game controller (such as a joystick), and other devices. USB enables you to connect up to 127 devices to a host, which is far more than most users ever dream of connecting. When shopping for USB devices, make sure you purchase devices that your PC supports. Most PCs sold after 2002 support USB 2.0, which is 40 times faster than the old USB 1.0. If you're not sure, click **Start**, right-click **Computer**, and click **Properties, Device Manager**. Click the plus sign next to Universal Serial Bus controllers. If you see "Enhanced" anywhere in the list, your PC supports USB 2.0. Connecting a USB device to your PC is a snap—you just plug it in. You don't have to turn off your PC, because USB devices are *hot swappable.* However, some manufacturers may recommend installing software that came with the device first.

Definition

Hot swappable means you don't have to turn off the power to your computer to connect or disconnect the device.

Even if a device is hot swappable, just to be safe, perform the following steps when connecting a USB device for the first time:

- Install any software included with the device.
- If the device needs to be plugged into a power outlet (as in the case of a USB printer), plug in the device.
- Turn on the device, if necessary.
- Connect the device, using a USB cable, to your PC.

To safely disconnect a USB device, first eject it in Windows. Right-click the USB icon in the notification area and then click the **Eject** option for the device you want to disconnect, as shown in Figure. (You may need to click the up arrow to the left of the notification area to access the USB icon.) Wait for Windows to indicate when you can safely disconnect the device, and then unplug it. Ejecting is especially important when disconnecting an external hard drive or a flash drive, because unplugging it while Windows is using the device could damage or destroy files being stored on the device.

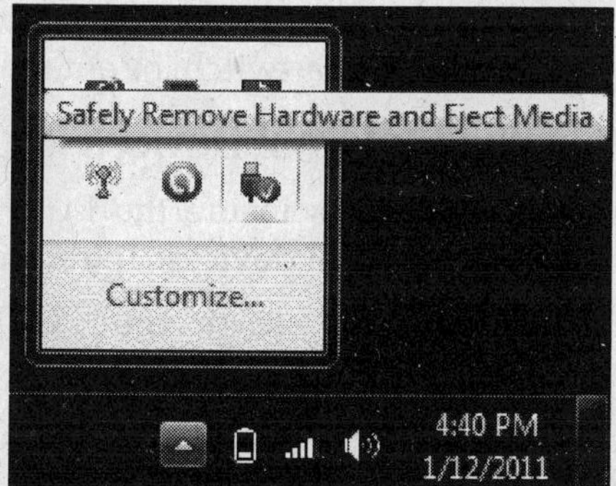

Disconnecting a USB drive

If you run out of USB ports, connect a USB hub, which enables you to plug numerous devices into a single port. Be aware, however, that hubs come in two types: powered and not powered. (All of the USB ports on your PC are powered.) Some devices, including USB hard drives and optical drives, require a powered USB port. Powered hubs require two connections: one to a power source and the other to an open USB port on your PC.

Wireless (Bluetooth and Wi-Fi)

Because wireless devices (Bluetooth and Wi-Fi) are cable-free, they're the easiest to connect:

- ❒ Make sure the device has power and is turned on. You may need to plug the device into a power outlet or install batteries.
- ❒ Make sure the device is in range of your PC's wireless adapter (typically 6 to 9 feet for Bluetooth and 100 feet for Wi-Fi).
- ❒ In Windows, click **Start**, **Control Panel**, **Add a device**. The Add a device window appears, and Windows searches for and detects the new device (assuming that all goes as planned).
- ❒ Click the icon for the device, click **Next**, and follow the onscreen instructions to complete the installation.

If Windows doesn't detect the wireless device, check the following:

- ❒ The device has power, is turned on, and is not in sleep mode. Try turning the device off and then on to bring it out of sleep mode.
- ❒ The device isn't already installed. Click **Start**, **Devices and Printers** to see if the device is already installed. (If Devices and Printers doesn't appear on your Start menu, click **Start**, **Control Panel**, **View devices and printers**.)
- ❒ The device is within range of your PC's wireless adapter. Try moving the device closer to your PC.
- ❒ No other wireless devices are interfering with this one. Try removing any cordless phones, microwave ovens, or other devices that commonly cause interference out of the vicinity.
- ❒ Your wireless adapter is properly connected and turned on, if necessary.
- ❒ Your PC's Bluetooth radio transmitter is on. Many portable PCs have an external switch for turning Bluetooth on or off.
- ❒ Your wireless device is set up to be discoverable. You may need to press a button on the device, flip a switch, or enter a menu setting to place the device in discoverable mode.

Installing Internal Devices and Upgrades

Installing devices inside the PC's system unit is a little more involved and riskier than installing external devices. To reduce the risk, take the following precautions:

- ❒ Back up the files on your PC. Turn off your PC and unplug it from the power source.
- ❒ Wear an antistatic wrist strap to protect sensitive electronic components from getting fried.
- ❒ Hold memory modules and expansion cards by their edges, to avoid touching any of the electronic components.

- Don't force anything.
- Make sure everything you plug in is securely plugged in before closing the case and turning on the power.

RAM Upgrades

To upgrade your PC's memory, you can add one or more memory modules. Depending on how your PC is configured, you may need to remove low-capacity memory modules before you can install higher-capacity modules. Consult your PC's documentation or manufacturer to determine the type of memory modules your PC can use—modules may look the same and be completely different. If you can't determine the type of memory from your manufacturer or your PC's documentation, an online memory dealer may be able to help. For example, www. crucial.com has a utility that can scan your PC and recommend the type of memory your PC uses, along with other useful information, including the maximum amount of memory your PC can have. Installing RAM is pretty easy. Following all precautions given earlier, proceed as follows:

- Open the case (system unit), following your manufacturer's instructions.
- Locate the memory modules on the motherboard, and note the position of the modules so that you can insert the new modules in the same position.
- If all the slots are occupied, remove one or more modules to make room for the new ones. This typically requires moving the clips on either side of the module away from the module and then pulling the module out of the slot. (The clips hold the module securely in place.)

RAM

- Insert the new memory modules into the slots, press them securely in place, and then hold down the module while pushing the clips back into place.
- Close the case. You may want to hold off on securing the case with screws until you're sure the memory upgrade works.

Expansion Cards

On desktop PCs, the motherboard has several expansion slots for installing expansion cards (also referred to as adapters). Common cards enable you to add USB and FireWire ports to your PC, upgrade its audio and video capabilities and performance, add a network adapter (wireless or LAN), and add Bluetooth capability. To install an expansion card, follow all the precautions given earlier and then proceed as follows:

- Install the software included with the device if the device documentation instructs you to do so.
- Turn off and unplug your PC.

- ❒ Open the case (system unit), following your manufacturer's instructions.
- ❒ Remove the metal cover plate (one screw) near the open expansion slot you want to use.
- ❒ Insert the new card so that the contacts on the card match up with the contacts in the expansion slot, and press down firmly on the card until it is fully seated.
- ❒ Replace the screw you removed in Step 4 to anchor the card in place, and then close the case.

ISA SCSI Expansion Card
http://www.computerhope.com

Expansion card

- ❒ If you installed the card to connect an external device, connect the device to the card.
- ❒ Turn on your PC and log on to Windows. Windows should identify the card and load any drivers it needs to use the card.

Upgrading Laptops, Notebooks, and Netbooks

Laptop, notebook, and netbook PCs tend to be limited in terms of their ability to upgrade. You may be able to upgrade the PC's memory and add an external monitor, but it's not likely to have an open drive bay and expansion slots. The best option is to look for a USB device that provides your PC with the desired functionality. If your portable PC has an ExpressCard slot, you may also be able to use ExpressCard devices to improve audio output, add USB and/or FireWire ports, add Wi-Fi apability, install an eSATA port for a high-speed external hard drive, and more. When purchasing ExpressCard devices, make sure you're getting the right card for your PC. Standard ExpressCards are 54mm wide and can accept 34mm cards. The 34mm slots are often used on smaller portable PCs to save space and consume less battery power.

Points to Remember

- ☆ If your PC is only one to three years old, you can probably upgrade it for less than the cost of a new PC and have it do everything you need it to.
- ☆ Adding RAM is one of the easiest ways to improve your PC's performance, particularly if your PC slows down when you're running multiple programs.
- ☆ The easiest way to upgrade a PC is to add an external device that plugs into one of the PC's USB ports.
- ☆ Desktop PCs have expansion slots into which you can plug expansion cards that can add to or improve upon your PC's features.
- ☆ Although portable PCs have limited upgrade options, a number of add-ons are available as USB devices.

Windows Inbuilt Games, Applications, Accessories, Word Processors

Windows comes up with lots of cool features installed. Just look over these sections and master it, you will start enjoying it.

Using Inbuilt Applications and Accessories

Windows 7 comes up with exciting features which will make your computing experience pleasurble.

Here`s how to reach to acessories:

- Click on start button
- Click on all programs
- Click on Acessories

You are There! Now checkout how to use these application on your own.

Calculator

Windows has always had a calculator, but for the most part it was a pretty cheap calculator. Windows 7 has substantially improved the calculator, adding more functions. You can now use the calculator in Windows 7 for everything from calculating your recent gas mileage to statistical analysis.

To run the Calculator, choose **Start→All Programs→ Accessories→Calculator**. You'll probably see the standard, basic Calculator window.

Calculator

With the Calculator in standard mode and with the basic configuration, you can do simple mathematical operations by entering the values to be computed separated by the operators (+ for addition, - for subtraction, * for multiplication, and / for division) and then clicking the equal (=) key. Keep in mind that you can enter your numbers and mathematical operators into the Calculator by either clicking the onscreen buttons or using the number keys or numeric keypad on your keyboard. The Calculator has three separate modes that you can switch to by selecting them from the View menu (or pressing the shortcut keys shown in parentheses):

- **Scientific (Alt+2):** Adds keys for performing trigonometric calculations — great for all the engineers out there.
- **Programmer (Alt+3):** Adds keys for performing programming calculations in different number systems, including hexadecimal, octal, and binary number systems, along with the usual decimal system using different word and byte sizes (and if you don't know what that is, you probably don't need this mode).
- **Statistics (Alt+4):** Adds keys for doing statistical calculations involving linear regression. The Calculator also offers specialized configurations (also available from the View menu) designed for more complex calculations:

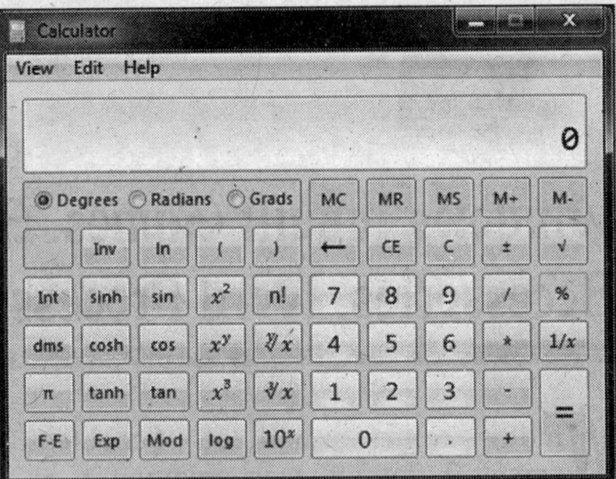

Scientific calculator

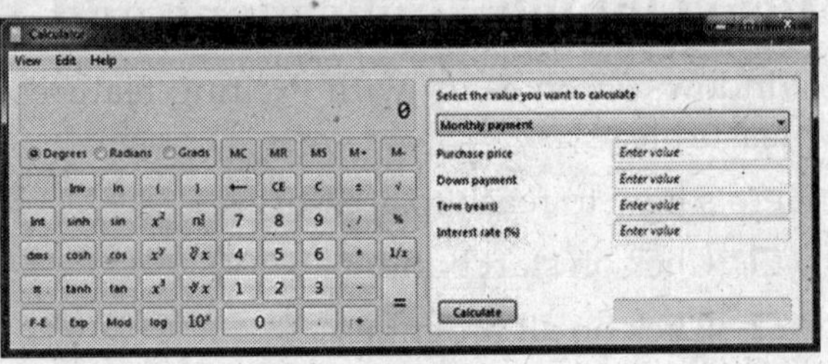
Statistics calculator

- **Unit Conversion (Ctrl+U):** Adds fields for converting all sorts of measurements (angles, pressures, temperatures, weights, time, velocities, mass, and so on) from one set of units to another.
- **Date Calculation (Ctrl+E):** Adds fields for performing calculations between two dates.
- **Worksheets:** Adds fields for calculating results, such as finding the necessary down payment or your monthly mortgage payment; the residual value of a leased vehicle; or the fuel economy of your vehicle.

Note....

Press Alt+1 to return the Calculator immediately to standard mode from any of the other three modes and press Ctrl+F4 to return to the basic configuration from any of the other available configurations.

Sticky Notes

The Sticky Notes accessory enables you to plaster the electronic equivalent of good old-fashioned Post – It notes all over your Windows 7 desktop. You can use Sticky Notes in Windows 7 as onscreen reminders: you can even colour code them to help you stay organized. They remain securely wherever you put them on the desktop until you delete them!

- To create a Sticky Note, click Start→All Programs→Accessories→Sticky Notes. Windows opens a new blank note on the desktop, positioning the cursor at the beginning of the note.
- Type the text of the note.
- You can also format the note text if you want.
- Just select the desired text and then press the appropriate shortcut key: Ctrl+B for bold text, Ctrl+I for italics, and Ctrl+U for underlining.
- You'll notice that the text automatically wraps to a new line, and if your text doesn't fit on the note, Windows automatically expands the height of the note to accommodate the length of your note.
- When you finish entering the note text, simply click somewhere on the desktop outside the sticky note itself.
- Alternatively, you can click the New Note button (the one with the plus sign) to start a new sticky note. The note you create will stay on the desktop.
- If you use sticky notes, you'll want to get acquainted with the Sticky Notes Quick Launch button on the taskbar. Click it once to temporarily hide all the sticky notes on your desktop. To bring all of your sticky notes back to the desktop or to the top of the windows on the desktop, click it again.
- To colour-code a sticky note, right-click the note and then click the colour you want. Your choices here are Blue, Green, Pink, Purple, White, or Yellow.
- To delete a note that you no longer need, click its Delete button in the upper-right corner.
- The first time you delete a note, Windows asks you to confirm the deletion. If you don't want to see this alert again, select the Don't Display This Message Again check box before you click Yes. When you open an Explorer window that overlaps a note, you can bring the sticky note to the top of the pile by clicking any visible part of the sticky note. If nothing is visible, click the Sticky Notes Quick Launch button on the taskbar.

Sound Recorder

Sound Recorder lets you record a sound and save it as an audio file on your computer. This will show you how to open and use Sound Recorder in Windows 7

You can record sound from different audio devices, such as a microphone that's plugged into the sound card or motherboard audio line in jack on your computer. The types of audio input sources you can record from depend on the audio devices you have and the input sources on your sound card or motherboard.

To use Sound Recorder, you must have a sound card or motherboard with an audio line in jack and speakers installed on your computer. If you want to record sound, you will also need a microphone or some other audio input device.

- Open the Start Menu, click on **All Programs**, **Accessories** folder, and double click on **Sound Recorder**. (See screenshot below)

Note....

The Sound Recorder exe file is located at ***C:\Windows\system32\SoundRecorder.exe.***

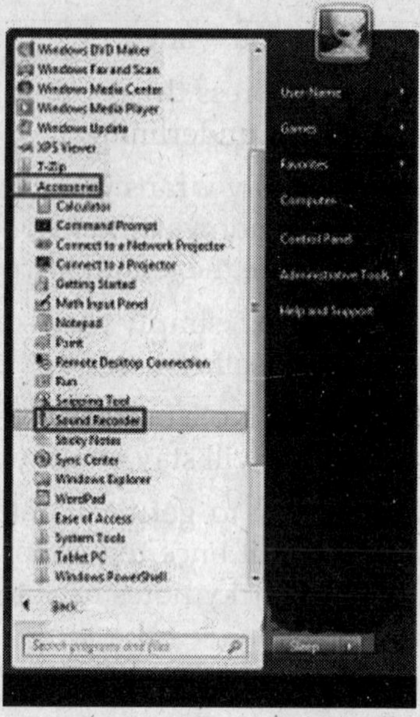

To Start Recording

A) Click on **Start Recording**. (See screenshot below)

To Stop Recording and Save

A) Click on **Stop Recording**. (See screenshot below)

B) Navigate to where you want to save this **.wma** file, type in a name for the file, then click on the **Save** button. (See screenshot below)

Note....

In this Save As window you can also specify information for the ***Contributing artists*** *name,* ***Album*** *title, or* ***Genre*** *by clicking on each one of them and typing the information before clicking on Save.*

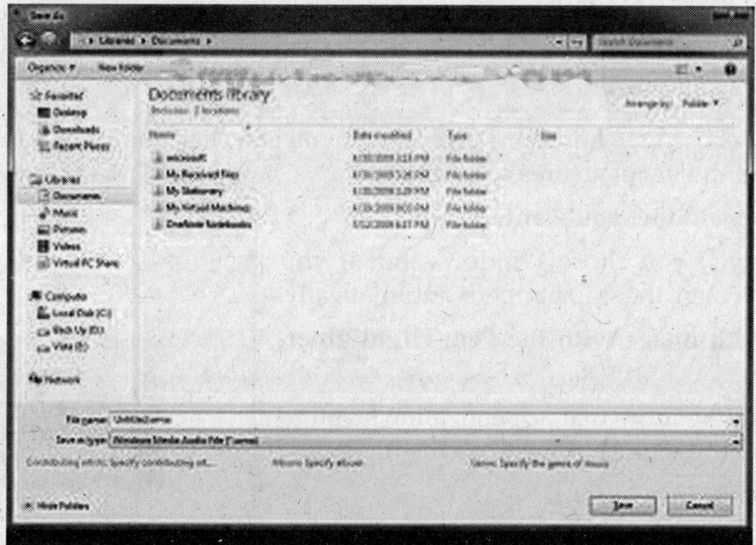

Saving recorded sound file

> **Tip...**
>
> *If you decide to continue recording audio instead of saving it to file right now, then click on the **Cancel** button instead. (See screenshot above)*

When ready to continue recording, click on **Resume Recording**. (See screenshot below)

When finished, close Sound Recorder.

Snipping Tool

Window 7 includes a neat tool — the Snipping Tool — that allows you to capture a screen shot of any object on your screen. Although capturing screen shots, or snipping, isn't a new concept, Windows 7 has made it easier and more functional with the snipping tool. Just follow these steps to see how easy snipping with the Snipping Tool in Windows 7 can be.

- ❒ **Choose Start.**

  Go to All Programs→Accessories→Snipping Tool.

- ❒ **Click the down-arrow on the New button.**

  Choose a snip mode from the drop-down list: Free Form Snip lets you draw any old kind of line you like, such as a triangle, to define what you want to snip; Rectangular Snip does what it says — when you click and drag over a region, it forms a

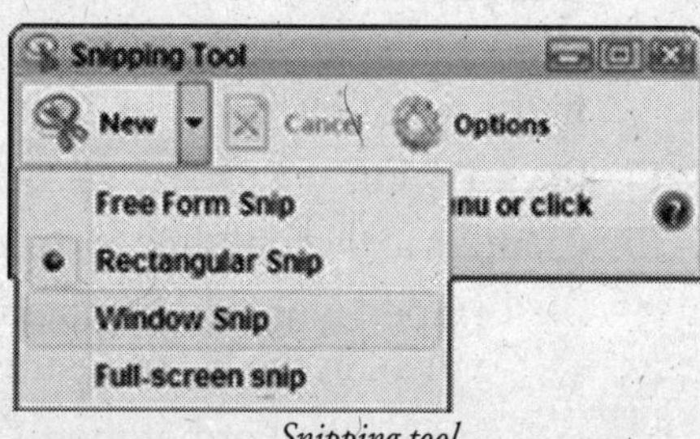

Snipping tool

rectangular snip; Window Snip allows you to select an active window to snip; and Full-Screen Snip takes the entire enchilada, capturing the whole screen in the wink of an eye.

- ❒ **Click and drag.**

  Only if you chose Free Form or Rectangular, you can click and drag on the desktop or in a document to form an area to snip.

- ❒ **Click on the window you want to snip.**

  Do this only if you chose Windows, but if you chose Full-Screen, the snip happens automatically.

- ❒ **Mark up with image with the Pen, Highlighter, and Eraser.**

  The mark-up window that appears allows you to choose from these tools to mark up the image.

- ❒ **Click the Save Snip button.**

  The Save Snip button looks like a computer disk and will display the Save As dialog box. The Save As dialog box is where you can enter a filename, specify the location to save the file to, and then click Save.

Snipping too

Playing Inbuilt Games

There are many games in the Windows 7 games folder. Follow the route map up to My programs & then click on Games.

Click the game you want to play. You can press F1 or read game instructions to learn how to play games.

Games

Using a Notepad

- ❒ Notepad is a basic text-editing program and it's most commonly used to view or edit text files. A text file is a file type typically identified by the .txt file name extension.
- ❒ Open Notepad by clicking the Start button . In the search box, type Notepad, and then, in the list of results, click Notepad.
- ❒ Start Typing
- ❒ Changes to the font style and size affect all the text in the document can be made in this way-.
  - Open Notepad by clicking the Start button. In the search box, type Notepad, and then, in the list of results, click Notepad.
  - Click the Format menu, and then click Font.

- Make your selections in the Font, Font style, and Size boxes.
- When you are finished making font selections, click OK. (See Part 3)

Using Paint

Windows Live Paint, Windows 7's improved drawing program, has been expanded to include a ribbon panel that makes drawing a picture easier than ever. Using the new Scenic Ribbon in Paint, you can access a variety of virtual pens and brushes for drawing whatever you can dream up.

Although there's an added hassle to obtain Paint, the program includes several new features to enhance your ability to draw and edit photos.

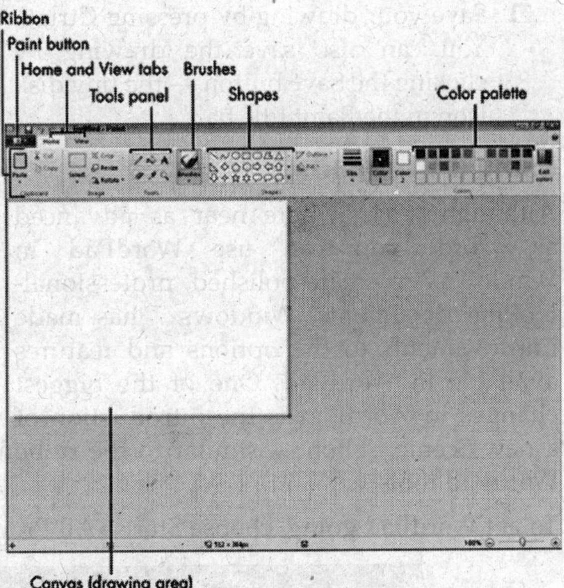

- ☐ Click the Start button, type paint, and click Paint in the search results. The Paint window opens. Maximize the window, if it isn't already.
- ☐ Click and drag your mouse over the white canvas to draw a black squiggle using the default brush and colour; then release the mouse button.
  - The canvas is the area you draw on, below the Ribbon.
  - If your computer uses a pen or has a touch screen, you may be able to draw directly on your screen.
- ☐ Click the down arrow on the Brushes button in the Ribbon to see a panel of brushes. Select one you like.

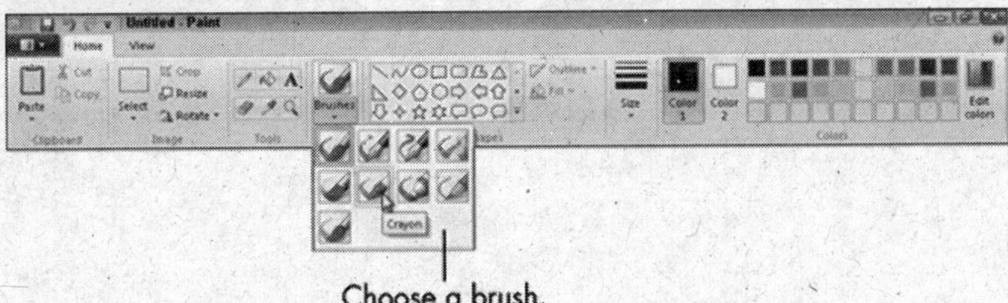

Choose a brush.

Hover your mouse pointer over each brush to see a tooltip that describes it.

- ☐ Click one of the small colour boxes at the right end of the Ribbon to select that colour.
- ☐ Click and drag your mouse over the canvas again. The new line will reflect the new brush and colour you chose. You can also use Paint's premade Shapes tools. Click the Shapes button on the Ribbon; click a shape on the panel that drops down; and click and drag in the canvas to draw that shape. Then click the paint-bucket icon on the Tools panel to change the inside (or *fill colour*) of the shape.

- ❒ To add text to your drawing, click the A button on the Tools panel; then click the canvas and start typing in the text box that appears. Notice that a new Text tab opens above the Ribbon.
- ❒ Select the text you just typed and choose options in the Text tab to size and format your text. You can change fonts, colours, sizes, and so on.
- ❒ Save your drawing by pressing Ctrl+S. You can also save the drawing by clicking the Save button — the tiny disk icon in the Paint title bar.

Using a WordPad

Although it's nowhere near as advanced as Word, you can use WordPad in Windows 7 to create polished, professional-looking documents. Windows 7 has made improvements to the options and features available in WordPad. One of the biggest changes in WordPad is the introduction of a new Scenic ribbon — similar to the ribbon interface in Word — that holds most of the WordPad tools.

To get WordPad going, choose Start→All Programs→Accessories→WordPad.

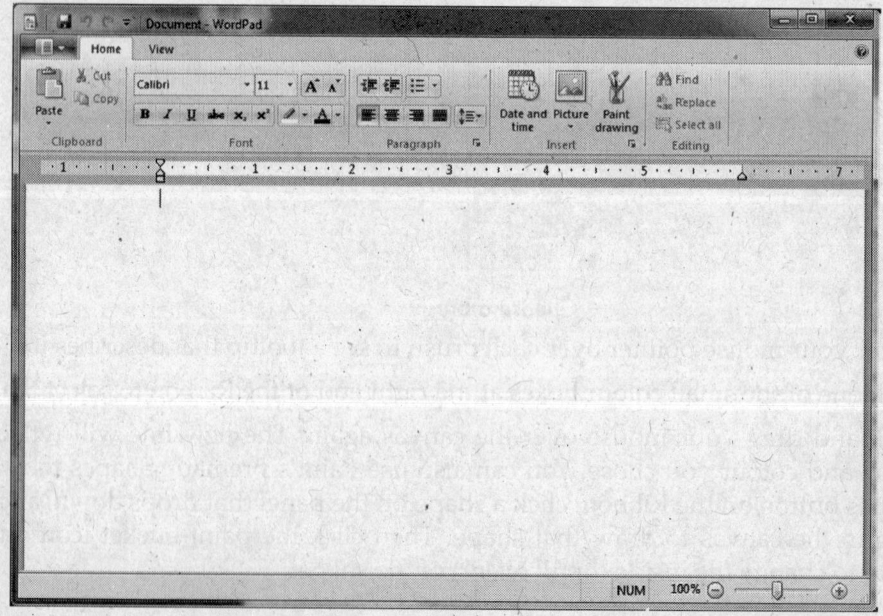

WordPad is primarily intended for typing. But if you need to do some formatting, you can use the tools on the ribbon. Here are a few things to keep in mind:

- To format text, select the text you want to format; then choose the formatting you want from the Ribbon. For example, to change the font, click the down arrow next to the font name and choose the font you like.
- To format a paragraph, simply click once inside the paragraph and choose the formatting from the Paragraph part of the Ribbon.
- To change the page layout (such as margins and whether the page is printed vertically or horizontally, for example), use the Page Setup dialog box. To open it, click the down arrow next to the icon that looks like a piece of paper. Then choose Page Setup.
- Tabs are complicated. Every paragraph has tab stops set every half inch. To insert a new tab, just press the Tab key. Add additional tab stops by clicking where you want in the ruler.
- You can also set tabs by clicking the tiny side arrow to the right of the word *Paragraph* and then clicking the Tabs button.
- If you create a tab stop, it only applies to the selected paragraph. So, select all the paragraphs you need before adding a tab stop.

WordPad allows you to save your documents in formats that will hold on to the new formatting. You can choose from the following formats:

- Rich Text Format (RTF) preserves basic formatting when read by a variety of word processors. RTF documents can have some simple formatting, but nothing nearly as complex as Word 97, for example.
- OOXML Text Document (.docx) is the new Microsoft document standard file format, introduced in Word 2007.
- Although WordPad can read and write .docx files, it doesn't apply formats in the same way that Word does. If you're not careful, WordPad will clobber much of the original Word formatting.
- ODF Text Document (.odt), the OpenDocument format, is the native format for OpenOffice.
- Text Document (.txt) strips out all pictures and formatting and saves the document in a Notepad-style regular old everyday text format.

Points to Remember

- ☆ To reach to inbuilt accessories click or start button, click on all programes, then click on accessories.
- ☆ Press Alt+1 to return the calculator to standard mode
- ☆ Word pad allows you to save your documents in formats that will hold on to the new formatting.

Networking and Basics of Internet

People generally network their PCs for two reasons:

- To share files and other resources, including a printer, a high-speed Internet connection, and a backup drive among two or more computers, to establish a connection with a *Wi-Fi hotspot*. A *hotspot* is a location that offers a wireless network connection for connecting to the Internet. You're likely to find hotspots in coffee shops, hotels and motels, and airports.
- To allow friends, roommates, or family members to play multiuser games. In this chapter, you discover the four most common ways to network computers, how to use the Windows networking features to set up a network and share files and resources, and how to connect to a Wi-Fi hotspot when you're on the road with your PC.

Exploring Your Networking Options

When planning your network, the first step is to decide which type of networking hardware you want to use. The following sections discuss your options and some important considerations for making the best choice for your situation and needs. The costs involved are comparable for each option.

Wireless

Wi-Fi networks enable computers to communicate via radio waves. The biggest advantages of wireless are that you can set up a network without having run cables, and you can move the computers almost anywhere in your home or office without losing your connection. The three main drawbacks are that wireless is generally slower than the other three options; Wi-Fi networks are less secure (because data is transmitted through airwaves); and signal interference can be caused by walls, pipes, electrical wiring, cordless phones, and microwave ovens. Still, Wi-Fi is almost always the most attractive choice for most homes and small businesses.

Note....

Some Wi-Fi signals can reach pretty far—150 to 350 feet—so be sure to secure your network to keep unauthorized users (such as your neighbours) from accessing your data or using your broadband Internet service Wi-Fi data transfer rates vary depending on the standard, as you'll see later. A maximum data transfer rate (under ideal conditions) of 54 megabits per second (Mbps) is pretty standard. At that rate, it takes about 1.5 seconds to download a 10MB file. The newest Wi-Fi standard can transfer data at speeds up to 600Mbps under ideal conditions.

Ethernet

Fast, reliable, secure, and inexpensive, Ethernet networks are an excellent choice if all your computers are in one room or you don't mind running network cables throughout your home or business.

Ethernet

Ethernet networks have data transfer rates of 10, 100, or 1,000Mbps, depending on the type of cables. Transferring a 10MB file over a 100Mbps connection takes about 1 second.

HomePNA

Secure and potentially inexpensive, Home Phoneline Networking Alliance (HomePNA) enables you to network computers over existing phone lines. HomePNA 2.0 is relatively slow, with a data transfer rate of 10Mbps—about the same speed as a slow wireless network. HomePNA 3.0 features data transfer rates of up to 128Mbps—about double the speed of most wireless networks.

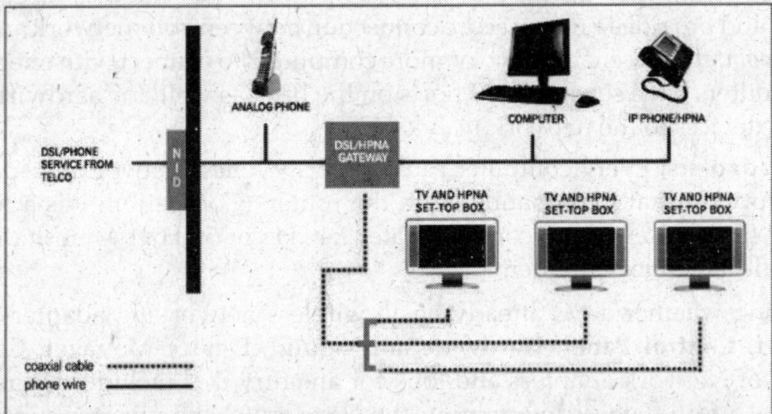

Home PNA

Powerline

Fast (up to 200Mbps), reliable, secure, and inexpensive, Powerline networking enables you to connect computers using existing electrical wiring in your home or business. The main drawback of powerline networks is that electrical "noise" on the line can interfere with the signal.

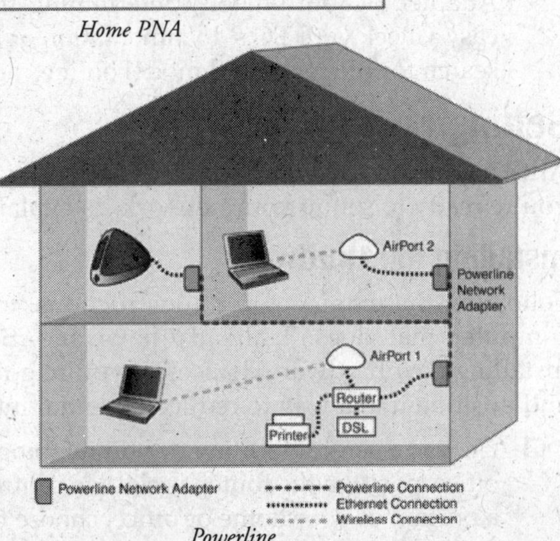

Powerline

Hybrid

You can combine the networking technologies discussed here to create a hybrid network. For example, you can build an Ethernet network that connects all the computers in your office and then use a wireless or phone line.

Networking Hardware Checklist

Chances are good that if the computers you plan to network are relatively new, some or all of them have a LAN port (for an Ethernet network) or some sort of Wi-Fi capability. Knowing which hardware you already have on hand may influence your choice of networking configuration. In the following sections, you take inventory of the hardware you already have and determine which hardware you need for each of your networking options.

Wireless Networking Hardware

To set up a wireless network, you need two things:

- **Wireless router or access point:** A *wireless router* is best and essential if you plan to share an Internet connection, because it can assign an Internet address to each networked computer and provides a more secure connection between your network and the Internet. An *access point* merely enables two or more computers to connect with one another. (Most wireless routers have several LAN ports on the back as well, for hardwiring computers and other devices to the network.)
- **Wireless adapters:** Every computer must have a wireless networking adapter or built-in Wi-Fi support that's compatible with the router. (Compatibility is a function of the frequency the devices use to communicate: 2.4GHz or 5GHz.) Almost all portable PCs have a built-in wireless adapter.
- Determining whether a PC already has a wireless networking adapter is pretty easy. Click **Start**, **Control Panel**, **Hardware and Sound**, **Device Manager**. Click the arrow to the left of Network adapters and look for an entry that includes "Wireless Network Adapter." Unfortunately, determining the standard(s) the adapter supports is not so easy. Check your PC's documentation or the box it came in, contact the manufacturer, or search for the make and model online.

Setting Up Your Network

After you've decided on the type of network you want and gathered the requisite hardware, you're ready to set up your network, as explained in the following sections.

Installing the Hardware

Following the manufacturer's instructions, install or connect a network adapter to every computer that doesn't already have one. See Chapter 10 for more information about installing new hardware devices. If you're going to use a wireless router, choose a location and position it in a way to reduce potential interference:

- Choose a central location. If you're going to be using computers all over your home or office, position the router as close to centre as possible. If you're using computers in only a portion of your home or office, choose the centre location in that portion.

- Reduce potential obstructions. Choose a location off the floor and away from walls, metal filing cabinets, and anything else that might block the signal.
- Reduce potential interference. Position your router away from microwave ovens and the most common areas where you use a cordless phone, if possible. Networking equipment that uses a 5GHz frequency can help reduce interference from cordless phones and microwaves. 802.11a and 802.11n devices are less susceptible. If your network primarily uses 802.11g (2.4GHz) networking equipment, shop for phones and other devices that operate at a higher frequency, such as 5.8GHz.

Setting Up Your Internet Connection

If you plan to share an Internet connection, now is a good time to set it up. Chances are pretty good that if you have high-speed Internet service, your service provider sent a technician to set up the modem on one of your computers and establish the connection for you. All you have to do is disconnect the modem's cable from the PC and plug it into the designated Internet port on the back of the router—the port is typically labeled "Internet," "WAN" (wide area network), or "WLAN" (wireless local area network). Some services supply a combination modem/router, which makes your job even easier—just plug the device into the designated port on any of your networked computers.

Connecting the Cables and Cords

The process for connecting the computers and other devices on your network varies, depending on the type of network.

Make the following connections based on your network configuration:

- **Wireless:** Plug the wireless router into your surge protector.
- **Ethernet:** Connect the Ethernet cable from each computer's LAN port to the router, hub, or switch, and then plug the router, hub, or switch into your surge protector.
- **HomePNA:** Using standard telephone cables, connect each computer's HomePNA network adapter to a phone jack.
- **Powerline:** Plug each computer's Powerline adapter into an electrical outlet.

Connecting a Printer

Now you should have everything connected except, perhaps, the printer. This varies based on the type of printer you have and how you want to connect it:

Network printer, wired: If your printer has a LAN port, you can connect it to the router. All computers on the network can then use the printer independently through the router.

Network printer, wireless: This printer is similar to a wired network printer, but it connects to the network through the wireless router. (Some wireless network printers also include a LAN port.)

USB printer: Connect the printer to a USB port on the computer from which you'll do most of your printing. The other computers can then access the printer through this computer. The only drawback is that the computer attached to the printer must be turned on for the other computers to use it.

Bluetooth printer: If all your networked computers are Bluetooth enabled and within range, they can connect to the printer independently. Otherwise, the computer must connect to the printer through one of the Bluetooth enabled computers.

Turning Everything On

In certain cases, you can turn on all the computers and the modem, printer, router, and other devices in any sequence, and everything works fine. Sometimes, however, something doesn't work—for example, if you turn on the computer and router before turning on the modem, the modem may have trouble establishing an Internet connection.

The proper sequence for powering up your network is to work from the outside (peripherals) back to the computer:

- ❒ Turn on the modem and wait for the lights to indicate that the modem has established a connection.
- ❒ Turn on the router and wait about 30 seconds for it to detect the modem.
- ❒ Turn on the computer you want to use.

If you're setting up a wired network (Ethernet, HomePNA, or Powerline), all computers on the network that are turned on should be connected, but you may still need to set up your router to establish an Internet connection. Check the installation instructions included with your router. Setting up a wireless network is more involved, as explained in the following section

Setting Up a Wireless Router

Most routers include a setup disc. After turning on the router and at least one of the computers on the network, insert the disc into one of the computers that's up and running. Windows should automatically launch the router setup routine from the disc. If it doesn't, find the Setup or Install file on the disc and double-click it. The steps for setting up a router for the first time vary depending on the router and the manufacturer's setup routine. However, they all require that you do the following:

- ❒ Establish an Internet connection. Because all of your computers will connect to the Internet through the router, you may need to provide the router with the username and password your ISP has assigned to you.
- ❒ Give your network a name. Most routers initially use a default network name, but for security purposes, assigning a unique name is a good idea. Network names are case sensitive, and every computer on the network needs to use the same network name to connect.
- ❒ Choose an encryption level, such as WiFi Protected Access (WPA) or WPA-2. This secures the network by blocking unauthorized access and encrypting data as it flows through the network.
- ❒ Specify a passphrase (password). A secure passphrase includes a mix of upper- and lowercase letters, numbers, and symbols (-, _, &, $, and so on). Initially, all computers on your network will use the same passphrase.

Write down the network name, encryption level, and passphrase, because you'll need to enter this information on all of the computers you want to include in the network.

Running the Set Up a Network Wizard

Running the Set Up a Network Wizard If your router did not include a disc, you can use Windows to set up your network. Windows features a Set Up a Network Wizard that leads you step by step through the process of configuring all computers on your wireless network to establish a connection with the network:

- Click Start, Control Panel to display the Control Panel.
- Click Network and Internet and then Network and Sharing Centre.
- Below Network and Sharing Centre, click Set up a new connection or network.
- Click Set up a new network, and then follow the wizard's instructions to set up your network.

The Set Up a Network Wizard can save the network settings to a USB drive to make it easier to add other computers to the network. You can then insert the USB drive into another computer and, in the AutoPlay dialog box, select Wireless Network Setup Wizard to have Windows automatically configure the computer to connect to the network. Otherwise, take the following steps to add another computer to the network:

- Click Start, Control Panel, Network and Internet.
- Below Network and Sharing Centre, click Connect to a network.
- Click the wireless network from the list that appears and click Connect, as shown in Figure.
- Follow the onscreen instructions to enter whatever information is required, such as the network name, encryption level, or passphrase/security key.

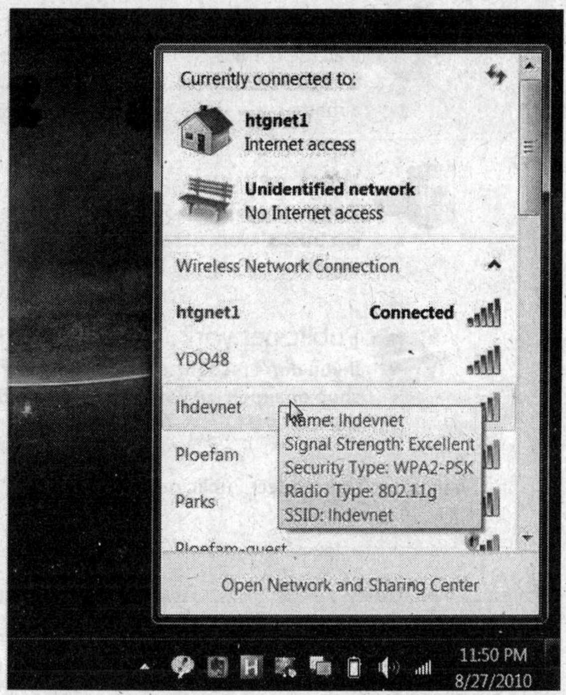

Setting up a network wizard

Choosing a Network Location

Networking computers increases their exposure to unauthorized access and to malware (viruses, spyware, and so on), especially if the computers share an Internet connection. The risk level varies depending on the network. A home network is relatively safe, whereas a Wi-Fi hotspot outside your home poses a greater risk. Whenever you connect to a network for the first time, Windows prompts you to choose a network location, which contains security settings appropriate for the type of network you're connecting to. To choose a network location, click **Start, Control Panel, Network and Internet, Network and Sharing Centre**.

Below View your active networks, click your current network location (**Home**, **Work**, or **Public**) and then choose the desired location:

- ❐ **Home network:** On a home network, you know all the networked computers and users, so Windows can let down its guard. Computers on a home network can join a homegroup, and network discovery is turned on, so networked computers and devices can identify one another and access shared resources.

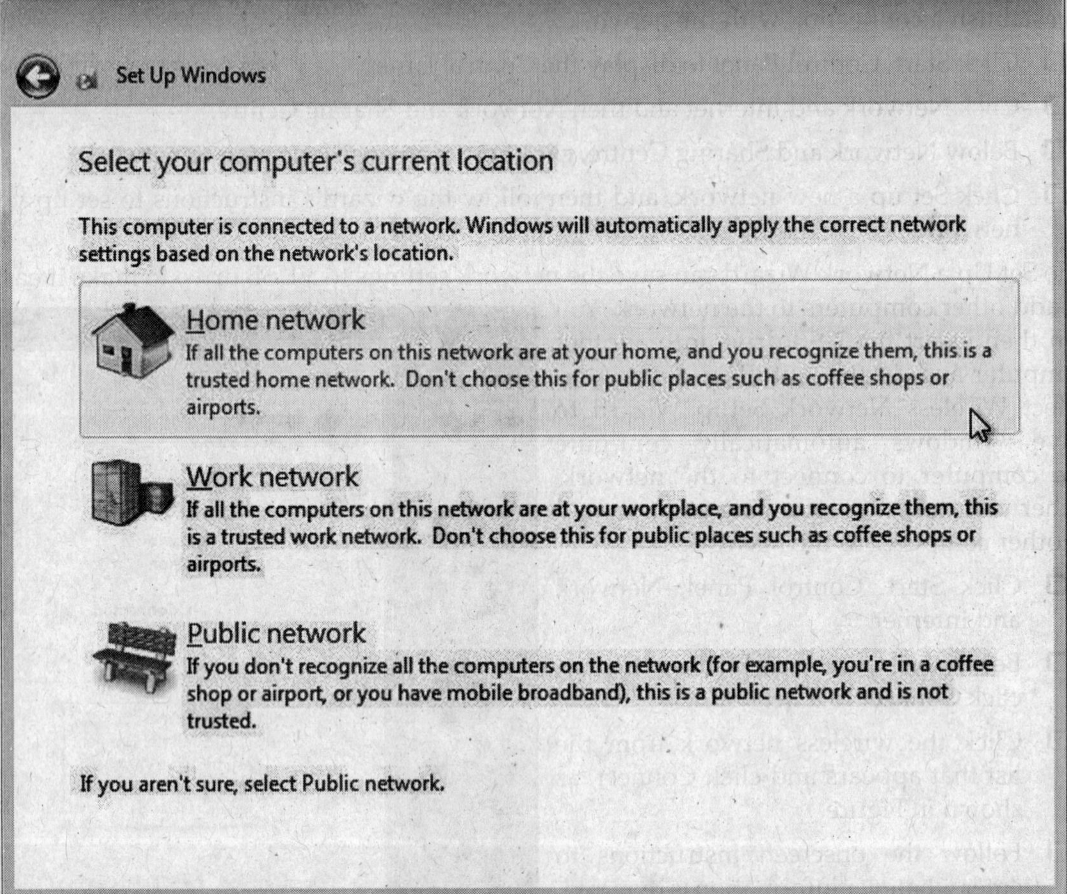

- ❐ **Work network:** Network discovery is enabled, so networked computers can see shared resources on your computer and vice versa, but you can't create or join a homegroup.
- ❐ **Public network:** This option attempts to keep your PC and any shared resources invisible and inaccessible when connecting in a public place, such as a coffee shop, or connecting directly to the Internet without the protection of a router.

Testing Your Network

To test your network, make sure everything is turned on, and then click **Start**, **Computer**, **Network**. You should see an icon for every computer on the network.

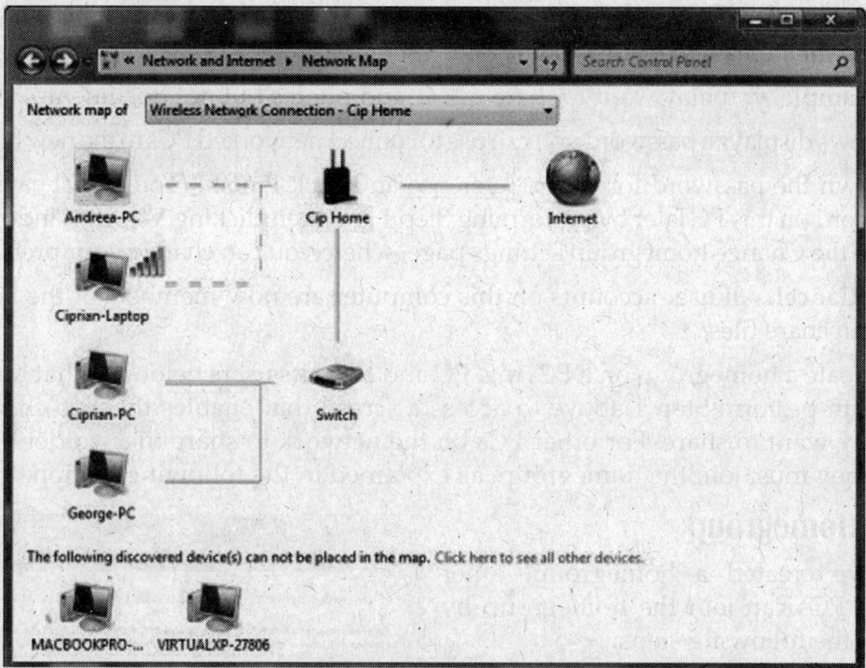

Testing your network

If you don't see icons for the other networked computers, run the Network troubleshooter:

- Click Start.
- Type network trouble (in the Search box).
- Click Identify and repair network problems. This runs the Network troubleshooter, which tries to diagnose the problem.
- Follow the onscreen instructions to diagnose and correct the problem. You can also check the status of your network at any time, from any of the computers on the network. Click Start, Control Panel; then below Network and Internet, click View network status and tasks. Near the top of the window, Windows displays a graphic showing your computer connected to the network, which is connected to the Internet (assuming you set up an Internet connection).

Creating a Homegroup

You can set up a homegroup in Windows, and each user can choose which folders and files to share with other users and networked computers that join the homegroup.

(Only PCs running Windows 7 Premium or Ultimate can create homegroups, but if a networked PC is running the Basic or Starter edition, it can still join a homegroup.)

To create a homegroup, here's what you do:

- Click Start, Control Panel, Choose homegroup and sharing options (below Network and Internet).

- ❒ Click Create a homegroup.
- ❒ Choose the items you want to share, and click Next.

  For example, you may want to share music and photos but not documents.

  Windows displays a password you can use to connect networked PCs to the new homegroup.
- ❒ Jot down the password for future reference and click **Finish**. (You can always view the password on this PC later by performing Step 1 and then clicking **View**.) Windows returns you to the Change homegroup settings page, where you can change your preferences.
- ❒ Click **Cancel**. All user accounts on this computer are now members of the homegroup and can share files.

After you create a homegroup on a PC, this PC and all of its users belong to that homegroup. Each user can perform Step 1 above to access a screen that enables them to choose which libraries they want to share. For other PCs on the network to share files, folders, and other resources, they must join the homegroup, as explained in the following section.

Joining a Homegroup

After you've created a homegroup, other Windows 7 PCs can join the homegroup by performing the following steps:

- ❒ Click **Start**, **Control Panel**, **Choose homegroup and sharing options** (below Network and Internet).
- ❒ Click the **Join now** button.
- ❒ Follow the onscreen instructions to enter the homegroup password and choose the libraries you want to share.

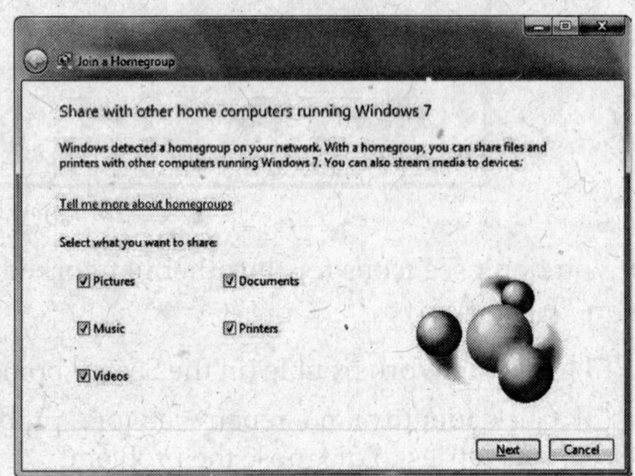

Joining a homegroup

Sharing Files in a Homegroup

These steps work well for sharing the entire contents of your library folders, but say you want to share only certain files or you create a new folder you'd like to share. In such cases, you can choose specifically what you'd like to share (or not share) and how much control over those items other users will have:

- ❒ Click Start, Computer.
- ❒ Navigate to the folder that contains the item(s) you want to share or prohibit other users from sharing. (See Chapter 8 for details about navigating disks and folders.)
- ❒ Click the file or folder to select it. (To select additional items, hold down the Ctrl key while clicking them.)
- ❒ Click Share with (in the toolbar near the top of the window).
- ❒ Click the desired share option: Nobody (to block access), Homegroup (Read), Homegroup (Read/Write), or Specific people.

- If you chose Specific people, use the File Sharing dialog box to select the people to share with and specify the level of access for each person; then click Share and then Done.

Checking an Item's Share Setting

To determine whether a resource is shared, click it and then check the details pane (shown in Figure), which shows whether the item is shared and with whom.

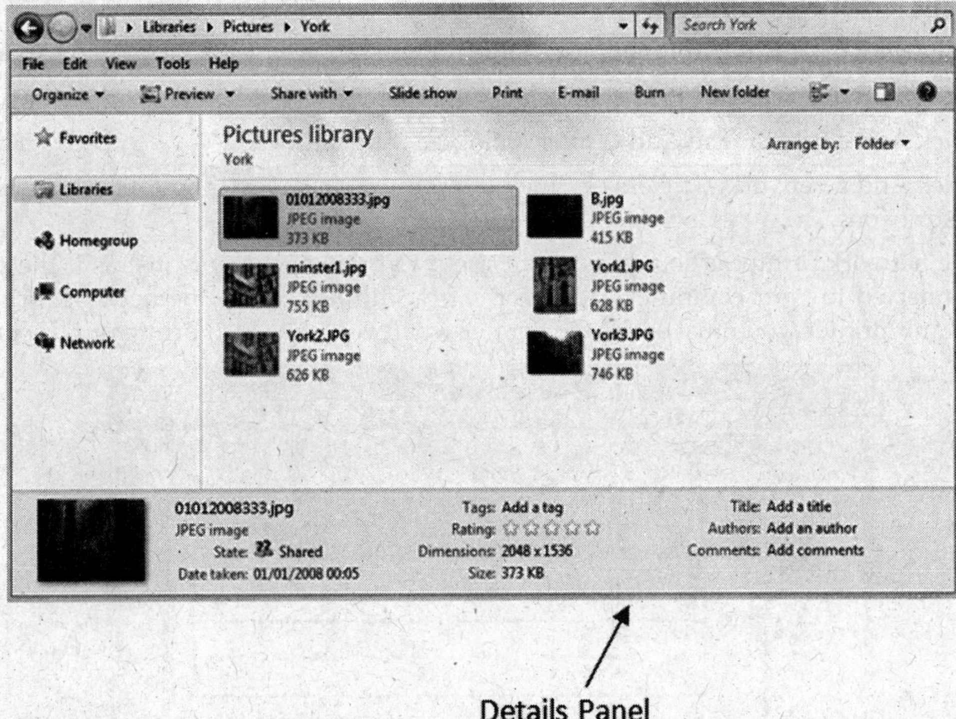

Accessing Shared Disks, Folders, and Files

Your network is up and running and you've chosen to share libraries or folders on the networked computers. Now, how do you get to those shared files and folders? Simply click **Start, Computer**. In the navigation pane (left), below Network, click the desired homegroup or computer. The folder pane (right) displays the shared folders or files in the homegroup or on the computer you selected. You can navigate the folders just as if they were stored on this computer,

Printer

You already know what a printer is, now checkout how to install it on web.

Installing a Printer on Your Network

The steps for installing a printer on your network depend on the printer and how it's connected to the network:

- **Network printer**: If your printer is connected to the router or is a wireless printer, you install it as a *network printer,* meaning all networked computers access the printer independently (not through another computer).

- **Shared printer**: If your printer is connected to one of your networked computers—for example, with a USB cable—you can set it up as a *local printer* and then share it. Other computers on the network can then access the printer through this computer.

Installing a Network Printer

To install a network printer, follow these steps:

- Click Start, Devices and Printers.
- Click Add a Printer. The Add Printer dialog box appears.
- Click Add a network, wireless or Bluetooth printer, click Next, and follow the onscreen instructions.

After the network printer is set up, you can use it to print documents just as if the printer were connected to your computer. However, if you did not set up the network printer as your default printer, you must select the printer when you choose to print your document

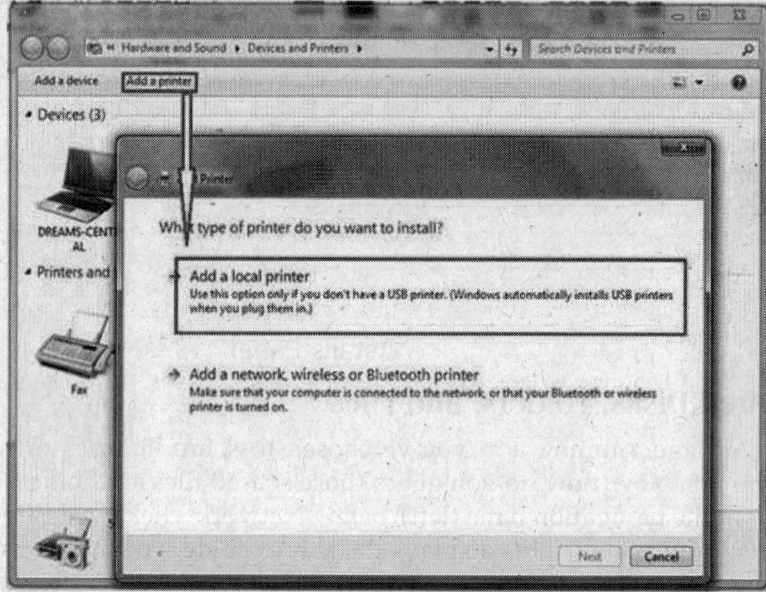

Installing a network printer

Sharing a Printer

To share a printer, first install it as a local printer on one of your networked computers, as explained in earlier . Assuming that the computer that's connected to the printer has joined the network's homegroup, the printer should be available to all computers in that homegroup. If the printer is not available, make sure it's shared:

- Click **Start, Devices and Printers**.
- Right-click the printer you want to share and click **Printer properties**.

❒ Click the **Sharing** tab, select the **Share this printer** check box, and click **OK**.

Just like Printer there are other devices also which work like scanner.

Securing Your Network

A broadband Internet connection is typically an *always-on* connection. That is, as long as you leave your modem, router, and computer on, you're connected to the Internet. This makes your network more vulnerable to attacks from snoopy people and perhaps even Internet vandals. With the proper know-how, someone on the Internet can connect to your computer, peek at your documents, and even destroy valuable data. You can't completely protect your computer or network from such threats, but you can significantly deter potential break-ins by implementing various security measures. For details on how to protect your computer and your network from online threats

Points to Remember

- ☆ To network your computers, install a single, centralized router and make sure each computer you want on the network has a compatible network adapter or LAN port.
- ☆ Learn how to adjust your router settings to enable its firewall, enter encryption settings, and specify a passphrase that all computers need to log on to the network.
- ☆ To share files, folders, and other network resources, create a homegroup and have all networked computers join the homegroup.
- ☆ To access a shared folder, click Start, Computer, and then click a homegroup or computer (below Network).
- ☆ When using your PC in a public Wi-Fi hotspot, change your network location to Public.
- ☆ Always have at least one firewall running: the router's firewall when you're home and the Windows firewall when you're on the road

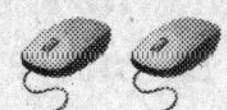

Disk Operating System (DOS)

As the name suggests, the operating System is used for operating the system or the computer. It is a set of computer programs and also known as DOS (Disk Operating System). The main functions of DOS are to manage disk files, allocate system resources according to the requirement. DOS provides features essential to control hardware devices such as Keyboard, Screen, Disk Devices, Printers, Modems and programs.

Basically, DOS is the medium through which the user and external devices attached to the system communicate with the system. DOS translates the command issued by the user in the format that is understandable by the computer and instruct computer to work accordingly. It also translates the result and any error message in the format for the user to understand.

Brief introduction to DOS and its need

Disk Operating System - is an old operating system prior to Windows that manages everything on your computer: hardware, memory, files...

Many people consider DOS ancient history, with the presence of graphic driven operating systems (GUI - Graphic User Interface) such as Windows, MacOS, I bet no one is running DOS as an operating system. However, the black box becomes useful when you're stuck with Windows, so it's sometimes necessary to know the basics of DOS. Even during the reign of Windows, DOS is still involved in many tasks. Another reason why you should learn DOS is to overwhelm your friends with a bunch of cryptic commands just like in the movies ! DOS isn't that complicated, all you need to know is few commands to list your files, copy, delete, rename, and other stuff...

Getting Started with DOS

Now DOS is known as Command Prompt.

C ommand Prompt is a feature of Windows that provides an entry point for typing MSDOS (Microsoft Disk Operating System) commands and other computer commands. The most important thing to know is that by typing commands, you can perform tasks on your computer without using the Windows graphical interface. Command Prompt is typically only used by advanced users.

When you're using Command Prompt, the term command prompt also refers to the right angle bracket (>, also known as the greater than character) that indicates the command line interface can accept commands. Other important information, such as the current working directory (or location) where the command will be run, can be included as part of the command prompt. For example, if you open the Command Prompt window and see the C:\> command prompt with a blinking cursor to the right of the right angle bracket character (>), you know that the command you enter will be run on the entire C drive of your computer.

Starting and Working with DOS in Windows 7

Open the Command Prompt window by clicking the Start button, clicking All Programs, clicking Accessories, and then clicking Command Prompt.

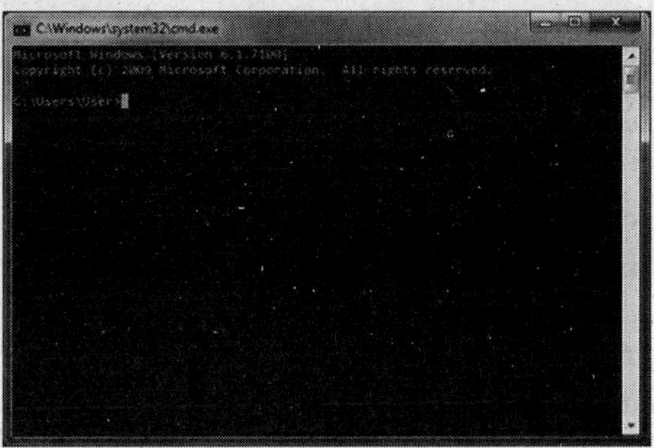

DOS Commands 'cd\,' 'time,' 'date,' and 'cls'

There are set of Command written in DOS for use, some of them, as the name suggests, they are similar to their functions.

Cd: Change Directory - move to a specific Folder

CD (Change Directory) is a command used to switch directories in MS-DOS. For example, if you needed to run Windows 3.11 from DOS, you would type:

cd windows - Changing the directory to Windows;

win - To run the win.com file within the windows directory.

Syntax

Windows XP and later syntax

CHDIR [/D] [drive:][path]

CHDIR [..]

CD [/D] [drive:][path]

CD [..]

.. Specifies that you want to change to the parent directory.

Type CD drive: to display the current directory in the specified drive.

Type CD without parameters to display the current drive and directory.

Use the /D switch to change current drive in addition to changing current directory for a drive.

If Command Extensions are enabled CHDIR changes as follows:

The current directory string is converted to use the same case as the on disk names. So CD C:\TEMP would actually set the current directory to C:\Temp if that is the case on disk.

CHDIR command does not treat spaces as delimiters, so it is possible to CD into a subdirectory name that contains a space without surrounding the name with quotes. For example:

cd \winnt\profiles\username\programs\start menu is the same as:

cd "\winnt\profiles\username\programs\start menu" which is what you would have to type if extensions were disabled.

Windows 98 and earlier syntax

CHDIR [drive:][path]

CHDIR[..]

CD [drive:][path]

CD[..]

Examples

cd

Goes to the highest level, the root of the drive.

cd..

Goes back one directory. For example, if you are within the C:\Windows\COMMAND> directory, this would take you to C:\Windows>

Windows 95, 98, and later versions have a feature in the CD command that allows you to go back more than one directory when using the dots. For example, typing: **cd...** with three dots after the cd would take you back two directories.

cd windows

If present, would take you into the Windows directory. Windows can be substituted with any other name.

cd\windows

If present, would first move back to the root of the drive and then go into the Windows directory.

cd\windows\system32

If present, would move into the system32 directory located in the Windows directory. If at any time you need to see what directories are available in the directory you're currently in use the dir command.

cd /d e:\pics

If, for example, you were on the C: drive, typing the above command with the /d option would first switch the E: drive letter and then move into the pics directory.

cd

Typing cd alone will print the working directory. For example, if you're in c:\windows> and you type the cd it will print c:\windows. For those users who are familiar with Unix or Linux this could be thought of as doing the pwd (print working directory) command.

Time: Display or set the system time

Syntax

Displays or sets the system time.

TIME [time]

Type TIME with no parameters to display the current time setting and a prompt for a new one. Press ENTER to keep the same time.

Example

time 12:00

Set the time to 12:00

Date: Display or set the date

Syntax

Displays or sets the date.

DATE [date]

Type DATE without parameters to display the current date setting and a prompt for a new one. Press ENTER to keep the same date.

Example-

date

Display the current date and prompt for a new one. If no date is entered, the current date will be kept.

Cls: Clear the screen

Syntax

CLS

Example-

cls

Running the cls command at the command prompt would clear your screen of all previous text and only return the prompt.

Acquiring Elevated or Administrative Privileges

Some commands that you can run using Command Prompt might require elevated or administrative privileges. To run these commands, you can use the Run as administrator command:

- Click the Start button.
- In the Search box, type command prompt.
- In the list of results, right-click Command Prompt, and then click Run as administrator. If you are prompted for an administrator password or confirmation, type the password or provide confirmation.

Changing Current file type

To convert an existing FAT or FAT32 volume to NTFS, follow these steps:

- ❒ Click Start, point to All Programs, point to Accessories, and then click Command Prompt.
- ❒ At the command prompt, type the following, where *drive letter* is the drive that you want to convert:
  - convert *drive letter*: /fs:ntfs
  - For example, type the following command to convert drive E to NTFS:
  - convert *e*: /fs:ntfs

Note....

If the operating system is on the drive that you are converting, you will be prompted to schedule the task when you restart the computer because the conversion cannot be completed while the operating system is running. When you are prompted, click YES.

- ❒ When you receive the following message at the command prompt, type the volume label of the drive that you are converting, and then press ENTER:
  - The type of the file system is FAT.
  - Enter the current volume label for drive *drive letter*
- ❒ When the conversion to NTFS is complete, you receive the following message at the command prompt:
  Conversion complete
- ❒ Quit the command prompt.

Creating a File Using the DOS Command 'copy con filename'

Syntax

Copies one or more files to another location.
COPY [/A | /B] source [/A | /B] [+ source [/A | /B] [+ ...]] [destination] [/A | /B]] [/V] [/Y | /-Y]

source	Specifies the file or files to be copied.
/A	Indicates an ASCII text file.
/B	Indicates a binary file.
destination	Specifies the directory or filename for the new file(s).
/V	Verifies that new files are written correctly.
/Y	Suppresses prompting to confirm you want to overwrite an existing destination file.
/-Y	Causes prompting to confirm you want to overwrite an existing destination file.

The switch /Y may be preset in the COPYCMD environment variable. This may be overridden with /-Y on the command line.

To append files, specify a single file for destination, but multiple files for source (using wildcards or file1+file2+file3 format).

Examples

copy *.* a:

Copy all files in the current directory to the floppy disk drive.

copy autoexec.bat c:\windows

Copy the autoexec.bat, usually found at root, and copy it into the windows directory; the autoexec.bat can be substituted for any file(s).

copy win.ini c:\windows /y

Copy the win.ini file in the current directory to the windows directory. Because this file already exists in the windows directory it normally would prompt if you wish to overwrite the file. However, with the /y switch you will not receive any prompt.

copy "computer hope.txt" hope

Copy the file "computer hope.txt" into the hope directory. Whenever dealing with a file or directory with a space, it must be surrounded with quotes. Otherwise you'll get the "The syntax of the command is incorrect." error.

copy myfile1.txt+myfile2.txt

Copy the contents in myfile2.txt and combines it with the contents in myfile1.txt.

copy con test.txt

Finally, a user can create a file using the copy con command as shown above, which creates the test.txt file. Once the above command has been typed in, a user could type in whatever he or she wishes. When you have completed creating the file, you can save and exit the file by pressing CTRL+Z, which would create ^Z, and then press enter. An easier way to view and edit files in MS-DOS would be to use the edit command.

Using the DOS Commands 'type,' 'ren,' and 'del'

- Type: Displays the contents of text files.

  TYPE [drive:][path]filename

  Example-

  type c:\autoexec.bat

  This would allow you to look at the autoexec.bat

- Ren: Used to rename files and directories from the original name to a new name. In earlier releases of MS-DOS instead of using ren or rename you need to use the move command to rename your MS-DOS directories or files.

  Renames a file/directory or files/directories.

  RENAME [drive:][path][directoryname1 | filename1] [directoryname2 | filename2]

  REN [drive:][path][directoryname1 | filename1] [directoryname2 | filename2]

  Note that you cannot specify a new drive or path for your destination.

Examples

rename c:\chope hope

Rename the directory chope to hope.

rename *.txt *.bak

Rename all text files to files with .bak extension.

rename * 1_*

Rename all files to begin with 1_. The asterisk (*) in this example is an example of a wild character; because nothing was placed before or after the first asterisk, this means all files in the current directory will be renamed with a 1_ in front of the file. For example, if there was a file named hope.txt it would be renamed to 1_pe.txt.

rename "computer hope.txt" "example file.txt"

Rename the file "computer hope.txt" to "example file.txt". Whenever dealing with a file or directory with a space, it must be surrounded with quotes. Otherwise you'll get the "The syntax of the command is incorrect." Error

❑ Del: is a command used to delete files from the computer

Syntax:

Deletes one or more files.

DEL [/P] [/F] [/S] [/Q] [/A[[:]attributes]] names

ERASE [/P] [/F] [/S] [/Q] [/A[[:]attributes]] names

names	Specifies a list of one or more files or directories. Wildcards may be used to delete multiple files. If a directory is specified, all files within the directory will be deleted.
/P	Prompts for confirmation before deleting each file.
/F	Force deleting of read-only files.
/S	Delete specified files from all subdirectories.
/Q	Quiet mode, do not ask if ok to delete on global wildcard
/A	Selects files to delete based on attributes
attributes	R Read-only files S System files H Hidden files A Files ready for archiving - Prefix meaning not

If Command Extensions are enabled DEL and ERASE change as follows:

The display semantics of the /S switch are reversed in that it shows you only the files that are deleted, not the ones it could not find.

Windows 2000 and Windows XP recovery console syntax

Deletes one file.

del [drive:][path]filename

delete [drive:][path]filename

[drive:][path]filenameSpecifies the file to delete.

Delete only operates within the system directories of the current Windows installation, removable media, the root directory of any hard disk partition, or the local installation sources.

Del and delete do not support replaceable parameters (wild cards).

Examples

Notice: Users who are running Microsoft Windows 95 and are used to deleted items going to the recycle bin need to keep in mind that deleting files from MS-DOS does not send files to the recycle bin.

del test.tmp = Deletes the test.tmp in the directory that you currently are in, if the file exists.

del c:\windows\test.tmp = Delete the c:\windows\test.tmp in the windows directory if it exists.

del c:\windows\temp*.* = (* is for wild character(s)) *.* indicates that you would like to delete all files in the c:\windows\temp directory.

del c:\windows\temp\?est.tmp = (? is a single wild character for one letter) This command would delete any file ending with est.tmp such as pest.tmp or zest.tmp...

Points to Remember

- **The main functions of DOS are to manage disk files, allocate system resources according to the requirement.**
- **There are set of command written in DOS for use, some of then, as name suggests are similar to their functions.**

SECTION–III
GETTING DOWN TO
BUSINESS

Chapter 13

Installing MS Office 2010

The Most important thing is installing the Microsoft Office on your Systems first. You can do it by purchasing a genuine copy of Microsoft Office from nearest software outlet, or simply download it from the Microsoft's official website. Here we are discussing setup instructions for Microsoft Office Professional Plus 2010.

After buying CD/Downloading files, follow these Instructions:

- ❐ Go to the File directory where the Microsoft office setup is.

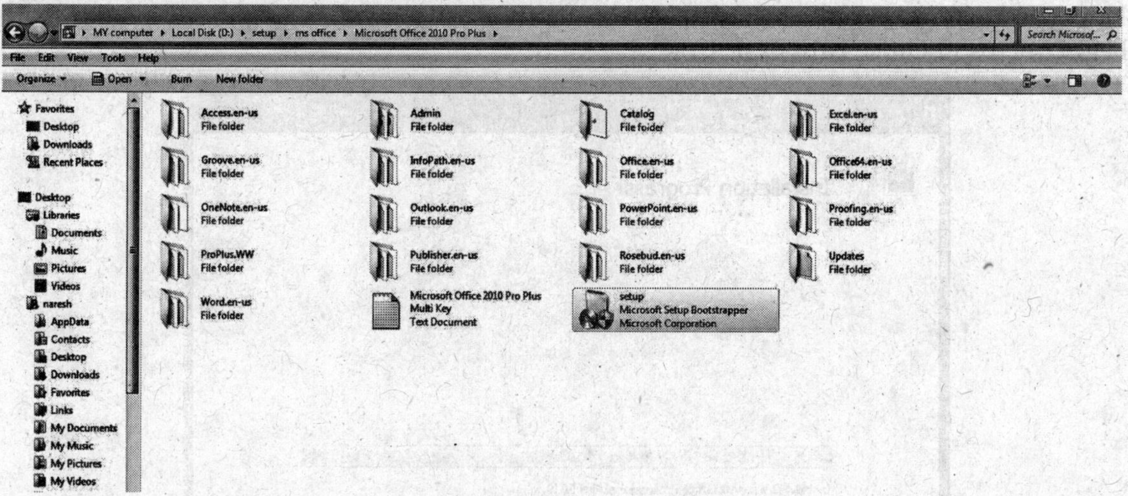

- ❐ Now click on Setup.exe and click on yes (In the case you are using Windows 7 or Vista).
- ❐ After sometime, the following dialog box will appear on your computer, Click "Install Now".
- ❐ The following box will appear on clicking "Install Now", wait for a few minutes and let Microsoft office 2011 be installed on your system.
- ❐ Then Click "Close" and Cheers; you are done!

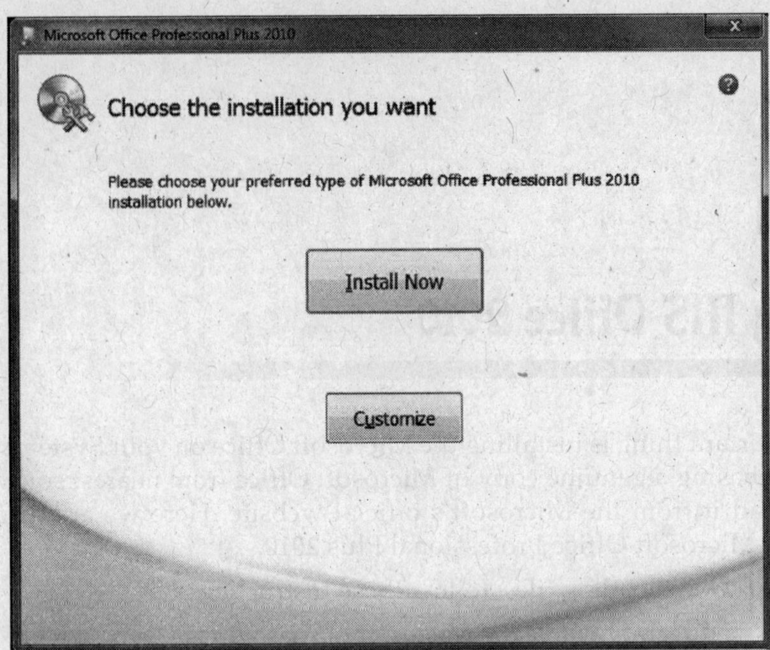

Now you have successfully Installed Microsoft office 2010 on your Computer. Now we shall begin Microsoft Office 2010 Basic Course.

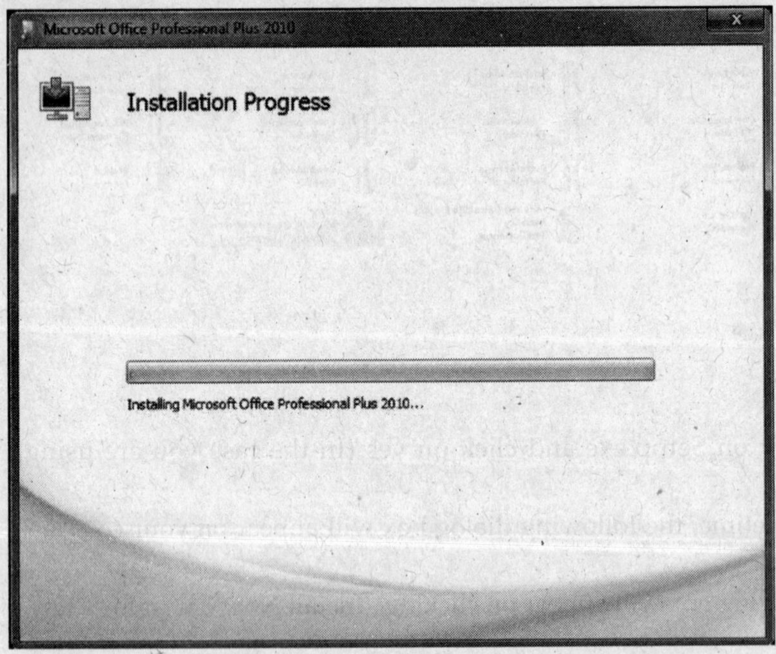

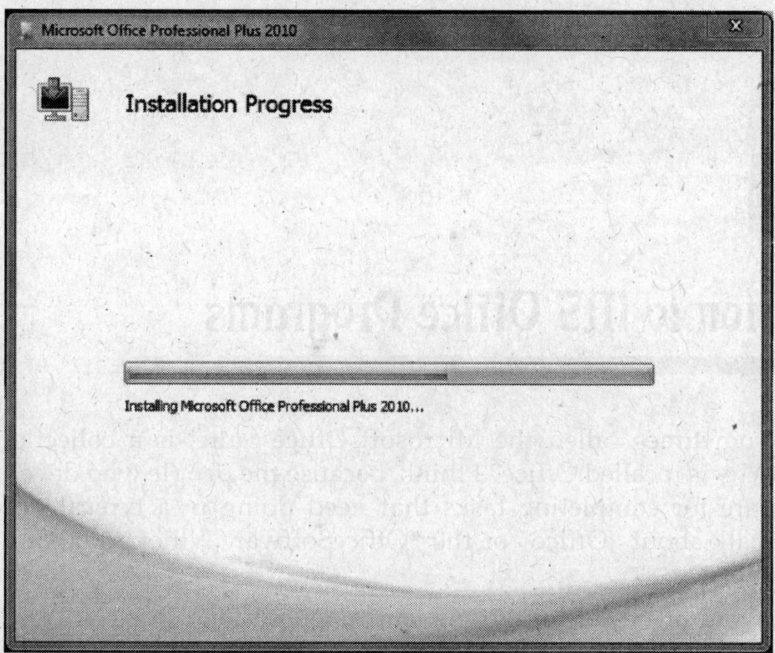

Points to Remember

- ☆ Always use genuine software from Microsoft. Pirated software may contain Viruses & other Malwares.
- ☆ Your Serial-Key is personal to you; don't share it with anyone before installing and activating the Product.
- ☆ Never download the Microsoft Product from any other website other than Microsoft. You can try beta versions before you buy.

Introduction to MS Office Programs

Office 2010, sometimes called the Microsoft Office Suite, is a collection of computer programs. Why is it called Office? I think, because the people who developed it wanted to make software for completing tasks that need doing in a typical office. When you hear someone talk about "Office" or the "OfficeSoftware," they're talking about several different programs:

- **Word:** A word processor for writing letters, reports, and so on. A Word file is called a document.
- **Outlook:** A personal information manager, scheduler, and e-mailer.
- **PowerPoint:** A means of creating slide presentations to give in front of audiences. A PowerPoint file is called a presentation, or sometimes a slide show.
- **Excel:** A Part of office for performing numerical analyses. An Excel file is called a workbook.
- **Access:** A database management program.
- **Publisher:** A means of creating desktop-publishing files — pamphlets, notices, newsletters, and even books!

If you're new to Office, don't study so many different computer programs. The programs have much in common. You find the same commands throughout Office. For example, the method of choosing fonts is the same in Word, Outlook, PowerPoint, Excel, Access, and Publisher. Creating diagrams and charts works the same way in Word, PowerPoint, and Excel.

Starting an Office Program

Unless you start an Office program, you can't create a document, construct a worksheet, or make a database. Learn how you can do that.

- Click the Start button, choose All Programs Microsoft Office, and then choose the program's name on the submenu.

User Interface in Microsoft Office

Interface, also called the user interface, is a computer term that describes how a software program presents itself to the people who use it.

The GUI

❒ File tab

In the upper-left corner of the window is the File tab, Go to the File tab to find commands for creating, opening, and saving files, as well as doing other file-management tasks. Noticethe Options command. You can choose Options to open the Options dialog box and tell the program you are working in how you want it to work.

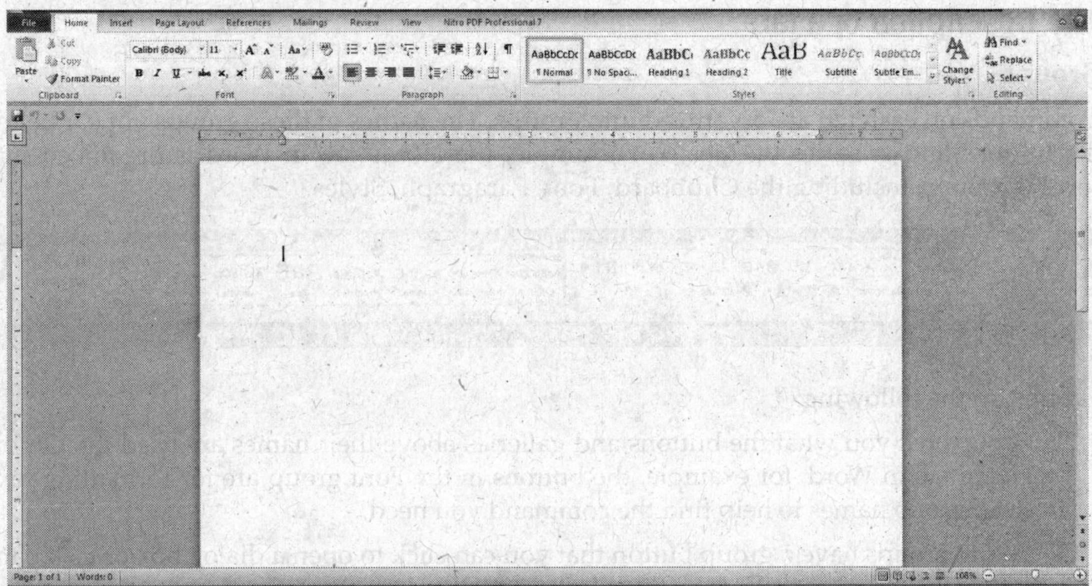

The Ribbon and its tabs

Across the top of the screen is the Ribbon, an assortment of different tabs; click a tab to undertake a task. For example, click the Home tab to format text; click the Insert tab to insert a table or chart.

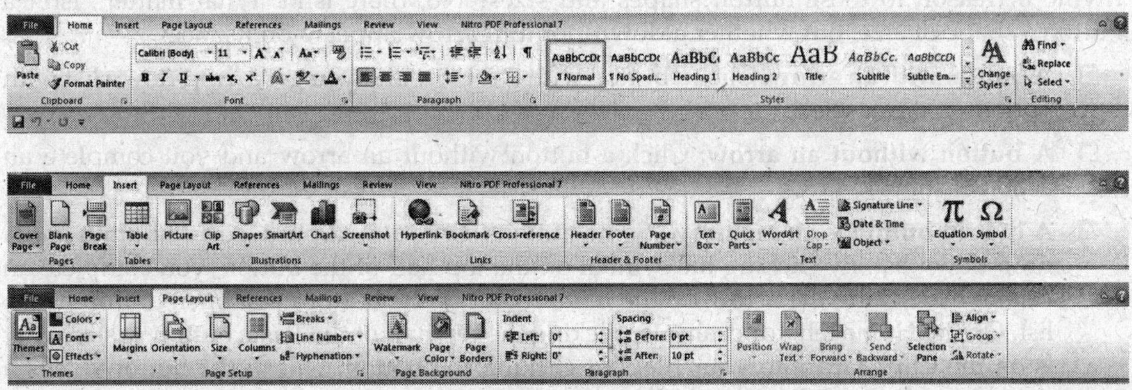

Your first step when you start a new task is to click a tab on the Ribbon. Knowing which tab to click takes a while, but the names of tabs — Home, Insert, View, and so on — hint as to which commands you find while you visit a tab.

To make the Ribbon disappear and get more room to view items on-screen, click the Minimize the Ribbon button (or press Ctrl+F1). This button is located on the right side of the Ribbon, to the left of the Help button. You can also right-click the Ribbon and choose Minimize the Ribbon on the shortcut menu, or double-click a tab on the Ribbon. To see the Ribbon again, click the Minimize the Ribbon button, press Ctrl+F1, double-click a Ribbon tab or right-click a tab name or the Quick Access toolbar and deselect Minimize the Ribbon on the shortcut menu. While the Ribbon is minimized, you can click a tab name to display a tab.

The Description of a tab

Groups

Commands on each tab are organized into groups. The names of these groups appear below the buttons and galleries on tabs. For example, the Home tab in Word is organized into several groups, including the Clipboard, Font, Paragraph, Styles.

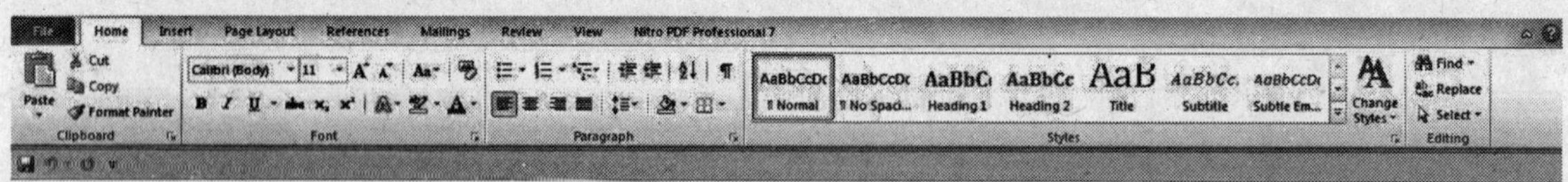

Groups do the following:

- ❒ Groups tell you what the buttons and galleries above their names are used for. On the Home tab in Word, for example, the buttons in the Font group are for formatting text. Read group names to help find the command you need.
- ❒ Many groups have a group button that you can click to open a dialog box or task pane (officially, Microsoft calls these little buttons dialog launcher).

Buttons

Go to any tab and you find buttons of all shapes and sizes. Square buttons and rectangular buttons; big and small buttons, buttons with labels and buttons without labels. Is there any rhyme or reason to these button shapes and sizes? No, there isn't. What matters isn't a button's shape or size, but whether a down-pointingarrow appears on its face:

- ❒ **A button with an arrow:** Click a button with an arrow and you get a drop-down list with options you can select.
- ❒ **A button without an arrow:** Click a button without an arrow and you complete an action of some kind.
- ❒ **A hybrid button with an arrow:** Some buttons serve a dual purpose as a button and a drop-down list. By clicking the symbol on the top half of the button, you complete an action; by clicking the arrow on the bottom half of the button, you open a drop-down list. On the Home tab, for example, clicking the top half of the Paste button pastes what is on the Clipboard into your file, but clicking the bottom half of the button opens a drop-down list with Paste options.

Keyboard Shortcuts

People who like to give commands by pressing keyboard shortcuts may well ask, "Is there keyboard shortcuts in Office?" The answer is: Yes, Office has shortcuts. For example, you can press Ctrl+B to boldface text and Ctrl+U tounderline text. Office offers Alt+key shortcuts as well.

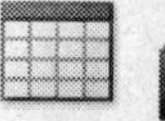

Saving Your Files

Soon after you create a file, be sure to save it. And save your file from time to time while you work on it as well. Until you save your work, it rests in the computer's electronic memory (**R**andom **A**ccess **M**emory), a precarious location. If a power outage occurs, you may lose all the work you did since the last time you saved your file. Make it a habit to save files every five Minutes or so or when you are doing an important task. Choose the folder where you want to save a file, declare where you want to save files by default, save files for use in 97–2003 editions of Office, and handle files that were saved automatically after a computer failure.

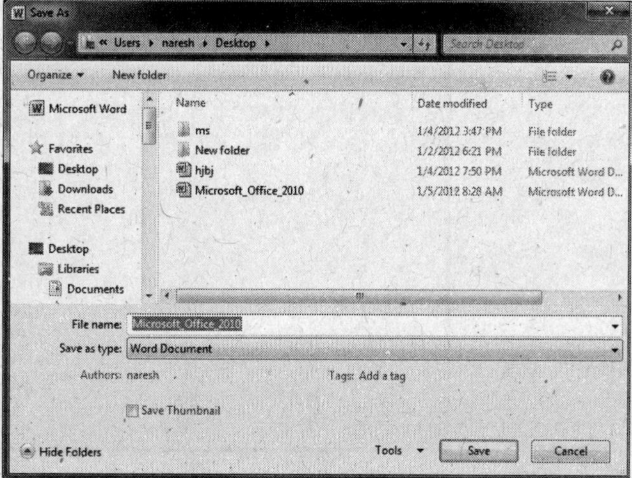

Saving your files

To save a file:

- ❒ Click the Save button (you find it on the Quick Access toolbar).
- ❒ Press Ctrl+S.
- ❒ Go to the File tab and choose Save.

Where you like to save files

To direct Office to the folder you like best and make it appear first in the Save As and Open dialog boxes, follow these steps:

- ❒ In Word, Excel, PowerPoint, or Access, go to the File tab and choose Options.

You see the Options dialog box. ➔

- ❒ In Word, Excel, and PowerPoint, select the Save category; in Access, select the General category.

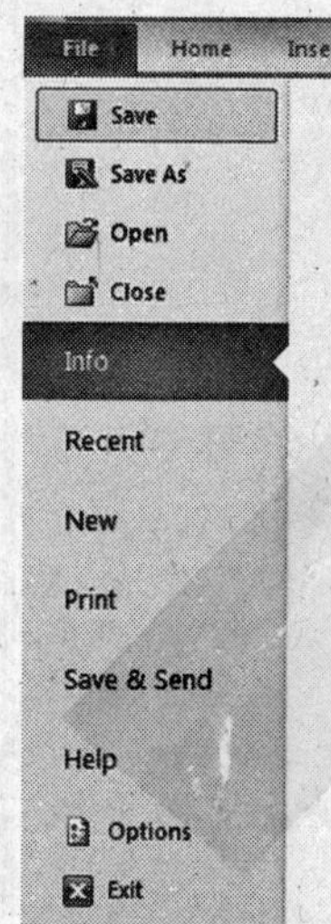

Options dialog box

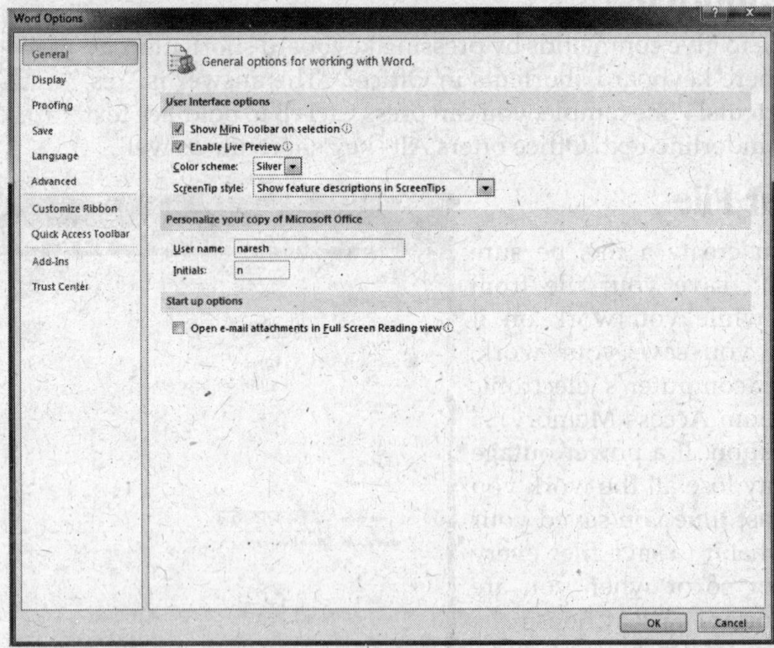

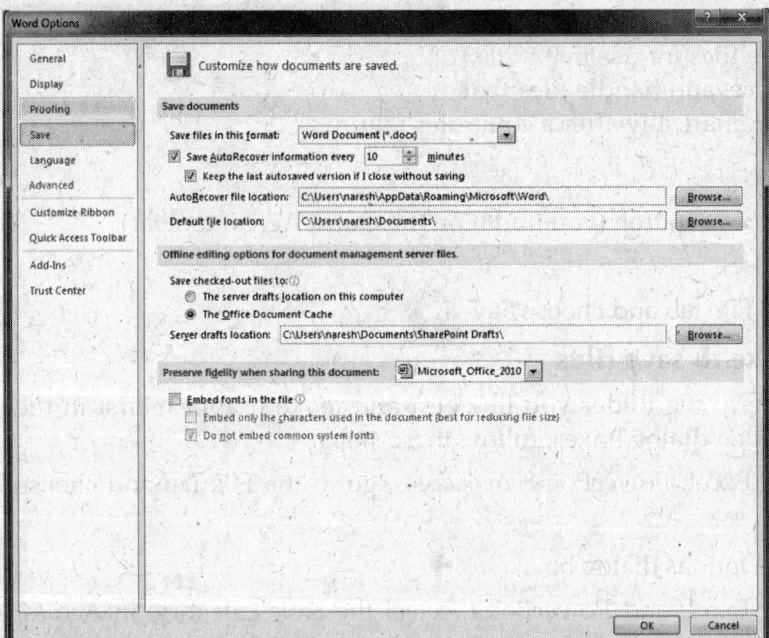

Saving files for use in earlier versions of an Office program

Before you pass along a file to a user who has Office 2003, XP, 2000, or 97, save your document in these versions so that the other person can open it. People with versions of Office prior to version 2010 and 2007 cannot open your Office files unless you save your files for earlier versions of Office.

Program	**2010, 2007**	**97–2003**
Access	.accdb	.mlb
Excel	.xlsx	.xls
PowerPoint	.pptx	.ppt
Publisher	.pub	.pub
Word	.docx	.doc

Saving a file for use in Office 97–2003

Follow these steps to save a file so that someone with Office 97, 2000, XP, or2003 can open it:

- ❒ Go to the File tab.
- ❒ Choose Save & Send.

You see the Share window.

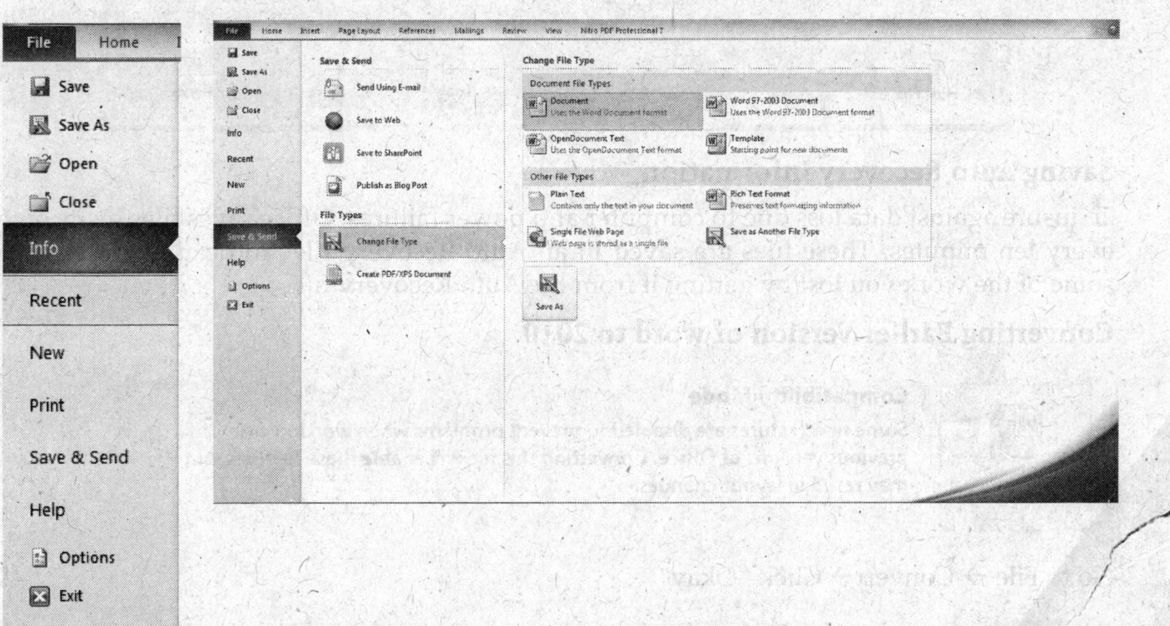

- ❒ Under File Types, choose Change File Type and then choose 97–2003 option for saving files.

The Save As dialog box opens.

- ❒ Enter a new name for the file, if necessary.
- ❒ Click the Save button.

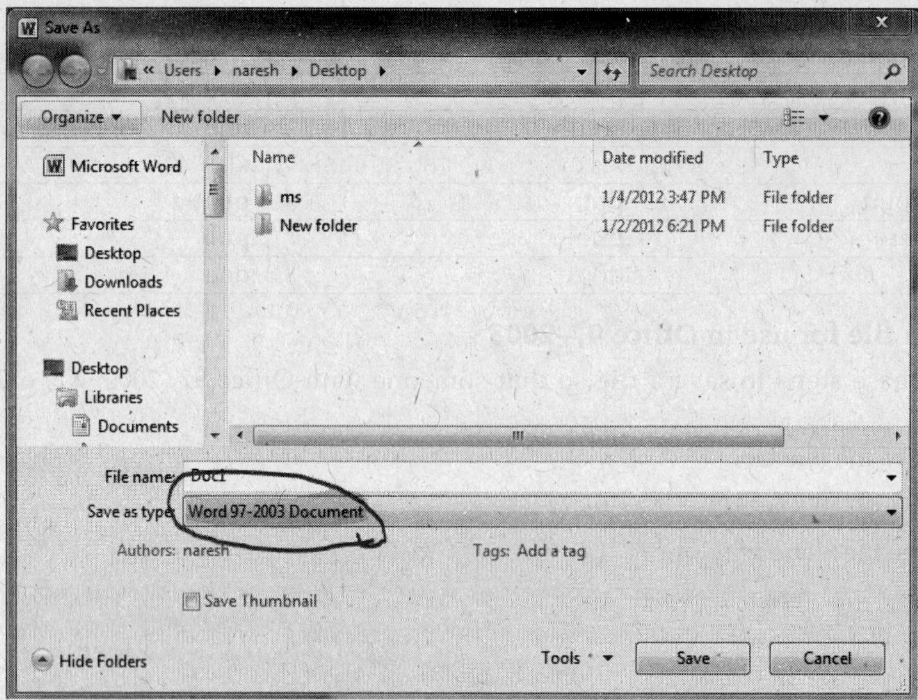

Saving Auto Recovery information

To insure against data loss due to computer and power failures, Office saves files on its own every ten minutes. These files are saved in an Auto Recovery file. You can try to recover some of the work you lost by getting it from the Auto Recovery file.

Converting Earlier Version of word to 2010

Compatibility Mode

Some new features are disabled to prevent problems when working with previous versions of Office. Converting this file will enable these features, but may result in layout changes.

Go to File → Convert→ Click "Okay"

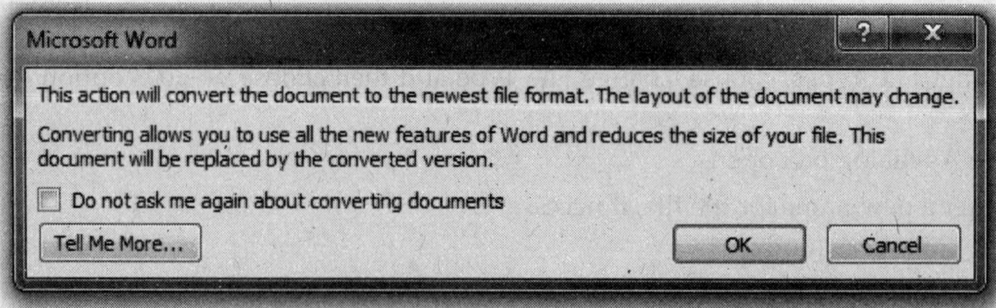

The Save As and Open Dialog Boxes

The Open dialog box and Save As dialog box offer a bunch of different ways to locate a file you want to open or locate the folder where you want to save a file.

Searching for files in a folder: Use the Search box to search for subfolders and files in the folder you is currently viewing. After you type the first few letters of a file name or subfolder, you see only the names of items that start with the letters you typed. To see all the files and subfolders again, click the Close button (the X) in the Search box.

Changing views: Display folder contents differently by choosing a view on the Views drop-down list (in Windows 7, look for the View arrow in the upper-right corner of the dialog box). In Details view, you see how large files are and when they were last edited.

Creating a new folder: Click the New Folder button to create a new subfolder for storing files. Select the folder that your new folder will be subordinate to and click the New Folder button. Then type a name forthe saved file.

Navigate to different folders: Click the Folders bar (in the lower-left corner of the dialog box) to open the Navigation pane and look for folders or presentations on a different drive, network location, or folder on your computer.

Opening a file

- ❒ On the File tab, choose Open (or press Ctrl+O).
- ❒ Locate and select the file you want to open.
- ❒ Click the Open button.
- ❒ Your file opens. You can also double-click a filename to open a file.

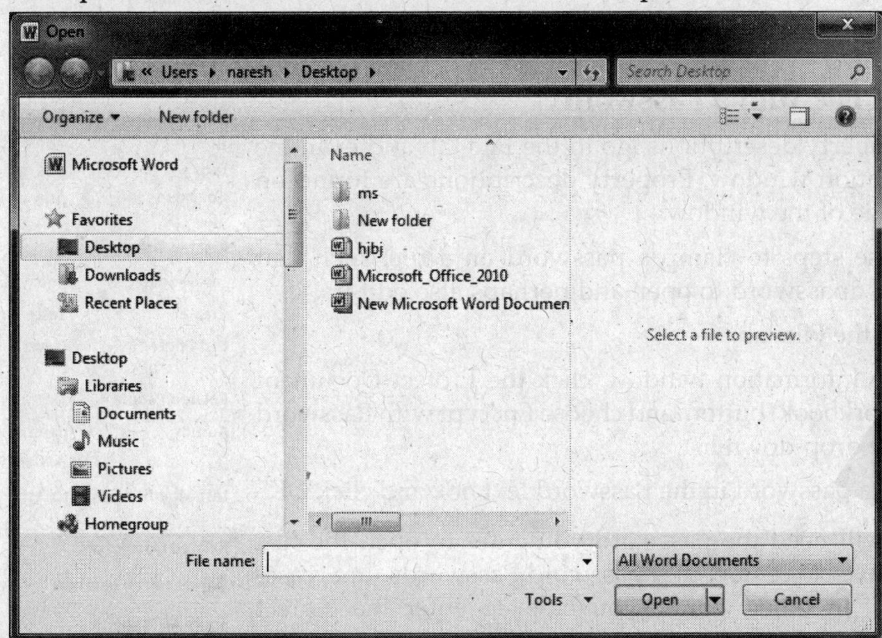

If you have recently accessed the file you can use recent button in file tab.

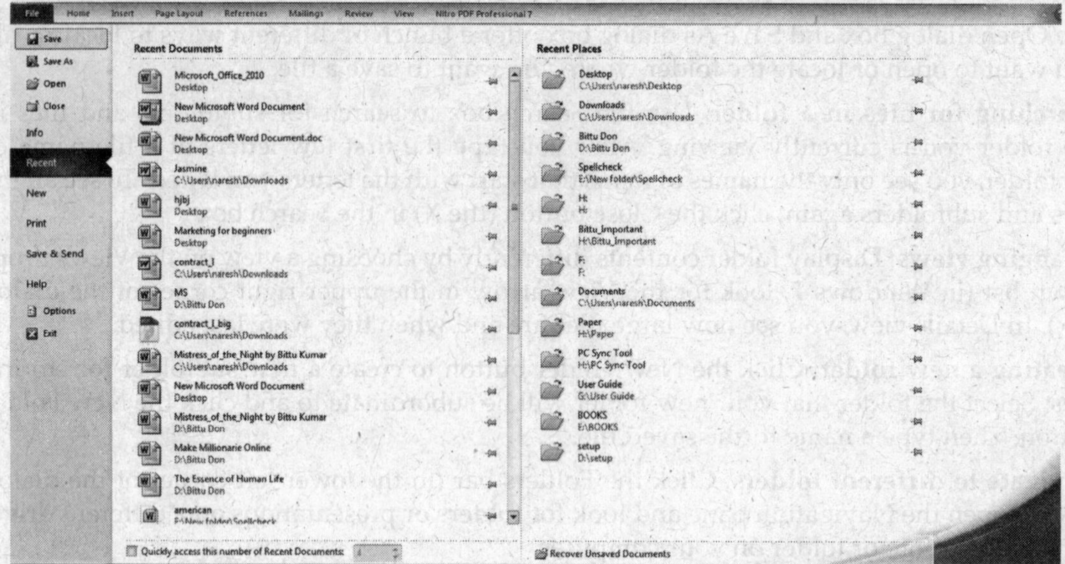

File Properties

Properties are a means of describing a file. If you manage more files, you owe it to yourself to record properties. You can use them later to identify files

Permissions

Anyone can open, copy, and change any part of this document.

Properties

Size	1.28MB
Pages	20
Words	2185
Total Editing Time	155 Minutes
Title	Add a title
Tags	Add a tag
Comments	Add comments

Related Dates

Last Modified	Today, 8:53 AM
Created	Yesterday, 9:25 PM
Last Printed	Never

Related People

Author	naresh
	Add an author
Last Modified By	naresh

Related Documents

Open File Location

Show All Properties

Locking a File with a Password

To read property descriptions, go to the File tab and examine the Information window. Property descriptions are found on the right side of the window.

Follow these steps to clamp a password on a file, such that others need apassword to open and perhaps also edit it:

- Go to the File tab.
- In the Information window, click the Protect Document (or Workbook) button, and choose Encrypt with Password on the drop-down list.
- Enter a password in the Password text box and click OK.

Others will need the password you enter to open the file. They have to enter the password.Passwords are case-sensitive. In other words, you have to enter the correct combination of upper- and lowercase letters to successfully enter the password. If the password is Apple (with an uppercase A), mentoring apple (with a lowercase a) is deemed the wrong passwordand doesn't open the file.

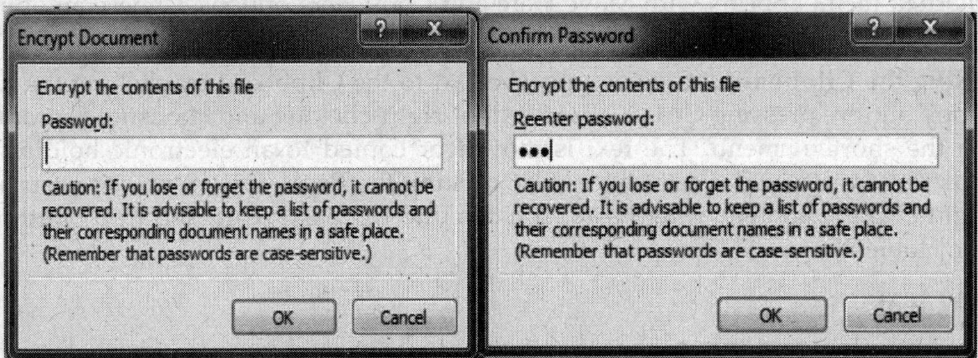

- In the Confirm Password dialog box, enter the password again.
- Click OK.

The Information window informs you that a password is required to open the file.

Removing Password

Follow these steps to remove a password from a file:

- Open the file that needs its password removed.
- Go to the File tab and in the Information window, click the Protect Document button, and choose Encrypt with Password.
- Delete the password and click OK.

Formatting Text

Before you can perform any activity to any text you have to select it.

To Select	Do This
A word	Double-click the word.
A few words	Drag over the words.
A paragraph	Triple-click inside the paragraph
A block of text	Click the start of the text, hold down the Shift key, and click the end of the text. In Word you can also click the start of the text, press F8, and click at the end of the text.
All text	Press Ctrl+A.

Moving and Copying text

- **Dragging and Dropping:** Move the mouse over the text and then click and drag the text to a new location. Drag means to hold down the mouse button while you move the pointer on-screen. If you want to copy rather than move the text, hold down the Ctrl key while you drag.

- **Dragging and Dropping with the right mouse button**: Drag the text while holding down the right, not the left, mouse button. After you release the right mouse button, a shortcut menu appears with Move Here and Copy Here options. Choose an option to move or copy the text.
- **Using the Clipboard**: Move or copy the text to the Clipboard by clicking the Cut or Copy button, pressing Ctrl+X or Ctrl+C, or right-clicking and choosing Cut or Copy on the shortcut menu. The text is moved or copied to an electronic holding tank called the Clipboard. Paste the text by clicking the Paste button, pressing Ctrl+V, or right-clicking and choosing Paste. You can find the Paste, Cut, and Copy buttons on the Hometab.

Deleting text

To delete a bunch of text, select the text you want to delete and press the Delete key.

Changing the Look of Text

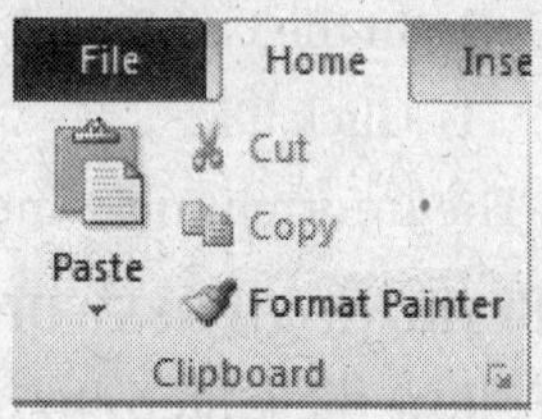

What text looks like is determined by its font, the size of the letters, the colour of the letters, and whether text effects or font styles such as italic or boldface are in the text. The text's appearance really matters in Word, PowerPoint, and Publisher because files you create in those programs are meant to be read by all and sundry. Even in Excel, Access, and Outlook messages, font choices matter because the choices you make determine whether your work is easy to read and understand.

A font is a collection of letters, numbers, and symbols in a particular typeface, including all italic and boldface variations of the letters, numbers, and symbols.

Choosing fonts for text

- **Mini-toolbar:** Move the pointer over the selected text. You see the mini toolbar. Move the pointer over this toolbar and choose a font in the Font drop-down list.
- **Shortcut menu:** Right-click the selected text and choose a new font on the shortcut menu.
- **Font drop-down list:** On the Home tab, open the Font drop-down list and choose a font.
- **Font dialog box:** On the Home tab, click the Font group button. You see the Font dialog box. select a font and click OK.

Changing the font size of text

- Font size is measured in points; a point is 1/72 of an inch.
- **Mini-toolbar:** Move the pointer over the text, and when you see the mini toolbar, move the pointer over the toolbar and choose a font size on the Font.
- **Shortcut menu:** Right-click the text and choose a new font size on the shortcut menu.
- **Font Size drop-down list:** On the Home tab, open the Font Size dropdown list and choose a font. You can live-preview font sizes this way.
- **Font dialog box:** On the Home tab, click the Font group button, and in the Font dialog box, choose a font size and click OK.

- **Increase Font Size and Decrease Font Size buttons:** Click these buttons (or press Ctrl+] or Ctrl+[) to increase or decrease the point size by the next interval on the Font Size drop-down list.

Applying font styles to text

- **Regular:** This style is just Office's way of denoting an absence of any font style.
- **Italic:** You can also italicize titles to make them a little more elegant. (Ctrl+I)
- **Bold:** Bold text calls attention to itself. (Ctrl+B)
- **Underline:** Underlined text also calls attention to itself, but use underlining sparingly. Later in this chapter, "Underlining text" discusses all the ways to underline text.
- **Strikethrough and double strikethrough:** By convention, strikethrough is used to show where passages are struck from a contract or other important document.
- **Subscript:** A subscripted letter is lowered in the text. In the chemical formula below, the 2 is lowered to show that two atoms of hydrogen are needed along with one atom of oxygen to form a molecule of water: H2O. (Press Ctrl+=.)
- **Superscript:** A superscripted letter or number is one that is raised in the text. Superscript is used in mathematical and scientific formulas, in ordinal numbers (1st, 2nd , 3rd), and to mark footnotes. In the theory of relativity, the 2 is superscripted: E = mc2. (Press Ctrl+Shift+plus sign.)

Changing the colour of text

- On the mini-toolbar, open the drop-down list on the Font Colour button and choose a colour.
- Right-click, open the drop-down list on the Font Colour button, and choose a colour on the shortcut menu.
- On the Home tab, open the drop-down list on the Font Colour button and choose a colour.
- On the Home tab, click the Font group button to open the Font dialog box, open the Font Colour drop-down list, and choose a colour. The Font Colour drop-down list offers theme colours and standard colours. You are well advised to choose a theme colour. These colours are deemed theme colours because they jive with the theme you choose for your file.

Changing Case

To change case in Word and PowerPoint, all you have to do is select the text, go to the Home tab, click the Change Case button, and choose an option on the drop-down list:

- **Sentence case:** Renders the letters in sentence case.

- ❒ lowercase: Makes all the letters lowercase.
- ❒ UPPERCASE: Renders all the letters as capital letters.
- ❒ Capitalize Each Word: Capitalizes the first letter of each word. If you choose this option for a title or heading, go into the title and lower case the first letter of articles (the, a, an), coordinate conjunctions (and, or, for, nor), and prepositions unless they're the first or last word in the title.
- ❒ TOGGLE CASE: Choose this option if you accidentally enter letters with the Caps Lock key pressed.

Entering Symbols and Foreign Characters

- ❒ On the Insert tab, click the Symbol button. (You may have to click the Symbols button first, depending on the size of your screen)
- ❒ If you're looking to insert a symbol, not a foreign character, choose Webdings or Wingdings 1, 2, or 3 in the Font drop-down list.
- ❒ Webdings and Wingdings fonts offer all kinds of weird and wacky symbols.
- ❒ Select a symbol or foreign character.
- ❒ Click the Insert button to enter the symbol and then click Close to close the dialog box.

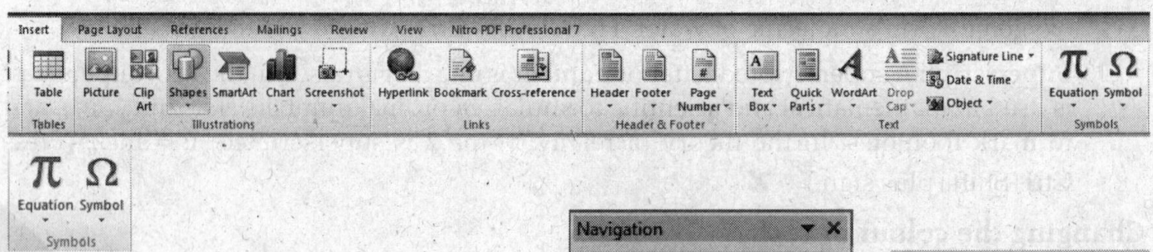

Finding and Replacing Text

- ❒ Press Ctrl+F or go to the Home tab and click the Find button. (In Excel, click the Find & Select button and choose Find on the dropdown list.)
- ❒ Enter the word or phrase in the Find What or Search Documenttext box.

After you enter the word or phrase in Word, the Navigation pane lists each instance of the term you're looking for and the term is highlighted in your document wherever it is found. You can click an instance of the search term in the Navigation pane to scroll to a location in your document where the search term is located. You can also remove the word using replace.

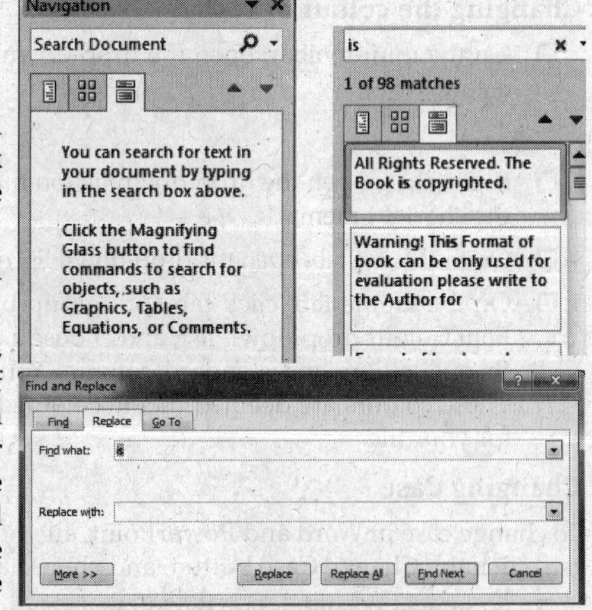

Finding and replacing text

Creating Hyperlinks

A hyperlink is an electronic shortcut from one place to another. Clicking hyperlinks on the Internet takes you to different web pages or different places on the same web page. In the Office programs, you can use hyperlinks to connect readers to your favourite web pages or to a different page, slide, or file.

Select the text or object that will form the hyperlink.

For example, select a line of text or phrase if you want viewers to be able to click it to go to a web page.

- On the Insert tab, click the Hyperlink button (or press Ctrl+K). Depending on the size of your screen, you may have to click the Links button before you can get to the Hyperlink button. You can also open this dialog box by right-clicking an object or text and choosing Hyperlink on the shortcut menu

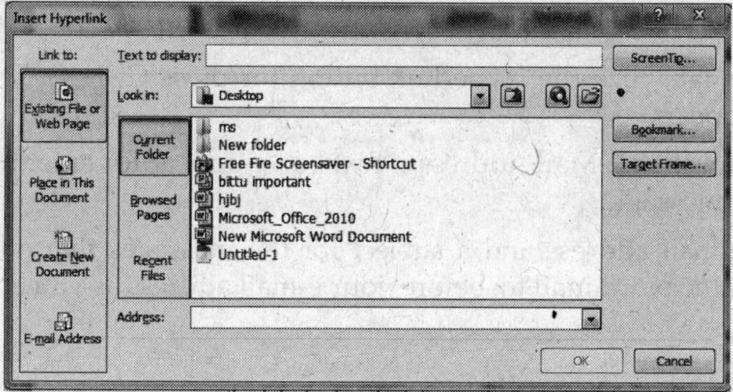

Creating hyperlinsk

- **Click Browse the Web button:** Your web browser opens after you click this button. Go to the web page you want to link to and return to your program. The web page's address appears in the Address text box.
- **Click Browsed Pages:** The dialog box lists web pages you recently visited after you click this button, Type (or copy) a web page address into the Address text box: Enter the address of the web page. You can right-click the text box and choose Paste to copy a web page address into the text box.
- Click the ScreenTip button, enter a ScreenTip in the Set HyperlinkScreenTip dialog box, and click OK.
- Click OK in the Insert Hyperlink dialog box.

Creating a hyperlink to another place in your file

Follow these steps to create a hyperlink to another place in your file:

- Select the text or object that will form the hyperlink.
- On the Insert tab, click the Hyperlink button (or press Ctrl+K). You see the Insert Hyperlink dialog box. Another way to open this dialog box is to right-click and choose Hyperlink in the shortcut menu.

- ❒ Under Link To, select Place in This Document. What you see in the dialog box depends on which program you're working in.
- ❒ Select the target of the hyperlink. Click the ScreenTip button.
- ❒ You see the Set Hyperlink ScreenTip dialog box.
- ❒ Enter a ScreenTip and click OK. When viewers move their pointers over the link, they see the words you enter. Enter a description of where the hyperlink takes you.

Creating an e-mail hyperlink

- ❒ An e-mail hyperlink is one that opens an e-mail program. These links are sometimes found on web pages so that anyone visiting a web page can conveniently send an e-mail message to the person who manages the web page. When you click an e-mail hyperlink, your default e-mail program opens. And If the person who set up the link was thorough about it, the e-mail message is already addressed and given a subject line.
- ❒ Select the words or object that will constitute the link.
- ❒ On the Insert tab, click the Hyperlink button (or press Ctrl+K). The Insert Hyperlink dialog box appears.
- ❒ Under Link To, click E-Mail Address. Text boxes appear for entering an e-mail address and a subject message.
- ❒ Enter your e-mail address and a subject for the messages that others will send you. Office inserts the word mail to: before your e-mail address as you enter it.
- ❒ Click OK.

Repairing and removing hyperlinks

- ❒ Repairing a link: Select a target in your file or a web page and click OK.
- ❒ Removing a link: Click the Remove Link button. You can also remove a hyperlink by right-clicking the link and choosing Remove.

Points to Remember

- ☆ Practice selecting skills at your best before creating custom documents
- ☆ While hyperlinking, double check that the directory exits
- ☆ While hyperlinking make sure that you don't hyperlink your files present at sensitive locations

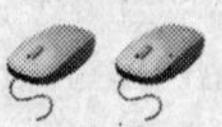

Chapter 15

Get more from MS Office

Undoing and Repeating Commands

Undo allows you to reverse actions you regret doing, and the Repeat repeats a previous action without you have to choose the same commands all over again. All is not lost if you make a big blunder because Office has a marvelous little tool called the Undo command. This command "Remembers" your previous editorial and formatting changes. As long as you catch your error in time, you can undo your mistake.

- ❒ Click the Undo button on the Quick Access toolbar (or press Ctrl+Z) to undo your most recent change. If you made your error and went on to do something else before you caught it, open the drop-down list on the Undo button.
- ❒ Click Redo to redo the change.

Zooming

You can find these controls in the lower-right corner of the window and on the View tab

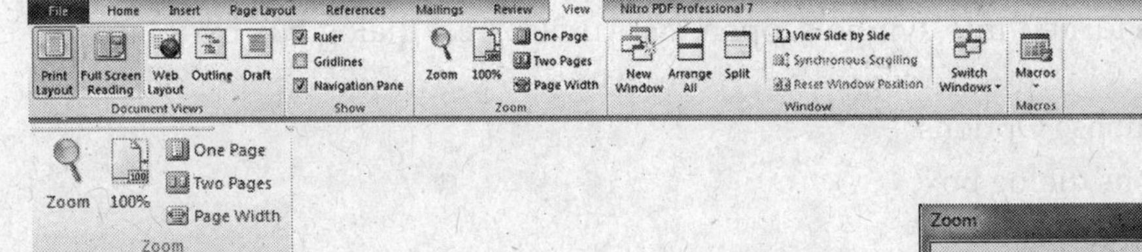

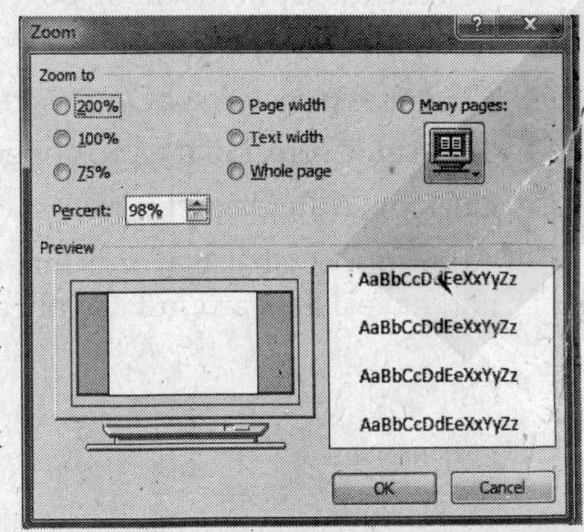

Zooming a file

- ❒ **Zoom dialog box:** Click the Zoom button on the View tab or the Zoom box (the % listing) to display the Zoom dialog box; you can select an option button or enter a Percent measurement.
- ❒ **Zoom button:** Click the Zoom In or Zoom Out button on the Zoom slider to zoom in or out in 10-percent increments.
- ❒ **Zoom slider:** Drag the Zoom slider left to shrink or right to enlarge what is on your screen.

- **Mouse wheel:** If your mouse has a wheel, you can hold down the Ctrl key and spin the wheel to quickly zoom in or out.

Viewing a File through more than One Window

- **New Window:** Opens another window on your file, so that you can view two places simultaneously in the same file. To go back and forth between windows, click a taskbar button or click the Switch Windows button and choose a window name on the drop-down list. Click window's Close button when you're finished looking at it.
- **Arrange All:** Arranges open windows side by side on-screen.
- **Switch Windows:** Opens a drop-down list with open windows so that you can travel between windows.
- **View Side by Side:** Displays files side by side so that you can compare and contrast them.
- **Synchronous Scrolling:** Permits you to scroll two files at the same rate so that you can proofread one against the other. To use this command, start by clicking the View Side by Side button. After you click the Synchronous Scrolling button, click the Reset Window Position button so both files are displayed at the same size on-screen.
- **Reset Window Position:** Makes files being shown side by side the same size on-screen to make them easier to compare.

Viewing a file through mare than one window

Opening Auto Correct dialog box

Office corrects common spelling errors and turns punctuation mark combinations into symbols as part of its AutoCorrect feature. To see which typos are corrected and which punctuation marks are turned into symbols, open the AutoCorrect dialog box by following these steps:

- On the File tab, choose Options.
- You see the Options dialog box.
- Go to the Proofing category.
- Click the AutoCorrect Options button.
- The AutoCorrect dialog box opens.
- Click the AutoCorrect tab.
- AutoCorrect tab lists words that are corrected automatically. Scroll down the Replace list and have a look around. Go ahead and make yourself at home.

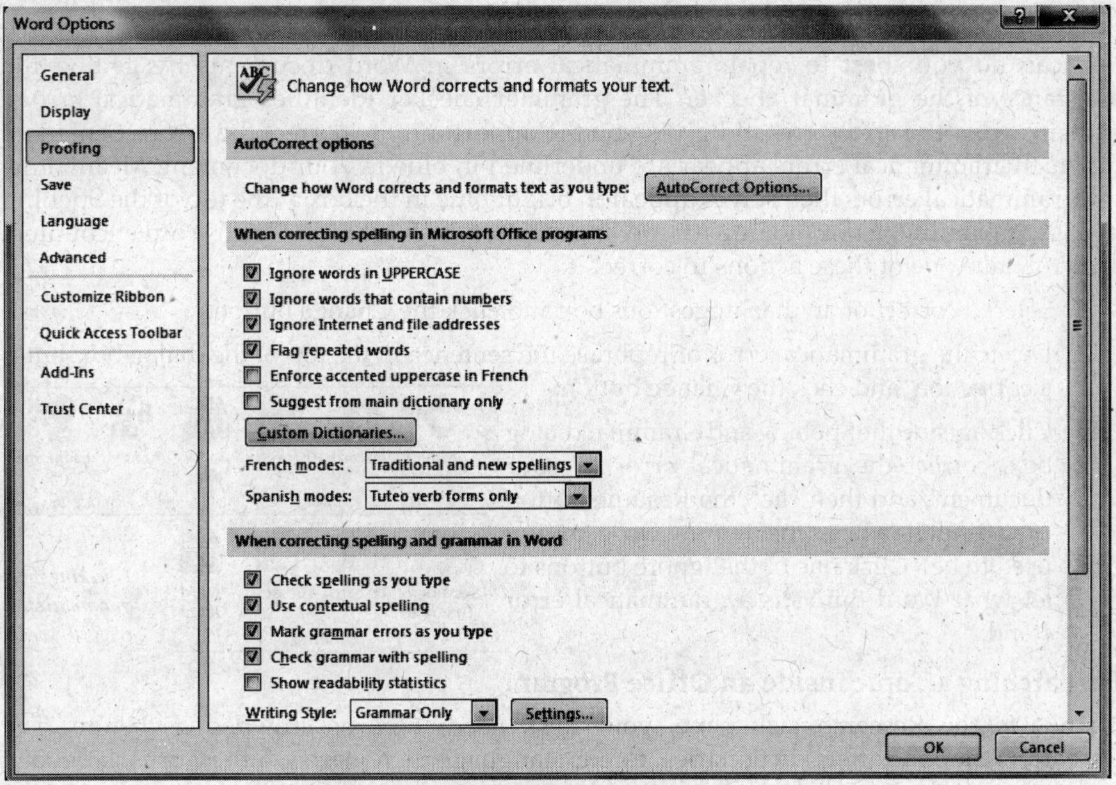

Word Options
General
Display
Proofing
Save
Language
Advanced
Customize Ribbon
Quick Access Toolbar
Add-Ins
Trust Center
Change how Word corrects and formats your text.
AutoCorrect options
Change how Word corrects and formats text as you type:
AutoCorrect Options...
When correcting spelling in Microsoft Office programs
Ignore words in UPPERCASE
Ignore words that contain numbers
Ignore Internet and file addresses
Flag repeated words
Enforce accented uppercase in French
Suggest from main dictionary only
Custom Dictionaries...
French modes: Traditional and new spellings
Spanish modes: Tuteo verb forms only
When correcting spelling and grammar in Word
Check spelling as you type
Use contextual spelling
Mark grammar errors as you type
Check grammar with spelling
Show readability statistics
Writing Style: Grammar Only
Settings...
OK
Cancel

Opening auto correct dialog box

AutoCorrect: English (U.S.)
AutoFormat
Actions
AutoCorrect
Math AutoCorrect
AutoFormat As You Type
Show AutoCorrect Options buttons
Correct TWo INitial CApitals
Exceptions...
Capitalize first letter of sentences
Capitalize first letter of table cells
Capitalize names of days
Correct accidental usage of cAPS LOCK key
Replace text as you type
Replace:
With: Plain text Formatted text
(c) ©
(e) €
(r) ®
(tm) ™
... …
:(☹
Add
Delete
Automatically use suggestions from the spelling checker
OK
Cancel

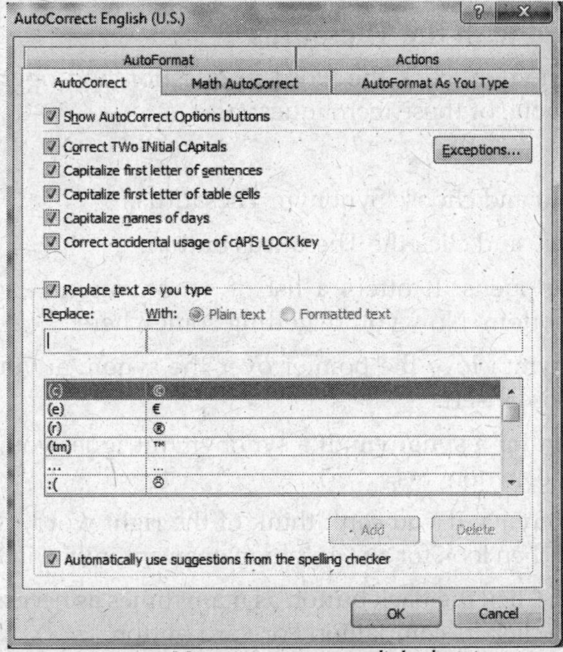

Managing auto correct dialog box

Checking for Grammatical Errors in Word

You can do your best to repair grammatical errors in Word documents by getting the assistance of the grammar checker. The grammar checker identifies grammatical errors, explains what the errors are, and gives you the opportunity to correct the errors. Sentences in which grammatical errors appear are underlined in blue in your document. Meanwhile, the grammatical errors themselves appear in bright blue in the box at the top of the Spelling and Grammar dialog box (alongwith spelling errors, which are red). When Word encounters an error, take one of these actions to correct it:

- Select a correction in the Suggestions box and click the Change button.
- Delete the grammatical error or rephrase the sentence in the top of the dialog box, enter a correction, and click the Change button.
- Click outside the Spelling and Grammar dialog box, correct the grammatical error in your document, and then click the Resume button (you find it where the Ignore Once button used to be). Click one of the Ignore buttons to let what Word thinks is a grammatical error stand.

Checking for grammatical erros in word

Researching a Topic inside an Office Program

Thanks to the Research task pane, your desk needn't be as crowded as before. The Research task pane offers dictionaries, foreign language dictionaries, a thesaurus, language translators, and encyclopedias, as well as Internet searching, all available from inside the Office programs.

Finding the Right Word with the Thesaurus

To search for a good synonym, click the word in question and open the thesaurus on the Research task pane with one of these techniques:

- Press Shift+F7.
- Right-click the word and choose Synonym Thesaurus.
- Go to the Review tab and click the Thesaurus button.

The Research task pane opens. It offers a list of synonyms and sometimes includes an artonym or two at the bottom. Now you're getting somewhere:

- **Choosing a synonym:** Move the pointer over the synonym you want, open its drop-down list, and choose Insert.
- **Finding a synonym for a synonym:** If a synonym intrigues you, click it. The task pane displays a new list of synonyms.
- **Searching for antonyms:** If you can't think of the right word, type its antonym in the Search For box and then look for an "antonym of an antonym" in the Research task pane.
- **Revisit a word list:** Click the Back button as many times as necessary. If you go back too far, you can always click its companion Forward button.

Telling Office which languages you will use

Follow these steps to inform Word, PowerPoint, Publisher, and Outlook that you will use a language or languages besides English in your files:

- On the Review tab, click the Language button and choose Language Preferences. The Options dialog box opens to the Language category.
- Open the Add Additional Editing Languages drop-down list, select a language, and click the Add button to make that language a part of your presentations, documents, and messages.
- Click OK.

Marking text as foreign language text

The next step is to tell Office where in your file you're using a foreign language. After you mark the text as foreign language text, Office can spellcheck it with the proper dictionaries. Follow these steps to mark text so that Office knows in which language it was written:

- Select the text that you wrote in a foreign language.
- Go to the Review tab.
- Click the Language button and choose Set Proofing Language on the drop-down list.
- Select a language and click OK.

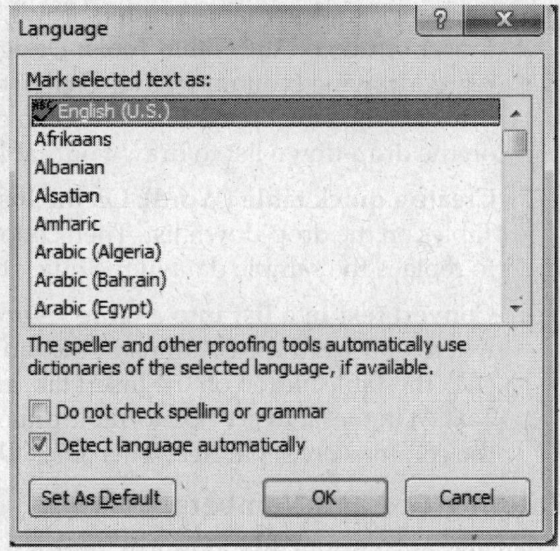

Marking text as language text

Tables

Before starting the Course you need to know the following terms:

- **Cell:** The box that is formed where a row and column intersect. Each cell holds one data item.
- **Header row:** The name of the labels along the top row that explain what is in the columns below.
- **Row labels:** The labels in the first column that describe what is in each row.
- **Borders:** The lines in the table that define where the rows and columns are.
- **Gridlines:** The gray lines that show where the columns and rows are.

Unless you've drawn borders around all the cells in a table, you can't tell where rows and columns begin and end without gridlines. To display or hide the gridlines, go to the (Table Tools) Layout tab and click the View Gridlines button.

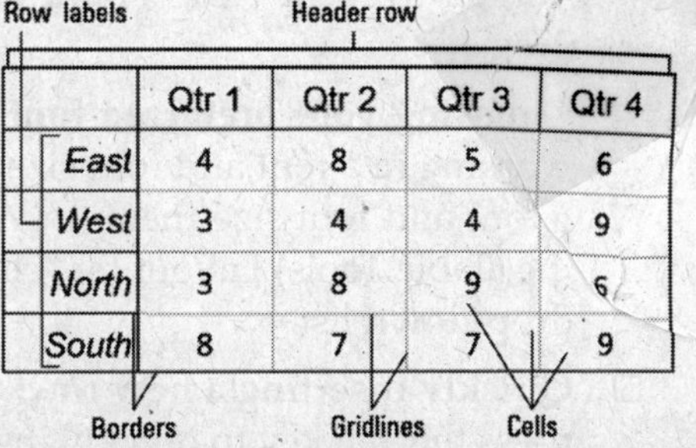

Creating a Table

- **Drag on the Table menu:** On the Insert tab, click the Table button, point in the drop-down list to the number of columns and rows you want, click, and let go of the mouse button.
- **Use the Insert Table dialog box:** On the Insert tab, click the Table button and choose Insert Table on the drop-down list. The Insert Table dialog box appears. Enter the number of columns and rows you want and click OK. In PowerPoint, you can also open the Insert Table dialog box by clicking the Table icon in a content placeholder frame.
- **Draw a table (Word and PowerPoint):** On the Insert tab, click the Table button and then choose Draw Table on the drop-down list. The pointer changes into a pencil. Use the pencil to draw table borders, rows, and columns. If you make a mistake, click the Eraser button on the (Table Tools) Design tab and drag it over the parts of the table you regret drawing (you may have to click the Draw Borders button first). When you finish drawing the table, press Esc. You can click the Pen Colour button and choose a colour on the drop-down list to draw your table in your favourite colour.
- **Create a quick table (Word):** On the Insert tab, click the Table button and choose Quick Tables on the drop-down list. Then choose a readymade table on the submenu. You have to replace the sample data in the quick table with your own data.
- **Convert text in a list into a table (Word):** Press Tab or enter a comma in each list item where you want the columns in the table to be. Select the text you'll convert to a table, click the Table button on the Insert tab, and choose Convert Text to Table. Under Separate Text At in the Convert Text to Table dialog box, choose Tabs or Commas to tell Word how the columns are separated. Then click OK.

Entering Text and Numbers

After you create the table, you can start entering text and numbers. All you have to do is click in a cell and start typing. Select your table and take advantage of these methods to make the onerous task of entering table data a little easier:

- **Quickly changing a table's size:** Drag the bottom or side of a table to change its overall size. In Word, you can also go to the (Table Tools) Layout tab, click the AutoFit button, and choose AutoFit Window to make the table stretch from margin to margin.
- **Moving a table:** In Word, switch to Print Layout view and drag the table selector (the square in the upper-left corner of the table). In PowerPoint and Publisher, move the pointer over the table's perimeter, and when you see the four-headed arrow, click and drag.
- **Choosing your preferred font and font size:** Entering table data is easier when you're working in a font and font size you like. Select the table, visit the Home tab, and choose a font and font size there. In Word and PowerPoint, you can select a table by going to the (Table Tools) Layout tab, clicking the Select button, and choosing Select Table on the drop-down list.
- **Quickly inserting a new row:** Click in the last column of the last row in your table and press the Tab key to quickly insert a new row at the bottom of the table.

Selecting different parts of a Table

- **Selecting cells:** To select a cell, click it. You can select several adjacent cells by dragging the pointer over them.
- **Selecting rows:** Move the pointer to the left of the row and click when you see the right-pointing arrow; click and drag to select several rows. You can also go to the (Table Tools) Layout tab, click inside the row you want to select, click the Select button, and choose Select Row on the drop-down list. To select more than one row at a time, select cells in the rows before choosing the Select Row command.
- **Selecting columns:** Move the pointer above the column and click when you see the down-pointing arrow; click and drag to select several columns. You can also start from the (Table Tools) Layout tab, click in the column you want to select, click the Select button, and choose Select Column in the drop-down list. To select several columns, select cells in the columns before choosing the Select Column command.
- **Selecting a table:** On the (Table Tools) Layout tab, click the Select button, and choose Select Table on the drop-down list. In PowerPoint, you can also right-click a table and choose Select Table on the shortcut menu.

Merging and Splitting Cells

Merge cells to break down the barriers between cells and join them into one cell; split cells to divide a single cell into several cells (or severalcells into several more cells).

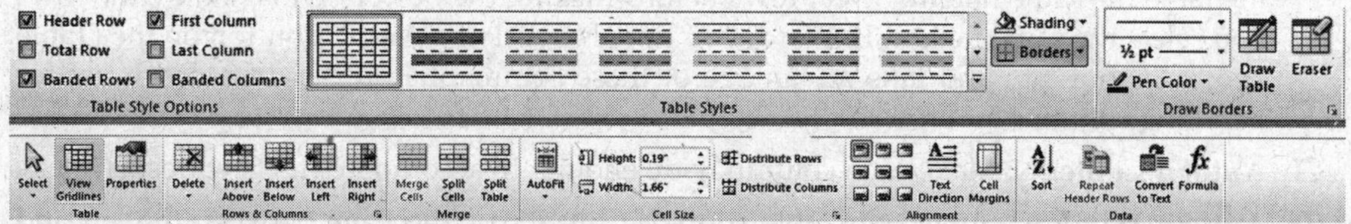

- Select the cells you want to merge or split, go to the (Table Tools) Layout tab, and follow these instructions to merge or split cells:
  - **Merging cells:** Click the Merge Cells button (in Word and PowerPoint, you can also right-click and choose Merge Cells).
  - **Splitting cells:** Click the Split Cells button (in Word and PowerPoint, you can also right-click and choose Split Cells). In the Split Cells dialog box, declare how many columns and rows you want to split the cell into and then click OK. In Publisher, you can only split cells that were previously merged.

Laying Out your Table

- **Column or row:** Move the pointer onto a gridline or border, and when the pointer changes into a double-headed arrow, start dragging. Tug and pull, tug and pull until the column or row is the right size. In Word and PowerPoint, you can also go to the (Table Tools) Layout tab and enter measurements in the Height and Width text boxes to change the width of a column or the height of a row. The measurements affect entire columns or rows, not individual cells.

- **A table:** Select your table and use one of these techniques to change its size in Word and PowerPoint:
- **Dragging:** Drag the top, bottom, or side of the table. You can also drag the lower-right corner to change the size vertically and horizontally.
- **Height and Width text boxes:** On the (Table Tools) Layout tab, enter measurements in the Height and Width text boxes. In Publisher, these text boxes are found on the (Table Tools) Design tab. In PowerPoint, click the Lock Aspect Ratio check box if you want to keep the table's proportions when you change its height or width.
- **Table Properties dialog box (Word only):** On the (Table Tools) Layout tab, click the Cell Size group button, and on the Table tab of the Table Properties dialog box, enter a measurement in the Preferred Width text box.

Adjusting Column and Row size

Resizing columns and rows can be problematic in Word and PowerPoint. For that reason, Word and PowerPoint offer special commands on the (Table Tools) Layout tab for adjusting the width and height of rows and columns:

- **Making all columns the same width:** Click the Distribute Columns button to make all columns the same width. Select columns before giving this command to make only the columns you select the same width.
- **Making all rows the same height:** Click the Distribute Rows button to make all rows in the table the same height. Select rows before clicking the button to make only the rows you select the same height. In Word, you can also click the AutoFit button on the (Table Tools) Layout tab, and take advantage of these commands on the drop-down list for handling columns and rows.
- **AutoFit Contents:** Make each column wide enough to accommodate its widest entry.
- **AutoFit Window:** Stretch the table so that it fits across the page between the left and right margin.
- **Fixed Column Width:** Fix the column widths at their current settings.

Inserting and deleting columns and rows

- **Inserting columns:** Select a column or columns and click the Insert Left or Insert Right button. If you want to insert just one column, click in a column and then click the Insert Left or Insert Right button. You can also right-click, choose Insert, and choose an Insert Columns command.
- **Inserting rows:** Select a row or rows and click the Insert Above or Insert Below button. If you want to insert just one row, click in a row and click the Insert Above or Insert Below button. You can also right-click, choose Insert, and choose an Insert Rows command on the shortcut menu. To insert a row at the end of a table, move the pointer into the last cell in the last row and press the Tab key.
- **Deleting columns:** Click in the column you want to delete, click the Delete button, and choose Delete Columns on the drop-down list. Select more than one column to delete more

than one. (Pressing the Delete key deletes the data in the column, not the column itself.)

- **Deleting rows:** Click in the row you want to delete, click the Delete button, and choose Delete Rows. Select more than one row to delete more than one. (Pressing the Delete key deletes the data in the row, not the row itself.)

Moving Columns and Rows

To move a column or row:

- Select the column or row you want to move. Earlier in this chapter, "Selecting Different Parts of a Table" explains how to select columns and rows.
- Right-click in the selection and choose Cut on the shortcut menu. The column or row is moved to the Clipboard.
- Insert a new column or row where you want the column or row to be. Earlier in this chapter, "Inserting and deleting columns and rows" explains how.

Move the column or row:

- Column: Click in the topmost cell in your new column and then click the Paste button or press Ctrl+V.
- Row: Click in the first column of the row you inserted and then click the Paste button or press Ctrl+V.

Designing a table with a table style

Click anywhere in your table and follow these steps to choose a table style:

- Go to the (Table Tools) Design tab.
- Open the Table Styles gallery and move the pointer over table style choices to "live-preview" the table. In Publisher, this gallery is called Table Formats.
- Select a table style. To remove a table style, open the Table Styles gallery and choose Clear (in Word) or Clear Table (in PowerPoint).

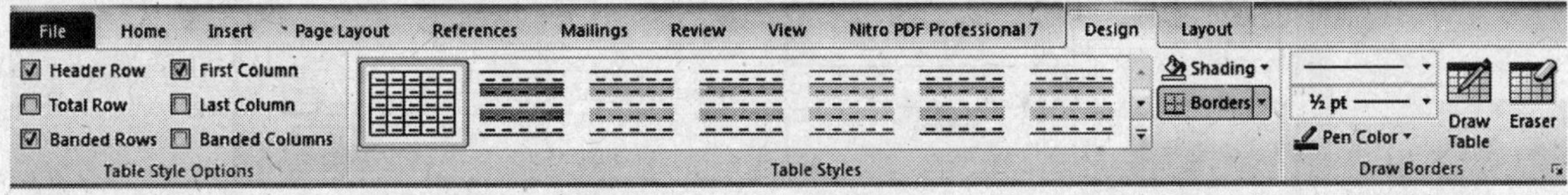

Designing borders for your table

Follow these steps to fashion a border for your table or a part of your table:

- Go to the (Table Tools) Design tab.
- Select the part of your table that needs a new border.

To select the entire table, go to the (Table Tools) Layout tab, click the Select button, and choose Select Table.

- Open the Line Style drop-down list (in Word) or the Pen Style drop down list (in PowerPoint) and choose a line style for the border (you may have to click the Draw

Borders button first, depending on the size of your screen). Stay away from the dotted and dashed lines unless you have a good reason for choosing one. These lines can be distracting and keep others from focusing on the data presented in the table.

- ❐ Open the Line Weight drop-down list (in Word and Publisher) or the Pen Weight drop-down list (in PowerPoint) and choose a thickness for the border (you may have to click the Draw Borders button first).
- ❐ If you want your borders to be of another colour apart from black, click the Pen Colour button (Word and PowerPoint) or the Line Colour button (Publisher) and choose a colour on the drop-down list (you may have to click the Draw Borders button first).
- ❐ Open the drop-down list on the Borders button and choose where to place borders on the part of the table you selected in Step 2.

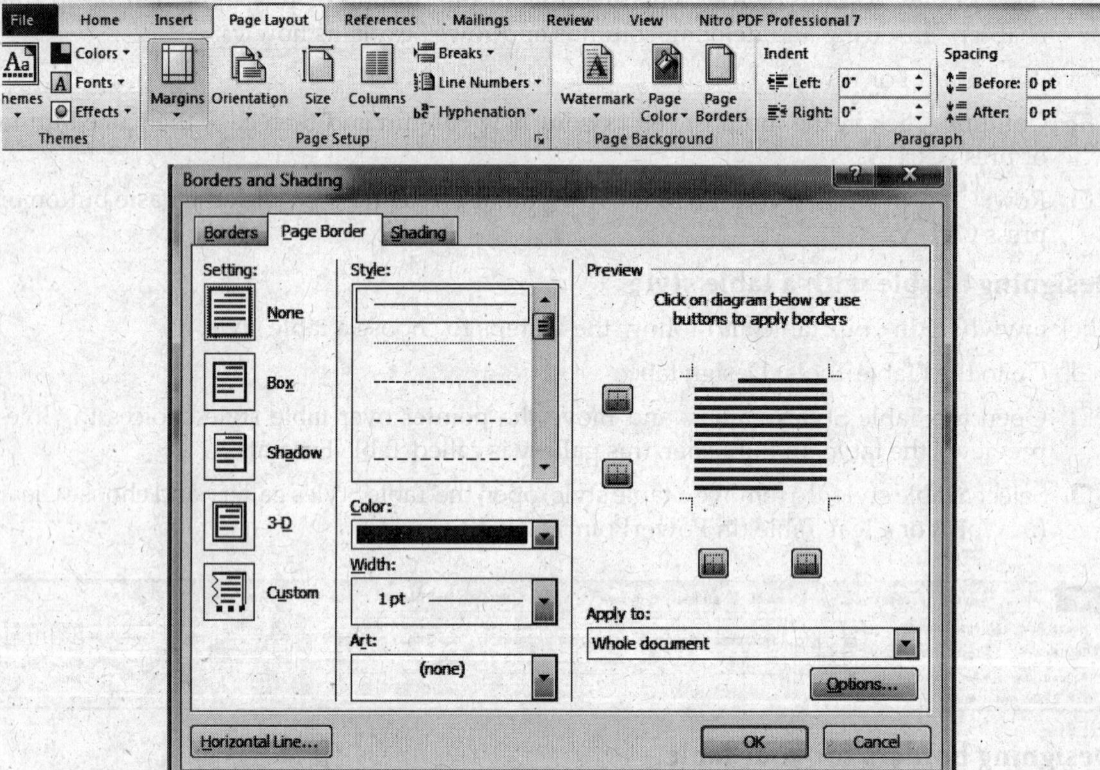

Using Math Formulas in Word Tables

You don't have to add the figures in columns and rows yourself; Word gladly does that for you. Word can perform other mathematical calculationsas well. Follow these steps to perform mathematical calculations and tell Word how to format sums and products:

- ❐ Put the cursor in the cell that will hold the sum or product of the cells above, below, to the right, or to the left.
- ❐ On the (Table Tools) Layout tab, click the Formula button.

Drawing diagonal lines on tables

Draw diagonal lines across table cells to cancel out those cells or otherwise make cells look different.

- Draw Table button: Click the Draw Table button (you may have to click the Draw Borders button first). The pointer changes into a pencil. Drag to draw the diagonal lines. Press Esc or click the Draw Table button a second time when you're finished drawing. Click the Pen Colour button and choose a colour before drawing on your table if you want the diagonal lines to be of certain colour.
- Borders button: Select the cells that need diagonal lines, open the dropdown list on the Borders button, and choose Diagonal down Border or Diagonal Up Border.

Drawing on a Table

- On the Insert tab, click the Shapes button and select the Oval shape on the drop-down list.
- On a corner of your page or slide, away from the table, drag to draw the oval.
- On the (Drawing Tools) Format tab, open the drop-down list on the Shape Fill button and choose No Fill.
- Open the drop-down list on the Shape Outline button and choose a very dark colour.
- Open the drop-down list on the Shape Outline button, choose Weight, and choose a thick line.
- Drag the oval over the data on your table that you want to highlight. If the oval is obscured by the table, go to the (Drawing Tools) Format tab, and click the Bring Forward button (click the Arrange button, if necessary,to see this button). While you're at it, consider rotating the oval a little way to make it appear as though it was drawn by hand on the table.

Charts

Anatomy of Charts

Before you start doing activities on charts, you need to know the following:

- **Plot area:** The center of the chart, apart from the legend and data labels, where the data itself is presented.
- **Values:** The numerical values with which the chart is plotted. The values you enter determine the size of the data markers — the bars, columns, pie slices, and so on — that portray values.
- **Gridlines:** Lines on the chart that indicate value measurements. Gridlines are optional in charts.
- **Worksheet:** Where you enter (or retrieve) the data used to plot the chart. The worksheet resembles a table. A worksheet is called a data table when it appears along with a chart.
- **Data series:** A group of related data points presented by category on a chart.

- **Categories:** The actual items that you want to compare or display in your chart.
- **Legend:** A text box located to the side, top, or bottom of a chart that identifies the chart's data labels.
- **Horizontal and vertical axes:** For plotting purposes, one side of the plot area.
- **Data point:** A value plotted on a chart that is represented by a column, line, bar, pie slice, dot, or other shape.
- **Data marker:** Shapes on a chart that represents data points.
- **Data label:** A label that shows the actual values used to construct the data markers.

The Basics: Creating a Chart

- Go to the Insert tab.
- If you're working in Excel, select the data you'll use to generate the chart.
- Select the kind of chart you want.
- To modify your chart, start by selecting it. Click a chart to select it. Selecting a chart makes the Chart Tools tabs appear in the upper-right corner of the window. Use these tabs — Design, Layout, and Format — to make your chart just-so. In Word, you must be in Print Layout view to see a chart.

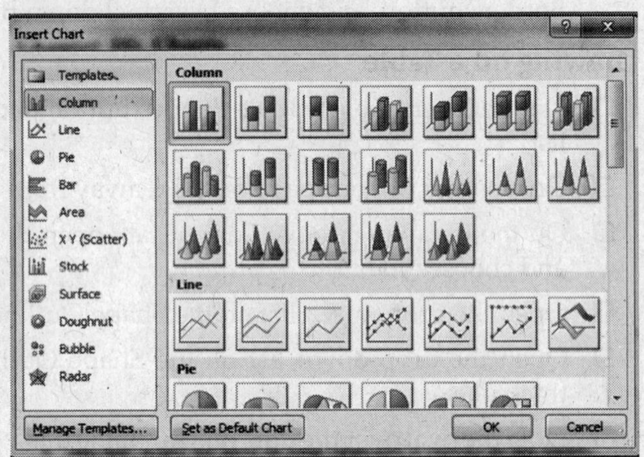

Creating a chart

- Select the (Chart Tools) Design tab when you want to change the chart's layout, alter the data with which the chart was generated, or select a different chart type.
- Select the (Chart Tools) Layout tab when you want to change the chart's title, labels, or gridlines. You can add or remove parts of a chart starting on the Layout tab.
- Select the (Chart Tools) Format tab when you want to change the appearance of your chart.

Changing chart layout

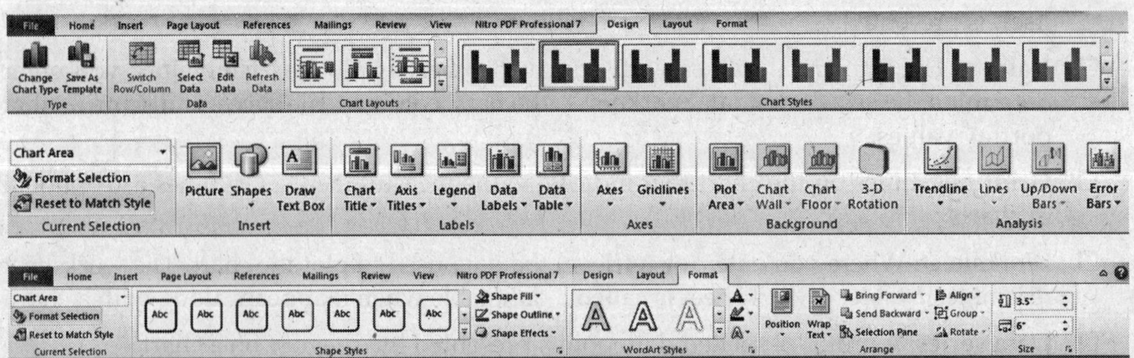

- **Design tab:** For quickly changing a chart's appearance, go to the Design tab. The ready-made gallery choices give you the opportunity to change a chart's layout and appearance in a matter of seconds. You can also choose a new chart type from the Design tab.
- **Layout tab:** For rearranging, hiding, and displaying various parts of a chart, including the legend, labels, title, gridlines, and scale, go to the Layout tab to tweak your chart and make different parts of it stand out or recede into the background.
- **Format tab:** For changing the colour, outline, font, and font size of various parts of a chart, including the labels, bars, and pie slices, you have to really know what you're doing and have a lot of time on your hands to change colours and fonts throughout a chart.

Changing Chart Type

- Click your chart to select it.
- On the (Chart Tools) Design tab, click the Change Chart Type button, or right-click your chart and choose Change Chart Type on the shortcut menu.
- Select a new chart type and click OK.

Changing Size and Shape of a Chart

To make a chart taller or wider, follow these instructions:

- Click the perimeter of the chart to select it and then drag a handle on the side to make it wider, or a handle on the top or bottom to make it taller.
- Go to the (Chart Tools) Format tab and enter measurements in the Shape Height and Shape Width boxes. You can find these boxes in the Size group (you may have to click the Size button to see them, depending on the size of your screen).

Relying on a Chart Style to change appearances

The easiest way to change the look of a chart is to choose an option in the Chart Styles gallery in the (Chart Tools) Design tab.

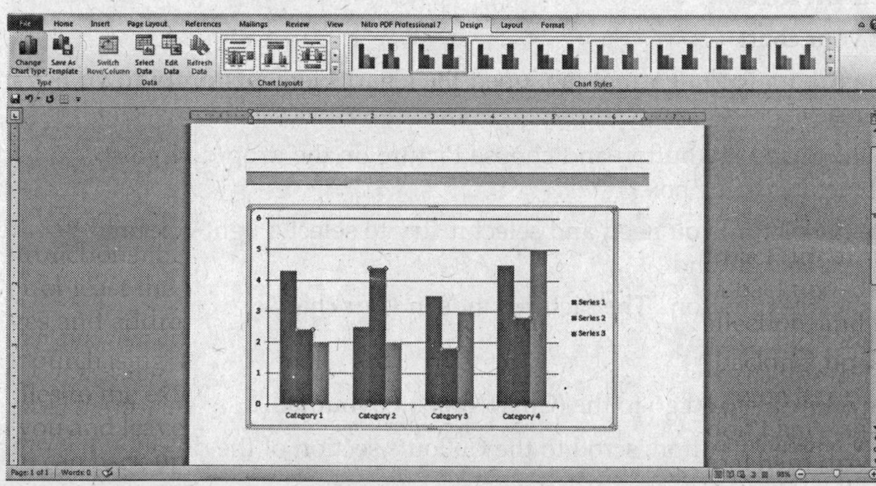

Changing a Chart elements' colour, font, or other particular

- ❐ Select the (Chart Tools) Format tab. The tools on the (Chart Tools) Format tab are very similar to the tools found on the (Drawing Tools) Format tab. You can find all the tools you need here to change the colour, outline, and size of a chart element.
- ❐ Select the chart element that needs a facelift. To select a chart element, either click it or choose its name on the Chart Elements drop-down.
- ❐ Format the chart element you selected.

Use one of these methods to format the chart element:

- ❐ Open a Format dialog box. The dialog box offers commands for formatting the element you selected.
- ❐ Do the work on your own. For example, to change fonts in the chart element you selected, right-click and choose a font on the shortcut menu. Or go to the Home tab to change font sizes. Or open the drop-down list on the Shape Fill button on the (Chart Tools) Format tab and select a new colour.

Saving a Chart as a Template

Follow these steps to make a template out of a chart:

- ❐ Save your file to make sure that the chart settings are saved on your computer.
- ❐ Select your chart.
- ❐ Go to the (Chart Tools) Design tab.
- ❐ Click the Save as Template button. You can find this button in the Type group. You will see the Save Chart Template dialog box.
- ❐ Enter a descriptive name for the template and click the Save button. Include the type of chart you're dealing with in the name. This will help you understand which template you're selecting when the time comes to choose a chart template.

Change Chart Type | Save As Template | Type

Inserting a picture

- ❐ Select your chart.
- ❐ On the (Chart Tools) Format tab, open the Chart Elements drop-down list and choose Plot Area.
- ❐ Click the Shape Fill button and choose Picture on the drop-down list. You will see the Insert Picture dialog box.
- ❐ Locate the picture you need and select it. Try to select a light-coloured picture that will serve as a background.
- ❐ Click the Insert button. The picture lands in your chart.

Annotating a chart

- ❐ Select your chart and go to the (Chart Tools) Layout tab.
- ❐ Click the Shapes button, scroll to the Callouts section of the dropdown list, and choose a callout.

- ❒ Depending on the size of your screen, you may have to click the Insert button to get to the Shapes button.
- ❒ Drag on your slide to draw the callout shape.
- ❒ Type the annotation inside the callout shape.
- ❒ Resize the callout shape as necessary to make it fit with the chart
- ❒ Drag the yellow diamond on the callout shape to attach the callout to the chart.

SmartArt

Creating a diagram

After you select a generic diagram in the Choose a SmartArt Graphic dialog box and click OK, the next step is to make the diagram your own by completing these tasks:

- ❒ **Change the diagram's size and position:** Change the size and position of a diagram to make it fit squarely on your page or slide. See "Changing the Size and Position of a Diagram," later in this chapter.
- ❒ **Add shapes to (or remove shapes from) the diagram:** Adding a shape involves declaring where to add the shape, promoting or demoting the shape with respect to other shapes, and declaring how the new shape connects to another shape. See "Laying Out the Diagram Shapes" later in this chapter.
- ❒ **Enter text:** Enter text on each shape, or component, of the diagram. See "Handling the Text on Diagram Shapes" later in this chapter. If you so desire, you can also customize your diagram by taking on some oral of these tasks:
- ❒ **Changing its overall appearance:** Choose a different colour scheme or 3-D variation for your diagram. See "Choosing a Look for Your Diagram" later in this chapter.
- ❒ **Changing shapes:** Select a new shape for part of your diagram, change the size of a shape, or assign different colours to shapes to make shapes stand out. See "Changing the Appearance of Diagram Shapes" later in this chapter.

Creating a diagram

Follow these steps to create a diagram:

- ❒ On the Insert tab, click the SmartArt button. You will see the Choose a SmartArt Graphic dialog box; you can also open the dialog box by clicking the SmartArt Icon in a content placeholder frame.

- ❐ Select a diagram in the Choose a SmartArt Graphic dialog box.

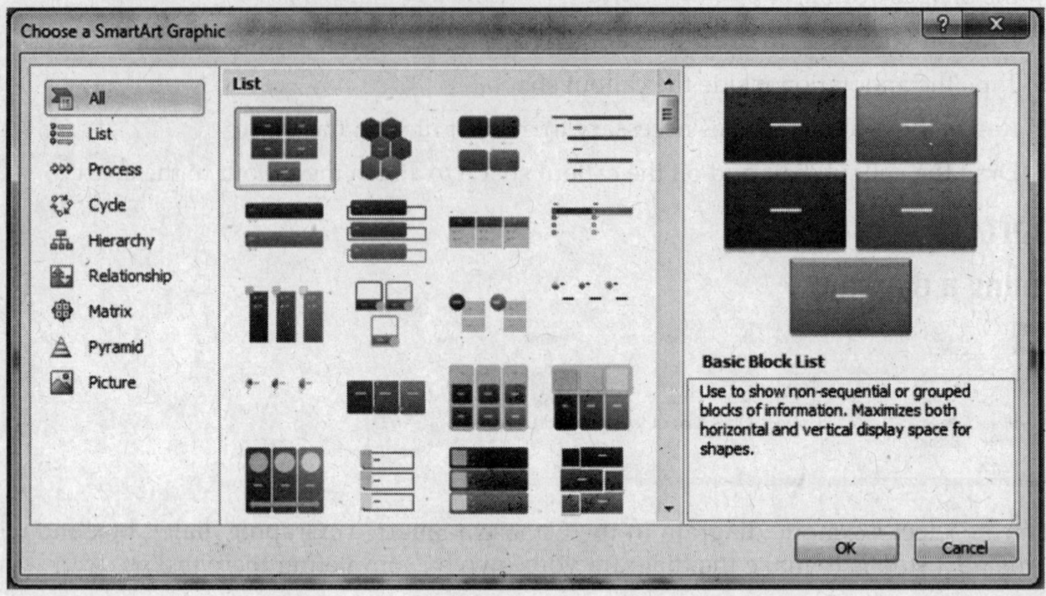

  - Click your diagram to select it.
  - Go to the (SmartArt Tools) Design tab.
  - Open the Layouts gallery (you may have to click the Change Layout button first). You will see a gallery with diagrams of the same type as the diagram you're working with. Select a new diagram or choose More Layouts to open the Choose a SmartArt Graphic dialog box and select a diagram there.

Changing Size and Position of a diagram

To make a diagram fit squarely on a page or slide, you have to change its size and position.

- ❐ **Resizing a diagram:** Select the diagram, move the pointer over a selection handle on the corner or side, and start dragging after the pointer changes into a two-headed arrow. You can also go to the (SmartArt Tools) Format tab and enter new measurements in the Width and Height boxes. (You may have to click the Size button to see these text boxes, depending on the size of your screen.)
- ❐ **Repositioning a diagram:** Select the diagram, move the pointer over its perimeter, and when you see the four-headed arrow, click and start dragging.

Adding shapes to diagrams apart from hierarchy diagrams

Follow these steps to add a shape to a list, process, cycle, relationship, matrix, or pyramid diagram:

- ❐ In your diagram, select the shape that your new shape will appear before or after.

- Choose the Add Shape After or Add Shape Before command. To get to these commands, use one of these methods:
  - On the (SmartArt Tools) Design tab, open the drop-down list on the Add Shape button and choose Add Shape After or Add Shape Before.
  - Right-click the shape you selected, choose Add Shape on the shortcut menu, and then choose Add Shape After or Add Shape Before on the submenu.

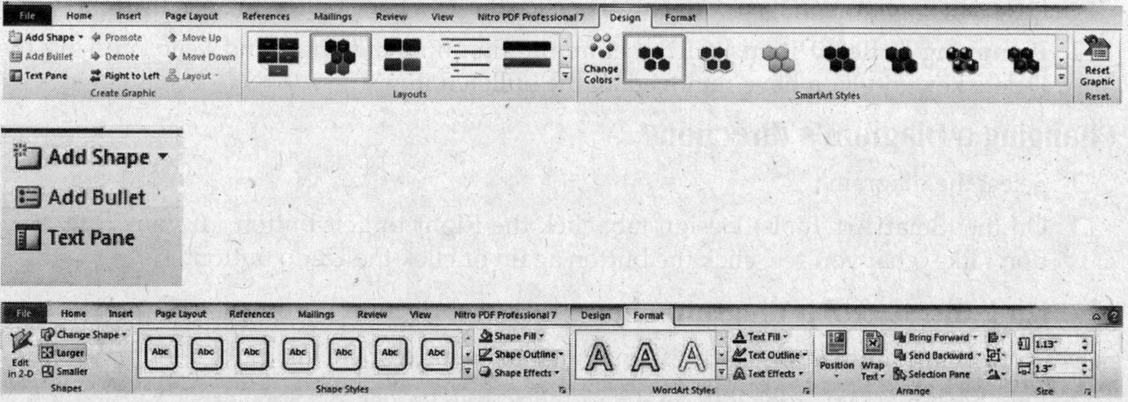

Adding an Organization Chart shape

Besides adding a shape after, before, above, or below a shape, you can add an assistant shape to an Organization Chart diagram. An assistant shape is an intermediary shape between two levels. Follow these steps to add a shape to an Organization Chart diagram:

- Select the shape to which you will add a new shape.
- Choose an Add Shape command.

You can choose Add Shape commands in two ways:

- On the (SmartArt Tools) Design tab, open the drop-down list on the Add Shape button and choose an Add Shape command.
- Right-click the shape you selected, choose Add Shape on the shortcut menu, and then choose an Add Shape command on the submenu.

Entering text on a diagram shape

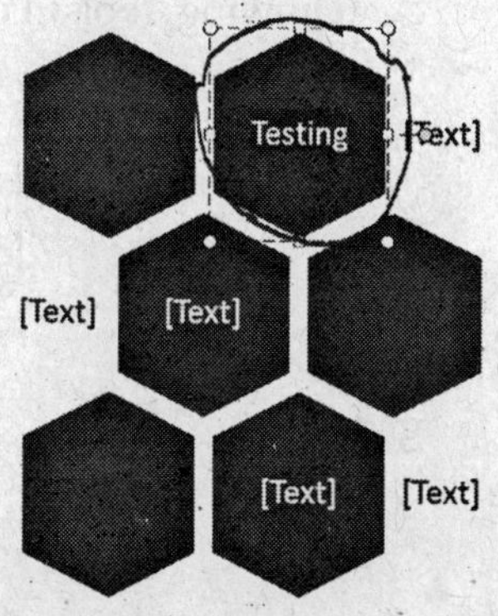

Use one of these techniques to enter text on a diagram shape:

- **Click on the shape and start typing:** The words you type appear.
- **Enter text in the Text pane:** Enter the text by typing it in the Text pane
- On the (SmartArt Tools) Design tab, click the Text Pane button.
- Click the Text Pane button on the diagram. This button is not labeled, but you can find it to the left of the diagram.

Entering bulleted lists on diagram shapes

Some diagram shapes have built-in bulleted lists, but no matter. Whether a shape is prepared to be bulleted or not, you can enter bullets in a diagram shape. Here are instructions for entering and removing bullets:

- **Entering a bulleted list:** Select the shape that needs bullets, and on the (SmartArt Tools) Design tab, click the Add Bullet button. Either enter the bulleted items directly into the shape (pressing Enter as you type each entry) or click the Text Pane button to open the Text pane.
- **Removing bulleted items:** Click before the first bulleted entry and keep pressing the Delete key until you have removed all the bulleted items.

Changing a Diagram's direction

- Select the diagram.
- On the (SmartArt Tools) Design tab, click the Right to Left button. If you don't like what you see, click the button again or click the Undo button.

Changing the size of a diagram shape

Change Shape
Larger
Smaller
Shapes

Select your shape and use one of these methods to enlarge or shrink it:

- On the (SmartArt Tools) Format tab, click the Larger or Smaller buttonas many times as necessary to make the shape the right size.
- Move the pointer over a corner selection handle, and when the pointer changes to a two-headed arrow, click and start dragging.

The Basics: Drawing Lines, Arrows, and Shapes

Follow these basic steps to draw a line, arrow, or shape:

- Go to the Insert tab.
- Click the Shapes button to open the Insert Shapes gallery.
- Select a line, arrow, or shape in the Shapes gallery.
- Drag on your page, slide, or worksheet. As you drag, the line, arrow, or shape appears.
- To alter your line, arrow, or shape—that is, to change its size, colour, or outline—go to the (Drawing Tools) Format tab. This tab offers many commands for manipulating lines and shapes.

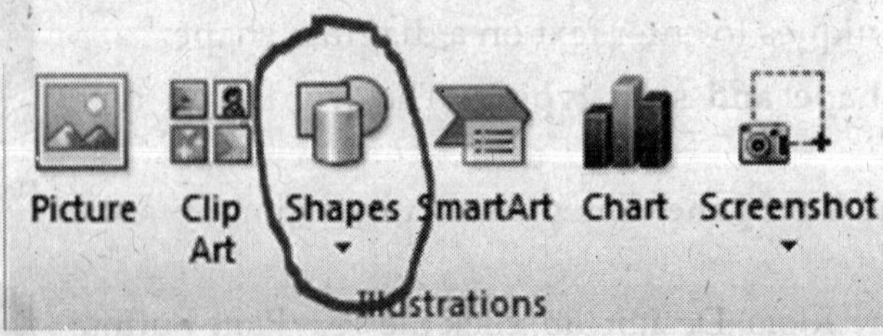

Handling Lines, Arrows, and Connectors

Changing the length and position of a line or arrow

To change anything about a line or arrow, start by clicking to select it. You can tell when a line has been selected because round selection handles appear at either end. Follow these instructions to move a line or adjust its length or angle:

- **Changing the angle of a line:** Drag a selection handle up, down, or sideways. A dotted line shows where your line will be when you release the mouse button.
- **Changing the length:** Drag a selection handle away from or toward the opposite selection handle.
- **Changing the position:** Move the pointer over the line itself and click when you see the four-headed arrow. Then drag the line to a new location.

Changing the appearance of a line, arrow, or connector

What a line looks like is a matter of its colour, its weight (how wide it is), its dash status (it can be filled out or dashed), and its cap (its ends can berounded, square, or flat). To change the appearance of a line, start by selecting it, going to the (Drawing Tools) Format tab, and opening the drop-down list on the Shape Outline button (this button is in the Shape Styles group).

- **Colour:** Select a colour on the drop-down list.
- **Width:** Choose Weight on the drop-down and then choose a line width on the submenu. You can also choose More Lines on the submenu to open the Format Shape dialog box and change the width there. Enter a setting in points to make the line heavier or thinner.
- **Dotted or dashed lines:** Choose Dashes on the drop-down list and then choose an option on the submenu. Again, you can choose More Lines to open the Format Shape dialog box and choose from many dash types and compound lines.
- **Line caps:** Click the Shape Styles group button to open the Format Shape dialog box. In the Line Style category, select a cap type (Square, Round, or Flat).

Making the connection

Before you draw the connections, draw the shapes and arrange them on the slide where you want them to be in your diagram. Then follow these steps to connect two shapes with a connector:

- Select the two shapes that you want to connect. To select the shapes, hold down the Ctrl key and click each one.
- On the (Drawing Tools) Format tab, open the Shapes gallery.
- Under Lines, select the connector that will best fit between the two shapes you want to link together.
- Move the pointer over a side selection handle on one of the shapes you want to connect. The selection handles turn red.
- Click and drag the pointer over a selection handle on the other shape, and when you see red selection handles on that shape, release the mouse button. Red, round selection

handles appear on the shapes where they're connected. These red handles tell you that the two shapes are connected and will remain connected when you move them.

Handling Rectangles, Ovals, Stars, and Other Shapes

Drawing a shape

Follow these steps to draw a shape:

- ❒ On the Insert tab, click the Shapes button to open the Shapes gallery. You can also insert shapes from the Shapes gallery on the (Drawing Tools) Format tab.
- ❒ Select a shape in the gallery. If you've drawn the shape recently, you may be able to find it at the top of the gallery under Recently Used Shapes.
- ❒ Click and drag slantwise to draw the shape. Hold down the Shift key as you drag if you want the shape to retain its proportions. For example, to draw a circle, select the Oval shape and Hold down the Shift key as you draw.

Changing a shape's size and shape

Selection handles appear on the corners and sides of a shape after you select it. With the selection handles showing, you can change a shape's size and shape:

- ❒ Hold down the Shift key and drag a corner handle to change a shape's size and retain its symmetry.
- ❒ Drag a side, top, or bottom handle to stretch or scrunch a shape.

Choosing a different shape

To exchange one shape for another, select the shape and follow these steps:

- ❒ On the (Drawing Tools) Format tab, click the Edit Shape button.
- ❒ You can find this button in the Insert Shapes group.
- ❒ Choose Change Shape on the drop-down list.
- ❒ Select a new shape in the Shapes gallery.

Changing a shape's symmetry

A yellow diamond, sometimes more than one, appears on some shapes. By dragging a diamond, you can change a shape's symmetry.

Follow these instructions to handle text box shapes:

- ❒ **Entering the text:** Click in the shape and start typing. In Word, you can right-click and choose Add Text if you have trouble typing in the shape.
- ❒ **Editing the text:** Click in the text and start editing. That's all there is to it. If you have trouble getting inside the shape to edit the text, select the shape, right-click it, and choose Edit Text on the shortcut menu.

- ❐ Changing the font, colour, and size of text: Right-click in the text and choose Font. Then, in the Font dialog box, choose a font, font colour, and a font size for the text.

WordArt for Bending, Spindling, and Mutilating Text

- ❐ Allowing the shape to enlarge for text: You can allow the shape to enlarge and receive more text. Click the Shape Styles group button, and in the Text Box category of the Format Shape dialog box, select the Resize Shape to Fit Text option button.

Creating a WordArt image

Follow these steps to create a WordArt image:

- ❐ On the Insert tab, click the WordArt button. A drop-down list with WordArt styles appears.
- ❐ Select a WordArt style.
- ❐ Enter the text for the image in the WordArt text box.

Editing a WordArt image

On the (Drawing Tools) Format tab, click the Edit Shape button, choose Change Shape, and then select a shape in the Shapes gallery. After the conversion, you usually have to enlarge the shape to accommodate the text. Usually, you have to wrestle with a WordArt image before it comes out right. Select the image, go to the (Drawing Tools) Format tab, and follow the steps:

- ❐ **Editing the words:** Click in the WordArt text box and edit the text there.
- ❐ **Choosing a new WordArt style:** Open the WordArt Styles gallery and select a style. Depending on the size of your screen and which program you're working in, you may have to click the Quick Styles button first
- ❐ **Changing the letters' colour:** Click the Text Fill button and choose a colour on the drop-down list.
- ❐ **Changing the letters' outline:** Click the Text Outline button and make choices to change the letters' outline.

Points to Remember

- ☆ To search for a good synonym, click the word in question and open the thesaurus or the research task pane
- ☆ Selection handles appear on the carness and sides of a shape after you select it.

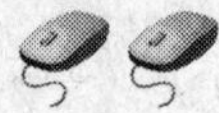

Welcome to MS Word 2010

Introducing the Word Screen

Easy description of the screen parts:

- **Word button:** In the upper-left corner of the screen, the Word button offers a menu for restoring, moving, sizing, minimizing, maximizing, and closing the Word window.
- **Quick Access toolbar:** This toolbar offers the Save, Undo, and Repeat buttons. Wherever you go in Word, you see the Quick Access toolbar.
- **Title bar:** At the top of the screen, the title bar tells you the name of the document you're working on.
- **Minimize, Restore, Close buttons:** These three magic buttons make it very easy to shrink, enlarge, and close the window you are working in.
- **File tab:** Go to the File tab to do file-management tasks.
- **The Ribbon:** Select a tab on the Ribbon to undertake a new task
- **Scroll bars:** The scroll bars help you get from place to place in a document.
- **Status bar:** The status bar gives you basic information about where you are and what you're doing in a document. It tells you what page and what section you're in, the total number of pages and words in your document, and what language the text is written in.
- **View buttons:** Click one of these buttons — Print Layout, Full Screen Reading, Web Layout, Outline, or Draft — to change your view of a document.
- **Zoom controls:** Use these controls to zoom in and out on your work.

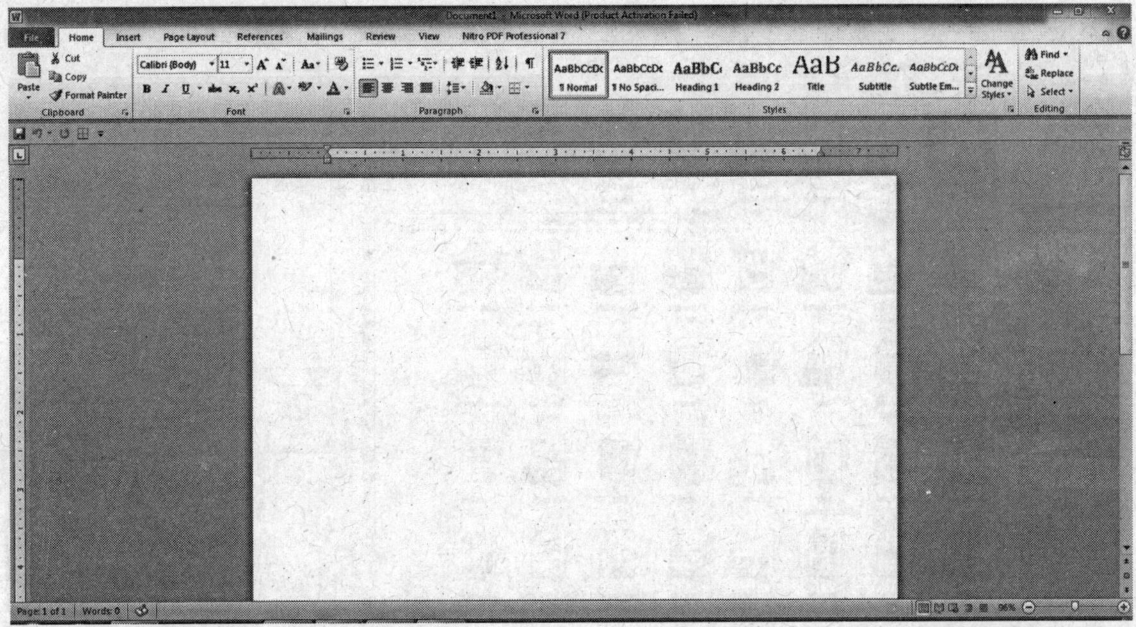

Creating a New Document

When you first start Word, you see a new, blank document with the generic name Document1. You can start working right away on this document, or you can create a new document by choosing a template.

A template is a special kind of file that is used as the starting point for creating documents. Each template comes with many preformatted styles. If your aim is to create an academic report, flyer, newsletter, calendar, résumé, see if you can spare yourself the formatting work by choosing the appropriate template when you create your document.

No matter what kind of document you want, start creating it by going to the File tab and choosing "New".

Click a template in this window to see, on the right side of the window, a preview of the document you will create. Double-click a template (or select it and click the Create button) to create a document.

Use these methods in the Available Templates window to create a document:

- ❒ **Create a blank document:** Choose the Blank Document icon to create a bare-bones document with few styles. Blank Document is the default template for creating documents. (By pressing Ctrl+N, you can create a new, blank document without opening the Available Templates window.)
- ❒ Create a brochure, form, invoice, or other specialty document.

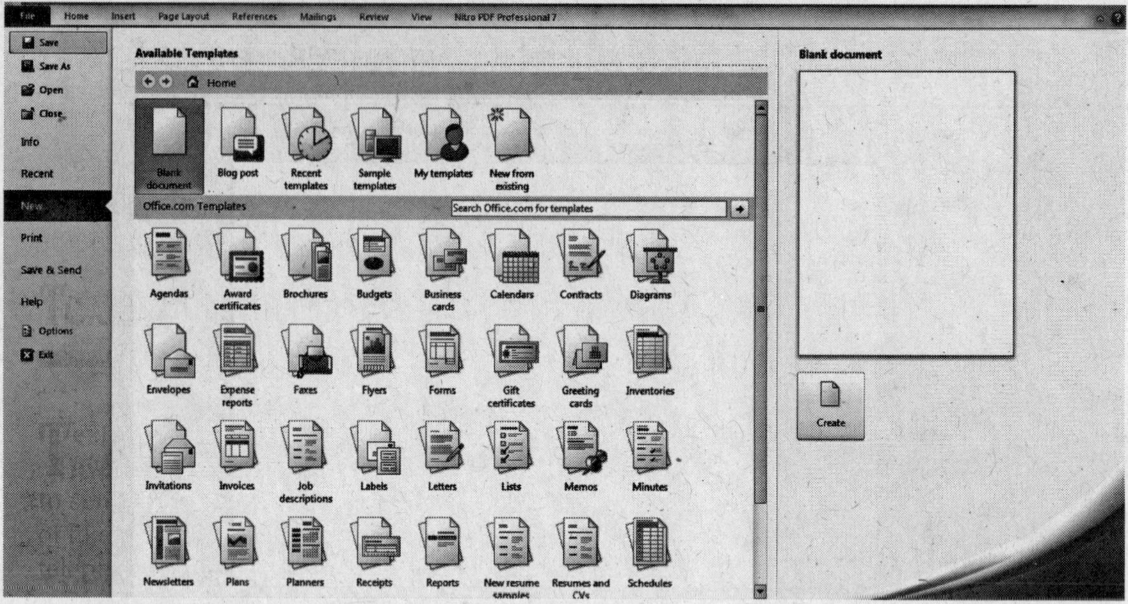

- **Use a template on your computer:** Choose Sample Templates. Templates that you loaded on your computer when you installed Office appear in the window.
- **Download a template from Microsoft:** Under Office.com Templates, do one of the following:
  - Choose the type of template you want, or
  - Make sure that your computer is connected to the Internet, enter a search term in the Search box, and click the Start Searching button (or press Enter). Choose a template and click the Download button to download it to your computer.
- **Use a template you created (or downloaded earlier from Microsoft or acquired from a third party):** Click the My Templates icon. The New dialog box appears so that you can choose a template.
- Create a document from a template you recently used, Templates icon and choose a template.
- **Create a document from another document:** If you can use another document as the starting point for creating a new document, click the New from Existing icon. In the New from Existing Document dialog box, select the document and click the Create New button.

Get a Better Look at Your Documents

In word processing, you want to focus sometimes on the writing, sometimes on the layout, and sometimes on the organization of your work. To help you stay in focus, Word offers different ways of viewing a document.

Changing views

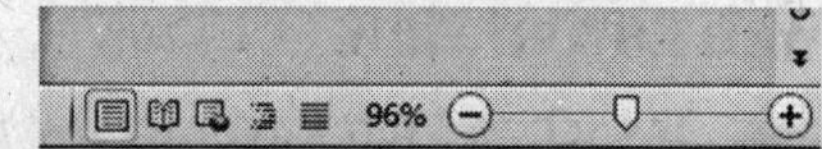

Use these techniques to change views:

- ❐ Click one of the five View buttons on the right side of the status bar.
- ❐ On the View tab, click one of the five buttons in the Document Views group.

Print Layout view

Switch to Print Layout view to see the big picture. In this view, you can see what your document will look like when you print it. You can see graphics, headers, footers, and even page borders in Print Layout view. You can also see clearly where page breaks occur (where one page ends and the next begins). In Print Layout view, you can click the One Page, Two Pages, or Page Width button on the View tab to display more or fewer pages on your screen.

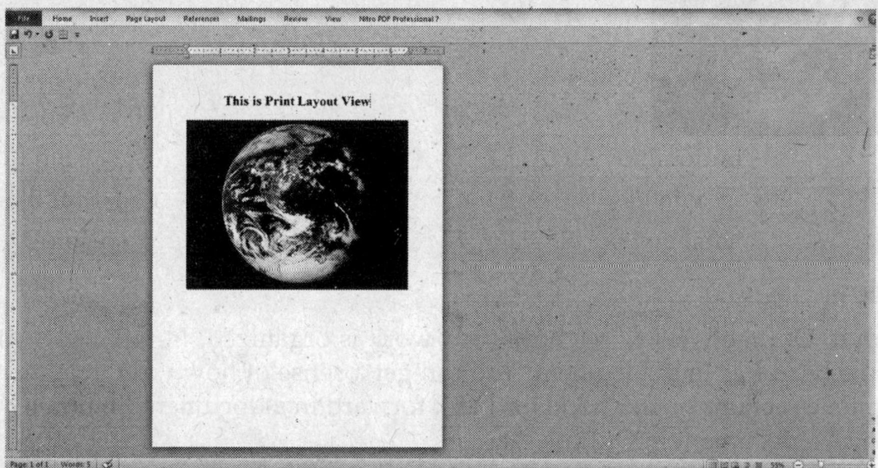

Full Screen Reading view

Switch to Full Screen Reading view to focus on the text itself and proofread your documents. In this view, everything gets stripped away — the Ribbon, scroll bars, status bar, and all. All you see is the text and artwork in your documents. You can't enter or edit text.

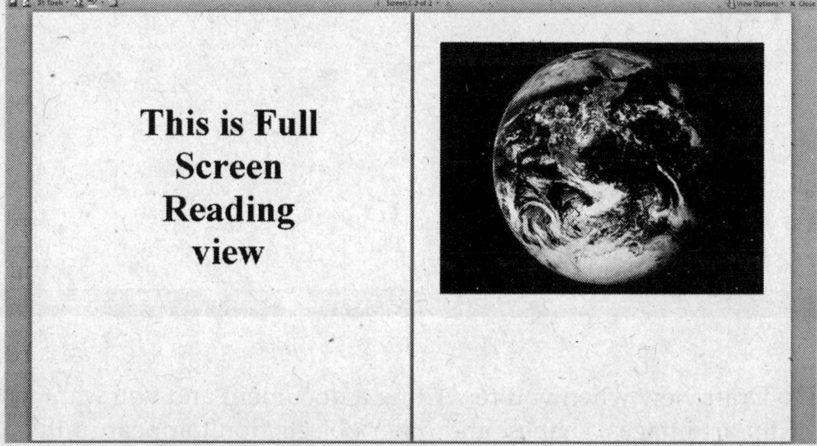

Web Layout view

Switch to Web Layout view to see what your document would look like as a web page. Background colours appear (if you chose a theme or background colour for your document). Text is wrapped to the window rather than around the artwork in the document.

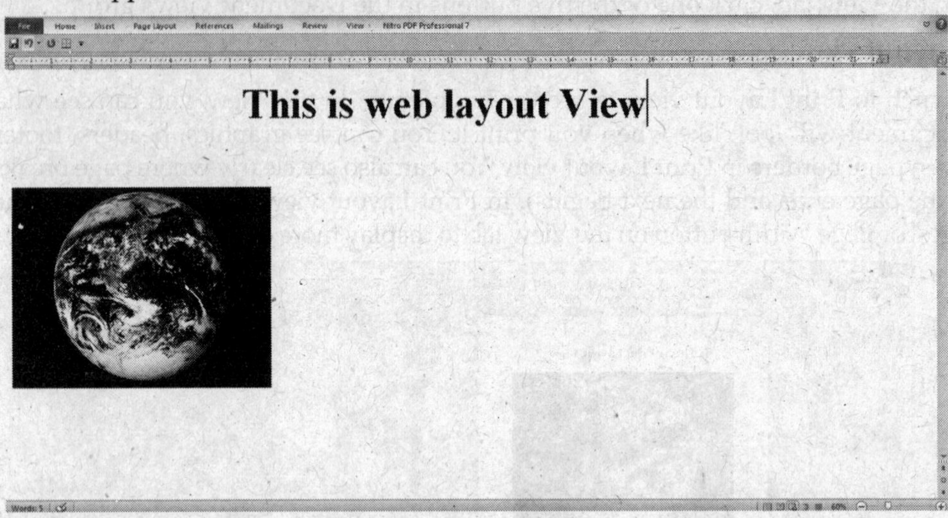

Outline view

Outline

Switch to Outline view to see how your work is organized. In this view, you can see only the headings in a document. You can get a sense of how your document unfolds and easily move sections of text backward and forward in a document. In other words, you can reorganize a document in Outline view.

Draft view

Draft

Switch to Draft view when you're writing a document and you want to focus on the words. Clip-art images, shapes, and other objects don't appear in this view, nor do page breaks (although you can clearly see section breaks). Draft view is best for writing first drafts.

Splitting the screen

Besides opening a second window on a document you can be two places at one time in a Word document by splitting the screen. Word offers two ways to split the screen:

- Move the mouse pointer to the split box at the top of the scroll bar on the right. Move it just above the View Ruler button. When the pointer turns into double arrows, click and drag the gray line down the screen. When you release the mouse button, you have a split screen.

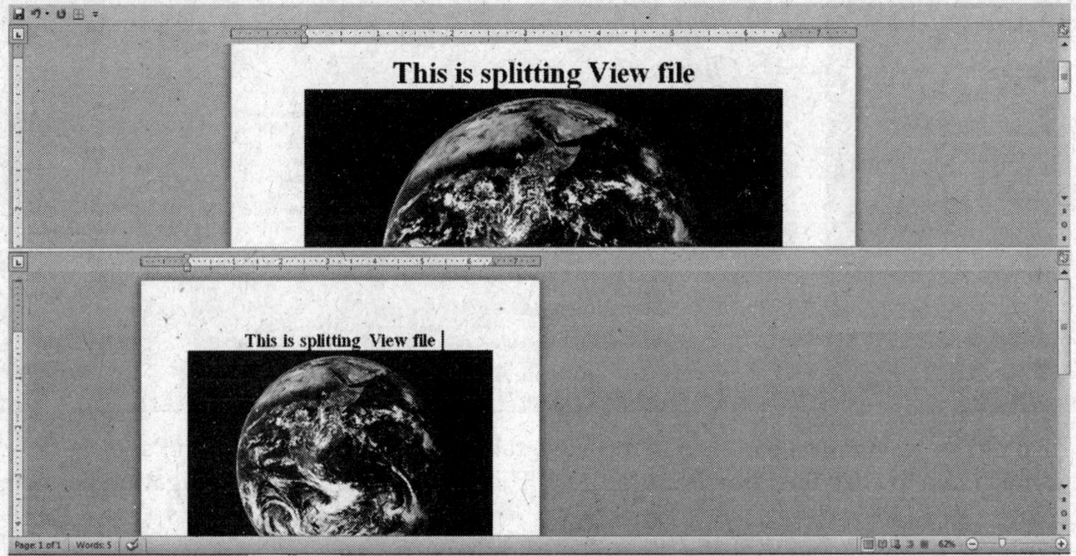

- On the View tab, click the Split button. A gray line appears on-screen. Roll the mouse down until the gray line is where you want the split to be, and click. You get two screens split down the middle.

Moving in Documents

Besides sliding the scroll bar, Word offers a handful of methods for navigation of documents

Keys for Navigation

Checkout this table:

Key to Press	Where it Takes You
PgUp	Up the length of one screen
PgDn	Down the length of one screen
Ctrl+PgUp	To the previous page in the document
Ctrl+PgDn	To the next page in the document
Ctrl+Home	To the top of the document
Ctrl+End	To the bottom of the document

Navigating from page to page or heading to heading

In lengthy documents such as the one in the best way to get from place to place is to make use of the Navigation pane.

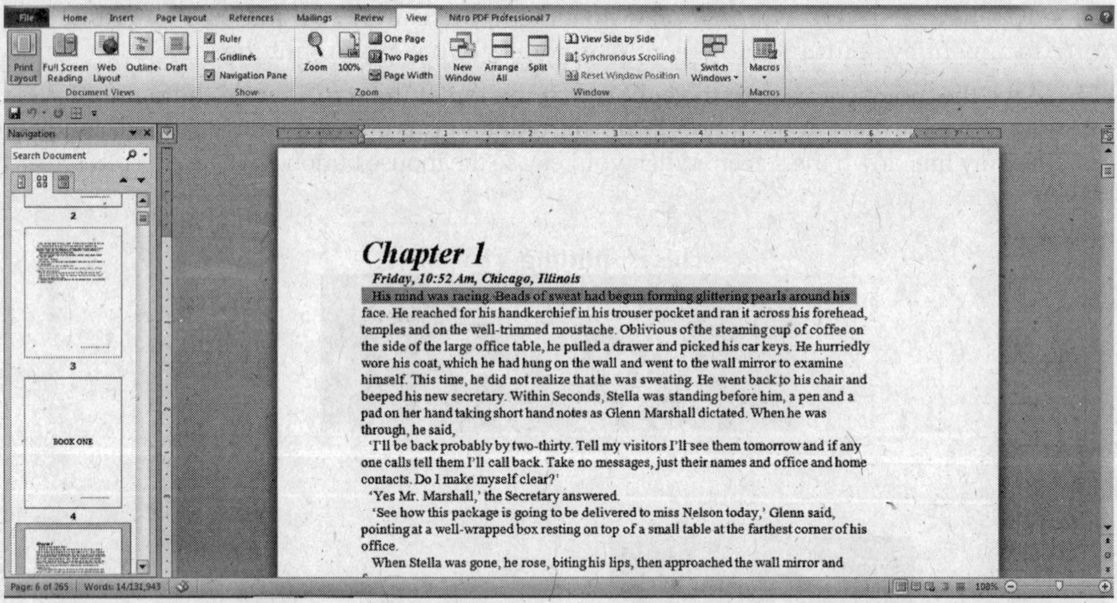

To display the Navigation pane, go to the View tab and click the Navigation Pane check box (you may have to click the Show button first). Then select a tab in the Navigation pane and go to it:

- ❒ **Going from heading to heading:** Select the Browse the Headings tab. Headings in your document appear (provided you assigned heading styles to headings). You can use the Navigation pane like a table of contents and click headings to get from place to place. Right-click a heading and choose a heading-level option on the shortcut menu to tell

Word which headings to display. You can also right-click a heading and choose Expand All or Collapse All to see or hide lower-level headings.

- **Going from page to page:** Select the Browse the Pages tab. A thumbnail image of each page in the document appears. To quickly move from page to page, use the scroll bar in the Navigation pane or click a page thumbnail. Each thumbnail is numbered so that you always know which page you are viewing.

Using 'Go To' command

- Another fast way to go from place to place in a document is to use the Go To command. On the Home tab, open the drop-down list on the Find button and choose Go To (you may have to click the Editing button first). You will see a box as shown below –

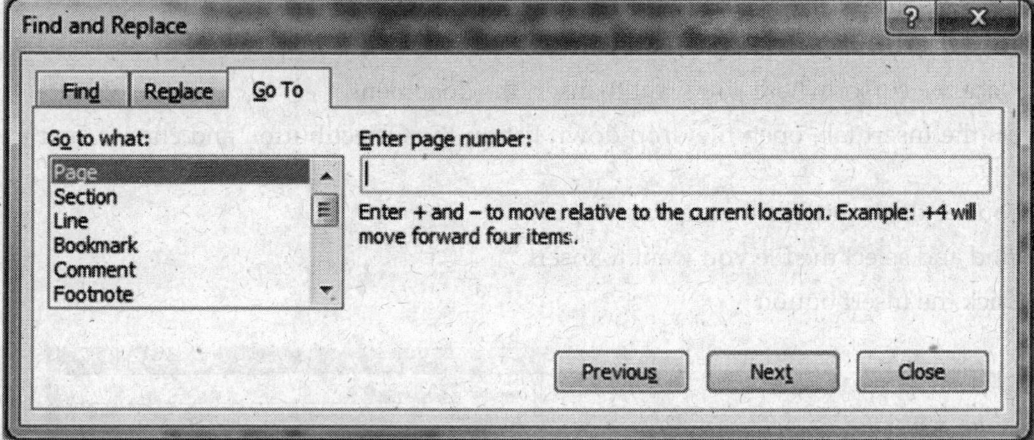

Bookmarks

Rather than press PgUp or PgDn or click the scroll bar to thrash around in a long document, you can use bookmarks. All you do is put a bookmark in an important spot in your document that you'll return to many times. To return to that spot, open the Bookmark dialog box and select a bookmark name.

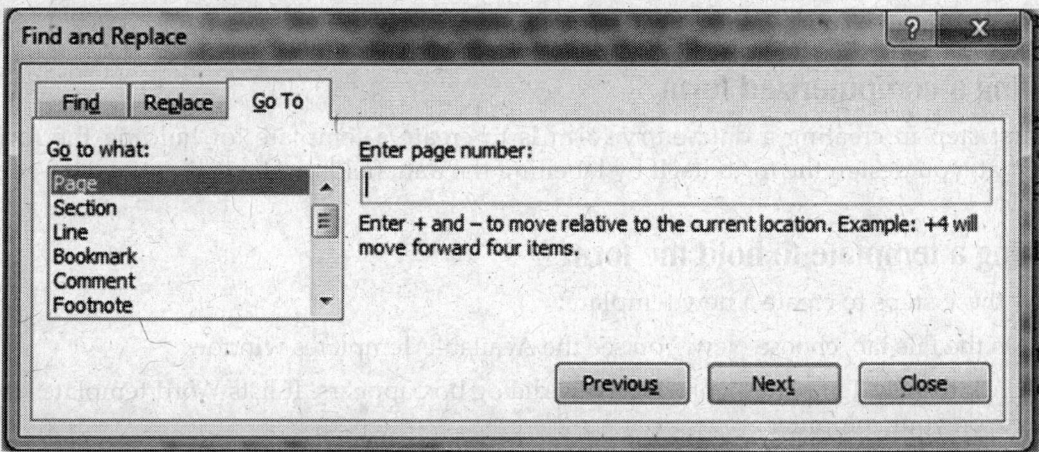

Follow these instructions to handle bookmarks:

- **Adding a bookmark:** Click where you want the bookmark to go, visit the Insert tab, and click the Bookmark button (you may have to click the Links button first, depending on the size of your screen). Then, in the Bookmark dialog box, type a descriptive name in the Bookmark Name box, and click the Add button. Bookmarks can't start with numbers or include blank spaces. You can also open the Bookmark dialog box by pressing Ctrl+Shift+F5.
- **Going to a bookmark:** On the Insert tab, click the Bookmark button (you may have to click the Links button first), double-click the bookmark in the Bookmark dialog box, and click the Close button.
- **Deleting a bookmark:** Select the bookmark in the Bookmark dialog box and click the Delete button.

Inserting a Whole File into a Document

- Place the cursor where you want to insert the document.
- On the Insert tab, open the drop-down list on the Object button and choose Text from File.
- You see the Insert File dialog box.
- Find and select the file you want to insert.
- Click the Insert button.

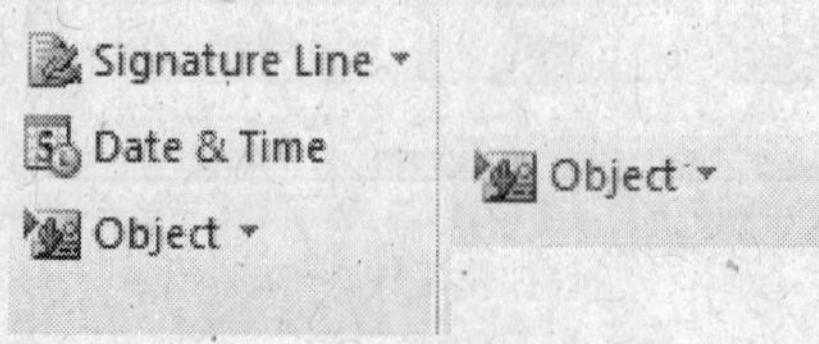

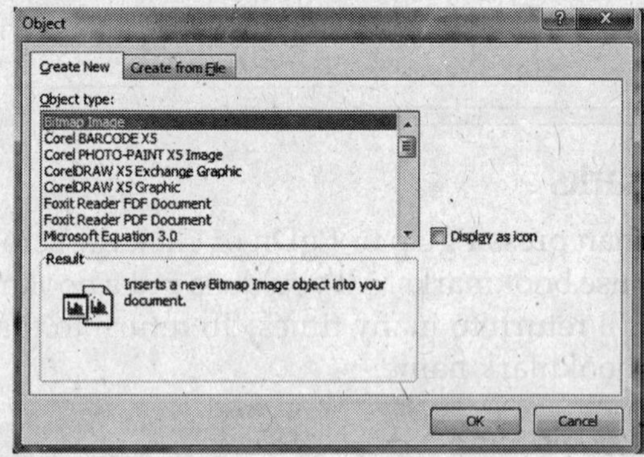

Creating a computerized form

The first step in creating a data-entry form is to create a template for holding the form. After that, you design the form itself by labelling the data fields and creating the data-entry controls.

Creating a template to hold the form

Follow these steps to create a new template:

- On the File tab, choose New. You see the Available Templates window.
- Click the My Templates icon. The New dialog box appears. It lists Word templates that are on your computer.

- ❐ Click the Template option button. You can find this button under Create New in the lower-right corner of the dialog box.
- ❐ Click OK.
- ❐ Click the Save button (or press Ctrl+S) to open the Save As dialog box.
- ❐ Enter a descriptive name for your template and click the Save button.

Creating the form and data-entry controls

Your next task is to create the form and data-entry controls for your template.

- ❐ Display the Developer tab, if necessary. If this tab isn't showing, go to the File tab, choose Options, and on the Customize Ribbon tab of the Word Options dialog box, select the Developer check box and click OK.
- ❐ Click where you want to place a control, and then create the control by clicking the Controls button followed by the Properties button on the Developer tab.

Entering Information Quickly in a Computerized Form

- ❐ **Combo box:** Like a drop-down list, a combo box "drops" to reveal choices. However, as well as choosing an option on the drop-down list, data-entry clerks can enter information in the box Click the Combo Box Content Control button and then the Properties button. In the Content Control Properties dialog box, enter option names the same way you enter them in a drop-down list.
- ❐ **Date picker:** A date picker is a mini-calendar from which data-entry clerks can enter a date. Click the Date Picker Content Control button and then the Properties button. In the Content Control Properties dialog box, choose a display format for dates and click OK. Click the Save button to save your template. Now you're ready to use your newly made form to enter data.

Entering data in the form

Now that you have the template, you or someone else can enter data cleanly in easy-to-read forms:

- ❐ On the File tab, choose New. You see the Available Templates window.
- ❐ Click the My Templates icon.
- ❐ The New dialog box opens and shows you Word templates on your computer.

Entering Information Quickly in a Computerized Form

- ❐ Double-click the name of the template you created for entering data in your form. The form appears.
- ❐ Enter information in the input fields.
- ❐ Press the up or down arrow, or press Tab and Shift+Tab to move from field to field. You can also click input fields to move the cursor there. When you're done, print the document or save it.

Composing Text and Pages

Format text and pages

Formatting text and pages gives a page an attractive look. Here we'll discuss formatting text and pages in detail.

Paragraphs and Formatting

Inserting a Section Break for Formatting Purposes

When you want to change page numbering schemes, headers and footers, margin sizes, and page orientations in a document, you have to create a section break to start a new section. Word creates a new section for you when you create newspaper-style columns or change the size of margins.

Follow these steps to create a new section:

- ❒ Click where you want to insert a section break.
- ❒ On the Page Layout tab, click the Breaks button. You open a drop-down list.
- ❒ Under Section breaks on the drop-down list, select a section break.

All four section break options create a new section, but they do so in different ways:

- ❒ **Next Page:** Inserts a page break as well as a section break so that the new section can start at the top of a new page (the next one). Select this option to start a new chapter, for example.
- ❒ **Continuous:** Inserts a section break in the middle of a page. Select this option if, for example, you want to introduce newspaper-style columns in the middle of a page.
- ❒ **Even Page:** Starts the new section on the next even page. This option is good for two-sided documents in which the headers on the left- and right-side pages are different.
- ❒ **Odd Page:** Starts the new section on the next odd page. You might choose this option if you have a book in which chapters start on odd pages. (By convention, that's where they start.) To delete a section break, make sure that you are in Draft view so that you can see section breaks, click the dotted line, and press the Delete key.

Breaking a Line

To break a line of text before it reaches the right margin without startinga new paragraph, press Shift+Enter.

Starting a New Page

Word gives you another page so that you can keep going when you fill up one page. But what if you're impatient and want to start a new page right away? Whatever you do, don't press Enter again and again until you fill up the page. Instead, create a hard page break by doing the following on the Insert tab:

- ❒ Click the Page Break button (or press Ctrl+Enter). Word starts a new page at the cursor position. (You can also go to the Page Layout tab, click the Breaks button, choose Page on the drop-down list.)

Page Break

- ❐ Click the Blank Page button. Word enters two hard page breaks to create an empty, blank page at the cursor position.

Setting Up and Changing the Margins

To set up or change the margins, go to the Page Layout tab and click the Margins button. You will see a drop-down list with margin settings. Either choose a setting or select Custom Margins to open the Margins tab of the Page Setup dialog box and choose among these commands for handling margins:

- ❐ **Changing the size of the margins:** Enter measurements in the Top, Bottom, Left, and Right boxes to tell Word how much blank space to put along the sides of the page.
- ❐ **Making room for the gutter:** The gutter is the part of the paper that the binding eats into when you bind a document. Enter a measurement in the Gutter box to increase the left or inside margin and make room for the binding. Notice on the pages of this book, for example, that the margin closest to the binding is wider than the outside margin. Choose Top on the Gutter Position menu if you intend to bind your document from the top, not the left, or inside, of the page. Some legal documents are bound this way.

Using mirror margins (inside and outside margins) in two-sided documents:

- ❐ In a bound document in which text is printed on both sides of the pages, the terms left margin and right margin are meaningless. What matters instead is in the inside margin, the margin in the middle of the page spread next to the bindings, and the outside of the page spread that isn't affected by the Choose Mirror Margins on the Multiple Pages drop-down list and adjust the margins accordingly if you intend to print on both sides of the paper.
- ❐ **Applying margin changes:** On the Apply To drop-down list, choose Whole Document to apply your margin settings to the entire document. This Section to apply them to a section; or This Point Forward to change margins in the rest of a document. When you choose This Point Forward, Word creates a new section.

© Bittu Kumar, December 2011

This Book is dedicated To-

Nirankari Baba Hardev Singh Ji Maharaj

Who, Inspired Me to Do something new something innovative.

Acknowledgements

I would like to express the deepest appreciation to my Parents. They constantly and convincingly conveyed a spirit of adventure in regard to writing. Without Their guidance and persistent help this publication would not have been possible.

In addition, a thank you to V&S Publishers. Who gave me the opportunity to develop this Book.

I must acknowledge as well the many friends, colleagues, teachers, other artists who assisted, advised, and supported my work and writing efforts over the years. Especially, I need to express my gratitude and deep appreciation to my maternal Uncle Narendra Kumar. Nirankari Mission's hospitality, knowledge, and wisdom have supported, enlightened, and entertained me; they have consistently helped me keep perspective on what is important in life and shown me how to deal with reality.

I am grateful too for the support of my Dear Friend Mukesh Kumar. I need to thank Maki Stanfield (Kyoto, Japan) and Texas Writers Foundation (USA) to advise me in this Project.

Thank You Once again...

Bittu Kumar

Author, Become Millionaire Online

Indenting Paragraphs and First Lines

Clicking an Indent button (for left-indents)

On the Home tab, click the Increase Indent or Decrease Indent button (or press Ctrl+M or Ctrl+Shift+M) to move a paragraph a half inch farther away from or closer to the left margin. If you created tab stops, text is indented to the next or previous tab stop as well as to the next or previous half inch. This is the fastest way to indent text, although you can't indent first lines or Indent from the right margin this way.

- **Indenting an entire paragraph from the left margin:** Drag the left-indent marker on the ruler to the right. Dragging the left-indent marker moves the first-line indent marker as well.
- **Indenting the first line of a paragraph:** Drag the first-line indent marker to the right. This marker determines how far the first line of the paragraph is indented.
- **Making a hanging indent:** Drag the hanging indent marker to the right. This marker determines how far the first line of the paragraph is indented.

Numbering the Pages

In which the first line of a paragraph appears to "hang" into the margin because the second and subsequent lines are indented to the right of the start of the first line. Bulleted and numbered lists employ hanging indents.

- **Indenting an entire paragraph from the right margin:** Drag the right indent marker to the left.

Indenting in Paragraph dialog box

Yet another way to indent a paragraph or first line is to visit the Paragraph dialog box. Click in or select the paragraph or paragraphs in question, go to the Home tab, and click the Paragraph group button. You see the Indents and Spacing tab of the Paragraph dialog box. Change the indentation settings.

If you want to indent the first line or create a hanging indent, choose FirstLine or Hanging on the Special drop-down list and enter a measurement in the By box.

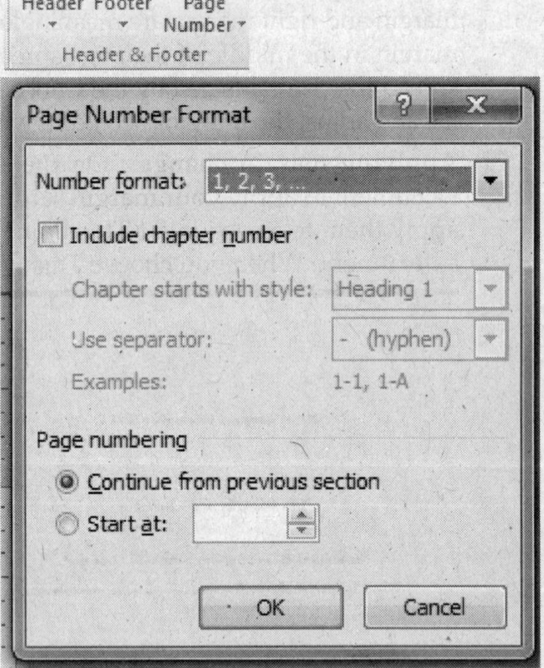

Numbering page numbers

Numbering with page numbers only

Follow these steps to insert page numbers by itself in the header, footer, or margin of the pages:

- On the Insert tab, click the Page Number button.

- On the drop-down list, choose where on the page you want to put the page number (Top of Page, Bottom of Page, or Page Margins).
- On the submenu that appears, choose a page number option. The farther you scroll on the submenu, the fancier the page number formats are.

Including a page number in header or footer

To put the page number part in a header or footer, click in the header or footer where you want the page number to appear (later in this chapter, "Putting Headers and Footers on Pages" explains headers and footers). Then follow these steps to insert page numbers:

- On the (Header & Footer Tools) Design tab, click the Page Numbers button.
- Choose Current Position. You see a submenu with page number choices.
- Scroll through the submenu and choose a page number format.

Header Footer Page Number
Header & Footer

Changing page number formats

Change page number formats in the Page Number Format dialog box. To display this dialog box, make sure that you're in Print Layout view and double-click your header or footer. Then use one of the following methods to change page number formats:

- On the Insert tab, click the Page Number button and choose Format Page Numbers.
- On the (Header & Footer Tools) Design tab, click the Page Number button and choose Format Page Numbers.

In the Page Number Format dialog box, make your page numbers just so:

- **Choosing a different number format:** Open the Number Format drop down list and choose a page-numbering format. You can use numbers, letters, or roman numerals.
- **Including chapter numbers in page numbers:** If your document generates chapter numbers automatically from headings, you can include the chapter number in the page number. Click the Include Chapter Number check box, choose a style, and choose a separator to go between the chapter number and page number.
- **Numbering each section separately:** Click the Start At option button (not Continue from Previous Section button) to begin counting pages anew at each section in your document. Earlier in this chapter, "Inserting a Section Break for Formatting Purposes" explains the same.
- **Start numbering pages at a number other than 1:** Click the Start At option button and enter a number other than 1.

Putting Headers and Footers on Pages

A header is a little description that appears along the top of a page so that the reader knows what's what. Usually, headers include the page number and a title, and often the author's name appears in the header as well. A footer is the same thing as a header except that it appears along the bottom of the page, as befits its name.

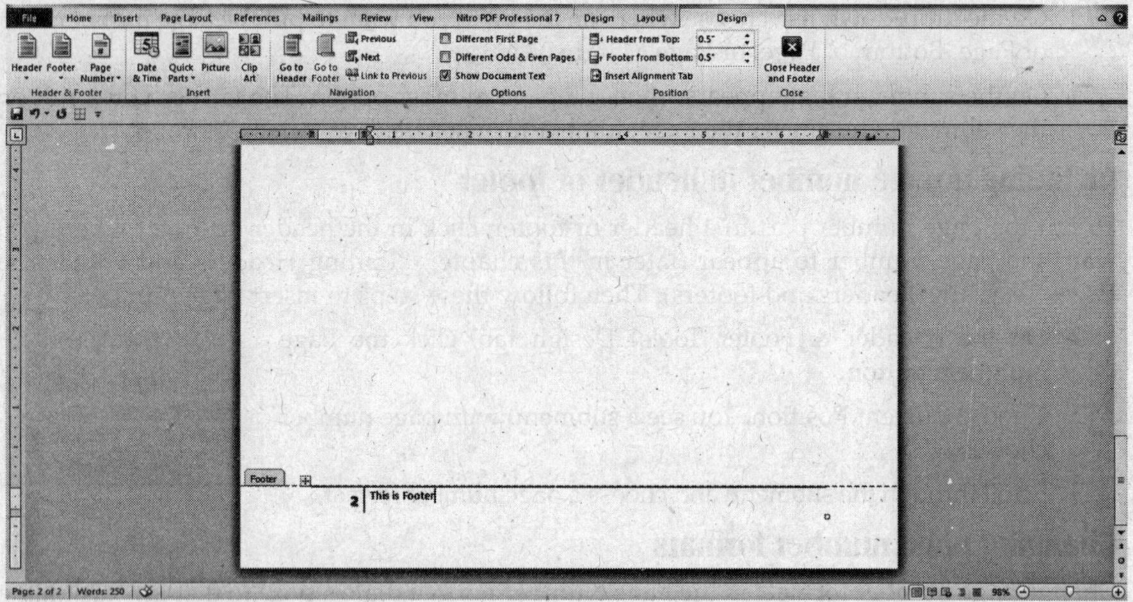

Here are rules how you can do it:

- ❒ **Switching to Print Layout view:** To enter, read, edit, or delete headers and footers, you must be in Print Layout view. You can't see headers and footers in the other views.
- ❒ **Displaying the (Header & Footer Tools) Design tab:** To display this tab after you create a header or footer, switch to Print Layout view and double-click a header or footer.
- ❒ **Closing the (Header & Footer Tools) Design tab:** Click the Close Header & Footer button or double-click outside the header or footer.
- ❒ **Placing different headers and footers in the same document:** To change headers or footers in the middle of a document, you have to create a new section.

Creating, editing, and removing headers and footers

Follow these instructions to create, edit, and delete headers and footers:

- ❒ **Creating a header or footer:** On the Insert tab, click the Header or Footer button, and choose a header or footer on the gallery. The gallery presents headers or footers with preformatted page numbers, dates, and places to enter a document title and author's name. Click More Headers (or Footers) from Office.com to download headers or footers from Microsoft.
- ❒ **Choosing a different header or footer:** If necessary, double-click your header or footer to display the (Header & Footer Tools) Design tab. Then click the Header or Footer button and choose a new header or footer from the gallery.
- ❒ **Editing a header or footer:** Click the Header or Footer button and choose Edit Header or Edit Footer on the drop-down list. The cursor moves into the header or footer so that you can enter or format text.

- **Changing the appearance of a header or footer:** Click a shape or text box in a header or footer and visit the (Drawing Tools) Format tab to change the shape or text box's colour, background, or size.
- **Removing a header or footer:** Click the Header or Footer button and choose Remove Header or Remove Footer on the drop-down list.

Fine-tuning a header or footer

Follow these steps for making a perfect header on the (Header & Footer Tools)Design tab:

- Inserting a page number: See "Including a page number in a header or footer" and "Changing page number formats" earlier in this chapter.
- Inserting the date and time: Click the Date & Time button, choose a date format in the Date and Time dialog box, and click OK. Click the Update Automatically check box if you want the date to record when you print the document, not when you created your header or footer.

Adjusting Space between Lines

To change the spacing between lines, select the lines whose spacing you want to change, or simply put the cursor in a paragraph if you're changing the line spacing throughout a paragraph. Then, on the Home tab, click the Line and Paragraph Spacing button and choose an option on the drop-down list. To take advantage of more line-spacing options, click the Paragraph group button on the Home tab or choose Line Spacing Options on the Line and Paragraph Spacing button drop-down list. You will see the Paragraph dialog box.

Select an option on the Line Spacing drop-down list:

- **At Least:** Choose this one if you want Word to adjust for tall symbols or other unusual text. Word adjusts the lines but makes sure that there is, at minimum, the number of points you enter in the At box between each line.
- **Exactly:** Choose this one and enter a number in the At box if you want a specific amount of space between lines.
- **Multiple:** Choose this one and put a number in the At box to get triple spaced, quadruple-, quintuple-, or any other number of spaced lines.

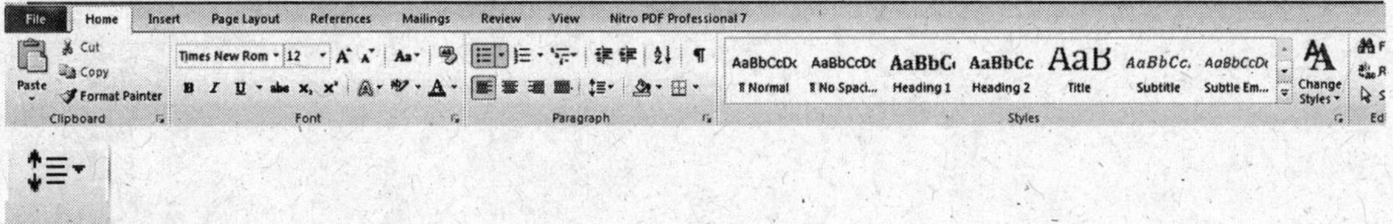

Creating Numbered and Bulleted Lists

Simple numbered and bulleted lists

Just press Enter at the end of each step or bulleted entry. When you're done, select the list, go to the Home tab, and click the Numbering or Bullets button. You can also click the

Numbering or Bullets button and start typing the list. Each time you press Enter, Word enters the next number or another bullet.

Meanwhile, here are some tricks for handling lists:

- **Ending a list:** Press the Enter key twice after typing the last entry in the list. You can also right-click the list, choose Bullets or Numbering, and choose None on the submenu.
- **Removing the numbers or bullets:** Select the list and click the Numbering or Bullets button.
- **Adjusting how far a list is indented:** Right-click anywhere in the list, choose Adjust List Indents, and enter a new measurement in the Text Indent box.
- **Resuming a numbered list:** Suppose that you want a numbered list to resume where a list you entered earlier ended. In other words, suppose that you left off writing a four-step list, put in a graphic or some paragraphs, click the Numbering a button to start numbering again. The Auto Correct Options button appears. Click it and choose Continue Numbering, or right-click and choose Continue Numbering on the shortcut menu.

Points to Remember

- Use all the tools for formatting for saving your time
- Pay attention to the spacing options
- Use custom designs for different purposes
- Adjust page Margins before printing to make sure that file is compatible for printing
- Use header & footer, numbering, Page layout tools for making page attractive
- Before finalizing the document review it in every formats & do necessary corrections if required

DTP using MS Word

Desktop publishing using word is essential part of overall desk top publishing learning. Let's learn in detail DTP on MS word.

Making Use of Charts, Diagrams, Shapes, Clip Art, and Photos

- **Charts:** A chart is an excellent way to present data for comparison purposes.
- **Diagrams:** A diagram allows readers to quickly grasp an idea, relationship, or concept.
- **Shapes and lines:** Shapes and lines can also illustrate ideas and concepts.
- **Clip-art images:** Clip-art images make a document livelier. They add a little colour to documents.
- **Photos:** A well-placed photo or two can make a newsletter or brochure that much more attractive.

Positioning and Wrapping Objects Relative to the Page and Text

Note....

"Object" is just Office's generic term for a shape, line, text box, clip-art image, photo, diagram, WordArt image, or chart that you insert in a document.

Wrapping text around an object

Select the object you want to wrap text around, go to the Format tab, and use one of these methods to wrap text around the object:

- Click the Wrap Text button and choose an option on the drop-down list.
- Click the Wrap Text button and choose More Layout Options on the drop-down list, or click the Size group button and select the Text Wrapping tab in the Layout dialog box. Then choose a wrapping style and side around which to wrap text.

Positioning an object on a page

To position an object in a Word page, you can drag it to a new location.

Use one of these methods to move your object precisely into place:

- Click the Position button and select a With Text Wrapping option on the drop-down list. These options position an object squarely in a corner, a side, or the middle of the page.
- Click the Position button and choose More Layout Options on the dropdown list, or click the Size group button and select the Position tab in the Layout dialog box. Then choose position options. Go to the Layout dialog box when you want to place objects in the very same position on different pages.

Working with Text Boxes

Put text in a text box when you want a notice or announcement to stand out on the page. Like other objects, text boxes can be shaded, filled with colour, and given borders. You can also lay them over graphics to make for interesting effects.

Inserting a text box

To create a text box, go to the Insert tab, click the Text Box button, and use one of these methods:

- **Choose a ready-made text box:** Scroll in the drop-down list and choose a preformatted text box.
- **Draw a conventional text box:** Choose Draw Text Box on the drop-down list, and then click and drag to draw the text box. Lines show you how big it will be when you release the mouse button.

Making text flow from text box to text box

You can link text boxes so that the text in the first box is pushed into the next one when it fills up. To link text boxes, start by creating all the text boxes that you need. You cannot link one text box to another if the second text box already has text in it. follow these directions to link text boxes:

- **Creating a forward link:** Click a text box and then click the Create Link button to create a forward link.
- **Breaking a link:** To break a link, click the text box that is to be the last in the chain, and then click the Break Link button.

Decorating a page with a border

Word offers a means of decorating title pages, certificates, menus, and similar documents with a page border. Besides lines, you can decorate the sides of a page with stars, pieces of cake, and other artwork. If you want to place a border around a page in the middle of a document, you must create a sectionbreak where the page is. Before you create your border, place the cursor on the page where the border is to appear. Place the cursor on the first page of a document if you want to put a border around only the first page. If your document is divided into sections and you want to put borders around certain pages in a section, place the cursor in the section — either in the first page if you want the bordersto go around it, or in a subsequent page.

With the cursor in the right place, follow these steps to decorate your page or pages with a border:

- ❐ Go to the Page Layout tab and click the Page Borders button.
- ❐ Under Setting, choose which kind of border you want. The Custom setting is for putting borders on one, two, or three sides of the page, not four. Use the none setting to remove borders.

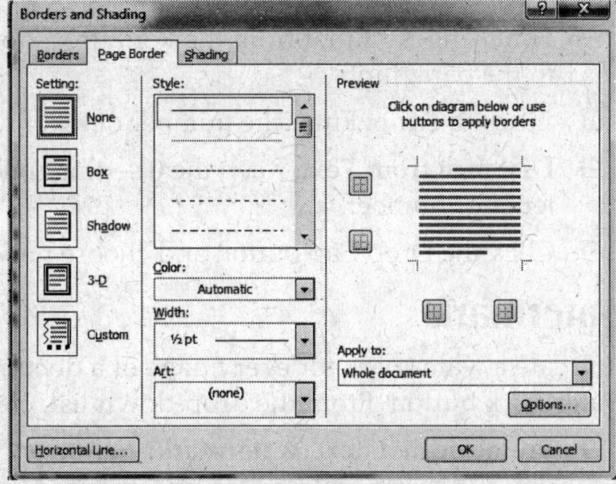

Decording a page with a border

- ❐ On the Apply To drop-down list, tell Word which page or pages in the document get borders.
- ❐ Select options to construct the border you want and then click OK.

Putting a background colour on pages

If you intend to save your Word document as a web page, you will be glad to know that putting a background colour on pages is easy. You can't, however, pick and choose which pages get a background colour. Putting background colours on the pages of a document is an all-or-nothing proposition.

To give a page with a background colour or gradient colour mixture, go to the Page Layout tab, click the Page Colour button, and choose a colour on the drop-down list. Choose Fill Effects to open the Fill Effects dialog box and apply gradient colour mixtures or patterns to the pages.

Dropping in a Drop Cap

To create a drop cap, start by clicking anywhere in the paragraph whose first letter you want to "drop." If you want to "drop" more than one character at the start of the paragraph, select the characters. Then go to the Insert tab, click the Drop Cap button, and choose Dropped or Drop Cap Options. You can configure the following:

- ❐ **Position:** Choose which kind of drop cap you want. In Margin, place the drop cap to the left of the paragraph, not in the paragraph itself.

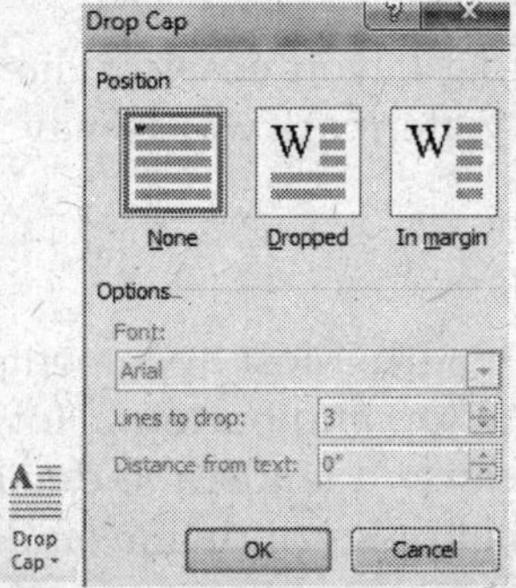

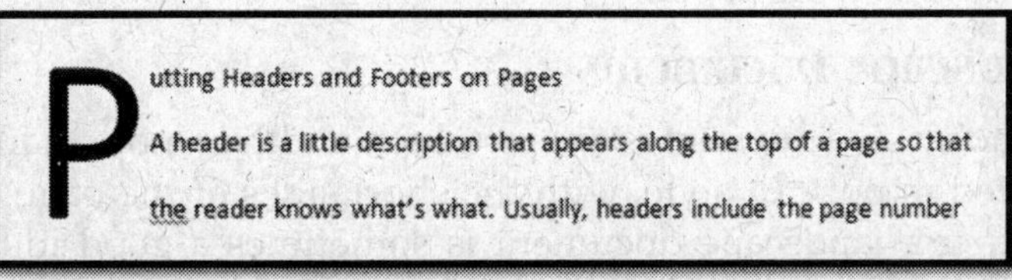

- **Font:** Choose a font from the Font drop-down list. Choose a different font from the text in the paragraph.
- **Lines to Drop:** Enter the number of text lines to drop the letter.
- **Distance from Text:** Keep the 0 setting unless you're dropping and I, 1, or other skinny letter or number.
- Click the Drop Cap button and choose none to remove a drop cap.

Watermark

To create a watermark for every page of a document, go to the Page Layout tab and click the Watermark button. From the drop-down list, create your watermark:

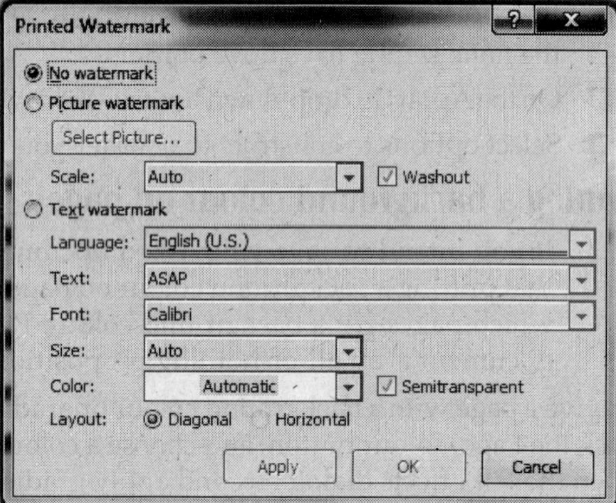

- **Prefabricated text watermark:** Scroll down the list and choose an option. You will find "Confidential," "Urgent," and other text watermarks.
- **Picture watermark:** Choose Custom Watermark, and in the Printed Watermark dialog box, click the Picture Watermark option button. Then click the Select Picture button. In the Insert Picture dialog box, select a graphic file to use for the watermark and click the Insert button. Back in the Printed Watermark dialog box, choose or enter a size for the graphic on the Scale drop-down list. I don't recommend deselecting the Washout check box — do so and your image may be so dark that it obscures the text.
- Watermark **Text watermark:** Choose Custom Watermark and, in the Printed Watermark dialog box, click the Text Watermark option button. Type a word or two in the Text box (or choose an entry from the drop-down list). Choose a font, size, colour, and layout for the words. If you deselect the semi-transparent check box, you do so at your peril because the watermark words may be too dark on the page.

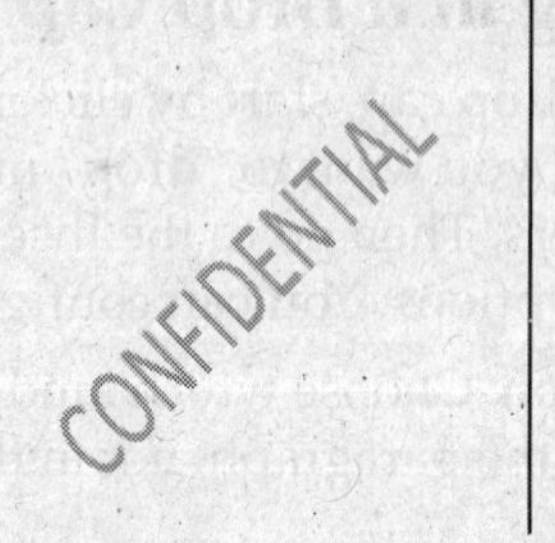

Landscape Documents

A landscape document is one in which width is more than the length. Most documents, are printed in portrait style, with the short sides of the page on the top and bottom. However, creating a landscape document is sometimes a good idea because a landscape document stands out from the usual crowd of portrait documents and sometimes printing in landscape mode is necessary to fit text, tables, and graphics on a single page.

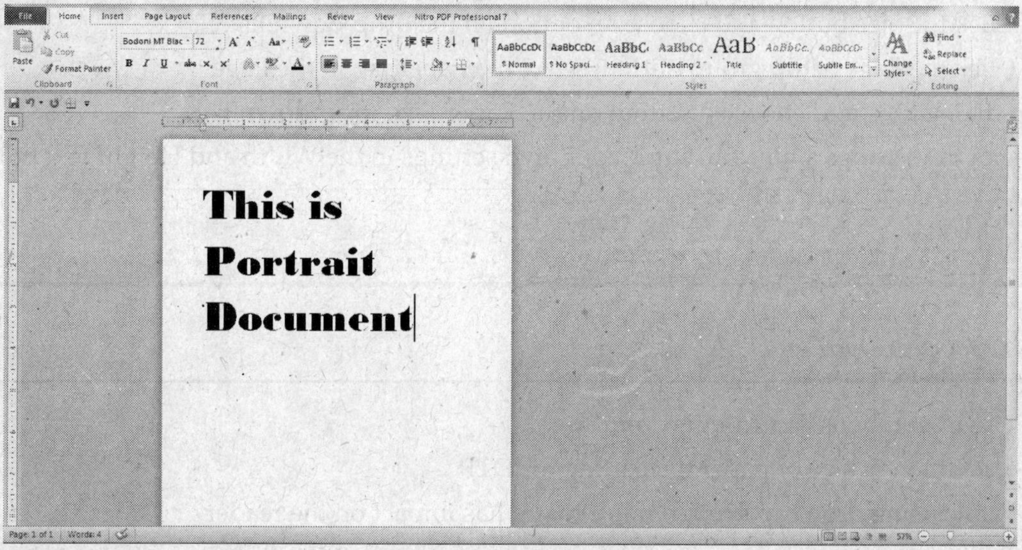

This is
Portrait
Document

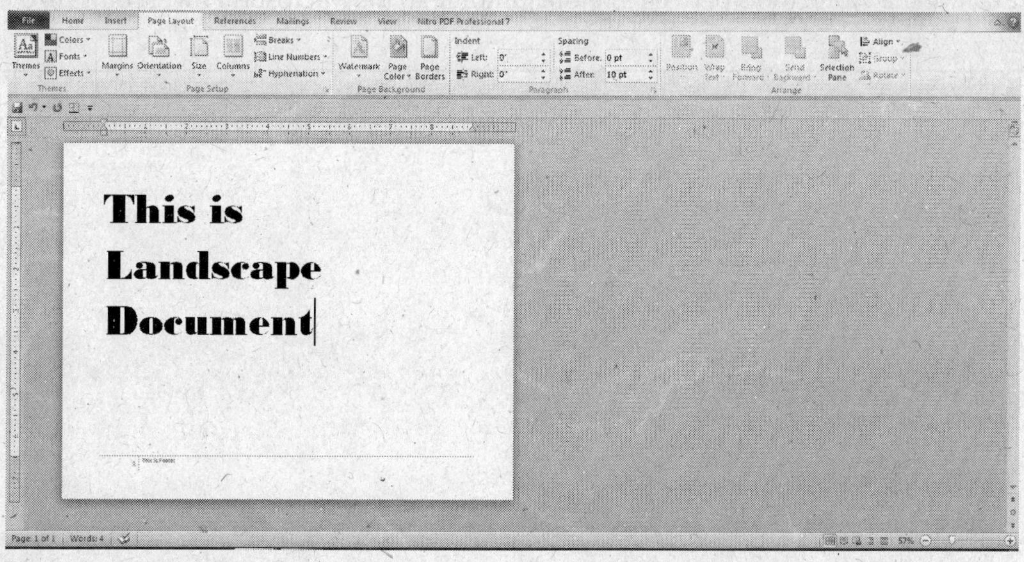

This is
Landscape
Document

Starting on the Page Layout tab, follow these steps to change the page orientation:

- **Landscape pages:** Click the Orientation button and choose Landscape on the drop-down list.
- **Portrait pages:** Click the Orientation button and choose Portrait on the drop-down list.

Printing on different sizes of paper

You don't have to print exclusively on standard 8.5-x-11 paper; you can print on legal-size paper and other sizes of paper as well. Go to the Page Layout tab and use one of these methods to change the size of the paper on which you intend to print a document:

- ❐ Click the Size button and choose an option on the drop-down list.
- ❐ Click the Page Setup group button, select the Paper tab in the Page

Set up dialog box, and choose a setting on the Paper Size drop-down list.

If none of the settings suits you, enter your own settings in the Width and Height text boxes.

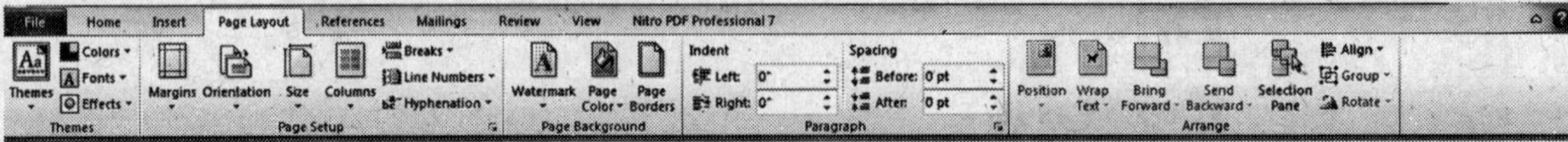

Points to Remember

- ☆ Use orientations according to your use
- ☆ Use different size of paper formatting for DTP
- ☆ While using drop cap keep in mind that it has impact on the reader
- ☆ Practice the Word Tools perfectly before jumping to the Microsoft PowerPoint 2010

Chapter 18

Welcome to Microsoft PowerPoint 2010

It is practically impossible to sit through a conference, seminar, or trade show without seeing at least one PowerPoint presentation. PowerPoint has found its way into nearly every office and boardroom.

Tip...

- **Presentation:** All the slides, from start to finish, that you show your audience. Sometimes presentations are called "slide shows." Presentations are saved in presentation files (.pptx files).
- **Slides:** The images you create with PowerPoint. During a presentation, slides appear on-screen one after the other. Don't be put off by the word slide and dreary memories of sitting through your uncle's slide show vacation memories. You don't need a slide

projector to show these slides. You can now plug a laptop or other computer into special monitors that display PowerPoint slides.

Creating PowerPoint Presentation

Creating a PowerPoint presentation entails completing these basic tasks:

- **Creating the slides:** Once you open the PPT Window, your next task is to create the slides. PowerPoint offers many preformatted slide layouts, each designed for presenting information a certain way.
- **Notes:** As you create slides, you can jot down notes in the Notes pane. You can use these notes later to formulate your presentation and decide what you're going to say to your audience while each slide is on-screen.
- **Designing your presentation:** After you create a presentation, the next step is to think about its appearance. You can change slides' colours and backgrounds, as well as choose a theme for your presentation, an all-encompassing design that applies to all (or most of) the slides.
- **Inserting tables, charts, diagrams, and shapes:** A PowerPoint presentation should be more than a loose collection of bulleted lists. Starting on the Insert tab, you can place tables, charts, and diagrams on slides, as well as adorn your slides with text boxes, WordArt images, and shapes.
- **"Animating" your slides:** PowerPoint slides can play video and sound, as well as be "animated". You can make the items on a slide move on the screen. As a slide arrives, you can make it spin or flash.
- **Delivering your presentation:** During a presentation, you can draw on the slides. You can also blank the screen and show slides out of order. In case you can't be there in person, PowerPoint gives you the opportunity to create self-running presentations and presentations that others can run on their own. You can also distribute presentations on CDs and videos.

Creating a New Presentation

No matter what kind of presentation you want to create, start creating it by going to the File tab and choosing New. You will see the Available Templates and Themes window. This window offers templates for creating many types of presentations. Click a template to preview it on the right side of the window. Double-click a template (or select it and click the Create button) to create a presentation. Apply following methods to create apresentation:

- **Blank presentation:** Double-click the Blank Presentation icon. A new presentation appears. Try visiting the Design tab and choosing a theme or background style to get a taste of all the things you can do to decorate a presentation. (By pressing Ctrl+N, you can create a new, blank Presentation without opening the Available Templates and Themes window.)
- **Recently used template:** Click the Recent Templates icon to use a template listed there.
- **Template on your computer:** Click the Sample Templates icon. Templates that you

loaded on your computer when you installed PowerPoint appear.

- **Template you created (or downloaded earlier from Microsoft):** Click the My Templates icon. The New Presentation dialog box appears. Select a template and click OK.

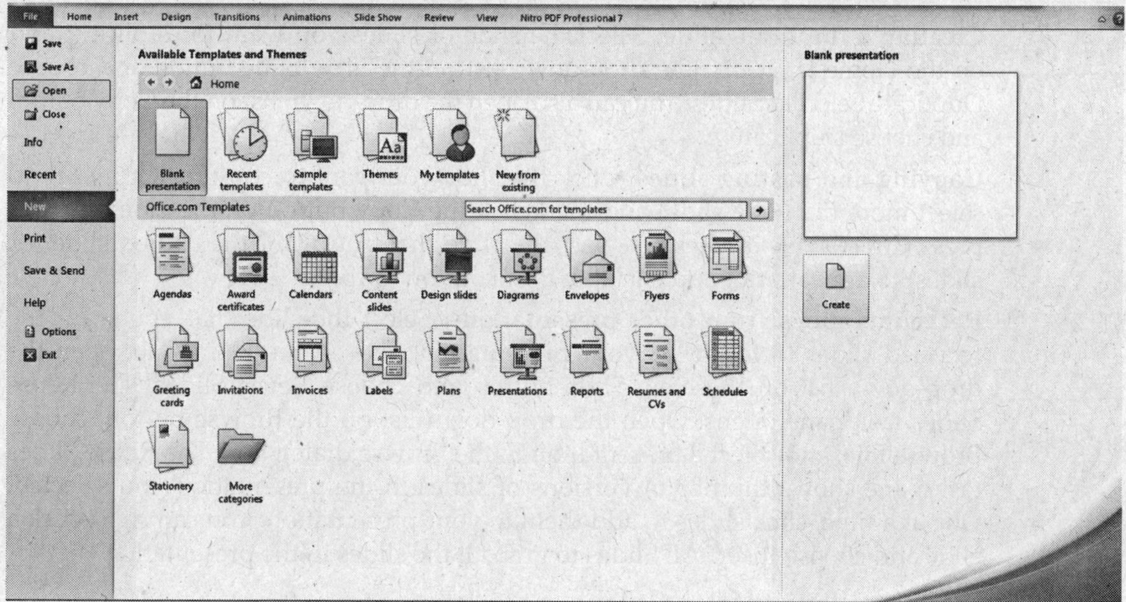

- **Template available online at Office.com:** Enter a search term in the Search box, make sure that your computer is connected to the Internet, and click the Start Searching button. Templates appear in the window. Double-click a template to download and use it to create a presentation.

- **Recycle another presentation:** If you can use another presentation as the starting point for creating a new presentation, nab slides from the other presentation. Click the New from Existing icon. In the New from ExistingPresentation dialog box, select the presentation and click the Open button.

Creating New Slides for Your Presentation

Inserting a new slide

Follow these steps to insert a new slide in your presentation:

- Select the slide that you want to insert. In Normal view, select the slide on the Slides pane. In Slide Sorter view, select the slide in the main window.
- On the Home tab, click the bottom half of the New Slide button. You see a drop-down list of slide layouts. (If you click the top half of the New Slide button, you insert a slide with the same layout as the one you selected in Step 1.)
- Select the slide layout that best approximates the slide you want to create.

New Slide

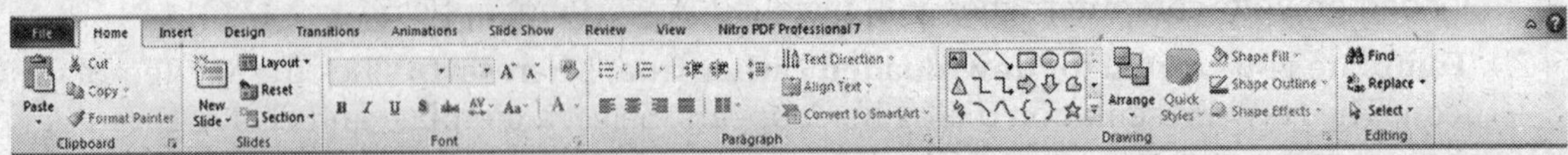

- **Creating a duplicate slide:** Select the slide or slides you want to duplicate, and on the Home tab, open the drop-down list on the New Slide button and choose Duplicate Selected Slides. You can also open the drop-down list on the Copy button and choose Duplicate.
- **Copying and pasting slides:** Click the slide you want to copy (or Ctrl+click to select more than one slide) and then click the Copy button on the Home tab (or press Ctrl+C). Next, click to select the slide that you want the copied slide (or slides) to appear after and click the Paste button (or press Ctrl+V).
- **Recycling slides from other presentations:** Select the slide that you want the recycled slides to follow in your presentation, and on the Home tab, open the drop-down list on the New Slide button and choose Reuse Slides. The Reuse Slides task pane opens. Open the drop-down list on the Browse button, choose Browse File, and select a presentation in the Browse dialog box. The Reuse Slides task pane shows thumbnail versions of slides in the presentation you selected. One at a time, click slides to add them to your presentation. You can right-click a slide and choose Insert All Slides to grab all the slides in the presentation.

Selecting a different layout for a slide

If you mistakenly choose the wrong layout for a slide, you can start all over. You can graft a new layout onto your slide with one of these techniques:

- On the Home tab, click the Layout button and choose a layout on the drop-down list.
- Right-click the slide (being careful not to right-click a frame or object), choose Layout, and choose a layout on the submenu.

You can use Reset command also.

Changing views

PowerPoint offers two places to change views:

- **View buttons on the status bar:** Click the View button — Normal, Slide Sorter, Slide Show, or Reading View — on the status bar to change views.
- **View tab:** On the View tab, click a button on the Presentation Views or Master Views group.

- 

Normal/Slides view for examining slides: Switch to Normal view, move the pointer to the Slides pane, and select the Slides tab when you want to examine a slide. In this view, thumbnail slides appear in the Slides pane, and you can see your slide in all its glory in the middle of the screen.

- **Slide Sorter view for moving and deleting slides:** In Slide Sorter view, you will see thumbnails of all the slides in the presentation (use the Zoom Slider to change the size of thumbnails). From here, moving slides around is easy, and seeing many slides simultaneously gives you a sense of whether the different slides are consistent with one another and how the whole presentation is shaping up. The slides are numbered so thatyou can see where they appear in a presentation.

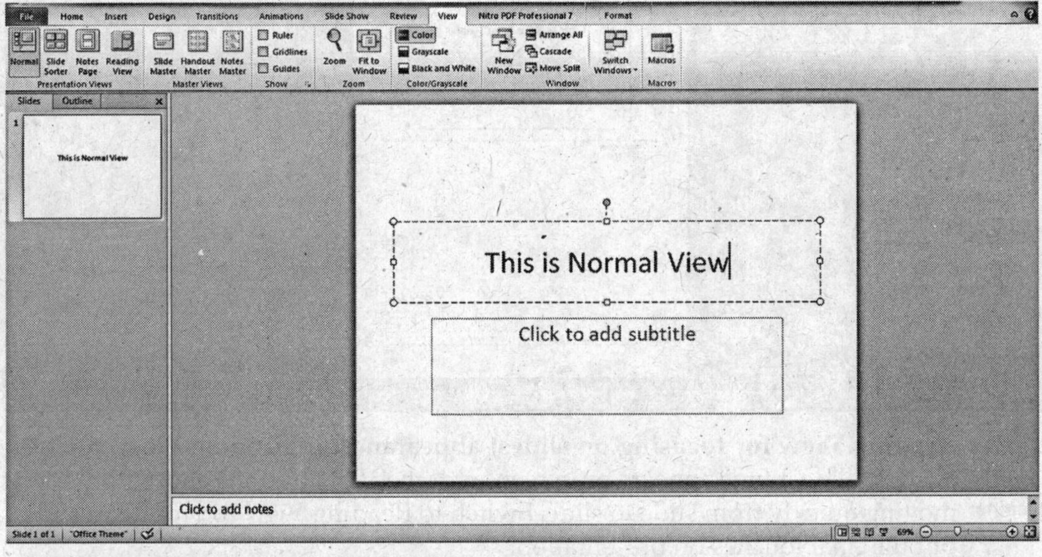

- **Notes Page view for reading your speaker notes:** In Notes Page view, you see notes you've written to aid you in your presentation, if you've written any. You can write notes in this view as well as in the Notes pane in Normal view.

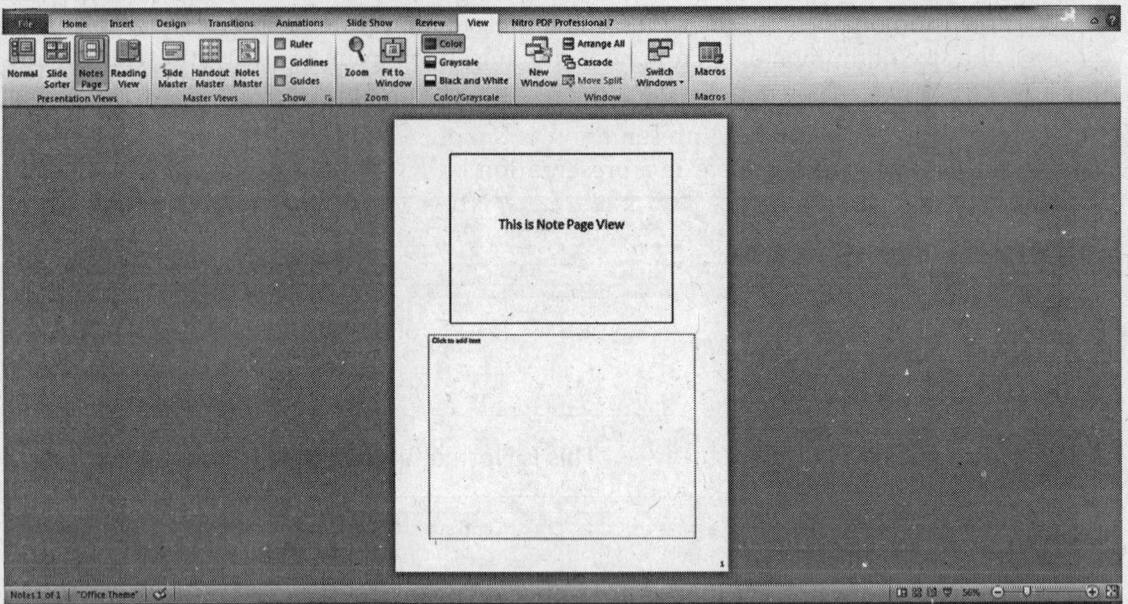

- 

Reading View for focusing on slides' appearance: In Reading View, you also see a single slide, but it appears on-screen with the View buttons and with buttons for moving quickly from slide to slide. Switch to Reading View to proofread slides and put the final touches on presentation.

- 
Slide Show view for giving a presentation: In Slide Show view, you see a single slide. Not only that, but the slide fills the entire screen. This is what your presentation looks like when you show it to an audience.

This is Slide Show View

❑ **The Master views for a consistent presentation:** The master views — Slide Master, Handout Master, and Notes Master — are for handling master styles, the formatting commands that pertain to all the slides in a presentation, handouts, and notes. To switch to these views, go to the View tab and click the appropriate button.

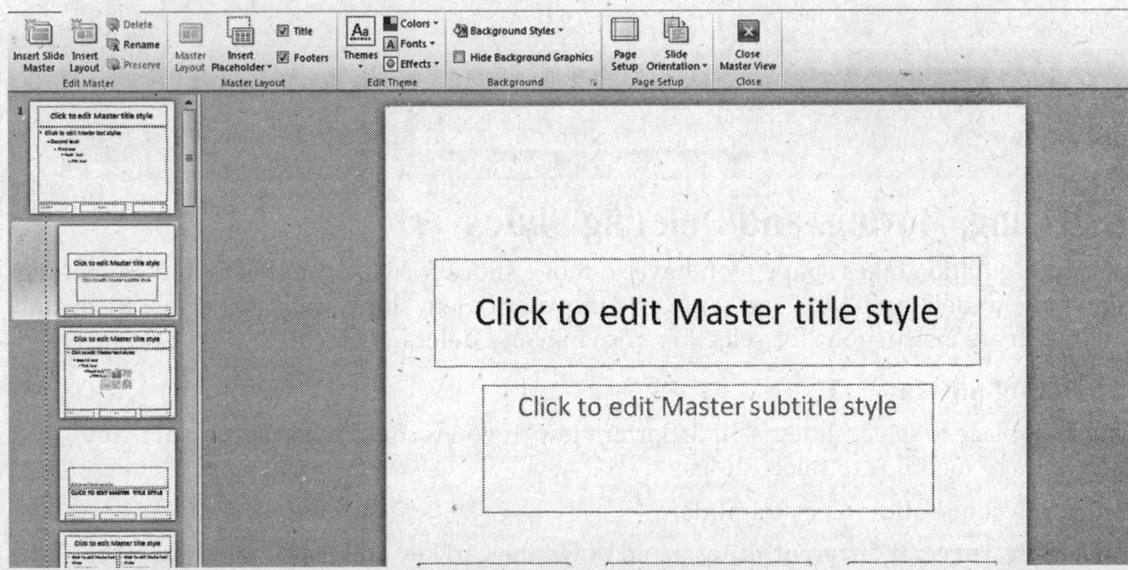

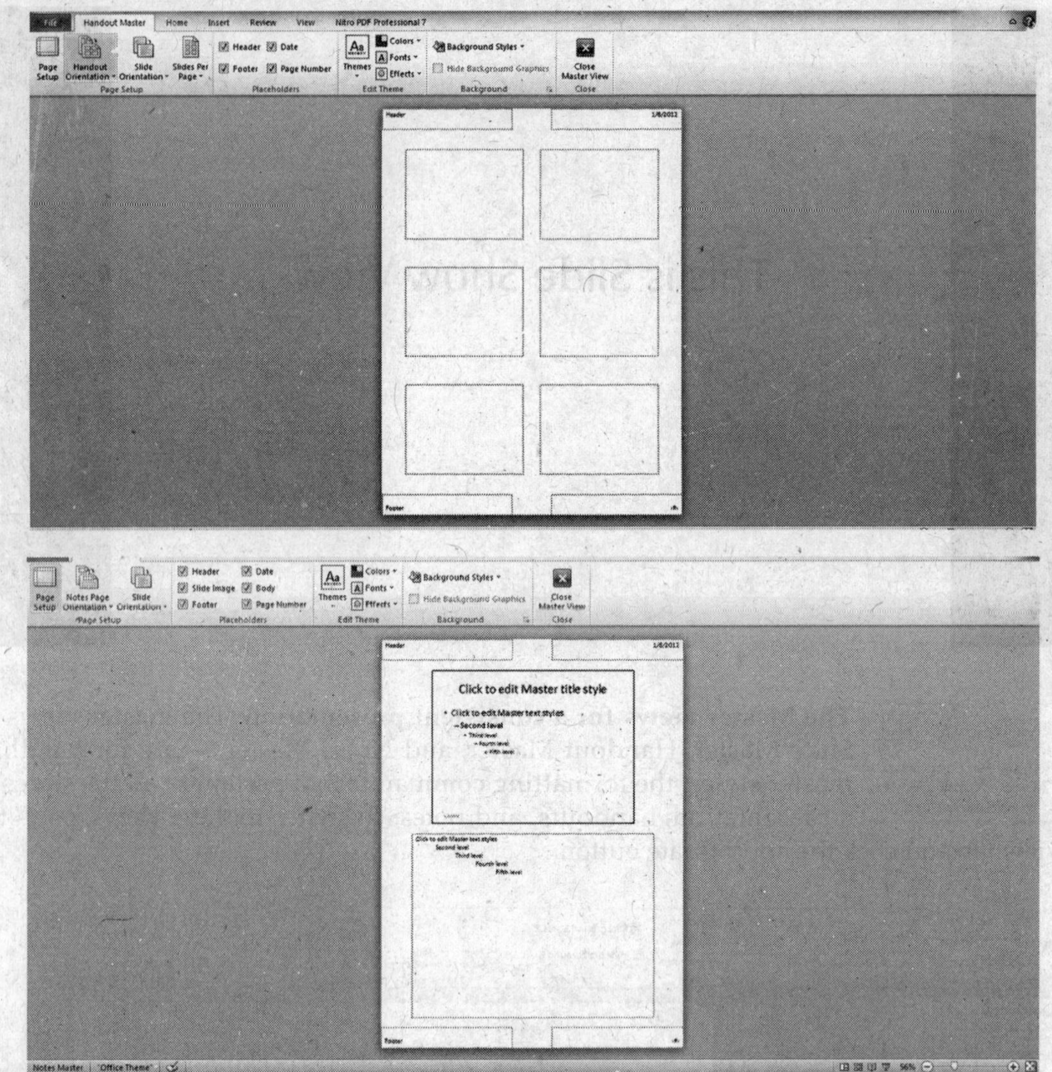

Selecting, Moving, and Deleting Slides

As a presentation takes shape, you have to move slides forward and backward. Sometimes you have to delete a slide. And you can't move or delete slides until you select them first. Herewith are instructions for selecting, moving, and deleting slides.

Selecting slides

The best place to select slides is Slide Sorter view (if you want to select several at a time). Use one of these methods to select slides:

- **Select one slide:** Click the slide.
- **Select several different slides:** Hold down the Ctrl key and click each slide in the Slides pane or in Slide Sorter view.

- Select several slides in succession: Hold down the Shift key and click the first slide and then the last one.

Moving slides

To move or rearrange slides, you're advised to go to Slide Sorter view. Select the slide or slides that you want to move and use one of these methods to move slides:

- **Dragging and dropping:** Click the slides you selected and drag them to a new location. You will see the drag pointer, and in Slide Sorter view, a vertical line shows you where the slide or slides will land when you release the mouse button. On the Slides pane, a horizontal line appears between slides to show you where the slide or slides will land when you release the mouse button.
- **Cutting and pasting:** On the Home tab, cut the slide or slides to the Windows Clipboard (click the Cut button, press Ctrl+X, or right-click and choose Cut). Then select the slide that you want the slide or slides to appear after and give the Paste command (click the Paste button, press Ctrl+V, or right-click and choose Paste). You can right-click between slides to paste with precision.

Deleting slides

Select the slide or slides you want to delete and use one of these methods to delete slides:

- Press the Delete key.
- Right-click and choose Delete Slide on the shortcut menu.

Let's Start PowerPoint

Choosing a Theme for Your Presentation

After you initially select a theme, you can do one or two things to customize it. These pages explain how to find and select a theme for your presentation and diddle with a theme after you select it. By the way, the name of the theme that is currently in use is listed on the left side of the status bar, in case you're curious about a theme you want to replace.

Selecting a theme

Use one of these methods to select a new theme for your presentation:

- **Selecting a theme in the Themes gallery:** On the Design tab, open the Themes gallery and move the pointer over different themes to "live preview" them. Click a theme to select it.
- **Borrowing a theme from another presentation:** On the Design tab, open the Themes gallery, and click Browse for Themes. Select and click the Apply button.

Tweaking a theme

Starting on the Design tab, you can customize a theme with these techniques and in so doing alter all the slides in your presentation:

- **Choosing a new set of colours:** The easiest and best way to experiment with customizing a theme is to select a different colour set. Click the Colours button, slide the pointer over the different colour sets on the dropdown list, and see what effect they have on your slides.
- **Change the fonts:** Click the Fonts button and choose a font combination on the drop-down list. The first font in each pair applies to slide titles and the second to slide text. You can also choose Create New Theme Fonts on the list and select theme fonts of your own.
- **Change theme effects:** Click the Effects button and choose a theme effect on the drop-down list. A theme effect is a slight refinement to a theme.
- **Choosing background style variation:** Most themes offer background style variations. Click the Background Styles button to open the Background Styles gallery and select a style.

Colors

Fonts

Effects

Background Styles

Hide Background Graphics

Background

Creating Slide Backgrounds on Your Own

Besides a theme or background style, your other option for creating slide backgrounds is to do it on your own. For a background, you can have a solid colour, a transparent colour, a gradient blend of colours, a picture, or a clip-artimage.

- **Solid colour:** A single, uniform colour. You can adjust a colour's transparency and in effect "bleach out" the colour to push it farther into the background.
- **Gradient:** A mixture of different colours with the colours blending into one another.
- **Clip art:** A clip-art image from the Microsoft Clip Organizer.
- **Picture:** A photograph or graphic.
- **Texture:** A uniform pattern that gives the impression that the slide is displayed on a material such as cloth or stone.

Using a solid (or transparent) colour for the slide background

Follow these steps to use a solid or transparent colour as the background for slides:

- On the Design tab, click the Background Styles button and choose Format Background on the drop-down list. You see the Fill category of the Format Background dialog box.
- Select the Solid Fill option button.
- Click the Colour button and choose a colour on the drop-down list. The muted theme colours are recommended because they look better in the background, but you can select a standard colour or click the More Colours button and select a colour in the Colours dialog box.
- Drag the Transparency slider if you want a "bleached out" colour rather than a slide colour. At 0% transparency, you get a solid colour; at 100%, you get no colour at all.
- Click the Apply to All button and then the Close button.

Follow these steps to create a gradient background for slides:

- On the Design tab, click the Background Styles button, and choose Format Background on the drop-down list. You see the Fill category of the Format Background dialog box. Drag this dialog box to the left side of the screen so that you can get a better view of your slide.
- Click the Gradient Fill option button.
- On the Type drop-down list, choose what type of gradient you want — Linear, Radial, Rectangular, Path, or Shade from Title. If you choose Linear, you can enter a degree measurement in the Angle box to change the angle at which the colours blend. At 90 degrees, for example, colours blend horizontally across the slide; at 180 degrees, they blend vertically.

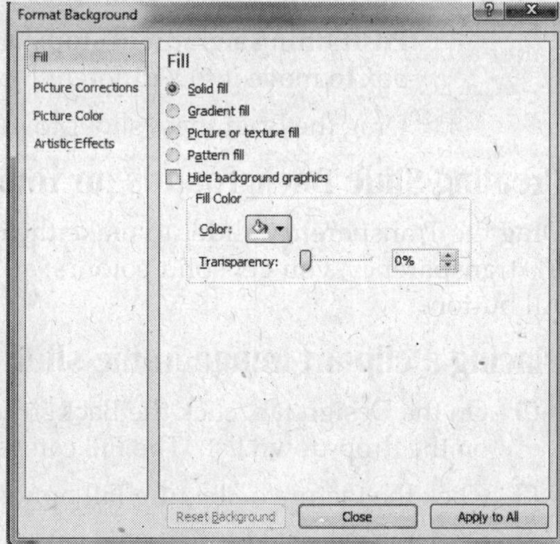

Creating a gradient background

- Create a gradient stop for each colour transition you want on yourslides. Gradient stops determine where colours are, how colours transition fromone to the next, and which colours are used. You can create as many gradient stops as you want. Here are methods for handling gradient stops:
    - **Adding a gradient stop:** Click the Add Gradient Stop button. A new gradient stop appears on the slider. Drag it to where you want the colour blend to occur.
    - **Removing a gradient stop:** Select a gradient stop on the slider and click the Remove Gradient Stop button.

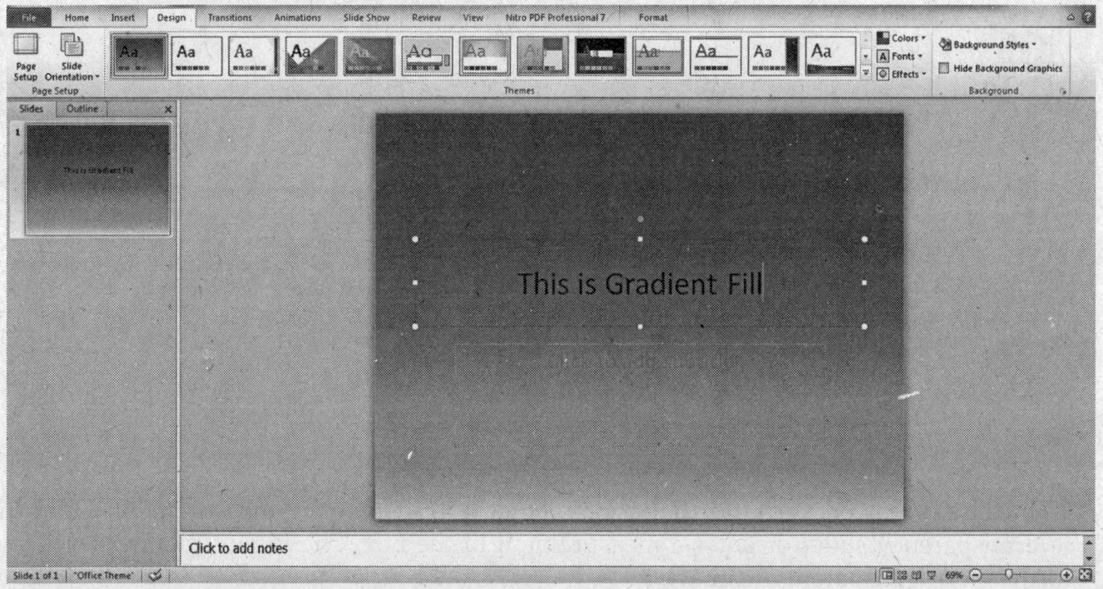

- **Choosing a colour for a gradient stop:** Select a gradient stop on the slider, click the Colour button, and choose a colour on the drop-down list.
- **Positioning a gradient stop:** Drag a gradient stop on the slider or use the Position box to move it to a different location.
- Drag the Brightness slider to make the colours dimmer or brighter.

Creating Slide Backgrounds on Your Own

Drag the Transparency slider to make the colours on the slides more or less transparent. At 0% transparency, you get solid colours; at 100%, you get no colour at all. Click the Apply to All button.

Placing a clip-art image in the slide background

- On the Design tab, click the Background Styles button and choose Format Background on the drop-down list. The Fill category of the Format Background dialog box appears
- Click the Picture or Texture Fill option button.
- Click the Clip Art button. You see the Select Picture dialog box.
- Find and select a clip-art image that you can use in the background of your slides. You can scroll through the clip-art images until you find a good one, enter a search term in the Search Text box and click the Go button (click the Include Content from Office Online check box to search online at Microsoft for a clip-art image), or click the Import button to get an image from your computer.

- In the Format Background dialog box, enter a Transparency measurement. Drag the Transparency slider or enter a measurement in the box. The higher the measurement, the more transparent the image is.

- ❒ Enter measurements in the Offsets boxes to make your clip-art image fill the slide.
- ❒ Click the Apply to All button and then click Close.

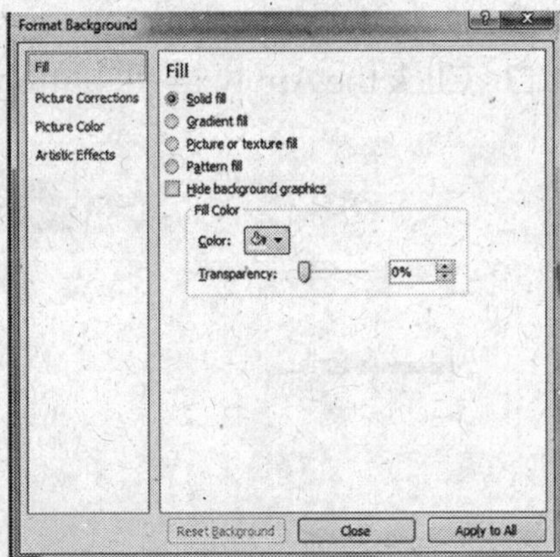

Follow these steps to use a picture as a slide background:

- ❒ On the Design tab, click the Background Styles button and choose Format Background on the drop-down list. You see the Fill category of the Format Background dialog box.
- ❒ Click the Picture or Texture Fill option button.
- ❒ Click the File tab. The Insert Picture dialog box appears.

- ❒ Locate the picture you want, select it, and click the Insert button. The picture lands on your slide.
- ❒ Enter a Transparency measurement to make the picture fade a bit in to the background. Using the Offsets text boxes, enter measurements to make your picturefit on the slides.
- ❒ Click the Apply to All button.

Using a texture for a slide background

- ❒ On the Design tab, click the Background Styles button and choose Format Background on the drop-down list.
- ❒ Click the Picture or Texture Fill option button.
- ❒ Click the Texture button and choose a texture on the drop-down list.
- ❒ Enter a Transparency measurement to make the texture less imposing.

- ❒ Drag the slider or enter a measurement in the Transparency box.
- ❒ Click the Apply to All button and then click Close.

Text & Powerpoint

Entering Text

Here we will discuss how to enter text in a slide in a Powerpoint presentation.

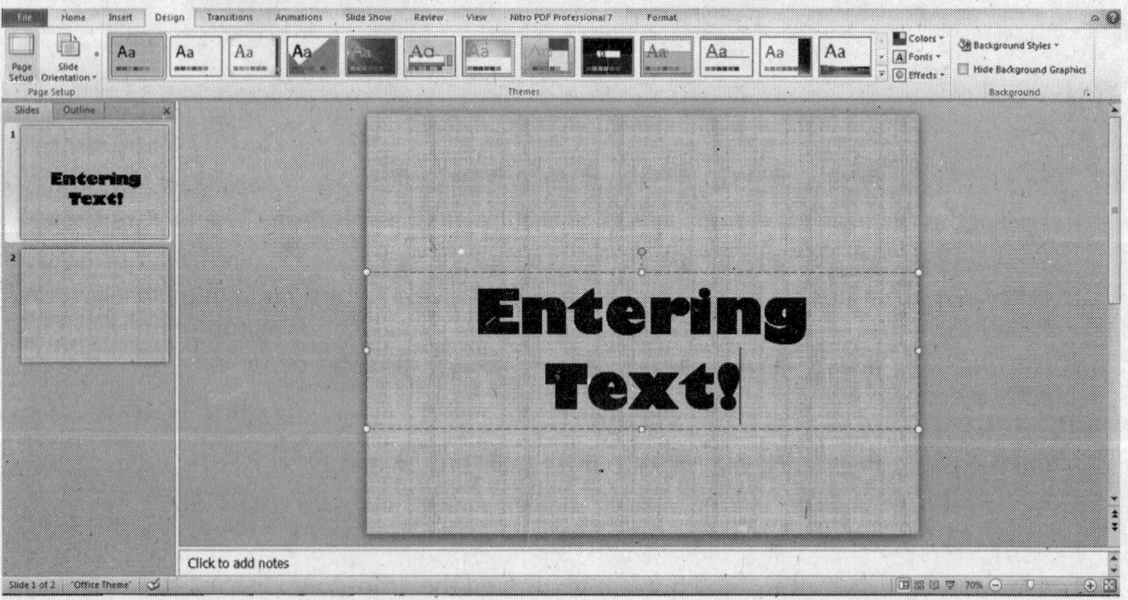

Text Boxes and Text Box Shapes

- ❒ **Creating a text box:** On the Insert tab, click the Text Box button and move the pointer to a part of the slide where you can see the text box pointer, a downward-pointing arrow. Then click and start dragging to create your text box, and enter the text.
- ❒ **Filling a text box with a colour style:** On the (Drawing Tools) Format tab, choose a style on the Shape Styles gallery.
- ❒ **Rotating a text box (text included):** Use one of these techniques to rotate a text box along with the text inside it.
  - Drag the rotation handle, the green circle above the text box.
  - On the (Drawing Tools) Format tab, click the Rotate button and choose a Rotate or Flip command on the drop-down list.
  - On the (Drawing Tools) Format tab, click the Size group button (you may have to click the Size button first) and, in the Size category of the Format Shape dialog box, enter a measurement in the Rotation box.
- ❒ **Turning a shape into a text box:** Create the shape, and then click in the shape and start typing.
- ❒ **Turning a text box into a shape:** Right-click the text box and choose Format Shape. In the Format Shape dialog box, click the Text Box category and under AutoFit, click the Do Not AutoFit option button. Then close the dialog box, go to the (Drawing Tools) Format tab, click the Edit Shape button, choose Change Shape on the drop-down list, and choose a shape on the Change Shape submenu.

Positioning Text in Frames and Text Boxes

- ❒ Align text commands control horizontal (left-to-right) alignments. On the Home tab, click the Align Left (press Ctrl+L), Center (press Ctrl+E), Align Right (press Ctrl+R), or Justify button.
- ❒ Align Text commands control vertical (up-and-down) alignments. On the Home tab, click the Align Text button and choose Top, Middle, or Bottom on the drop-down list.

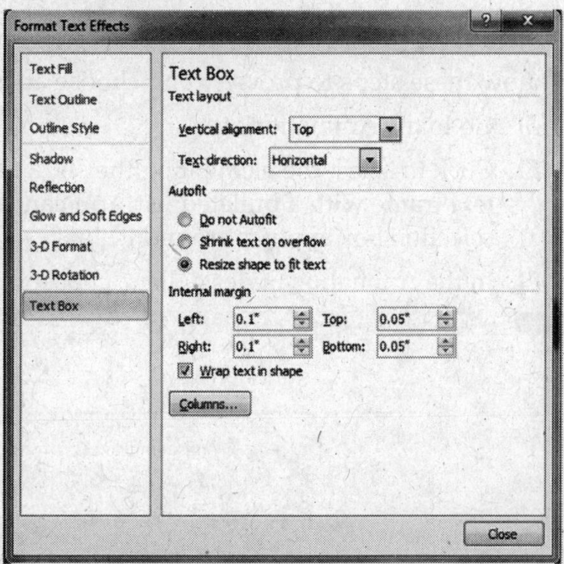

Formating text

Transition & Animations

In PowerPoint, a transition is a little bit of excitement that occurs as one slide leaves the screen and the next slide climbs aboard. An animation is movement on the slide.

Tools for tweaking a transition:

- **Effect Options:** Click the Effect Options button and choose an effect on the drop-down list. For example, choose From Top or From Bottom to make a transition arrive from the top or bottom of the screen. Not all transitions offer effect options.
- **Sound:** Open the Sound drop-down list and choose a sound to accompany the transition. The Loop Until Next Sound option at the bottom of the drop-down list plays a sound continuously until the next slide in the presentation appears.
- **Duration:** Enter a time period in the Duration box to declare how quickly or slowly you want the transition to occur. As mentioned earlier, you can click the Apply To All button to assign the same.

Altering and removing slide transitions

In the Slides pane and Slide Sorter view, the transition symbol, a flying star, appears next to slides that have been assigned a transition. Select the slides that need a transition change, go to the Transitions tab, and follow these instructions to alter or remove transitions:

- **Altering a transition:** Choose a different transition in the Transition to This Slide gallery. You can also choose different effect options and sounds, and change the duration of the transition.
- **Removing a transition:** Choose None in the Transition to This Slide gallery.

Animating parts of a slide

Follow these steps to preview and choose an animation scheme for slides:

- Go to the Animations tab.
- Click to select the element on the slide that you want to animate. For example, select a text frame with a bulleted list. You can tell when you've selected an element because a selection box appears around it.
- In the Animation Styles gallery, choose an animation effect.

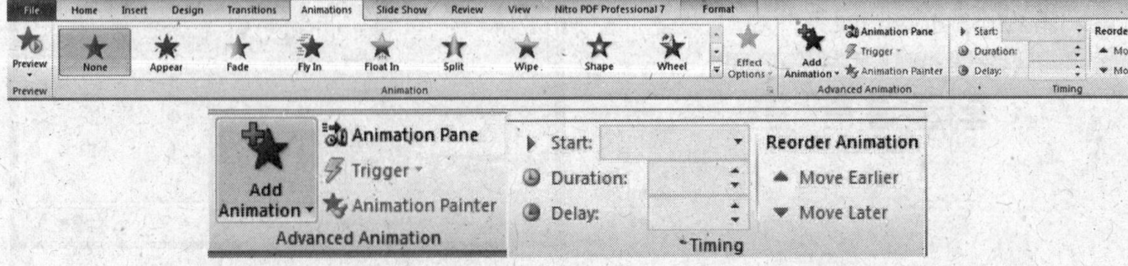

You can choose Entrance, Emphasis, and Exit animation effects. As soon as you make your choice, the animation springs to life, and you can click the Preview button at any time to see your animation in all its glory.

Animation pane

- Click the Effect Options button and experiment with choices on the drop-down list to tweak your animation. Which options are available depends on the animation you chose.
  - **All at Once:** All the text is animated at the same time.
  - **By Paragraph:** Each paragraph is treated separately and is animated on its own.

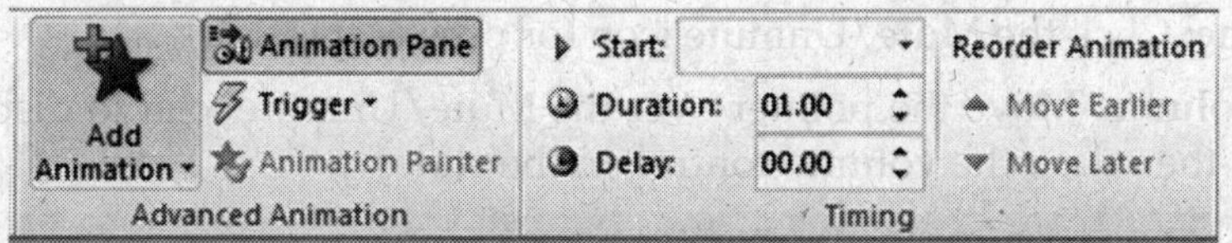

To remove an animation, return to the Animation Styles gallery and choose None.

Audio Part of Your Presentation

PowerPoint offers two ways to make audio part of a presentation:

- **As part of slide transitions:** A sound is heard as a new slide arrives on-screen. On the Transitions tab, open the Sound drop-down list and choose a sound.
- **On the slide itself:** The means of playing audio appears on the slide in the form of an Audio icon. By moving the mouse over this icon, you can display audio controls, and you can use these controls to play audio. You can also make audio play as soon as the slide arrives on-screen.

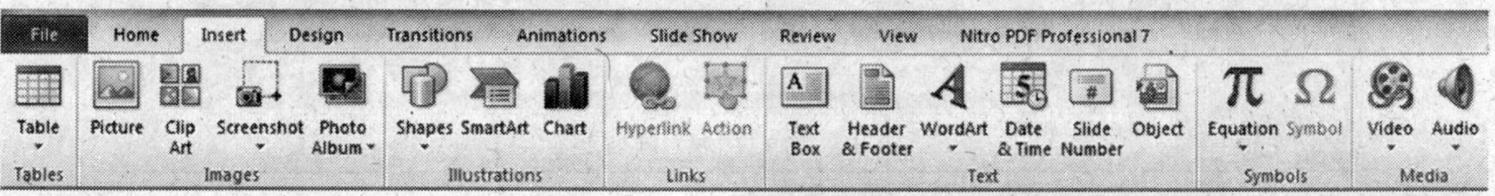

Inserting an audio file on a slide

Follow these steps to insert an audio file in a slide:

- Go to the Insert tab.
- Click the Audio button. You will see the Insert Audio dialog box.
- Locate and select a sound file and then click Insert.

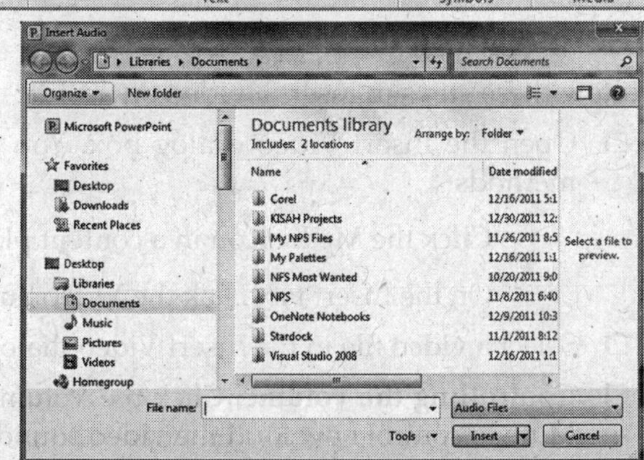

Inserting an audio file

Playing audio during a presentation

While an audio file is playing during a presentation, controls for starting, pausing, and controlling the volume appear on-screen.

Follow these instructions to start, pause, and control the volume of an audio recording during a presentation:

- ❒ **Starting an audio file:** Move the pointer over the Audio icon, and when you see the Audio controls, click the Play/Pause button (or press Alt+P).
- ❒ **Pausing an audio file:** Click the Play/Pause button (or press Alt+P). Click the button again to resume playing the audio file.
- ❒ **Muting the volume:** Click the Mute/Unmute icon (or press Alt+U).
- ❒ **Controlling the volume:** Move the pointer over the Mute/Unmute icon to display the volume slider and then drag the volume control on the slider.

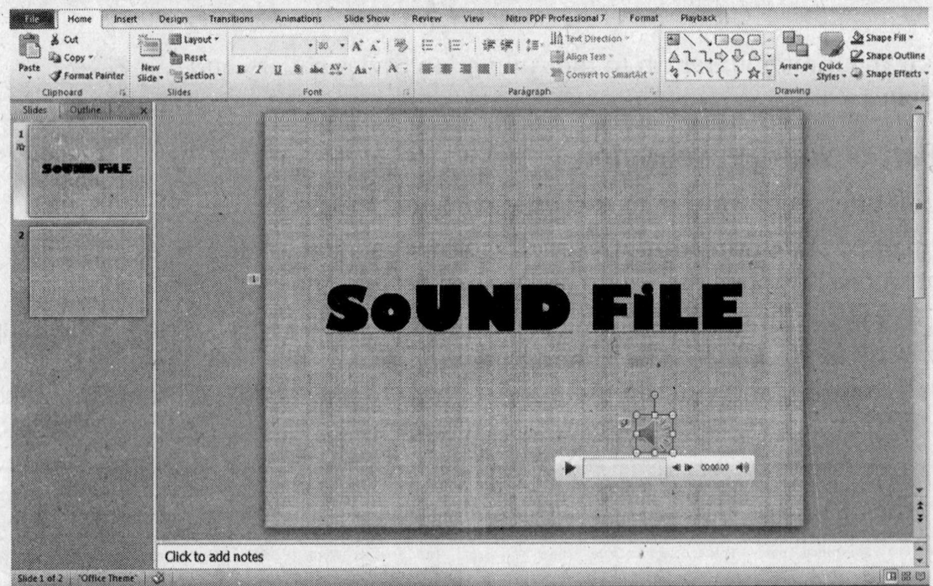

Inserting a video on a slide

Follow these steps to insert a video on a slide:

- ❒ Open the Insert Video dialog box. You can open the dialog box with one of these methods:
  - Click the Media icon in a content place holder frame.
  - On the Insert tab, click the Video button.
- ❒ Select a video file in the Insert Video dialog box and click Insert.
- ❒ **Controlling the volume:** Click the Volume button and choose Low, Medium, High, or Mute to control how loud the video sound is.

- **Playing the video automatically or when you click the Play/Pause button:** Open the Start drop-down list and choose Automatically or On Click to tell PowerPoint when to start playing the video.
- **Playing the video at full screen:** Make a video fill the entire screen by selecting the Play Full Screen check box. Be careful of this one. Videos can look terribly grainy when they appear on the big screen.
- **Hiding the video when it isn't playing:** You can hide the video until you start playing it by selecting the Hide While Not Playing check box. Be sure to choose Automatically on the Start drop-down list if you select this check box.
- **Continuously playing, or looping the video:** Play a video continuously or until you go to the next slide by selecting the Loop Until Stopped check box.
- **Rewinding the video when it's finished playing:** Rewind a video if you want to see the first frame, not the last, when the video finishes playing.

Showing Your Presentation

- On the Slide Show tab, click the From Beginning button.
- Select the first slide and then click the Slide Show view button
- Press F5

Going from slide to slide

In a nutshell, PowerPoint offers four ways to move from slide to slide in a presentation. Here we describe methods for navigating a presentation, using the four different ways:

- ❒ **Use the slide control buttons:** Click a slide control button — Previous, Next — in the lower-left corner of the screen.
- ❒ **Click the Slide button:** Click this button and make a choice on the pop-up menu.
- ❒ **Right-click on-screen:** Right-click and choose a navigation option on the shortcut menu.
- ❒ **Press a keyboard shortcut:** Press one of the numerous keyboard shortcuts. That PowerPoint offers for going from slide to slide (Spacebar, PgUp, PgDn…)

Wielding a pen or highlighter in a presentation

Follow these instructions so that you can draw on a slide:

- ❒ **Selecting a pen or highlighter:** PowerPoint offers Pen for writing on slides and Highlighter for highlighting text on slides. To select the Pen or Highlighter, click the Pen button and choose Pen or Highlighter. You can also right-click, choose Pointer Options, and make a selection on the submenu.
- ❒ **Choosing a colour for drawing:** After you select the Pen or Highlighter, click the Pen button, choose Ink Colour, and select a colour on the submenu

Follow these steps to make yours a kiosk-style, self-running presentation:

- ❒ Go to the Slide Show tab.
- ❒ Click the Set Up Slide Show button.

You will see the Set Up Slide Show dialog box.

- ❒ Under Show Type, select the Browsed at a Kiosk (Full Screen) option. When you select this option, PowerPoint automatically selects the Loop Continuously Until 'Esc' check box.
- ❒ Make sure that the Using Timings, If Present option button is selected.
- ❒ Click OK.

Packaging a presentation on a CD

Follow these steps to copy your presentation and the PowerPoint Viewer to a CD or a folder:

- ❒ Open the presentation you want to package.
- ❒ On the File tab, choose Save & Send.
- ❒ Choose Package Presentation for CD, and click the Package for CD button.
- ❒ Enter a name for the CD or folder in the Name of the CD text box. The name you enter will appear as the name of the CD if you view the CD on Computer; if you're copying your presentation to a folder, the name you enter will be given to the folder PowerPoint creates when it creates the packaged presentation file.

- ❒ Create the packaged presentation and copy it to a CD or to a folder on your computer. Copy the presentation to a folder if you want to send the presentation by e-mail rather than distribute it by CD.
  - **Copying to a CD:** Click the Copy to CD button.
  - **Copying to a folder:** Click the Copy to Folder button. In the Copy to Folder dialog box, click the Browse button, and in the ChooseLocation dialog box, select a folder for storing the folder where you will keep your packaged presentation. Then click the Select button and click OK in the Copy to Folder dialog box.

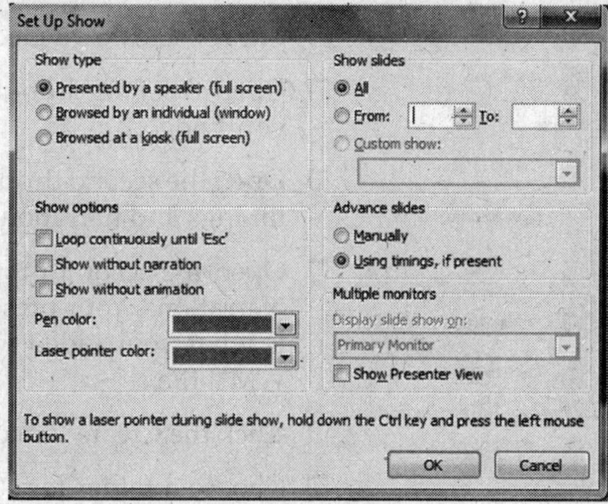

Set Up Slide Show button

- ❒ Click Yes in the message box that asks if you want to include linked content in the presentation. It can take PowerPoint several minutes to assemble the files and copy them to the CD or folder.

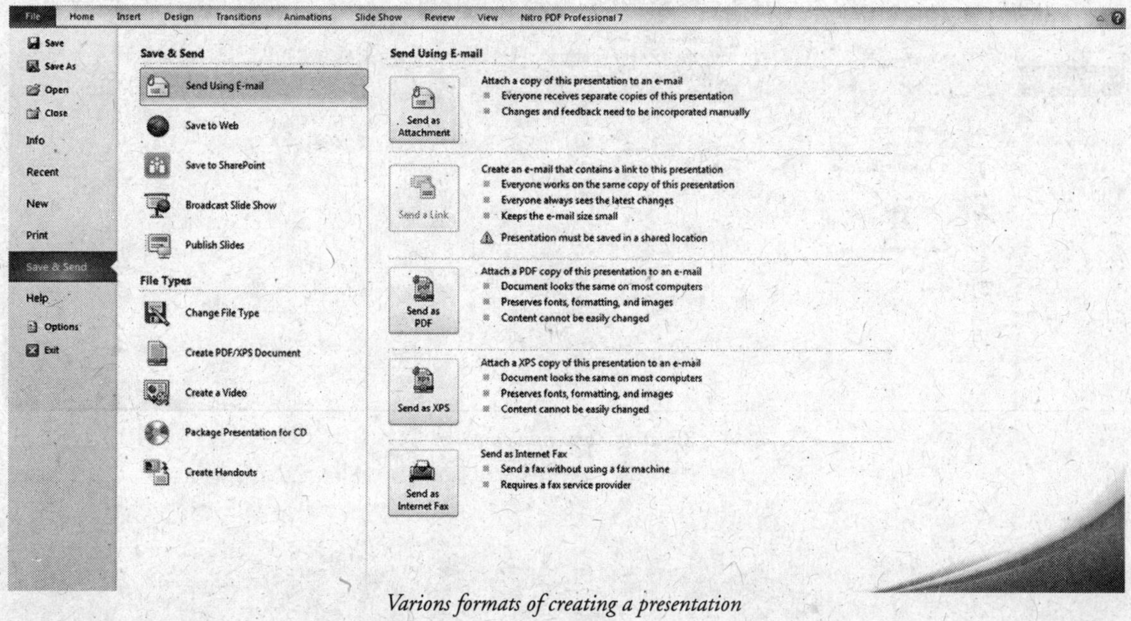

Varions formats of creating a presentation

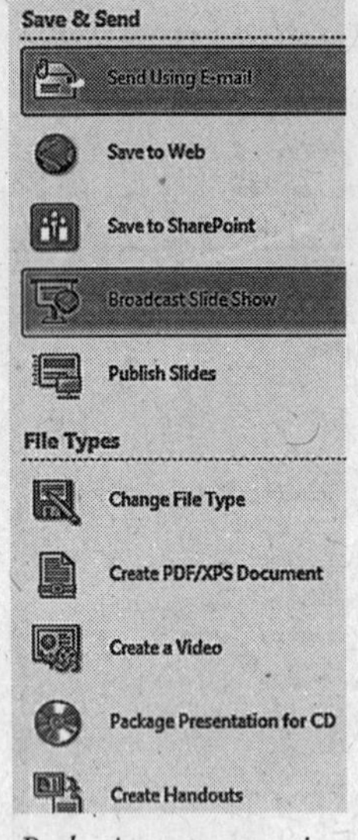

Packaging a presentation on a CD

Creating a presentation video

Follow these steps to create a WMV-file version of a PowerPoint presentation:

- ❒ On the File tab, choose Save & Send.
- ❒ Choose Create a Video. You see the Create a Video window.
- ❒ Open the first drop-down list and choose a display resolution for your video.
- ❒ Open the second drop-down list and choose whether to use recorded timings and narrations.
- ❒ Open the second drop-down list and choose Preview Timings and Narrations. Your presentation video plays. How do you like it? This is what your video will look and sound like after you save it in a WMV file.
- ❒ Click the Create Video button. The Save As dialog box opens.
- ❒ Choose a folder for storing the WMV file, enter a name for the file, and click the Save button.

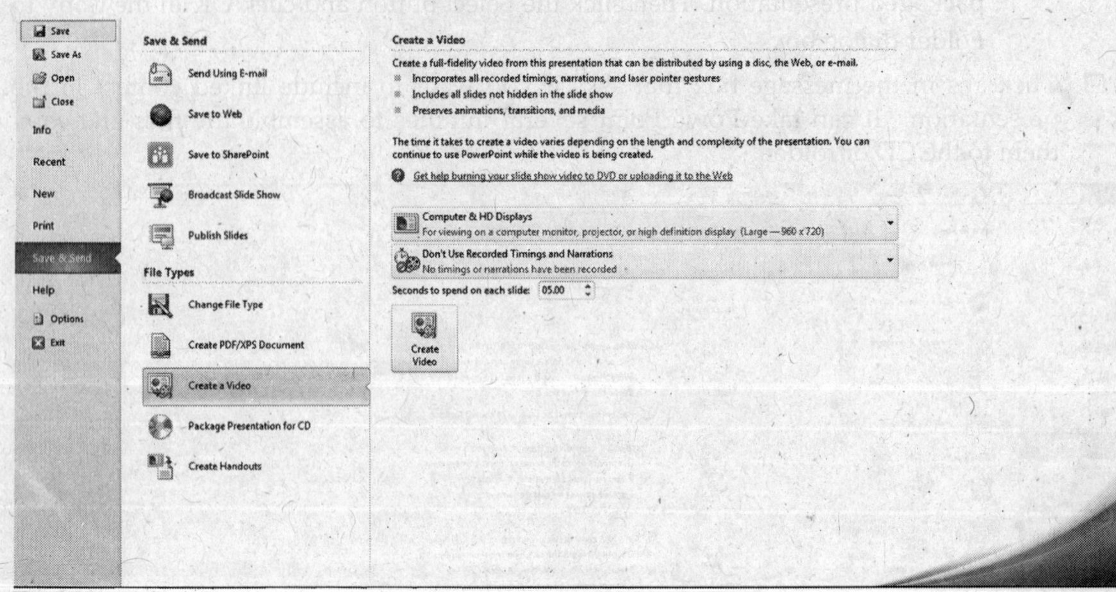

Creating a presentation video

Points to Remember

- ☆ Use Animation & transition with tools to ensure that which object will appear on click & which will appear automatically
- ☆ Use suitable frame for videos
- ☆ Your Sound clip button should appear on frame during slide show
- ☆ While converting the file into Video, please set the sound clips & Video playback in auto-mode by setting time limits

Welcome to MS Excel

Creating a New Excel Workbook

Use one of these methods in the Available Templates window to create a workbook:

- **Create a blank workbook:** Double-click the Blank Workbook icon. (By pressing Ctrl+N, you can create a new, blank workbook without opening the Available Templates window.)
- **Create a workbook from a template:** Use a template on your computer: Click Sample Templates. Templates that you loaded on your computer when you installed Office appear in the window.
- **Download a template from Office.com:** Under Office.com Templates, either choose the type of template you want or make sure that your computer is connected to the Internet, enter a search term in the Search box, and click the Start Searching button (or press Enter). Choose a template and click the Download button to download it to your computer.
- **Use a template you created (or downloaded earlier from Microsoft):** Click the My Templates icon. The New dialog box appears. Select a template and click OK.
- **Select a recently used template:** Click the Recent Templates icon and double-click on a template name.
- **Recycle another workbook:** If you can use another workbook as the starting point for creating a new one, click the New from Existing icon. In the New from Existing Workbook dialog box, select the workbook and click the Create New button.

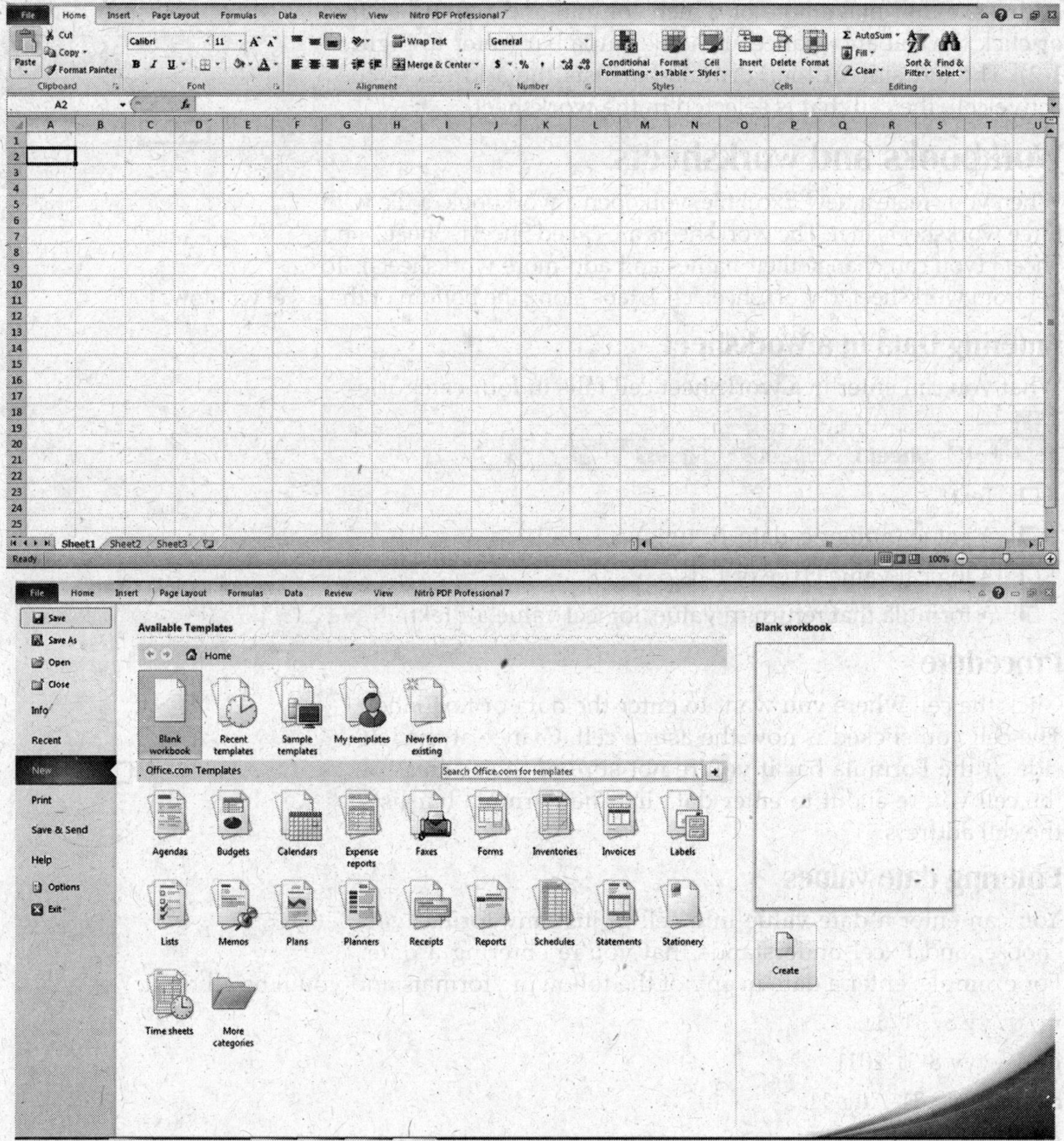

Creating a blank workbook

Rows, columns, and cell addresses

An Excel worksheet has numerous columns and over 1 million rows. The rows are numbered, and columns are labeled A to Z; then AA to AZ; then BA to BZ, and so on. The important thing to remember is that each cell has an address whose name comes from a column letter and a row number. The first cell in row 1 is A1, the second is B1, and so on. You need to enter cell addresses in the formula bar as to tell Excel which numbers to compute. To find a cell's address, either make note of which column and row it lies in, or click the cell and glance at the Formula bar (refer to Figure 1-2). The left side of the Formula bar lists the address of the active cell, the cell that is selected in the worksheet.

Workbooks and worksheets

When you create a new Excel file, you open a workbook, a file with three worksheets in it. The worksheets are called Sheet1, Sheet2, and Sheet3 (you can change their names and add more worksheets). To get from worksheet to worksheet, click tabs along the bottom of the Excel window.

Entering Data in a Worksheet

What you can enter in a worksheet cell falls in four categories:

- ❐ Text
- ❐ A value (numeric, date, or time)
- ❐ A logical value (True or False)
- ❐ A formula that returns a value, logical value, or text

Procedure

Click the cell where you want to enter the data or text label. The cell you clicked is now the active cell. Glance at the left side of the Formula bar if you're not sure of the address of the cell you're about to enter data in. The Formula bar lists the cell address.

Entering date values

You can enter a date value in a cell in just any format you choose, and Excel understands that you're entering a date. For example, enter a date in any of the following formats and you'll be all right:

m/d/yy 8/31/11

m-d-yyyy 8-31-2011

d-mmm-yy 31-Aug-11

Here are some basic things to remember about entering dates:

- ❐ Date formats: You can quickly apply a format to dates by selecting cells and using one of these methods:
  - On the Home tab, open the Number Format drop-down list and choose Short Date (m/d/yyyy; 8/31/2011) or Long Date (day-of-the-week, month, day, year; Saturday, Aug 31, 2011).
  - On the Home tab, click the Number group button to open the Number tab of the Format Cells dialog box.

- **Current date:** Press Ctrl+; (semicolon) and press Enter to enter the current date.
- **Current year's date:** If you don't enter the year as part of the date, Excel assumes that the date you entered is in the current year. For example, if you enter a date in the m/d (8/31) format during the year 2011, Excel enters the date as 8/31/11. As long as the date you want to enter is the current year, you can save a little time when entering dates by not entering the year, as Excel enters it for you.
- **Dates on the Formula bar:** No matter which format you use for dates, dates are displayed in the Formula bar in the format that Excel prefers for dates: m/d/yyyy (8/31/2010). How dates are displayed in the worksheet is up to you.

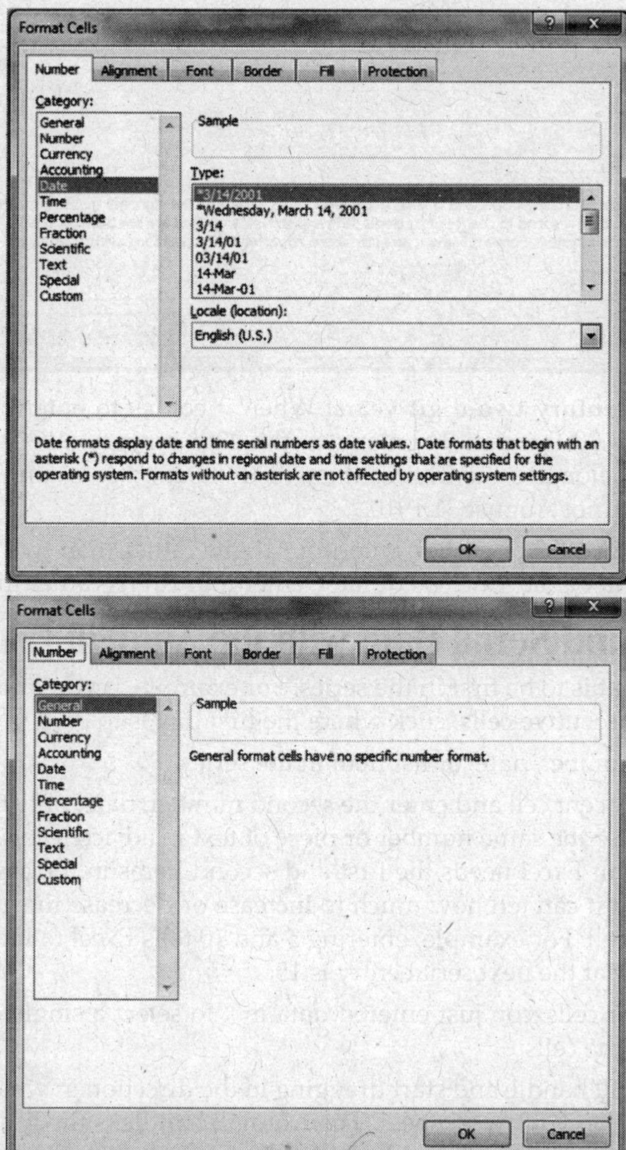

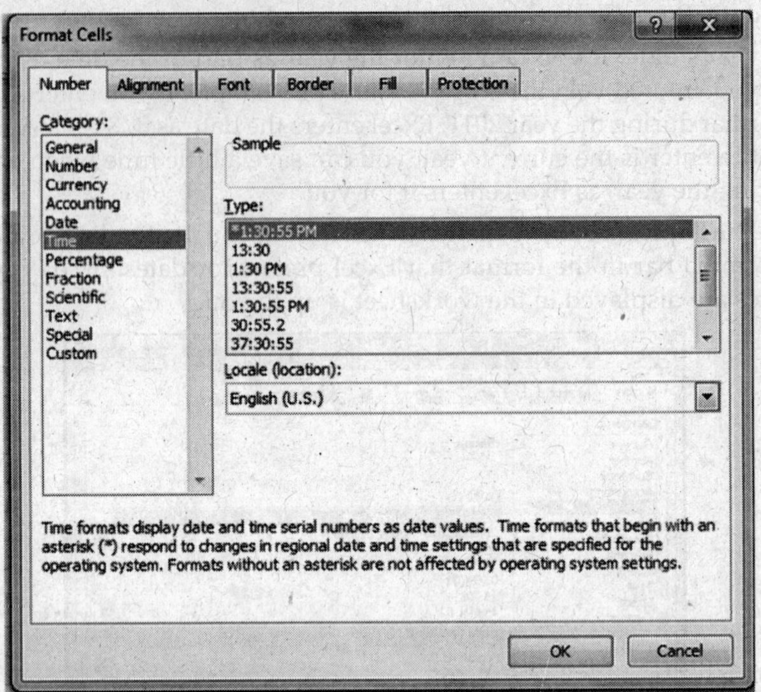

- **20th and 21st century two-digit years:** When it comes to entering two digit years in dates, the digits 30 through 99 belong to the 20th century (1930–1999), but the digits 00 through 29 belong to the 21st century (2000–2029). For example, 8/31/10 refers to August 31, 2010, not August 31,1910.
- To enter a date in 1929 or earlier, enter four digits rather than two to describe the year: 8-31-1929. To enter a date in 2030 or later, enter four digits rather than two: 8-31-2030.

Entering Lists and Serial Data with the AutoFill Command

- Click the cell that is to be first in the series. For example, if you intend to list the days of the week in consecutive cells, click where the first day is to go.
- Enter the first number, date, or list item in the series.
- Move to the adjacent cell and enter the second number, date, or list item in the series. If you want to enter the same number or piece of text in adjacent cells, it isn't necessary to take this step, but Excel needs the first and second items in the case of serial dates and numbers so that it can tell how much to increase or decrease the given amount or time period in each cell. For example, entering 5 and 10 tells Excel to increase the number by 5 each time so that the next serial entry is 15.
- Select the cell or cells you just entered data in. To select a single cell, click it; to select two, drag over the cells.
- Click the AutoFill handle and start dragging in the direction in which you want the data series to appear on your worksheet. The AutoFill handle is the little black square in the lower-right corner of the cell or block of cells you selected. Finding it can be difficult.

Carefully move the mouse pointer over the lower-right corner of the cell, and when you see the mouse pointer change into a black cross, click and start dragging. As you drag, the serial data appears in a pop-up box, 1.

Formatting Numbers, Dates, and Time Values

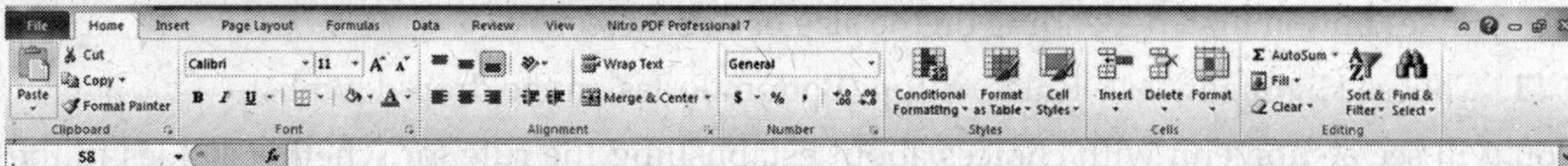

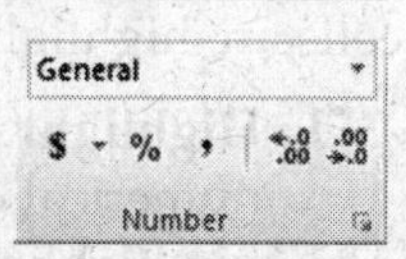

Excel offers five number-formatting buttons on the Home tab — Accounting Number Format, Percent Style, Comma Style, Increase Decimal, and Decrease Decimal. Select cells with numbers in them and click one of these buttons to change how numbers are formatted:

- **Accounting Number Format:** Places a dollar sign before the number and gives it two decimal places: You can open the drop-down list on this button and choose a currency symbol apart from the dollar sign.
- **Percent Style:** Places a percent sign after the number and converts the number to a percentage.
- **Comma Style:** Places commas in the number.
- **Increase Decimal:** Increases the number of decimal places by one.
- **Decrease Decimal:** Decreases the number of decimal places by one.
- To strip formats from the data in cells, select the cells, go to the Home tab,click the Clear button, and choose Clear Formats. Clear

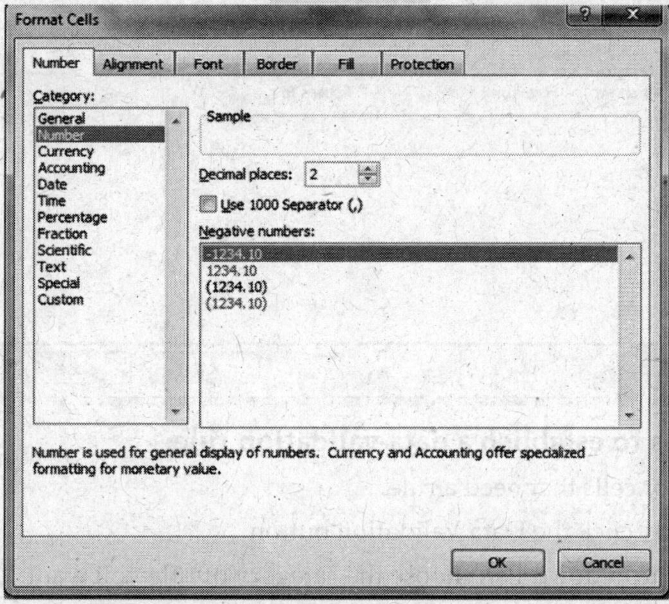

Formatting numbers

Conditional Formats

Select the cells that are candidates for conditional formatting and follow these steps to tell Excel when and how to format the cells:

- ❒ On the Home tab, click the Conditional Formatting button (you may have to click the Styles button first, depending on the size of your screen).
- ❒ Choose Highlight Cells Rules or Top/Bottom Rules on the drop-downlist.

You will see a submenu with choices about establishing the rule for whether values in the cells are highlighted or otherwise made more prominent:

- ❒ **Highlight Cells Rules:** These rules are for calling attention to data if it falls in a numerical or date range, or it's greater or lesser than a specific value. For example, you can highlight cells that are greater.
- ❒ **Top/Bottom Rules:** These rules are for calling attention to data if it falls within a percentage range relative to all the cells you selected.

For example, you can highlight cells with data that falls in the bottom 50 percent range.

- ❒ Choose an option on the submenu.
- ❒ On the left side of the dialog box, establish the rule for flagging data.
- ❒ On the drop-down list, choose how you want to call attention to the data.

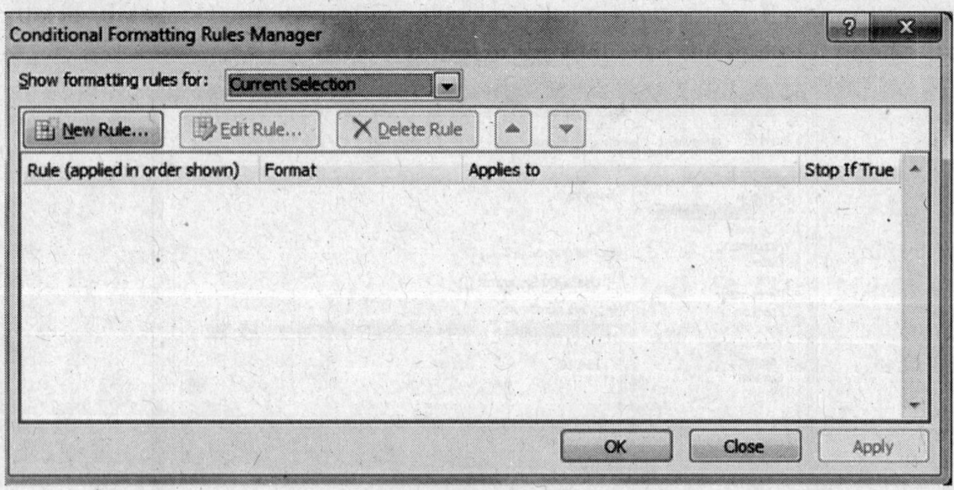

Follow these steps to establish a data-validation rule:

- ❒ Select the cell or cells that need a rule.
- ❒ On the Data tab, click the Data Validation button.
- ❒ On the Allow drop-down list, choose the category of rule you want.
- ❒ Enter the criteria for the rule.

What the criteria is depends on what rule category you're working in. You can refer to cells in the worksheet by selecting them. To do that, either select them directly or click the Range Selector button and then select them.

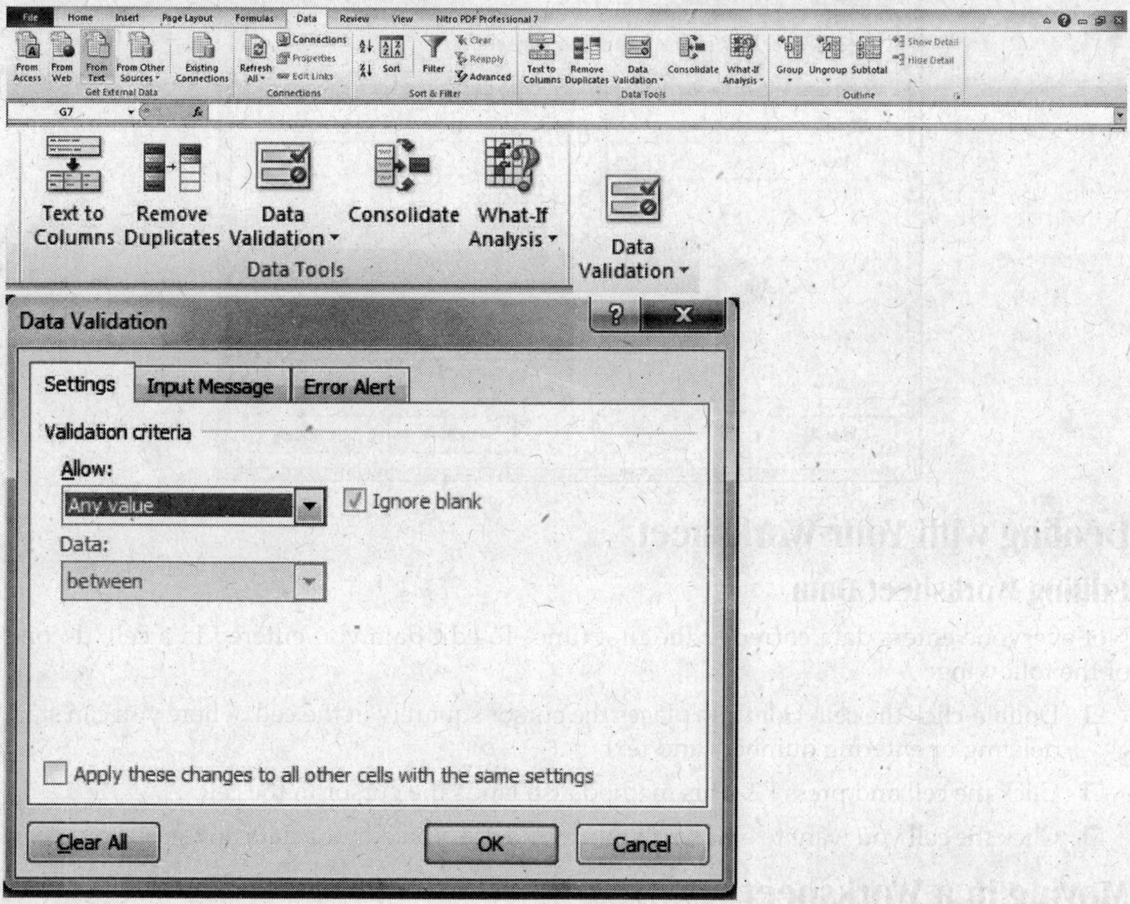

- ❒ On the Input Message tab, enter a title and input message.
- ❒ On the Error Alert tab, choose a style for the symbol in the Message Alert dialog box, enter a title for the dialog box, and enter a warning message.
- ❒ Click OK.

To remove data-validation rules from cells, select the cells, go to the Data tab, click the Data Validation button, and on the Settings tab of the Data Validation dialog box, click the Clear All button, and click OK.

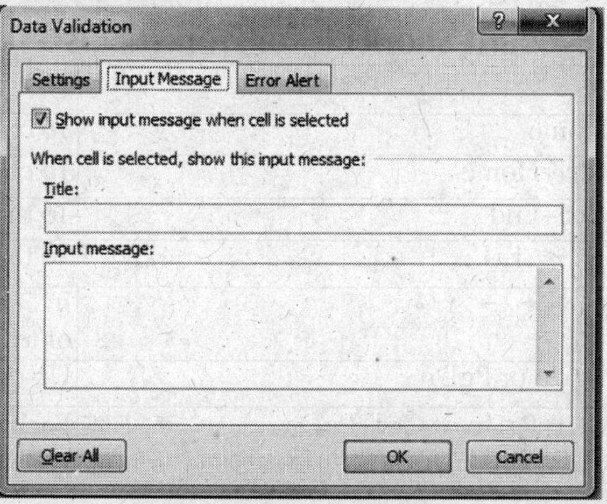

Entering title and input message

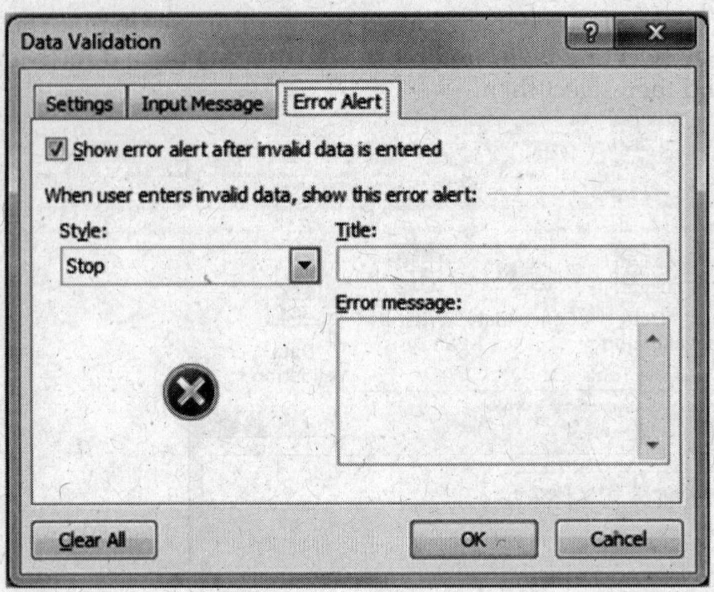

Dealing with Your Worksheet

Editing Worksheet Data

Not everyone enters data correctly the first time. To edit data you entered in a cell, do one of the following:

- Double-click the cell. Doing so places the cursor squarely in the cell, where you can start deleting or entering numbers and text.
- Click the cell and press F2. This method also lands the cursor in the cell.
- Click the cell you want to edit. With this technique, you edit the data on the Formula bar.

Moving in a Worksheet

Keyboard Shortcuts for Worksheets

Press	To Move the Selection
Home	To column A
Ctrl+Home	To cell A1, the first cell in the worksheet
Ctrl+End	To the last cell in the last row with data in it
←, →, ↑, ↓	To the next cell
Ctrl+←, →, ↑, ↓	In one direction toward the nearest cell with data in it or to the first or last cell in the column or row
PgUp or PgDn	Up or down one screen's worth of rows
Ctrl+PgUp or Ctrl+PgDn	Backward or forward through the workbook, from worksheet to worksheet

❐ **Scroll bars:** Use the vertical and horizontal scroll bars to move to different areas. Drag the scroll box to cover long distances. To cover long distances very quickly, hold down the Shift key as you drag the scroll box on the vertical scroll bar.

❐ **Scroll wheel on the mouse:** Turn the wheel to quickly scroll up and down.

❐ **Name box:** Enter a cell address in the Name box and press Enter to go to the cell. The Name box is found to the left of the Formula bar.

❐ **Go To command:** On the Home tab, click the Find & Select button, and choose Go To on the drop-down list (or press Ctrl+G or F5). You will see the Go To dialog box. Enter a cell address in the Reference box and click OK. Cell addresses you've already visited with the Go To command are already listed in the dialog box. Click the Special button to open the Go To Special dialog box and visit a formula, comment, or other esoteric item.

❐ **Find command:** On the Home tab, click the Find & Select button, and choose Find on the drop-down list (or press Ctrl+F). Enter the data you seek in the Find What box and click the Find Next button.

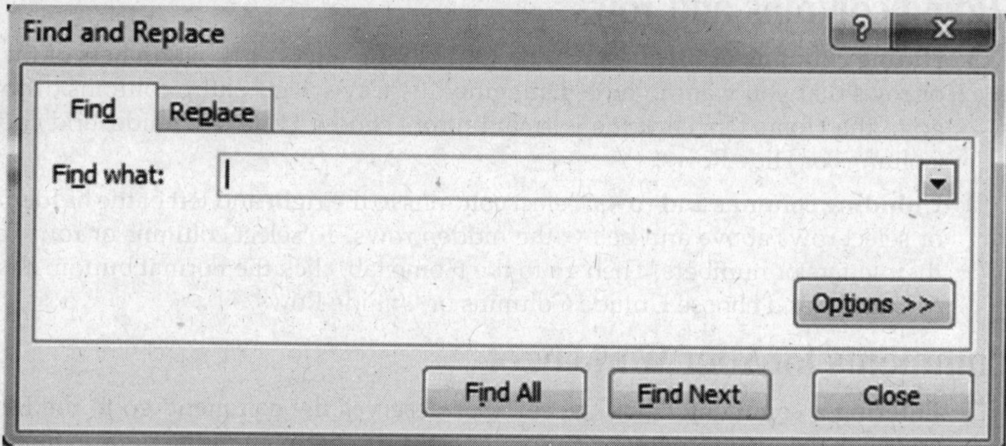

Giving the Split or Freeze Panes command

Follow these steps to split or freeze columns and rows on-screen:

❐ Click the cell directly below the row you want to freeze or split, and click in the column to the right of the column that you want to freeze or split. In other words, click where you want the split to occur.

❐ On the View tab, split or freeze the columns and rows. Go to the View tab and use one of these techniques:

- **Splitting:** Click the Split button and then click and drag the split bars to split the screen horizontally or vertically. The other way to split a worksheet is to grab hold of a split bar, the little division markers directly above the vertical scroll bar and directly to the right of the horizontal scroll bar (in the lower-right corner of your screen). You can tell where split bars are because the pointer turns into a double arrow when it's over a split bar.

Freezing: Click the Freeze Panes button and choose one of three Freeze options on the drop-down list.

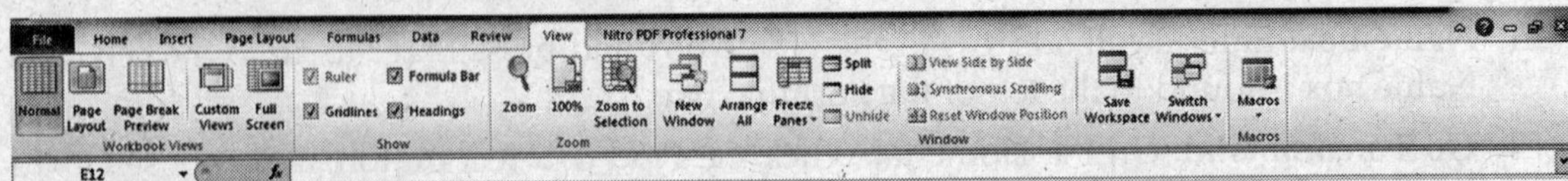

Unsplitting and unfreezing

- **Unsplitting:** Click the Split button again; double-click one of the split bars to remove it; or drag a split bar into the top or left side of the worksheet window.
- **Unfreezing:** On the View tab, click the Freeze Panes button and choose Unfreeze Panes on the drop-down list.

Hiding columns and rows

- **Hiding columns or rows:** Drag over the column letters or row numbers of the columns or rows that you want to hide. Dragging this way selects entire columns or rows. Then go to the Home tab, click the Format button, choose Hide & Unhide, and choose Hide Columns or Hide Rows.
- **Unhiding columns and rows:** Select columns to the right and left of the hidden columns, or select rows above and below the hidden rows. To select columns or rows, drag over their letters or numbers. Then go to the Home tab, click the Format button, choose Hide & Unhide, and choose Unhide Columns or Unhide Rows.

Comments for Your Worksheet

- **Entering a comment:** Click the cell that deserves the comment, go to the Review tab, and click the New Comment button. Enter your comment in the pop-up box. Click in a different cell when you finish entering your comment.
- **Reading a comment:** Move the pointer over the small red triangle and read the comment in the pop-up box.
- **Finding comments:** On the Review tab, click the Previous or Next button to go from comment to comment.
- **Editing a comment:** On the Review tab, select the cell with the comment, click the Edit Comment button, and edit the comment in the pop-upbox. You can also right-click the cell and choose Edit Comment.
- **Deleting comments:** On the Review tab, click a cell with a comment, and then click the Delete button, or right-click the cell and choose Delete Comment. To delete several comments, select them by Ctrl+clicking and then click the Delete button.
- **Deleting all comments in a worksheet:** Select all comments and then, on the Review tab, click the Delete button. You can select all comments by clicking the Find & Select

button on the Home tab, choosing Go To, and in the Go To dialog box, clicking the Special button and choosingComments in the Go To Special dialog box.

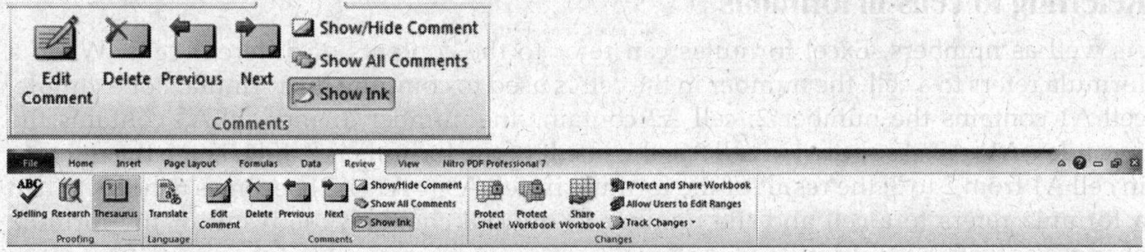

Hiding a worksheet

Follow these instructions to hide and unhide worksheets:

- **Hiding a worksheet:** Select the worksheet you want to hide, go to the View tab, and click the Hide button. You can also right-click the worksheet's tab and choose Hide on the shortcut menu. And you can also display the worksheet, go to the Home tab, click the Format button, and choose Hide &Unhide Hide Sheet.
- Hide Unhide **Unhiding a worksheet:** On the View tab, click the Unhide button, select the name of the worksheet you want to unhide in the Unhide dialog box, and click OK. To open the Unhide dialog box, you can also right-click any worksheet tab and choose Unhide; or go to the Home tab.

Protecting a worksheet

- Select the worksheet that needs protection.
- On the Review tab, click the Protect Sheet button.
- Enter a password in the Password to Unprotect Sheet box if you want only people with the password to be able to open the worksheet after you protect it.
- On the Allow All Users of This Worksheet To list, select the check box next to the name of each task that you want to permit others to do. For example, click the Format Cells check box if you want others to be able to format cells. Deselect the Select Locked Cells check box to prevent any changes from being made to the worksheet. By default, all worksheet cells are locked, and by preventing others from selecting locked cells, you effectively prevent them from editing any cells.
- Click OK.

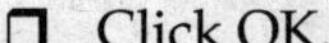

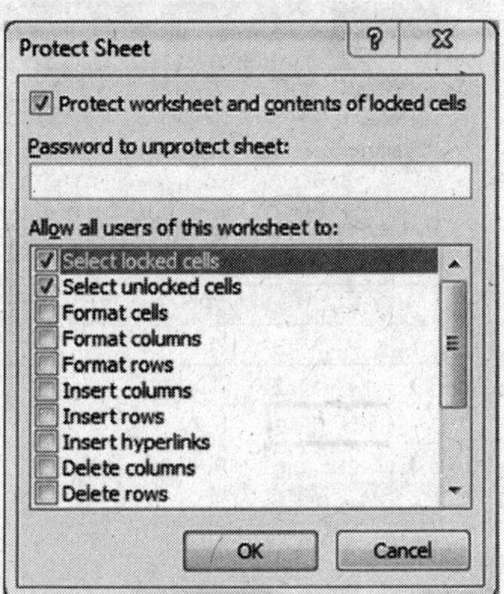

Protecting a worksheet

Formulas and Functions

Referring to cells in formulas

As well as numbers, Excel formulas can refer to the contents of different cells. When a formula refers to a cell, the number in the cell is used to compute the formula. For example, cell A1 contains the number 2; cell A2 contains the number 3; and cell A3 contains the formula =A1+A2. As shown in cell A3, the result of the formula is 5. If I change the number in cell A1 from 2 to 3, the result of the formula in cell A3 (=A1+A2) becomes 6, not 5. When a formula refers to a cell and the number in the cell changes, the result of the formula changes as well.

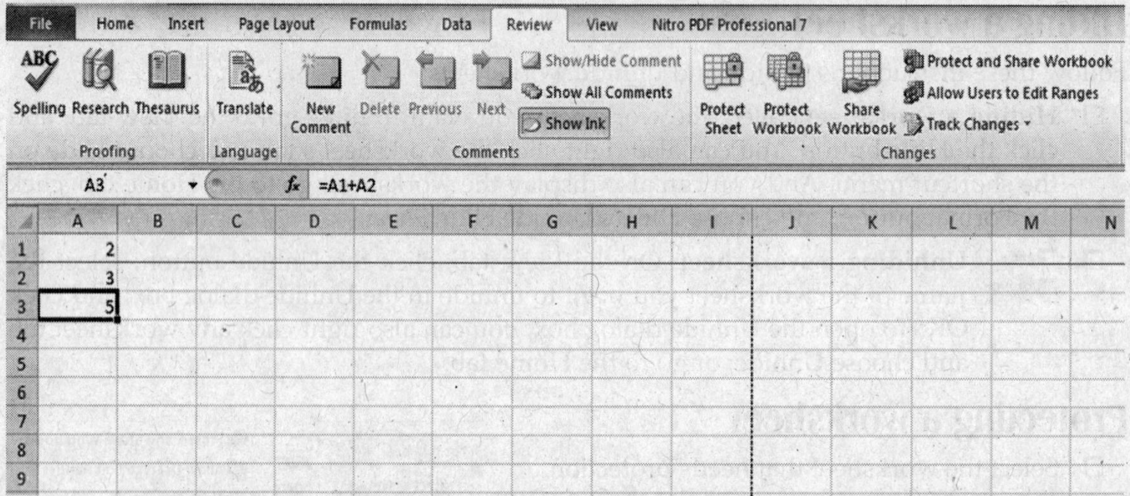

Similarly for Subtraction,

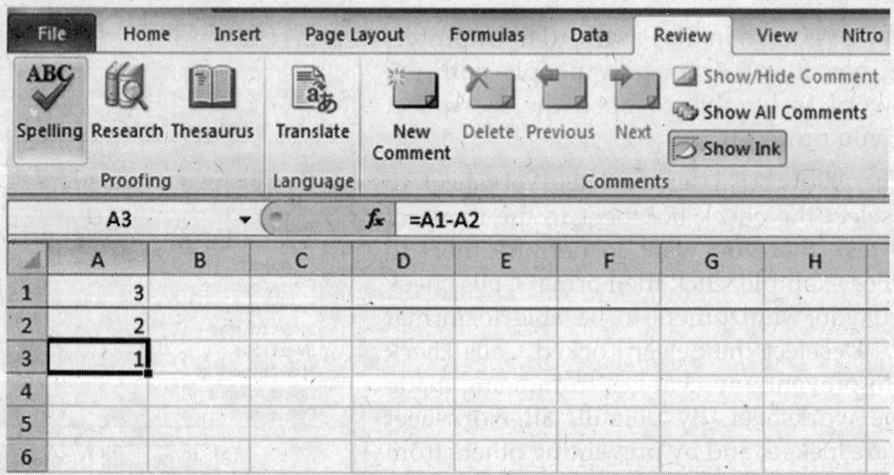

Similarly for Multiplication,

Operators Table

The formulas given in tabular format are very important. You'll need these formulas while doing important stuffs in Excel.

Operator	Example Formula
% (Percent)	=50%
^ (Exponentiation)	=50^2
* (Multiplication)	=E2*4
/ (Division)	=E2/3
+ (Addition)	=F1+F2+F3
– (Subtraction)	=G5–8
= (Equal to)	="Part No."&D4 =C5=4
<> (Not equal to)	=F3<>9
< (Less than)	=B9<E11
<= (Less than or equal to)	=A4<=9
> (Greater than)	=E8>14
>= (Greater than or equal to)	=C3>=D3

Creating a cell range name

Follow these steps to create a cell range name:

- Select the cells that you want to name.
- On the Formulas tab, click the Define Name button. You see the New Name dialog box.
- Enter a descriptive name in the Name box. Names can't begin with a number or include blank spaces.

- On the Scope drop-down list, choose Workbook or a worksheet name.
- Enter a comment to describe the range name, if you want.

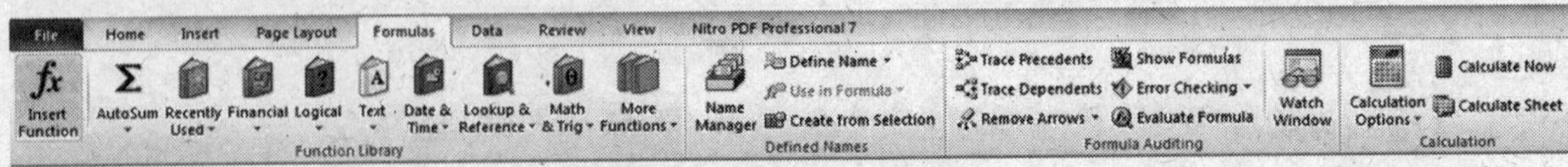

- Click OK.

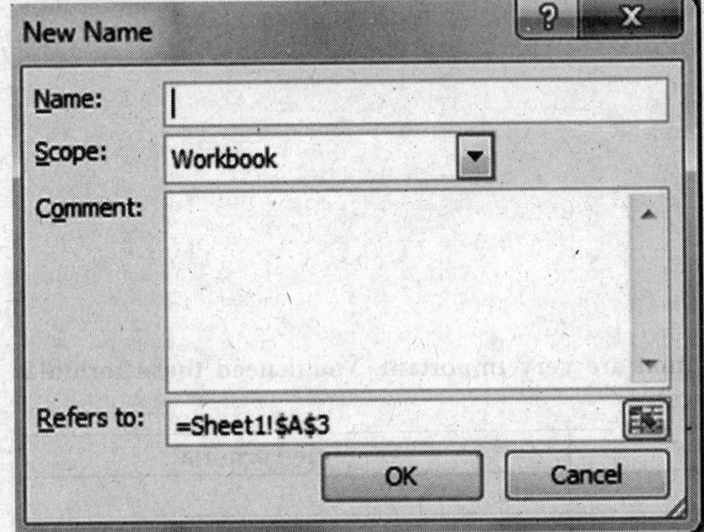

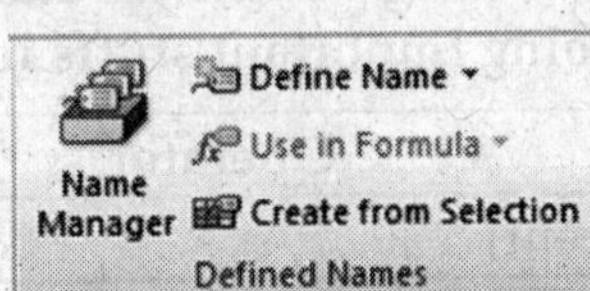

Entering a range name as part of a formula

To include a cell range name in a formula, click in the Formula bar where you want to enter the range name and then use one of these techniques to enter the name:

- On the Formulas tab, click the Use in Formula button and choose a cell range name on the drop-down list
- Press F3 or click the Use in Formula button and choose Paste Names on the drop-down list.

Managing cell range names

To rename, edit, or delete cell range names, go to the Formulas tab and click the Name Manager button.

- **Renaming:** Click the Edit button and enter a new name in the Edit Name dialog box.
- **Reassigning cells:** To assign different cells to a range name, click the Edit button. You see the Edit Name dialog box. To enter a new range of cells, either enter the cells' addresses in the Refers To text box or click the Range Selector button (it's to the right of the text box), drag across the cells on your worksheet that you want for the cell range, and click the Cell Selector button again to return to the Edit Name dialog box.
- **Deleting:** Click the Delete button and click OK in the confirmation box.

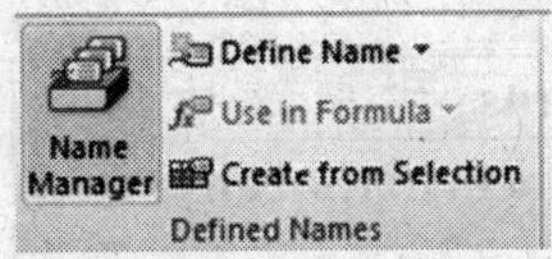

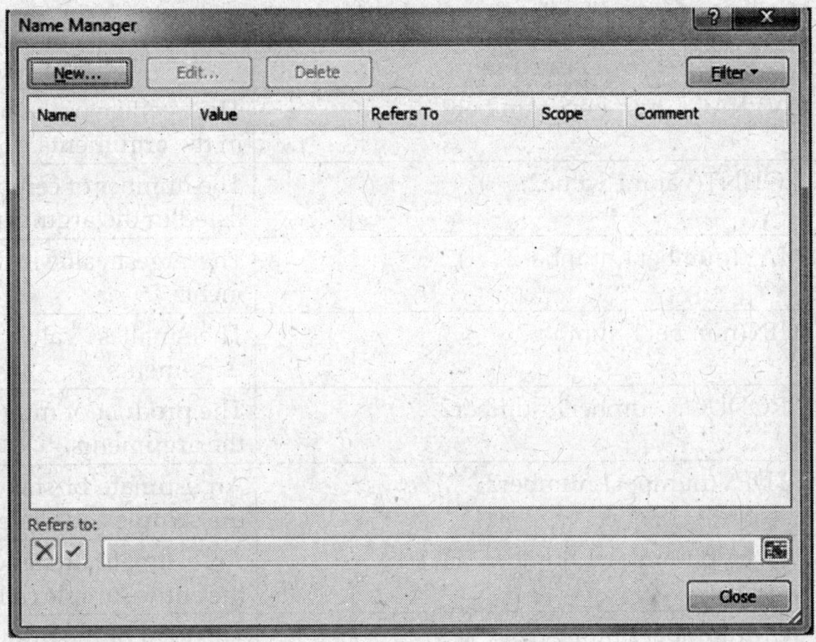

Common Formula Error Messages

Message	Mistake
#DIV/0!	You tried to divide a number by a zero (0) or an empty cell.
#NAME	You used a cell range name in the formula, but the name isn't defined.
#N/A	The formula refers to an empty cell, so no data is available for computing the formula. Sometimes people enter N/A in a cell as a place holder to signal the fact that data isn't entered yet. Revise the formula or enter a number or formula in the empty cells.
#NULL	The formula refers to a cell range that Excel can't understand. Make sure that the range is entered correctly.
#NUM	An argument you use in your formula is invalid
#REF	The cell or range of cells that the formula refers to aren't there.
#VALUE	The formula includes a function that was used incorrectly, takes an invalid argument, or is misspelt. Make sure that the function uses the right argument and is spelled correctly.

Common Functions and Their Use

Function	Returns
AVERAGE(number1,number2,. . .)	The average of the numbers in the cells listed in the arguments.
COUNT(value1,value2,. . .)	The number of cells that contain the numbers listed in the arguments.
MAX(number1,number2,. . .)	The largest value in the cells listed in the Arguments.
MIN(number1,number2,. . .)	The smallest value in the cells listed in the Arguments.
PRODUCT(number1,number2,. . .)	The product of multiplying the cells listed in the arguments.
STDEV(number1,number2,. . .)	An estimate of standard deviation based on the sample cells listed in the argument.
STDEVP(number1,number2,. . .)	An estimate of standard deviation based on the entire sample cells listed in the arguments.
SUM(number1,number2,. . .)	The total of the numbers in the arguments.
VAR(number1,number2,. . .)	An estimate of the variance based on the sample cells listed in the arguments.
VARP(number1,number2,. . .)	A variance calculation based on all cells listed in the arguments.

Entering a function in a formula

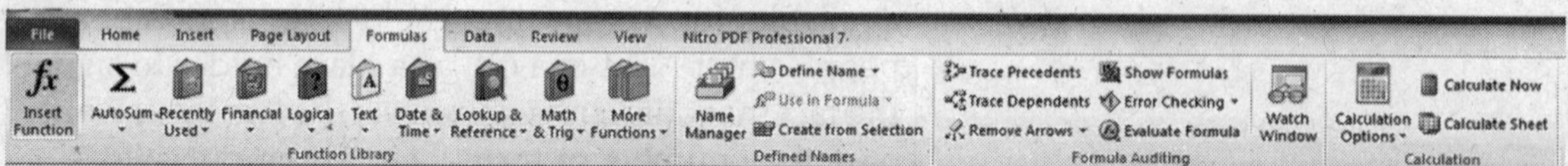

To enter a function in a formula, you can enter the function name by typingit in the Formula bar, or you can rely on Excel to enter it for you. Enter function names yourself if you're well acquainted with a function and comfortable using it.

No matter how you want to enter a function as part of a formula, start this way:

- Select the cell where you want to enter the formula.
- In the Formula bar, type an equals sign (=). Be sure to start every formula by entering an equals sign (=). Without it, Excel thinks you're entering text or a numbering the cell.
- Start constructing your formula, and when you come to the place where you want to enter the function, type the function's name.

Excel's help in entering a function as part of a formula:

On the Formulas tab, tell Excel which function you want to use.

You can do that with one of these techniques:

- ❒ **Click a Function Library button:** Click the button whose name describes what kind of function you want and choose the function's name on the drop-down list. You can click the Financial, Logical, Text, Date & Time, Lookup & Reference, Math & Trig, or More Functions buttons.
- ❒ **Click the Recently Used button:** Click this button and choose the name of a function you used recently.
- ❒ **Click the Insert Function button:** Clicking this button opens the Insert Function dialog box. Find and choose the name of a function. You can search for functions or choose a category and then scroll the names until you find the function you want.
- ❒ Enter arguments in the spaces provided by the Function Arguments dialog box. To enter cell references or ranges, you can click or select cells in your worksheet. If necessary, click the Range Selector button (you can find it to the right of an argument text box) to shrink the Function Arguments dialog box and get a better look at your worksheet.
- ❒ Click OK when you finish entering arguments for your function. I hope you didn't have to argue too strenuously with the Function Arguments dialog box.

Points to Remember

- ☆ Use correct formula operators & methods to ensure the genuine data
- ☆ Use correct Functions
- ☆ Use correct syntaxes & arguments while formatting the text.

Welcome to Publisher

Creating a Publication

Use one of these methods in the Available Templates window to create a publication:

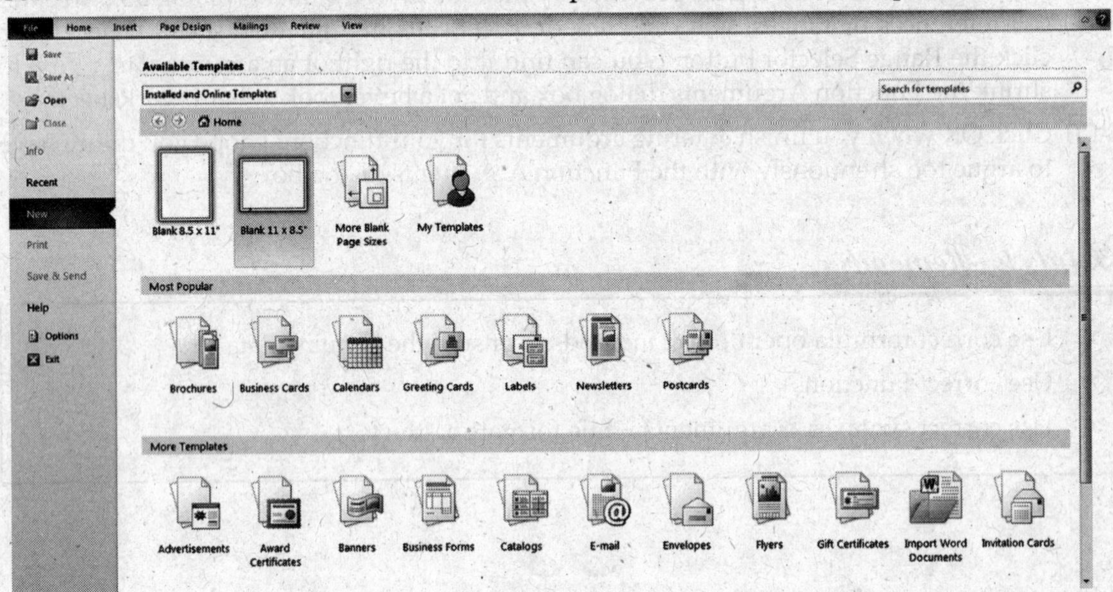

- ❒ **Start from a template category:** Select the icon representing a category (Brochures, Business Cards, and so on). You see a dozen or more templates. Scroll through the list and select a template.

- ❒ **Search for a template:** In the Search for Templates text box, enter the name of a publication type and click the Search button (or press Enter). Then select a template.
- ❒ **Use a template you created:** Click the My Templates icon and then select your template.

Setting up your pages

On the Page Design tab, visit the Page Setup group to determine the marginsize, orientation, and page size of your publication:

- ❒ **Margins:** Click the Margins button and choose an option on the dropdown list or click Custom Margins to enter margin measurements in the Layout Guides dialog box.
- ❒ **Orientation:** Click the Orientation button and choose Portrait or Landscape on the drop-down list to stand your publication upright or turn it on its side.
- ❒ **Size:** Click the Size button and select a page size on the drop-down list. You can choose Create New Page Size on the menu to declare a page size of your own for your publication in the Create New Page Size dialog box. Decide right away which page size to use for your publication. How large or small the page is determines how the headings, graphics, and text fit on the pages.

Margins Orientation Size
Page Setup

A Screen Shot of a Template

Entering Text on the Pages

The placeholder text that appears in publication designs has to go, of course. One of your first tasks is to replace the placeholder text with your own words. In the case of a story, you have a lot of writing and replacing to do (story is Publisher's term for an article that reaches across several textframes). If you're putting together a sign or greeting card, you have only a handful of words to write. If you have to replace more than two dozen words, follow these steps to replace the placeholder text in a text frame with text of your own:

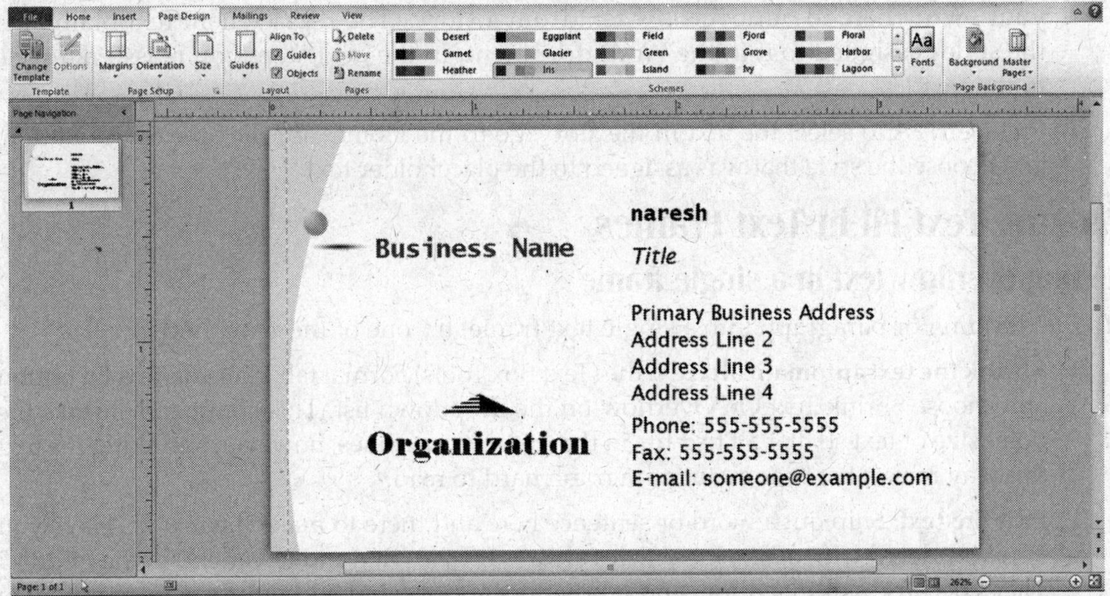

- ❒ Read the first paragraph of the placeholder text to see how many words can fit in the text frames that hold the story. Each placeholder story starts with a sentence describing roughly how many words are in the story. You can spare yourself a lot of time and trouble by making the replacement text roughly as many words as the placeholder text.

- In Word, write the text and save the text in a file. You can call on all the Word commands to edit the text. You can also copy text from elsewhere into the Word document. Later you will copy this file into Publisher. The status bar in Word tells you how many words are in a file. See if you can keep to the number of words that are in the place holder text.
- In Publisher, click in the placeholder text, go to the Home tab, click the Styles button, and note on the Styles drop-down list which style has been assigned to the place holder text. You can tell which style has been assigned to the text because it is selected on the Styles drop-down list. You will assign the style that is currently applied to the text to the replacement text you insert into the text frame.
- If necessary, press Ctrl+A to select the text in the story, and with the text selected, right-click and choose Change Text Text File. You see the Insert Text dialog box. You can also open this dialog box by going to the Insert tab and clicking the Insert File button.
- Select the Word file with the replacement text and click the OK button. Replacement text from the Word file "flows" into the text frame or frames. If the replacement text doesn't fit in the text frames allotted to the story, you see the Autoflow dialog box. You can click the Yes button to tell Publisher to flow the text into different text frames in the publication, but I recommend clicking No in the Autoflow dialog box. Later in this chapter, "Making text flow from frame to frame" explains how to decide on your own where to put overflow text from a story. The replacement text maintains the styles assigned to it in the Word document. In the next step, you reassign a style to the text.
- Press Ctrl+A to select the text in the story, go to the Home tab, click the Styles button, and choose the style that was assigned to the placeholder text.

Making Text Fit in Text Frames

Fitting overflow text in a single frame

To fit a heading or paragraph into a single text frame, try one of these methods:

- **Shrink the text automatically:** On the (Text Box Tools) Format tab, click the Text Fit button and choose Shrink Text On Overflow on the dropdown list. This command shrinks the point size of text so that all text fits in the frame. Sometimes, however, shrinking the text this way makes the heading or paragraph hard to read.
- **Edit the text:** Snip out a word or sentence here and there to make the text fit. Have you ever wondered why magazine articles always fill the page and never end in the middle? That's because skillful editors and typesetters remove and add words here and there to make the story fit the page.

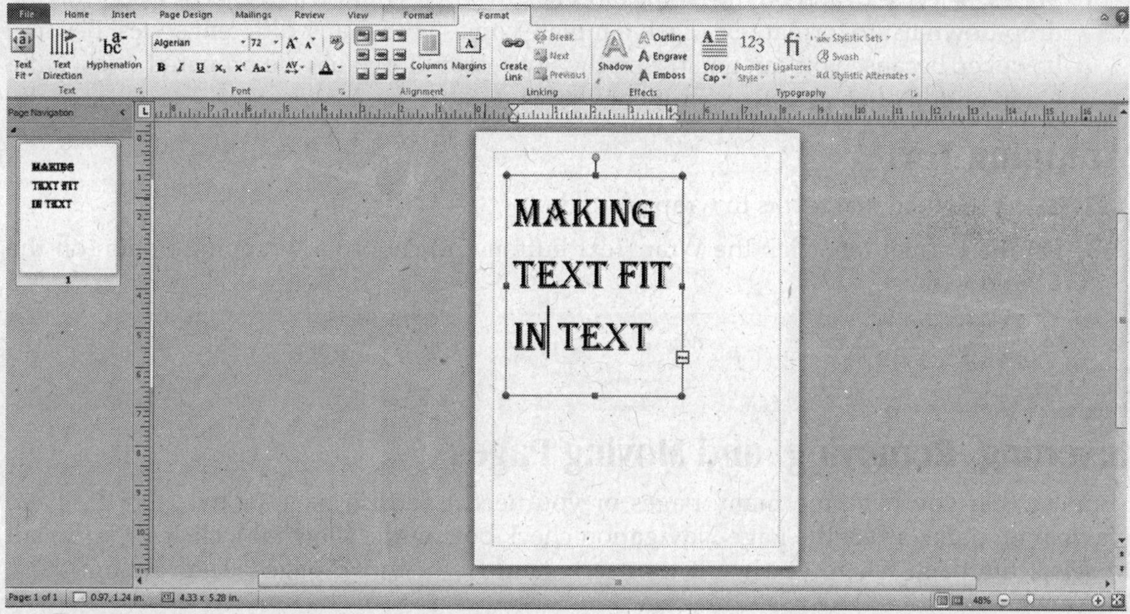

Making Text Fit in Text Frames

Make the text frame margins smaller: Like a page, text frames have internal margins to keep text from getting too close to the frame border. To shrink these margins and make more room for text, go to the (TextBox Tools) Format tab, click the Margins button, and choose Narrow onthe drop-down list. You can also choose Custom Margins, and on the Text Box tab of the Format Text Box dialog box, enter smaller measurements for the text box margins.

Making text flow from frame to frame

Create a new text box for the overflow text and follow these steps to direct text from one frame to another in your publication:

- Select the text frame with overflowing text. You can tell when text is overflowing because the Text in Overflow icon appears in the lower-right corner of the frame
- On the (Text Box) Formatting tab, click the Create Link button. The pointer turns into an overflowing pitcher after you click the button.
- Move the pointer over the box that you want the text to flow into. You may have to click a page navigation button to go to another page.
- Click in the target text box to make the text flow there.

Formatting Text

Use these methods to format the text in a publication:

- **Home tab font and paragraph commands:** The commands on the Home tab for changing the look of text and paragraphs are nearly identical to the Home tab commands in Word and PowerPoint.

- **Styles:** Select text, and on the Home tab, click the Styles button and choose a style on the drop-down list to format text. Each template comes with many different styles. Beware, however, because you can get lost on the Style drop-down list. Be prepared to click the Undo button often as you experiment with styles.

Wrapping Text

- Select the item that text is to wrap around.
- On the Format tab, click the Wrap Text button and choose a wrapping option on the drop-down list.

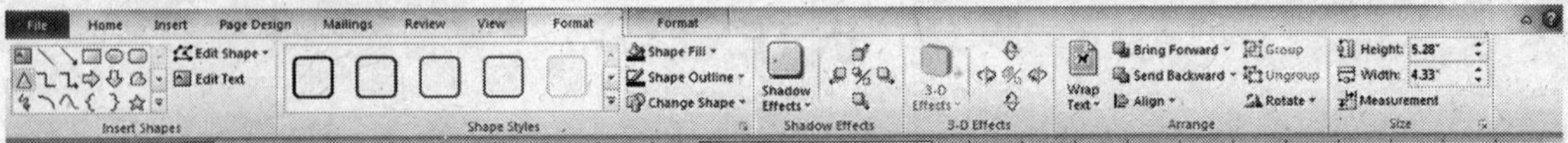

Inserting, Removing, and Moving Pages

Suppose that you have too many pages or you need to add a page or two. On the Page Navigation pane (select the Page Navigation check box on the View tab), click a thumbnail to select the page where you want to insert, remove, or move pages. Then follow these instructions:

- **Inserting a new page:** On the Insert tab, click the Page button and choose an option on the drop-down list:
- **Insert Blank Page:** Inserts an empty page.
- **Insert Duplicate Page:** Inserts a page identical to the thumbnail page you selected.
- **Insert Page:** Opens the Insert Page dialog box, where you can enter the number of pages you want to insert and click an option button to put the new pages before or after the page you selected. You can also tell Publisher what to put on the new page or pages.
- **Removing a page:** On the Page Design tab, click the Delete button. You can also right-click a page thumbnail and choose Delete.
- **Moving a page:** On the Page Design tab, click the Move button. Give instructions for moving the page in the Move Page dialog box and click OK.

Points to Remember

- ☆ Make custom frames to place different objects
- ☆ Use different types of frames as per your need
- ☆ Keep in mind that you do everything in the frame, since on printing & publishing the material in frame will appear

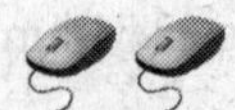

MS Outlook

What is Microsoft Outlook?

Microsoft Outlook 2010 offers premium business and personal e-mail management tools to more than 500 million Microsoft Office users worldwide. With the release of Outlook 2010, you get a richer set of experiences to meet your communication needs at work, home, and school.

From a redesigned look to advanced e-mail organization, search, communication and social networking features, Outlook 2010 provides you with a world-class experience to stay productive and in touch with your personal and business networks.

Add an e-mail account

Before you can send and receive e-mail messages using Outlook 2010, you must add and configure an e-mail account. If you have used an earlier version of Microsoft Outlook on the same computer where you have installed Outlook 2010, your account settings are automatically imported.

If you are new to Outlook or are installing Outlook 2010 on a new computer, the Auto Account Setup feature automatically starts and helps you configure account settings for your e-mail accounts. This setup requires only your name, e-mail address, and password. If your e-mail account cannot be automatically configured, you must enter the required additional information manually.

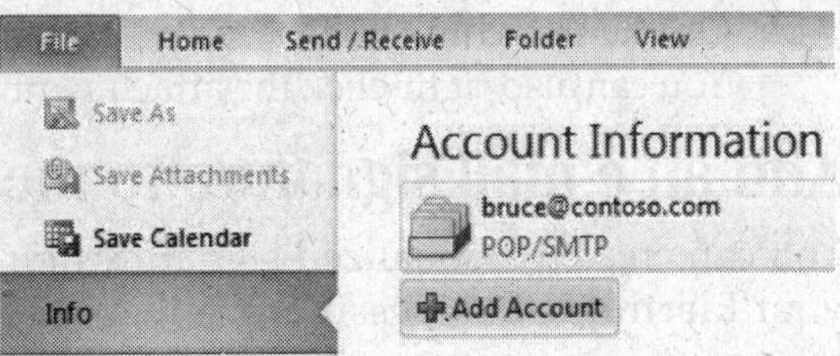

- Click the File tab.
- Under Account Information, and click Add Account.

Create a new e-mail message

Outlook 2010 enables you to communicate with one or more recipients with a rich set of features and customizations.

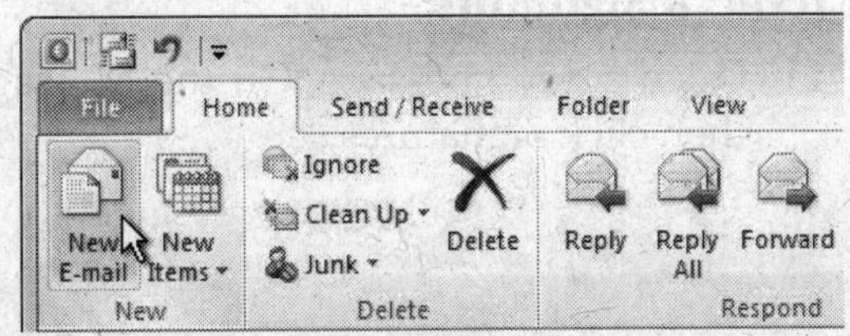

- In Mail, on the Home tab, in the New group, click New E-mail.

Keyboard shortcut: To create an e-mail message, press CTRL+SHIFT+M.

Forward or reply to an e-mail message

- On the Home or Message tab, in the Respond group, click Reply, Reply All, or Forward.

Note....

The name of the tab depends on whether the message is selected in the message list or opened in its own window.

To remove a name from the To and Cc lines, click the name and then press DELETE. To add a recipient, click in the To, Cc or Bcc box and enter the recipient.

Add an attachment to an e-mail message

Files can be attached to an e-mail message. Also, other Outlook items, such as messages, contacts, or tasks can be included with messages that you send.

- Create a message, or for an existing message, click Reply, Reply All, or Forward.
- In the message window, on the Message tab, in the Include group, click Attach File.

Open or save an e-mail message attachment

You can open an attachment from the Reading Pane, or from an open message. After opening and viewing an attachment, you may choose to save it to a disk drive. If a message has more than one attachment, you can save multiple attachments as a group or one at a time.

Open an attachment

- Double-click the attachment.

Save an attachment

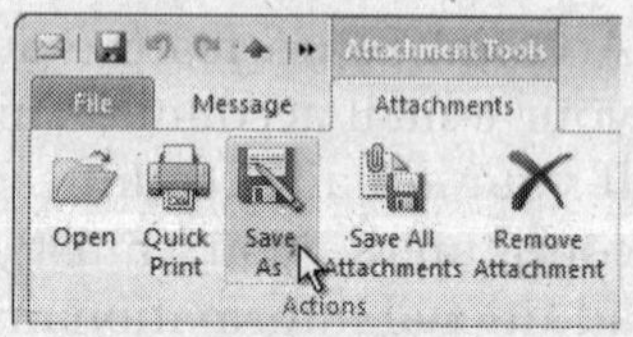

- Click the attachment in the Reading Pane or the open message.
- On the Attachments tab, in the Actions group, click Save As. You can also right-click the attachment, and then click Save As.

Add an e-mail signature to messages

You can create personalized signatures for your e-mail messages that include text, images, your **Electronic Business Card**, a logo, or even an image of your handwritten signature.

Create a signature

- Open a new message. On the Message tab, in the Include group, click Signature, and then click Signatures.

- ❐ On the E-mail Signature tab, click New.

Add a signature

- ❐ In a new message, on the Message tab, in the Include group, click Signature, and then click the signature that you want.

Create a calendar appointment

Appointments are activities that you schedule in your calendar that do not involve inviting other people or reserving resources.

- ❐ In Calendar, on the Home tab, in the New group, click New Appointment. Alternately, you can right-click a time block in your calendar grid, and then click New Appointment.

Keyboard shortcut: To create an appointment, press CTRL+SHIFT+A.

Schedule a meeting with other people

A meeting is an appointment that includes other people and can include resources such as conference rooms. Responses to your meeting requests appear in your **Inbox**.

- ❐ In Calendar, on the Home tab, in the New group, click New Meeting.

Keyboard shortcut: To create a new meeting request from any folder in Outlook, press CTRL+SHIFT+Q.

Set a reminder

You can set or remove reminders for a variety of items, including e-mail messages, appointments, and contacts.

For appointments or meetings

In an open item, on the Appointment or Meeting tab, in the Options group, in the Reminder drop-down list, select the amount of time before the appointment or meeting when you want the reminder to appear. To turn a reminder off, select None.

For e-mail messages, contacts, and tasks

- ❐ On the Home tab, in the Tags group, click Follow Up, and then click Add Reminder.

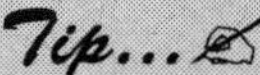

You can quickly flag e-mail messages as to-do items by using reminders. Right-click the Flag Status column in the message list. Or if you have the message open, on the Message tab, in the Tracking group, click Follow Up, and then click Add Reminder.

Create a contact

Contacts can be as simple as a name and e-mail address, or include additional detailed information such as street address, multiple phone numbers, a picture, birthdays, and any other information that relates to the contact.

- ❒ In Contacts, on the Home tab, in the New group, click New Contact.

Keyboard shortcut: To create a contact from any folder in Outlook, press CTRL+SHIFT+C.

Create a task

Many people keep a list of things to do — on paper, in a spreadsheet, or with a combination of paper and electronic methods. In Microsoft Outlook you can combine various lists into one, get reminders and track task progress.

- ❒ In Tasks, on the Home tab, in the New group, click New Task.

Keyboard shortcut: To create a new task, press CTRL+SHIFT+K.

Create a note

Notes are the electronic equivalent of paper sticky notes. Use notes to jot down questions, ideas, reminders, and anything you would write on paper.

- ❒ In Notes, in the New group, and click New Note.

Keyboard shortcut: To create a note, press CTRL+SHIFT+N.

Print an e-mail message, contact, calendar item, or task

You can print individual items, such as e-mail messages, contacts, or calendar items, or larger views, such as calendars, address books, or content lists of Mail folders.

The procedure for printing is the same in Mail, Calendar, or any other folders in Microsoft Outlook — all printing settings and functions are found in the Backstage view. Click the File tab to open the Backstage view.

- ❒ Click an item or folder in Outlook that you want to print.
- ❒ Click the File tab.

Points to Remembe

- ☆ Always write the right email id of the person you want to send an email to.
- ☆ Check attachment if any before you click the send button.

Adobe Photoshop

Are you interested in creating, modifying, combining and/or optimising digital images on your computer? This chapter introduces you to Abode Photoshop CS5, a popular software application for working with digital images.

Installing Photoshop

Look for Trial Versions of Adobe Programs, visit www.adobe.com/downloads to download trial versions of the software. Get up to 30 days testing period & then you can purchase the same.

Minimum Requirement needed:

Windows

- Intel® Pentium® 4 or AMD Athlon® 64 processor
- Microsoft® Windows® XP* with Service Pack 3 or Windows 7 with Service Pack 1
- 1GB of RAM
- 1GB of available hard-disk space for installation; additional free space required during installation (cannot install on removable flash storage devices)
- 1024x768 display (1280x800 recommended) with 16-bit colour and 256MB (512MB recommended) of VRAM
- OpenGL 2.0–capable system
- DVD-ROM drive

This software will not operate without activation. Broadband Internet connection and registration are required for software activation, validation of subscriptions, and access to online services. Phone activation is not available.

Lets Install Photoshop on our system.

Setups:

- Browse for the setup.exe in your DVD/ Downloaded Package (Here a single Example to install Photoshop)

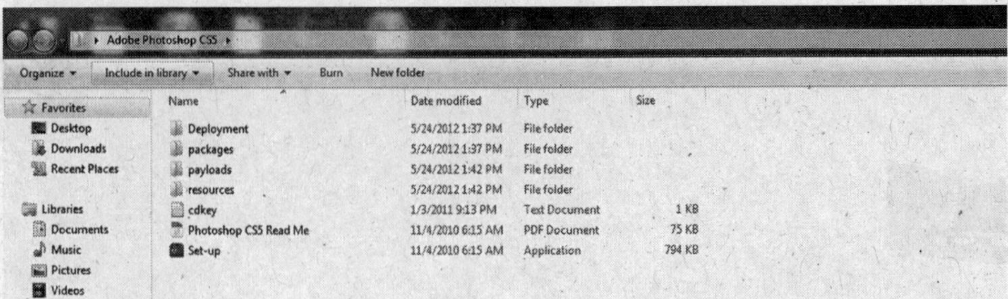

- ❒ Run Setup.exe

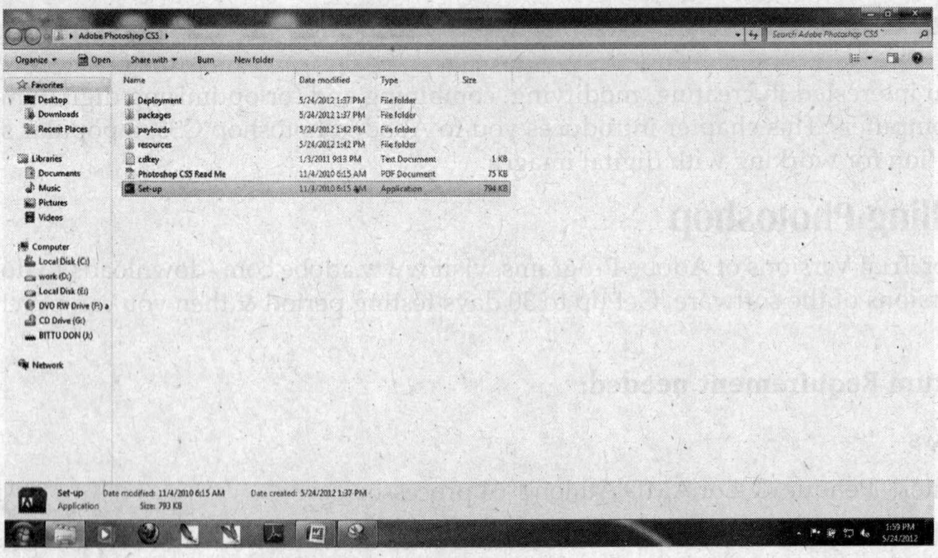

- ❒ Wait for setup to start, a dialog box will open

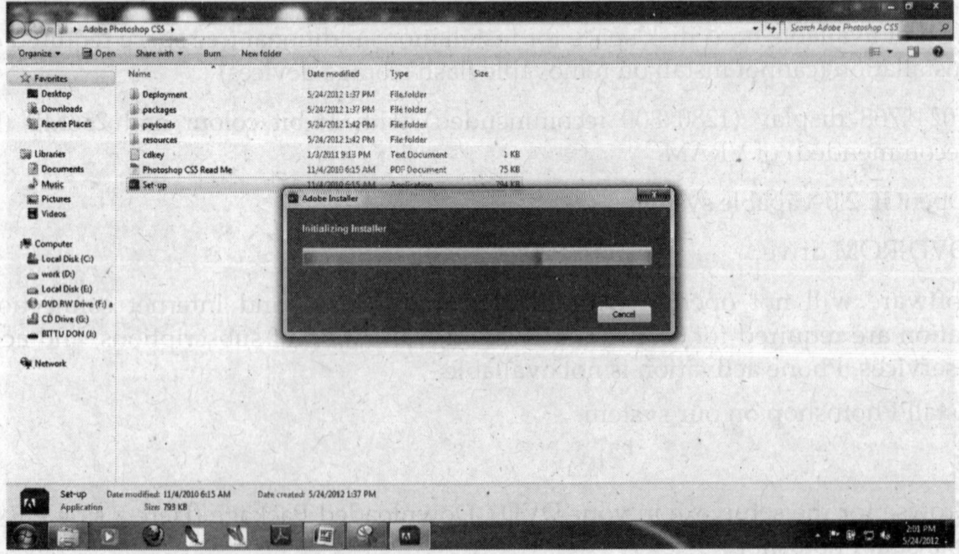

- ❒ Read the agreement and click install

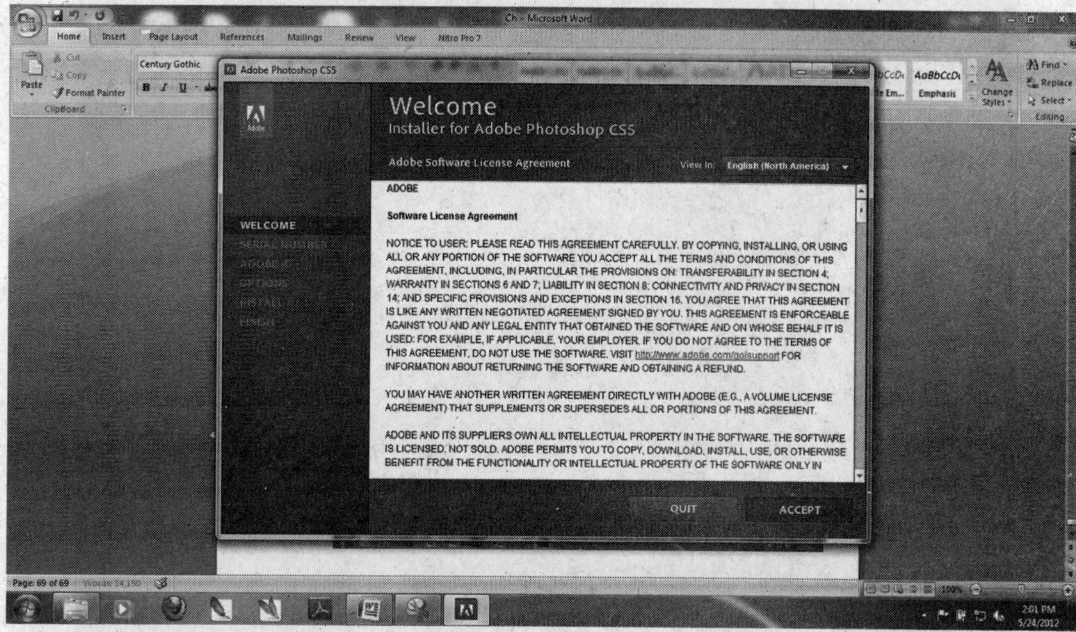

- ❒ Enter your license number or click to install as trial, select your Language & continue

- ❒ Create your adobe ID or skip if you like

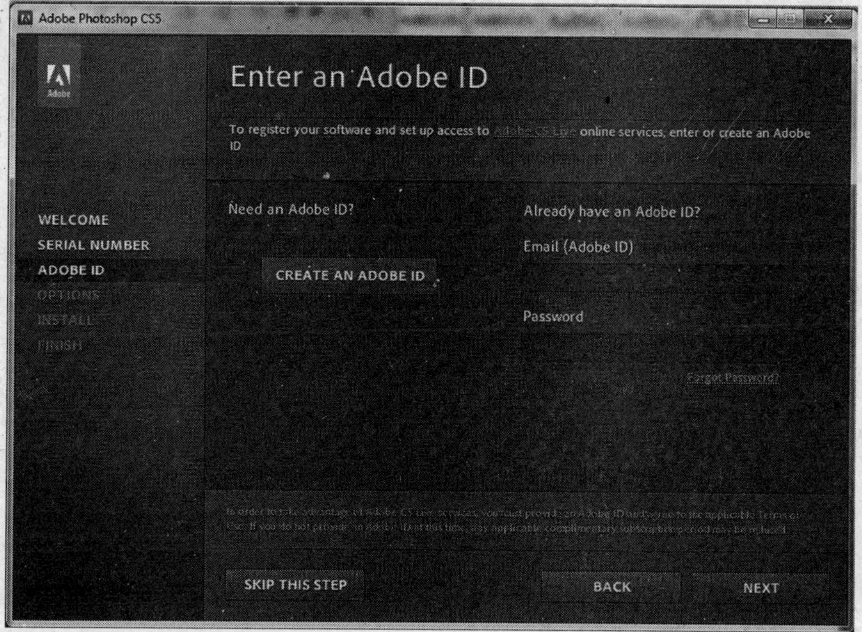

- Choose directory to install your product

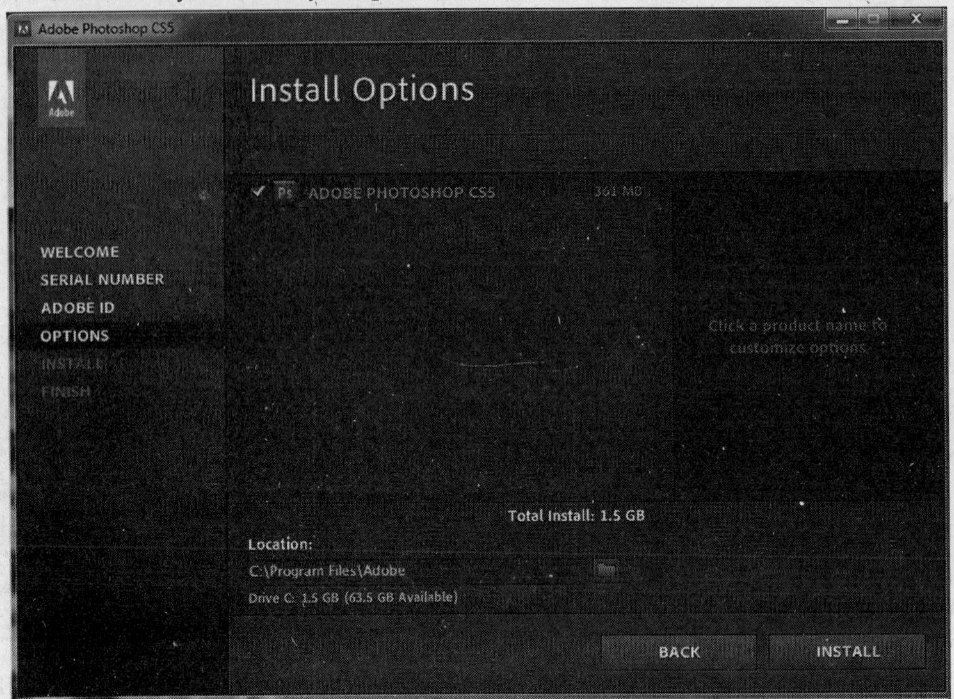

- Click on button Install, the following screen will appear. Wait for sometime & you are done

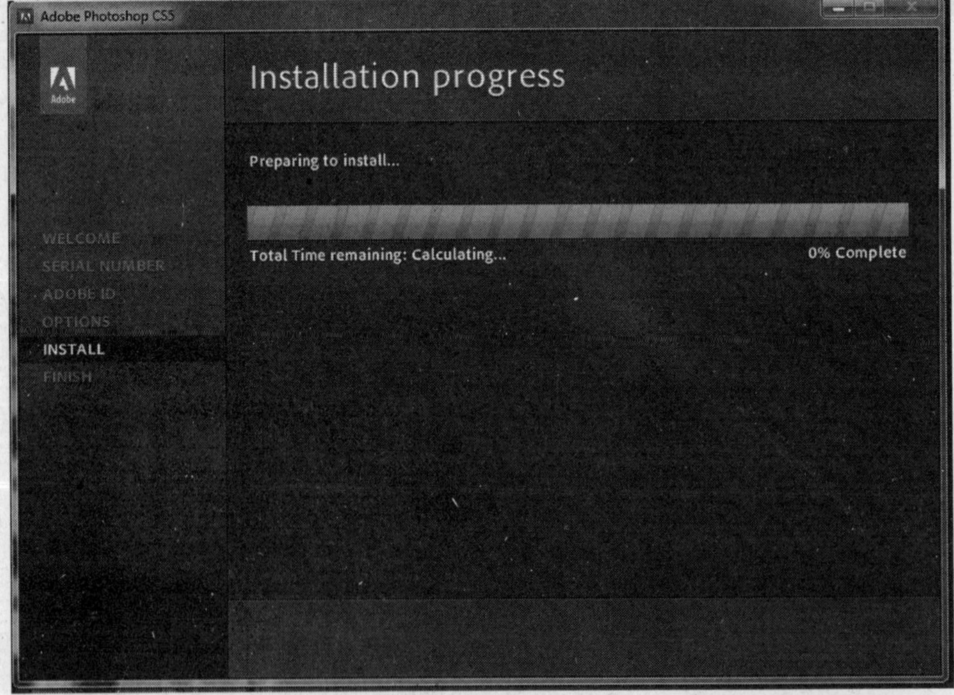

Continue your Experience online.

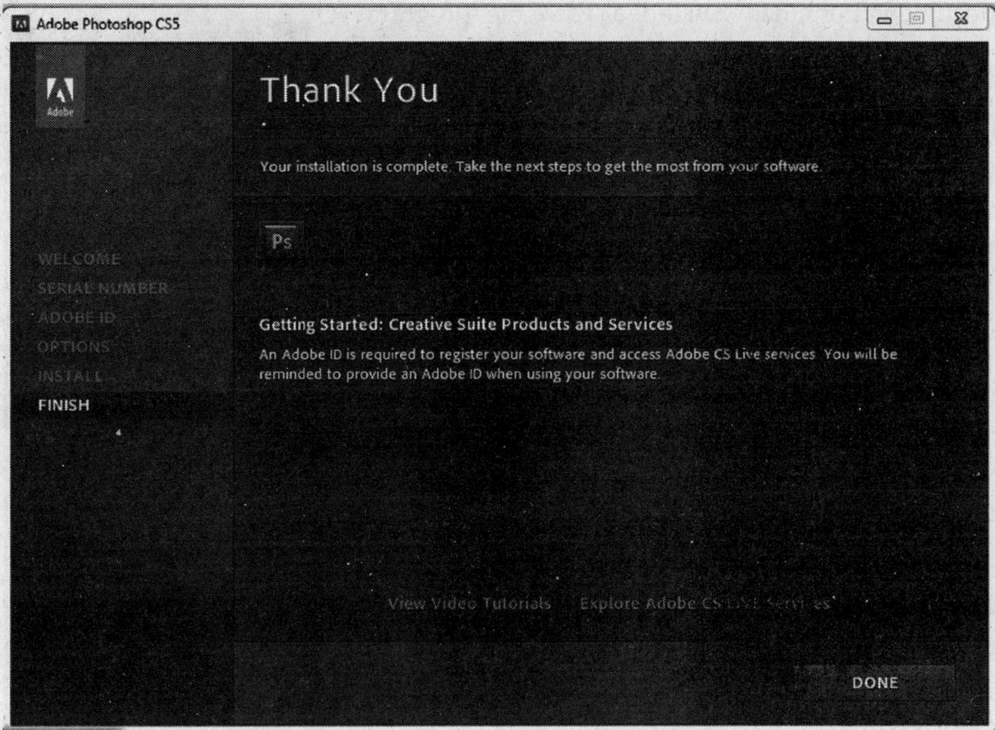

You are done! Now we can begin….!

Menus & their Working

Menus

Menus that appear in the CS5 programs:

- **File:** Contains many commands that control the overall document, such as creating, opening, saving, printing, and setting general properties for the document. The File menu may also include options for importing or exporting data into or from the current document.
- **Edit:** Contains options and commands for editing the current document. Commands include copying, pasting, and selecting as well as options for opening preferences and setting dialog boxes that are used to control parts of the document. Commands for spell-checking and transforming objects are also common parts of the Edit menu.
- **View:** Contains options for changing the level of magnification of the document. The View menu also sometimes includes options for viewing the workspace in different ways, showing rules, grids, or guides, and turning snapping on and off.
- **Window:** Contains options primarily used to open or close whatever panels are available in the program. You can also choose how to view the workspace and save a favourite arrangement of the workspace.

- **Help:** Contains the option to open the Help documentation that's included with the program. This menu may also include information about updating the software, registration, and tutorials.

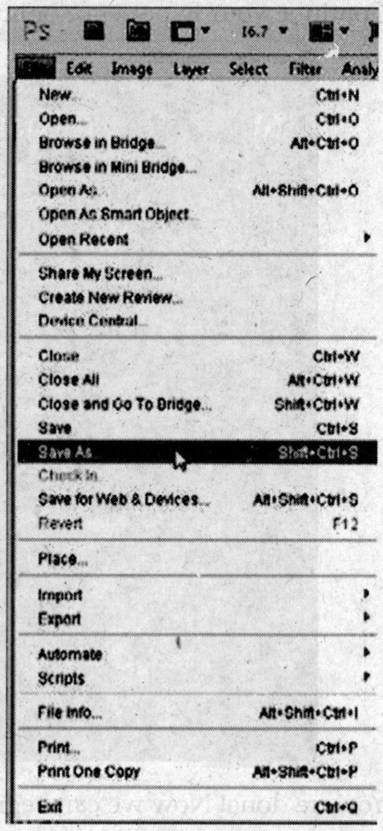

Dialog Boxes

A *dialog box* is a window that contains a combination of options formatted as drop-down lists, panes, text fields, option buttons, check boxes, and buttons that enable you to make settings and enter information or data as necessary.

It helps in controlling the files. Some tasks you perform by using dialog boxes:

- Save a new version of a file.
- Specify printing or page-setup options.
- Set up preferences for the software you're using.
- Check the spelling of text in a document.
- Open a new document.

Menu Options

The following menu options are found in several CS5 programs, and these commands either perform similar (or the same) functions or they open similar dialog boxes:

- **New:** Creates a brand-new document in the native file format. For example, in InDesign, a new *INDD* (the extension for InDesign documents) file is created by choosing File⇨New⇨Document. You can sometimes choose the type of new file you want to create.
- **Open:** Opens a dialog box where you can choose a (supported) file to open on your hard drive or a disk.
- **Close:** Closes the current document. If it has unsaved changes, you're prompted to save those changes first.
- **Save:** Saves the changes you've made to the current document.
- **Save As:** Saves a new copy of the current document.
- **Import:** Imports a file, such as an image or sound file, into the current document.
- **Export:** Exports the current data to a specified file format. You can sometimes select several different kinds of file formats to save the current data in.
- **Copy:** Copies the selected data to the computer's Clipboard.
- **Paste:** Pastes the data from the Clipboard into the current document.
- **Undo:** Undoes the most recent task you performed in the program. For example, if you just created a rectangle, the rectangle is removed from the document.
- **Redo:** Repeats the steps you applied the Undo command to. For example, if you removed that rectangle you created, the Redo command adds it back to the document.

- ❒ **Zoom In:** Magnifies the document so that you can view and edit its con- tents closely.
- ❒ **Zoom Out:** Scales the view smaller so that you can see more of the document at a time.
- ❒ **Help:** Opens the Help documentation for the current program.

Keyboard Shortcuts

Command	Shortcut
New	Ctrl+N
Open	Ctrl+O
Save	Ctrl+S
Undo	Ctrl+Z
Redo	Shift+Ctrl+Z
Copy	Ctrl+C
Paste	Ctrl+V
Print	Ctrl+P
Preferences (General)	Ctrl+K
Help	F1 or sometimes Ctrl+?

Panels

Panel is an integral part of working with most of the programs in Adobe Creative Suite 5 (CS5) because it contains many of the controls and tools you use when you're creating or editing a document.

- ❒ **To expand tools to two columns:** Click the right-facing double arrows on the gray bar on top of the tools.
- ❒ **To collapse tools to a single column:** Click the left-facing double arrows on the gray bar on top of the Tools panel.
- ❒ **To expand a docked panel:** Simply click the icon in the docking area, the panel you selected expands but goes away when you select a different panel.
- ❒ **To expand all docked panels:** Click the left-facing double-arrow icon at the top of the docking area; put away the panels by clicking the right- facing double-arrow icon in the gray bar above them.
- ❒ **To undock a panel:** Simply click the tab (where the panel name is located) and drag it out of the docking area. You can re-dock the panel by dragging the panel back into the docking area.

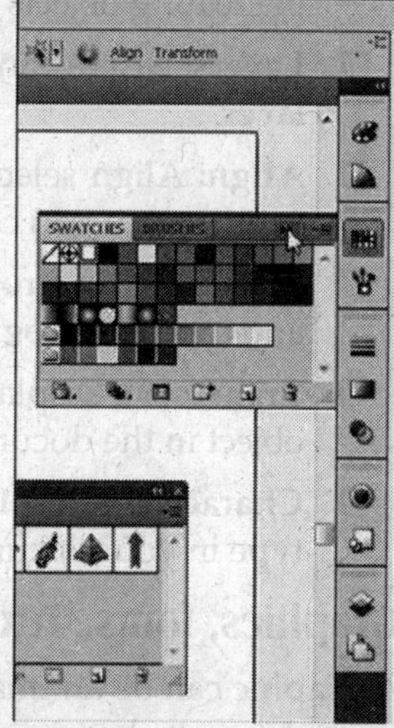

Panels in the Workspace

- ❒ **Open a panel:** Open a panel in a Creative Suite program by using the Window menu: Choose Window and then select the name of a panel. For example, to open the Swatches panel (which is similar in many programs in the suite), choose Window Swatches.

- **Close a panel:** If you need to open or close a panel's tab or panel altogether, just choose Window *Panel's Tab Name.* Sometimes a panel contains a close button.
- **Access the panel menu:** Panels have a panel menu, which opens when you click the arrow in the upper-right corner of the panel. The panel menu contains a bunch of options you can select that relate to the selected tab when you click the panel menu. When you select an option from the panel menu, it may execute an action or open a dialog box. Sometimes a panel menu has few options, but particular panels may have a bunch of related functionality and therefore many options on the panel menu. 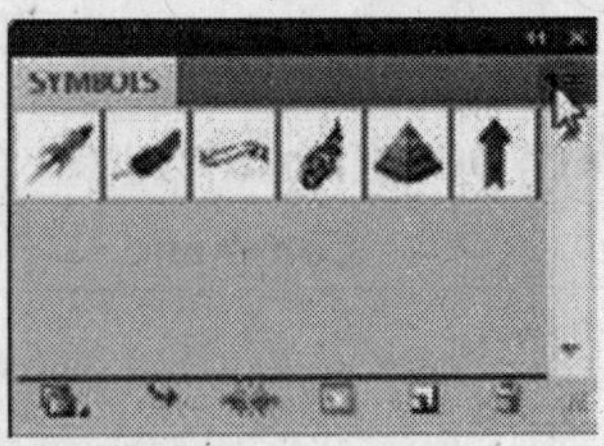
- **Minimize/maximize:** All you need to do to minimize a selected panel is click the Collapse to Icons double-arrow button on the title bar of the panel.

Some Common panels

- **Colour:** Select or mix colours for use in the document you're working on. You can use different colour modes and several ways of mixing or choosing colours in the Colours panel.
- **Info:** See information about the document itself or a particular selection you've made. The Info panel includes information on the size, positioning, and rotation of selected objects. You can't enter data into the Info panel: It only displays, not accepts, information, so you have to use the Transform panel (described in this list) to make these modifications, if necessary.
- **Swatches:** Create a swatch library, which can be saved and imported into other documents or other programs. You can store on the Swatches panel any colours and gradients you use repeatedly.
- **Tools:** You use this important panel, sometimes called the toolbox (and not available in all Creative Suite programs), to select tools — such as the Pencil, Brush, or Pen — to use in creating objects in a document.
- **Layers:** Display and select layers, change the layer order, and select items on a particular layer.
- **Align:** Align selected objects to each other or align them in relation to the document itself so that you can arrange objects precisely.
- **Stroke:** Select strokes and change their attributes, such as colour, width/ weight, style, and cap. The program you're using determines which attributes you can change.
- **Transform:** Display and change the shear (skew), rotation, position, and size of a selected object in the document. You can enter new values for each transformation.
- **Character:** Select fonts, font size, character spacing, and other settings related to using type in your documents.

Graphics, fonts, Texts & Printing

A graphic can be an image, a drawing, or a vector object. You can create graphics manually by making marks on a page or create them electronically using software.

Bitmap images

Bitmap images are pictures made up of many tiny squares, or bits, on an invisible grid. When these dots are next to each other, the picture is formed. Common kinds of bitmap files are BMP, GIF, JPEG, PICT, and TIFF

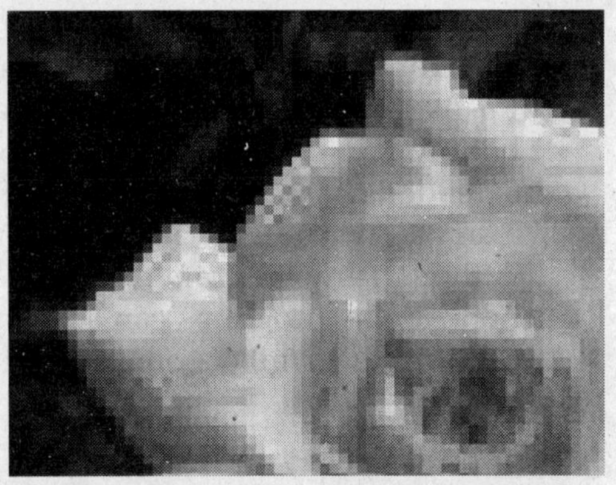

Bitmap images

Vector graphics

A vector image (or graphic or drawing) is quite different from a bitmap image. A vector image is created by a series of mathematical calculations or code that describes how the image should be formed. These calculations tell the computer how the lines should display and render on the page.

Vector graphics

Paths and Strokes

Paths are the vector lines and outlines you create in a document. You can use paths to outline an image, separate areas of text, or be part of an illustration you create.

A stroke is the colour, width, and style of the line that makes up the path you create.

Adding Text

You can add text to a document by using the Text tool or by importing the text from another source, such as Microsoft Word.

fonts

A font refers to the typeface of a set of characters. See Microsoft Office 2010 crash course to learn more.

Types of fonts

- ❐ **TrueType:** Like other digital typefaces, the *TrueType* font file contains information, such as outlines, hinting instructions, and character map- pings (which characters are included in the font). Available for both the Mac and Windows formats, the TrueType fonts designed for each oper- ating system have slight differences; therefore, Mac and Windows users can't share TrueType fonts.
- ❐ **PostScript (Type 1):** The scalable *PostScript* font system is compatible with PostScript printers; users can see fonts on the screen the same way the fonts would be printed. Type 1 font files consist of two files —- a screen font with bitmap information for onscreen display and a file with outline information for printing. For high-end printing, both parts of the Type 1 font files (Printer and Screen fonts) must be included with the file. Because of differences in their structure, Mac and Windows PostScript Type 1 fonts aren't cross-platform compatible.

- **OpenType:** The *OpenType* font technology was created in a joint effort between Adobe and Microsoft and is an extension of the TrueType font format that can also contain PostScript data. OpenType fonts are *cross- platform* — the same font file works under both Macintosh and Windows operating systems. This digital type format offers extended character sets and more advanced typographic controls. As with TrueType, a single file contains all the outline, metric, and bitmap data for an OpenType font. Although any program that supports TrueType fonts can use OpenType fonts, not all non-Adobe programs can access the full features of the OpenType font format. You can find the symbols on the Font menus of many of the CS5 programs representing the type of font.

Colour

RGB

RGB (Red, Green, Blue) is the colour mode used for onscreen presentation, such as an image displayed on the Web or a broadcast design for TV. Each colour displayed onscreen has a certain level (between 0 and 100 percent) of red, green, and blue to create the colour.

CMYK

CMYK — Cyan, Magenta, Yellow, and Key (or Black) — is the standard colour mode for print media, particularly in commercial printing such as what a service provider does.

grayscale

Grayscale refers to the different shades of gray that can be used when printing using only black ink on a white page.

swatches

A swatch is a good way to choose a colour. The Swatches panel in Creative Suite programs contains colours and sometimes gradients.

Mixing colours

A colour mixer, found in the Colour panel, helps you choose colours. You can use the Eyedropper tool to choose a colour.

Follow these steps to choose a colour in a specified colour mode:

- In a program that has a Colour panel, choose Window Colour to open the Colour panel (if it's not open already). The Colour panel is available in Illustrator, InDesign, and Photoshop.
- Click the Colour panel menu to choose a new colour mode. Open this menu by clicking the arrow button in the upper-right corner of the Colour panel.
- Choose the RGB colour mode from the panel menu that opens. The panel switches to RGB colour mode.
- In the Colour panel, click either the Fill box (solid square) or the Stroke box (hollow square) to choose the colour you want to change. If you click the Fill box, you can modify

the colour of a fill (the colour inside a shape). If you click the Stroke box, you can modify the colour of a stroke (the outline of a shape or a line).

- ❒ Use the sliders in the Colour panel to change the colour values. You can also change the percentage values to the right of each slider.
- ❒ After you choose a colour you're happy with, return to your document and create a new shape that uses the colour.

Printing Documents

To print a file as a PDF from Photoshop CS5, follow these steps:

- ❒ Choose File⇨Print. The Print dialog box opens, as shown below

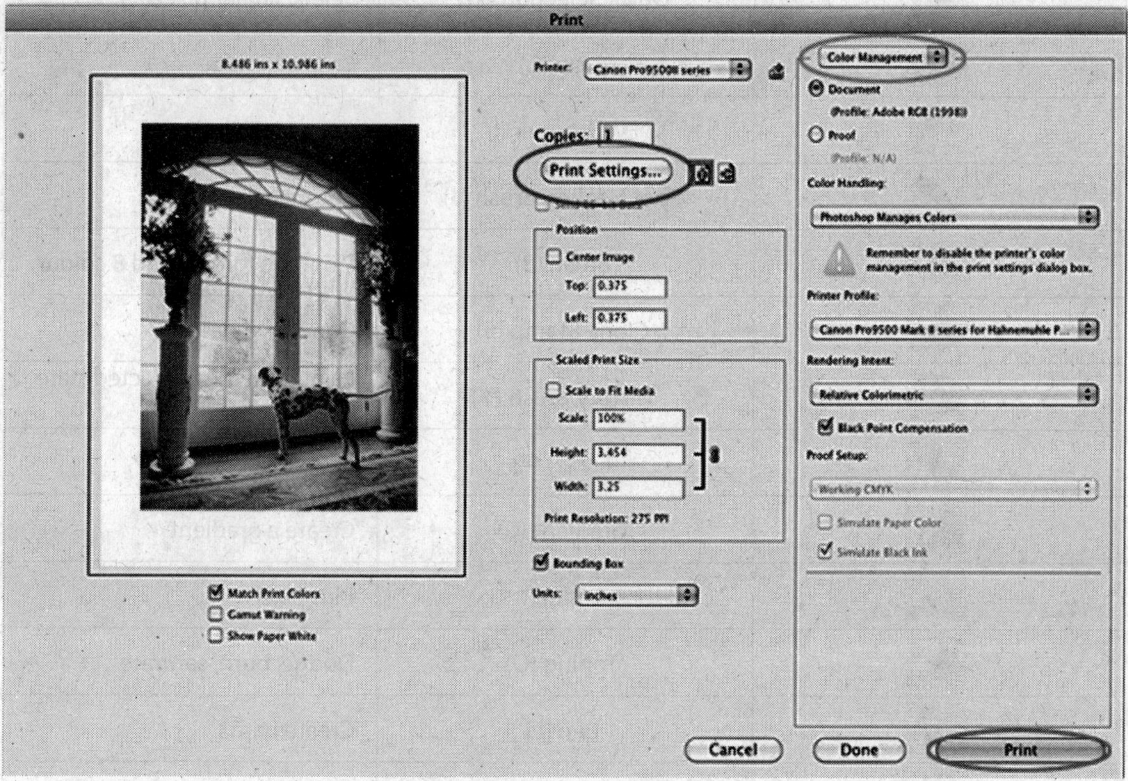

- ❒ From the Printer drop-down list, choose Adobe PDF. If you want to choose the settings for an installed printer, you can also select it here.
- ❒ If necessary, scale the image to fit the paper and then click the Print Settings button.
- ❒ From the Printer drop-down list, choose Adobe PDF.
- ❒ If you want to choose the settings for an installed printer, you can also select it here.
- ❒ If necessary, scale the image to fit the paper and then click the Print Settings button.

Photoshop CS5 Basics

This table lists the Photoshop tools, describes what each one is used for:

Button	Tool	What You Can Do with It
	Move (V)	Move selections or layers
	Marquee (M)	Select the image area
	Lasso (L)	Make freehand selections
	Quick Selection (W)	Select similar pixels
	Crop (C)	Crop an image
	Eyedropper (I)	Create HTML slices
	Spot Healing Brush (J)	Retouch flaws
	Brush (B)	Paint the foreground 8 colour
	Clone Stamp (S)	Copy pixel data
	History Brush (Y)	Paint from the 8 selected state
	Eraser (E)	Erase pixels
	Gradient (G)	Create a gradient
	Blur	Blur pixels
	Toning (O)	Dodge, burn, saturate
	Pen (P)	Create paths
	Type (T)	Create text
	Path Selection (A)	Select paths
	Vector Shape (U)	Create vector shapes
	3D Object Rotate (K)	Rotate 3D objects
	3D Camera Rotate (N)	Rotate 3D objects

Button	Tool	What You Can Do with It
	Hand (H)	Navigate page
	Zoom (Z)	Increase or decrease 2 the view

Opening an image

You can open an existing Photoshop image in one of several ways:

- Choose File⇨Open, select the file in the Open dialog box, and then click the Open button.
- Choose File⇨Browse. By selecting Browse instead of Open, you launch the Adobe Bridge application. Read more about Adobe Bridge later in this section.
- Double-click an image in the Mini Bridge panel.

Cropping an image

A simple but essential task is to crop an image. Cropping means to eliminate all parts of the image that aren't important to its composition.

Cropping is especially important in Photoshop. Each pixel, no matter what colour, takes up the same amount of information, so cropping eliminates unneeded pixels and saves on file size and processing time. For that reason, you should crop images before you start working on them.

You can crop an image in Photoshop CS5 in two ways:

- Use the Crop tool.
- Select an area with the Marquee tool and choose Image⇨Crop.

To crop an image by using the Crop tool, follow these steps:

- Press C to access the Crop tool and drag around the area of the image you want to crop to.
- If you need to adjust the crop area, drag the handles in the crop- bounding area.
- When you're satisfied with the crop-bounding area, double-click in the centre of the crop area or press the Return or Enter key to crop the image.
- If you want to cancel the crop, press the Esc key.

Working with Bitmap Images

Modes in Photoshop for images

Bitmap

Bitmap mode offers little more than the ability to work in black and white. Many tools are unusable, and most menu options are grayed out in this mode. If you're converting an image to bitmap, you must convert it to gray- scale first.

Grayscale

Use Grayscale mode, if you're creating black-and-white images with tonal values, specifically for printing to one colour. Grayscale mode supports 256 shades of gray in 8-bit colour mode. Photoshop can work with grayscale in 16-bit mode, which provides more information, but may limit your capabilities when working in Photoshop.

Duotone

Use Duotone mode when you're creating a one- to four-colour image created from spot colours (solid ink, such as Pantone colours). You can also use Duotone mode to create monotones, tritones, and quadtones. If you're producing a two-colour job, duotones create a beautiful solution to not having full colour.

The Pantone Matching System (PMS) helps keep printing inks consistent from one job to the next. By assigning a numbered Pantone colour, such as 485 for red, you eliminate the risk of one vendor (printer) using fire engine red and the next using orange-red for your company logo.

To create a duotone, follow these steps:

- Choose Image⇨Mode⇨Grayscale.
- Choose Image⇨Mode⇨Duotone.
- In the Duotone dialog box, choose Duotone from the Type drop-down list.

  Your choices range from *monotone* (one-colour) up to *quadtone* (four- colour). Black is assigned automatically as the first ink, but you can change it, if you like.
- To assign a second ink colour, click the white swatch immediately under the black swatch.

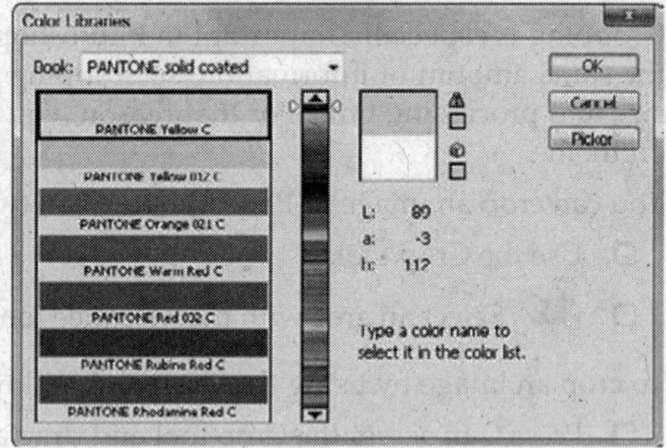

Creating a duotone

- Now **comes the fun part: Type (quickly!) the Pantone or PMS number you want to access and then click OK.**

  There's no text field for you to enter the number, so don't look for one. Just type the number while the Colour Libraries dialog box is open.

  Try entering 200, to select PMS 200. You can already see that you've created a tone curve.
- Click the Curve button to the left of the ink colour to further tweak the colours.
- Click and drag the curve to adjust the black in the shadow areas, perhaps to bring down the colour overall. Then experiment with the results.
- Click OK when you're finished

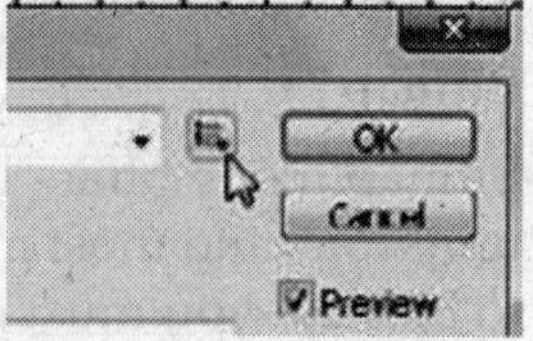

Index colour

Even if you don't work in Index colour, you probably have saved a file in this mode.

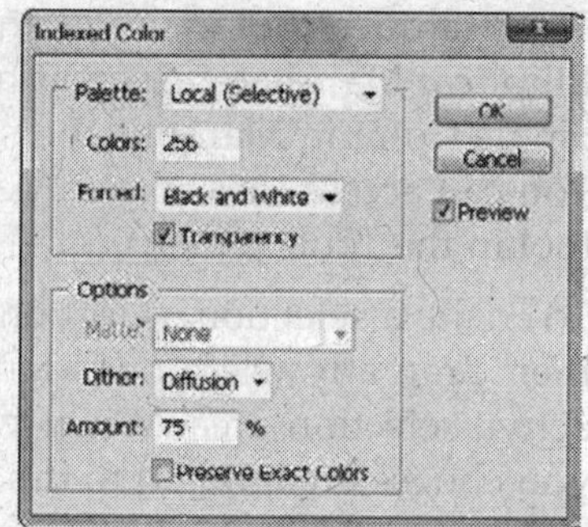

Working in Index colour

RGB

RGB (Red, Green, Blue) mode is the standard format you work in if you import images from a digital camera or scan images on a scanner. For complete access to features, RGB is probably the best colour mode to work in. If you're working on images for use on the Web, colour copiers, desktop colour printers, and onscreen presentations, stay in RGB mode.

CMYK

CMYK (Cyan, Magenta, Yellow, Black) mode is used for final separations for the press. Use a good magnifying glass to look closely at anything printed in colour and you may see the CMYK colours that created it. A typical four-colour printing press has a plate for each colour and runs the colours in the order of cyan, magenta, yellow, and then black.

LAB colour

The LAB (Lightness, A channel, and B channel) colour mode is used by many high-end colour professionals use because of its wide colour range. Using LAB, you can make adjustments to luminosity (lightness) without affecting colour. In this mode, you can select and change an L (lightness or luminosity) channel without affecting the A channel (green and red) and the B channel (blue and yellow).

Multichannel

Multichannel is used for many things; you can end up in this mode and not know how you got there. Deleting a channel from an RGB, a CMYK, or a LAB image automatically converts the image to Multichannel mode. This mode supports multiple spot colours.

Creating a Selection

You create selections by using selection tools. Think of *selections* as windows in which you can make changes to pixels. Areas not selected are masked, which means that they're unaffected by changes, much like when you tape window and door frames before painting the walls. In this section, we briefly describe the selection tools and show you how to use them. You must be familiar with these tools in order to do *anything* in Photoshop.

If you move a selection with the Move tool, pixels move as you drag, leaving a blank spot in the image. To clone a selection (to copy and move the selection at the same time), Alt+drag (Windows) or Option+drag (Mac) the selection with the Move tool.

Marquee tool

The Marquee tool is the main selection tool; by that, we mean that you use it most often for creating selections. The exception, of course, is when a special situation calls for a special tool — the Lasso, Magic Wand, Quick Selection, or new Refine Radius tool (located in the Refine Edge dialog box). Throughout this section, we describe creating (and then deselecting) an active selection area; we also provide you with tips for working with selections.

The Marquee tool includes the Rectangular Marquee (for creating rectangular selections), Elliptical Marquee (for creating round or elliptical selections), and Single Row Marquee or Single Column Marquee tools (for creating a selection of a single row or column of pixels). You can access these other Marquee tools by holding down the default Rectangle Marquee tool in the Tools panel.

To create a selection, select one of the Marquee tools (remember that you can press M) and then drag anywhere on your image. When you release the mouse button, you create an active selection area. When you're working on an active selection area, whichever effects you choose are applied to the whole selection.

To deselect an area, you have three choices:

- Choose Select⇨Deselect.
- Press Ctrl+D (Windows) or Ô+D (Mac).
- While using a selection tool, click outside the selection area.

Creating rectangular and elliptical selections

How you make a selection is important because it determines how realistic your edits appear on the image. You can use the following tips and tricks when creating both rectangular and elliptical selections:

- Add to a selection by holding down the Shift key; drag to create a second selection that intersects the original selection. The two selections become one big selection.
- Delete from an existing selection by holding down the Alt (Windows) or Option (Mac) key and then drag to create a second selection that intersects the original selection where you want to take away from the original selection.

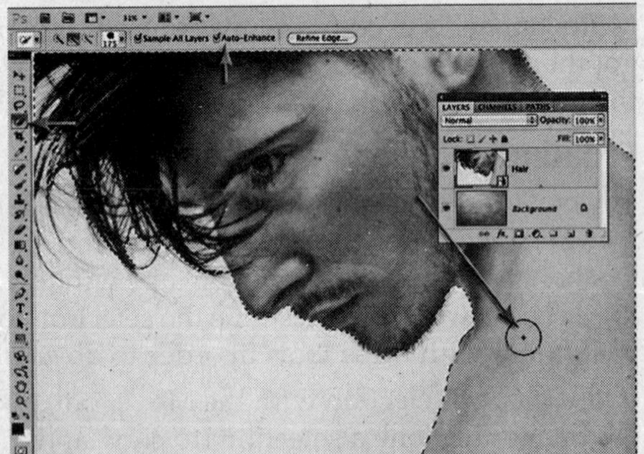

- Constrain a rectangle or an ellipse to a square or circle by Shift+dragging; make sure that you release the mouse button before you release the Shift key. Holding down the Shift key makes a square or circle only when there are no other selections. (Otherwise, it adds to the selection.)
- Make the selection from the centre by Alt+dragging (Windows) or Option+dragging (Mac); make sure that you release the mouse button before releasing the Alt (Windows) or Option (Mac) key.
- Create a square or circle from the centre outward by Alt+Shift+dragging (Windows) or Option+Shift+dragging (Mac). Again, make sure that you always release the mouse button before releasing the modifier keys.
- When making a selection, hold down the spacebar before releasing the mouse button to drag the selection to another location.

Setting a fixed size

If you've created an effect that you particularly like — say, changing a block of colour in your image — and you want to apply it multiple times throughout, you can do so. To make the same selection multiple times, follow these steps:

- ❒ With the Marquee tool selected, select Fixed Size from the Style drop-down list on the Options bar. You can also select Fixed Ratio from the Style drop-down list to create a proportionally correct selection not fixed to an exact size.
- ❒ On the Options bar, type the Width and Height values into the appropriate text fields. You can change ruler increments by choosing Edit⇨Preferences⇨Units and Rulers (Windows) or Photoshop⇨Preferences⇨Units and Rulers (Mac).
- ❒ Click the image. A selection sized to your values appears. With the selection tool, drag the selection to the location you want selected.

Making floating and non-floating selections

When you're using a selection tool, such as the Marquee tool, your selections are floating by default, which means that you can drag them to another location without affecting the underlying pixels.

The Lasso tool

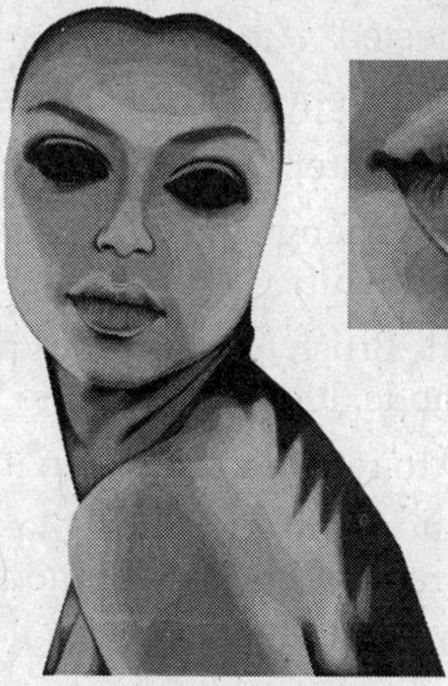

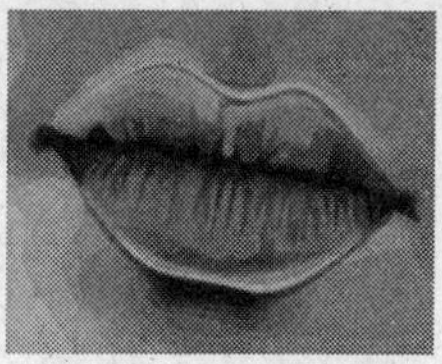

Use the Lasso tool for freeform selections (selections of an irregular shape). To use the Lasso tool, just drag and create a path surrounding the area to be selected. If you don't return to the starting point to close the selection before you release the mouse button, Photoshop completes the path by finding the most direct route back to your starting point.

Hold down the Lasso tool to show the hidden Lasso tools:

Polygonal Lasso tool: Click a start point and then click and release from point to point until you come back to close the selection.

Magnetic Lasso tool: Click to create a starting point and then hover the cursor near an edge in your image. The Magnetic Lasso tool is magnetically attracted to edges; as you move the cursor near an edge, the Magnetic Lasso tool creates a selection along that edge. Click to manually set points in the selection; when you return to the starting point, click to close the selection.

The Magic Wand tool

The Magic Wand tool is particularly helpful when you're working on an image of high contrast or with a limited number of colours. This tool selects individual pixels of similar shades and colours. Select the Magic Wand tool, click anywhere on an image, and hope for the best — the Magic Wand tool isn't magic. You decide how successful this tool is. What we mean is that you control how closely matched each pixel must be in order for the Magic Wand tool to include it in the selection. You do so by setting the tolerance level on the Options bar.

When you select the Magic Wand tool, a Tolerance text field appears on the Options bar. As a default, the tolerance is set to 32. When you click with a setting of 32, the Magic Wand tool selects all pixels within 32 shades (steps) of the colour you clicked. If it didn't select as much as you want, increase the value in the Tolerance text field (all the way up to 255). The number you enter varies with each individual selection. If you're selecting white napkins on an off-white tablecloth, you can set the number as low as 5 so that the selection doesn't leak into other areas. For coloured fabric with lots of tonal values, you might increase the tolerance to 150.

Quick Mask tool

To enter Quick Mask mode, create a selection and then press Q. (Pressing Q again exits you from Quick Mask mode.) You can also click the Quick Mask button at the bottom of the Tools panel. If you have a printing background, you'll notice that the Quick Mask mode, set at its default colour (red), resembles something that you may want to forget: rubylith and amberlith. (Remember slicing up those lovely films with Exacto blades before computer masking came along?) In Quick Mask mode, Photoshop shows your image as it appears through the mask. The clear part is selected; what's covered in the mask isn't selected.

To create and implement a quick mask, follow these steps:

- ❒ Press Q to enter Quick Mask mode.
- ❒ Press D to change the foreground and background colour boxes to the default colours of black and white.
- ❒ Select the Brush tool and start painting with black in the clear area of the image in Quick Mask mode. It doesn't have to be pretty; just get a stroke or two in there.
- ❒ Press Q to return to Selection mode.

  You're now out of Quick Mask mode. Notice that where you painted with black (it turned red in Quick Mask mode), the pixels are no longer selected.
- ❒ Press Q again to reenter Quick Mask mode and then press X.
- ❒ With the Brush tool, paint several white strokes in the red mask area. The white strokes turn clear in Quick Mask mode.
- ❒ Press Q to return to Selection mode.

Points to Remember

- ☆ Dialog box is a window that contains a combination of options and button that unable you to make setting and enter information or data as necessary
- ☆ Panel is an integral part of working with most of the programs in Adobe Creative Suite 5 (CS5) because it contains many of the controls and tools you use when you're creating or editing a document.

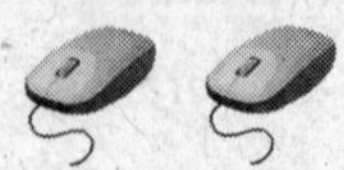

Tally 9 Basics

Tally 9 is a wonderful accounting software. It got good reputation in the field of business. A businessman wanted an accounting software which can be handled easily. Tally 9 fulfils this desire of a businessman. From a small sole trade business to large scale multinational companies accounts can easily keep in tally 9 data base. There is no difficulty in operating tally 9, accounting software. It uses 3 fundamental formulae for recording.

1st formula is to record different companies' creation, display and alteration.

2nd formula is to record all ledger accounts vie create, display and alter under different head or master accounts. 3rd formula à is to record all voucher entries.

Tally 9 the accounting software includes different data base of tds items, and service tax rate, etc. Tally 9 can easily be operated by non-commerce background persons also .In the bill wise voucher entries there no need of journal entry .That is good point of tally 9 and it goes to the favors who do not know double entry system. Education of tally 9 is very simple. All work in this software is under good discipline. Suppose if you want to pass voucher entry but, and you have not create ledger account of that voucher entry, then tally will not pass the voucher entry at that time. Tally 9 gives you facility to make ledger account in accounting vouchers. For this just press Alt +C for creating ledger account in accounting voucher.

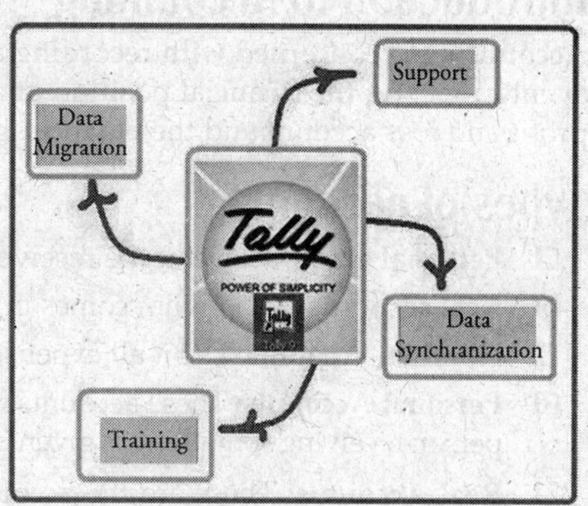

Tally 9 provides good accounting environment. Imports, export, print, email, web publishing direct from tally 9 software is the one of major reason of its popularity. If we compare tally 9 with other accounting software in India, the tally 9 gets No. 1 position in market. We can do comparison of its extra large facility regarding its VAT calculation, automatic interest calculation and fringe benefit tax calculation.

In tally 9 we can easily record of sale trade, partnership firm, MNC, business of commission agents, share market and money market business records and other service and professional sector records.

Tally 9 is becoming torch-bearer for all businessmen who were facing difficulty to record all their branches transactions. Tally 9's simple cost centre feature solve all problems regarding record of transaction more than one job, machine, process, department, branches and sub-branches .

The World's First Concurrent Multi-lingual Business Accounting & Inventory Management Software

Speed can be increased in tally 9 up to 30 to 40% from simple voucher entry passing through the following way:

- ❒ Multiple ledger creation
- ❒ Effective use of shortcut commands of tally 9
- ❒ Effective utilization of configuration button.

Let's start learning Accounting. Before we start learning Tally, lets learn what accounting is...!

Tally is the most popular financial accounting software in India and abroad.

Introduction to Accounting

Accounting is concerned with recording and processing all transactions with outsiders and events affecting the financial position of a firm. This leads to the preparation of the annual profit and loss account and the balance sheet.

Types of accounts

- ❒ **Personal accounts**: Debit the receiver, Credit the giver
- ❒ **Real accounts**: Debit what comes in, Credit what goes out
- ❒ **Nominal accounts**: Debit all expenses and losses, Credit all incomes and gains
- ❒ **Personal Accounts:** These accounts record a business dealing with persons or firms. The person receiving something is given debit and the person giving something is given credit.
- ❒ **Real Accounts:** These are the accounts of assets. Asset entering the business is given debit and asset leaving the business is given credit.
- ❒ **Nominal Accounts:** These account deal with expenses, incomes, profits and losses. Accounts of expenses and losses are debited and accounts of incomes and gains are credited.

Types of Journal book

Journal is derived from the French word "Jour" which means a day. **Journal**, therefore, means daily record of business transactions. **Journal** is a book of original entry because transactions are first written in the journal from which it is posted to ledger at any convenient time.

In small business firms, the volume of transactions is also small and hence, all of them can be recorded in one **subsidiary book** namely, the journal. But in large business houses since the number of transactions if large, it is impossible to enter them in one subsidiary book. Therefore, it is desirable to sub-divide the transactions according to their nature. And it is customary to keep each division of transactions in one book. The book in which the transactions are entered at first time are known as subsidiary books.

Kinds of subsidiary books/Journals are:

- ❐ Cash book to record cash receipts and payments.
- ❐ Purchase book for recording credit purchase of goods.
- ❐ Sales book or day book for recording all goods sold on credit
- ❐ Purchases Returns book for recording all goods sold on credit.
- ❐ Purchases Returns book or Returns outwards book for recording all purchases returned to the creditors.
- ❐ Sales Returns book or Returns Inwards book for recording all sales returned by the customers.
- ❐ Bills receivables book to keep record of bills received from customers.
- ❐ Bills payable book to keep record of bills payable to creditors.
- ❐ Journal proper to keep a record of those transactions for which there is no separate book.

The stages in book-keeping are:

- ❐ Recording the transactions in subsidiary books or books of prime entry.
- ❐ Posting the entries into the appropriate accounts in the main book called ledger.
- ❐ Preparing the Trial balance, thereby profit and loss account and Balance sheet.

Configuring a Company and setting Features

Company Creation

Installation of Tally 9

Different versions of Tally use different Installation methods. Previous versions will work by simply copying folders to hard driver. Newer versions are coming with MSI Installer setup. There are licensing methods for various versions which we will discuss later.

After Installing Tally you can open Tally by clicking Tally Icon on the Desktop. You will get the Gateway of Tally Screen.

On the Left hand side is 'List of Selected Companies' which lists name of the companies selected and Date of Last voucher Entry for those companies. Right hand bottom side has two buttons – features and Configure.

(F11) Features will help you enable or disable Accounting, Inventory and Statutory Features. These features are company specific, that means it will be applied only to the current company you are working with.

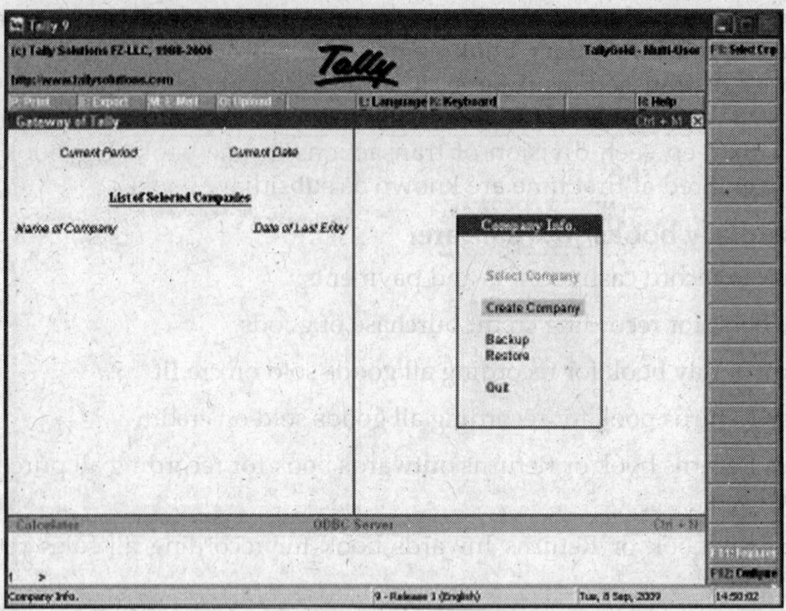

(F12) Configure is used to change Reporting, Printing and numerical styles, etc. This is applied to all companies in the DATA folder.

At the bottom of the screen there is a calculator option which can be used for arithmetic calculations.

Menu Selection in Tally

You can use keyboard up and down arrow keys for navigation. Also use the Hot Keys (Red colour letter). Use **ENTER** key to select and item.

Freshly Installed Tally has no Companies created. So you need to create company first.

Simply select '**Create Company**' and you will be taken to the next screen '**Company Creation**'.

Provide the following Details:

Name: Type the name of the company. The maximum characters for name field are 51.

Mailing Name: This will used to print name in all statements of accounts that are used to give parties outside of company.

Address: Address of the company

Statutory compliance: India for Indian companies

State: Respective state where your company operates

PIN code: Postal code

Telephone: Company phone number

E-Mail: Email ID if available

Currency Symbol: Rs. For Indians

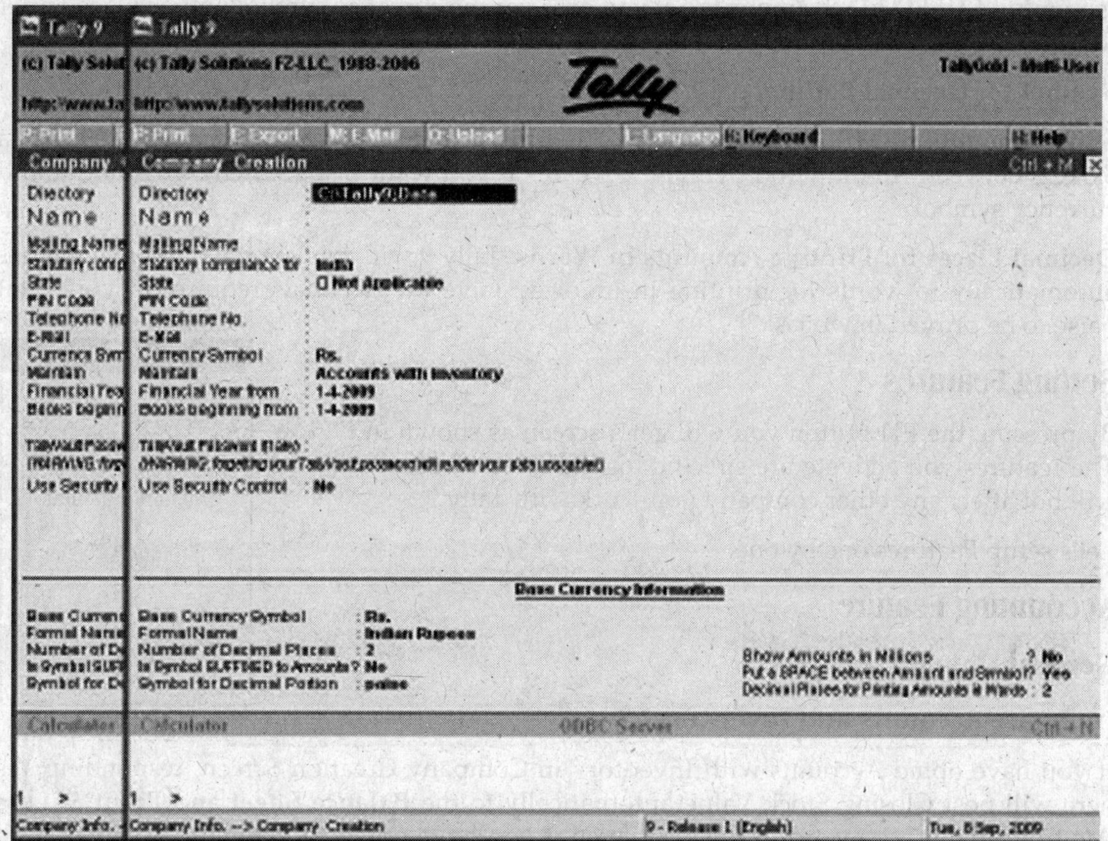

Maintain: In Tally 9 there are two options: 1. Account Only; 2. Accounts with inventory

Financial Year From: Enter beginning date of the financial year for which you wish to keep accounts. Books are closed exactly 12 months after this date.

Books Beginning from: The date from which you actually wish to maintain your accounts in Tally. By default this is the date you specify for the Financial year Beginning. You may, however, give a different date to maintain books only from that date. This must be a date further to the Beginning of the financial year. In such case, you give the opening balances for accounts as at the new date and start your entries from that date.

For example, you start maintaining accounts on tally from 01-09-2009; give that date for Books Beginning from and give the closing Balance on that date for ledger opening balances.

Use Security Control: If want to protect data with security control give Yes and you will be required to enter Name of Administrator and password (15 characters max.)

Base Currency Symbol: Rs. For India

Formal Name: Indian Rupees for India

Number of Decimal Places: 2 for India

Is Symbol SUFFIXED to amounts?: If you give yes the currency symbol will be placed after the amount. For example 100 Rs. instead of Rs. 100

Symbol for Decimal Portion: paise for India

Show amounts in Millions: Amount is shown in millions. For example, 1,000,000. Put a SPACE between Amount and Symbol: Give Yes if you want a space between amount and currency symbol.

Decimal Places for Printing Amounts in Words: Tally 9 will convert the numerical values automatically to words for printing in Invoices. Give the decimals required if you want paise to be printed in words.

Setting Features

By pressing the F11 button you will get a screen as shown in Figure. The features you activate are specific for the selected company and will not affect any other company you work with Tally 9.

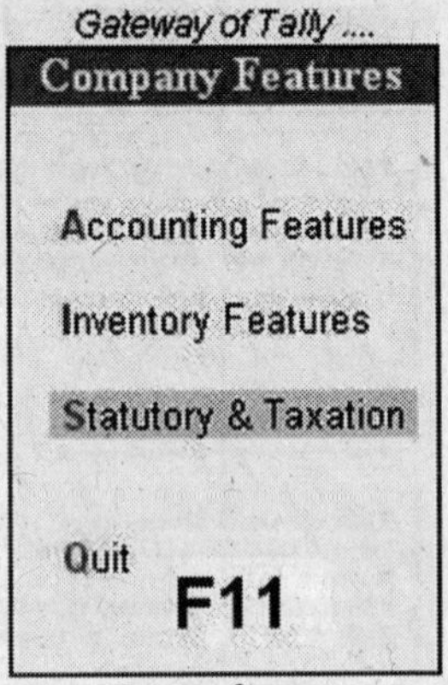

Let's setup Features one by one.

Gateway of Tally ....

Company Features
Accounting Features
Inventory Features
Statutory & Taxation
Quit

F11

Setting features

Accounting Feature

General

Integrate Accounts and Inventory?

If you have opted Accounts with Inventory in Company Creation Screen, responding Yes here will post Closing Stock Value automatically to the **Balance Sheet and Profit & Loss A/c** from Inventory records. However, even if you have opted to maintain Accounts with Inventory for the Company but want to input Closing Stock value on your own respond No, which will not post the stock valuation and you will have the option to manually put the figure in stock Ledger(s).

Income/Expense Statement instead of P & L?

Instead of Profit & Loss Statement it will give as Income/Expense Statement

Allow Multi-Currency?

If you work with Multi-Currency in the Company, respond Yes.

Maintain Budgets and Controls?

If you want to maintain Budgets, Credit Limits, respond Yes

Invoicing

Allow Invoicing?

Bills can be entered either in Voucher mode or in Invoice Mode. The elementary difference is: In Voucher mode, first accounting entries are done followed by Inventory allocation requiring prior computation of Bill Value whereas in Invoice mode, first Inventory entries

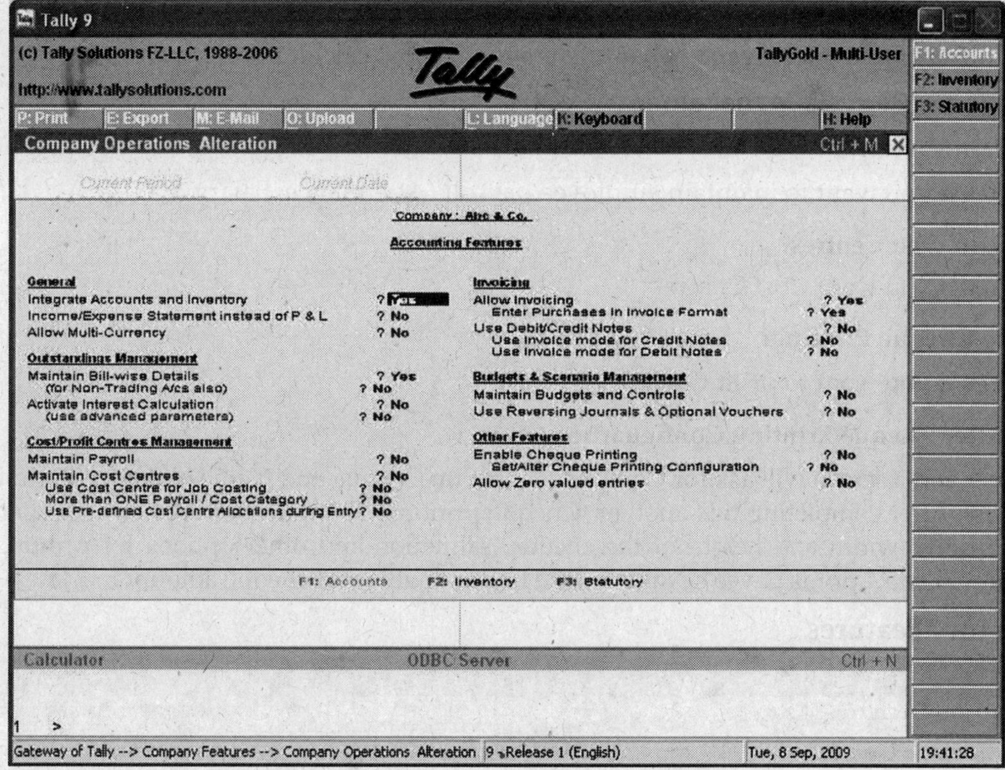

are made and the Bill Value is auto computed and Tax & Additional charges are also auto-computed. If you want Invoicing, give Yes.

Enter purchases in Invoice format?

If you want to enter **Purchase Bills** in Invoice format, give Yes.

Use Debit / Credit Notes?

If you want to generate **Debit Note** and **Credit Notes** you can enable this feature by giving **Yes**

Outstandings Management

Maintain Bill-Wise Details?

Set to Yes if you want to track bill-by-bill outstanding.

(for Non-Trading A/cs also?)

If you want bill-wise tracking for other accounts apart from sundry Creditors and Sundry Debtors, give yes

Activate Interest Calculation?

If you want to calculate Interests for Ledger Accounts, give Yes.

(Use advanced parameters?)

If you want to activate advanced parameters for Interest calculations, give Yes

Cost/Profit Centres Management

Maintain Payroll?

Give Yes if you want to maintain employee payroll (Attendance, Salary & Wages)

Maintain Cost Centres?

Give Yes if you want Cost Centres

Enable Cheque Printing?

Give Yes if you want to print Cheques.

Set / Alter Cheque Printing Configuartion

Give yes and a screen will ask for Company Name on Cheque and Name of Banks (From Bank Ledgers). After completing this another 'Cheque printing Configuration' Screen will open up. You can give width and height of the cheque, salutation and other options for printing the cheque. (Tally 5.4 prints payee's Name in one line and will print cheque amount in 2 lines).

Inventory Features

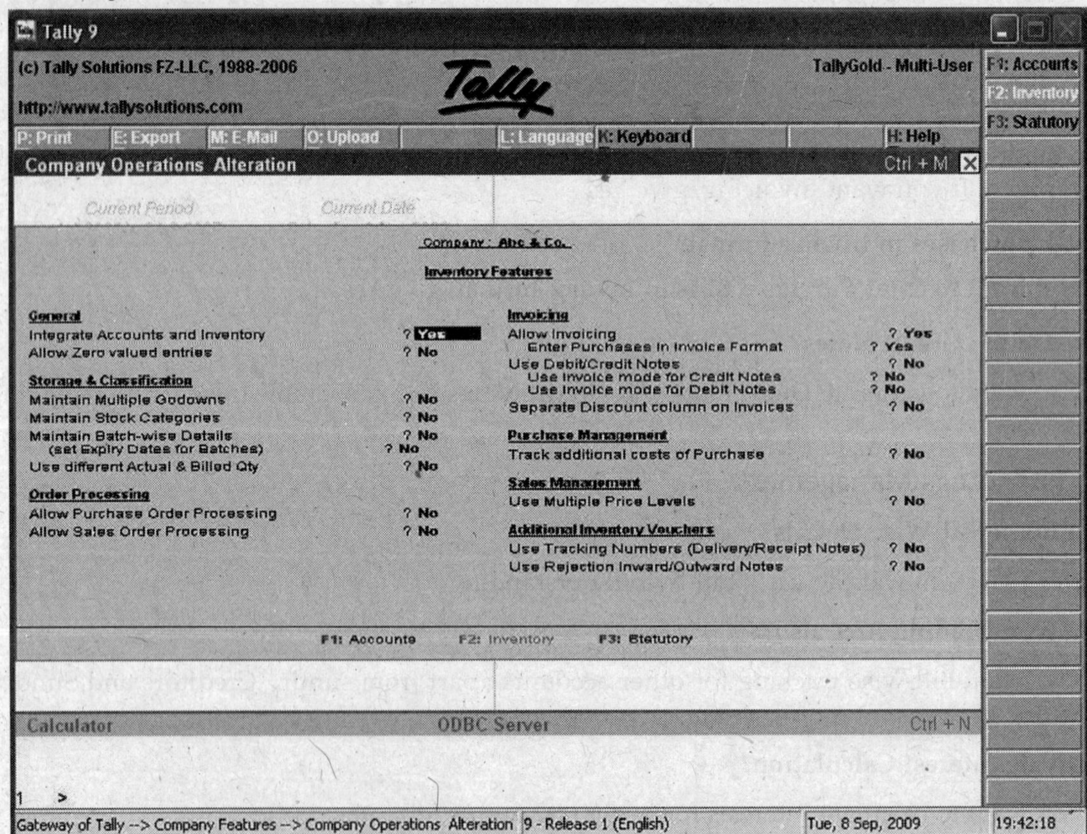

Allow zero valued entries?

Give Yes to allow zero valued entries.

Maintain Multiple Godowns?

Give Yes if you want to maintain more than on Godown/Warehouse.

Maintain Stock Categories?

Apart from Stock Groups, if you want to have secondary classification of items into Stock Categories, give Yes.

Maintain Batch-wise Details?

If you require Batch/Lot-wise details for items, give Yes

(Set Expiry Dates for Batches)?

Set to Yes if you require Manufacturing and Expiry Dates for the batches (applies to Medical drugs/medicines)

Use different Actual and Billed Qty?

If your billing quantity is different from actual quantity set this option to Yes, which will allow to input different quantity for Actual and Billed. Actual quantity will update stock and Billed Quantity will be used to compute Invoice.

Order Processing:

Allow purchase order processing?

Give Yes if you want to generate purchase order (PO)

Allow Sales order processing?

Give Yes if you want to generate Sales order

Use Tracking Numbers?

If goods move without Invoice and if you require Goods Inward or Goods Outward vouchers give Yes.

Use Rejection Inward/Outward Note?

If you require separate document for rejected items, i.e, Rejection-In for Goods returned to you by Buyers and Rejection-Out for Goods returned by you to sellers to record movement of goods without Accounting documents, set this option to Yes.

Statutory & Taxation

Enable Dealer – Excise?

Give Yes to enable Excise duty

Set/Alter Dealer Excise Details

Give Yes and a screen will pop up asking for ECC/PAN based Regn/Code No, Range and Division Name and Address and commissionerate.

Enable Value Added Tax (VAT)?

Give yes to enable VAT

Set/Alter VAT Details

Give Yes and a screen will popup asking for State and applicable date for VAT

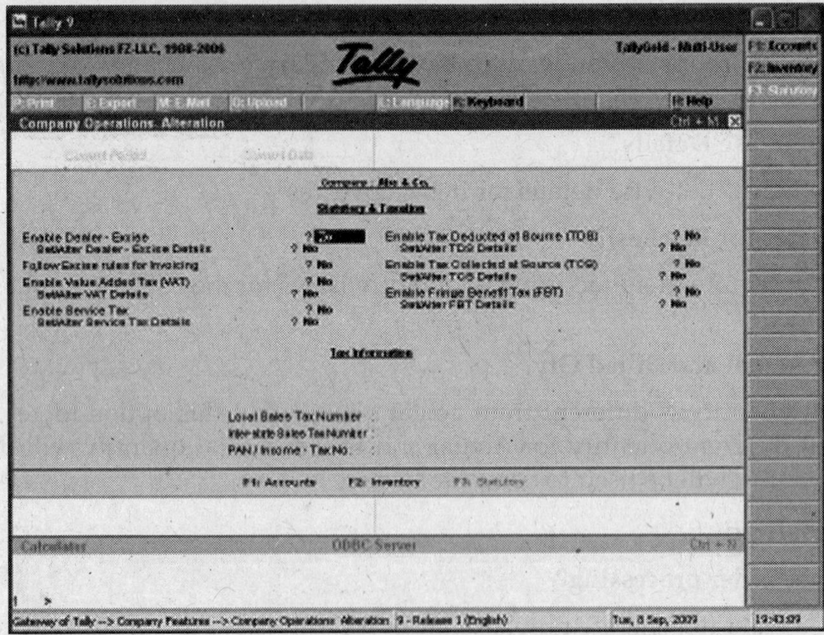

Enable Service Tax?

Give Yes to enable service TAX

Set/Alter Service Tax Details:

Give Yes and a screen will pop up asking for service Tax Registration No, Date of Registration, Assessee code, Division, Range and commissionerate.

Enable Tax Deducted at Source (TDS)?

Give Yes to activate **TDS in Tally 9.**

Set/Alter TDS Details

Give Yes and a screen will pop up asking for Tax Assessment Number, Income Tax Circle Etc.,

Enable Tax Collected at Source (TCS)?

Give Yes to enable TCS

Set/Alter TCS Details

Give Yes to alter TCS Details

Enable Fringe Benefit Tax (FBT)?

Give Yes to enable FBT Tax

Set / Alter FBT Details:

Give Yes and a screen will pop up asking for PAN/Income Tax Number etc.

Tax information:

Local Sales Tax Number: _________

Inter-State Sales Tax Number: ___________

PAN / Income Tax No: ______________

Ledgers and Groups

The **ledger** is the main book of account. The Journal is a subsidiary book. The word subsidiary means 'giving additional help to.' The journal helps a businessman to take the various transactions to the right place, i.e. to the appropriate accounts. The journal is the base, the ledger is the middle. The **Balance sheet** and **Profit and loss account** can be prepared from the main book of account, namely Ledger.

The entries are posted under appropriate accounts. All similar transactions must be brought together. Transactions relating to cash are grouped under cash account. Similarly the transactions with customers and suppliers (debtors and creditors) are grouped under appropriate personal accounts. Ledger is the main book of the business containing personal, Real and Nominal accounts of the business.

Account Groups provide you the ability to organize your Accounts. You can classify all ledger based on their functions. When you create a ledger, you have to put it in an appropriate Group depending on its nature of function. This classification is known as Grouping of Ledgers which determines whether the ledger goes into the Profit and Loss account into the Balance Sheet. Grouping of ledger determines the type and amount of Information you can get.

Tally 9 provides a set of pre-defined Groups. You can use these Groups readily for classification of ledgers, without creating new Groups or you can create Groups under and of these Groups and place ledger under these Group or create new primary Group. You create multi-level Group one under another to any level.

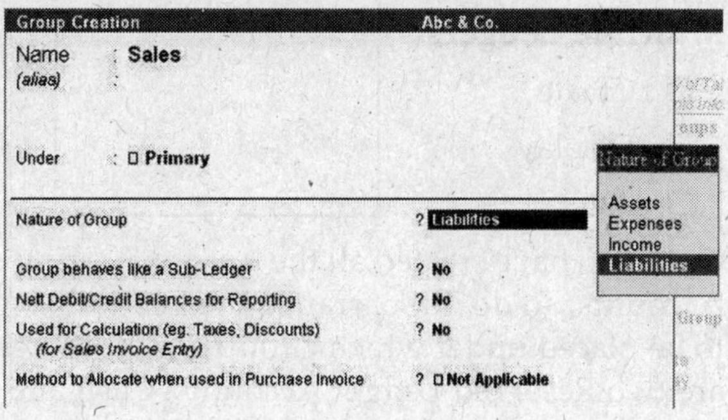

Group Creation — Abc & Co.

Name : Sales
(alias) :

Under : Primary

Nature of Group ? Liabilities

Nature of Group: Assets, Expenses, Income, Liabilities

Group behaves like a Sub-Ledger ? No
Nett Debit/Credit Balances for Reporting ? No
Used for Calculation (eg. Taxes, Discounts) (for Sales Invoice Entry) ? No
Method to Allocate when used in Purchase Invoice ? Not Applicable

Create New Group

Select Create under Single Group menu Groups menu, a screen appears to create a new Group with following fields as in picture.

Name: Type the name of the Group. You can not give duplicate name.

Alias: Give additional name(s) for the Group. When you select Group you can refer to it either by Name or by Alias. Alias is optional but Name is compulsory.

Under: When you reach this field a pop-up window will open and show all the existing Group heads. Select the parent group under which the Group being created should be placed. You may select any from the existing Group by pressing ALT+C which will bring Group Creation screen to create parent group of the group you are currently creating.

Creation of Primary Group

You can create a Primary Group if Allow Advanced Entries in Masters is set to Yes. While creating New Group, select Primary at Under, then select the nature of Group from the following 4 items:

- ❒ Assets
- ❒ Expenses
- ❒ Income
- ❒ Liabilities

If you select Expenses or Income, you have to additionally specify whether this Group affects Gross Profit or not by appropriately responding Yes / No.

For example, you may crate Groups like Depreciation, Interest on Loan, Selling Expenses, etc. in primary Group. The advantage of Primary Group is that you can configure the Group nearer to your requirements than the default Reserved Groups provided by Tally 9.

Creating ledger Accounts

Ledgers

Single Ledger

- ❒ Create
- ❒ Display
- ❒ Alter

Multiple Ledgers

- ❒ Create
- ❒ Display
- ❒ Alter

Gateway of Tally ....
Accounts Info. ....
Ledgers

Single Ledger
Create
Display
Alter

Multiple Ledgers
CReate
DIsplay
AlTer
Credit Limits

Quit

Once you have created all the Accounts Groups, you are now ready to make entry for Ledger Accounts. To do, first arrange the Ledger Accounts and note down which ledger account is to be placed under which Group. Previous year's Final Accounts may also be of help. There are two Reserved Ledger Accounts, Cash and Profit & Loss a/c. that are created by **Tally 9** when you create a Company which you can not delete nor you can move them under any other Group.

Single Ledger Creation

Name: Type the new Ledger's name here. Duplicate in name is not permitted.

Alias: Alternate names for you ledgers. This is optional.

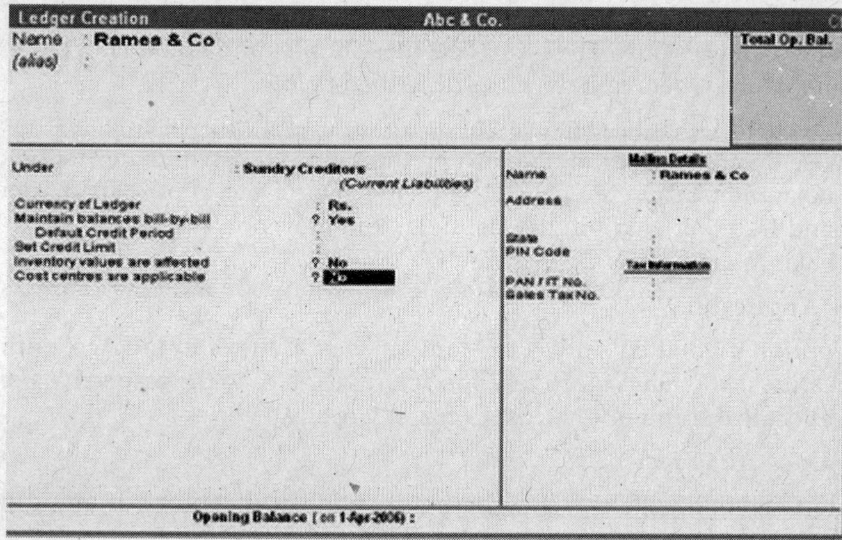

Under: Select the Group under which this Ledger Account falls. You will get a pop-up window from which you can select the appropriate Group. To create a new Group press **ALT+C** which will bring Group Creation Screen. When you have created the Group, cursor will return to this place accepting newly created Group as default.

Opening Balance: Enter the opening Balance as on the date of Books Beginning From. Normally the Opening Balance of Revenue Accounts will be Zero unless you start from middle of the Financial Year. If your books begin at mid-year, i.e. dates from Financial year from and Books beginning from are different, enter closing balance of previous date as opening balance here for all capital and Revenue accounts.

Cr/Dr: If opening Balance figure is not zero, specify whether the amount is Debit or Credit.

Mailing & Related Details

If you have set Yes to *'Allow Addresses for Ledger Accounts'* under F12: Configure, you can enter Mailing & related details for Ledger accounts under Sundry Debtors, Sundry Creditors, Branch/Divisions, Loan, Loan & Advances groups.

If you have set Yes at the *'Use Contact Details for Ledger Accounts'* Under F12: configure, you get additional prompts to input Contact Person, Telephone, Fax Numbers, etc.

Advanced information

If you have set Yes to *'Allow Advanced Entries in masters under F12: Configure'*, you get a screen with options configured by you.

Maintain balances bill-by-bill?

If you have set Yes in F11: Features to Maintain bill-wise details, then this option appears:

- While creating any ledger placed under Sundry Debtors or Creditors Group, you may specify yes to keep bill-wise details for the ledger
- Similarly, you can specify Yes to other ledger accounts also, if you had specified Yes to For Non –Trading A/c also in Accounting Features under F11: Features.

Specify No, when you do not need to maintain bill-wise details of outstanding balance but like to get ledger balances only. The input becomes simpler and you do not have to enter the bill-wise details of the Opening Balance as described below.

If you have specified Opening Balance and have opted for bill-wise details, then you may specify bill-wise details of Opening Balance in the popup box where in first field you enter date of Bill, next enter Bill Reference, Credit Days/Due Date in next field, amount of Bill outstanding and Debit or Credit in the last field. You may, however, leave the full or part of the opening balance amount as On Account.

Cost Centres Applicable?

You get this option if you had set yes to Maintain Cost Centres in the Accounting Features under F11: Features. You may selectively specify Yes (or No) to the respective ledgers where you want to allocate the amount to Cost Centres/Cost Categories.

Inventory Values are Affected?

Specify Yes to ledgers like Sales / Purchase which affect Inventory. If any duty of Direct Expenses affects your inventory, you may set to Yes for such ledgers.

Percentage of Calculation

If you have set Allow Invoicing in the Accounting Features under F11: Features and if the Ledger is placed under Duties & Taxes Group or any other Group for which you responded to yes to the Query Used fro Calculation? Then you may specify the rate of Tax (%). On specifying rate, you have to select the Method of Calculation from the list of Types of Duties.

- Additional Duty
- On Total Sales
- Surcharge on Tax
- Tax based on Item Rate

Additional Duty

Under F11: Features, if you disable Excise Rules, Additional Duty and Surcharge on Tax functions similarly. If enabled, Additional Duty is added to the Tax based on Item Rate in the Invoice to reflect the Total Duty Payable.

On Total Sales

As the term suggests, this type of Duty will be calculated on the Total value of individual items ignoring the rate of Duty specified for each item in Stock Item Master.

Note....

If you have responded yes to the question Calculate Tax on Current sub-total? in the Invoice/ orders settings under F12: Configure, then the calculation will be on current sub-total and if set to No, it will calculate on Total value of Inventory Only.

Surcharge on Tax

A surcharge is treated as a percentage of the duty levied and is computed on immediately preceding entry. The Tally software presumes that the preceding line in the Invoice is the

Duty on which surcharge is to be computed. This is suitable for taxes or duties like of Additional Excise Duty that is computed on the Tax (or Duty) amount.

Tax Based on Item Rate

If rate of Tax or Duty is directly associated with items which again differs from item to item, this type of Duty will be most suitable.

While creating Stock items, you get a field to specify Rate of Duty, where you may specify rate of Duty applicable for the Item.

When you select this Type of Duty for the Ledger, while preparing Invoice the rate of duty specified in each item will be picked up and computed. If more than one rate of Duty is applicable in single Invoice amount for similar rate of duty will be clubbed.

During Invoice Entry, the Tally software will automatically compute the Tax/Duty at the specified rate as per specified method which can however be modified.

Activate Interest Calculation?

This prompt appears if you responded Yes to the question Activate Interest Calculations? At F11: Features for the Company. If your response is Yes to that question, you will get another question: Use Advanced Parameters? Giving Yes will activate Advanced Mode and No will restrict to Normal Mode.

Effective Date for Reconciliation:

When you create any Ledger under Bank Accounts (or Bank OCC) Group, this prompt appears displaying books beginning date as default. Enter here the date from which you want to reconcile the Bank Accounts.

Specifying Closing Stock Value

In Case of creating new ledger Accounts under stock-in-hand, you can enter only Opening Balance. You should enter figures of closing stock through Alteration mode which allows you to specify date and closing balance for that date.

Note....

Date wise closing Balance is available only in Ledger Alter menu only. Once you create the stock ledger, go to alter select the ledger and give closing stock values.

If you maintain non-integrated accounts, Balance Sheet as on this date will reflect the closing balance that you specify here. However, if you maintain integrated accounts, you can not enter closing stock value through this option.

Credit Limit

For Ledger created under Sundry Creditors, Sundry Debtors and Branch / Divisions you get additional option *'Set credit Limit:'* you can specify the credit limit amount for such ledgers.

Default credit period (in days) will be asked for these ledgers if you have given **yes** to *Maintain balances bill-by-bill?*

Alter

In this option you can change the contents of any existing ledger.

Note....

To enter, opening balance in an of the built-in ledger Accounts (Cash A/c, Profit & Loss A/c) select the Ledger in Alter mode and type opening balance.

To **Delete a Ledger**, first select the ledger from the pop-up in Alter mode, then press **ALT+D** keys, a confirmation box will appear. To confirm, press Y, the item will be deleted. However, if any voucher has been placed under the ledger, it can not be deleted as long as any Voucher is associated with the ledger. If you still want to delete the Ledger, list the vouchers which are associated with the Ledger through and option in Display mode, alter the voucher or delete the voucher. When there is no voucher contain the ledger to be deleted, you will be permitted to delete the Ledger. This Deletion concept applies to all masters.

Making Voucher Entries

Tally 9.0 by default provides 18 types of vouchers (Excluding payroll vouchers introduced in this version) for recording different natures of transactions. You can create your own voucher types.

For example, you can classify payment vouchers for Traveling Expenses, Advance, and Payment to Creditors against Purchase, etc. You can easily generate report for Traveling expense alone.

Voucher Class

What is voucher class?

Voucher class permits you to automate accounting allocations during invoice entry. For example, in sales invoicing you can define the nominal ledger account to be credited for each item of sale, so the accounting credits for items sold, Tax, Freight and other charges are posted to the respective ledgers automatically.

For Sales voucher you can create voucher classes for Cash Sales, Credit Sales, and Export Sales etc.

These permits,

- ❒ Automatic posting of entries to predefined ledger accounts
- ❒ Automatic rounding off to preset value limits
- ❒ Automating other calculations

Optional Voucher

Optional Voucher is a temporary voucher that will not reflect in regular accounts. Once the transaction is authorized and completed you can convert the optional voucher into regular voucher. This eliminates the need to maintain manual records before the transaction is complete.

For example in order to issue a payment you have to create a payment voucher and get the signature from appropriate authorities. Once the payment process is completed you have to enter it in Tally as payment voucher. Using optional vouchers you can create temporary payment voucher that is not counted for accounting and after the actual transaction is completed you can convert it to a regular voucher.

Viewing and Deleting Vouchers

By default **Tally 9 provides 18 types of Vouchers** (with out counting payroll vouchers) for recording different natures of transactions. However, if you require further Voucher Types that function like the one of the existing type, you can create New Voucher Types and give different Voucher Numbering series.

The Voucher Type facility is great as you can make several alternates of each pre-fixed Voucher Type. For example, for Sales Voucher, it may be convenient to have several Voucher Types like Cash Sales, Credit Sales, Sales To Registered Dealers, Sales to Unregistered Dealers, Export Sales, etc. By creating separate voucher types for them, you can independently configure their numbering scheme, layout, etc.

Creating New Voucher Type

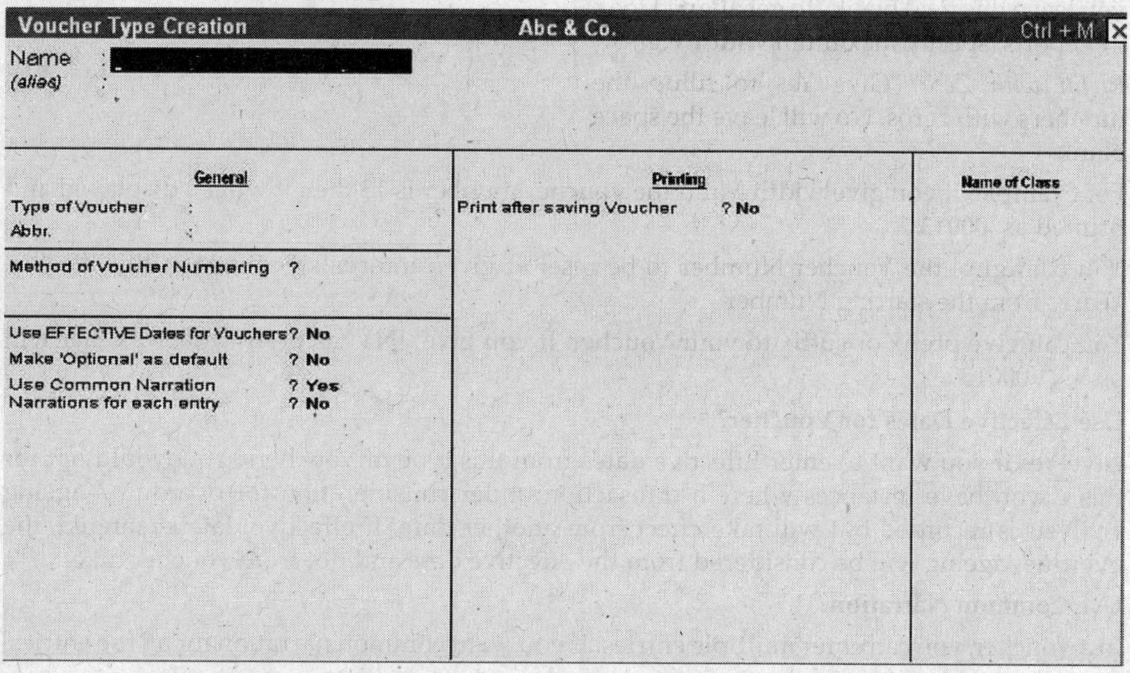

Voucher Type Creation Abc & Co. Ctrl + M

Name :
(alias) :

General

Type of Voucher :
Abbr. :

Method of Voucher Numbering ?

Use EFFECTIVE Dates for Vouchers? No
Make 'Optional' as default ? No
Use Common Narration ? Yes
Narrations for each entry ? No

Printing

Print after saving Voucher ? No

Name of Class

Select Create from the Voucher Types menu.

Name: Enter a name for your new Voucher Type.

Type of Voucher: Select the Type of Voucher from the List of Voucher Types. The Voucher you are creating will have similar functions that you select here.

Abbr.: Enter abbreviated short name for the new type of Voucher, preferably within 5 Characters.

Method of Numbering: Select from the list of Types of Numbering that displays following options:

- Automatic
- Manual
- None

If you want to get system-generated numbering, select Automatic. On selection of this option, and giving Yes to Use advance Configuration? You will get the following prompts.

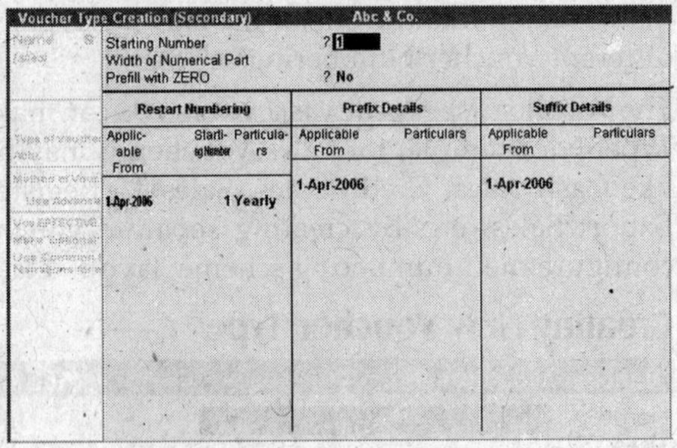

Voucher Type Creation (Secondary) Abc & Co.

Starting Number ? 1
Width of Numerical Part :
Prefill with ZERO ? No

Restart Numbering			Prefix Details		Suffix Details	
Applicable From	Starting Number	Particulars	Applicable From	Particulars	Applicable From	Particulars
1-Apr-2006	1	Yearly	1-Apr-2006		1-Apr-2006	

Starting Number: Give the Starting number you wish. By default 1.

Width of Numerical Part: Tally 9 on it's own adjusts the width according to the number if you leave this field blank. To get aligned look in Reports, specify maximum width, e.g., 5

Prefill with Zero? Give Yes to fillup the numbers with zeros. No will leave the space blank.

For example, if you give width 5 and the voucher number is 13 then it will be displayed and printed as: **00013**

You configure the Voucher Number to be reset at given intervals Daily, Monthly, Weekly, Yearly from the starting Number

You can give prefix or suffix to your Voucher. If you give 'INV' as prefix your voucher will be 'INV00013'

Use Effective Dates for Voucher?

Give Yes if you want to enter Effective dates from this type of Vouchers. You would opt for this if you have instances where a transaction under consideration for overdue / ageing analysis is recorded but will take effect from another date. If effective date is entered, the overdue/ageing will be considered from the effective date and not from voucher date.

Use Common Narration?

In a Voucher, you can enter multiple entries. If you want common narration for all the entries, set to Yes and No if you do not want common Narration.

Narrations for each entry?

If you want separate narration for each entry, set it to Yes, after each entry in Voucher, you will be prompted to enter narration for the entry. Give No if you don't want separate narration for every entry.

Print after Saving Voucher?

If you want to print Voucher after saving, give Yes. You will require it for Sales Voucher / Payment Voucher.

Accounting voucher in Tally

If you create Accounts voucher

In this field you should specify Dr or Cr. Type the letter D or Dr over the existing prompt to change, then select the ledger name from the pop-up list that Tally opens. There may be multiple Debit and Credit entries in one single voucher.

If you create Inventory voucher

If you are creating inventory voucher in Tally you will give information about the stock item you receive or issue and item related details like the Godown/warehouse, Batch Details, Quantity, Rate, Amount etc.

Gateway of Tally ....
Configuration ....
Voucher Printing

General

PUrchase Transactions
Payment Voucher

Sales Transactions
Receipt Voucher

Journal/Contra
Debit/Credit Note

REminder Letters
Confirmation Statements

Quit

Debit / Credit Amount:

This field appears in Accounts voucher only. Enter the amount of transaction and press Enter key. Tally will update current balance of the ledger and display it. This will happen only if you gave 'Yes' to the question 'Show Ledger Current Balance?' under Accounting Voucher in Vouchers Entry under F12: configure option. The total will appear on the bottom of the Debit and Credit columns. If both credit and Debit totals are not equal Tally will prompt to enter further Credit / Debit to balance the voucher. If both are equal Tally will move the cursor to Narration field.

The Narration field

The last field of Voucher is Narration, here you enter details of the transaction entered in the voucher. It is not mandatory / compulsory to give narration. You can type anything about the transaction or just leave this field blank. You can turn off narration by responding No to the question 'Use Common Narration?' at voucher creation/alteration screen.

Saving the Voucher:

After entering narration, when you press Enter key a confirmation prompt will appear Asking 'Accept Yes/No?'. Press Y or Enter to save the voucher or press N to return cursor to the first entry allows you to alter any data in the voucher. If you give Y Tally will save the voucher and blank screen will appear next to continue voucher entry.

Voucher Types in Tally:

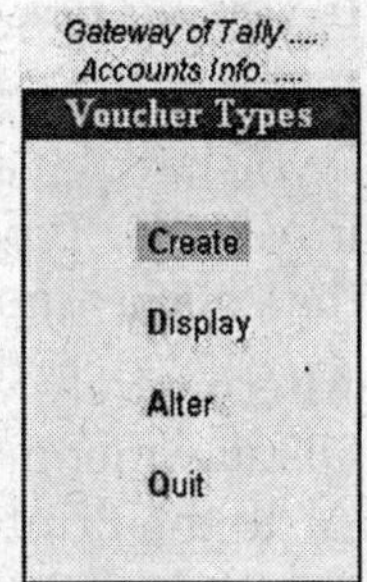

Payment voucher:

The payment voucher is for all payments you make through cash or Bank. These payments can be towards expenses, purchases, to trade creditors, etc. Follow the below procedure to create a payment voucher.

All payment vouchers must have first entry a debit and at least one credit to a Cash or a Bank Account. You can have any number of debit and credit entries. However, if you do not credit one cash or bank account and still try to accept the voucher a message appears asking for a cash or bank account.

If configured, Fund Transfer entries can also be made in payment voucher.

If you have given Yes to 'Print After Saving Voucher?' in Voucher Type creation/Alteration Tally will print the voucher immediately after saving.

Payment Printing Setup

Height of Voucher (inches)	: 7
Width of Voucher (inches)	: 5
Space to leave on top (default 0.25)	: 0.25
Space to leave on left (default 0.75)	: 0.75
Payment Mode on Top of Voucher	: No
Print Bill-wise Details	: Yes
Space for Checked/Verified initials	? No
Print Foreign Currency Symbol	? No

Invoice Printing Configuration

Title of Document	:		
(for Optional Voucher)	: *PROFORMA INVOICE*		
Sub Title (if any)	:		
Height of Normal Invoice (inches)	: 10	Simple:	10
Width of Normal Invoice (inches)	: 7.50	Simple:	7.50
Space to leave on top (default 0.25)	: 0.25	Simple:	0.25
Space to leave on left (default 0.5)	: 0.50	Simple:	0.50

Number of Copies to Print	: 1	Print Quantity Column	? Yes
Print in Simple Format	? No	Print Actual Quantity Column	? No
		Print Rate Column	? Yes
Print Voucher Reference	? Yes		
Print Order Details	? Yes	Print Batch Details	? Yes
Print Terms of Payment and Delivery	? Yes	Print Rate of Duty with Items	? No
Print details of Despatch	? Yes		
		Print Sub-Totals after each line	? No
Print Tax Analysis of Items	? No	Print Narration	? No
Print Company's Tax Regn. Numbers	? Yes		
Print Buyer's Tax Regn. Number	? Yes		

Method to use for Stock Item Name : **Name Only**
Jurisdiction :

Receipt Voucher

The receipt voucher in Tally is for all receipts into the Cash/Bank account. The voucher is similar to the payment voucher except that you debit cash or bank A/cs and credit the ledger from which you receive. The first entry in receipt must be credit and at least one debit to a cash or bank account. There can be any number of debit and credit entries. If you do not debit one Cash or bank account, a message appears asking you to rectify the entry.

If you have given Yes to 'Print After Saving Voucher?' in Voucher Type creation/Alteration Tally will print the voucher immediately after saving.

Receipt Printing Setup

Height of Voucher (inches)	: 7
Width of Voucher (inches)	: 5
Space to leave on top (default 0.25)	: 0.25
Space to leave on left (default 0.75)	: 0.25
Receipt Mode on Top of Voucher	: No
Print Bill-wise Details	: Yes
Space for Checked/Verified initials	? No

Details of Formal Receipt

Height of Receipt (inches)	: 6
Width of Receipt (inches)	: 5
Space to leave on top (default 0.25)	: 0.25

Alternatively you can print any voucher later by going to Voucher Alteration screen using Display menu. Open the voucher and press Alt-P to display the 'Print Voucher' Screen. Give 'Y' to the Print? Prompt.

Sales Voucher

The first entry must be a debit involving any debtor, bank or cash account and second should be a credit to ledger placed under sales account group. Rest of the accounts may be any Revenue account or any account under the Group current liabilities. Thus you can include Duties & Taxes from 3rd entry onwards.

Purchase voucher

The first entry must be a credit involving any creditor, Cash or Bank account and second entry should be a debit to a ledger placed under purchase account group. Rest of the accounts may be any revenue account or any account under the Group Current Liabilities.

Purchase Printing Configuration

Title of Document	: INVOICE		
(for Optional Voucher)	: *INVOICE*		
Sub Title (if any)	:		
Height of Normal Invoice (inches)	: 10	Simple/Voucher :	10
Width of Normal Invoice (inches)	: 7.50	Simple/Voucher :	7.50
Space to leave on top (default 0.25)	: 0.25	Simple/Voucher :	0.25
Space to leave on left (default 0.5)	: 0.50	Simple/Voucher :	0.50

Number of Copies to Print	: 1	Print Quantity Column	? Yes
Print in Simple Format	? No	Print Actual Quantity Column	? No
		Print Rate Column	? Yes
Print in Voucher Format	? No		
Print Cost Allocations in Voucher Format	? No	Print Batch Details	? Yes
		Print Rate of Duty with Items	? No
Print Voucher Reference	? Yes		
Print Order Details	? No	Print Sub-Totals after each line	? No
Print Company's Tax Regn. Numbers	? Yes	Print Narration	? No
Print Supplier's Tax Regn. Numbers	? Yes		

Method to use for Stock Item Name : **Name Only**
Jurisdiction

Contra Voucher

The contra voucher is for Fund transfers between cash and Bank accounts only. The following is the rule:

For example, if you pay Rs. 10000 cash into State bank Account, your contra entry should be like this,

Particulars	Debit/credit
Cr. Cash	Credit - 15000
Dr. State bank ac	Debit - 15000

Credit Note

Credit Note is raised when a buyer returns some goods that you sold him. or you give him credit due to rate difference or discount/rebate or when there is an excess debit to any party

Debit Note

You create a Debit Note when you make purchase return or when you have short billed a customer or you are granted credit by your supplier due to rate difference, discount, etc.

Memo Voucher

This is purely Non-accounting voucher. These entries will not affect your accounts nor does affect your final results. You can alter and convert a Memo Voucher into a regular voucher when you decide to bring the entry into your books.

You can use memo vouchers to make suspense payments, vouchers not verified at the time of entry, Items given on approval.

Trading, Profit and Loss account

Trading account: This account is prepared to know the trading results of the business, i.e. how much gross profit the business has earned from buying and selling during a particular period. The difference between the sales and cost of goods sold is gross profit.

Profit and loss account: This account is prepared to calculate the net profit or net loss of the business. There are certain items of incomes and expenses of the business which must be taken into consideration for calculating net profit of the business.

Balance sheet

As the Name suggests it's the record of all balances maintained.

To begin:

- Go to Gateway of Tally→Balance Sheet→F12: Configure
- Set Balances Sheet according to the Mentioned Fields, or Click Alt+F1 to see the detailed Balance sheet (If You had Made Earlier).

To View Balance Sheet of www.Tally9Book.Com with Percentage Column.

1. Go to **Gateway of Tally → Balance Sheet → F12: Configure**

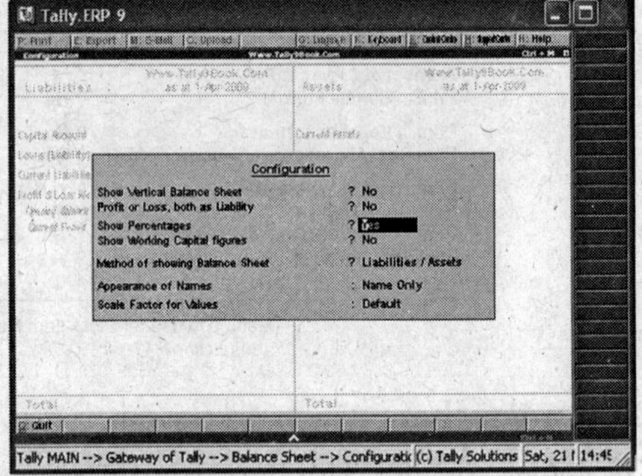

2. Set Show Percentage to Yes in the Balance Sheet configuration screen.
3. Press **ALT+F1** to view the detailed Balance Sheet.

Balance Sheet
1-Apr-2005 to 31-Mar-2006

Liabilities		as at 31-Mar-2006	Assets		as at 3[illegible]2006
Capital Account		**72,48,461.88** *28.77 %*	**Fixed Assets**		**65,24,993.74** 25.90%
Bhabesh Kumar Panda	*23,47,886.93*		*Building*	*1,17,145.85*	
Biresh Kumar Panda	*12,86,247.56*		*Computer*	*947.08*	
Harish Chamdra Panda	*16,17,783.46*		*Furniture & Fittings*	*4,025.49*	
Manorama Panda	*19,96,543.94*		*Land*	*2,93,121.50*	
			Plant & Machinery	*24,89,147.45*	
Loans (Liability)		**6,32,614.69** *2.51 %*	*Vehicle*	*36,20,606.37*	
ICICI BANK LTD.	*6,32,614.69*				
			Current Assets		**1,86,66,668.65** 74.10%
Current Liabilities		**1,61,81,793.55** 64.23%	INVESTMENT(C.A.)	1,07,75,278.00	
Sundry Creditors	1,23,62,425.57		Closing Stock	34,31,261.20	
Audit Fee Payable	*10,000.00*		Loans & Advances (Asset)	34,45,447.06	
SBI, Main Branch-Adhoc A/c	*14,70,114.33*		Sundry Debtors	9,16,745.15	
SBI, Main Branch-CC A/c	*23,39,253.65*		Cash-in-hand	67,411.68	
			Bank Accounts	30,625.56	
Term Loan					
Profit & Loss A/c		**11,28,792.27** *4.48 %*			
Opening Balance					
Current Period	*11,28,792.27*				
Total		**2,51,91,662.39** 100 %	**Total**		**2,51,91,662.39** 100 %

In this view, each group is expressed as a percentage of the total of the Balance Sheet.

Bank reconciliation

What is BRS? In accounting terminology BRS stands for Bank Reconciliation Statement. For example, you make a payment by issuing a bank check to a party / supplier. What will happen to the check. The transaction will not reflect immediately in your bank. The party will first deposit the check on or after the date mentioned on the check. Then it will take further one-three days for the check to clear depending on the bank. But your voucher entry in Tally is on prior date. So your bank ledger in tally may be showing wrong balance, not the actual balance. You don't know what happened to the check. Whether it is cleared or not? After getting your bank statement you will make reconciliation entry. Thus you will get actual bank balance.

In Tally 9 there is an option to enter the bank date. Tally will show two balances in reconciliation statement. The Balance as per company books, and amount not reflected in Bank, and Balance as per Bank.

Whatever voucher entries you make (Payment/Receipt/Contra etc) will be reflected in Balance as per company books. For whatever vouchers you make BSR entry will be shown in Balance as per bank. The difference between the two is given as Amount not reflected in Bank.

We will see this with the following examples and screen shots.

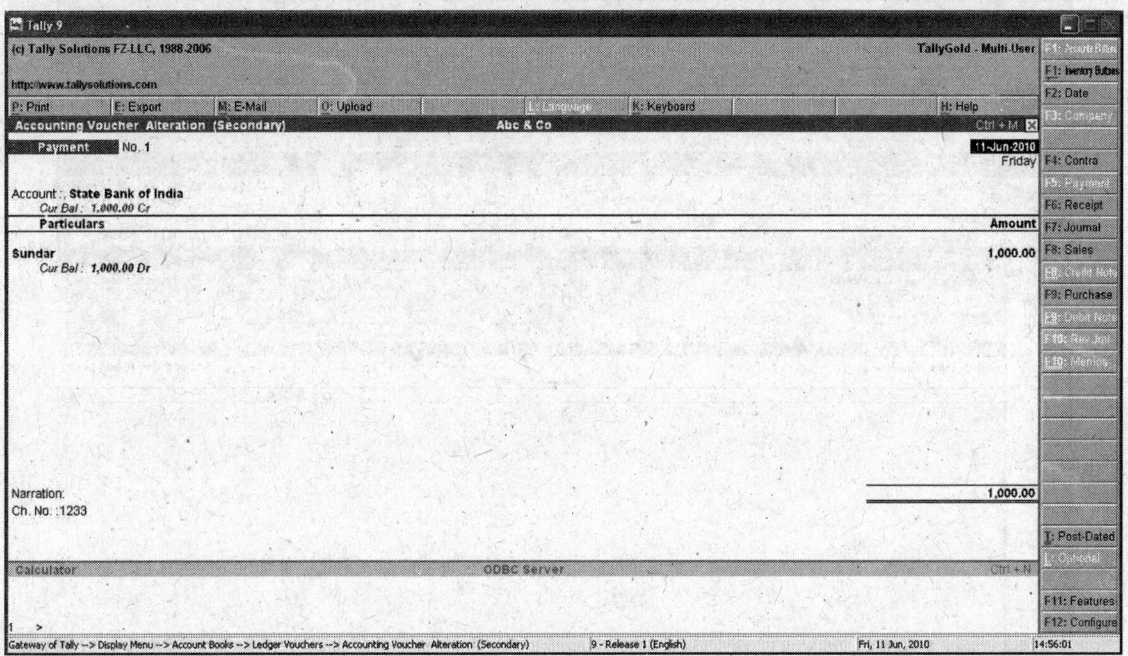

Now will go to Display menu -> Accounts Books -> Ledger -> State bank of India. Then Click Reconcile button on the right hand side. (Short cut : F5) [Figure A].

Now the Balance as per company books is Rs. 1000

Amounts not reflected in Bank is Rs.1000

Balance as per Bank is Rs.0

I gave the check on 11 June.10. If the check clears on 13 June.10, I give that date under Bank Date column. Now the Bank account will tally [Figure B].

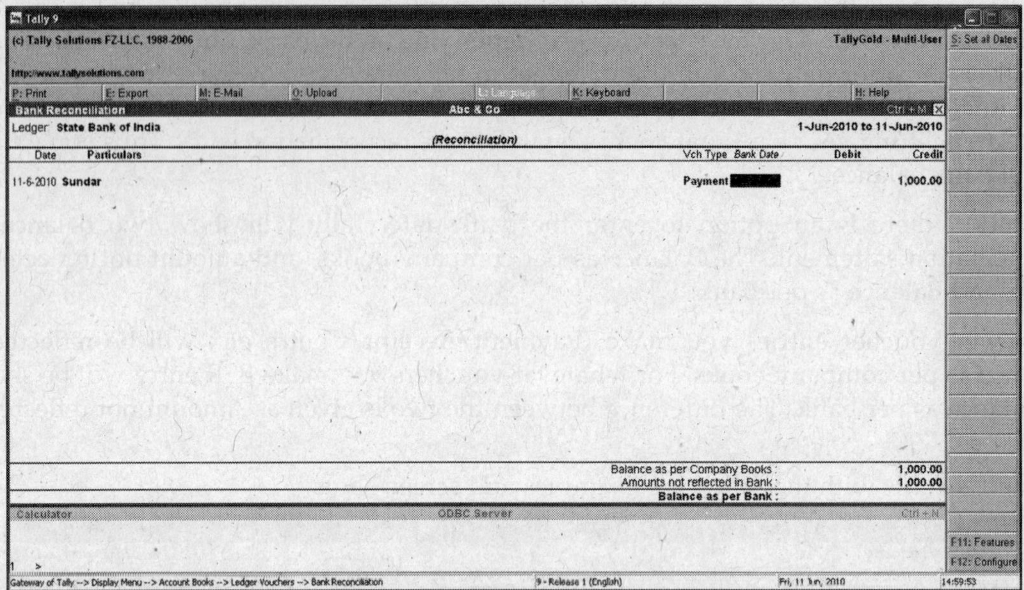

Figure A

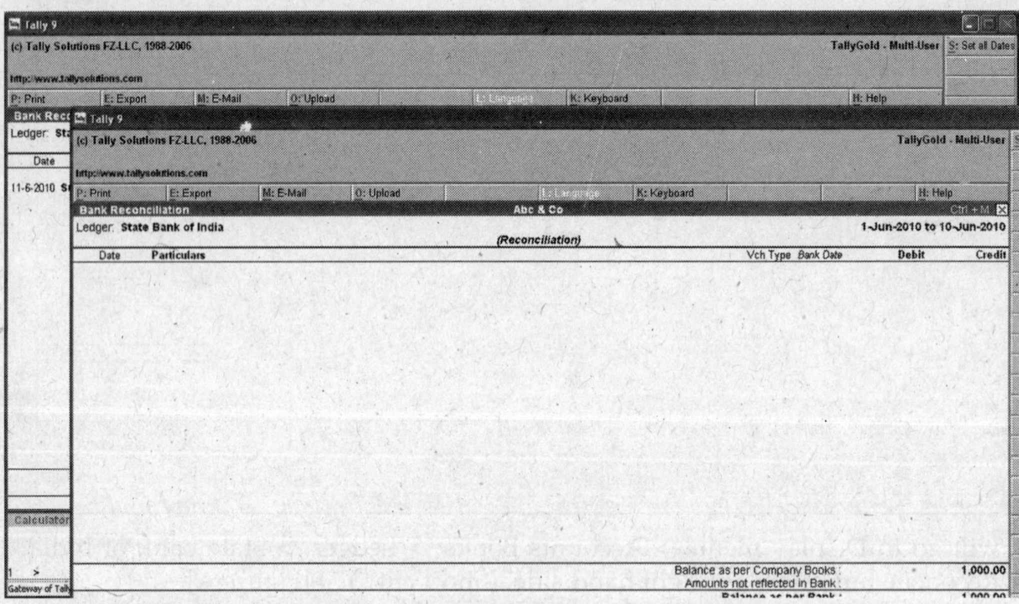

Figure B

Debit and Credit: Double Entry Bookkeeping

Configure single/double entry for payment, receipt and contra:

Somebody asked me he is not getting debit credit entry fields in payment/receipt vouchers. Tally 9 by default is set to single entry for payment, receipt and contra. That means you will

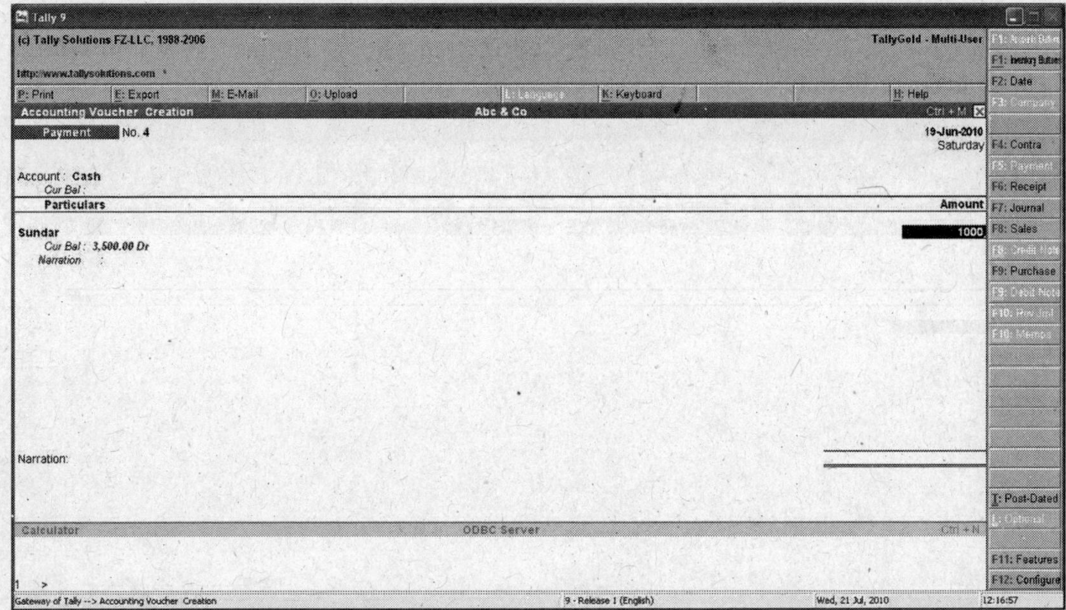

select a single that is to be credited or debited (for payments credited, for receipts debited) then you will select the accounts to be credited (for receipts) or debited (for payments). This is the single entry mode in Tally.

For example, if you are making a payment you will first select a Cash or bank account and in the particulars you will select a supplier (for example), and on the right hand side you will enter the amount of payment. This method is simple and convenient. However, if you want double entry system you can still use it by configuring Tally.

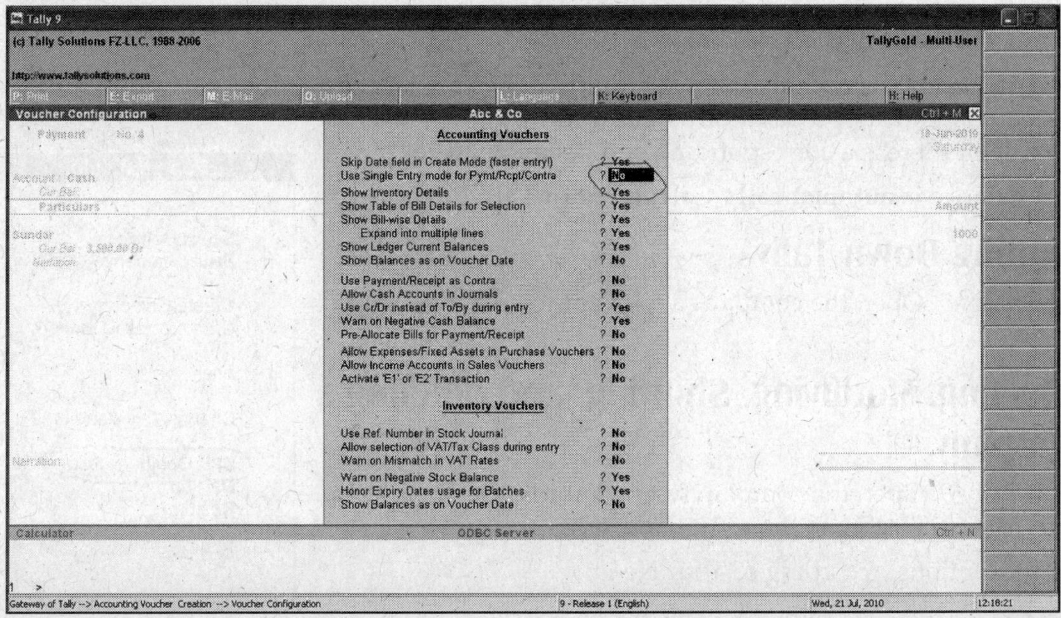

To do this open Accounting Vocher Creating screen (F5: Payment, F6: Receipt). Press F12: Configure. Give No to Use Single Entry mode for Pymt/Rcpt/Contra. Now you will have both debit and credit fields.

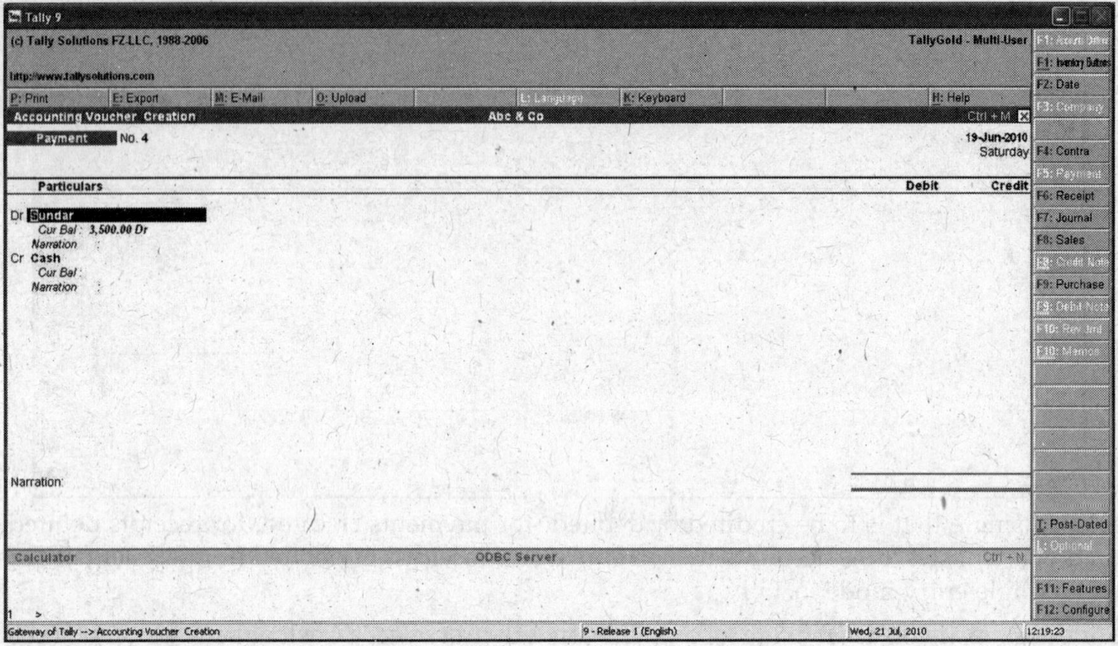

Trial Balance

The balances standing in the various accounts in the ledger at the end of a period are listed down in the form of a statement, showing debit balances in one column and credit balances in the other, known as a **Trial balance**.

The Trial Balance is nothing but a summary of the various transactions entered in the books of accounts and its preparation is based on the rule that 'for every debit there is a corresponding and equal credit'.

Trial balance is automatically Calculated in Tally!

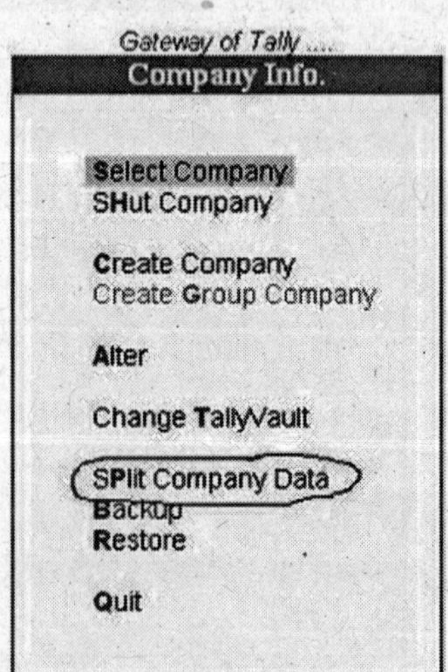

Shutting Down Tally

Open Tally 9. Open the company you want to split. Press Esc./ Alt+F4

Selecting, Modifying, Shutting, and deleting a Company

Open Tally 9. Open the company you want to split. Press **Cmp. Info** (Alt+F3) button on the right hand side.

Use the Options According to Your Need.

Points to Remember

- ☆ Speed can be increased in Tally 9 up to 30 to 40% from simple voucher entry
- ☆ Different version of Tally use different installation methods
- ☆ Tally 9 by default provides 18 types of vouchers for recording different natures of transactions

SECTION–IV
Going Digital with Music,
Photos, and Video

Music

Playing, Growing, and Managing Your Music Collection

If you thought the move from LPs to CDs was impressive (if you're old enough to even remember that!), you're going to love the latest in audio and video technology. With your PC, a *CD drive,* a sound card, and a decent set of speakers, you can create your own computerized jukebox that can play hundreds of your favourite songs. With an Internet connection, you can download music to add to your collection. With a portable music player, you can take your favourite tunes wherever you go. And if you have a recordable disc drive, you can even "burn" your own custom CDs and play them on any CD player! This chapter shows you how to do all this and more with Windows Media Player.

Digital Music Basics

Digital music is music stored in files rather than as grooves on the surface of vinyl records. Recordings on audio CDs, computers, and digital music players (MP3 players) are all forms of digital music. Digital music offers several advantages:

- You can create your own custom mixes and burn them to CDs.
- You can copy music to a portable digital audio player and take it with you wherever you go.
- You have less clutter than you do with CDs.
- You can buy and listen to only the songs you like instead of having to buy an entire CD.
- You can buy and download music and listen to it right now instead of waiting for CDs to arrive in the mail.
- You don't need to worry about scratches rendering your favourite CDs useless.

Digital Players, Rippers, and Burners

One of the complications of digital music is that different devices store and play music in different, often incompatible formats. For example, CDs store music in a format that most portable digital players can't play. Fortunately, various programs can handle the required format conversions for you:

- A *digital music player* plays audio in one or more digital formats. The player may be a program on your PC, such as Windows Media Player, or a portable digital music player, often referred to as an MP3 player.

- A *CD ripper* converts audio clips from a CD into a format you can play on your PC or MP3 player.
- A *CD burner* copies digital audio clips from your PC to a recordable CD. You can then play the CD in a standard audio CD player.

Choosing the Right Recordable Discs

- With digital music, you don't need discs unless you plan to burn music to recordable CDs. You can download digital clips, copy them to your MP3 player, and use your MP3 player as the stack of CDs you would otherwise carry around with you or play in your car. On some newer cars, you can plug your MP3 player into the car's sound system. On older cars, you can purchase an adapter that enables you to play recordings from your MP3 player through the car's sound system.
- If you want or need to burn music to CDs, however, make sure you purchase CD-R, not CD-RW, discs. You can record to CD-R discs only once, but they're more reflective, making them a better choice for storing digital music. (Some audio CD players have a tough time reading a CD-RW disc.) Also make sure the maximum recording speed of the discs is at least as fast as that of your CD-R drive. If you have a drive that can print labels on the CDs and you want to do that, look for printable discs that support the same print technology the drive uses.

Playing, Ripping, and Burning with Windows Media Player

If you insert an audio CD into your PC's disc drive, Windows should display the Audio CD dialog box, prompting you to specify which action you want Windows to perform: **Play Audio CD** (with Windows Media Player), **Rip Music from CD** (with Windows Media Player), **Open Folder to View Files** (in Windows Explorer), or perform another action with some other audio program that's installed on your PC. To start listening to the CD, click one of the options for playing it. (The audio CD may begin to play automatically when you insert the CD, depending on how your system is configured.)

Playing, ripping, and burning with windows media player

If Windows Media Player starts playing the CD, you'll see a small window like the one in. This is how Windows media player appears in Now Playing mode, a streamlined version of Media Player. To see Windows Media Player in its full glory, click the **Switch to Library** button. (You can switch back by clicking the **Switch to Now Playing** button in the lower-right corner of the Library window.)

Ripping Tracks from CDs

Playing an audio CD makes your PC little more than an overpriced CD player. To make your PC a *superior* overpriced CD player, record your favourite audio clips to your PC's hard drive as files. This provides you with a virtual jukebox, which you can program to play only the songs you want to hear in the order you want to hear them. It also allows you to copy the clips to your MP3 player, but we'll get to that later.

- ❐ Establish a connection to the Internet, if possible. If your PC is connected to the Internet, Media Player can automatically download the title of the album, the name of the artist, and track titles for most CDs so that you don't have to enter this information manually.
- ❐ Run Windows Media Player by selecting **Start**, **All Programs**, **Windows Media Player**.
- ❐ Insert a CD that has one or more tracks you want to record into your PC's CD player. Media Player displays a list of the tracks stored on the CD, as shown in Figure, with all tracks on the CD selected.
- ❐ 4. (Optional) Click the check box next to each track you do *not* want to record to remove the check mark from the box.
- ❐ Click **Rip CD**. Media Player begins ripping the selected tracks from the CD and displays its progress.
- ❐ When Media Player is done ripping the selected tracks, eject the CD.

Creating a Playlist

With Media Player, you can mix tracks from various CDs and downloads by creating *playlists*. Here's how:

- ❒ Click **Create Playlist**, type a name for the playlist, and press **Enter**.
- ❒ In the list pane (on the left), below Music, click **Album**. A collection of ripped CDs appears on the right.
- ❒ Double-click an album that contains tracks you want to add to your playlist.
- ❒ Select the tracks you want to add to your playlist.
- ❒ Drag and drop any one of the selected tracks onto the name of the new playlist, as shown in Figure.

Creating a playlist

- ❒ Repeat steps 2 to 5 to add tracks to your playlist from other CDs.
- ❒ Click the name of the playlist.
- ❒ Drag items up or down in the list to rearrange the tracks in the desired order.

  To play your clips, click the clip you want to start playing and then click Media Player's **Play** button (near the bottom of the window). Media Player plays the selected song and then the remaining songs in your playlist.

Burning an Audio CD

You can burn a CD, a playlist, or a new collection of audio tracks to a CD. Take the following steps:

- ❒ Click the **Burn** tab (upper right).
- ❒ Click the **Burn Options** button (below and to the right of the Burn tab) and click **Audio CD**.
- ❒ Insert a blank CD-R disc into your CD drive. (If the AutoPlay dialog box appears, close it.)
- ❒ If the burn list contains tracks from a previous session, click the **Clear list** button to remove the tracks.

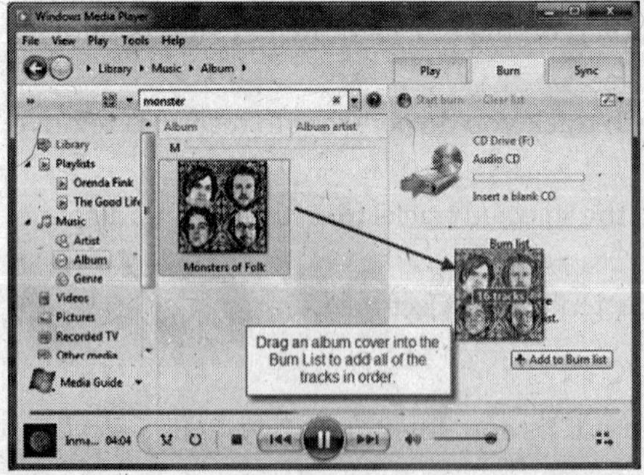

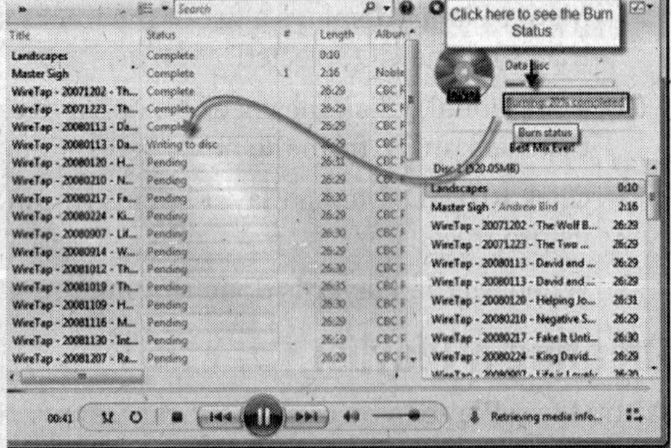

- Select the album, artist, or playlist that contains tracks you want to burn to the CD.
- Drag the tracks from the details pane (centre) to the list pane (right) and drop them in place. (You can drag individual track or an entire album or playlist. If you drag more tracks than will fit on the CD, Media Player creates a new list for another CD.)
- To change the order of tracks in the burn list, drag a track up or down. To remove a track from the burn list, right-click the track and click **Remove from list**.
- When you're ready to burn the CD, click **Start burn**.

Downloading Music from the Web

The web is buzzing with companies that sell downloadable music, audio books, and other digital audio. You can go to any number of online music stores and pack your shopping cart with tracks for under a buck each. You might even be able to legally pick up a few tracks for free. You can then burn the tracks to CDs, copy them to your MP3 player, and add them to your PC's growing audio library.

Keep in mind that downloading and "sharing" music without paying for it (unless you're downloading a free promotional track) is against the law. Downloading any file is pretty easy. You click a link and follow the onscreen instructions to tell your browser where to save the file. However, before you can download audio clips, you have to find some tunes that are worth downloading. The following sites are popular online stores where you can purchase individual tracks:

- iTunes (www.apple.com/itunes) is the home of one of the most popular music stores on the Internet. Here you can download and install a free copy of iTunes so that you can listen to your favourite tunes, preview recent releases, and purchase and download quality clips online for less than $1 per tune.
- Rhapsody (www.rhapsody.com) is where the creators of RealPlayer host their own online music store. Here you can purchase and download individual tracks to play on your RealPlayer, transfer to portable players, or burn to CDs.
- Yahoo! Music (new.music.yahoo.com) is one of the most popular online music sites, featuring Internet radio stations. If the station is playing a song you like, you can jump to the online store, order it, download it, add it to your playlist, and transfer it to your portable music player or burn it to a CD.
- AOL Music Now (music.aol.com) features on-demand Internet radio and customizable, commercial-free listening; you can order individual tracks online for less than a buck.

Copying Music to a Portable Music Player

Building a huge music library on your PC is cool, but your PC may be a bit too bulky to carry around in certain situations. How do you take your music collection (or at least a portion of it) on the road? The easiest and lightest way is to purchase a portable music player, often called an MP3 player. Portable music players come equipped with enough storage to hold gobs of music. Typically, you can rip tracks from CDs or download them from various sources on the Internet and then transfer (copy) them to your player. Portable music players are usually equipped with the software you need to transfer clips from your PC to your player. Many of the music stores discussed earlier in this chapter also offer free software that can handle the file transfers. However, this software may not enable you to rip music from the CDs you already own. An alternative is to use Windows Media Player or Apple iTunes to perform both jobs. This assumes, of course, that you have a portable music player one of these programs supports. If you don't, you may need to purchase additional software.

The process of transferring clips to your player is fairly straightforward. The following steps show you how to copy files from your PC to your portable music player using Windows Media Player. If you're using other software, the steps should be similar:

- ❒ Connect your portable music player to your PC as instructed in the player's documentation, and turn it on.
- ❒ Run Windows Media Player, as explained earlier in this chapter.
- ❒ Click the Sync tab. A pane appears on the right, instructing you to drag tracks into the pane to add them to the Sync list. (If your portable music player or a drive letter for it does not appear, Windows Media Player may not support your player.)
- ❒ Use the navigation pane (left) and the details pane (centre) to display tracks you want to copy to your portable music player.
- ❒ Drag and drop one of the selected tracks into the Sync pane (on the right).
- ❒ Repeat steps 4 and 5 to copy any remaining tracks to the Sync pane.
- ❒ Click the Start Sync button (near the bottom of the Sync pane).
- ❒ When the sync is complete, exit Media Player and disconnect your portable music player as instructed in its documentation.

Points to Remember

- ☆ To play an audio CD, insert it into your PC's CD-ROM drive. When a dialog box pops up asking what you want to do, click **Play Audio CD** and click **OK**.
- ☆ To run Windows Media Player, click **Start**, **All Programs**, **Windows Media Player**.
- ☆ To copy all the tracks from an audio CD to the Windows Media Library, run Windows Media Player, insert the audio CD, and click **Start Rip**.
- ☆ To create a new playlist in Media Player, click **Create playlist**, type a name for the playlist, and press **Enter**. Drag and drop tracks over the name of the new playlist to add them to the playlist.
- ☆ To burn an audio CD, run Media Player, click the **Burn** tab, drag and drop albums and/or tracks into the Burn pane, and then click **Start burn**.
- ☆ To transfer music to a portable music player, run Media Player, click the **Sync** tab, drag and drop albums and tracks into the Sync pane, and then click **Start sync**.

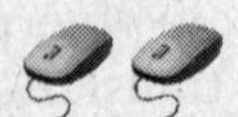

Photos

With a digital camera, you get instant gratification. Right after you take a picture, you can check out the results on the LCD display and delete the photo and retake it if it didn't turn out right. You can plug your camera into a TV set and view the picture, or connect your camera to your computer and print the photo. In addition, digital photography enables you to e-mail photos to your friends and relatives, post them on your website or blog or an online photo album, and pack them away on CDs or DVDs. Perhaps best of all, you can airbrush out any imperfections before sharing your photos.

In this chapter, you learn the basics of digital photography, including how to take photographs, enhance your photographs with digital imaging software, share photos online in places like Facebook, and print and e-mail photos.

Managing Digital Photos & Images

Digital cameras are modeled off standard 35mm cameras, so snapping a picture is easy: you just point and shoot. If the camera has an autofocus feature, you may need to hold down the button halfway to focus the camera and then press down all the way to snap the shot.

Before you snap too many pictures, check the following camera settings:

- **Resolution, image size, or megapixels:** Most cameras enable you to adjust the size and quality of the image. If you plan to print the photos, choose a higher setting. If you're going to e-mail the photos or place them on a web page, a setting of 640 480 pixels is usually sufficient. Larger images are higher quality, but they're also larger files, requiring more storage space and taking longer to transfer on the Internet.
- **Mode or environment:** Many cameras feature an assortment of modes or environments that automatically adjust the camera settings for different types of photos—for example, parties, landscapes, sporting events, daytime or nighttime portraits, and so on.
- **Flash:** In most cases, leave the flash setting on Auto. If you're taking all your pictures outside, turn off the flash. For backlit scenes, turn on the flash, if this option is available on your camera.
- **Exposure:** Many cameras enable you to bump the exposure up or down for very dark, very light, or high-contrast subjects. (When you're first starting out, you may want to leave this setting alone.)

- **Date imprint:** Some cameras can add a date imprint to your photos so that you can later tell the date you snapped them. If you find the date imprint more annoying than helpful, turn it off.

Some digital cameras can capture audio and short video clips as well as take photographs.

Check your camera's documentation to determine any additional features it may have. The procedure for checking the camera settings varies from one digital camera to another. Some cameras have two buttons: one for changing to a feature (such as flash, image quality, timer, and audio) and another for changing the settings. You change to the desired feature (for instance, flash) and then press the other button to change the setting (for instance, Autoflash or Flash On).

> **Tip...**
>
> *Carry an extra memory card and battery with you ... especially the battery. Most digital cameras use a lot of battery power, especially when you're using the flash.*

Getting Windows Live Photo Gallery

You can find numerous programs for managing and editing your photos and converting them into slide shows with background music or other audio. Your digital camera or even your printer may have come with its own photo-management software. You can also pick up free software on the web, such as Google's Picasa (picasa.google.com), or use free online photo-editing and sharing services, such as Flickr (www.flickr.com) and Photobucket (www. photobucket.com). I use Picasa for photo management and editing.

- If you want to stick with a Microsoft product that has the look and feel of Windows 7, a good choice is Windows Live Photo Gallery. You can download it from download. live. com. I use Photo Gallery throughout this chapter to illustrate common photo editing and management tasks. I use Windows Live Movie Maker (explore.live. com/windows-live-movie-maker) to transform my photos into DVD slide shows, you can use Windows DVD Maker instead.
- After installing Photo Gallery, you can run it by selecting **Start, All Programs, Windows Live, Windows Live Photo Gallery**.

Managing and Editing Your Photos

You have a bunch of photos on your camera. Now what? How do you transfer those photos to your PC, organize them, and edit them to improve their quality? The following sections answer all of these questions by showing you how to perform these essential tasks with Windows Live Photo Gallery.

Transferring Photos from Camera to PC

To transfer the images from your camera to your PC, connect the cable to your camera and to the specified port on your PC, and turn on the camera. (Most cameras connect to a PC via a

USB cable.) Windows should detect the camera and display a dialog box, like the one shown in Figure, prompting you to select the program you want to use to import photos from the camera to your PC.

Note....

Many new printers and some PCs, especially portable PCs, are equipped with memory card readers. Instead of connecting the camera to your PC with a cable, you remove the memory card from your camera and plug it into the memory card slot on the PC or printer. The memory card reader typically appears as another storage drive on your computer.

If Windows does not detect the camera, try running your photo-management program and clicking the button to import photos. If you're using Windows Live Photo Gallery to import images, here's what you do:

- Click **Start**, **All Programs**, **Windows Live**, **Windows Live Photo Gallery**.
- Connect your digital camera to your PC and turn on the camera.
- Click **File**, **Import from camera or scanner**. Photo Gallery displays a list of sources from which you can import photos. (Your camera may appear as a drive letter rather than a camera.)
- Click the icon for your camera and then click **Import**. The Import Photos and Videos dialog box appears with **Review, organize, and group items to import** selected by default.
- Click **Next**. All photos on the camera are selected and grouped by date taken, as shown in Figure. Unless you specify otherwise, each group will be saved to a different folder.
- Click **Import**. Photo Gallery starts importing the photos and displays its progress. You can click **Erase** after importing to have the photos removed from the camera when Photo Gallery has finished.

Editing and Enhancing Your Photos

To edit a photo in Photo Gallery, double-click the photo. The photo appears, as shown in Figur. You can then click the icon for the desired quick fix:

- **Auto adjust:** Automatically adjusts colour and contrast so that you don't have to mess with it.
- **Adjust exposure:** Enables you to adjust the brightness and contrast, correct for shadows, and mute or accentuate highlights.
- **Adjust colour:** Allows you to adjust the colour temperature (drag left for more blue, right for more yellow and red), tint, and saturation.

- **Straighten photo:** Allows you to straighten a photo by dragging a slider left or right to pivot the photo around its centre point.

- **Crop photo:** Enables you to choose a preset crop or drag a box to define the area you want included in the photo. (Anything outside the box will be cropped out.)
- **Adjust detail:** Allows you to sharpen the photo or reduce "noise."
- **Fix red eye:** Corrects red-eye problems. Click this option and then drag a small box around each red eye you want to repair.
- **Black and white effects:** Enables you to convert a colour photo into various black-and-white renditions.

Resizing Your Photos

Before you share photos via e-mail or on the web, you may want to make the photo files smaller so that they consume less storage space and transfer faster over the Internet. To make a smaller copy of a photo, right-click the photo in Photo Gallery (not in photo edit mode) and click **Resize**. Open the **Select a size** drop-down list, click the desired size, and then click **Resize and Save**, as shown in Figure. Photo Gallery resizes the photo and saves it.

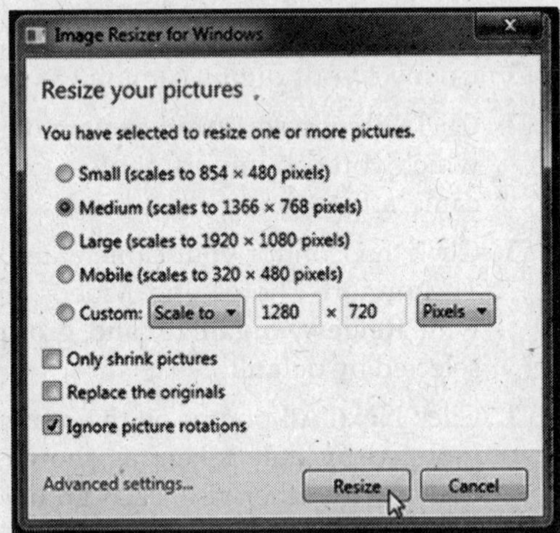

Copying Photos to a Recordable CD

After you transfer the photos to your computer's hard drive, consider copying them to a CD for safekeeping, just in case anything bad happens to your hard drive. Be sure to label the CD with a title and date so that you can tell what's on it. If you simply want to copy the photos to a disc for safekeeping or share them with someone else, for viewing on a PC, here's what you do:

- In Windows Live Photo Gallery, select the photos you want to copy to a CD.
- Open the **Make** menu and click **Burn a data CD**. Photo Gallery prompts you to load a recordable CD.
- Insert a recordable CD into your PC's CD-R drive.
- Type a descriptive name for the disk, choose how you want to use it, click **Next**, and follow the onscreen cues to complete the operation. Windows formats the CD, and Photo Gallery copies the selected photos to the CD.

Sharing Your Photos on the Internet

One of the best features of digital cameras is that they create graphic files you can immediately use on web pages and in e-mail messages. You don't have to scan the picture after taking it, because it's already in a digital format.

Creating a Photo Slide Show and Burning It to a DVD

If you're in a hurry and need something more basic, consider using Windows DVD Maker instead. Windows DVD Maker, included as a part of Windows 7, is a little less feature rich. It doesn't allow you to add video clips (photos and music only), and you can't insert text slides between groups of photos as you can in Windows Live Movie Maker. Nevertheless, Windows DVD Maker is an excellent program that suits most users' needs.

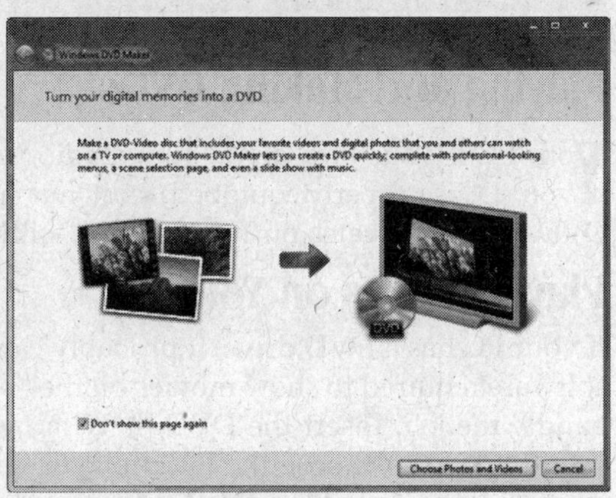

You can run Windows DVD Maker directly from Photo Gallery. Simply select the photos you want to burn to the DVD, and then click **Make, Burn a DVD**. Windows runs Windows DVD Maker and adds the selected photos to the list of photos to be burned to the DVD.

Click **Next** and use the options on the resulting screen to select a menu style, edit the text on the menu, customize the menu, and add slide show features—add background music, adjust the time each slide appears, and control the transitions between slides.

Click **Change Slide Show** to save your preferences. You can then click **Preview** (near the top) to play the slide show and make sure everything is just right before you burn it to a disc.

When you're ready to burn the slide show to a disc, click **OK** to end the preview (if it's still playing). Insert a blank DVD-R into your PC's recordable DVD drive, and then click the **Burn** button. Depending on the number, size, and quality of the photos; the amount of music; and the performance of your PC, Windows DVD Maker can take quite a while to produce the video and burn it to the disc.

Points to Remember

- ☆ Download and install Windows Live Photo Gallery at download.live.com.
- ☆ To transfer photos from your digital camera to your PC, connect the camera to the PC, turn on the camera, and follow the onscreen cues.
- ☆ Double-click a photo in Windows Live Photo Gallery to display it in edit mode. To transform a collection of photos into a movie, select the photos in Windows Live Photo Gallery, open the **Make** menu, and click **Burn a DVD**.

Videos and Media

Playing and Making DVDs

Your PC is your own digital film studio, where you can watch DVD movies (even Blu-ray, if your PC is properly equipped), edit, manage, and share your own video clips; and even make DVD movies to watch on TV and share with family and friends. This chapter shows you how.

Playing DVDs on Your PC

If your PC has a DVD drive, it probably came equipped with its own DVD video player—the software required to show movies on the "big" screen. If it didn't, Windows Media Player can handle the job. Insert the DVD. If Windows prompts you to choose the DVD player you want to use, click **Play DVD Movie using Windows Media Player**. Media Player begins to play the movie. You can use the controls at the bottom of the screen to stop, pause, play, skip forward or back, or access the DVD menu, as shown in Figure. If you change to full-screen mode, the controls at the bottom of the screen disappear when you stop moving the mouse. To bring the controls back into view, simply move the mouse.

Enjoying video or PC

Transferring Video to Your PC

The procedure for transferring video from a digital camera or camcorder, a memory card reader, or a disc (CD or DVD) is relatively easy, because you're merely transferring a file from one device to the other.

Your camcorder probably came with its own video transfer / editing program, and chances are pretty good that it's better than Windows Live Movie Maker. If you don't have a specialized program or simply need to transfer video from a memory card reader, CD, or DVD, you can use Windows Live Movie Maker to perform the transfer.

To transfer video from a digital camera or camcorder, a memory card reader, or a disc (CD or DVD) using Windows Live Movie Maker, here's what you do:

- Connect the device to your PC, if it's not already connected, and turn it on.
- Click **Start**, **All Programs**, **Windows Live**, **Windows Live Movie Maker**.
- Click the **Movie Maker** menu button (to the left of the Home tab) and click **Import from device**. A dialog box appears, indicating "Photos and videos will be imported into Windows Live Photo Gallery."
- Click **OK**. A list of devices you may be able to import video from appears.
- Click the device that contains the video and click **Import**. The Import Photos and Videos dialog box appears, indicating the number of new photos and videos found on the device.
- Click **Next**. All videos and any photos on the device are selected and grouped by date taken, as shown in Figure. Unless you specify otherwise, each group will be saved to a different folder.

Transferring video to PC

- Click **Import**. Movie Maker starts importing the videos and photos and displays its progress. You can click **Erase** after importing to have the items removed from the device (if possible) when the transfer is complete.

Converting Old Tapes into Digital Video

If you already have an analog camcorder and/or old camcorder or VHS tapes, consider adding a video capture device to your PC. You have several options here. The most convenient is to purchase an external unit that connects to your PC's USB or FireWire (IEEE-1394) port, or into a circuit board that comes with the unit.

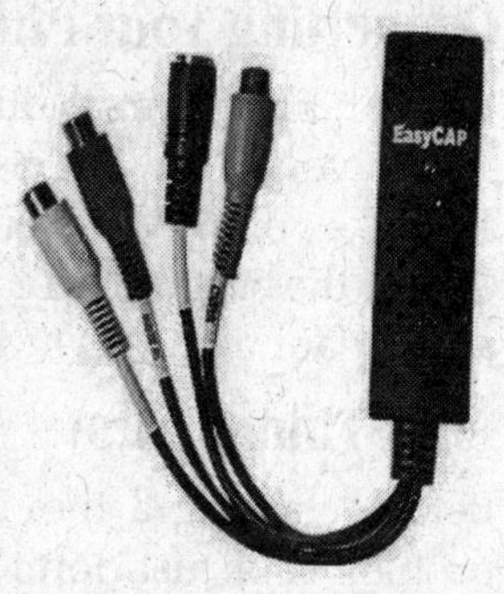

Video capture boards and external units have special ports that let you connect your camcorder to your PC. They typically capture video at a rate of 15 or more frames per second (fps) (30 fps is better), and they do a fairly good job of converting your analog clips into a digital format. If you're looking for a way to convert your collection of old camcorder or VHS tapes into a digital format and store them on DVDs, this is the way to go. To transfer video from an analog camcorder or VCR to your PC, you must connect your analog-to-digital converter to your PC and connect the camcorder or VCR to the converter. In the case of an external converter, you connect it to the PC with a USB or FireWire cable. You use a composite or S-Video cable to connect the camcorder or VCR to the converter:

- **Composite video** combines the colour and brightness data in a single signal, resulting in a lower-quality display. A composite cable typically has three RCA connectors: yellow (video), red (right audio), and white (left audio).

- **S-video** divides the video into two signals—one for colour and one for brightness—generating a high-quality image. An S-video cable has a male connector with four pins that plugs into a female connector.
- **Audio jacks** carry the audio portion of the recording. Most analog-to digital converters have two audio jacks: right (red) and left (white). However, most cameras have a single audio output jack. You can connect the audio output jack on the camera to either the left or right audio-input jack on the converter.

Your digital camcorder or video capture device probably came with its own program for recording and editing your video footage. Most of these programs are similar and follow the same overall procedure for recording video. Here's a quick overview of the process:

- Connect your camcorder or VCR to your PC through the converter, as instructed in the previous section.
- Use your camcorder or VCR controls to play the video to the point at which you want to start transferring the video to your PC.
- Run your video transfer/conversion program.
- Start playing the video and immediately click the **Start Record** button in your video transfer program to start capturing the video. When you're ready to stop recording, click the **Stop Record** button in your video transfer program. Depending on the length of the video, the video transfer program may chop the recording into separate files to make them more manageable.

Windows Movie Maker

Converting Your Photos and Videos into a DVD Slide Show

You can transform a collection of photos and/or videos into a slide show and burn it to a DVD so that you or anyone else can view your photos on a TV equipped with a standard DVD player. To make your DVD even more engaging, you can add music tracks that play in the background. One of the best tools for transforming a collection of photos into a slide show DVD with musical accompaniment is Windows Live Movie Maker. (Picasa also has a Movie Maker.)

First Things First

Before creating a movie, correct any photos that are too dark, are too light, have red-eye problems, or just don't look right for some reason. If your photos look bad, your movie will look bad, too. Also rotate any images as necessary to display them in the proper orientation. (Movie Maker can rotate the photos for you, but you're better off having them look just as you want them to appear in the movie before you begin.)

Tip...

*You can start your movie from Windows Live Photo Gallery and then skip the next section on adding photos and videos. Select the photos and videos you want to include in your movie, open the **Make** menu, and click **Make a Movie**. Photo Gallery runs Movie Maker and adds the selected photos and videos.*

Adding Photos and Videos to Create a Movie

To start making the movie using Windows Live Movie Maker, take the following steps:

Click **Start, All Programs, Windows Live, Windows Live Movie Maker**.

Adding photos to create a movie

- ❒ Click the **Home** tab and click **Add videos and photos**.
- ❒ Change to the folder that contains the photos and/or videos you want to include in your movie, select all the items you want to include, and click **Open**. Movie Maker adds the selected items to your movie, as shown in Figure .
- ❒ 4. (Optional) To move an item, drag and drop it where you want it to appear in the movie. To remove an item, right-click it and click **Remove**.

After choosing the photos and videos to include in your movie and arranging them in the order you want, you can have Movie Maker do the rest, and you can skip the rest of this chapter. Just click the **Home** tab and click **Auto Movie** to have Movie Maker create a movie for you. Auto Movie adds a title slide, credits, and transitions. All you need to do is add background music (assuming that you want background music).

Adding a Title, Credits, and Captions

To give your movie a professional touch, consider adding a title slide and credits. (You can add a title slide at the beginning to introduce the movie or between sections to transition from one series of related photos and videos to another.) You can also add captions to your photos and videos. Click the **Home** tab and then add the desired text object:

Adding a title, credits and captions

- ❒ **Title:** Click the slide before which you want the title slide to appear, type the desired text, and then use the options near the top of the screen to format the title slide and specify the time it remains onscreen, as shown in Figure.
- ❒ **Caption:** Click the photo you want to caption, click **Caption**, type the desired text, and use the options near the top of the screen to format the caption.
- ❒ **Credits:** Click the slide after which you want the credits to appear, type the names of the people you want to credit (pressing Enter after each name), and then use the options near the top of the screen to format the credits and specify the amount of time to display the credits. To change the background colour for a title or credit slide, click the slide, click the Edit tab, open the Background colour list, and click the desired colour.

Controlling Slide Transitions

To add cool, smooth transitions between slides, right-click anywhere in the collection of photos and click **Select all**, click the **Animations** tab, and select the Transition and Pan and zoom options you want to use. It's tough to tell what each option does, so choose an option and then play a portion of your movie to see the effect in action.

Adding Background Music

Once you have some audio clips stored in one or more folders on your computer's hard drive, you can import them into Movie Maker and add them to your movie:

- Click the slide where you want the audio track to begin playing.
- On the Home tab, click the musical note icon above Add music.
- Change to the folder that contains the audio track you want to include in your movie, select the track, and click **Open**. Movie Maker imports the selected track and displays a green bar above the photos indicating that photos will be displayed during the track, as shown in Figure .
- Repeat Steps 2 and 3 to add tracks.
- 5.(Optional) Move a track by dragging and dropping it where you want it tom begin playing. To remove a track, right-click it and select **Remove**.

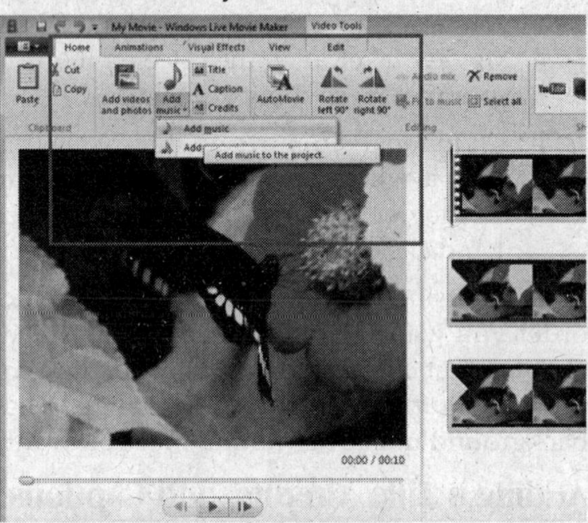

Adding background music

Previewing Your Movie

Before burning (recording) your movie to a DVD, preview it to make sure it contains all the photos, videos, and music you want it to include in the order in which you want them to play.

To preview your movie, click the first slide in your show (probably the Title slide, if you added a title to your movie) and then click the **Play** button.

Saving Your Project

To save your project so that you can edit it later, open the **Movie Maker** menu (to the left of the Home tab) and click **Save Project**, or press **Ctrl+S** and then save the file as you would save any file on your PC. This simply saves your project; it doesn't allow you to play the movie on a TV DVD player. To do that, you need to save your project as a *movie*.

Burning Your Movie to a DVD

To publish your movie to a DVD, your computer must be equipped with a recordable DVD player and you must use DVD-R discs. To burn your movie to a disc, take the following steps:

- Insert a blank DVD-R in your PC's recordable DVD drive.
- Open your movie project in Windows Live Movie Maker, if it's not already open.
- Click the **Home** tab.
- Click the DVD icon.
- Choose a folder in which to save the movie, type a name for the movie file, and click **Save**. Movie Maker saves the project as a movie. (This can take quite a bit of time, depending on the movie length and your PC's speed.)
- Click **Next**. Movie Maker displays a dialog box for creating an opening menu for your movie.
- Click the desired menu style (on the right) and then click **Customize menu**, use the resulting options to make additional changes, and click **Change Style**. (The Foreground and Background video options are a little misleading; you can use videos or photos for the opening menu, in addition to the photos and videos already included in the movie. You may also want to add a separate music track for the menu.)
- Click **Menu text**, use the resulting screen to edit and format the opening menu text, and click **Change Text**.
- Click the **Burn** button. Movie Maker encodes the movie to play on a TV DVD player and burns the movie onto the recordable DVD, which can take quite some time. When the process is complete, Movie Player ejects the disc and offers you the option to make another copy of the DVD or close (exit).

Points to Remember

- As long as your PC is equipped with a DVD player, Windows Media can use it to play DVD movies on your PC.
- You can connect a digital camcorder directly to your PC via a USB port.
- With an analog-to-digital converter, you can transfer video from old VHS and analog camcorder tapes to your PC.
- You can pick up a free copy of Windows Live Movie Maker at download.live.com.
- To add photos and videos to your movie in Movie Maker, click the Home tab, click Add videos and photos, use the resulting dialog box to select the photos and videos you want to add, and click Open.
- To burn your movie to a DVD in Windows Live Movie Maker, make sure the project is open; then click the Home tab, click the DVD icon, and follow the onscreen cues.

Gaming

Understanding Game's system requirements and Buying Game

Games are of different types; different manufactures make different variants of game for different users, but on an average we can conclude following minimum gaming PC requirement:

- HD Video Graphics Support (At least 256 MB)
- Dedicated Video Graphics (At Least 128 MB)
- RAM (At least 2 GB)
- Processor (At least 2.0 GHz)
- Sound Cards. Monitors & Other Input Device

You can buy lots of game from the marketplace. But be careful of the following things:

- Never buy Pirated Games
- Always make sure that you have the sufficient PC Requirement
- Be sure to ask for serial Key & Licenses.

Installing Games

You can install Games in very easy manner, just like you did to install programs. Most of the Games Distributor will provide you with setup manuals.

Serial Keys

Serial keys define that your product is original. You will require them to install your game & for the Authentication process in Games. Make Sure you have these Keys.

Your Serial Keys Look like this: XXXXXXXXXXXXXXXXXXXXXX

Downloading Games

Downloading Games is as simpler as downloading photos from internet. Many Manufactures of Games will provide you free Trial Versions & Free Games. Just follow their Downloading instructions.

Playing Games Online

You can Play games online as well. Just look out for websites offering online gaming.

Gaming Consoles and Equipments

Besides playing Games on your PC, You can play them on different consoles such as:

- Sony® Play stations®
- Nintendo®
- Xbox®
- BlackBerry® Playbook®
- Mobile Phones®
- Apple® I Pad®

Cheat Codes

Cheat codes are the codes/shortcuts/combinations of keys that help you significantly in the game. You can get a cheat book easily available online. Make sure you download Hex-Editor, An Advanced Cheating Program.

GTA- Vice City Stories Cheat Codes (PSP)

Cheat
DOWN, LEFT, UP, L1, R1, TRIANGLE, CIRCLE, X
RIGHT, RIGHT, CIRCLE, CIRCLE, L1, R1, DOWN, X
L1, R1, L1, R1, LEFT, CIRCLE, UP, X
DOWN, UP, RIGHT, TRIANGLE, L1, TRIANGLE, L1, TRIANGLE
RIGHT, L1, DOWN, L1, CIRCLE, UP, L1, SQUARE
RIGHT, UP, LEFT, DOWN, TRIANGLE, TRIANGLE, L1, R1
UP, DOWN, LEFT, RIGHT, X, X, L1, R1
LEFT, LEFT, CIRCLE, CIRCLE, DOWN, UP, TRIANGLE, X
LEFT, LEFT, R1, R1, UP, TRIANGLE, DOWN, X
UP, L1, DOWN, R1, LEFT, CIRCLE, RIGHT, TRIANGLE
DOWN, TRIANGLE, UP, X, L1, R1, L1, R1
R1, L1, L1, DOWN, LEFT, CIRCLE, DOWN, L1
UP, DOWN, LEFT, RIGHT, SQUARE, SQUARE, L1, R1
UP, DOWN, LEFT, RIGHT, CIRCLE, CIRCLE, L1, R1
UP, RIGHT, SQUARE, SQUARE, DOWN, LEFT, CIRCLE, CIRCLE
LEFT, DOWN, R1, L1, RIGHT, UP, LEFT, CIRCLE
LEFT, DOWN, R1, L1, RIGHT, UP, LEFT, X
LEFT, DOWN, L1, R1, RIGHT, UP, LEFT, SQUARE
LEFT, DOWN, L1, R1, RIGHT, UP, LEFT, TRIANGLE
LEFT, DOWN, TRIANGLE, X, RIGHT, UP, LEFT, L1
UP, L1, DOWN, R1, LEFT, L1, RIGHT, R1

Have Fun!!

Installing Resident Evil-5

Resident Evil is an Action Game, here is how to install this game.

Here are the steps to install and activate Resident Evil V, from Electronics art Website.

Click "**Ready to Install**" from *Origin*:

- The Resident Evil 5 Installer Wizard should prepare to install. Once it appears, click **Next**.

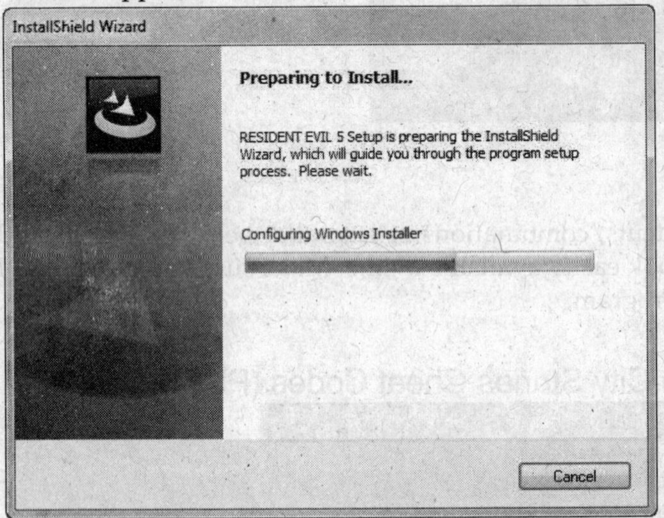

- To accept the license agreement, click on "**I accept the terms in the license agreement**", then click **Next**.

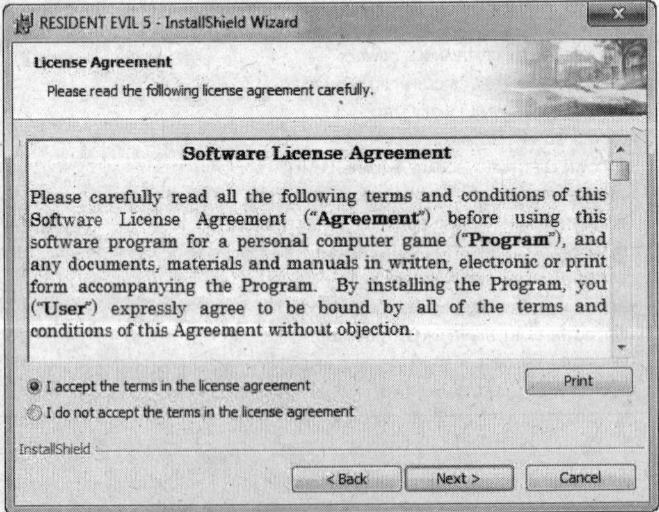

❒ Select your **Destination Folder.** Click **Change** to select a different folder, then click **Next**.

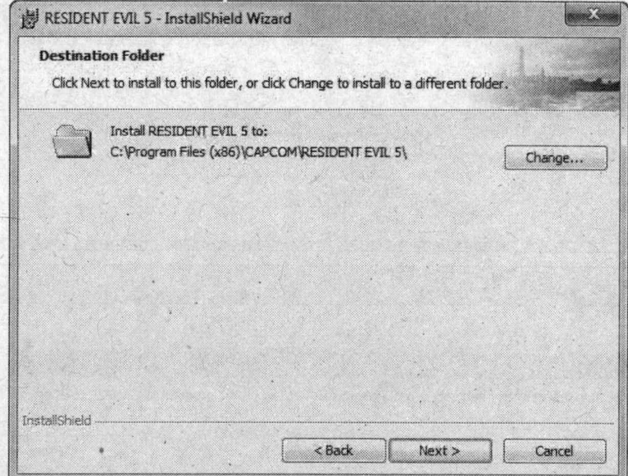

❒ After the installation completes, click **Finish**.

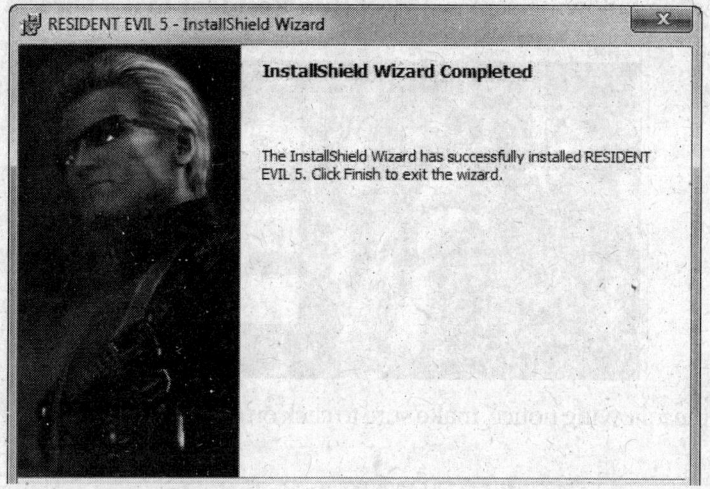

❒ A Welcome screen should appear. Click **Next**.

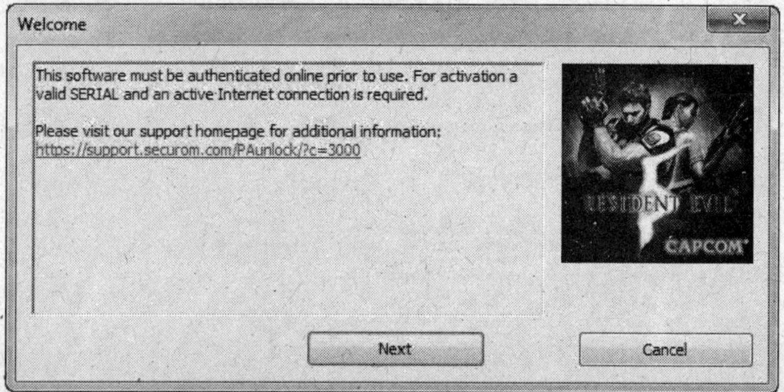

- The Activation should begin and complete successfully.

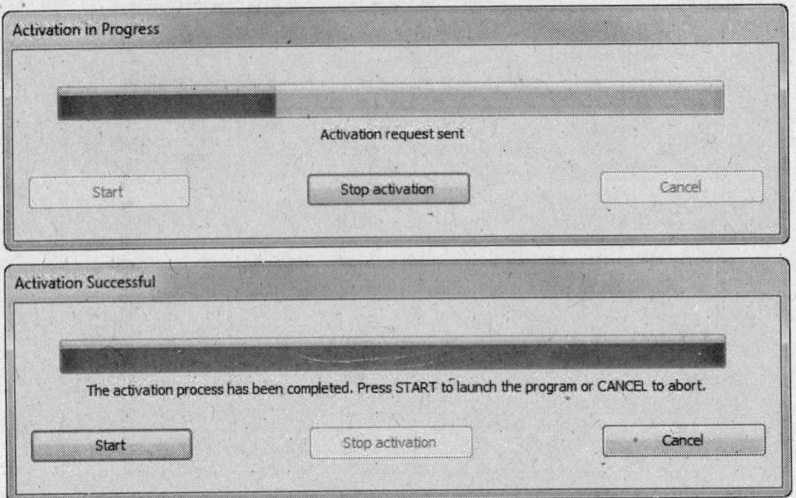

- You should see the following screen. Select **Run Resident Evil 5 DirectX9 Version**.

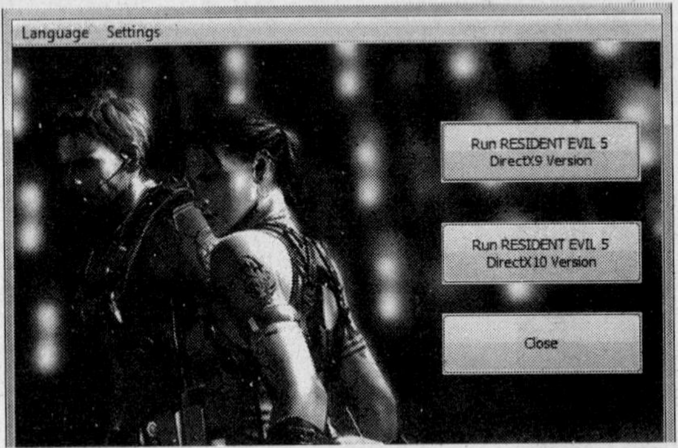

- When you see the following notice, make sure to click on **Copy To Clipboard,** then click **Install**.

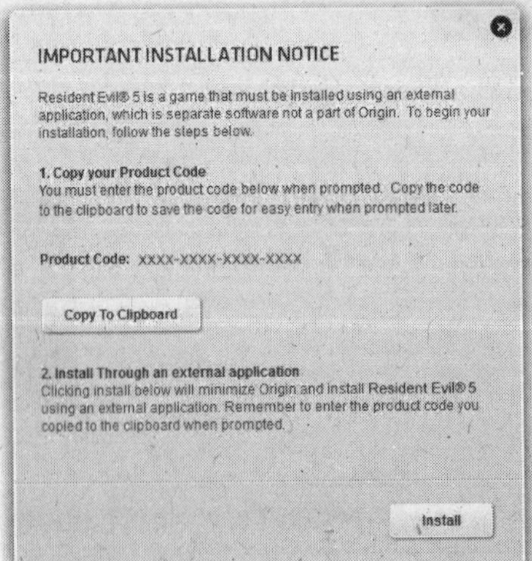

- In this screen, you will enter your **Product Code** that was copied to your clipboard in an earlier step. Click **Activate**.

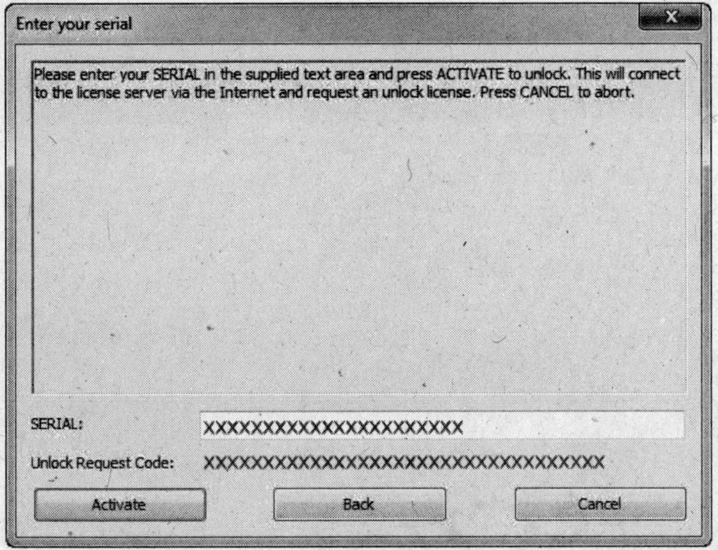

- You should now be ready to play Resident Evil V!

Understanding and playing games increases your mental sharpeners and speed of reciprocation. However, always do remember to check the time you devote to playing games.

Points to Remember

- ☆ Always remember that serial keys define that your product is original.
- ☆ You can buy lots of game from the marketplace. But never buy pirated games and always remember that you name the sufficient PC requirement.

SECTION–V
Tapping the Power of the Internet

Getting Wired to the Internet

Understanding How Internet Works

The Internet is a worldwide network of computers that can communicate with one another and share resources. The computers are all interconnected by a massive collection of fiber-optic cables, phone lines, and wireless signals that facilitate data transfer at lightning-fast speeds. For your computer to plug into this network and tap its resources, it needs a modem and an Internet service provider (ISP). The modem is the hardware your computer uses to send and receive data on the Internet—it's sort of like a telephone for your computer. The ISP functions as a communications hub between your computer and the Internet. Using the modem, your computer connects to the ISP, and the ISP connects to the Internet.

Picking a Connection Type

Although myriad options are available for connecting to the Internet, they boil down to two choices: dial-up or broadband. Dial-up is a slow connection, but it's available wherever you have access to a phone line, which is pretty much everywhere. Your options may be limited because of your location. Broadband is a fast connection, which you can get through some cable companies, digital satellite services, phone companies, and wireless ISPs, but keep in mind that fast is a relative term. A dedicated (leased) line is typically the fastest, followed by fixed wireless (as opposed to mobile wireless), cable, Digital Subscriber Line (DSL), and satellite, but several factors can affect the actual speed at which your computer connects. One user's DSL connection may be faster than another user's cable connection. If you live in a major metropolitan area, you have plenty of Internet connection types from which to choose: dial-up using a standard modem over your existing phone line, DSL modem, cable modem, satellite, and perhaps even some type of wireless connection (fixed or mobile). Your choice hinges on the following three factors:

- **Availability**: You might not have cable or DSL service in your area, so that can significantly limit your choices. Dial-up service over an existing phone line and satellite service are almost universally available.
- **Speed**: Choose the fastest connection you can afford. You may think you won't use the Internet that much, but when Windows or your other programs need to download huge software updates, you'll be wishing you had a faster connection.

- **Price**: Monthly service charges range from about Rs. 100 per month for dial-up service (plus the cost of local phone service) to more than Rs. 25000 a month for cable or satellite service. (Satellite also costs about Rs. 40000 up front for the installation, although satellite Internet companies often offer special deals if you make a long-term commitment.)

The following sections provide a brief overview of your choices, but you need to shop around to find out what's available in your area and compare prices.

Tip...

Connection speeds are measured in kilobits per second (Kbps), which is equivalent to 1,000 bits per second; and megabits per second (Mbps), which is roughly equivalent to 1 million bits per second.

Turbo-Charging Your Connection with a Cable Modem

Like cable television connections, a cable Internet connection supports high-speed data transfers to your PC, enabling you to cruise the Internet at the same speed you can flip TV channels:

- **Speed**: Rates range from 4Mbps to 20Mbps, although you're likely to experience download rates of 3Mbps to 6Mbps.
- **Cost**: Service depends on speed, plus rent for the modem, which you may get for free or be able to rent from the cable company for a few bucks a month.
- **Drawbacks**: You share bandwidth with other users in your area, so the speed of your connection can fluctuate depending on how many users are currently using the service and how much data they're transferring.

Another Speedy Option: DSL

DSL may be a little more available than cable and cost a little less, but it's also slower:

- **Speed**: Rates range from 768Kbps to 7.1Mbps.
- **Cost**: Service costs depending on the speed, plus for the modem, which you may get for free or be able to rent from the phone company for a few bucks a month.
- **Drawbacks**: Your PC must be within about 3 miles of the phone company's switching station.

Connecting from the Boonies via Satellite

If you can't get cable or DSL, you may need to settle for satellite broadband. Here's how it stacks up:

- **Speed**: Rates range from 500Kbps to 6Mbps but are typically much slower, especially when you're sending data (uploading) from your computer to the Internet.
- **Cost**: Service costs, depending on speed and bandwidth limit, plus Rs. 40000 for the hardware and installation (although the satellite company may waive the installation fee if you make a long-term commitment).

- **Drawbacks**: Satellite service is slower, pricier, and less reliable than cable or DSL service, but it's still way better than dial-up. Also ask whether you have to stick one of those ugly satellite dishes on the side of your house or in your yard.

> **Tip...**
>
> *If you choose satellite, consider using a dial-up account as a backup for when you can't connect in storms or dense cloud cover.*

On the Go with Wireless Internet

Wireless Internet comes in two basic forms: fixed and mobile. With fixed wireless, you install an antenna on your home or workplace and connect to a specific signal tower. Fixed wireless is beginning to compete with cable, DSL, and satellite, especially in rural areas. Mobile wireless is more like the wireless Internet you might have for an iPhone or similar device. You can connect to the Internet wherever your service provides coverage. Here's how wireless stacks up:

- **Speed**: Speeds vary greatly, typically from 256Kbps to 1Mbps for residential use. With the latest wireless technologies, speeds top out at about 100Mbps for mobile users and 1Gbps for fixed wireless (wireless service for users at stationary locations), but residential users will see speeds more in the range of 1Mbps to 10Mbps.
- **Cost**: Costs vary about as much as speeds and are almost always linked to speed. For example, you may pay Rs.100 per month for a 256Kbps connection and Rs.500 for a 1Mbps connection. I've seen ISPs that charge hundreds of bucks per month for 1Mbps service in areas where the only other broadband option is satellite.
- **Drawbacks**: Distance from the communications tower, any obstacles between the tower and your PC, and other factors can negatively affect the reliability and speed of the connection. Most services limit you to a certain number of megabytes or gigabytes per month and charge you for any number of megabytes over that amount.

When shopping for a WISP (wireless Internet service provider) and a wireless modem (adapter), keep the following standards and terminology in mind:

- **Wi-Fi**: For connecting to a wireless network at home or an Internet hotspot, look for modems that support the 802.11g (up to 54Mbps) or 802.11n (theoretically, up to 600Mbps) standard.
- **WiMAX**: This is like Wi-Fi, but potentially faster and with a much greater range. Through a wireless ISP that supports WiMAX (802.16), you can connect to the Internet whenever you're in the ISP's coverage area.
- **LTE**: Long Term Evolution (LTE) is similar to and in competition with WiMAX.
- **3G**: 3G is short for 3rd Generation wireless communications technology. WiMAX and LTE both support 3G standards.
- **4G**: This high-performance wireless technology supports downloads of up to 1 gigabyte per second (1GBps) for fixed wireless and 100Mbps for mobile users. This is about 10 times faster than with 3G. As of the writing of this book, WiMAX and LTE were evolving toward the

4G standard, and many communications companies were offering the LTE version of 4G. When you're in the market for a WISP, check out the major providers first, including AT&T, Verizon, and Sprint. Visit their websites and enter your phone number or location to determine whether the WISP provides coverage for your location and whatever areas you travel to most.

Chugging Along with Dial-Up

Because dial-up is the least expensive and most universally available of the lot, the dial-up modem has managed to hang on, but dial-up really can't compete when it comes to speed:

- **Speed:** You'll get 56Kbps tops, but you're likely to see speeds in the range of 28Kbps to 44Kbps for downloads and slower for uploads.
- **Cost**: Expect to pay Rs.500 to Rs.1000 per month.
- **Drawbacks**: S-L-O-W.

Dial-up modems are fairly standard, so any new 56Kbps V.92/V.44 modem from any of the major manufacturers (3Com, Zoom, or U.S. Robotics) can handle the job. If you have an open expansion slot in your PC, consider buying an internal modem. If you'd rather use your PC's expansion slots for something else, purchase a USB model.

Most dial-up modems support voice applications, fax, and videophone, but check the product description if you plan to use those features.

Shopping for an Internet Service Provider

The best way to shop for an ISP is to ask your neighbours and/or local business associates which ISP they use and how they like it. This way, you know the service is available in your area and you can find out about any customer service issues the company may have.

The second-best way to shop for an ISP is to connect to the Internet and search the web for services in your area. You can use a friend or relative's computer, or head down to the public library and use one of its computers.

If you have no way to shop for an ISP online, employ one of the following old-fashioned techniques:

- Call your phone company. Most phone companies offer DSL and wireless Internet service—and if they don't, they'll be able to refer you to a company that does. Also, ask about package deals.
- Call your cable or satellite company. If you have cable or satellite TV service, your cable or satellite company probably offers Internet service, too. Ask about package deals, especially if you're already a customer.
- Look in your Yellow Pages under "Internet." Most phone books list the ISPs in the area.

Establishing a Connection

If you're getting a broadband connection through your ISP (such as cable, satellite, or DSL), your ISP is going to schedule a date and time for installation, and the installer will set up your connection for you. You'll have an "always on" connection, in which you remain connected as long as your PC, broadband modem, and router (if you use a router) are turned on. If you choose dial-up service, the ISP provides you with Internet connection settings you must enter to establish a connection, including a phone number, login name, and password. You must then enter the connection settings in Windows:

- Click Start, Control Panel, Network and Internet, Network and Sharing Centre.
- Below Change your network settings, click Set up a new connection or network.
- Click Set up a dial-up connection and click Next.
- Follow the Create a Dial-up Connection wizard's instructions to enter the settings required to establish a connection with your ISP.

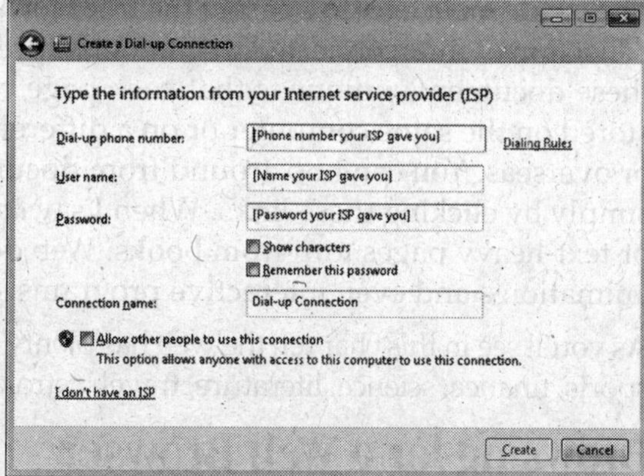

Establishing a dial-up connection

With a dial-up connection, your modem must dial in to the ISP and log on to connect before you can access the Internet. When you install software for most ISPs, the installation places an icon on the desktop that you can click or double-click whenever you want to connect. If you don't see an icon for connecting to the service, here's what you do:

- Click Start, Control Panel, Network and Internet, Network and Sharing Centre.
- Double-click the icon for your dial-up ISP. Windows dials in and automatically enters your username and password to log you in. After you've established a connection, a Dial-Up icon typically appears in the system tray (in the lower-right corner of the Windows desktop). It looks like two overlapping computers. Rest the mouse pointer on the icon to check out your connection speed, or click the icon for additional details. You can right-click the icon and click Disconnect to hang up.

Testing Your Connection Speed

No matter how your computer connects to the Internet, connection speeds can vary depending on the speed of your modem, the condition of the phone and fiber-optic cables, the amount of traffic on the network, and various other factors outside your control. If your Internet connection seems more sluggish than usual, you can check your connection speed at any of several websites:

- Click the Internet Explorer button in the taskbar. The Internet Explorer window appears and then downloads and displays the page it's set up to load upon startup.
- Click in the address bar near the top of the window, type http://us.mcafee. com/root/speedometer/default.asp, and press Enter. This connects you to McAfee's Internet Connection Speedometer.
- Click the Click here to Test Now link. The Internet Speedometer sends data to your computer to test your connection speed and then displays the results.

You can test your actual connection speed on the web.

Poking Around on the World Wide Web

The single most exciting part of the Internet is the World Wide Web (or web, for short), a loose collection of interconnected documents stored on computers all over the world. What makes these documents unique is that each page contains a link to one or more other documents stored on the same computer or on a different computer down the block, across the country, or overseas. You can hop around from document to document, from continent to continent, simply by clicking these links. When I say *documents*, I'm not talking about dusty old scrolls or text-heavy pages torn from books. Web documents contain pictures, sounds, video clips, animations, and even interactive programs.

As you'll see in this chapter, the web has plenty to offer, whatever your interests is – music, movies, sports, finance, science, literature, travel, astrology, body piercing, shopping, you name it.

Browsing for a Web Browser

To navigate the web, you need a special program called a *web browser*, which works through your Internet service provider (ISP) to pull up documents on your screen. Windows 7 includes a web browser called Internet Explorer, but plenty of other (free) browsers are available, including Mozilla Firefox (www.mozilla.com), Google Chrome (www.google.com/chrome), Apple Safari (www.apple.com/safari), and Opera (www. opera.com).

To keep things simple, I use Internet Explorer in the examples throughout this chapter. However, if you're using a different browser, don't fret. Most browsers offer the same basic features and similar navigation tools. Be flexible, and you'll be surfing the web in no time.

Steering Your Browser in the Right Direction

To run Internet Explorer, click its icon (in the taskbar). When your browser starts, it immediately opens a page that's set up as its starting page. You can begin to wander the web simply by clicking links. You can tell when the mouse pointer is over a link because the pointer changes from an arrow into a pointing hand. Click the **Back** button to flip to a previous page, or click the **Forward** button to skip ahead to a page you've visited but backed up from (see Figure). Click on link to flip to a page.

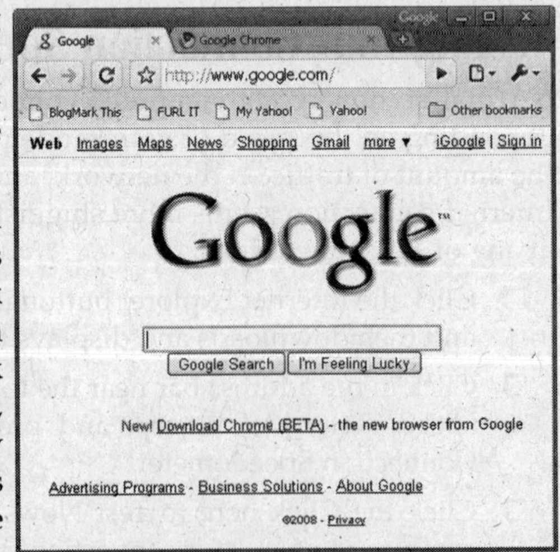

A web browser displays and helps you navigate web pages

If you click a link and your browser displays a message that it can't find the page or that access has been denied, don't freak out. Just click the **Back** button and try the link again. If that doesn't open the page, try again later. In some cases, the link may have a typo, the page was moved or deleted, or the service hosting the page is temporarily down. On the ever-changing web, this happens quite often. Be patient, be flexible, and don't be alarmed.

Note....

If you're not connected to the Internet when you start your browser, it might display a message indicating that it cannot find or load the page. If you have a standard modem connection, reestablish your connection.

A Word about Web Page Addresses

Every website has an address that defines its location, such as www.si.edu for the Smithsonian Institution or www.walmart.com for Walmart. The next time you watch TV or flip through a magazine, listen and keep your eyes peeled for web addresses.

Web addresses are formally called *URLs* (uniform resource locators). URLs allow you to open specific pages. You enter the address in your web browser, usually in a text box near the top of the window, and your web browser loads the page. Every web page URL starts with http://. Newsgroup sites start with news://. FTP sites (where you can get or upload files) start with ftp://. You get the idea. HTTP (short for Hypertext Transfer Protocol) is the coding system used to format web pages. The rest of the address identifies a specific site or page. You can omit the http:// at the beginning, and in almost all cases, you can omit the www. as well. The domain name (site address) is not case sensitive, so joekraynak.com and JoeKraynak.com will both take you to my site, but everything after that might be case sensitive; joekraynak.com/about opens my About page, but joekraynak.com/About results in an error.

Finding Stuff with Google and Other Search Tools

The web has loads of information and billions of pages, and this vast amount of information can make it difficult to track down anything specific. The web often seems like a big library that gave up on the Dewey Decimal System and piled all its books and magazines in the centre of the library. How do you sift through this massive mess of information to find what you need?

The answer: use an Internet search tool. You simply connect to a site that has a search tool, type a couple of words that specify what you're looking for, and click the **Search** button (or its equivalent). The following are the addresses of some popular search sites on the web:

www.google.com www.yahoo.com

www.ask.com www.bing.com

Most web browsers have a Search option that connects you to various Internet search tools. Internet Explorer, for example, displays a Search box near the upper-right corner of the window.

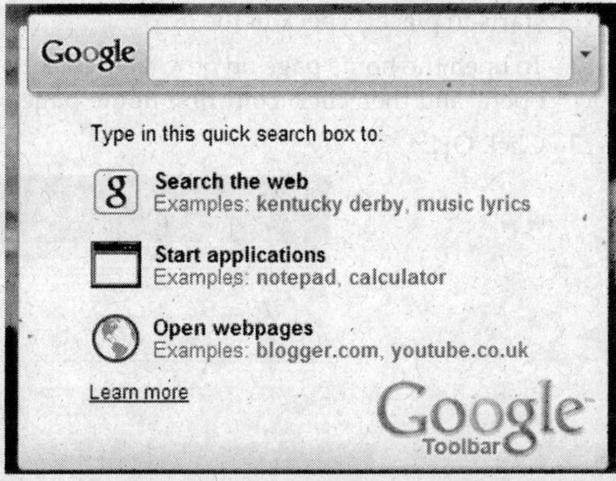

Use the Search box to find the desired web content

Simply click in the Search box, type a couple of key words that describe what you're looking for, and click the **Search** button.

Type your search word or Click phrase in the Search box Search

Locating People Online

You can also use special search tools to find long-lost relatives and friends on the Internet. These search tools are electronic telephone directories that can help you find mailing addresses, phone numbers, and even e-mail addresses. To search for people, check out the following sites: www.whitepages.com; www.pipl.com

www.spokeo.com; www.anywho.com

www.peekyou.com

The best way to find long-lost friends and relatives, however, is through Facebook.

Navigating Multiple Pages with Tabs

Most web browsers, including Internet Explorer, have tabs that enable you to keep multiple web pages open in a single window. You can then quickly switch to a page by clicking its tab. To open a new tab, click the **New Tab** button, as shown in Figure, or press **Ctrl+T**. By default, Internet Explorer opens a blank tab. You can then click in the address box and enter a website address to open the desired page. If you'd rather have Internet Explorer display the page it opens upon startup rather than displaying a blank tab, take the following steps:

- ❒ Click **Tools, Internet Options**. If you don't see "Tools," click >> on the right end of the toolbar.
- ❒ Under Tabs, click the **Settings** button.
- ❒ Click the check box next to **Open only the first home page when Internet Explorer starts** to place a check in the box.
- ❒ To open the home page on new tabs, click the button below "When a new tab is opened, open" and then click **Your first home page**.
- ❒ Click **OK**.

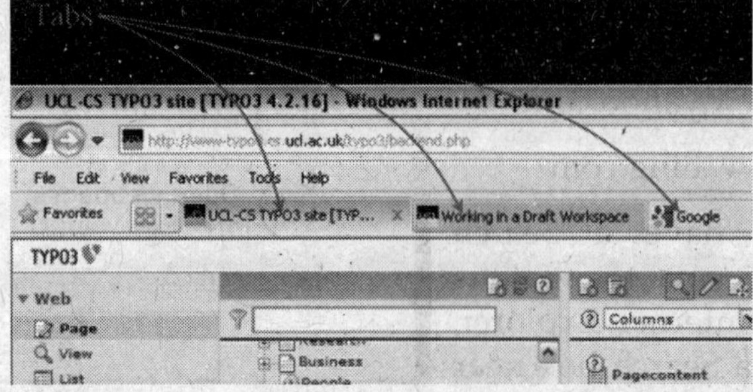

Tabs enable you to open several web pages in a single window

> ***Tip...***
>
> *When clicking links, you can choose to have a link's contents open in a new tab or window. Right-click the link and click* **Open in New Tab** *or* **Open in New Window***.*

Going Back in Time with the History List

Although the Back and Forward buttons eventually take you back to where you were, they don't get you there in a hurry or keep track of pages you visited yesterday or last week. For faster return trips and a more comprehensive log of your web journeys, check out the history list.

Click the **Favourites** button (to the left of the tabs) and click **History**. Click the day or week when you visited the website, and click the website's name to see a list of pages you viewed at that site. To open a page, click its name, as shown in Figure.

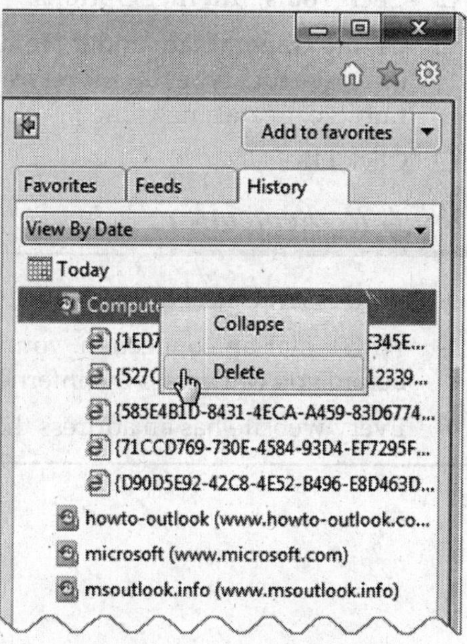

Use the history list to retrace your steps

If you share your computer with someone, you might not want that person to know where you've been on the web. To cover your tracks, do one of the following:

- Click **Favourites**, **History**; right-click the page, site, day, or week you want to remove; and click **Delete**.
- Click **Tools**, **Internet Options**, **Delete**. Click to place a check box next to each group of items you want to remove and click **Delete**.

Marking Your Favourite Web Pages

You can add your favourite sites and pages to the Favourites menu for quick return trips. To mark a page, right-click a blank area of the page and select **Add to Favourites**. You can then add and edit the name of the page as it appears in your favourites list, create a new folder (submenu) to store related favourites, and choose the folder where you want to insert your new favourite. When you're done entering your preferences, click the **Add** button. (Other browsers have similar features but may refer to favourites as *bookmarks*.)

> ***Tip...***
>
> *Right-click a blank area of the page and click* **Create Shortcut***. This places a shortcut icon for the page on your desktop. To quickly open a favourite page, click* **Favourites***, click the folder in which you saved the favourite, and then click the page's name. You can rearrange items on your Favourites menu by dragging and dropping them. If you drag an item over a folder and wait a moment, Internet Explorer opens the folder. You can then drag and drop the item in place.*

Changing the Starting Web Page

Whenever you fire up your browser, it opens with the same page every time. If you have a page you'd like your browser to load upon startup, just let your browser know.

To change your starting page in Internet Explorer, take the following steps:

- ❒ Open the page you want to view upon startup.
- ❒ Click **Tools, Internet Options**.
- ❒ On the **General** tab, under **Home page**, click **Use Current**. To open two or more pages upon startup, type the addresses in the Home page text box, one address per line. (Press **Enter** to create a new line.)
- ❒ Click **OK**.

Points to Remember

- ☆ Wireless Internet comes in two basic forms.: fixed and mobile
- ☆ With a dial-up connection, your modem must dial in to the ISP and log an to connect before you can access the internet
- ☆ Every website has an address that defines its location.

Google Search, Email and more

Google is a search engine—sort of like a web librarian. It finds stuff on the web, indexes it, and then enables people like you and me to search its index to find what we're looking for, including web pages, photos, video clips, maps, and documents. Performing a basic search on Google is easy and straightforward, but there's much more to it than most people realize.

Performing a Basic Search

To "google" a topic, go to www.google.com, type a brief description of what you're looking for, and click the **Search** button. Google displays links to web pages it deems are most relevant to what you searched for, as shown in Figure. Each item in the search results includes a title, description, address, link to a cached page, and link to similar pages. You can click the title to access the site or page. (A cached page is a backup of a page.) If nothing on the first page of search results looks promising, you can revise your search or scroll to the bottom of the page, where you'll find links to related searches or the next page of search results.

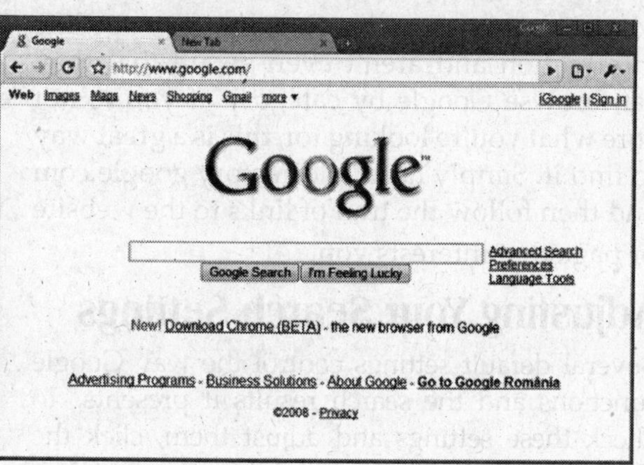

Google a topic of interest

> **Tip...**
>
> *If your search phrase contains a typo, Google displays search results for pages that include the typo, along with a link (above the search results) that you can click to perform the search again with the correct spelling. Click the link for more accurate results.*

Focusing on Specific Content

You can narrow your search by focusing it on specific content, including images, video clips, blog posts, books, scholarly articles, definitions, and even patents. Before or after performing a search, click one of the content links near the top of the page:

Images, **Videos**, **Maps**, **News**, or **Shopping**. You can click **More** (to the left of the search results) for additional filter options.

Performing an Advanced Search

Unless you specify otherwise, Google uses all the words in your search phrase to present you with what it deems most relevant. You can take more control over the results by performing an advanced search. Go to www.google.com and then click **Advanced Search** (to the right of the Search box). Google's advanced search options appear, as shown in Figure. Enter your search instructions and then click the **Advanced Search** button.

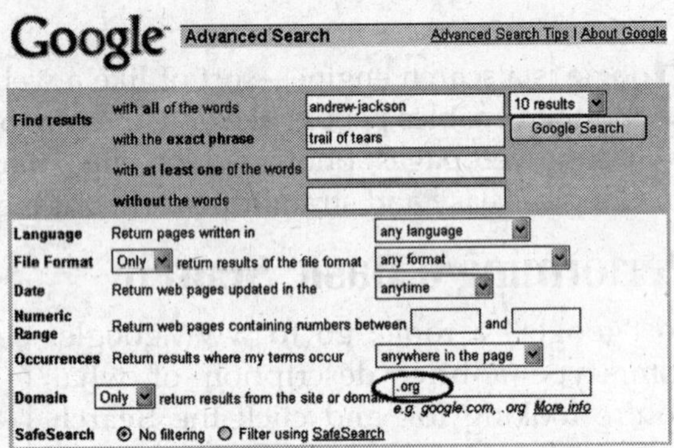

Perform an advanced search

Browsing the Website Directory

Most people search Google for specific information and aren't even aware that they can browse Google by category. If you're not sure what you're looking for, this is a great way to find it. Simply head to directory google.com and then follow the trail of links to the website or page that interests you.

Browse Google's directory

Adjusting Your Search Settings

Several default settings control the way Google functions and the search results it presents. To check these settings and adjust them, click the **Settings** link in the upper-right corner of any Google page and then click **Search settings.** The Google Preferences page appears, allowing you to enter your preferences for the following options:

- **Interface Language:** Choose the language you want Google to use when displaying text, tips, and messages.
- **Search Language:** Choose the language of the pages you want to see in the results.
- **Safe Search Filtering:** Specify how strict you want Google to be in blocking links to sexually explicit content, including photos and video.

- **Number of Results:** Specify the number of search results you want Google to display per page.
- **Results Window:** You can click the check box to have Google display the search results in a new browser window.
- **Query Suggestions:** You may notice that as you type a search phrase, Google displays a list of search phrases you can choose from so you don't have to keep typing. You can enable or disable this feature.
- **Subscribed Links:** You can subscribe to certain sites to give their content priority in the search results when your search phrase contains specific words. For example, if you subscribe to CalorieLab.com, whenever you include a food item in your search, CalorieLab.com content related to that food item appears at the top of the search results.

When you're done entering your preferences, click the **Save Preferences** button.

Cool Google Search Tips and Tricks

Google's Search box can perform all sorts of tricks, including presenting the weather for a specific city, displaying conversion rates for different currencies, converting inches into centimeters, and much more.

To Look Up ...	Type (For Example) ...
Weather for specific	⇨ city weather Chicago, IL
Stock quote	⇨ ticker BBY
Time in city/country	⇨ time France
News for sports team	⇨ New York Yankees
Calculation result	⇨ (34+27+75)/3
Book author or title	⇨ Ralph Waldo Emerson
Earthquake activity	⇨ earthquake
Temperature conversion	⇨ 65 Fahrenheit in Celsius
Public data	⇨ population WY
People profile	⇨ Sally Strapinski
Definition	⇨ define: quadruped
Local business/restaurant	⇨ pizza Hut
Movie showtimes	⇨ movies Spice
Health issue	⇨ allergy
Poison Control Centre	⇨ poison control
Airline departure/arrival	⇨ Cleartrip
Currency conversion rate	⇨ 300 USD in EUR
Map	⇨ Delhi map
Tracking number for package	⇨ 1X8888Z99999999
Patent number	⇨ patent 4345679
Location based on area code	⇨ 812

Creating a Google Account

Google has numerous features that require you to have a free Google account, including Gmail (web-based e-mail), iGoogle (personal home page), Picasa Web Albums (for photo sharing), Talk (online chat), and Calendar. To tap Google's full potential, I encourage you to create your own Google account:

- ❒ Head to www.google.com.
- ❒ Click **Sign in** (upper-right corner).
- ❒ Below Don't have a Google Account?, click **Create an account now**.
- ❒ Enter the requested information and word verification, review the Terms of Service, and (if you agree to the Terms of Service), click **I accept. Create my account**.

You can now sign in to Google whenever you like, to take advantage of features and tools of Google.

Feature Website Address

Alerts www.google.com/alerts

Free blog www.blogger.com

Bookmarks www.google.com/bookmarks

Calendar www.google.com/calendar

Docs docs.google.com

Gmail mail.google.com

Groups groups.google.com

Customizable home page www.google.com/ig

Maps maps.google.com

Notes www.google.com/notebook

Social network www.orkut.com

Photo sharing picasaweb.google.com

Web aggregator www.google.com/reader

Subscribed links google.com/coop/subscribedlinks

Chat www.google.com/talk

Videos video.google.com

Checking Out Other Search Sites and Tools

Google is the most popular search engine, but it's not the only one. Some of the other search engines are comparable, while others perform specialized searches. Following are some notable search engines you may want to check out:

- ❒ **WhitePages.com** (www.whitepages.com) is excellent for tracking down phone numbers and addresses of individuals and businesses.

- **Yahoo!** (www.yahoo.com) is comparable to Google in connecting you with Yahoo! resources, news, trends, and search.
- **Bing** (www.bing.com) is Microsoft's search engine.
- **Open Directory** (www.dmoz.com) is a hand-crafted, no-frills search directory.

Sending and Receiving E-Mail

How would you like to send a message to a friend and have it arrive in a matter of seconds? Send dozens of messages every day without paying a single cent in postage?

Never again stare out your window waiting for the mail carrier?

Well, your dreams are about to come true. When you have a connection to the Internet and an e-mail program, all these benefits are yours. Here, you learn how to start taking advantage of them.

Before you set sail on your maiden voyage, you have a choice to make: do you want to use an e-mail client installed on your computer, access your e-mail via the web, or both? Using an e-mail program installed on your computer allows you to download all incoming messages to your computer and read them at your leisure—regardless of whether you're connected to the Internet. E-mail programs also provide enhanced tools for managing messages. Web-based e-mail offers the advantage of being able to access your e-mail from any computer. You simply use a web browser installed on any computer to connect to the site, log in, and send and receive your messages.

Using an E-Mail Program

An e-mail program runs on your computer and connects to your Internet mail server to send messages from and receive messages to your PC. You can use any of several programs to access e-mail, including Outlook, Windows Live Mail (download.live.com/wlmail), Eudora (www.eudora.com), and Thunderbird (www.mozilla.com/thunderbird), to name a few. Versions of Windows prior to Windows 7 include an e-mail program—Outlook Express, Windows Messenger, or Windows Mail. Microsoft Office also includes an e-mail program called Outlook. If you're running Windows 7 and don't have Office, go to one of the websites mentioned in the previous paragraph to download and install the e-mail client of your choice.

Setting Up Your Account

The hardest part about using an e-mail program is setting it up to connect to your mail server—an electronic post office that routes your incoming and outgoing messages to their proper destinations. To set up your e-mail program, you need the following information from your ISP:

- **E-mail address:** Your e-mail address contains some version of your name or nickname followed by the @ sign and your e-mail server's domain name—for example, jsmith@iway.com.
- **Password:** You pick the password or have one assigned to you.
- **Outgoing mail (SMTP):** The Simple Mail Transfer Protocol (SMTP) server is the mailbox where you drop your outgoing messages. It's actually your Internet service provider's

computer. The address usually starts with "mail" or "smtp," as in mail.iway.com or smtp. iway.com.

- **Incoming mail (POP3):** The Post Office Protocol (POP) server is like your neighbourhood post office. It receives incoming messages and places them in your personal mailbox. POP server addresses commonly start with pop or mail, as in mail.google.com, but check to make sure. When you have the preceding information, you must enter it into your e-mail program. To enter e-mail settings in Outlook 2010, click **File**, **Add Account**, and then follow the onscreen instructions to enter your name, e-mail address, password, and any other information required to establish a connection with your e-mail provider. Figure shows the first dialog box in the Add New Account wizard in Outlook 2010. Using your e-mail address and password, Outlook can usually obtain the other settings it requires to access your e-mail server. If it can't connect, you may need to start over and click the option to manually configure your server settings (lower-left corner of the dialog box shown in Figure).

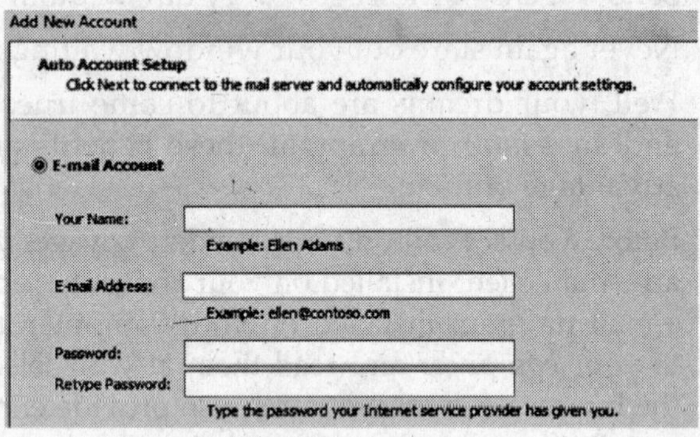

Setting uyp an account

Before you can use your e-mail program, you must set up an account.

Addressing an Outgoing Message

The procedure for sending messages over the Internet varies, depending on which e-mail program or online service you're using. In most cases, you first click the button for composing a new message. For example, in Outlook 2010, you click the **Home** tab and then the **New E-mail** button and use the resulting dialog box, as shown in Figure, to address, compose, and send your message.

Note....

*Most e-mail programs, including Outlook, feature an e-mail address book or list of contacts. If a contact is in the address book, you simply start typing the person's name or e-mail address in the To box, and the program completes the entry for you. Or, you can click **To** and select the address from the list.*

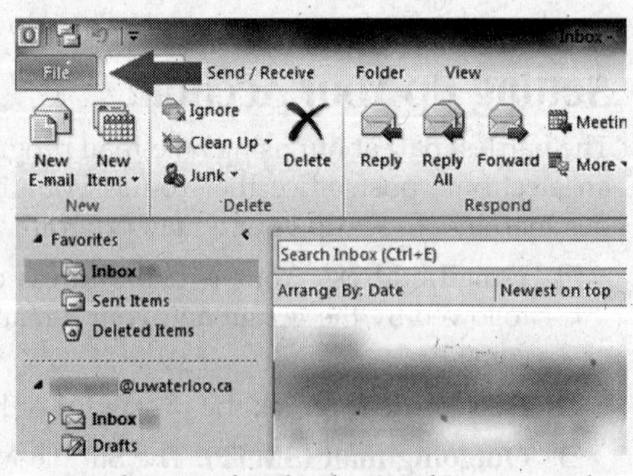

Here's how to send mail with a typical Internet e-mail program (Outlook)

Type the person's e-mail address

- Click to send the message
- Type your message – Type a brief description of the message

Checking Your E-Mail

Most e-mail programs check for messages automatically on startup or display a button you can click to fetch your mail (the Send/Receive button in Outlook or the Sync button in Windows Live Mail). The program retrieves your mail and then displays a list of message descriptions. To preview a message, click it, as shown in Figure. To view the message in its own window, double-click it. Most e-mail programs use several folders to help you keep your messages organized. For example, Outlook features folders named Inbox, Outbox, Sent Items, and Deleted Items.

To switch from one folder to another, click the desired folder.

Click the message to preview its contents. The contents of the message appear in the preview pane

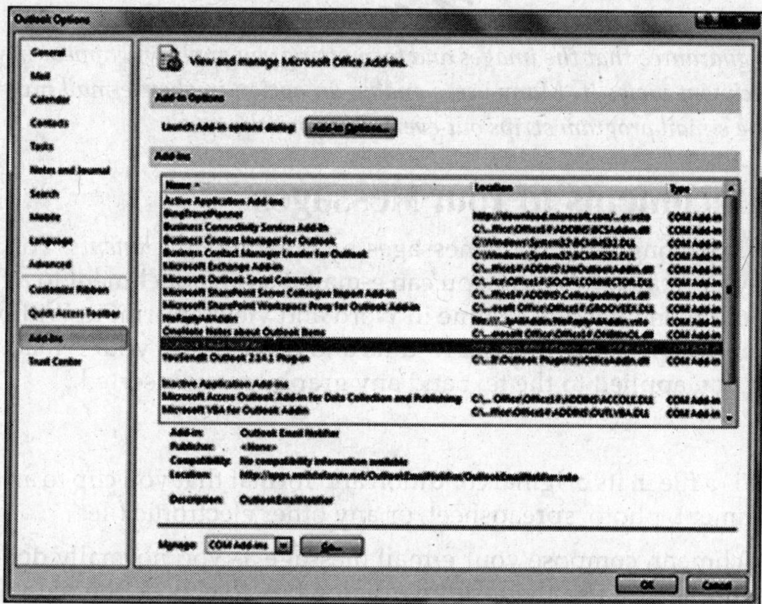

You can quickly display the contents of messages you receive.

Sending Replies

To reply to a message you received, double-click the message, click the **Reply** button, type your reply, and click **Send**. If you received a message that you want to pass along to other recipients, you can *forward* the message. Double-click the message you want to forward, and click the **Forward** button. In the To text box, enter the e-mail addresses of the people to whom you want to forward the message. If you want to add an introduction to or comment about the original message, type this text in the message area. When you're ready to forward the message, click the **Send** button.

Adding Photos and Other Cool Stuff

Almost all e-mail programs, including Outlook, offer a toolbar with buttons for the most common enhancements. You can use the toolbar to make text bold or italic; add bulleted and numbered lists; and insert pictures, horizontal lines, links, and other objects. (If the toolbar does not appear, check the **Format** menu and click the **HTML** or **Rich Text** option. HTML stands for Hypertext Markup Language, the coding system used to format web pages. Rich Text is another specification that allows for fancy formatting in e-mail messages.)

The buttons for inserting pictures and hyperlinks and formatting text work the same way as in your word processing and desktop publishing programs.

To share a link, type the e-mail address or address of the web page you want it to point to and press the **spacebar** or **Enter** key. Most e-mail programs automatically convert web page and e-mail addresses typed in the message area into links. You can also drag links from a web page into the message area and drop them in the message area.

Note.... ✍

You have no guarantee that the images and formatting you apply will appear in your message when the recipient views it. Many users enable an option in their e-mail programs to view text only. The e-mail program strips out everything but the text.

Attaching Documents to Your Messages

You can send files along with your messages by creating *attachments.* For instance, if you have a resume you created in Word, you can e-mail it as an attachment to a friend to review. That person could then open the resume in Word and view or print it. Without attachments, you would need to copy the text of the resume and paste it into your e-mail message, losing any formatting you applied to the text and any graphics you inserted.

DEFINITION

An **attachment** is a file in its original condition and format that you clip to an e-mail message. It can be a document, photo, spreadsheet, or any other electronic file.

To send an attachment, compose your e-mail message as you normally do; click the **Attach** or **Insert File** button; and use the resulting dialog box to choose the file you want to send. When you're ready to send the message, along with the attachment, click the **Send** button.

Many word processing and spreadsheet programs have built-in support for e-mail, allowing you to send a document right from the program. In Word 2010, for instance, you can open the document you want to send, open the **File** menu, click **Share**, click **Send Using E-mail**, and click **Send as Attachment**.

If you receive a message that contains an attached file, your e-mail program usually displays some indication that a file is attached. For example, Outlook displays a paperclip icon. If you double-click the message (to display it in its own window), an icon appears at the bottom of the window or in an attachments text box. You can double-click the icon to open the file, or right-click and choose **Save** to save the file to a separate folder on your hard drive.

Note.... ✍

When you receive an attachment, use an antivirus program to scan the file before opening it (if it's a document) or running it (if it's a program). Programs are especially notorious for carrying viruses, but documents may contain macro viruses, which can cause as much havoc. (Most antivirus programs are set up to run in the background and automatically scan attachments when you choose to open them or save them to disk.)

What About Free, Web-Based E-Mail?

You've probably heard of "free e-mail" services, such as Gmail (Google Mail), Yahoo!, and Hotmail, and wondered why anyone would need free e-mail. Isn't all e-mail free?

Does your ISP charge extra for it? Of course, your e-mail account is included with the service that your ISP provides; your ISP does not charge extra for it. But there are several good reasons to explore these free e-mail services:

- Free e-mail is typically web-based, allowing you to send messages and check your mail from anywhere in the world using any computer that's connected to the Internet.
- Free e-mail lets everyone in your home or business have his or her own e-mail account.
- Free e-mail is good to use when you register "anonymously" for free stuff, keeping your real e-mail address private.
- Free e-mail also provides you with a stable e-mail address so that when you change ISPs, you don't have to change your e-mail address.

To get a free e-mail account, connect to any of the following sites, click the link for free e-mail, register, and follow the instructions at the site to start using your free e-mail account:

- Gmail – mail.google.com
- Yahoo! – mail.yahoo.com
- Windows Live – signup.live.com
- AOL Mail – mail.AOL.com

Emoticons and E-Mail Shorthand

If you want to look like an e-mail veteran, you can pepper your messages with emoticons (pronounced *ee-mow-tick-ons*). These icons look like facial expressions or act as abbreviations for specific emotions. (You might need to turn your head sideways to see the tiny faces.) You can use these symbols to show your pleasure or displeasure with a particular comment, to take the edge off a comment you think might be misinterpreted, and to express your moods.

Emoticon Meaning

:) or :-) I'm happy, or it's good to see you, or I'm smiling as I'm saying this.

(You can often use this to show you're joking.)

:D or :-D I'm really happy or laughing.

;) or ;-) Winking.

:(or :-(Unhappy. You hurt me, you big brute.

;(or ;-(Crying.

:| or :-| I don't really care. Straight face. Neutral.

:/ or :-/ Skeptical. Annoyed.

:# or :-# My lips are sealed. I can keep a secret.

:> or :-> Devilish grin.

:p or :-p Sticking my tongue out.

<g> Grinning. (Usually takes the edge off whatever you just said.)

<lol> Laughing out loud.

<jk> Just kidding.

In addition to the language of emoticons, Internet chat and e-mail messages are commonly seasoned with a fair share of abbreviations. The following table offers samples of the abbreviations you'll encounter and be expected to know.

Abbreviation Meaning

AFAIK – As far as I know.

AFK – Away from keyboard.

BRB – Be right back.

BTW – By the way.

CUL8R – See you later.

F2F – Face to face (usually in reference to meeting somebody in person).

Abbreviation Meaning

FAQ – Frequently asked questions. (Many sites post a list of often asked questions, along with the answers. They call this list a FAQ.)

FTF – Another version of "face to face."

FYI – For your information.

IDK – I don't know.

IMHO – In my humble opinion.

IMO – In my opinion.

IOW – In other words.

KISS – Keep it simple, stupid.

LOL – Laughing out loud.

NM, NVM – Never mind.

OIC – Oh, I see.

ROTFL – Rolling on the floor laughing.

TTFN – Ta ta for now.

TTYL – Talk to you later.

E-Mail No-No's

To avoid getting yourself into trouble by unintentionally sending an insulting e-mail message, be sure you use the proper protocol for composing e-mail messages.

The most important rule is to NEVER, EVER TYPE IN ALL UPPERCASE CHARACTERS. This is the equivalent of shouting, and people become edgy when they see this text on their screen. Likewise, take it easy on the exclamation points!!! Avoid sending bitter, sarcastic messages (flames) via e-mail. When you disagree with somebody, a personal visit or a phone call is usually more tactful than a long e-mail message that painfully describes how stupid and inconsiderate the other person is.

Besides, you never know who might see your message; the recipient could decide to forward your message to a few choice recipients as retribution.

Also in a business or educational e-mail, use correct spelling and grammar. Abbreviations for words or sentences, such as CUL8er (for "see you later"), and emoticons may be acceptable in text messaging and e-mailing friends, but they're taboo in formal circles.

If you're in marketing or sales, avoid sending unsolicited ads and other missives. Few people appreciate such advertising. In fact, few people appreciate receiving anything that's unsolicited, cute, "funny," or otherwise inapplicable to their business or personal life. In short, don't forward every little cute or funny e-mail message, "true" story, chain letter, joke, phony virus warning, or free offer you receive. Finally, avoid forwarding warnings about the latest viruses and other threats to human happiness. Most of these warnings are hoaxes, and when you forward a hoax, you're just playing into the hands of the hoaxers. If you think the warning is serious, check the source to verify the information before you forward the warning to everyone in your address book. Virus hoaxes are posted at www.symantec.com/avcentre/hoax.html and vil.nai.com/vil/hoaxes.aspx.

Points to Remember

- ☆ To set up a new e-mail account in Outlook, click **File**, **Add Account**, and follow the onscreen instructions.
- ☆ To create a new e-mail message, click the **Compose Mail** or **New Message** button or its equivalent in your e-mail program.
- ☆ incoming e-mail messages are often stored in the Inbox. Simply click the **Inbox** folder and click the desired message to display its contents.
- ☆ To reply to a message, select the message and click the **Reply** button.
- ☆ To attach a document to an outgoing message, click the button for attaching a file and select the desired document file.
- ☆ DON'T TYPE IN ALL UPPERCASE … and follow all the other rules of proper e-mail etiquette.

You Tube

Forget about ABC, CBS, and NBC. YouTube is way more popular, providing you with free access on demand to an unlimited selection of video clips 24/7. Simply head to www.youtube.com, click a link for a video that looks interesting, and then kick back and watch. Of course, you can do a lot more on YouTube, which is what this chapter is all about.

Searching and Browsing on YouTube

When you go to www.youtube.com, the opening screen displays a sample collection of video clips that members recently added, none of which you may find particularly interesting. If nothing catches your eye, or if you're looking for a specific type of video, you can search for items or browse YouTube's video collection.

Searching for Specific Video Footage

When you know what you're looking for, or at least have a vague notion, click inside the Search box (near the top of the page), type one or more words describing what you're looking for, and then click the Search button. YouTube displays a collection of video clips that match your description, as shown in Figure. Click a clip to play it.

Searching for videos

Browsing YouTube's Video Collection

To browse YouTube's video collection by category, click the Browse button near the top of any YouTube page and then click the double down arrow button to the right of Videos/All categories. Click the category of your choice and then use the resulting screen to browse the videos in the selected category. (See Figure.)

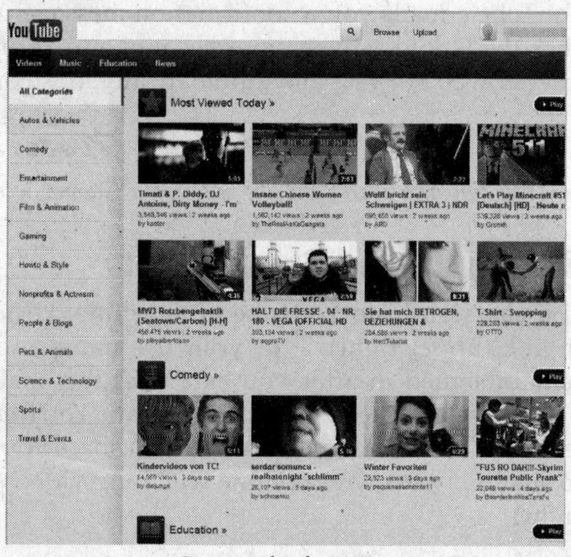

Browse videos by category

If you click any of the major categories near the bottom of the Categories list, such as Shows or Movies, the Search button changes, so you can limit your search to the selected category. For example, if you click Movies, the Search button changes to Search Movies. Click in the Search box, type one or more words describing the movie, and click Search Movies.

> **Tip...**
>
> *To return to YouTube's opening page, click the YouTube logo in the upper-left corner of any YouTube page.*

Doing more through a YouTube Account

You can watch most videos without joining YouTube, but if you want to do more than that, create an account, which allows you to do the following:

- Enable YouTube to keep track of the videos you watched so it can recommend other videos you might enjoy.
- Flag videos as your favourites, so you can quickly return to them later.
- Rate (thumbs up or down) and comment on videos.
- Subscribe to channels. (A channel is a collection of videos uploaded by a specific individual on YouTube.)
- Customize your YouTube home page.
- Upload and share your own videos with millions of other YouTube users.

Creating an Account

To create an account, click the Create Account link (upper-right corner), complete the form, and click I accept. When YouTube prompts you for your e-mail address, complete the form by entering your e-mail address and the password you want to use (and confirming it), typing the word verification, and then clicking the Create New Account and Finish.

YouTube e-mails you a confirmation message. When you receive it, open the message and click the link to activate your account and verify your e-mail address. This opens YouTube in your web browser and automatically logs you into your account.

Note....

You can sign in to YouTube with your Google account and password.

Signing In and Signing Out

You can sign in to YouTube at any time. Head to www.youtube.com and click the Sign In link (upper right). Type your username and password in the corresponding boxes. To remain signed in after you exit YouTube, make sure the Stay signed in box is checked, or remove the check mark if you want YouTube to sign you out automatically when you leave. Click the Sign in button. If you share your computer with other users, you may want to sign out when you're done watching videos. To sign out, click the Sign Out link (upper right).

Saving Your Favourites

When you come across an amazing video that you're probably going to want to watch again or share with others, add it to your list of favourites. Click the Save to button (below the video) and click Favourites, as shown in Figure.

To view a video on your Favourites list, click your username (upper right) and click Favourites. This displays a list of your favourites. Click the Play button for the favourite you want to watch. (You can remove a video from your list of favourites by clicking the Remove button, to the lower right of the favourite.)

Creating Additional Playlists

Your list of favourites is your default playlist. You can create additional playlists to more effectively organize your favourite videos. To create a playlist, pull up a video you want to add to the playlist, click the Save to button (below the video), and click Create a new playlist, as shown in Figure. Type a name for the new playlist and press Enter. To add a video to your new playlist, pull up the video, click the Save to button, and then click the name of the playlist you want the video added to.

Subscribing to a Channel

If you really like a video, chances are good that you'll enjoy other videos the person has

Subscribing to a channel

uploaded. Just above the video, click the member's username to access his or her channel. Here you'll find links to any other videos the member has uploaded, along with the member's favourites and playlists (assuming that the person is not preventing them from being shared). To subscribe to the member's channel, click the Subscribe button at the top of the page or above any video the member has uploaded.

To manage your subscriptions, click the YouTube logo (upper left), click your username (upper right), and click Subscriptions.

Sharing a Video with Others

When you see an incredible (or incredibly funny) video, your first impulse may be to share it with others you think will like it. YouTube provides options that make it easy to share videos via e-mail and on numerous social networking sites, including Facebook and Twitter. To share a video, click the Share button, click the desired share option, and follow the onscreen cues to complete the process.

Sharing a video with others

Rating and Commenting on Videos

Below every video are a thumbs up (Like) button, thumbs down button, and Respond to this video box. Click the thumbs up or thumbs down button to cast your vote for or against the video. To comment on the video, click in the Respond to this video box, type your comment, and press Enter.

If you feel the video is inappropriate, click the Flag button (off to the right), select the reason you think the video is inappropriate, and then click the Flag this video button.

Sharing Your Videos

You may not be Celebrity, but you can play a more active role on YouTube by contributing (uploading) your own video footage taken using a camcorder, digital camera, or even cell phone. You shoot the video, copy it to your computer, edit it, save it as a file, and then upload the file on YouTube. The following sections show you how to deal with the uploading step. If you have a functional webcam attached to your computer, YouTube also enables you to record video on the fly directly into YouTube.

Note....

YouTube has a detailed list of rules and regulations governing the content users can post. Don't post sexually explicit video or video that shows bad stuff, including child or animal abuse, drug abuse, underage drinking or smoking, bomb making, gratuitous violence, racist comments, and so on. I encourage you to read YouTube's Community Guidelines at www.youtube.com/t/ community_guidelines before uploading any videos.

Prepping a Video for Uploading

Before uploading a video, edit and save your video to a file that adheres to YouTube's video specifications:

- No longer than 10 minutes
- No larger than 2 gigabytes
- Saved in one of the following file formats:
  - .WMV (Windows Media Video) .3GP (cellphones)
  - .AVI (Windows) .MOV (Mac)
  - .MP4 (iPod/PSP) .MPEG
  - .FLV (Adobe Flash) .MKV (h.264)

Your video editing program, such as Windows MovieMaker or Apple iMovie, enables you to edit and compress video, and should allow you to save the video in one of the acceptable formats. (Keep in mind that compression negatively affects the quality of the video.)

Uploading Your Video to YouTube

After you've prepped your video and have a suitable file to upload, the actual process of uploading it is a snap:

- Click the Upload link (near the top of the page). If the Upload link isn't there, click the YouTube logo in the upper-left corner of any YouTube page to go to your home page, and then click the Upload link.
- Click the Upload video button.

Uploading a video

- ❒ Choose the video file you want to upload, and click Open.
- ❒ Complete the Video information and privacy settings section.

Recording a Video with a Webcam

If you have a functioning webcam connected to your PC, you can use it to record live video and instantly upload it to YouTube. Here's how:

- ❒ Click the Upload link near the top of the page.
- ❒ Click Record from webcam.
- ❒ If an Adobe Flash Player Settings box appears, click Allow to give it access to your webcam, click Remember, so that you won't be asked again, and then click Close. Whatever's in front of the camera should now appear in the record area on the screen.
- ❒ Position yourself or whatever you want to "film" in front of your webcam, click the Record button, and do the recording.
- ❒ If something bad happens while you're recording, click Stop and then Restart.
- ❒ When you're done recording, click the Stop button.

Getting Help

You can do more on YouTube than this chapter covers. To learn about additional features or to obtain assistance using a feature, check out YouTube's help system. Scroll to the bottom of almost any YouTube page and click the Help link. You can then search the help system for a specific topic or browse to learn more about YouTube.

Points to Remember

- ☆ To search for videos on YouTube, click in the Search box (top of the page), type one or more words to describe what you want, and then click the Search button.
- ☆ To browse YouTube's video collection, click the Browse link (to the right of the Search button).
- ☆ Register for a free account so that you can save your favourite videos for future viewing and personalize YouTube.
- ☆ To save a video as a favourite, click the Save to button (below the video) and click Favourites.
- ☆ To upload a video of your own, click the Upload link (at the top of almost every YouTube page) and follow the onscreen cues to complete the process.
- ☆ To get help, scroll to the bottom of almost any YouTube page and click the Help link.

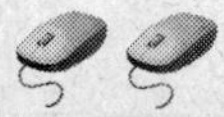

Chapter 31

Twitter

In the twenty-first century, hearing it through the grapevine usually means reading it on Twitter. Twitter is a social networking tool that enables users to share very brief text messages (140 characters or less), commonly referred to as *tweets*. At any time of the day or night, hundreds of millions of Twitter users are in the process of sharing tweets with one another, creating a global buzz. This chapter shows you how to join in the chorus of tweeters round the world.

Creating a Twitter Account

To create a Twitter account, head to twitter.com and click the **Sign Up** button. Complete the Join the Conversation form, shown in Figure. If you don't want to receive e-mail updates from Twitter, click the check box next to **I want the inside scoop** to remove the check mark. Click the **Create my account** button.

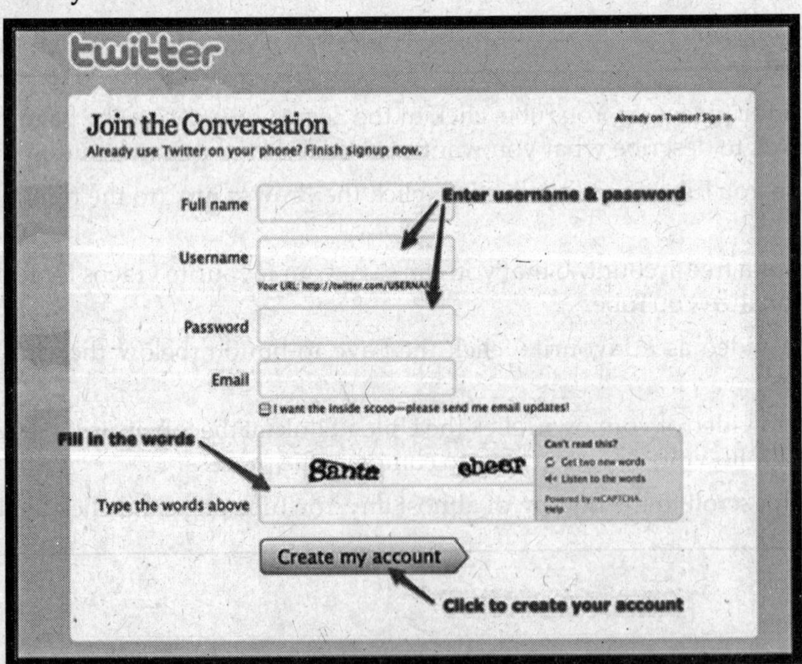

When Twitter asks "Are you human?" click in the **Type the words above** box, type the validation text displayed on the page, and click **Finish**. Twitter creates your account, signs you in, and displays a list of topics you can explore. Before you do that, however, confirm your account. Check your e-mail for a confirmation message from Twitter. When you receive the message, open it and then click the link for confirming your account. Twitter grants you full access to the service and displays its home page.

Signing In and Signing Out

To sign in to Twitter, go to twitter.com, click the **Sign in** button (upper right), enter your username or e-mail address and password in the designated text boxes, and click the **Sign in** button.

When you're done on Twitter, consider signing out, especially if you're sharing the PC—you don't want just anyone tweeting using your username and identity. To sign out, click the **Sign out** link (upper-right corner).

Fleshing Out Your Profile

Unless you add more information about yourself, the only thing identifying you on Twitter is your Twitter name. To give yourself more of a presence and improve your chances of connecting with more people, consider fleshing out your profile with a picture, location, website address, and bio. Click **Settings** (upper right), **Profile**, and use the Profile Settings screen, as shown in Figure, to upload a profile picture and add details about yourself. When you're done, click the **Save** button.

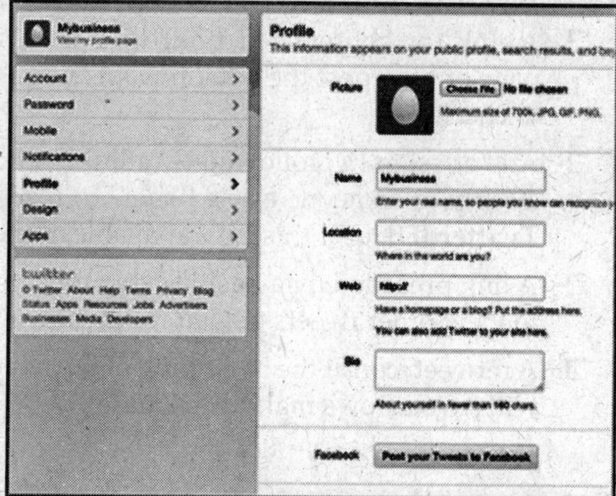

Add a picture and details to your profile.

Tweaking Your Account Settings

Before you post any of your own tweets, you may want to check out your account settings and perhaps make some adjustments. Click **Settings** (upper right) and then **Account**. You can use the Account Settings screen to change your username, e-mail address, language preference, time zone, location, and tweet privacy preference. You can also choose to let others find you by searching for your e-mail address. Enter your preferences and click the **Save** button.

Reading and Replying to Tweets

To get a feel for the Twitter community and tweeting, read some tweets and perhaps reply to a tweet or two before posting your own tweets. The following sections show you how.

Reading a Tweet

When you're interested in learning what others think about a particular topic, you can read all about it on Twitter. On twitter.com, click in the search box, type one or more words describing the topic, and then click the search button, as shown in Figure.

Twitter displays a list of recent tweets (most recent first) that match the topic description you searched. To see more tweets on this topic, scroll to the bottom of the list and click **more**.

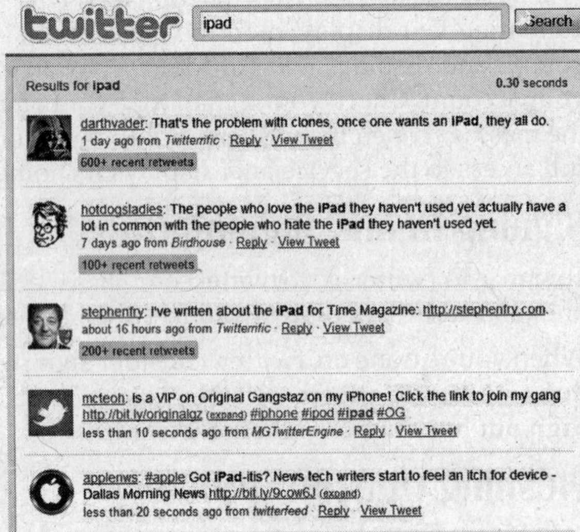

Searching for twitter

Search for tweets:

Every tweet contains the name of the person who posted it, followed by a brief message. You can click the member's name to view more tweets by that individual. Below each message is an indication of the time that has passed since the message was posted. A tweet may also contain any of the following:

- A link (or abbreviated link) to a web page or blog post the person wants you to check out.
- An "at" sign (@) followed by a link, indicating that the tweet you're reading is actually a reply to someone else's tweet. To read the original tweet, click **in reply to [person's Twitter ID]**, or if this isn't available, click the link to the right of the @ sign.
- A link preceded by a hashtag (#), indicating a group or extra information. Click the link to view other tweets tagged for inclusion in this group.
- A retweet icon at the beginning of the tweet (just to the right of the person' profile picture with two arrows making a square).

Tip...

If you're probably going to search for this same topic in the future, click ***Save this search*** *(above the list of tweets that match your search phrase). Saved searches appear in the navigation bar on the right—simply click the link for the saved search whenever you want to repeat it.*

Replying to a Tweet and Retweeting

Twitter is all about interacting with others—engaging in conversations. If a tweet inspires you to respond in some way, mouse over the tweet and click **Reply**, as shown in Figure. The What's happening? box becomes the Reply to so-and-so box, and Twitter starts you off by adding the @ sign followed by the member's username. Type your reply and then click the **Tweet** button.

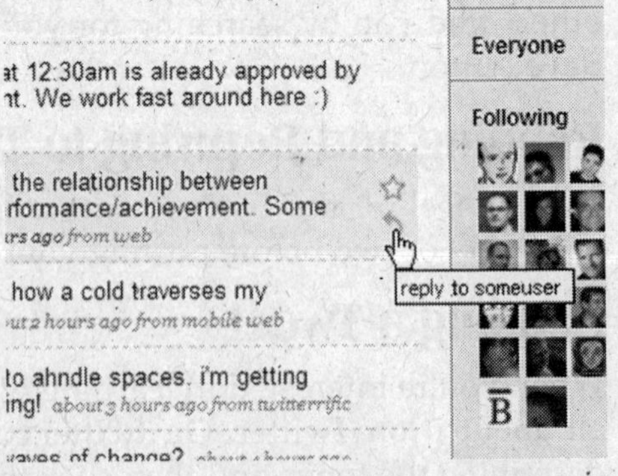

Reply or retweet

Another way to respond to a message is to retweet it—spread the word by passing the tweet along to all of your followers. Of course, when you're just starting out, you probably have few (if any) followers, so retweeting may not make much sense right now. When you do have some followers, here's how you retweet: put the mouse over the tweet you want to retweet, click **Retweet**, and then click **Yes** to confirm.

You can always delete a reply or undo a retweet. To delete a reply you posted, put the mouse over the reply and click **Delete**. To undo a retweet, put the mouse over the tweet you retweeted and click **Undo**.

Flagging a Tweet as a Favourite

When you come across a tweet you'll probably want to return later, mark it as a favourite. Simply put the mouse over the tweet and click the hollow star that appears to the upper right of it. The star turns solid gold, and Twitter adds the tweet to your list of favourites. To view your favourites, click **Favourites** (in the navigation bar on the right).

Posting Tweets

Posting a tweet is a snap. Click in the **What's happening?** box and type a message (140 characters or less). As you type, Twitter displays the number of characters remaining, as shown in Figure—a negative number means you're over the limit.

When you're done typing, click the **Tweet** button. Twitter posts your tweet and displays it on your home page.

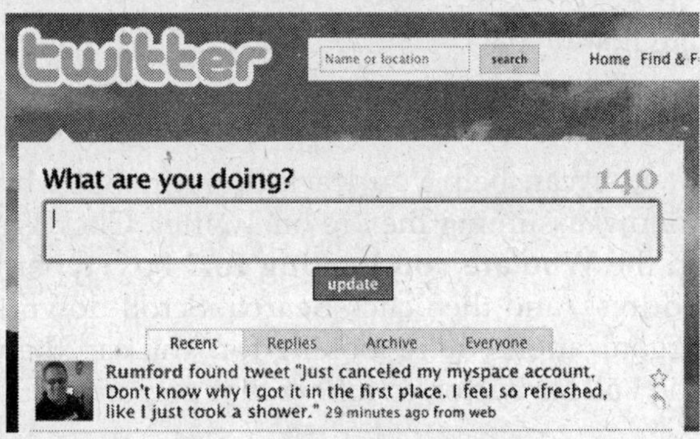

Your Twitter home page

Adding a Link

Many tweets consist of a brief message that introduces a web page or blog entry followed by a link to that page or entry. To insert a link into your tweet, type the web page address or copy the address from your browser's address box and paste it in your message. (You do not need to include the http:// at the beginning of the address.) When you click the **Tweet** button, Twitter automatically converts the address into a link prior to posting your tweet, so anyone reading it can simply click the link.

A long URL can consume a huge portion of your allotted 140 characters. Consider using a free URL abbreviation service, such as bit.ly, to truncate the URL for you. Visit bit.ly for details.

Deleting a Tweet

You can't edit a tweet, so if you make a mistake or want to remove your tweet for any reason later, delete it. Sign in to Twitter and rest the mouse pointer on the tweet you want to delete. In the lower-right corner of the tweet, a trash can icon appears with the Delete link next to it. Click **Delete** and then click **OK** to confirm.

Following Users on Twitter

Follow someone on Twitter

Twitter users who share common interests can choose to follow one another. Friends often use Twitter sort of like Facebook to keep in touch with one another. You and your friends can choose to follow one another—whenever you post a tweet, all your friends are notified. You can also follow complete strangers or politicians, celebrities, athletes, and anyone else who chooses to tweet in public. To follow someone on Twitter, put the mouse over his or her username and click the **Follow** button, as shown in Figure. Whenever you want to check the person's tweets, click **following** (near the top of the navigation bar).

Searching for People on Twitter

Twitter can help you track down people, businesses, or organizations you may want to follow, assuming they're on Twitter. Click **Find People** (near the top of any Twitter page). In the **Who are you looking for?** box, type the person's or organization's name or e-mail address, and then click **Search**. Scroll down the list, if necessary, to find the individual or organization you're looking for. You can then click the user's name to read tweets or click the **Follow** button to follow that person.

Seeing Who's Following You

If you have friends on Twitter or post such interesting tweets that complete strangers take an interest, you may begin to gather a following. To see who's following you, click **followers** (near the top of the navigation bar). For each follower, Twitter displays the following three buttons:

- The Follow button enables you to follow the person who's following you.
- The list button enables you to add users to lists to make them more manageable.
- The third button opens a menu with options for mentioning so-and-so in a tweet, sending the person a direct message (sort of like e-mail), following the person, blocking the person, or reporting the person for spamming you.

Exchanging Direct Messages in Private

You can send a direct message privately to anyone who's following you. Direct messages are sort of like a cross between an e-mail and a tweet. They're private like e-mail, but brief like tweets. To send a direct message, do one of the following actions:

- From your home page, click **Direct Messages** (right navigation bar), open the **Send ______ a direct message** list, select the desired recipient, type a message in the box, and click **Send**.

- ❒ Click **followers** (right navigation bar), click the button to the far right of the desired recipient's name, and click **Direct message so-and-so**. Type your message and click **Send**.
- ❒ Click in the **What's happening?** box and type **d+username+message**, dropping the @ symbol; for example, **d bittudon4 What are you working on?** Click the **Tweet** button. As soon as you type **d** followed by a space, the "What's happening?" changes to "Direct message."

> **Tip...**
>
> *To reply to a follower's tweet with a private message instead of a public response, click **Reply** (below the tweet you want to respond to), replace the @ sign with a d followed by a space, type your message after the person's username, and click **Tweet**.*

Learning More About Twitter

This chapter provides you with all you need to know to start using Twitter, but the more you know, the more you'll get out of it. I encourage you to check out Twitter's help system. Just click **Help** near the top of any page to access Twitter's Help Centre.

Points to Remember

- ☆ To search for tweets about a specific topic, click in the search box (right navigation bar), type a topic description, and click the search button.
- ☆ To post a tweet, click in the **What's happening?** box, type your message (140 characters or less), and click **Tweet**.
- ☆ To reply to a tweet, put the mouse over it, click the **Reply** button, type your reply, and click **Tweet**.
- ☆ To follow someone on Twitter, put the mouse over the person's username and then click the **Follow** button.
- ☆ To personalize Twitter, edit your profile, change your account settings, and more, click **Settings** at the top of most Twitter pages and use the resulting options to enter your preferences

Chapter 32

Communicating One-on-One in Real Time

Your PC is no replacement for an iPhone or Android, but when you're sitting in front of a PC equipped with a webcam and microphone, you can do everything you can do with a cellphone and then some ... and for less money. Using programs like AOL Instant Messenger (AIM), Google Talk, and Skype, you can communicate in real time with anyone, anywhere in the world via texting, Internet phone, and even video calling, all for free. This chapter shows you how.

Instant Messaging with AIM

America Online's Instant Messaging program, AIM, is the most popular program of its kind. Millions of people, probably including some of your friends and relatives, use it daily to keep in touch with one another. In the following sections, you learn how to download a free copy of AIM to your PC, install it, and start using it to communicate with your other computer-savvy pals.

Getting Started with AIM

Most IM programs, including AIM, are free for the taking. You don't even need an AIM account. You can use an existing e-mail address, including the address you use to sign in to Facebook. To download and install a copy of AIM and (optionally) create a username that identifies you on the AIM network, take the following steps.

- ❒ Connect to the Internet and start your web browser.
- ❒ Click in the Address bar, type **www.aim.com**, and press **Enter**. AIM's home page appears.
- ❒ Click **Download AIM.**
- ❒ When asked whether to run or save the installation file, click the **Run** button.
- ❒ Follow the onscreen instructions to download and install AIM and set a username and password. (I recommend doing a custom installation so that you can see a list of optional components and choose whether to install them.)

AIM starts automatically after you install it and whenever Windows starts. If you exit the program and decide to restart it later, click **Start**, **All Programs**, **AIM**, and click the icon for running AIM. When AIM starts, it prompts you to enter your username and password.

Type your username and password in the appropriate boxes. To have AIM remember your password so that you don't have to enter it next time, click **Remember me** and **Remember**

my password to place a check in each box. You can also click **Automatically sign me in** and/ or **Sign in as invisible** (so your buddies won't know you're online until you want them to). Click the **Sign In** button to go online. At this point, anyone who knows your username can contact you by sending you a message, assuming that you're not invisible.

You can make yourself visible or invisible after signing on. Click the button to the left of your username and choose the desired online status:

- **Available** lets your buddies know that you're online and taking calls.
- **Away** lets your buddies know that you're online but away from your PC right now.
- **Mobile** enables you to set up and turn on IM forwarding so that any instant messages your buddies send you are forwarded to your cellphone.
- **Invisible** keeps you hidden so that your buddies don't know you're online.

Building a Buddy List

AIM provides a feature called the *buddy list* that enables you to keep track of the people with whom you most commonly interact. To add a buddy to your list, click the **Buddy List** tab, and then click the **+Add** button (just below the tabs) and click **Add Buddy**. The New Buddy window appears. Enter the necessary contact information and your buddy's AIM username and click **Save**. (If you're wondering what an ICQ number is, ICQ is another instant messaging program AIM supports.)

Click the **Buddy List** tab, and then click the **+Add** button (just below the tabs) and click **Add Buddy**. The New Buddy window appears, as shown in Figure.

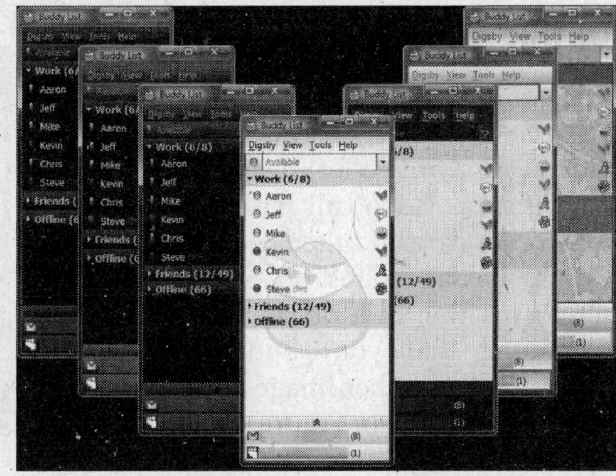

Add a buddy to your buddy list

> **Tip...**
>
> *If you have loads of buddies, create your own buddy groups to make your buddy list less crowded and overwhelming. To create a new group, click the* ***+Add*** *button, click* ***Add Group****, type a descriptive name for the group, and click* ***Save****.*

Instant Messaging

Whenever you sign on to AIM, AIM checks to see which of the people on your buddy list are currently online and willing to accept messages. When a buddy is online, you simply double-click that person's username in your buddy list and start chatting.

In addition to typing text, you can format the text to use a different type style, shrink or enlarge the text, add enhancements such as bold and italics, apply highlighting, insert a link to a web page, or even insert small icons that represent your current emotional state. Click the smiley face icon to display a list of available icons for expressing your mood. Click the **A** icon to view formatting tools.

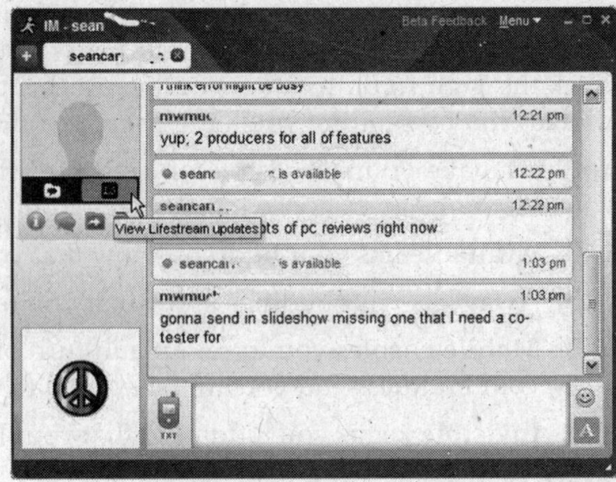

Start sending instant messages!

Audio Instant Messaging

To engage in audio instant messaging with a buddy who has the proper equipment (speakers and a microphone), double-click your buddy's name; then click the camcorder icon and click **Start an Audio IM**. Your buddy then needs to click **Accept** to answer the "phone."

Video Instant Messaging

By equipping your computer with an affordable webcam, you can engage in video calls with colleagues and loved ones. To initiate a video call with AIM, click the camcorder icon and then click **Start a Video IM**. A message pops up on your buddy's screen inviting him or her to a video chat. Assuming that your buddy accepts the invitation, his or her image appears on your screen, as shown in Figure, and your image appears on your buddy's screen.

With video chat, you and your buddy can see and hear one another chat

Texting a Buddy's Mobile Phone

If your AIM buddies have mobile devices with Internet access, you can text them right from AIM, and they can text you back. First, you must enter your buddy's mobile phone number. Right-click your buddy's name and click **Edit Buddy**. Click in the **Mobile Number** box, type the person's 10-digit phone number, and click **Save**.

To text the person, right-click his or her name and click **Text Message (SMS)** or press **Alt+Shift+T**, type your message, and press **Enter**. AIM sends the text message to your buddy's mobile device, and the person can then reply to you.

Getting AIM for Your Cellphone

You can stay in touch with your buddies when you're away from your PC by opening the availability list (to the left of your username) and clicking **Mobile**. When a buddy sends an instant message to your username, the message is automatically forwarded to your cellphone; you can text back a reply, but you can't initiate a discussion.

Sampling Other Chat/Instant Messaging Clients

Although AIM may still be the most popular instant messaging client and chat network around, it's certainly not the only option—and it's not necessarily the best. Following are some other online chat/instant messaging clients you may want to check out, along with website addresses where you can go to learn more about them:

- Yahoo! Messenger, at messenger.yahoo.com
- Google Video Chat and Google Talk, at www.google.com/talk
- Windows Live Messenger, at download.live.com/messenger
- Facebook Chat

If you have a diverse group of friends all using different instant messaging clients, conversing with all of them may mean installing and juggling several different clients. Fortunately, apps that let you access and use multiple services within a single app are available, enabling you to manage and communicate with all your buddies and friends from one account. Following are a few multiprotocol clients you may want to check out:

EBuddy (www.ebuddy.com)

Digsby (www.digsby.com)

KoolIM (www.koolim.com)

Meebo (www.meebo.com)

Miranda (www.miranda-im.org)

Pidgin (www.pidgin.im)

Trillian Astra (www.trillian.im)

Placing Really Cheap (or Free) Phone Calls with Skype

If you're travelling to foreign lands or have friends on the opposite side of the globe, the best way to talk to them is to use Skype or an instant messaging program that supports PC-to-PC and PC-to-phone calling.

For quite a while, the only game in town was Skype, and I think it's still the best, but other players are now competing in this space, including Windows Live Messenger and Yahoo! Messenger. The following sections introduce you to the basics of Skype. Competing services function pretty much the same way.

Note....

If you're wondering what's free and what's not, Skype offers free PC-to-PC calls (audio and video) and instant messaging for Skype users. Skype charges for PC-to-phone calls, and calling a mobile phone costs significantly more. Check www.skype.com for more pricing details and special deals.

Getting Skype

To get Skype on your PC, head to www.skype.com, click **Get Skype**, click **Get Skype for Windows**, and follow the onscreen cues to download and install Skype. (When you click the button to download Skype, a security bar may appear near the top of your browser window. If it does, click the bar to proceed with the download.) When asked whether to run or save the downloaded file, click the **Run** button. When the installation is complete, Skype leads you through the process of creating a new Skype account, creating a Skype username, and entering the e-mail and password you want to use to sign in.

To sign in to Skype, click **Start**, **All Programs**, **Skype**, **Skype**, type your login name and password in the appropriate boxes, and then click **Sign in**. The first time you sign in, a welcome screen appears with buttons you can click to learn the basics, test and set up your equipment (speakers, microphone, and webcam), and find Skype members you may know. If the people you want to call don't have Skype accounts, encourage them to sign up.

Adding Contacts

Skype features several ways to add contacts using a person's Skype username, e-mail address, or phone number:

- **Find people using a list of contacts:** Click **Directory** and then click the **See friends who are already on Skype** link. Use the resulting dialog box to find friends on Facebook, AOL, or Gmail, or in your Microsoft Outlook address book, and then add them as contacts.
- **Find someone you know:** Click **Directory**, click in the **Type Skype name** box, type the person's full name or e-mail address, and click **Search**. If the name of the person you're looking for appears in the list near the bottom of the window, double-click it to add it as a contact.
- **Add a phone number:** Click **New**, **New Contact**. Click the **Save a phone number in your contact list** link (near the bottom). Type the contact's name in the **Name** box, as shown in Figure. Open the drop-down list and choose Mobile, Home, Office, or Other. Click the flag and select the country you'll be calling. Click in the phone number box and type the person's phone number. Click **Save phone number**.

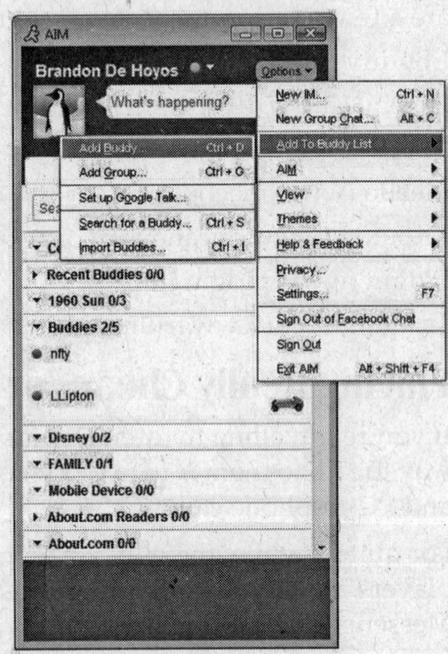

Add a contact's phone number

Making Free Skype-to-Skype Calls

You can call, video-call, or instant-message any of your contacts who also use Skype for free, assuming that the person is online, signed on to Skype, and sitting at his or her computer. To place a Skype-to-Skype (PC-to-PC) call, click the person's name in your Contacts list, click the **Skype** tab (if it's not already selected), and then click the Skype places the call, and a notification appears on the screen of the person you called.

Place a Skype-to-Skype call for free

He or she can then answer with or without video or deny the call. Use the buttons near the top or bottom of the call pane to mute your microphone, adjust the volume, turn video on or off, adjust other settings, or hang up, as shown in the figure.

Manage your call session

Cheap Long Distance with PC-to-Phone Calls

Prior to placing PC-to-phone calls, you need to place some money in your account. Click the **View account** button (upper left) or open the **Skype** menu and click **Account**; then use the resulting screen to buy credits or a subscription:

- **Buy more credit:** For the pay-as-you-go plan, click **Buy more credit** and use the resulting screen and your credit card to add money to your account. As you make calls, money is deducted from your balance.
- **Buy a subscription:** Click the link to find out more about subscriptions and use the resulting web page to purchase a monthly subscription. This enables you to make unlimited calls for a month for a flat monthly fee at a considerably lower per-minute rate.
- To place a PC-to-phone call, click the name of the person you want to call in your Contacts list, click the tab for the phone you want to dial, and click the **Call** button, which may appear as Call Phone, Call Home, Call Mobile, or Video Call. When the person answers (or you get the message machine), start talking. When you're done, click the **End call** button (the red button with the phone on it).

Points to Remember

- ☆ Most instant messaging programs allow you to send instant messages to others who use the service and talk with them for free via voice and video.
- ☆ To get started with AIM, download the instant messaging client from www.aim. com.
- ☆ To add a contact in AIM, click the **+Add** button and then **Add Buddy**, use the resulting dialog box to enter contact information, and click **Save**.
- ☆ To contact a buddy who's online, double-click your buddy's name and use the resulting window to exchange text messages or initiate a voice or voice+video call.
- ☆ To make free PC-to-PC calls and cheap long-distance calls worldwide, try Skype, at www.skype.com

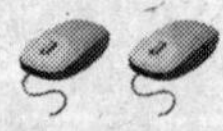

Saving and Making Money Online

The World Wide Web is home to one of the largest free-market economies in the world. At any time of the day or night, 7 days a week, 365 (and sometimes 366) days per year, you can find millions of people buying, selling, and giving stuff away online. And because the competition is so stiff among sellers, you can often find better deals online than what local brick-and-mortar discount stores offer. In this chapter, I introduce you to the wonderful world of online shopping and reveal some of the best places to go and strategies to use to find great deals online.

Note....

Don't automatically assume that just because you're buying something online, you're getting a better deal than what local stores are offering. You must still perform your due diligence and compare prices. In addition, buying online usually means you pay shipping fees, which can boost the price of goods higher than what you'd pay locally.

Is It Safe?

Generally speaking, shopping online is about as safe as shopping offline. If you head out to your local shopping mall, for example, you take the risk that someone will break into your car, steal your purse or wallet, or even sneak a peak at the name and number on your credit card. You face similar risks online, but you face these risks whether you shop online or not.

You can reduce the risks by taking the following precautions:

- Shop only on sites you trust. Buying merchandise from a reputable online retailer is generally much safer than placing an order on an individual seller's website.
- If you're buying from a little-known company, search the web to find out anything you can about the company. If other shoppers have been burned by that company, they usually post something on the web warning others. enter your name, credit card number, and other sensitive information only on secure websites. You can tell whether a site is secure by looking at the address bar in your browser. The address of a secure site begins with "https" rather than "http." Your web browser may also display a lock icon near the top or bottom of the browser window to indicate that a site is secure.
- If you receive an e-mail message asking for account information, be highly skeptical. Legitimate companies rarely request account information via e-mail or ask that you log in to a website to verify account information.

- Don't place orders on a shared computer. Any information you enter on the shared computer could be stored for future use. If it is, someone else can log into the site where you placed the order and access your account information.
- Pay for orders with a credit card or an escrow service such as PayPal, rather than using a debit card, so you have the opportunity to cancel the order or at least file a dispute if you don't receive your order or are dissatisfied with it. Credit card companies are usually pretty cooperative and successful in ensuring customer satisfaction.
- Overall, trust your instincts. If a deal sounds too good to be true, it probably is. If a website asks for your UID, birthday, driver's license number, or other information that's rarely needed to process a transaction, it's probably up to no good.

Comparison-Shopping for the Real Deals

Savvy shoppers always compare prices, and you can compare prices online, too. However, several comparison-shopping sites can do all the legwork for you and display a list of merchants who offer the same or similar products.

Myntra is one of many comparison-shopping sites you can find online

Check out the following popular comparison-shopping sites; many also offer product reviews to help you make your decision:

www.flipkart.com

www.naaptol.com

www.myntra.com

Buying Online

The procedure for shopping at most online stores is fairly standard—you find the product you want, check out the product details and what other consumers have to say about it, click a button to order the product or place it in your shopping cart, and check out by entering your payment and shipping information. The Figure pretty much captures the online shopping experience, except for the part when you have to enter your credit card and shipping information. Most dedicated shopping sites make finding and ordering items very intuitive. Select a product category. Go to Myntra.com; Describe the product; Click Go Products that match your product description.

After you've successfully placed your order, the site sends you a confirmation e-mail describing what you ordered, the price of each item, the shipping cost, and your grand total.

You can search for specific products on Myntra.com

Booking Travel Reservations Online

If you do any travelling, whether for business or pleasure, you can often save considerable amounts of money by serving as your own travel agent and booking your reservations online. Several companies offer one-stop shopping for airline tickets, hotel and motel accommodations, and car rental. Visit the following sites to see what they have to offer:

www.irctc.co.in (Railways)

www.cleartrip.com

www.via.com

Don't stop at simply making reservations online. Plenty of websites offer free information and resources on just about any destination you can imagine. You can go online and check rail routes and schedules and buy your rail pass online.

visit museum websites to plan which exhibits you'd like to see, explore an area's hottest attractions to figure out what you'd like to do, find the best restaurants and entertainment, and much more.

Tip...

Some websites specialize in providing information about your preferred mode of travel. For example, Cleartrip (www.cleartrip.com) can show you how to travel around the world even if you have no travel budget to speak of. If you're looking to trim your travel budget by staying in lower-priced accommodations, via, where you can obtain information about hostels located in just about every country. You can also find sites that specialize in timeshare rentals, cruises, and other special travel opportunities.

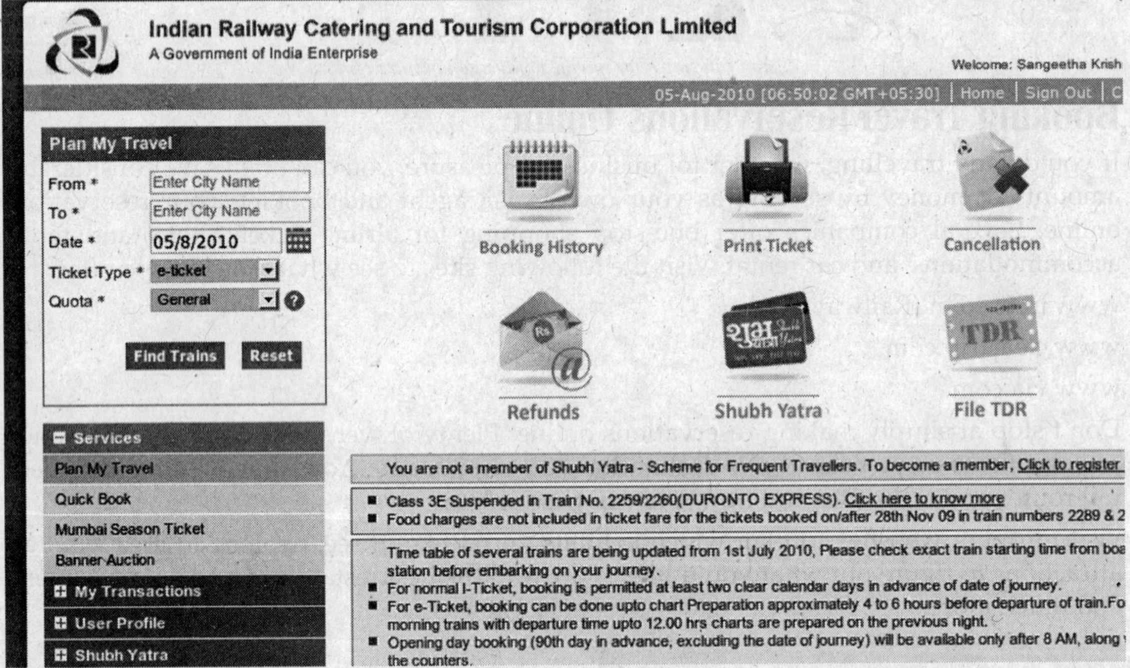

Buying and Selling on eBay

Even if you've never placed a bid or purchased anything on eBay, you've probably heard about it. eBay bills itself as "The World's Marketplace," where its eager community of online sellers and buyers from all around the world gather to buy, sell, and trade products every day. When most people think of eBay, however, they think "online auction," and even though eBay now has its own eBay Stores, it still serves primarily as an online auction.

In the following sections, I step you through the process of buying and selling stuff on eBay, including how you pay for items you buy and collect money for items you sell.

Buying Stuff on eBay

Most people get their first taste of eBay by bidding on and eventually purchasing an item. The process is very similar to buying a product on Amazon.com or from any online store, except that you set the maximum price you're willing to pay for an item. In the following sections, I step you through the process of buying something on eBay. (You can also buy some stuff without bidding if the seller enables the Buy It Now option.)

You don't need to be an eBay member to window-shop on eBay. Point your web browser to www.ebay.in. A Search bar appears at the top of the opening page. Click in the Search box and type one or more words to describe what you're looking for.

To narrow the search to a specific category of products, open the Categories list and click the desired category. Now click the **Search** button. eBay displays a list of items that match your description, as shown in Figure.

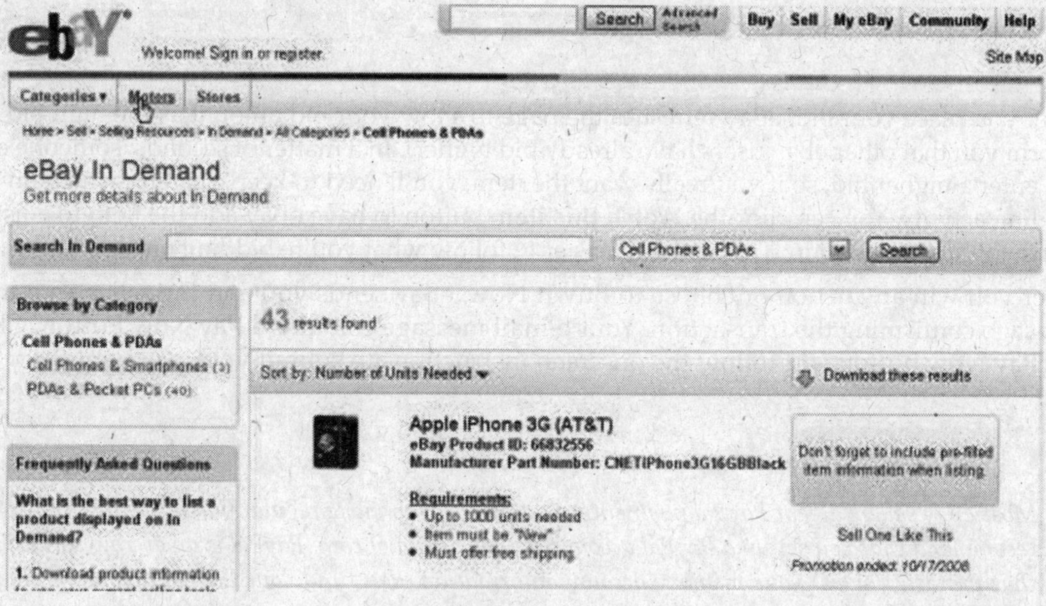

eBay can help you find what you're looking for

Before placing a bid on an item, click the item that interests you to display more information about it. Check the product description to determine whether the item looks and sounds like the product you want.

Also click on the seller's feedback score to view information about the person who has listed the product for sale. eBay encourages buyers to rate sellers and provide feedback so that future buyers know how trustworthy or untrustworthy a particular seller may be. You'll also find a link you can click to ask the seller questions about the product or about payment, shipping, or customer service.

Placing a bid is very easy. Click in the **Your maximum bid** box, type your bid amount, and click the **Place bid** button, as shown in Figure below. (The Your maximum bid box is the minimum amount you can enter to place a bid.

You can learn more about the item and the seller and place a bid

After you place your bid, eBay refreshes the page to show your bid amount as the high bid (or inform you that other eBay users have already bid higher). In a matter of seconds, someone else can enter a higher bid, so if you really want the item, you'll need to keep a careful watch on the bidding activity. You can click the **Watch this item** button to have eBay add the item to a list of items you're interested in. This makes it easier to follow what you're bidding on.

After you win an auction or choose to Buy It Now, eBay sends you and the seller an e-mail message confirming the transaction. Your e-mail message contains a Pay Now button. Click the **Pay Now** button and follow the onscreen instructions to submit your payment.

Tip...

Most eBay sellers accept PayPal payments, so if you plan to make regular purchases, I strongly recommend that you set up a PayPal account at www. paypal.com. PayPal is an escrow service that protects (hides) your primary account information. You fund your PayPal account from your bank or credit card account and use PayPal to buy products, pay vendors, send money to relatives or friends, and so on. The person you pay never sees your bank account or credit card information. PayPal also protects against fraud and insures you against unauthorized payments from your account

After you receive the item(s) you purchase, remember to return to eBay to rate and provide feedback to the seller. Not only do these ratings and feedback help other eBay buyers determine whom they can trust, but positive feedback helps sellers become more successful. Sellers often succeed or fail based on their feedback ratings.

Selling Stuff on eBay

eBay began as a tool to help collectors of Pez dispensers swap dispensers online. From there, it evolved into more of an online flea market, where people would try to sell their collectibles and anything else they no longer wanted to store in their basements or attics. (There's still a lot of that going on.) Now eBay also provides a forum where professional retailers can sell brand-new products.

Note....

Before you list an item for sale, do some research to find out the going price of the item or similar items and see how other sellers are marketing these items online. Using other sellers' marketing materials (photos and product descriptions) is a no-no, but existing product listings can give you some ideas of what works and what doesn't. When you have something for sale, all you have to do is take a photo of it, write a description of it, log on to eBay, and list the item. Keep in mind, however, that eBay charges listing fees, whether or not your item sells. You pay an insertion fee to list an item for sale. This fee varies depending on the type of item and the starting bid or reserve price (the lowest bid you'll accept). The final value fee is calculated as a percentage of the purchase price (rates vary; check eBay's help system, where you can find a link to learn more about seller fees). To sell something on eBay, rest the mouse pointer on **Sell** *(upper-right corner of the page), click* **Sell an Item**, *and follow the onscreen instructions as eBay steps you through the process. eBay assists you in determining how much the item you're selling is probably worth, choosing a category for the item, entering a description, uploading photos, specifying the shipping fee, and so on. After you list an item, you can monitor your auctions to observe the bidding process. When the auction is over, you receive an e-mail message informing you of the winning bid. The buyer then submits the payment, and you package and ship the product.*

Points to Remember

- ☆ To shop safely online, stick with well-established stores and place orders only on secure websites, indicated by the closed lock in your browser's notification area, until you gain more experience.
- ☆ Comparison-shopping sites such as Flipkart and Naaptol can help you track down the best deals.
- ☆ Buying something online usually consists of finding what you want, checking the product details, adding the item to your shopping cart, and checking out.
- ☆ On eBay you can buy and sell items through an auction, the Buy It Now option, or an eBay Store.

Blogs & Web Page

Surfing the web is nice, but you want more. You want to establish a presence on the web, publish your own stories or poems, place pictures of yourself or your family online, show off your creativity, and communicate your ideas to the world.

Where do you start? Right here. This chapter shows you how to whip up your first web page or blog right online, without having to learn any special programs or deal with any cryptic web page formatting codes (unless you really want to). And because you create the page online, you don't have to worry about publishing your web page when you're done.

Behind the Scenes with a Web Page

Behind every web page is a text document that includes codes for formatting the text, inserting pictures and other media files, and displaying links that point to other pages. This system of codes (commonly referred to as *tags*) is called *HTML* (Hypertext Markup Language). Most codes are paired. The first code in the pair turns on the formatting, and the second code turns it off. For example, to type a heading such as "Apple Dumplin's Home Page," you use the heading codes like this:

1]&36eeaZ 9jbea^c h =dbZ EV\Z1$]&3

The <h1> code tells the web browser to display any text that follows the code as a level-one heading. The </h1> code tells the web browser to turn off the level-one heading format and return to displaying text as normal. Unpaired codes act as commands; for instance, the <img> code inserts a graphic, so <img src='http://www.sample.com/horse.jpg' /> inserts a graphic file named horse.jpg that's stored in the root directory of the website www.sample.com.

Forget About HTML

A basic introduction to HTML is helpful in understanding how the web works, troubleshooting web page formatting problems, and customizing web pages with fancy enhancements, but don't worry—you don't need a certification in HTML to create your first web page. Many companies have developed specialized programs that make the process of creating a web page as easy as designing and printing a greeting card.

Professional web designers use industrial-strength tools like Dreamweaver to design and create websites. If your website needs are modest, however, you can create and format your web pages right on the web simply by specifying your preferences and using forms to enter your text. The next section shows you just how easy it is to create and publish your own web page online with Google Sites.

Tip...

If you want your own unique domain name with an address like www.yourname.com, a matching e-mail address like bill@yourname.com, and a site with a custom design that's easy to maintain, I recommend starting an account with a web hosting provider—such as Bluehost, HostGator, or GoDaddy.com—and using WordPress to create and maintain your site. (These hosting providers enable you to register a domain name, and they feature numerous tools for creating and maintaining websites and blogs.) It costs around about Rs. 2000 per year to start and maintain, plus Rs. 1500 one-time fee for the Thesis Theme.

Creating a Free Website with Google Sites

Here's what you do to publish a simple web page (for free) using Google Sites:

- Using your web browser, go to **sites.google.com**.
- If you have a Google account, log in. If you don't have a Google account yet, get one: Click **Create an account now** and follow the onscreen cues to enter your desired e-mail address and password.
- Click the **Create site** button.
- Click the template you want to use, as shown in Figure. (For more templates, click **Browse the gallery for more.**)

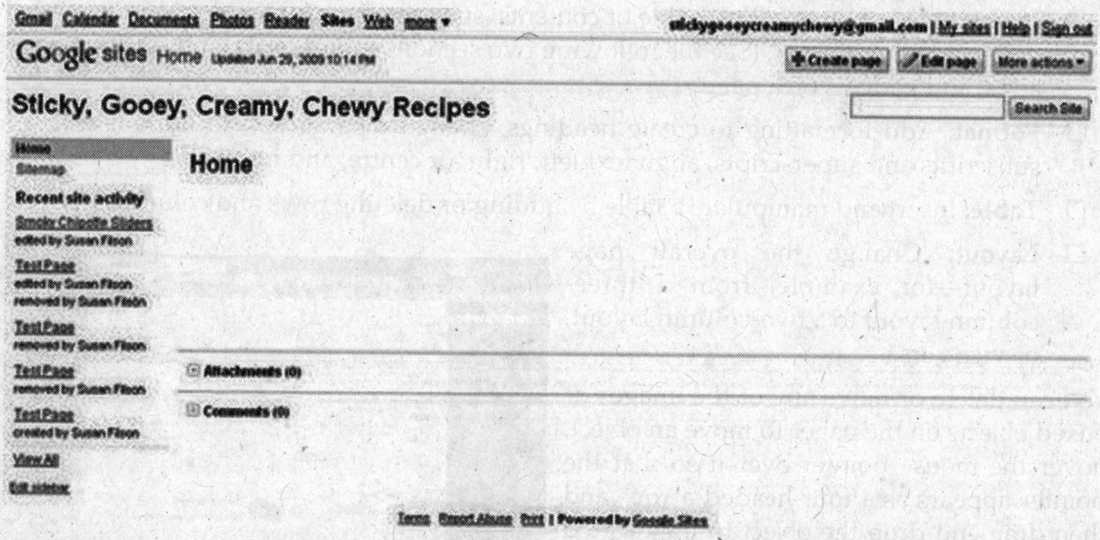

- ❒ Click in the **Name your Site** box and type a name for your site. Google Sites automatically assigns your site a URL (address) based on the name you typed. You can edit the address, if desired.
- ❒ Click **More Options**.
- ❒ Click in the Site description box and type a brief description of your site's content.
- ❒ Under Share with, click **Everyone in the world can view this site** or **Only people I specify can view this site**.
- ❒ If your site contains adult-only content, click **This site contains mature content only suitable for adults**.

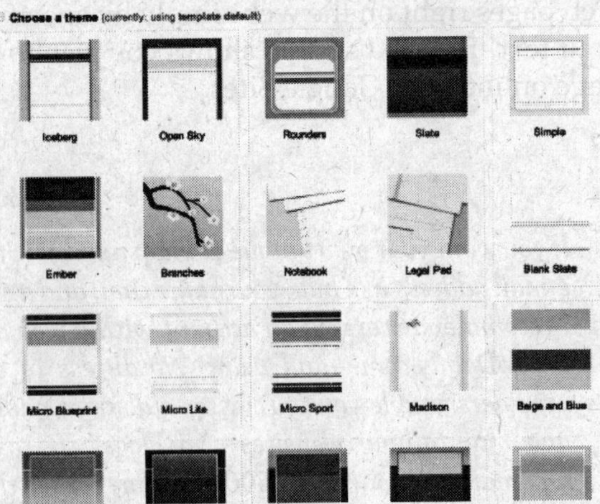

Select a template and enter a name for your site

- ❒ Click in the verification text box and type the verification code that's displayed.
- ❒ Click the **Create site** button. Google Sites creates your website and displays it. The page contains a bunch of placeholder text and graphics you can replace with your own text and graphics. The page also contains links you can click to learn how to replace images, text, and other objects with your own; click one of these links for complete instructions.

Editing Your Google Site

To edit your site, click the **Edit page** button (upper right). The page appears in edit mode, as shown in Figure. To replace text, drag over it and then type your own text. You can use the four buttons in the blue toolbar near the top to do the following:

- ❒ **Insert:** Insert an image, link, table of contents, subpage listing, Google calendar, Google map, and other objects. (See the following two sections for more about inserting objects, apps, and gadgets on a page.)
- ❒ **Format:** Add formatting to create headings; change a paragraph to normal text; add subscripts and superscripts; align text left, right, or centre; and more.
- ❒ **Table:** Insert and manipulate a table by adding or deleting rows and columns.
- ❒ **Layout:** Change the overall page layout—for example, from a three-column layout to a two-column layout, or vice versa.

You can delete or move any of the images or boxed objects on the page. To move an object, hover the mouse pointer over it so that the pointer appears as a four-headed arrow, and then drag and drop the object to the desired location. To delete an object, click it and press the **Delete** key.

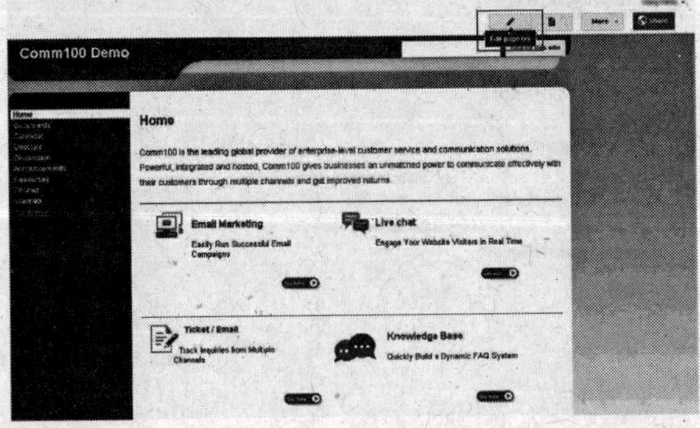

Edit and format text and objects on your site.

The gray toolbar (just above the page) displays buttons for applying standard formatting, such as bold and italic; choosing a type size; creating numbered or bulleted lists; and aligning text left, right, or centre.

Inserting Objects and Apps

Using the Insert menu, you can insert a variety of objects and apps (applications) to make your site more feature rich. Click on the page where you want the object or app inserted, and then follow the instructions for the type of object or app you want to insert (this list includes a small selection of available objects and apps):

- **Image:** Click **Insert**, **Image** and use the resulting dialog box to upload an image from your PC or use an image from a specific web address. After the image appears in the Add an Image box, click **OK**. Click the image and use the options below it to select an alignment (left, centre, or right), size (small, medium, or large), and word wrap preference (on or off),
- **Video:** Upload the video you want to insert to Google Video or YouTube, and then copy its web address (URL). Click **Insert**, **Video**, **Google Video** or **YouTube**. In the resulting dialog box, right-click in the **Paste the URL** box and click **Paste**. Enter any other preferences and click **Save**.
- **Horizontal line:** Click where you want the horizontal line to appear, and then click **Insert**, **Horizontal Line**.
- **Google Map:** Click **Insert**, **Map**. In the Search box, type the address of the location you want mapped (including city, state, and zip code) and click **Search**. You can use the controls on the upper left of the map to zoom in or out or pan left, right, up, or down. When the area you want shown appears, click **Select**, enter your preferences in the resulting dialog box, and click **Save**.
- **Picasa Photo:** If you use Picasa to store and manage your digital photos Online, you can easily insert photos from your online photo albums into a Google Sites web page. Click **Insert**, **Picasa Photo**, use the resulting dialog box to choose the photo to insert, and click **Select**.
- **Picasa Web Slideshow:** If you use Picasa, you can insert an entire photo album to have your Google Site web page display it as a slide show. Copy the web address of the Picasa photo album you want to use. Click **Insert**, **Picasa Web slideshow**. Right-click the **Paste the URL** box near the top of the resulting dialog box and click **Paste**. Enter your preferences and click **Save**.

Inserting Gadgets

Google includes gadgets you can add to your site to improve navigation and add features to your site. To add a gadget, click where you want the gadget inserted; then click the **Insert** menu, scroll down to near the bottom, and click the desired gadget.

A dialog box pops up requesting additional details. For example, the Recent posts gadget

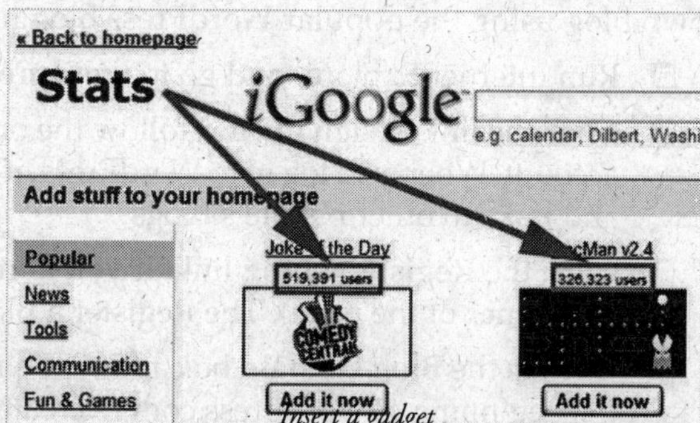

Insert a gadget

displays a list of the most recently published posts, so that visitors can quickly find out what's new on your site. When you choose to add the Recent posts gadget, the dialog box prompts you to specify the type of post, post length, number of posts, and so on.

Saving or Cancelling Your Changes

When you're done making changes to your Google site, you have the option to save the changes or cancel them. To save the changes, click the **Save** button (upper right). To cancel changes, click the **Cancel** button (next to the Save button).

Blogging Your Way to Internet Fame

Relatively recently (sometime in the late 1990s), self-publishing on the web became easier with the introduction of *web logs,* or *blogs* for short. These relatively simple web pages are primarily text based, and you can create and update them by filling out a form. You type a message, comment, or other text and then *post it* to the blog. The most recent posting appears at the top of your blog, followed by prior postings. As your list of posted messages grows, old messages are pushed off the main blog and archived.

The first blogs focused on news and commentary. Bloggers would read an article online and then post a link to the article along with their comments, insights, questions, and sometimes corrections or additional facts concerning the article. Over the years, the scope of blogs has broadened considerably. Now people commonly use blogs to publish their own poetry and fiction; broadcast news stories the mainstream media has overlooked; share business expertise; communicate with family members, friends, and colleagues; promote grassroots movements; keep an online journal; and much more.

Definition

A **blog** (short for **web log**) is a publicly accessible personal journal that enables an individual to voice his or her opinions and insights, keep an online record of experiences, and gather input from others. People also use blogs to share photos with friends and family and set up their own online clubs.

Launching Your Blog

To start blogging, you need a *blogging platform*—an application that provides the tools you need to post messages to your blog and maintain it. Several developers offer platforms for free and can even host your blog for you. The following steps show you how to launch your own blog using the popular WordPress blogging platform:

- ❒ Run Internet Explorer and go to **wordpress.com**.
- ❒ Click the link to sign up and follow the onscreen instructions to sign up for a WordPress account. When you log in to WordPress, it displays a page that's packed with information and links to other people's blogs.
- ❒ Click the **Register a blog** link. If you don't see the link, click the **My Blogs** link (upper-left corner of the page). The Register a Blog page appears.
- ❒ Click in the **Blog Domain** box and type a name for your blog. This name will be added to the beginning of wordpress.com to create your blog's domain name. You won't be able

to change this later, although you can delete the blog later and create a new one.

- ❒ Click in the **Blog Title** box and type the title you want to appear at the top of every page of your blog.
- ❒ If you want to prevent search engines from indexing your blog, click the check box next to the Privacy option to remove the check mark.
- ❒ Click the **Create Blog** button. As long as the domain name you entered is not already in use, WordPress displays a message indicating that the domain name is now yours and showing you the username to use to log in.

Register a new WordPress blog for free

You can now visit your blog by entering its address (for example, **yourblogname.wordpress.com**) into Internet Explorer, but it consists of only an opening page that contains a welcome message.

To log in to your blog, launch Internet Explorer, type **yourblogname.wordpress.com/wp-admin** in the address box near the top of the window, and press **Enter**.

You're already logged in, so this displays the WordPress Dashboard for your blog. However, if you log out and then try to use Internet Explorer to go to **yourblogname.wordpress.com/wp-admin** later, WordPress displays a page prompting you to enter your username and password. When you enter the correct information, WordPress displays the Dashboard.

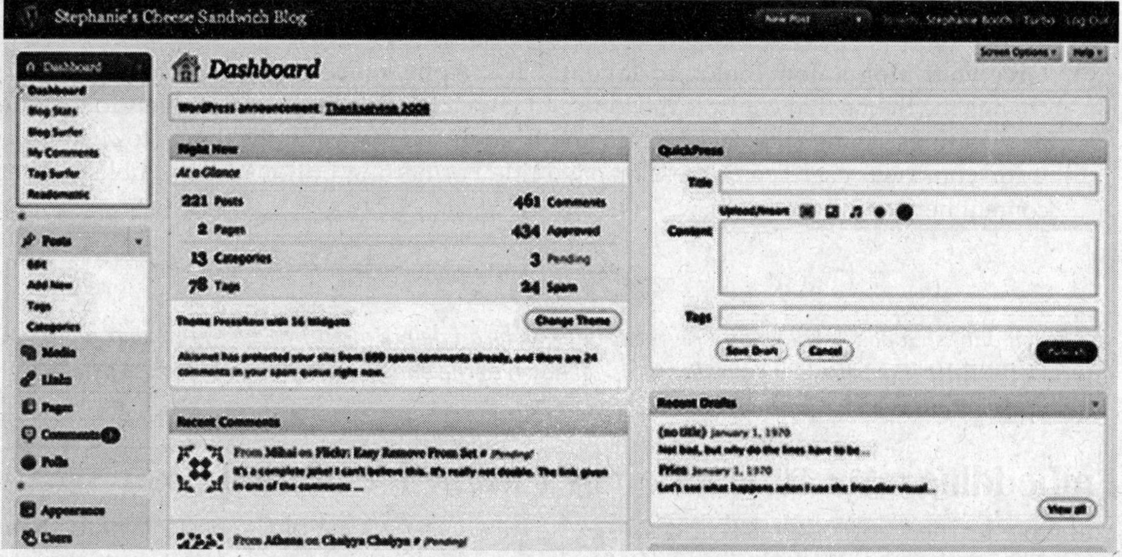

The WordPress Dashboard gives you access to the tools you need to post messages and manage your blog

Making Your Own Blog

The WordPress Dashboard provides all the tools you need to post content to your blog, redesign it, and manage it:

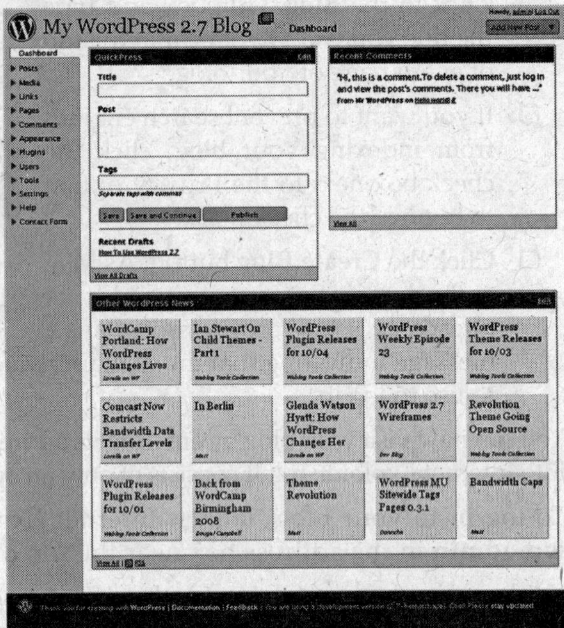

Posting content to your blog is as easy as filling out a form and clicking Publish

- **Write a new post:** Writing a post is as easy as typing in a word processing application. Click **Posts** (left menu), **Add New**, and then simply type a title for the post, type and format your content, add a photo or other graphic, and click **Publish**. Posts appear on your opening page with the newest post first.
- **Create a page:** Pages are almost identical to posts, but they're used for static content. In other words, they function more like web pages. Links for the pages you create appear under "Pages" in your blog's navigation bar. To create a page, click **Pages** (left menu), **Add New**, and use the resulting form to create your page.
- **Manage your blog:** The Dashboard contains everything you need to manage your blog, and all of it is accessible through the left menu. You can install WordPress upgrades, create and edit posts and pages, create your own media library with digital graphics and video, approve and reject comments others have posted, check your site statistics, and much more.
- **Give your blog a new look and layout:** Click **Appearance** (left menu) for options to change the theme that controls the look and layout of your blog, add widgets to include new features, change the background and header, and even edit the theme to customize it for your own use. Type a post or page title Formatting buttons Click Publish Enter content here.

Note....

*If you publish a post or page and regret it later, you can delete or edit it. Log in to your blog, click the **Edit** link below Pages or Posts, scroll down to the end of the entry you want to delete, and click **Remove** or click **Edit** to change your entry.*

Embedding a YouTube Video in a Web Page or Blog Post

You have learned how to watch and share YouTube videos. One of the best ways to share a YouTube video is to include it on a web page or blog. YouTube makes this very easy to accomplish with its *embed* code. The embed code provides a link that pulls the video from

YouTube and plays it on a web page. To embed a video in a web page or blog post, here's what you do:

- ❒ Head to YouTube and display the video you want to embed in your web page or post.
- ❒ Click the **<Embed>** button below the video.
- ❒ Enter your preferences,
- ❒ Click in the box that contains the embed code, and then right-click the code and select **Copy**.
- ❒ Open the post or page you want to add the video to and display it in HTML mode. (This works only if you paste the code into the page's or post's HTML.)
- ❒ Right-click where you want the video inserted and click **Paste**.
- ❒ Save your changes. Now whenever someone opens this page or views this post, they'll see a box in which they can click the play button to view the video. Click to highlight code Enter preferences first.

Points to Remember

- ✫ Hypertext Markup Language (HTML) is a system of codes used to format web pages.
- ✫ You don't need to master HTML to create your own attractive web pages.
- ✫ Google Sites, at sites.google.com, provides an easy (and free) way to build a website.
- ✫ An easy way to establish and maintain a presence on the Internet is to create your own blog.
- ✫ You can place a YouTube video on a web page or blog post by copying and pasting the video's embed code into the HTML for the web page or post.

Internet Safety

The Internet is a virtual city packed with shopping malls, libraries, community centres, museums, newsstands, meeting rooms, and other valuable offerings. But like any city, the Internet has its dark side—a section of town ruled by vandalism, theft, and other criminal behaviour. You want access to all the positive features the Internet offers, but you need to protect your system, data, and confidential information from the riffraff and from viruses and other *malware.* (Malware is short for "malicious software"—any computer code designed to do something bad.) This chapter shows you how to protect yourself and your PC from various Internet threats.

Keeping Out Viruses and Other Malware

Picking up a virus on the Internet is like coming home from vacation with some exotic illness. You were having so much fun; how could this happen? And how can you prevent it from happening again? By following a few simple rules:

- Download programs, plug-ins, and add-ons only from reputable and known sites. If you know the company that created the program, go to its web page or FTP server and download the file from there. Most reputable sites regularly scan their systems to detect and eliminate viruses.
- Don't accept copies of a program from another person (for example, by e-mail). Although the program might not have contained a virus when your buddy downloaded it, your buddy's computer could have a virus that infected the program. Ask your friend where he or she got the file and then download the file from its original location.
- If your web browser displays a message indicating that a program it's being asked to download is unsigned or from a questionable source, cancel the download.
- If you receive a file attachment from someone you don't know or from a questionable source, delete the message along with the attachment. Do *not* open it.
- Keep an antivirus program running at all times. Antivirus programs scan any incoming files for viruses and scan your computer regularly to identify viruses before they can damage files. Two of the best antivirus programs around are also free for home users—Avast (www.avast.com) and Microsoft Security Essentials (www.microsoft.com/

security_essentials/). All you do is download and install them. Either one runs in the background, constantly monitoring activity and incoming files; warns you when they detect anything suspicious; and provides options for dealing with each incident.

Note....

If you receive e-mail, you'll eventually receive virus warnings indicating that a nasty new virus is infecting thousands of computers all over the world and wiping out hard drives or stealing confidential information. Most of these warnings are hoaxes, and you should not forward the message as it instructs you to do. Check the source of the hoax first. Virus hoaxes are posted at http:// home.mcafee.com/virusinfo (open the ***View*** *drop-down menu below Virus Information and click* ***Hoax****).*

Detecting and Eliminating Spyware

Spyware is unauthorized software that works in the background to collect information about you or what you type (such as usernames and passwords) and transmits the information to another computer. Fortunately, Windows 7 is equipped with Windows Defender to deal with spyware before it has a chance to do much harm. To access Windows Defender and scan your system for spyware, click **Start** and type **defender** in the **Search programs and files** box. Click **Windows Defender** to run the utility and then click the **Scan** button.

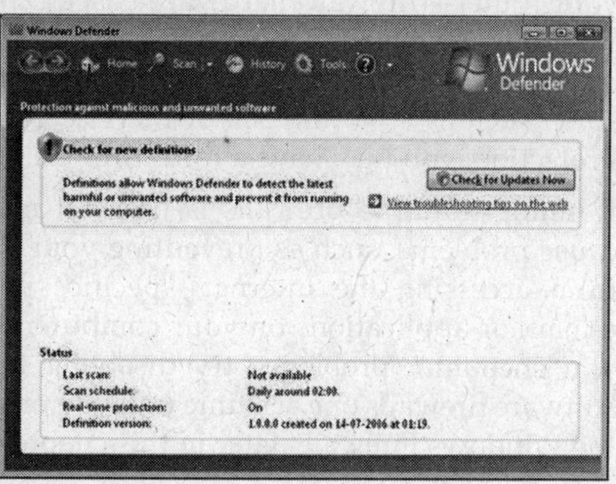

You can scan your PC for spyware

Keeping Hackers at Bay with a Firewall

Whenever you're connected to the Internet, you run the risk of having a mischievous hacker break into your system, steal information, and even damage files. Hackers rarely break into home PCs that are connected to the Internet by a dial-up modem (via a phone line), because you typically disconnect when you're done working. If you have a DSL or cable modem connection, which keeps your computer connected to the Internet at all times, consider installing a *firewall* to prevent unauthorized access to your system.

A firewall stands between your PC and the Internet, enabling your PC free access to the Internet but limiting access to your PC from outside sources (including hackers).

It does this by monitoring activity between your PC or network (*trusted* network) and the Internet (*untrusted* network). As long as the trusted network initiates contact, the firewall allows the connection. If the untrusted network (another PC on the Internet) initiates contact, the firewall blocks the connection.

If you have two or more computers that share an Internet connection through a router, the best option is to use your router's firewall to limit outside access to your networked computers. If your PC is connecting directly to the Internet through a modem or a Wi-Fi connection (not through a router), turn on the Windows Firewall. If your PC works fine with both firewalls on, you have added protection.

Configuring Your Router's Firewall

Your router should have come with instructions that show you how to configure it or at least access the configuration settings. In most cases, you can access the configuration settings by running your web browser and then entering the IP address of your router.

After accessing your router's configuration settings, select the Security or Firewall option and enable the firewall, if it's not already enabled. (It's probably already enabled.)

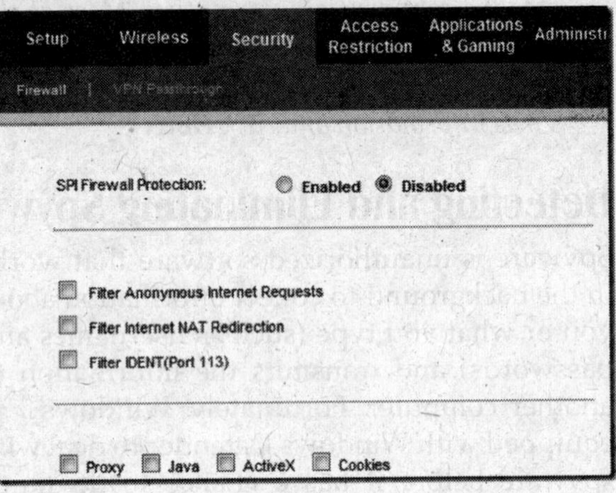

Configure your router's firewall and security settings

You can have two or more firewalls in place—your router's firewall (hardware based) and Windows Firewall (software based), for example. If you have an Internet security suite, such as a Norton 360 or McAfee Total Protection, you may have a third firewall.

Running multiple firewalls is fine but may cause problems, such as preventing your PC from accessing the Internet, specific sites, e-mail, or applications on your computer. If you encounter problems, try disabling the software firewalls one at a time until the problem is resolved. See "Activating or Deactivating the Windows Firewall" later in this chapter.

Note....

Your PC should always have at least one firewall running when connecting to the Internet—your router's firewall if you're connecting through a router with firewall protection, or Windows Firewall if you're connecting via a Wi-Fi hotspot or other public network.

Limiting Access to Your Wireless Network

Restrict access to your network by enabling encryption and entering a passphrase that all computers on the network must use to establish a network connection.

Check your router's wireless settings to determine whether it has an option to allow the network name to be broadcast. If it does, you can improve security by disabling this option so the router won't broadcast the network name, making your network less visible.

Activating or Deactivating the Windows Firewall

One of the best ways to protect your computer from break-ins is to install a firewall. A firewall is security software that stands between your computer and the Internet, enabling your computer to freely exchange data with the Internet but blocking access to your computer or network from other users on the Internet.

If you're using a router to connect to the Internet, it probably has its own firewall, which is usually superior to any software firewall, such as the Windows firewall.

Activate both your router's and the Windows firewall. (Check your router documentation to determine how to enable/disable its firewall.) If you run into problems connecting to the Internet, try enabling the router's firewall and disabling the Windows firewall. To turn the Windows firewall on or off, follow these steps:

- Click **Start**, **Control Panel**.
- Click **System and Security** and then **Windows Firewall**.
- Click **Turn Windows Firewall on or off**. Enter your log-on password, if prompted to do so, and click **Yes**.
- Below Home or work (private) network location settings, click the desired setting: **Turn on Windows Firewall** or **Turn off Windows Firewall (not recommended)**. Click **OK**.

Note....

Always have at least one firewall running whenever your network is connected to the Internet. For most people, this means all the time.

Making Exceptions for Certain Programs

A firewall can cause Internet connection problems for some features, including instant messaging, especially when you're trying to share files or videoconference. If you experience a connection problem when Windows Firewall is on, you may need to set up exceptions to allow specific programs free access to the Internet.

To set up an exception, click **Start**, **Control Panel**, **System and Security**, **Allow a program through Windows Firewall** (below Windows Firewall). Click the file or program you want to exempt from Windows Firewall protection, and click **OK**.

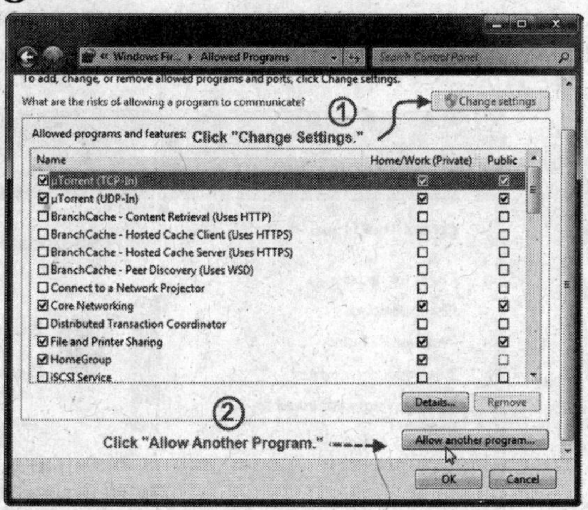

Allow a program to bypass Windows Firewall

Securing Your Portable PC in Public Hot Spots

Wi-Fi is great. You can spend the entire day at Starbucks drinking your caffe latte and playing on your Wi-Fi–enabled laptop. Unfortunately, this makes your PC vulnerable to anyone else in the vicinity who may log on to the Wi-Fi network looking to view or steal information either stored on your computer or passing between your computer and the network. Consider a few tips to protect yourself:

- When you're ready to head out, change your network location to Public: Click **Start, Control Panel, Network and Internet, Network and Sharing Centre**. Below View your active networks, click your current network location and then click **Public network**.
- Be sure you send and receive your e-mail over a secure connection. If you use a web-based e-mail program, you can usually tell whether the connection is secured by looking at the web-based e-mail services address in your web browser. If it starts with "https" instead of "http," you're on a secure site.
- If you use a separate e-mail account, check with your e-mail service provider to determine whether it offers a secure connection. This is usually referred to as SSL (Secure Socket Layer). You'll need to enter special settings in your e-mail program to send and receive e-mail over these secure connections. Your e-mail service provider can give you detailed instructions.
- Don't lug around sensitive data on your notebook computer. None of the other precautions listed here will protect your data if someone walks off with your computer or steals it out of your car. The only protection is to keep sensitive data at home, although this isn't always practical.

Updating Windows 7

Microsoft is constantly improving Windows in all sorts of ways and tweaking it to repair security holes. Assuming that you didn't mess with the Windows update feature, Windows automatically downloads updates when your PC is connected to the Internet and installs those updates either automatically or after receiving your okay.

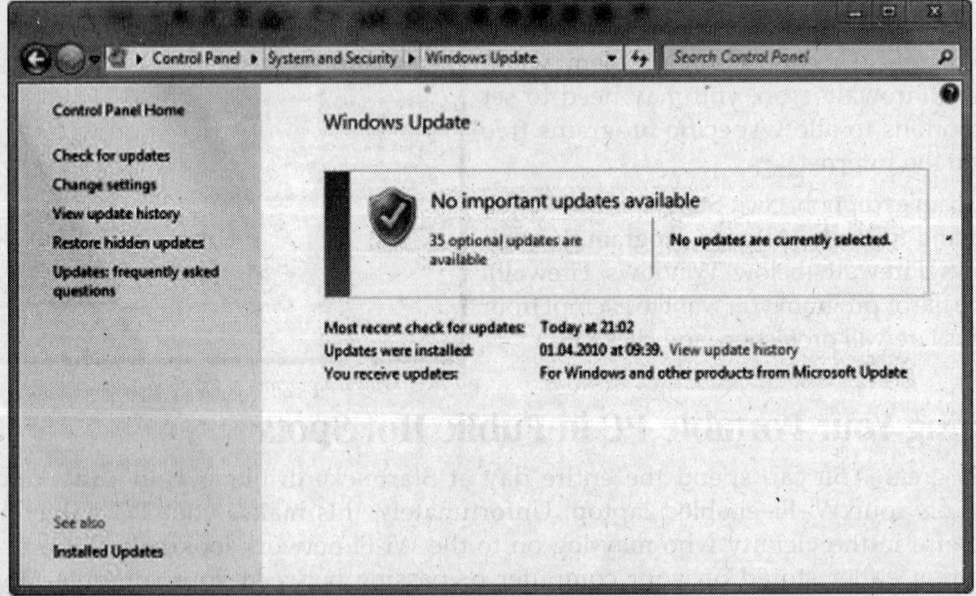

Check for Windows updates

If you disabled automatic updates, be sure to check for and install updates regularly to ensure that you have the latest security updates in place.

To check for updates, click **Start**, **All Programs**, **Windows Update**. Click **Check for updates** (on the left). Windows connects to the Internet, checks for updates, and (if it finds any) displays a link showing the number of updates available, as shown in Figure. Click the link to check out the available updates. You can then choose the updates you want to download and install, and click **OK** to install them. To enable or disable automatic updates and adjust the feature's settings, click **Start**, **Control Panel**, **System and Security**, **Windows Update**, **Change settings**. The Choose how Windows can install updates screen appears, which allows you to enable or disable automatic updates, choose when Windows checks for updates, and adjust other settings.

Opting for a Standard User Account

We have introduced three types of user accounts: Administrator, Standard, and Guest. An administrator account gives you complete control over your PC, but it also poses a security risk. If other users (or hackers) gain access to your PC when any user is logged on as an administrator, they can cause all sorts of trouble.

Consider creating only one password-protected administrator account and using a standard user account for daily PC use. If someone happens to gain access through the standard user account, he won't be able to change settings, create or delete other user accounts, or damage system files. When you're logged on as a standard user, you can still perform administrative tasks, as long as you know the administrator's password.

And if Windows prevents you from performing a specific administrative task, you can switch to your administrator account to proceed with whatever you want to do and then log out when you're done.

Dealing with E-Mail Threats and Annoyances

Many of the most serious threats to your PC come in the form of e-mail or e-mail attachments. By knowing what to watch out for and what to do or not do, you can steer clear of most problems.

Avoiding Infected E-Mail Attachments

The cardinal rule for avoiding viral infections from e-mail attachments is this: never open an e-mail attachment unless you know and trust the source. Your antivirus program will scan incoming e-mail messages and attachments, providing you with some protection, but if the attachment contains a brand-new virus your antivirus program doesn't recognize, or the sender figured out a way to hide the virus's true identity, your antivirus program may not catch it.

Don't Even Preview Junk Mail

You can recognize most junk mail just by looking at the sender's name or the message description, so don't even look at it. Some messages may contain images or other objects that send a message back to the sender, letting the person know that the message arrived and someone looked at it. This tells a spammer that your e-mail address is legitimate.

To avoid looking at junk mail, take the following precautions:

- Turn off your e-mail client's preview pane. Check your e-mail program's help system for details.
- Use your e-mail client's junk mail feature to automatically route suspected spam to the junk mail folder. You can then pick through the junk to find legitimate messages and delete the rest.
- Open e-mail only from known and trusted sources, and immediately delete all the rest.

Avoiding Phishing Scams

Phishing scams are commonly initiated via e-mail. *Phishing* is a fraudulent means of obtaining someone's username and password. The con artist/identity thief sends an e-mail that appears to originate from a bank, credit card company, or other such company warning of a serious issue you must address *right now* by clicking a link and logging into your account. The link takes you to an official-looking site complete with text boxes for entering your username and password. If you enter this sensitive information, the con artist has what he or she needs to log in to your real account.

To avoid falling victim to e-mail phishing scams, take the following precautions:

- Play it safe and go to the website yourself without clicking the e-mail or a link in the message. (You should be able to identify the website from the subject line or the address from which the e-mail originated.) If the website is legitimate and the message did in fact originate from it, you should be able to find something on the website about it; otherwise, it's most likely a scam.
- If your e-mail program features phishing protection, enable it. Check your e-mail program's help system for details.
- Be aware that most legitimate companies do not send alarming e-mail messages with links to click to resolve issues. If you receive such a message, it's probably not from the source it claims to come from.
- Put the mouse over the link and look in the status bar at the bottom of the window to see the address the link will take you to. Chances are, the link indicates one destination while the address takes you somewhere else entirely. This is a sure sign of a phishing scam.
- If you think the e-mail message is legitimate, head to the company's website to obtain legitimate contact information, and then contact the company to verify that someone at the company sent the message.
- If you determine that an e-mail message is fraudulent, report it to the legitimate company from which it supposedly originated so that the company can take action.

Phishing scams are most common but not exclusive to e-mail. Con artists may try to obtain login information in chat rooms, via instant messaging programs, and in social networking venues (including Facebook). A good rule of thumb is this: provide sensitive information only if *you* initiated contact.

Avoiding, Filtering, and Blocking Spam

Spam is unsolicited, unwanted e-mail—junk mail. When you first get an e-mail account, you receive very little spam. The spam starts to flow when you post your e-mail address on the web or sign up for free offers with companies that pass your e-mail address to others. Once your e-mail address lands on a spam list as a legitimate address, the spam is almost impossible to stop. When it comes to spam, an ounce of prevention is worth a kilo of cure. Here are a few tips for preventing spam:

- ❐ Don't use your primary e-mail address to register for anything on or off the web. Get a free e-mail account from Gmail, Yahoo!, or Hotmail and use this disposable e-mail address to register for stuff. If you start receiving too much junk e-mail, you can dump the address and use a different one.
- ❐ If you receive a spam message, don't reply to it. Replying verifies your e-mail address to the spammer and encourages more spam.
- ❐ Don't put your primary e-mail address on the web—for example on your website or blog. Spammers scan the web for e-mail addresses.

If you're receiving an overwhelming amount of spam, try the following solutions to slow the flow:

- ❐ Log in to your Internet service provider's website to find out whether it uses a spam blocker and whether you can configure it to make it more aggressive in identifying spam.
- ❐ If you have the e-mail account through a hosting provider (a business that hosts your website), log in to your account to find out about available options.
- ❐ Purchase and install a spam blocker of your own. You can find plenty of good spam filters/blockers out there, including SPAMfighter (www.spamfighter.com), ChoiceMail (www.digiportal.com), and Spameater Pro (www.spameaterpro.com), to name a few.

Most newer e-mail programs offer some sort of spam protection (perhaps in the form of a Junk Mail folder) and enable you to enter settings to make the program more or less aggressive in identifying spam. In addition, you can usually create lists of safe senders and blocked senders and block e-mail from certain domains or countries. Search your e-mail program's help system for "spam" to determine what, if any, spam protection features are available.

Checking Your Browser's Security Settings

Your web browser has its own security guard on duty that checks incoming files for potential threats. If you try to enter information such as a credit card number on a form that's not secure, the web browser displays a warning message asking if you want to continue. If a site attempts to install a program on your PC, your browser displays a confirmation dialog box or a warning near the top of the window asking for permission to download and install the program.

With most browsers, the default security settings are fine, but they may be a little on the aggressive side, warning you too much. In any event, checking your browser's security settings is usually a good idea, just in case your browser has a setting you'd like to change. To check security settings in Internet Explorer, click **Tools**, **Internet Options**, and then the **Security** tab.

If you use a browser other than Internet Explorer, check the browser's help system for information on how to enter your security preferences. All browsers have security features, although they all handle them a little differently.

Points to Remember

- ☆ To protect your PC against viruses, purchase and install a good antivirus program, and keep it updated with the latest virus definitions.
- ☆ To prevent unauthorized access to your PC, enable the Windows firewall or configure your router's firewall settings.
- ☆ Update Windows 7 regularly to ensure that you have the latest security updates installed.
- ☆ Log in to a standard user account for your daily activities to limit access to your PC in case a hacker breaks in and takes control of it.
- ☆ To avoid potential virus infections from e-mail attachments, install an antivirus program and open attachments only from trusted sources

SECTION–VI
MAINTAINING AND
TROUBLESHOOTING YOUR
COMPUTER

Maintenance/Troubleshooting/ Backup – Play Safe

One of the best clean-air machines on the market is a computer. The cooling fan constantly sucks in the dusty air and filters out the dust. A monitor acts like a dust magnet, pulling in any airborne particles unfortunate enough to get close to it. And the keyboard and mouse act like vacuum cleaners, sucking crumbs and other debris from your desk.

Unfortunately, the dust and smoke that your computer filters out eventually build up on the mechanical and electrical components inside it. When enough dust and debris collect on your computer and accessories, it's time for a thorough cleaning.

Tools of the Computer-Cleaning Trade

Before you start cleaning, turn off your computer and any attached devices, and gather the following cleaning equipment:

- **Screwdriver or wrench:** This is for taking the cover off your system unit. (If you don't feel comfortable going inside the system unit, take your computer to a qualified technician for a thorough annual cleaning. It really does get dusty in there.)
- **Computer vacuum:** Yes, there are vacuum cleaners designed especially for computers.
- **Can of compressed air:** You can get this at a computer or electronics store. Compressed air is great for blowing the dust out of tight spots, such as between keyboard keys.
- **Soft brush:** A clean paintbrush with soft bristles will do. Use this to dislodge any stubborn dust the vacuum won't pick up.
- **Toothpick:** This is the only tool you need to clean your mouse.
- **Cotton swabs:** Another good tool for cleaning your mouse, it's great for swabbing down your keyboard, too.
- **Paper towels:** Use these for wiping dust off your equipment and for cleaning the monitor.
- **Alcohol:** This is not the drinking kind; save that for when you're done.
- **Distilled water:** You can get special wipes for your monitor, but paper towels and distilled water do the trick.

Tip…

You've probably seen floppy disk or CD-ROM cleaning kits, but most likely you don't need one. If your drive is having trouble reading disks, buy a cleaning kit and clean it. If it's running smoothly, let it be.

Vacuuming and Dusting Your Computer

Work from the top down and from the outside in—with the power off and the pieces unplugged. Start with the monitor. You can use your regular vacuum cleaner for this part; if you have a brush attachment, use it. Run your vacuum hose up and down all the slots at the top and sides of the monitor. This is where most of the dust settles. Work down to the tilt-swivel base and vacuum that, too. You might need a narrow hose extension to reach in there.

Next, vacuum your printer, speakers, and any other devices. If dust is stuck to a device, wipe it off with a damp (not soaking-wet) paper towel. The system unit comes next. When vacuuming, be sure you vacuum all the ventilation holes and any gaps that allow air to flow into the system unit, including the power button, the DVD drive, open drive bays, and so on.

Now take the cover off the system unit and vacuum any dusty areas. You can't just poke your vacuum hose in there, though. Use only a vacuum designed for computers. Don't use a DustBuster, your regular vacuum cleaner, or your ShopVac. These can suck components off your circuit boards and can emit enough static electricity to fry a component. A computer vacuum is gentle and grounded. Also be careful not to suck up any loose screws. Before you begin, touch a metal part of the case to discharge any static electricity from your body, and keep your fingers away from the circuit boards.

Dust likes to collect around the fan, ventilation holes, and disk drives. Try to vacuum the fan blades, too. If you can't get the tip of the vacuum between the blades, gently wipe them off with a cotton swab. Some fans have a filter where the fan is mounted. If you're really ambitious, remove the fan (be careful with the wires) and clean the filter.

(Alternatively, take your PC outside and blow the dust out using your can of compressed air. Be careful spraying the air against internal components. Compressed air can be very cold and can cause condensation to form on sensitive electrical components.)

You can use a can of compressed air to blow dust off external peripheral devices as well, such as your keyboard and speakers.

Cleaning Your Monitor

If you can write "Wash Me" on your monitor with your fingertip, the monitor needs cleaning. Check the documentation that came with your computer or monitor to see if it's okay to use window cleaner on it. The monitor might have an antiglare coating that can be damaged by alcohol- or ammonia-based cleaning solutions. If it's not okay or if you're not sure, use water.

With your monitor turned off and unplugged, spray the window cleaner (or water) on a paper towel, just enough to make it damp; wipe the screen; and wipe with a dry paper towel to remove excess moisture. *Don't* spray window cleaner or any other liquid directly on the monitor; you don't want moisture to seep in.

You can also purchase special antistatic wipes for your monitor. These not only clean your monitor safely, but they also discharge the static electricity to prevent future dust buildup.

If you don't want to spend money on antistatic wipes, wipe your monitor with a *used*dryer sheet. A new dryer sheet might smudge the screen with fabric softener.

Shaking the Crumbs Out of Your Keyboard

Your keyboard is like a big placemat, catching all the cookie crumbs and other debris that fall off your fingers while you're working. Unlike a placemat, however, the keyboard isn't flat; it's full of nooks and crannies that are perfect hiding spots for crumbs and debris and are nearly impossible to reach to clean. And the suction from a typical vacuum cleaner just isn't strong enough to pull up the dust (although you can try it). The easiest way I've found to clean a keyboard is to turn it upside down and shake it gently. Repeat two or three times to get out any particles that fall behind the backs of the keys when you flip it over. If you don't like that idea, take your keyboard outside, get your handy-dandy can of compressed air, and blow between the keys.

Note....

Rubbing alcohol is an excellent cleaning solution for most electronic devices because it cleans well and dries quickly. Use it for your keyboard, plastics, and most glass surfaces (except for some monitors). Avoid using it on rubber (for example, the rubber rollers inside a printer), because it tends to dry out the rubber and make it brittle.

For a more thorough cleaning, shut down your computer and disconnect the keyboard. Dampen a cotton swab with rubbing alcohol and gently scrub the keys. Wait for the alcohol to evaporate completely before reconnecting the keyboard and turning on the power. If you spill a drink on your keyboard, try to save your work and shut down the computer fast but properly. Flip the keyboard over and turn off your computer. If you spilled water, let the keyboard dry out thoroughly. If you spilled something sticky, give your keyboard a bath or shower with lukewarm water. Take the back off the keyboard, but do not flip over the keyboard with the back off, or parts will scurry across your desktop. Let it dry for a couple of days (don't use a blow dryer), and put it back together. If some of the keys are still sticky, clean around them with a cotton swab dipped in rubbing alcohol. If you still have problems, you may have to buy a new keyboard.

Making Your Mouse Cough Up Hairballs

If you can't get your mouse pointer to move where you want it to, you can usually fix the problem by cleaning the mouse. Most new mice are optical or laser mice and use light to detect motion, so they have no moving parts to clean. I've never had a problem with an optical mouse getting gunked up. The only part you may need to clean are the little raised areas on the bottom of the mouse that come in contact with your desk or mouse pad, because these can get sticky. Simply dab a lint-free cloth in alcohol and gently wipe the pads.

Note.... ✍

Whatever you do, don't allow any cleaning solution or your cleaning cloth to come in contact with your mouse's light sensor, as this could negatively affect its operation. If you have a mouse with a ball in it (a mechanical mouse), forget about cleaning it. Take the plunge and purchase an optical mouse. And don't forget to clean your mouse pad or the area of your desk where your mouse scurries about. If the mouse was dirty, there's a good chance it picked up the dirt from your desk or mouse pad.

Cleaning Your Printer

Printer maintenance varies so widely from one printer to another that I recommend referring to the manual that came with your printer. In some cases, for example, cleaning the print heads means wiping them off with a damp, lint-free cloth; other printers may have a control panel option for cleaning the print heads, and if you touch the print head, you void the warranty. If you don't have the printer manual, you can usually visit the manufacturer's website and obtain an electronic version of the manual. If no manual is available, search the website for general instructions on printer cleaning and maintenance, or try to find a manual for a similar make and model.

Note.... ✍

Toner used in laser printers can be hazardous to your health. Using compressed air to blow toner out of the printer or a standard vacuum cleaner to suck it out can launch a lot of toner dust into the air. You can buy a special toner vacuum, but they're fairly expensive. You're better off hiring out the job to someone who has the right equipment and experience. Even with these variables, there are a few things the average user can do to keep the printer in peak condition and ensure high-quality output.

When turning off the printer, always use the power button on the printer or press the **Online** *button to take the printer offline (don't use the power button on your power strip). This ensures that the print head is moved to its rest position. On inkjet printers, this prevents the print head from drying out. Avoid touching the print heads unless the manufacturer or a tech support person tells you specifically to do so.*

If the ink starts to streak on your printouts (or you have frequent paper jams in a laser printer), see if your printer has an option for cleaning the print heads. If it doesn't, get special printer-cleaner paper from an office supply store and follow the instructions to run the sheet through your printer a few times. Using a damp cotton cloth, wipe paper dust and any ink off the paper feed rollers. Do not use alcohol. Do not use a paper towel; fibers from the paper towel could stick to the wheels.

What About the Disk Drives?

Don't bother cleaning your CD or DVD drives unless they're giving you trouble. If one of these drives is having trouble reading a disc, the disc is usually the cause of the problem. Clean the disc and check the bottom of the disc for scratches. If the drive has problems reading every disc you insert, try cleaning the drive using a special drive-cleaning kit. The kit usually consists of a disc with some cleaning solution. You squirt the cleaning solution on the disc, insert it, and remove it, and your job is done.

Giving Your PC a Tune-Up

Over time, you'll notice that your PC has slowed down. Windows takes a little longer to start up, programs that used to snap into action now seem to crawl, scrolling becomes choppy, and your PC locks up more frequently. You might begin to think that you need a new processor, more RAM, a larger hard disk drive, or even a whole new PC. Before you take such drastic action, work through this chapter to give your PC a tune-up. By eliminating useless files from your disk drive, reorganizing files, and reclaiming some of your PC's memory, you can boost your PC's performance and save a lot of money at the same time.

Eliminating Useless Files

Your hard disk probably contains *temporary files* and backup files that your programs create without telling you. These files can quickly clutter your hard drive, consuming space you need for new programs or new data files you create. You can easily delete most of these files yourself.

The easiest way to clear useless files from your hard drive in Windows is to let the Windows Disk Cleanup utility manage the details:

- Click **Start**, **All Programs**, **Accessories**, **System Tools**, **Disk Cleanup**. If your PC has more than one hard drive, Windows prompts you to select the drive you want to clean.
- If prompted to select a drive, click the arrow to the right of the Drives box, click the desired drive, and click **OK**. The utility scans your PC's hard drive for useless files and displays a list of file types you probably won't ever need, as shown in Figure.
- Check the box next to each file type you want Disk Cleanup to sweep off your PC's hard drive, and uncheck the box next to any items you want to keep.
- Click **OK** to commence the proceedings. The Cleanup utility removes the files you selected in Step 3.

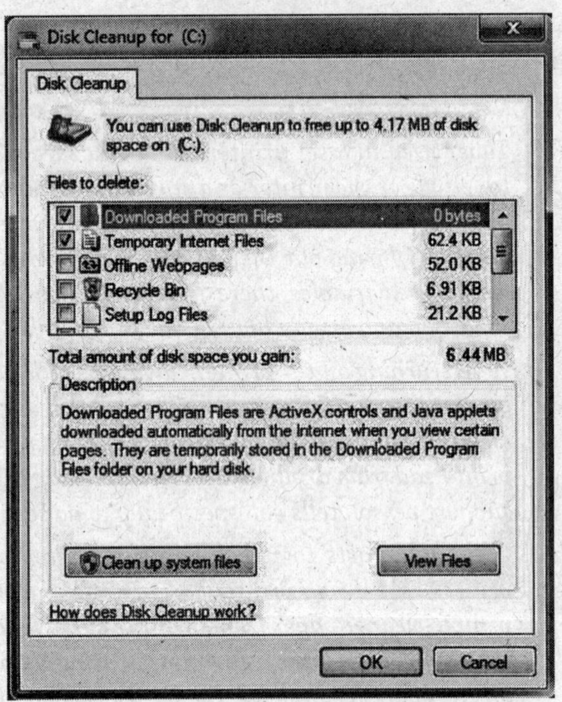

Disk Cleanup can remove useless files from your hard drive

Definition

Temporary files, those files that end in .TMP, are files that your programs create but often forget to delete. You can safely delete them to make more room on your PC.

For a more thorough and aggressive cleaning, perform Steps 1 and 2 and then click the **Clean up system files** button. Windows displays a Disk Cleanup dialog box. Click the **More**

Options tab, and then click the **Clean up** button under Programs and Features or System Restore and Shadow Copies to clear additional items from the disk. Confirm you're sure you want to delete by clicking **Delete**.

Tip...

You can clear temporary Internet files off your hard drive without having to perform a full disk cleanup. In Internet Explorer, click **Tools, Internet Options**. *Under Browsing history, click* **Delete**; *use the resulting options to choose the items you want to delete, or click the* **Delete All** *button to delete everything. Disk Cleanup does not remove copies of old digital photos you never look at, video clips you never watch, or music clips you never listen to. These are the items that really gobble up hard drive space in a hurry. Track down the folders where these files are stored and delete them or move them to CDs or DVDs. For more about managing files and folders, skip back to Part 4. While you're at it, open your e-mail program and delete any e-mail messages you no longer need, including copies of messages you sent. When you delete e-mail messages, some e-mail programs stick the deleted messages in a separate folder (usually called Deleted Items). Be sure to delete the messages from that folder, too.*

Checking for and Repairing Damaged Files

Windows comes with a utility called ScanDisk that can test a disk, repair most problems on it, and refresh it if needed. What kind of problems? ScanDisk can find defective storage areas on a disk, retrieve any recoverable data, and block those areas to prevent your PC from using them. ScanDisk can also find and delete misplaced (usually useless) file fragments that might be causing your PC to crash. Run ScanDisk regularly, at least once every month, and whenever your PC seems to be acting up and crashing for no apparent reason.

To run ScanDisk, follow these steps:

- ❒ Click **Start**, **Computer**.
- ❒ Right-click the icon for the drive you want to scan and click **Properties**.
- ❒ Click the **Tools** tab and (under Error-Checking) click the **Check now** button. The Check Disk Local Disk dialog box appears.
- ❒ Click the check box next to **Automatically fix file system errors**.

Note....

Disk Cleanup can dump your Recycle Bin and open up a lot of disk space. If you already did this, that's fine, but know that you can dump the Recycle Bin at any time. Just be sure it doesn't contain something you might need. Open the **Recycle Bin** *by double-clicking its icon on the desktop, and scroll down the list of deleted files to be sure you don't need anything in the Bin. If you find a file you might need, drag it onto the Windows desktop for safekeeping, or rightclick the file and select* **Restore** *to restore the file to its original location. Then click the* **Empty the Recycle Bin** *button.*

- To check for bad areas on the disk, click the check box next to **Scan for and attempt recovery of bad sectors**. Checking this option tells ScanDisk to do a thorough job, which might take several hours; turn on this option only if you don't plan to use your PC for a while.
- When you're ready to begin the scan, click **Start**. ScanDisk either automatically starts to scan the drive or displays a message indicating that it will scan the drive the next time you restart Windows.

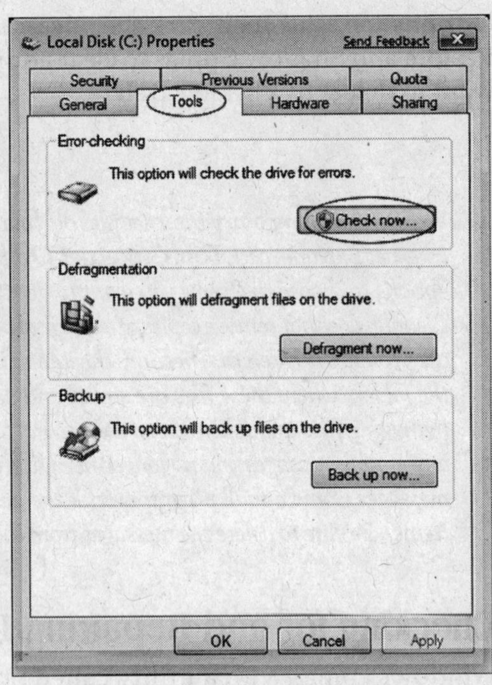

ScanDisk can repair most disk problems

Defragmenting Files

Whenever you delete a file from your hard disk, you leave a space where another file can be stored. When you save a file, your PC stores as much of the file as possible in that empty space and stores the rest of the file in other empty spaces. The file is then said to be *fragmented,* because its parts are stored in different locations on the disk. This slows down your disk drive and makes it more likely that your PC will lose track of a portion of the file or the entire file. Every month or so, run Windows Disk Defragmenter to determine the fragmentation percent and defragment your files, if necessary.

Before you start Disk Defragmenter, it's a good idea to disable any power-management utilities that might interfere with Defragmenter and any antivirus programs you're using. It's also a good idea to run Disk Cleanup before defragmenting your drive, as discussed in "Eliminating Useless Files," earlier in this chapter. Save and close all open documents and exit any programs currently running. To disable an antivirus program, right-click its icon in the notification area (right end of the taskbar), and click the option to disable the security features or exit the program.

When you're ready to have Disk Defragmenter defragment your files, follow these steps:

- Click **Start, All Programs, Accessories, System Tools, Disk Defragmenter**. Disk Defragmenter appears, as shown in Figure. You can also run Disk Defragmenter by right-clicking the drive icon and then selecting **Properties, Tools, Defragment now**. Click the disk to Schedule a disk defragmentation.

  Click to defragment now.

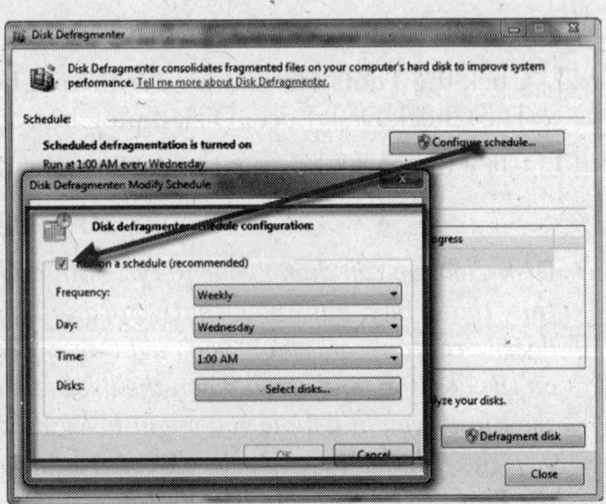

Defragmenter prompts you to select the drive(s) you want to defragment

- ❒ If your PC has more than one hard drive, click the icon for the drive you want to defragment.
- ❒ 3. (Optional) Click **Analyze disk** to display the percentage of file fragmentation on the disk and determine whether you need to defragment the disk.
- ❒ When you're ready for Defragmenter to start working, click the **Defragment disk** button. Defragmenter starts defragmenting the files on the disk.

Wait until the defragmentation is complete. It's best to leave your PC alone during the process. Otherwise, you might change a file and cause Defragmenter to start over. Don't run any programs or play any PC games. When defragmentation is complete, Defragmenter displays a message telling you so. Another issue that can significantly slow down your PC is having numerous programs and processes running in the background. Many programs install automatic update options, for example, that frequently check for updates on the Internet and download and install updates without notifying you. You can use the Windows System Configuration Utility to choose which programs are allowed to run on startup.

Note....

I recommend avoiding any registry "fixes" that optimize your system. I've had registry optimizers severely mess up my system. If you choose to try the registry fixes, make a system restore point first.

PC Problems: Preparation and Troubleshooting

Your PC can be quite moody. One day, all the components run fine and all tasks proceed without a glitch. The next day, your mouse pointer won't budge, your printer refuses to print a document, Windows locks up, your PC refuses to connect to the Internet, or valuable documents simply disappear.

In this chapter, I help you prepare in advance so that you can recover from serious problems, and I reveal troubleshooting techniques that can help you track down the solutions to nearly any PC issue without having to call a technician.

This chapter won't transform you into a professional PC technician, but with a little practice and a lot of patience, you should be able to solve the most common problems and even help your friends with their PC woes.

Backing Up and Restoring Files

Your PC's hard drive may be very reliable, but it's not totally immune to virus attacks, hardware malfunctions, or human error. Because of this, you should back up all the files on your PC, or at least the files you can't reasonably recover without a backup—data files, e-mail messages and addresses, digital photos, your video or music collection, and so on.

I recommend purchasing an external hard drive for your PC and backing up all your irreplaceable files to the external hard drive at least once a week. If you go on a trip, take the backups with you and leave the originals at home, or vice versa. (If you don't have an external hard drive, you can back up files to recordable CDs or DVDs or an internal hard drive.)

Backing Up Files

Take the following steps to back up files with Windows Backup's recommended settings:

- ❒ Click **Start, All Programs, Maintenance, Backup and Restore**.
- ❒ Under Backup, do one of the following:
  - If this is the first time you're running Windows Backup and Restore, click **Set up backup** and then proceed to Step 3 to enter your backup settings.
  - If you already entered your backup settings and want to use those same settings, click **Back up now**.
  - If you already entered your backup settings and want to use different settings, click **Change settings** and proceed with Step 3.
- ❒ Click the drive you want to use to store your backup files and click **Next**. (I recommend backing up to recordable DVDs or a removable hard drive so that you can store your backup in a safe location away from your PC.)
- ❒ When asked "What do you want to back up?" do one of the following:
  - Click **Let Windows choose (recommended)** and click **Next** so that Windows can decide which files to back up—all data files saved in libraries, on the desktop, or in Windows default folders. Windows also creates a system image that you can use to restore your PC if it stops working.
  - Click **Let me choose**, use the resulting dialog box to choose the folders and files you want included in the backup, and click **Next**. (Use this option if you store your data files in folders outside the Windows libraries and default folders—for example, in a folder named C:\Data.)
- ❒ Click **Save settings and run backup**. (You can stop the backup operation at any time by clicking **View Details** and then clicking **Stop backup** and **Stop backup** again to confirm.)

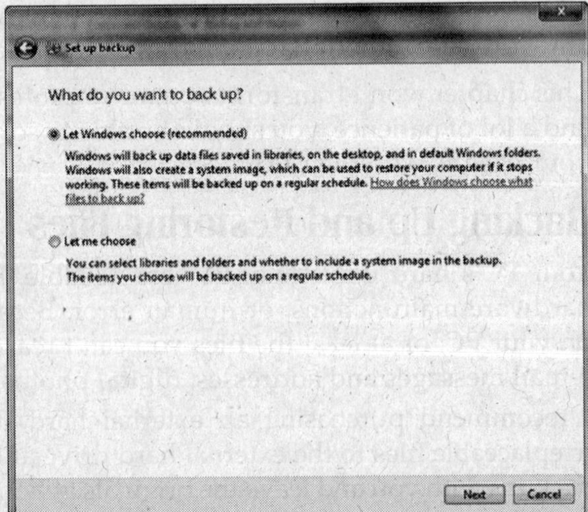

Select disk drives, folders, and files to back up

If you choose to select what to back up, selecting items is the only tricky part. If you click the check box next to a drive or folder that's not expanded (in other words, you can't see the folders below the drive letter or the subfolders below a folder), you select everything on the drive or in the folder. To select specific folders or files, first click the arrow to the left of the drive letter or folder in which the items are stored. This expands the listing for the selected file or folder. You can then select individual files or folders.

As you modify files included in your backup, Windows either adds those files to your Backup the next time you perform a backup or automatically backs up files according to the schedule settings. This ensures that you have up-to-date backups.

Restoring Files

If disaster strikes and you lose valuable files, you can restore your files from your backups. Before restoring files, make sure they're really gone. Backup files tend to be older than the originals, and you usually don't want to replace a new file with an older version. Windows will warn you if you're about to replace a file with a file of the same name and ask you to confirm.

To restore folders or files from your backups, here's what you need to do:

- Click **Start**, **All Programs**, **Maintenance**, **Backup and Restore**.
- Click **Restore my files**. The Restore Files dialog box appears.
- Click one of the following options:
  - **Search**, to search your backups for specific files and folders.
  - **Browse for files**, to selectively restore specific files within one or more folders.
  - **Browse for folders**, to selectively restore one or more folders and their entire contents.
- Follow the onscreen cues to find and select the file(s) and/or folder(s) you want to restore and add them to the list of items you want restored.
- 5.(Optional) Repeat Steps 3 and 4 to select additional files and folders.
- Click **Next**. Windows prompts you to choose the location where you want to restore the items.
- Click **In the original location** or choose **In the following location**, and then click the **Browse** button and choose the disk drive and folder in which to restore the items.
- Click **Restore**.

Creating a System Image

Windows enables you to create a system image, which essentially clones the hard drive on which Windows is installed. If that drive ever stops working, you can then restore the system image, in its entirety, to return your PC to the time when the system image was created. This returns Windows 7 and all your programs installed on that drive. (You can't selectively restore items from a system image.)

Note....

Store the system image on a separate disk drive. If the original drive stops working, your system image will be of no use. You can store the system image on another hard drive or on DVDs.

To create a system image, click **Start**, **All Programs**, **Maintenance**, **Backup and Restore**. In the left column, click **Create a system image**. Click the drive on which to store the system image and click **Next**. Choose the drives you want to include and click **Next**. Click **Start backup**.

If your PC's system files are damaged to the point of rendering your PC inoperable, you can recover by restoring the system image to your PC. (If the hard drive on which the system files are stored is not working, you must replace the hard drive first. The hard drive must be the same size or larger than the original drive.) Do one of the following:

- If your PC is working and you can access the Control Panel or you want to restore your system image to another Windows 7 PC, click **Start, Control Panel, System and Security, Action Centre, Recovery, Advanced recovery methods**. Click **Use a system image you created earlier to recover your computer**, and then follow the onscreen cues to complete the operation.
- If you can't access the Control Panel and you don't have a Windows installation or system repair disc, restart your computer and keep tapping the **F8** key to start Windows in Safe mode. On the Advanced Boot Options screen, use the arrow keys to highlight **Repair your computer**, and press **Enter**. Select a keyboard layout and click **Next**. Select a username, type the password, and click **OK**. On the System Recovery Options menu, click **System Image Recovery** and then follow the instructions.

Creating and Using a System Repair Disc

Viruses or other malware can attack system files and bring your Windows PC to its knees. One way to protect your PC is to prepare for the worst by creating a system repair disc and backing up your files. This section shows you how to create a system repair disc. The following section shows you how to back up and restore files. To create a system repair disc, click **Start, All Programs, Maintenance, Create a System Repair Disc**. If you have more than one disc drive, open the **Drive** menu and click the drive you want to use. Insert a blank disc into the drive and click **Create disc**. When Windows has completed the disc, it displays a message instructing you to label the disc. Eject the disc, label it as instructed, click **Close**, and then click **OK**.

To use the repair disc, here's what you need to do:

- Insert the repair disc into your PC's disc drive.
- Restart your PC using your PC's power button and watch the screen carefully; it should display a message telling you to press a certain key to access the boot menu. (If you don't see such a message, check your PC's manual to determine how to boot from the disc drive.)
- Press the designated key and then choose the option to boot from the disc drive instead of the hard drive.
- Choose your language settings and click **Next**.
- Choose the desired recovery option and click **Next**.
- Follow the onscreen instructions to repair or restore your system.

Troubleshooting Problems

When you run into a problem that doesn't have an obvious solution, the best course of action is inaction—that is, don't do anything. If you're fidgeting to do something, take a walk or grab a snack. Doing the wrong thing can often make the problem worse. After you've calmed down a little, come back and work through this list:

- ❒ **Are there any onscreen messages?** Look at the monitor for any messages that indicate a problem.
- ❒ **Is everything plugged in and turned on?** Turn off everything and check the connections. Don't assume that just because something looks connected, it is. Wiggle all the plugs.
- ❒ **When did the problem start?** Did you install a new program? Did you enter a command? Did you add a new device?
- ❒ **Is the problem limited to one program?** If you have the same problem in every program, the problem is probably caused by your PC or Windows. If the problem occurs in only one program, focus on that program.
- ❒ **When did you have the file last?** If you lost a file, it probably didn't get sucked into a black hole. It's probably somewhere on your disk, in a separate folder.
- ❒ **Realize that it's probably not the PC, and it's probably not a virus.** The problem is usually in the software—Windows or one of your programs. Of the problems that people blame on PC viruses or the PC itself, 95 percent are actually bugs in the software or problems with specific device drivers (the instructions that tell your PC and Windows how to use the device). Only about 5 percent prove to be caused by viruses.

Tip...

Keep a running log of the changes you make to your system. Every time you install a new device or new software, install updates, or change settings, jot down the date and what you did. It takes a little extra time, but it enables you to retrace your steps later. You may also want to check out a free tool called Belarc Advisor (belarc.com/free_download.html), which creates a detailed profile of your installed software and hardware and displays the results in your web browser. It's a good idea to print an update every quarter.

Enlisting the Assistance of a Windows Troubleshooter

Windows has a collection of troubleshooters that can help you track down the cause of common issues and resolve them. To run a troubleshooter, click **Start**, **Control Panel**, and (below System and Security) click **Find and fix problems**. Click the link for the program or feature group that's giving you problems (for example, **Programs**, **Network and Internet**, or **System and Security**) and then click the specific item.

This launches the troubleshooter for that item. Click **Next** and then follow the troubleshooter's lead, as shown in Figure.

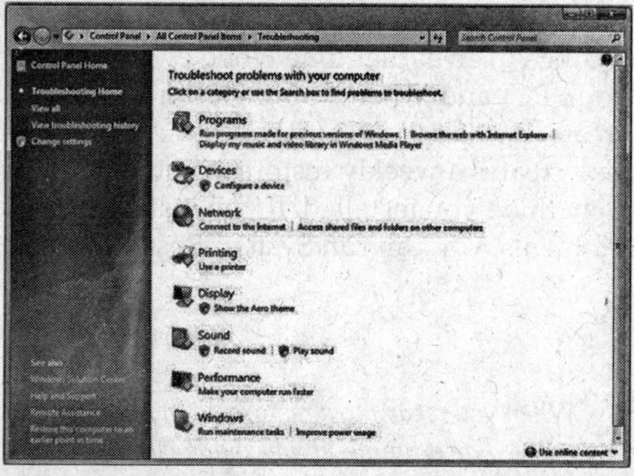

The Windows troubleshooters can help track down problems and resolve issues

Searching for Solutions Online

If you can connect to the Internet and access the web, you can often find solutions to common PC problems simply by using your favourite search engine, such as Google or Yahoo!. Run your web browser, access the search engine, type a description of the problem, and press **Enter**. The search likely returns a bunch of links to pages that may or may not contain the solution to the problem you're experiencing.

If Windows or one of your applications displays a specific error message, jot down the message and then enter it as your search phrase enclosed in quotes—for example, "Network Path Not Found".

Checking the Manufacturer's Website

Every PC hardware and software company has a website and almost always provides technical support, software or driver updates, and online forums where you can find help. If you have an inkling that a particular hardware device or program is causing problems, head directly to the manufacturer's website. Often the manufacturer's website will not appear near the top of the search results when you search for a specific problem, but it will pop up immediately when you search the manufacturer's website.

If you can't find the answer on the website, you can usually find contact information, a contact form, or a link to online technical support. Learn how to find website addresses and contact information for numerous PC, component, and software manufacturers.

Getting Remote Assistance

I had already told you how to use the Windows 7 Remote Assistance feature to obtain help from a friend or relative over the Internet. Many manufacturers also have their own remote assistance programs and technology that enable technicians to take control of your PC and help you resolve issues. Be sure to check the manufacturer's website for a link to live technical support.

Thank Goodness for System Restore!

Windows includes a nifty utility called System Restore that can help you return your PC's settings to an earlier time when everything was working properly. System Restore monitors your PC, and when you install a program or a new peripheral device or component, it creates a *restore point* and saves the current settings to your PC's hard drive. System Restore also creates a weekly restore point, just in case something goes wrong that's not a result of something you installed. If you install a program or change a setting in Windows that causes problems, you can run System Restore and pick the desired restore point.

Tip...

When you return to a restore point, you don't lose any of the work you've done since that restore point. For example, if you made changes to a Word document, those are safe. However, if you installed a device or a program after Windows created the restore point, you'll probably need to reinstall it after you complete the restoration.

Restore System Using a Restore Point

To return Windows to a previous state using one of the restore points it created, take the following steps:

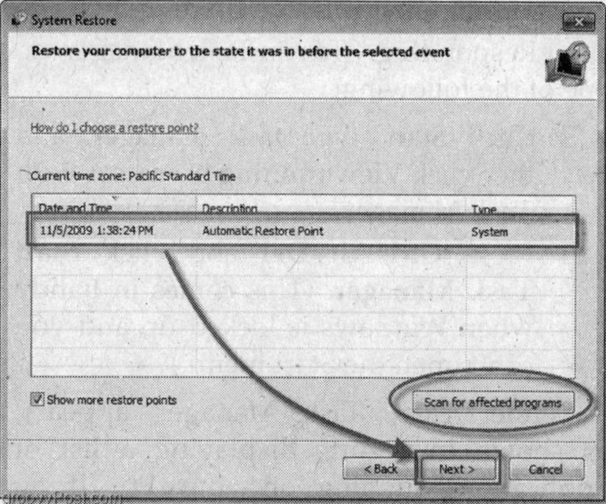

System Restore enables you to return your system to an earlier time

- Click **Start, All Programs, Accessories, System Tools, System Restore**. The System Restore window appears.
- Click **Next**. System Restore displays available restore points. A list of recent restore points appears, as shown in Figure.
- Click the desired restore point, click **Next**, and follow the onscreen instructions to complete the operation. Windows restarts your PC as part of the restoration process.

After System Restore restarts your PC, it displays a message indicating that you can undo the restoration. Cancel out of this window and test a few of the applications you normally use, to be sure the restoration didn't mess up your system. If the restoration made things worse instead of better, you can run System Restore again and undo the restoration.

Create a Restore Point

If you plan to change any system settings in Windows, delete device drivers, or install applications, run System Restore and create your own restore point before you begin. If something goes wrong, you can immediately return your PC to its previous condition.

- Click **Start, Control Panel, System and Security, System**.
- Click **System protection** (left column). The System Properties dialog box appears.
- Click **Create** (near the bottom of the dialog box).
- Type a name for the restore point and click **Create**.

Identifying Troublesome Software

Although Windows is responsible for its fair share of problems, applications, drivers, and other software are often responsible. Windows provides a couple of utilities for helping track down problems with other software—Task Manager and the System Configuration Utility.

Note....

Don't assume that the programs you run are the only programs running on your PC. Many programs that you install or that came already installed on your PC run in the background. You won't see buttons for them on the Windows taskbar or even in the system tray, but they're running just the same and can cause conflicts with Windows and your other programs. They can also consume processor and memory resources.

Using Task Manager

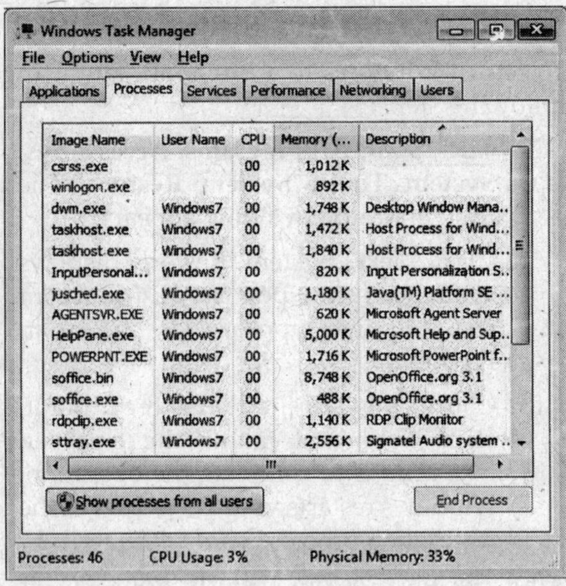

Task Manager displays all the applications and processes running on your PC

Task Manager is most useful for identifying programs that have locked up or are "Not Responding." To run Task Manager, do one of the following:

- Click **Start**, type **task manager**, and then click **View running processes with Task Manager**.
- Press **Ctrl+Alt+Del** and click **Start Task Manager**. (This comes in handy when Windows is locked up and you can't open the Start menu.)

In either case, Task Manager appears, as shown in Figure, displaying a list of applications running on your PC. If an application is shown as "Not Responding," you can exit the application, although you may lose any recent changes to what you were working on in that application. To exit the application, click its name, click **End Task**, and then confirm your request.

If your PC is running very slowly, you can also use Task Manager to help identify the problem. Click the **Processes** tab and check the CPU and Memory columns, which show the percentage of resources the process is using. (The number in the CPU column is most important.) If the number is consistently high for a program (over, say, 50), you may need to do some additional troubleshooting to find out why it's so high.

Troubleshooting with the System Configuration Utility

The System Configuration utility enables you to disable programs that automatically run when Windows starts. You can disable most of the programs to prevent them from running and then enable each program to identify the one that's causing problems.

To determine which programs are running on startup and to pick and choose which programs you want to run, perform a diagnostic startup:

- Click **Start**, type **system con**, and click **System Configuration** (near the top of the Start menu).
- Click the **Services** tab and click **Hide all Microsoft services**, as shown in Figure. By hiding Microsoft services, you avoid accidentally disabling a service that's critical for the operation of Windows.
- Click the check box next to each *service* you don't want Windows to run on startup, being careful not to disable services that are crucial for securing your computer, such as antivirus services. (You can click the **Disable all** button and enable the items you do want Windows to run on startup.)

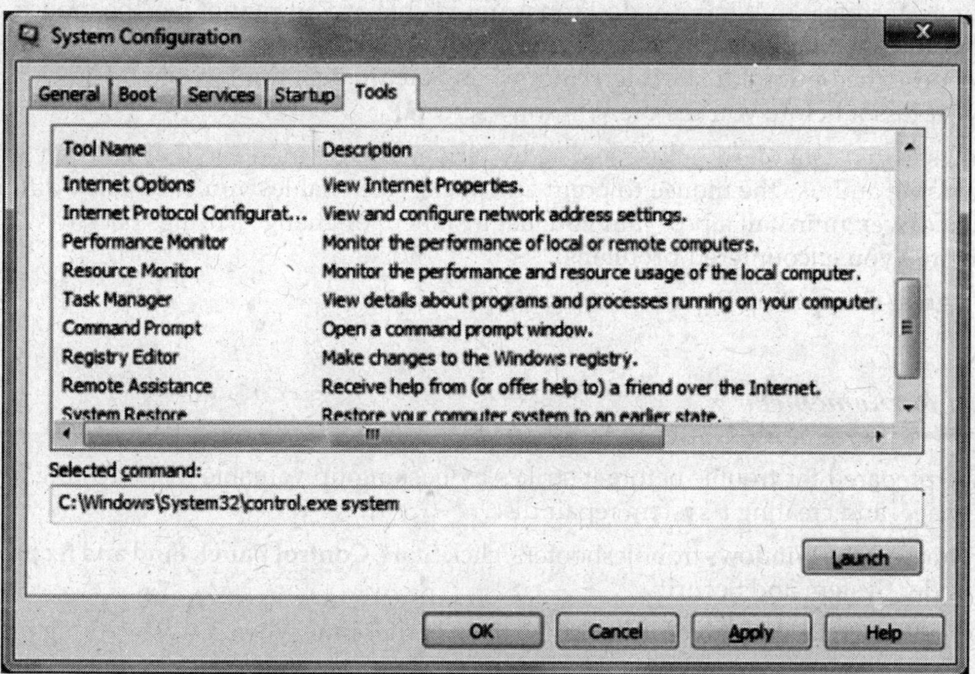

System Configuration enables you to safely disable programs and services that might cause problems

- ❒ Click the **Startup** tab. A list of all the background programs that run on startup appears.
- ❒ Click the check box next to each *program* you don't want Windows to run on startup, being careful not to disable programs that are crucial for securing your computer, such as antivirus services. (You can click the **Disable All** button and enable the programs you do want Windows to run on startup.)
- ❒ Click **OK**. The System Configuration dialog box appears, prompting you to restart your computer.
- ❒ Exit any currently running programs and click the **Restart** button. Windows restarts. A message appears in the lower-right corner of the screen, reminding you that you blocked some programs.

If the problem is no longer present, you now know that one of the services or programs you disabled is causing the problem and you can enable one or two services and programs at a time to narrow the list of possibilities. If the problem is still present, run the System Configuration utility again, disable more startup programs, and restart your PC. Using this strategy, you can focus on the program or service that's causing the problem.

Starting Windows in Safe Mode

Windows typically starts in Safe mode if you install a wrong device driver (especially a wrong video or mouse driver). In Safe mode, "Safe Mode" appears at each corner of the desktop. In most cases, you can simply restart Windows to have it load the previous driver.

If, upon restarting, the Windows desktop is not visible or you cannot use the mouse, restart your PC and keep tapping the **F8** key every second or so until you see the Safe Mode screen. Then choose the option for starting Windows in Safe mode. (You have to be quick with the F8 key—press it before you see the Windows screen.)

Windows loads a standard mouse and video driver in Safe mode so that you can see what you're doing and use the mouse to point and click. This enables you to install a different or updated driver, uninstall a program you just installed, or change settings back to what they were before you encountered problems.

Have a great Computing Experience!

Points to Remember

- Be prepared for trouble before it strikes by backing up valuable files, creating a system image, and creating a system repair disc.
- To access the Windows troubleshooters, click **Start**, **Control Panel**, **Find and fix problems** under System and Security.
- Use System Restore to return your PC to an earlier time when it was working properly.
- If a program stops responding or Windows freezes up, press **Ctrl+Alt+Del**, click **Start Task Manager**, and end any programs that are "Not Responding."
- Use the System Configuration utility to troubleshoot problems caused by programs that run in the background.
- Don't go into shock when Windows starts in Safe mode. Shutting down and restarting your PC usually corrects the problem

SECTION–VII
ADD-ONS

Texting Slang

Texting: Only a few short years ago, no one knew what that was. Now, everyone is doing it. **Texting involves using a phone, or other device, to send a text message to another mobile device.** In other words, it is sort of like instant messaging for your phone. However, because you are using a telephone, you don't usually have a full keyboard at your disposal. Instead, you have to type your message using the numbers on your phone, each of which is associated with a letter. To save time and energy and avoid carpal tunnel of the thumbs, hundreds of different texting slang words and abbreviations have come into play. The problem is, there's so many, if you don't know them all you might think someone is speaking a foreign language! Never fear, though, because here is a list to help you figure out just what on earth you BFF texted you!

Texting Slang

Texting slang involves both symbols, and special abbreviations that mean certain things. Here some of the most popular texting slang words:

Texting Symbols

❒ :) Smiley face / happy	❒ :(Sad	❒ :-* Kiss
❒ =) Happy	❒ =(Sad	❒ :-D Laughing
❒ :-) Happy	❒ :') Happy Tears	

Texting Words and Phrases Explained

A	
❒ ABT About	❒ ADDY Address
❒ ABT2 About to	❒ AEAP As early as possible
❒ ACDNT Accident	❒ AF April Fools
❒ ACK Acknowledge	❒ AIGHT Alright
❒ ACPT Accept	❒ AKA Also known as
❒ ADD Address	❒ AMAP As much as possible

❒ AML All my love	❒ ATB All the best
❒ AMOF As a matter of fact	❒ ATEOTD At the end of the day
❒ ASAP As soon as possible	❒ AYT Alright / Are you there?
B	
❒ B2W Back to work	❒ BLNT Better luck next time
❒ B/F Boyfriend	❒ BM Bite me
❒ B4 Before	❒ BOYF Boyfriend
❒ BDAY Birthday	❒ BRB Be right back
❒ BF Boyfriend	❒ BTW By the Way
❒ BF Best friend	❒ BYOB Bring Your Own beer
❒ BFF Best friends forever	
C	
❒ CIAO Good-bye	❒ CU See you
❒ CM Call me	❒ CUA See you around
❒ CMB Call me back	❒ CUL See you later
❒ CMON Come on	❒ CUL8R See you later
❒ CR8 Create	❒ CYA See you
❒ CTC Care to chat?	❒ CYAL8R See you later
D	
❒ DIY Do it yourself	❒ DL Download
❒ DKDC Don't know, don't care	❒ DNT Don't
❒ D/L Download	
E	
❒ EMA E-mail address	❒ EZ Easy
❒ EOM End of message	❒ EZY Easy
❒ ETA Estimated time of arrival	

F	
❒ FAQ Frequently asked questions	❒ FWIW For what it's worth
❒ FBM Fine by me	❒ FWM Fine with me
❒ FC Fingers crossed	❒ FYEO For your eyes only
❒ FTW For the win	❒ FYA For your amusement
❒ FW Forward	❒ FYI For your information
G	
❒ G/F Girlfriend	❒ G2G Got to go
❒ G2CU Good to see you	❒ G2R Got to run

❒ GB Goodbye	❒ GNIGHT Good night
❒ GBTW Get back to work	❒ GNITE Good night
❒ GBU God bless you	❒ GR8 Great
❒ GF Girl friend	❒ GRATZ Congratulations
❒ GG Gotta Go	❒ GTG Got to go
❒ GJ Good job	❒ GUD Good
❒ GL Good luck	❒ GUDNYT Goodnight
❒ GN Good night	
H	
❒ H8 Hate	❒ HF Have fun
❒ HAK Hug and kiss	❒ HFAC Holy flipping animal crackers
❒ HAU How about you?	❒ HRU How are you?
❒ HAV Have	❒ HTH Hope this helps
❒ H&K Hugs & kisses	❒ HUB Head up butt
❒ H2CUS Hope to see you soon	❒ HUYA Head up your ass
❒ HAND Have a nice day	❒ HV Have
❒ H-BDAY Happy Birthday	❒ HW Homework
I	
❒ IB I'm back	❒ ILY I love you
❒ IC I see	❒ IM Instant message
❒ IDC I don't care	❒ IMO In my opinion
❒ IHNI I have no idea	❒ IMS I am sorry
❒ IK I know	❒ IMU I miss you
❒ ILU I love you	❒ IUSS If you say so
J	
❒ JAC Just a sec	❒ JLMK Just let me know
❒ JK Just kidding	
K	
❒ K Okay	❒ KIT Keep in touch
❒ KK Okay, Okay!	❒ KUTGW Keep up the good work
❒ KEWL Cool	
L	
❒ L8R Later	❒ LOL Lots of love
❒ LOL Laugh out loud	❒ LUVYA Love you

M	
❒ MC Merry Christmas	❒ MTF More to follow
❒ MIRL Meet in real life	❒ MUSM Miss you so much
❒ MKAY "Mmm, okay"	❒ MWAH To give a kiss
❒ MSG Message	❒ MYOB Mind your own business
N	
❒ N1 Nice one	❒ NM Never mind
❒ N2M Nothing too much	❒ NOYB None of your business
❒ NBD No big deal	❒ NP No problem
❒ NE Any	❒ NT Nice try
❒ NE1 Anyone	❒ NVM Never mind
❒ NIMBY Not in my back yard	❒ NVR Never
❒ NM Nothing much	❒ NW No way
O	
❒ OB Oh baby	❒ OMG Oh my God
❒ OB Oh brother	❒ OMW On my way
❒ OI Operator indisposed	❒ ONL Online
❒ OIC Oh, I see	❒ OTB Off to bed
❒ OJ Only joking	❒ OTL Out to lunch
❒ OM Oh, my	❒ OTOH On the other hand
❒ OMDB Over my dead body	❒ OVA Over
P	
❒ P2P Peer to peer	❒ PM Private Message
❒ PEEPS People	❒ POV Point of view
❒ PIC Picture	❒ PPL People
❒ PL8 Plate	❒ PROLLY Probably
❒ PLMK Please let me know	❒ PRT Party
❒ PLS Please	❒ PZ Peace
❒ PLZ Please	
Q	
❒ QIK Quick	❒ QT Cutie
❒ QL Quit laughing	❒ QTPI Cutie pie
R	
❒ RIP Rest in peace	❒ RU Are you?
❒ RLY Really	❒ RUOK Are you okay?
❒ RME Rolling my eyes	❒ RX Regards

S	
❐ SBT Sorry 'bout that	❐ SOS Meaning help
❐ SC Stay cool	❐ SRSLY Seriously
❐ SIT Stay in touch	❐ SRY Sorry
❐ SK8 Skate	❐ SS So sorry
❐ SK8NG Skating	❐ STR8 Straight
❐ SK8R Skater	❐ SUL See you later
❐ SK8RBOI Skater Boy	❐ SUP What's up?
❐ SO Significant other	❐ SUX sucks or "it sucks"
❐ SOAB Son of a B*tch	❐ SYL See you later
❐ SOL Sooner or later	❐ SYS See you soon
T	
❐ TBC To be continued	❐ TMTH Too much to handle
❐ TBD To be determined	❐ TOJ Tears of joy
❐ TBL Text back later	❐ TTFN Ta ta for now
❐ TC Take care	❐ TTLY Totally
❐ TGIF Thank God it's Friday	❐ TTUL Talk to you later
❐ THX Thanks	❐ TU Thank you
❐ THNX Thanks	❐ TTYL Talk to you later
❐ TMB Text me back	❐ TTYS Talk to you soon
❐ TMI Too much information	❐ TY Thank you
U	
❐ UFB Un "freaking/f-ing" believable	❐ UOK You ok?
❐ UFN Until further notice	❐ UR Your / You're
❐ UL Upload	❐ URW You are welcome
❐ U-L Meaning "You will"	❐ UW You're welcome
V	
❐ VBS Very big smile	❐ VN Very nice
❐ VIP Very important person	❐ VRY Very
❐ VM Voice mail	
W	
❐ W@ What?	❐ WAM Wait a minute
❐ W/ With	❐ WAYF Where are you from?
❐ W8 Wait	❐ W/B Write back
❐ WAH Working at home	❐ WB Welcome back

❐ WBU What about you?	❐ WRK Work
❐ WC Who cares	❐ WRU@ Where are you at?
❐ W/E Whatever	❐ WTF What the freak
❐ W/END Weekend	❐ WTG Way to go
❐ WE Whatever	❐ WTH What the heck? What the hell?
❐ WIU Wrap it up	❐ WTM Who's the man?
❐ WK Week	❐ WU What's up?
❐ WKD Weekend	❐ WUF Where are you from?
❐ W/O Without	❐ WUP What's up?
X	
❐ X Kiss	❐ XOXOXO Hugs & Kisses
❐ XME Excuse Me	❐ XLNT Excellent
Y	
❐ Y? Why?	❐ YNK You never know
❐ Y2K You're too kind	❐ YR Your
❐ YARLY Ya, really?	❐ YR Yeah right
❐ YBS You'll be sorry	❐ YW You're welcome
❐ YGG You go girl	
Z	
❐ ZUP Meaning "What's up?"	❐ ZZZZ Bored or asleep

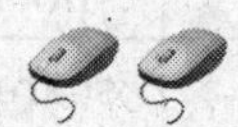

Emoticons

Smiley	ASCII	Traditional		Horsey	
happy	:-)		:smile:		:hsmile:
sad	:-(		:sad:		:hsad:
crying	:'(		:cry:		:hcry:
winking	;-)		:wink:		:hwink:
laughing	:-D		:laugh:		:hlaugh:
tongue	:-P		:tongue:		:htongue:
uncertain	:-/		:uncertain:		:huncertain:
eyes popping	8-)		:pop:		:hpop:
surprised	=-o		:surp:		:hsurp:
shocked	=-O		:shock:		:hshock:
scared	8-o		:scared:		:hscared:
glaring	>:-|		:glare:		:hglare:
mad	>:-[		:mad:		:hmad:
halo	O:-)		:halo:		:hhalo:
oops	:-.		:oops:		:hoops:
blushing	8-.		:blush:		:hblush:
punchy	S-o		:punchy:		:hpunchy:
kissing	:-*		:kiss:		:hkiss:
yawning	:-O		:yawn:		:hyawn:
sick	X-o		:sick:		:hsick:
devious	>:->		:devious:		:hdevious:

crafty	:-}		:crafty:		:hcrafty:
hot	:-{		:hot:		:hhot:
cold	:-#		:cold:		:hcold:
anime	^_^		:anime:		:hanime:
dog	U^_^U		:dog:		:dog:
cat	>^_^<		:cat:		:cat:
mouse	^x^		:mouse:		:mouse:
orc	8-{		:orc:		:orc:

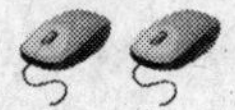

Youtube Video Tutorials

Youtube Link: https://www.youtube.com/watch?v=1e6ZprqDETA

The book comes with 34 Video Tutorials on Youtube for better understanding of some useful applications discussed in the book. For convenience of the reader we divide the videos section wise, such as Computer Basics, MS Word, MS Excel, MS PowerPoint, MS Publisher and MS Access.

Computer Basics:

1. **What is a Computer:** This video acquaints you with a computer and various hardware and software of a computer, different types of computers, basic difference between a PC and a MAC, Servers, various uses of Servers, etc.
2. **Basic Parts of a Desktop Computer:** This video tutorial will show you the basic parts of a desktop computer, such as Computer Case or Tower Case, Monitor, Keyboard, Mouse, and also familiarizes you with important roles each part plays in working of a computer.
3. **Inside a Desktop Computer:** This video will show you the various components that make a computer work, such as the CPU, Motherboard, Ram, Hard Drive, etc., along with the roles each component plays in a computer.
4. **Buttons and Ports on Computer:** In this video you will get to know the various buttons and ports appearing in the front and back of a desktop computer, such as the Power button, Optical disc Drive or CD Drive or DVD Drive button, Audio Port, USB Port, Power Socket in the back, Ethernet port, Monitor Port, etc.
5. **Getting to Know Laptop Computers:** This video will show the various ways a laptop differs from a desktop computer which will help you decide to the right computer to meet your needs.
6. **Setting up a Desktop Computer:** This short video tutorial will show step by step how to set up a desktop computer putting all the basic parts in the right order.
7. **Understanding Operating System:** This video tutorial covers the roles played by the Operating system in working of a computer. The video also discusses about different

operating systems such as Microsoft Windows, MAC OS, iOS, etc. and elaborates how an operating system works in a computer.

8. **Getting started with Windows:** This video tutorial familiarizes you with the Windows operating system along with its various features of windows 7 and shows you how to customize its features, such as the working of the taskbar, how to open, save and delete a folder and file, the start menu and its importance, and many more.
9. **Connecting to the Internet:** In this tutorial you will get the know how to connect your computer to the internet. You will also find a discussion on different types of internet connections that are available in the market, such as Dial-up, Broadband, 3G, 4G, and also get the mention of wireless home connection.
10. **Protecting your Computer**: This video tutorial guides you on how to protect your computer from various malware, viruses, spywares and Trojan horses. It also shows how to have backup of files using Windows back up or time machine. Using of online backup service like Mozy or Carbonite is also discussed.
11. **Cleaning your Computer**: This video tutorial will show you how to clean up the various parts of your desktop computer such as Monitor, Computer case, Keyboard and mouse properly and safely.

MS Word:

1. **New Features:** This video tutorial guides you through the new features Word 2010 has added its domain, such as Ribbon Improvements, Photo Editing and Smart Art, Editing & Productivity and many more.
2. **Word Environment:** This video tutorial familiarizes you with the basics of word environments and teaches you how to use and customize various features of Word 2010 before you start working on a word document.
3. **Creating Documents:** In this video you will get to know how to open a new document, and open an existing document that is already saved in your computer.
4. **Formatting Text:** In this video tutorial you will learn the various methods of formatting text so that you can communicate your message to readers better.
5. **Working with Text:** This video tutorial guides you on the basics of working with text which includes cut, copy and paste; drag and drop; find and replace.
6. **Working with Tables:** This video will teach you how to work on tables in Word using various features to organize text in tabular format and make things comprehensible and organized.
7. **Printing Documents**: This video will takes you through a short tutorial on how to print a finished document, view print preview and adjust margins of a document before clicking the print command.

8. **Saving Documents:** This video tutorial guides you on how to save a document for the first time, how to open an auto saved document, how to save a document in previous versions like word 2003, 2007, and how to save a document in PDF format and other formats.

MS Excel:

1. **New Features:** This video tutorial covers improvements and new features of MS Excel 2010 over the previous versions, such as Ribbon Improvements, Spark lines & Conditional formatting, Slicers, etc.
2. **Excel environment:** This video tutorial guides you on how to explore the Excel environment and customize various features of MS Excel.
3. **Creating workbooks:** This tutorial teaches you how to open a new file in Excel and open an existing file that is already saved in your computer.
4. **Simple formulas:** This video tutorial guides you on using simple formulas to work with numerical data such as Auto Sum, Average, Etc.
5. **Pivot tables part1:** This important video tutorial shows you how to manage large volume of data using Excel's special feature called pivot table.
6. **Pivot tables part 2:** This video tutorial teaches you how to make report vouchers, slicers, etc., using pivot table.

MS PowerPoint:

1. **PowerPoint Environment:** This video tutorial guides you on how to explore the PowerPoint environment and customize various features of PowerPoint.
2. **Creating Presentations:** In this tutorial you will learn how to open a new file in PowerPoint and open an existing file that is already saved in your computer, selecting templates, etc.
3. **Slide Basics:** This video covers how to work in PowerPoint using placeholders, layouts and PowerPoint slides and templates and backgrounds, etc.
4. **Working with text:** This video tutorial guides you on the basics of working with text such as formatting, adding text boxes to your slides and modifying text boxes to change the size and location.
5. **Presenting a slide show:** This video takes you through a tutorial covering how to present a smooth professional PowerPoint presentation using various presentation tools.

MS Publisher:

1. **Know it:** This video will guide you on how to create publications such as name badges, business card, brochures, menus, etc., using MS publisher 2010.
2. **Printing and Publishing:** This video will show you several different ways of printing and publishing a document created in MS Publisher.

MS Access:

1. **Database Introduction:** This video covers how you can manage your own database to meet the needs of your business or the company you work for.
2. **Working with database:** In this video tutorial you will get to know how to open and save databases and objects in MS Access 2010. This video also teaches step by step different methods of working in MS Access.